Good Schools for Young Children

Good Schools for Young Children

A GUIDE FOR WORKING WITH THREE-, FOUR-,
AND FIVE-YEAR-OLD CHILDREN

Fifth Edition

Sarah Hammond Leeper

University of Maryland

Ralph L. Witherspoon

University of South Carolina

Barbara Day

University of North Carolina

Macmillan Publishing Company
NEW YORK

Collier Macmillan Publishers
LONDON

Copyright © 1984, Macmillan Publishing Company, a division of Macmillan, Inc.

Printed in the United States of America

Earlier editions copyright © 1963, 1968, and 1974, copyright © 1979 by Macmillan Publishing Company.

Macmillan Publishing Company
866 Third Avenue, New York, New York 10022

Collier Macmillan Canada, Inc.

Library of Congress Cataloging in Publication Data

Leeper, Sarah Hammond, Date:
  Good schools for young children.

  Bibliography: p.
  Includes index.
    1. Education, Preschool—United States—Curricula.
2. Child development.   3. Day care centers—United States.
I. Witherspoon, Ralph L. (Ralph Leo),
II. Day, Barbara,   III. Title.
LB1140.23.L43   1984   372′.21   83-11362
ISBN 0-02-369380-0

Printing: 7 8   Year: 9 0 1 2

ISBN 0-02-369380-0

Preface

Changing concerns in the society and economy, in theories of learning and child development, increased knowledge gained through research, new insights regarding exceptionality, technological advances, and subject matter content have all had their influence on this fifth edition of *Good Schools for Young Children*, which includes an examination of those changes and their effect on both content and methods of teaching. Pervading the text of this edition is the consideration of such changes and their effects on teaching and learning in the early years.

All persons who guide the development of young children need an understanding of the child, the world, and the forces that influence him or her as well as the basic principles on which decisions are made regarding instruction and practice. This fifth edition has been prepared to fulfill the need of the undergraduate students in Early Childhood Education and teachers who are inexperienced or who have little training in working with young children. The graduate student should also find this book valuable for study and reference in regard to research and practice. Parents, volunteers, and aides who are interested in the development and education of young children will likewise find this book a helpful guide.

The interdisciplinary approach in this volume draws upon the documented research of many disciplines as they affect the educational development of young children. Respect for the child is reflected throughout this book. The interrelationship of the culture, the research relating to children, the goals sought, and the practices employed is emphasized. As a basis for planning the program for young children, the findings of research in biological, sociological, and psychological areas are utilized. Factors in the social scene that influence children, their homes, and their changing family life, along with their implications for programs for young children, are included. Examples of activities and procedures are emphasized.

Extensive lists of related reading and of suggested activities are to be found at the end of each chapter. The photographs and illustrations depict typical situations and activities. They are used to clarify and extend concepts.

The book is divided into three parts:

Part I, entitled "Early Education and the Young Child," considers the young child as a person and the importance of the early years of life. The impact of social changes is interpreted in the light of program needs. Research related to growth, development, play, and learning is presented. Each major component of early childhood education is placed in historical perspective to show the development of current trends.

Part II, "The Curriculum and Young Children," develops the school and center program within the framework of the concepts presented in Part I. Each subject area is planned to take these factors into account. Suggested approaches to teaching, activities, and learning encounters are discussed, and examples are presented for each subject area. Plans for developing units (key concepts) are included. In planning and teaching, however, the subject areas are not isolated; they are interrelated in treating the concerns that young children have and wish to pursue.

Part III, "Early Childhood Education: Making It Work," concentrates on information relating to physical facilities and equipment, working with children who have uniquely different needs, parental involvement, guidance and discipline, and a look to the future.

The fifth edition has many new photographs. The reference list has been updated and expanded. The number of "Suggested Activities" has been increased as have the titles of films. A listing of organizations and agencies providing educational and related services to young children is also included.

Much of the material of earlier editions has been rewritten. However, a conscious effort has been made to preserve the qualities that have made the book distinctive. *Good Schools for Young Children* continues to be a comprehensive and practical guide for those working with young children.

S. H. L.
R. L. W.
B. D. D.

Acknowledgments

In the development of each edition of *Good Schools for Young Children*, the authors are deeply indebted to their families, friends, and professional associates at the Florida State University, the University of Maryland, the University of South Carolina, and the University of North Carolina, Chapel Hill.

Grateful appreciation is expressed to all those who helped in developing the fifth edition: Robert R. Leeper for guidance, inspiration, and editorial assistance; Kathleen M. Witherspoon for patience and encouragement; Douglas C. and Susan Day for their love and inspiration; Lloyd C. Chilton, Jr., for continuing guidance and counsel; William H. Green for technical assistance and encouragement; Marilyn Church, the Center for Young Children, University of Maryland, College Park; and the Decatur Presbyterian Kindergarten, Decatur, Georgia, for illustrative material; Mabel Jean Morrison for help in securing information; Ann Sanford, The Chapel Hill Training-Outreach Project; The Chapel Hill Public Schools; Ann Overton's Preschool Program; The Chapel Hill Montessori Day School; and to Pat Sullivan of Chapel Hill.

Appreciation for photographs is expressed to: Joseph Sparling, The Frank Porter Graham Child Development Center and Dr. Richard Brice, The University of North Carolina at Chapel Hill; *The Chapel Hill Newspaper*; Chapel Hill Training-Outreach Project, Overton Preschool, Glenwood School, Pod 1, Seawell School, Chapel Hill Montessori Day School, and Beatrix Potter School all of Chapel Hill, N.C.; Jean C. Findley; Tommy and Elizabeth G. Yates; and Robert R. Leeper.

Contents

PART TWO
Curriculum and Young Children   132

Good Schools for Young Children

PART ONE

Early Education and the Young Child

CHAPTER 1

Education and the Early Years: Past and Present

The early years of a child's life may well be the most crucial as far as opportunities for effective educational experiences are concerned. Awareness of the importance of educational programs for young children as an integral part of the educational system has developed slowly and over a long period of time.

Recently, the mother of a five-year-old started a conversation in the following manner: "Is it true that the first few years of a child's life are the most important?" Without waiting for a reply, she added, "I feel so helpless now that Mary is five years old. I'm afraid I have made too many mistakes and that there is nothing I can do about them now!" Such concepts often stem from only partially understanding what is written in popular articles about the young child and far too often from the rather perfunctory treatment given child psychology in many introductory textbooks on psychology and child development. Emphasis on the futility of aiding the child's personality after the age of five could easily arise as a result of reading some of the popular interpretations of Freudian psychology. On the other hand, until the impact of Freud's theories began to be felt in the early part of the present century, it was all too commonly believed that the early years were unimportant as long as the physical needs of the child were met.

The questions asked by Mary's mother and by many young mothers today reveal the fears mothers have of frustrating their children by disciplining them or of developing overdependent children by not giving them enough attention. Many have developed guilt feelings about not being "good mothers." It is generally agreed that the present generation of parents is more concerned about the personality development of their children than was shown by any previous generation of parents. Parents' misconceptions of how personality is influenced and the lack of understanding on the part of adults in general as to what to expect developmentally from children point dramatically to the need for study and planning by all persons who teach or interact with young children.

To some, the education of young children means very little other than what the child happens to learn before starting school, usually at the age of six. To many, education begins with the entrance to a public school. Others realize that there are nursery schools and kindergartens for younger children, but to many it is not necessary that they be "real" schools. Most parents, however, are unaware that play schools, day care and child development centers, nursery schools, and kindergartens are not just different names for the same services. They tend to think of them all as "schools." The importance of understanding these differences will be considered later in this chapter.

EARLY EUROPEAN LEADERS

Interest in schools for young children is not a modern innovation. In 1657, Comenius, in *The Great Didactic*,[1] advocated the Mother's School for the first six years of life. There was to be a Mother's School in every home for every child. He also advocated prenatal education for mothers. The course of study prescribed in his *School of Infancy*, first published in German in 1633, contained "Simple lessons in objects, taught to know stones, plants, and animals; the names and uses of the members of the body; to distinguish light and darkness and colors; the Geography of the cradle, the room, the farm, the street, and the field; trained in moderation, purity and obedience, and taught to say the Lord's Prayer,"[2] Comenius wrote the first picture book for children in 1658, the famous *Orbis Pictus*.[3] This book has been widely used and translated into every major language in the world. In addition, he maintained that a school, whatever the age group, must train the heart as well as the head. One must be sensitive to his or her own feelings as well as to the emotions of others.

Seventeenth-century Frenchmen also were concerned that warm and human feelings be displayed in young children. François de Salignac de la Mothe Fénelon

[1] J. A. Comenius (Komensky), *The Great Didactic*, de Geer Family, Amsterdam, 1657.
[2] W. S. Monroe (ed.), *Comenius' School of Infancy* (Boston: Heath, 1908), p. ix.
[3] J. A. Comenius (Komensky), *Orbis Pictus*, Nuremberg, 1658 (Syracuse, N.Y.: C. W. Bardeen, 1887).

prescribed a relationship of complete trust and honesty between adults and children. He believed that children could not learn to trust each other or adults unless they were first trusted. As early as 1681 in *The Education of Daughters*, Fénelon described a theory of education by play.

> I have known many children who have learned to read whilst they were at play . . . We should give them a book well ornamented, even on the outside, with the most beautiful pictures, and characters well formed; everything which pleases the imagination facilitates study. We should endeavor to choose a book full of short and marvellous histories; this done, be not in trouble about the child's learning to read correctly.[4]

Published in 1762, Rousseau's *Emile* gave great impetus to the importance of beginning education early.[5] Rousseau felt education should commence at birth and be continued until twenty-five years of age. He stressed the need for allowing natural development rather than preparation for later life—"the first of all blessings is not authority, but liberty. This is my fundamental maxim. We have but to apply it to childhood, and all the rules of education will flow from it." Rousseau's fundamental concept was that sense perception is the only true foundation of human knowledge.

During the early years of the nineteenth century, Friedrich Froebel, influenced by the earlier work of Pestalozzi, became convinced that the most needed educational reform concerned the early childhood years.[6] He considered carefully planned play materials essential to the proper education of the young. His gifts and occupations were not mere materials used in play for the sake of play. Rather, proper use of the gifts or material objects and the occupations or play activities expressed spiritual principles of deep philosophic significance essential to the child's proper development. Society is indebted to Froebel for the kindergarten idea, which recognized the educational value of play. The first kindergarten was established in Blackenberg in 1842, and the first kindergarten training college was founded by Baroness Bertha von Marenholtz Bülow-Wendhausen, a disciple of Froebel, in 1870 at Dresden.

DEVELOPMENT OF AMERICAN SCHOOLS

Mrs. Carl Schurz, a pupil of Froebel, established the first kindergarten in the United States at Watertown, Wisconsin, in 1855. This was a German-speaking kindergarten. The first English-speaking kindergarten in the United States was privately operated by Miss Elizabeth Peabody in Boston in 1860. A significant event in the history of education in the United States occurred in 1873, when Susan E. Blow

---

[4] E. S. Lawrence, *Origins and Growth of Modern Education* (New York: Penguin Books: paperback, 1970).

[5] J. J. Rousseau, *Emile*, trans. Barbara Foxley (London: Dent, 1911), p. 48.

[6] F. Froebel, *The Education of Man* (New York: Appleton, 1903).

(with William T. Harris) established the first public school kindergarten in St. Louis, Missouri. The following decade witnessed rapid developments in kindergarten education. Since the 1880s the kindergarten movement has had its ups and downs, often giving way to the pressures of the times for public education at other levels. Today public school kindergartens have become a reality in most states. Many of the states have passed legislation that permits the funding and operation of comprehensive developmental programs for select four- and five-year-olds. The trend has been to make the implementation permissive rather than mandatory except for kindergarten and for children with handicapping conditions.

Nursery schools

Nursery schools were first introduced into the United States at Teachers College, Columbia University, and at the Merrill Palmer School of Motherhood and Home Training in Detroit as experimental centers where children could be thoughtfully cared for and observed.[7] These schools emphasized educational guidance of parents and children in contrast to programs of custodial care hitherto considered adequate for children of working mothers. The Iowa Child Welfare Research Station was established under a state legislative grant in 1917. Through a trust fund left by Lizzie Pitts Merrill Palmer of Detroit, the Merrill Palmer School was established in 1920. In 1922 a nursery school demonstration center for student study and practice was opened at the Merrill Palmer School. Through the Laura Spelman Rockefeller Memorial, grants were made available in 1923 whereby child study centers were developed or expanded at various universities. These and many other centers established soon after have given stimulus to the growing interest in child development research, and education has assumed much larger significance in the programs for young children.

During the period from 1920 to 1932 the number of nursery schools reported to the United States Office of Education increased from 3 to 203. There were many more nursery schools that did not report. During this same decade the evidence supporting the need for schools for young children centered on the needs of the only child, limited play space for children at home, women seeking employment outside the home and needing care for their children, and parents seeking the best environment for the development of their children. Between periods of social crises, nursery and kindergarten education continued in a limited way, usually without public support.

Because the heavy emphasis beginning in the 1960s[8] on compensatory and intervention programs for children from low-income and culturally different families has

---

[7] Mary Dabney Davis, *Nursery Schools, Their Development and Current Practices in the United States,* Bull. 9 (Washington, D.C.: U.S. Office of Education, 1932).
[8] Discussed later in this chapter.

continued, the traditional nursery school has become much less prominent on the early childhood education scene. Nevertheless, prekindergarten enrollments increased rapidly during the 1960s and early 1970s: 0.7 million prekindergarten children enrolled in 1967 as compared to 1.6 million by 1974. Of the latter number, 422,000 were enrolled in public facilities against 1,182,000 in nonpublic centers.[9]

Among three- to four-year-old children, enrollment in schools doubled between 1968 (16 per cent) and 1978 (34 per cent) despite a 22 per cent decline in that age population.[10] This burgeoning increase grew primarily out of the belief in the importance of the programs as compensation for early social and economic disadvantages. Emphasis was also placed on acceleration of cognitive development, especially in research and so-called model programs.

In the United States the early 1960s witnessed a revival of Early Childhood Education for exactly the same reason that early education had been advocated so often in the past by such leaders as Froebel, Montessori, the McMillan sisters, and many others. Conditions of the times had created slum cultures that produced serious social problems.

In the search for panaceas and quick results, the Montessori approach promised an answer. Montessori schools quickly became popular and were glamorized by magazines, television, and the news media. Maria Montessori began her work with slum children in Rome in 1907. A medical doctor by profession, she developed methods and accompanying materials that are used in today's schools exactly as she prescribed in the early 1900s. Her principal contributions lie in the emphasis on learning and the importance of the environment in the learning process. However, today's teacher of young children should be familiar enough with the total field of Early Childhood Education to choose which of the Montessori concepts, materials, and procedures will best serve children in the context of today's individual and cultural needs. The pros and cons of Montessori are objectively set forth in *Montessori in Perspective*.[11]

Today, as was often true in the past, the largest number of publicly supported programs for children is predicated on the principle that child care must be worked out satisfactorily if the family is to maintain itself in society.

The inadequate provision on the part of public schools to meet the growing need for extensive care and early educational experiences for preschool-age children has meant heavy reliance on private care centers and schools. The rapid progress these

---

[9]*1976 Databook the Status of Education Research and Development in the United States* (Washington, D.C.: The National Institute of Education, U.S. Department of Health, Education and Welfare, 1976), p. 6.

[10]*The Status of Children, Youth, and Families 1979* (Washington, D.C.: U.S. Department of Health and Human Services, Office of Human Development Services, 1980), p. 67.

[11]Evelyn Beyer et al. (eds.), *Montessori in Perspective* (Washington, D.C.: NAEYC, 1971). See also Steven R. Yussen, Samuel Mathews, and Jacqueline W. Knight, "Performance of Montessori and Traditionally Schooled Nursery Children on Social Cognitive Tasks and Memory Problems," *Contemporary Educational Psychology*, **5** (April 1980), pp. 133–137.

The early years of a child's life may well be the most crucial as far as opportunities for effective educational experience are concerned.

have made raises questions as to what types of schools, program quality, and adult personnel qualifications, including teachers, are needed. Although many provide excellent facilities, have a good adult–child ratio, and employ properly trained personnel, there are some that do not maintain standards necessary for the well-being of the children involved.

National emergencies and care programs

Since 1930, two national emergencies—the Great Depression of 1929 and World War II—greatly increased the demand for care services for young children. The provision in 1933 for children's centers as a part of the Federal Emergency Relief Administration was the first time that center programs for young children had become a part of a federally supported program. Although the legislation was designed to help relieve unemployment and to supplement existing educational programs, the increasing concern for the welfare of the young child gave direction to the development of children's centers. Since then, many varied laws and guidelines have resulted from what was learned in the implementation of these programs. As women were mobilized for war emergency work and to replace men in service, attention was focused on the need for legislation to ensure that schools for young children provided an educational experience in a satisfactory environment. This was made possible through funds made available by the Lanham Act.[12] To put this act into operation,

> the War Manpower Commission issued a directive in August, 1942, instructing the Office of Defense Health and Welfare Services to present plans for the development and coordination of federal programs for the care of children of working mothers. Very soon thereafter the President made $400,000 of emergency funds available for transmittal to the U.S. Office of Education and the U.S. Children's Bureau to assist the states in establishing needed services. By June, 1943, 39 states had developed plans for extended school services to be developed under state and local educational agencies, and thirty states had similar plans for child-welfare programs to be administered by welfare agencies.

These war-created emergency programs were developed through the cooperative endeavor of the Federal Emergency Relief Administration and the U.S. Office of Education, assisted by the three professional organizations concerned with the education of young children—the National Association for Nursery Education, the Association for Childhood Education, and the National Council of Parent Education—to provide adequate care for children of working mothers. This program was

---

[12] Bess Goodykoontz, Mary Dabney Davis, and Hazel F. Gabbard, "Recent History and Present Status of Education for Young Children," *Early Childhood Education* (46th Yearbook), Part II, NSSE (Chicago: U. of Chicago, 1947), p. 61.

later administered by the Work Projects Administration and the Federal Works Agency.[13]

In a democracy, the right of every child to have an equal opportunity is recognized. Therefore, it is essential to provide a good environment for each child; this means that an inadequate home environment must be compensated for by a rich and varied preschool curriculum.[14]

Between periods of social crises, nursery and kindergarten education continued in a limited way, usually without public support but for quite different reasons. Middle- and upper-class parents believed that early education was essential to later school success or at least necessary to maintaining family status in the community.

COMPENSATORY AND INTERVENTION EDUCATION PROGRAMS

During the 1960s, the realization that one fourth of the children entering first grade were academically retarded by one to three years called for a reevaluation of the educational system. Children primarily from low-income families had been denied the early experiential opportunities so necessary for normal cognitive growth enjoyed by their counterparts from middle- and upper-income families. Early (preschool) education for the first time in the history of the nation became the priority educational concern of educators, communities, and government.

The ever-increasing affluence of American economic life and of the demands of a complex technological society made it apparent that those who lacked special skills and advanced education were at a great disadvantage. The public school, with its relatively late entrance age, had become less and less able to cope with the two or three years' learning retardation present at school entrance in children from low-income homes and from some culturally different homes. Researchers had found that young children lacking the opportunity to experience a learning environment common to middle-class children had great difficulty in bridging the gap. They often became early school dropouts, later joining the ranks of the unemployed.

In an effort to break the poverty cycle thus engendered, the federal government beginning in the mid-1960s set up unprecedented funds for the education of children from such homes—especially for preschool-age children. Thus the value of early education quickly became popular, and the young child was "rediscovered" by educators, the public, and the parents. The public schools have worked to accept the challenge and to meet the unique needs of these children as well as those of the great majority for whom the conditions of nature and nurture have been more favorable. It is important to clarify terms frequently used during this period.

[13] Ibid., p. 60.
[14] M. L. Goldschmidt. "Early Cognitive Development and Preschool Education" *Internatl. J. Early Child. Educ.*, 3:1 (1971), pp. 5–6.

A brief but inclusive definition of the culturally disadvantaged (the low-income deprived) is that these are individuals or a group of people who lack social amenities and cultural graces associated with the majority middle-class society. This goes back to the overwhelming numbers of the culturally deprived, who began to appear around 1860, when the population changed largely to rural-urban with the rural living in urbanized communities for which they were not vocationally equipped. Large groups of culturally deprived children were found in the slums of large cities, certain rural areas, Indian reservations, and migrant workers camps.

Today we do not think of these groups as culturally deprived or disadvantaged, for it has been shown that each has an exceedingly rich heritage that is different from, but not inferior to, that of the majority group. When compared to commonly accepted norms, many groups deviate because of their own backgrounds and values. Therefore, it is more appropriate to speak of culturally different, than of culturally disadvantaged, people, even though these differences may put some at a disadvantage competitively in the everyday requirements of work and conduct. *Different* does not carry the negative and inferior connotations that *disadvantaged* does.

The importance of language to the child's early development cannot be overemphasized. Language development is treated in detail elsewhere in this text.

Early compensatory education for children from culturally different and low-income families is an attempt through direct intervention to enable such children to "catch up" in school learning. Previous experience and child-development research and theory would indicate a pessimistic outlook for much success. The availability of funds for such programs in the early 1960s spurred a vast amount of controlled research in this field. Notable is the work of Bereiter and Engelmann,[15] Bloom,[16] Deutsch,[17] and Hunt.[18] Whereas early reports indicate a high level of achievement success by using direct methods and by eliminating other developmental areas common in most preschool programs, follow-up studies will be necessary to determine the effectiveness of such programs. A review of many studies done two to five years following intensive educational efforts would seem to cast doubt on the effectiveness of compensatory programs. However, some report sustained gains.[19] It is highly possible that gains may not be manifest until later childhood or adolescence.

It must be kept in mind that most children involved in these efforts continue to

[15] C. Bereiter and S. Engelmann, *Teaching Disadvantaged Children in the Preschool* (Englewood Cliffs, N.J.: Prentice-Hall, 1966).

[16] B. S. Bloom, A. Davis, and R. Hess, *Compensatory Education for Cultural Deprivation* (New York: Holt, 1965).

[17] M. Deutsch, "Facilitating Development in the Preschool Child: Social and Psychological Perspectives," *Merrill-Palmer Quart.*, **10**:3 (1964), pp. 249–263.

[18] J. McV. Hunt, "The Psychological Basis for Using Pre-School Enrichment as an Antidote for Cultural Deprivation," *Merrill-Palmer Quart.*, **10**:3 (1964), pp. 209–248.

[19] *Educational Programs That Work*, 3d ed. (San Francisco: Far West Laboratory for Educational Research and Development, 1976).

live in the same environments that brought about the deprivation in the first place. It seems highly unrealistic to expect a child to maintain gains resulting from short intensive learning programs without rather drastically restructuring the home and community living conditions and bringing about greatly improved family life. Obviously, much social learning occurs very rapidly during the preschool years. It is felt by many that the attitudes toward others and toward right and wrong developed during these years strongly persist throughout childhood and adolescence and even during the entire life span. The implications for the need of well-qualified teachers and caregivers of irreproachable character for preschool children are clear.

The Economic Opportunity Act of 1964 provided for varied ways through which children might derive the best possible benefits from child development, social welfare, teaching methods, and motivational techniques.[20] It authorized the establishment of programs for economically deprived children of preschool age designed to prepare them to enter public school. These programs were called Head Start Child Development Programs.

The goal of Head Start was and continues to be that of reaching children of low-income families between the ages of three and five through a comprehensive preschool program. It provides language opportunities (speaking and listening), a wide variety of experiences, and adequate behavior models for the children. It was and is an attempt to break the poverty cycle in early ages because evidence indicates that the early years of childhood are the most crucial in educational development. Bloom pointed out that environment can mean as many as 20 IQ points in the developing child and is most critical in preschool years because children go 50 per cent of the way in organizing their thinking patterns by the time they are four years of age and the next 30 per cent by the time they are eight.[21]

Head Start is a total program to meet children's mental and emotional needs in preparing them to find success in their first school experience. It has many component parts—medical and dental examinations and corrections, immunizations, social services, nutritional care, and psychological services. The parents are involved in all aspects of the program, including decision making and often filling many nonprofessional positions. Other people interested in the community are encouraged to work as volunteers. Activities are planned by the center to help parents deal with general and specific problems of making a home and bringing up a family.

The planning for Head Start programs was based on first looking at the needs of children and then setting up appropriate goals. It was found that many children were lacking in language development and often had difficulty in expressing themselves because of limited vocabulary and inability to speak so as to be heard. Because of limited experiences, they did not fit into social groups and were often unable to use simple toys or scissors, crayons, paper, pencils, and such, which are

---

[20] D. Brieland, "Cultural and Social Change," *Young Children*, **20**:4 (1965), pp. 223–229.
[21] B. S. Bloom, *Stability and Change in Human Characteristics* (New York: Wiley, 1964), p. 88.

readily accessible to privileged children. The program that emerged placed emphasis on improving language, healthful living, developing curiosity, building self-image, and respecting authority as a means to self-discipline.

The 1965 summer program of Head Start began at 13,344 centers in 2,000 communities with an attendance of approximately 500,000 children.[22] One of every two economically deprived children eligible to enter public school in the fall of 1965 was helped. Forty thousand teachers and 500,000 volunteers were involved in the eight-week program. Local communities paid 10 per cent (either in cash or in kind). The federal government paid up to 90 per cent of the cost.

This 1965 summer program was so successful that in August of that year it was announced that Project Head Start would become a year-round program. There were the following three types of programs:[23]

1. Programs, including health, education, social service, and parent activities, during the school year for the children who participated in summer Head Start.
2. Full-year programs for preschool children who would enter school in the fall of the year.
3. Short-term summer programs for children who would enter school in the fall of the year.

The local programs were conducted by a Community Action Agency or were delegated to a group that had the capacity to organize and operate the program, such as the public schools, other public agencies, private nonprofit organizations, or institutions of higher education. In communities without a Community Action Agency other provisions were made for sponsorship of a Head Start program. Children were selected on the basis of an index of whether a family was earning a minimum-standard income, where the family lived (farm or nonfarm family), and number of children in the family. At least 90 per cent of the children came from families that fell below the poverty line. The other 10 per cent could come from the community at large but could not share in the medical benefits.

Groups were limited to fifteen to twenty children per teacher. The Office of Economic Opportunity financed an eight-week teacher training course for a limited number of local people who were to teach in the program. Short-term courses were planned for other teachers.

Such programs as Institutional Development Studies,[24] the program in New Rochelle, New York,[25] the Early School Admission Project in Baltimore,[26] Early

[22] Irwin Ross, "Head Start Is a Banner Project." *The PTA Magazine,* **60**:7 (1966), p. 3.
[23] Keith Osborn, "Project Head Start—An Assessment," *Educ. Leadership,* **23**:98 (1965), pp. 18–103.
[24] M. Deutsch, "Early Social Environment: Its Influence on School Adaptation," *Pre-School Education Today* (Garden City, N.Y.: Doubleday, 1966).
[25] Thelma G. Wolman, "A Preschool Program for Disadvantaged Children—The New Rochelle Story," *Young Children,* **21**:2 (1965), pp. 98–111.
[26] Catherine Brunner, "Deprivation—Its Effects, Its Remedies," *Educ. Leadership,* **23**:2 (1965), pp. 103–107.

Training Project at Murfreesboro,[27] Tennessee, and the New York Housing Authority Project[28] had given direction to the development of preschool programs before the need for compensatory education had attained such national scope.

Some educators questioned whether an eight-week program or even a year-round program could make up for four years of deprivation. Some leaders in the field suggested that emphasis in these programs be placed only upon academic learning. Others believed that the broader program would ensure greater achievement in academic learning and contribute more to the cultural development of the child.[29] Spodek raised the questions of the value of "massive intervention" and quality control of programs for such large groups of disadvantaged children.[30]

Jenny W. Klein states that it took almost one hundred years before a comprehensive, federally sponsored intervention program emerged for preschoolers. Experimental and pilot programs, planned variations of Head Start, and other models provide information to show that early intervention may raise the quality of children's lives before the effects of poverty are established into a self-perpetuating cycle.[31]

Some medical findings of the first 2 million children participating in Head Start were: 180,000 failed a vision test and 60,000 needed eye glasses; 60,000 had bad skin disease; 180,000 had anemia; 40,000 had mental retardation or a learning problem requiring specialist evaluation; 20,000 had a bone or joint problem; 1,300,000 had dental disease; and 1,200,000 had not been vaccinated against measles. More than two thirds of these children received the medical and dental services they required through Head Start.[32]

The evaluative studies of Project Head Start are divided into census surveys, research, educational testing service, longitudinal studies, and national evaluation studies. The studies showed the need for more careful instrumentation, particularly in research designs; the need to study long-term interventions; and the need to avoid quick judgments on the basis of data or the art of Early Childhood Education.[33]

In a review of the effect of Head Start programs, Moore[34] summarizes the following earlier findings:

[27] R. A. Klaus and Susan W. Gray, "Murfreesboro Preschool Program for Culturally Deprived Children," *Child. Educ.*, **42**:2 (1965), p. 92.

[28] Alice M. Brophy, "Children's Centers—Three Decades of Progress," *J. of Nursery Educ.*, **13**:3 (1964), pp. 173–177.

[29] "Project Head Start," *NEA J.*, **54**:7 (1965), p. 58.

[30] B. Spodek, "Is Massive Intervention the Answer?" *Educ. Leadership*, **23**:2 (1965), p. 109.

[31] Jenny W. Klein, "Head Start: Intervention for What?" *Educ. Leadership*, **39**:1 (1971), pp. 16–19.

[32] Project Head Start, *A Child Development Program* (Washington, D.C.: U.S. Government Printing Office, 1970), p. 3.

[33] Lois-Ellen Datta, "A Report on Evaluation Studies of Project Head Start." *Internatl. J. of Early Child. Educ.*, **3**:2 (1971), pp. 58–68.

[34] Shirley M. Moore, "The Effects of Head Start Programs with Different Curricular and Teaching Strategies," *Young Children*, **32**:6 (1977), pp. 54–60.

1. Gains are short-lived, whatever the model, once the program is over.
2. Head Start children are less likely to be placed in special rooms or to be retained in the same grade than are similar non-Head Start children.
3. Early intervention is a complex process. It must involve the home and family and requires unusual resources.
4. Variation of results using the same model suggests that forces other than the model used are influential.
5. The more structured academically oriented models seem to produce the best results, at least temporarily.
6. The answer as to long-term effects of early programs is not in, and awaits much clarification from long-term efforts now under way.

Since Head Start began, the effectiveness of compensatory and early intervention programs in producing lasting gains has been debated. New evidence based on longitudinal studies begun in the sixties, suggests that advantages of early childhood compensatory and intervention programs have been retained by most children over a period of years.[35] The "sleeper effects" were not evident in the scores of children participating in the original preschool program the first few years following the program. However, there is now evidence of gains that seem somewhat permanent.[36]

Seitz and colleagues[37] followed the academic progress of children from economically disadvantaged families living in the inner city. One group of children participated in Head Start and Follow Through programs whereas the control group received no special attention. For those children who responded positively there was no fade-out of gains. The gains evident when the program ended were still found four to five years later—these children were still performing at a higher level than were those in the control group in mathematics, general information, vocabulary, and IQ scores.

Several studies have reported that early compensatory and intervention programs produced marked reductions in the number of children placed in special education classes or retained in the grade. For example, Guinagh and Gordon found that 10 per cent of the children in the treatment group were placed in special education classes, as compared with 30 per cent of the control group.[38]

According to Royce, "The problem for Head Start evaluators became which goals

---

[35] *Education Daily*, February 25, 1977, p. 6.

[36] B. Brown, "Long-Term Gains from Early Intervention: An Overview of Current Research," mimeographed (Paper presented at the 1977 Annual Meeting of the American Association for the Advancement of Science, Denver, Colorado, February 23, 1977).

[37] Victoria Seitz, Nancy Apfel, and Carol Efron, "Long-Term Effects of Early Intervention: A Longitudinal Investigation." mimeographed. (Paper presented at the 1977 Annual Meeting of the American Association for the Advancement of Science, Denver, Colorado, February 23, 1977).

[38] B. J. Guinagh and I. J. Gordon, *School Performance as a Function of Early Stimulation* (Final Report, Grant No. NIH-HEW-OCD-90-C-638), Institute for Development of Human Resources, University of Florida, 1976.

had highest priority and which outcome criteria would be the 'best' measure of Head Start's effectiveness."[39]

Although findings of the early Head Start evaluations were disappointing, in many ways they provided valuable cues for the development of programs with specific characteristics and goals. Furthermore, teachers generally report Head Start children as being better prepared for school than like children who had not attended Head Start. Head Start children also repeat fewer grades than children not in the program, and, of course, the value of better health and personality adjustment resulting from the health and social services program to later learning is hard to estimate.

By the fall of 1977, more than 5.5 million children had participated in Head Start programs. Despite the fact that 37 per cent of preschoolers' mothers work outside the home, 10,000 Head Start parents have become certified teachers.[40] In addition to its standard program, Head Start has consistently allocated a portion of its funds to research and development. Three significant programs emerged as a result, namely, Follow Through, Parent-Child Centers, and Home Start.

The objectives of the Follow Through program were twofold: comparing short-term and long-term effects of well-defined approaches to Early Childhood Education and assessing the cumulative impact of a continuous, systematically different program from preschool to primary grades.[41] The operation of the Follow Through program was delegated to the U.S. Office of Education. Selected school districts were asked to choose a model that had been shown promising as a vehicle for meeting the objectives of Head Start and for continuing that model program for former Head Start children into the early elementary grades. This study was done in order to determine the effectiveness of the program through time.

A recent study involving 352,000 Follow Through and comparison group children over a nine-year period conducted originally by Stanford Research Institute and continued by Abt Associates found Follow Through ineffective in increasing test scores in the basics. Sixty-seven per cent of Follow Through programs failed to produce gains in the program children over those not in the program. However, the basic skills models were superior as far as test results were concerned over the cognitive/conceptual skills and affective/cognitive models. The study also showed great variations within the use of the same models from site to site with the best results in middle-sized communities rather than in large cities or small communi-

[39] J. M. Royce, H. W. Murray, I. Lazar, and R. B. Darlington, "Methods of Evaluating Program Outcomes," in *Handbook of Research in Early Childhood Education*, ed. by B. Spodek (New York: Free Press, and London: Collier Macmillan, 1982), p. 619.

[40] Dorothy Levenson, "Whatever Happened to Early Childhood Education?" *Instructor* (Oct. 1977), p. 71.

[41] *Implementation of Planned Variations in Head Start, 1969–70* (Washington, D.C.: Institute of Child Study, University of Maryland, and Office of Child Development, DHEW).

ties. This is an important finding, as it points to significant influences on learning other than the model program used.[42]

A critique of the Abt Report made by House and others reached different conclusions.[43] These workers found that models that emphasize basic skills are not necessarily better than other models or methods. However, one approach was not demonstrated to be better than another, and participation in the Follow Through classes was neither superior nor inferior to regular schooling. Many of the goals of the Follow Through models were not measured, even though the development of effective evaluative instruments had been promised. House and his team agree with the Abt Report that the effectiveness of a teaching model varies from one community to the next. Individual teachers, schools, neighborhoods, and homes seem to influence children's achievement far more than the method used.

Parent-Child Centers were established in 1967 as an early intervention demonstration project involving 36 communities. Thirty-three of these were managed by the Office of Child Development, DHEW, and three were retained by the Office of Economic Opportunity as research demonstration programs. Head Start for children from three to five years of age had clearly shown that environmentally caused developmental deficits present by age three were difficult to overcome. In an effort to alleviate this problem, Parent-Child Centers (PCC) enrolled only children below the age of three and "graduated" them when they reached their third birthday. In reality, the family of the target child in each case was an active part of the program. In many cases, in order to assure the most profitable impact of the program, these centers accepted target children before birth.

PCC is a Head Start program with all components receiving maximum attention. It operates on the concept that normal learning and development must have a normal environment in which to function if critical early developmental processes are to proceed on schedule and without causing later retardation. Consequently, heavy emphasis is placed on working with the entire family, encouraging home improvement, and an all-out effort to bring target families into the mainstream of American life while still retaining their unique cultural and ethnic characteristics. Every effort is made in the interest of the target child in order that he or she be provided optimum opportunities for all aspects of growth and development. It will be interesting to see how these children fare later in middle and high school because they were originally, almost without exception, at high educational risk.

Home Start, a three-year demonstration Head Start project involving sixteen programs, was conducted from 1972 to 1975, buttressed by certain continuing efforts thereafter. Basically, Home Start, like PCC, provided all the services of Head

---

[42] "Value of Federally Funded Programs in Basics Disputed," *ASCD News Exchange* **19**:4 (1977), pp. 1–13.

[43] E. R. House, G. V. Glass, L. D. McClean, and D. F. Walker, "No Simple Answer: Critique of the 'Follow Through' Evaluation," *Educ. Leadership*, **35**:6 (1978).

Start except that the programs focused on home rather than on a center operation, thus enabling parents to become "child development specialists" providing for the maximum education, growth, and development of their own children. A major goal was to demonstrate the effectiveness of providing support for parents in their major child-rearing efforts through home-based programs as well as to assess the financial feasibility of such efforts.[44]

During the 1970s several carefully designed program development projects were funded by the Program Development Branch of the U.S. Office of Education Bureau of Education for the Handicapped. Many have become renowned for the quality of their work.[45] Some of the well-established major projects and centers that were established to study certain aspects of education of the disadvantaged child include (1) A Parent Education Project in Gainesville, Florida; (2) Frank Porter Graham Child Development Center in Chapel Hill, North Carolina; (3) Nurseries in Cross Cultural Education in San Francisco, California; (4) Bank Street Early Childhood Center in New York City; (5) A Piaget Derived Curriculum in Ypsilanti,

[44]*The Home Start Demonstration Program: An Overview* (Washington, D.C.: U.S. Department of HEW, Office of Child Development, 1973).
[45]*Program Description, Handicapped Children's Early Education Program* (Program Development Branch, Division of Educational Services, Bureau of Education for the Handicapped, U.S. Office of Education, October 25, 1971).

When one considers the importance of language throughout life, education during the foundation years becomes increasingly important.

Michigan; (6) an integrated nursery school in Wayne State University; (7) Parent Participation Nursery Schools and Children's Centers in Berkeley, California; (8) University of Chicago Laboratory Nursery School in Chicago, Illinois; (9) Pre-Kindergarten Demonstration Center in Rochester, New York; and (10) Early Childhood Education Study in Newton, Massachusetts.[46]

Social and educational trends

The 1970s witnessed larger public expenditures for Early Childhood Education than were made in this field prior to the mid-1960s. By the mid-1970s, in keeping with other economic trends, funding for Early Childhood Education had stabilized, and in some cases it had decreased. Evaluation and accountability had become important components of the process as those in charge of the purse strings attempted to find ways to assure taxpayers of the best possible results for each dollar spent. The result was that academic achievement became a major objective, and more structured activities began to take shape in the daily schedules. Combination care and educational programs with more flexible hours to meet the time schedules of the families involved became commonplace. Because parents were still recognized as the prime child-rearing agents in society, they were encouraged to become involved in every activity of the educational process. Such involvement included a decision-making role regarding what their children were to be taught, under what conditions, and by whom.

Continuing inflationary trends, an ever-increasing national debt, and unstable economic conditions in the sixties and seventies all had increased the need for assistance in many areas of life. More than half the mothers of young children were gainfully employed outside the home. In almost all cases, the father in intact families was employed as well. These conditions called for alternate means of providing for the health, safety, education, and nurturance of very young children, often infants less than a year old. By 1977, widely publicized government findings indicated that more than half the households consisted of one or two persons only. Elementary and middle schools were feeling the impact of these population trends toward fewer or no children in young families. Birthrate patterns and population statistics were changing so rapidly in the direction of fewer children that conflicting statements regarding family size, divorce rates, number of gainfully employed mothers of young children, and family structure were constantly appearing in the news media, college texts, popular books, and magazine articles intended for lay consumption.

An assessment of developments in Early Childhood Education during the 1970s revealed clearly emerging trends. As a natural consequence of a decrease in birthrate in the United States, elementary school enrollments were generally lower than

[46] Evelyn Weber, *Early Childhood Education: Perspectives on Change* (Worthington, Ohio: Charles A. Jones Publishing Co., 1970), pp. 71–95.

formerly, making once-scarce space available for kindergartens, federally sponsored Early Childhood Education programs, or Child Development Centers. This fact, coupled with a broader acceptance of the value of early educational experiences for later success in school, encouraged the establishment of more opportunities for kindergarten experiences in the public schools. Even more dramatic was the development of comprehensive child development programs for three- and four-year-old children. Pilot programs for even younger children, including infants, were cropping up. Although most of the programs for prekindergarten children sponsored by various federal agencies were not administered by the public schools, many were found in public school facilities, often in close cooperation with school programs. At the same time, more and more schools were developing programs for children below the kindergarten level. The designation Child Development Center rather than "school" has gained popular acceptance for such programs.

Some Child Development Center personnel, especially for the educational component, were not trained or "certified" in Early Childhood Education. However, many centers were adding qualified teachers, especially in supervisory roles, because earlier experience had shown a particular need for those in leadership positions. In an effort to provide properly prepared teachers a pilot program for training Child Development Associates was begun in 1972. This program is discussed in Chapter 18.

Although most federally funded programs for young children were basically limited to children of low-income families, there was a growing demand for early education for all children. States and local governments were responding by making provision for such programs, especially public school kindergartens. The education of young children was fast becoming the responsibility of the public and private sectors of society, including business and industry. The importance of health and nutrition, family and personal development, and agency cooperation in providing services for young children and their families had been established. Program staffing patterns included parents, aides, and volunteers from the community and were truly interdisciplinary in nature. A coordinated educational effort never before known in American education, making effective use of various levels and types of competencies was emerging. Most significant to teachers and educators was the development of pilot and model programs with built-in research components to determine the effect of various curriculum approaches, teaching strategies, and newly developed materials of instruction on the immediate and long-range cognitive and learning abilities of young children.

THE CURRENT SCENE

Benjamin Spock has expressed some considerations of children in the 1980s.[47] Children now, he believes, "face subtle yet serious problems." Among those prob-

[47]*The Chapel Hill Newspaper*, Feb. 1, 1983, p. 5B.

lems he cites the disappearance of the extended family, the loss of community because of frequent moves, the high divorce rate, and the increasing incidence of child abuse. He also believes the American school system "has lost sight of its real job—very simply, to help children grow up."

Statistics vital to those involved in planning programs for young children are reported periodically by the U.S. Bureau of the Census. In 1970, of the 54 million children under fourteen years of age in the United States more than 17 million were under five years of age. The next eight years witnessed a dramatic change: The number of children under the age of fourteen had dropped to about 47 million, and the number under the age of five was down to a little over 15 million, representing decrements of 13.2 per cent and 10.5 per cent, respectively.[48]

Nevertheless the Census Bureau anticipates a reversal in the birth statistics some time in the late seventies to the year 2000. According to this projection, by the turn of the century there will be 70,577,000 children under the age of fourteen (up 40.1 per cent) and 24,654,000 under the age of five (up 51.2 per cent).[49] By 1978 there had been several news reports that the trend in the number of births had started upward as predicted, with the largest increase in number of live births in twenty-five years occurring during 1977. This does not necessarily mean that the birthrate has changed. The increase in the number of births was likely due to the fact that there were a large number of women of childbearing age who were born during or toward the end of the baby boom years. The average number of children in the family remains small compared to earlier years in America's history.

When mothers of young children work outside the home, a need for alternate forms of child rearing is created. It is interesting to note that the female labor force as a percentage of the total female population increased from 33.9 per cent in 1950 to 50.8 per cent in 1979. By 1979 women comprised 41.2 per cent of the total labor force, and married women with husband present comprised 47.6 per cent. Between 1970 and 1979, the participation rate of divorced women in the labor force had increased from 71.5 per cent to 74.0 per cent. And by 1979, more than half of all women with school-age children were working, as well as over 30 per cent of mothers with children under six years of age.[50]

What effect does the fact that there are so many working mothers have on this generation of preschool children? With their mothers working outside the home, most of these children may receive little or no education other than that provided by maids, relatives, or the numerous day care centers and babysitting services, many of which are inadequate and, in some instances, are actually harmful to the normal development of the children involved.[51] The situation remained much the

[48]*The Status of Children, Youth, and Families 1979*, op. cit., p. 5.
[49]*Statistical Abstracts of the United States 1976* (Washington, D.C.: U.S. Department of Commerce, Bureau of the Census, 1976), p. 6.
[50]*The Status of Children, Youth, and Families 1979*, op. cit., pp. 130, 159.
[51]*Profiles*, White House Conference on Children, 1970 (Washington, D.C.: Superintendent of Documents, U.S. Government Printing Office, 1970), p. 85.

same in 1977, for large numbers of families still needed educational, as well as care, opportunities for their children.

In 1978, the usual weekly earnings of women were $166; and for men, $272, with women earning 61 per cent as much as men. The same percentage differential in 1970 was 62 per cent.[52] The lower wages of women create especially burdensome problems when a woman is a single parent.

In a discussion of today's population profile, it should be noted that as the more dependent over-65 age group continues to increase, there will be a need for more children to replace the labor force to balance the scale. On the basis of previous patterns, it is predicted that the birthrate will increase and that children will be more valued by society than they were at the time of this writing.

The time period under consideration has seen continuing improvement in opportunities for culturally different groups. Integrated housing and schools, innovative and adequately funded educational programs, better health and other human need delivery systems, guaranteed equal opportunity employment, equal rights in other areas, and the women's liberation movement have all enabled hitherto denied provisions for decision making. Such provisions have resulted in more creative participation of the many culturally different groups in the mainstream of American life and society.

Public acceptance of altered life-styles brought about by these changes has brought about a need for adequate care and improved educational opportunities for large numbers of America's young below the traditional public school-age children. Despite the preceding conditions and trends, the provision for the care and education of young children outside the home by other than family members is far from adequate.

However, children continue to need protection. By 1974 all states had licensing laws for day care centers. Procedures for effective enforcement of the laws are being developed and some states have successfully moved against programs that were not in compliance with the regulations. Nevertheless at this time regulatory policy is fragmented and does not have the public commitment necessary for vigorous enforcement.[53]

Responsibility for preprimary education and services

The American public has generally accepted responsibility for the education of all children age six and above and has been willing to support such efforts with tax dollars. When it comes to like responsibilities for the education of children below that age, the story is somewhat different. There are two significant beliefs rather

---

[52] *The Status of Children, Youth, and Families 1979*, op. cit., p. 131.
[53] Gwen Morgan, "Regulating Early Childhood Programs in the Eighties," in B. Spodek (ed.), op. cit., pp. 387–389.

firmly ingrained in the minds of most people that account for this situation. First, educational psychology has led us to believe that it takes a certain amount of maturity to be able to achieve the tasks expected of the school. Though there is some validity to this belief, there is considerable evidence, as pointed out elsewhere in this text, that perhaps the child's most significant learning occurs prior to that time. Second, the American cultural and religious heritage suggests that the responsibility for the care and education of infants and preschool-age children belongs to, and is the responsibility of, the child's family. Yet families continue to have difficulty in fulfilling this role.

Beginning in 1909 and every ten years thereafter the President of the United States has called a national conference on the needs of children and youth attended by citizens and professionals from all walks of life. It is of value to look at the recommendations made over the last three decades by these White House Conferences on Children and Youth.

At the 1950 White House Conference, the citizens attending expressed their approval of education for young children by this recommendation: "As a desirable supplement to home life, nursery schools and kindergartens, provided they meet high professional standards, should be included as a part of public opportunities for all children."[54]

At the 1960 conference, three forums recommended that free public education be extended downward to include kindergartens as a part of the school system. It was further recommended that every organized group of young children away from home be under the supervision of at least one person qualified in the field of Early Childhood Education.[55]

The 1970 conference had certain unique features, namely (1) the division into two groups, one conferring on children and another on youth so that the problems of children not become secondary to the problems of youth; and (2) the multidisciplinary approach, by bringing together groups from both inside and outside educational circles.[56] The conference participants recommended that each state set up community-coordinated child-care committees. These committees were to be composed of parents and professionals (both public and private) who serve in the field of child development.

The 1980 White House Conferences on Families were held in Baltimore, Minneapolis, and Los Angeles. During the present decade there is need for child and family advocates to become active in identifying priorities, initiating and supporting policies and programs which are essential for children and their families.[57]

[54] *Conference Proceedings* (Washington, D.C.: Midcentury White House Conference on Children and Youth, 1950).

[55] *Conference Proceedings* (Washington, D.C.: The Golden Anniversary White House Conference on Children and Youth, 1960).

[56] *Report to the President, White House Conference on Children* (Washington, D.C.: U.S. Government Printing Office, 1970), pp. 5–15.

[57] Carol Levin," White House Conferences on Families," *Child. Educ.*, **57**:1 (1980), pp. 32-L–32M.

National programs

The U.S. Office of Education (OE) did not come into the "big time" in education until the early 1960s with the passage of federal legislation involving substantial appropriations. The major purpose of most education legislation at that time was to enable the public schools to provide quality education for children of low-income families and to find and research innovative and alternative ways of improving the instructional process.

An important source of information is the Educational Resources Information Center, commonly known as ERIC. Although originally sponsored by the U.S. Office of Education, ERIC is now a function of the National Institute of Education, and has several clearinghouses, one of which is the ERIC Clearinghouse on Early Childhood Education, located at the University of Illinois. The current address of the ERIC/ECE Clearinghouse and *Newsletter* is College of Education, University of Illinois, Urbana-Champaign, Urbana, Illinois 61801.

The Economic Opportunity Act of 1964 and the Elementary and Secondary Education Act (ESEA) of 1965 brought the federal government increasingly into the educational scene. For the first time, funds in unprecedented amounts were made available to every community in the nation. Both of these acts and their subsequent implementation placed major emphasis on early education, particularly for children of disadvantaged families. The tremendous and immediate public response to Head Start pointed up the urgent need for such a program.

The influence of this federal legislation during the mid-1960s has given impetus to the changing trends in Early Childhood Education and should prove beneficial to children of all socioeconomic levels. The prospects for kindergartens in all public school systems are brightened. In addition, the child care centers are rapidly changing to carefully planned educational programs under the direction of trained teachers.

In crowded situations, however, there has been a tendency for the teacher to teach two groups, one in the morning and one in the afternoon, and to increase the size of the group to as many as forty-five to fifty pupils. Inability to meet the cost involved may prevent many children from attending a private school, thereby depriving them of the opportunity to attend preschool or kindergarten unless schools are made available through public funds.

Integrated schools and centers for young children have been established in most sections of the country. In many instances, this has meant busing children away from their residential neighborhoods, often eliminating within-walking-distance neighborhood schools and other neighborhood community facilities. In those communities in which mixed racial housing is now a fact, the opportunity for a return to neighborhood children's programs and to neighborhood schools is becoming possible.

Federal Public Law 94-142, enacted November 29, 1975, is designed to assure

Federal Public Law 94-142 assures all handicapped children between the ages of three and eighteen a free appropriate public education.

that all handicapped children between the ages of three and eighteen will have available to them a free appropriate public education.

The Social Security Act, as amended in 1981 as Public Law 97-35, established social services block grant programs. This program, usually referred to as Title XX, replaced among other titles, Title IV, which was of greatest concern to Early Childhood Education. The act provides for local and state planning and accountability. Funding requires the prior approval of a state plan. Because approval of state plans is prerequisite to funding, as would be expected, care programs vary in number and quality from state to state and from program to program.

Legislative trends

The trend toward provision of educational opportunities for greater numbers of children under the age of six has focused attention on the need to ensure that schools and centers for young children meet acceptable standards. Parents have faith in the term *school;* therefore, they frequently place their child in a center called a school without further investigation.

As early as 1879 state legislators began to enact laws permitting local school authorities to establish kindergartens. In a 1928 survey, Davis found that children's centers were expanding in number and enrollment at a rapid rate. This survey indicated that parents were seeking the best possible environment for their children; in addition, it indicated that parents desired guidance and cooperation in the supervision of the child's development.[58]

However, the strongest demand for provision and protection of schools for young children has come since 1940. Many states have taken legislative action regarding standards for schools for young children.

Legislative and federal action that pertains only to schools supported through public funds is not adequate. Many of the leaders of nonpublicly financed programs are giving aggressive leadership toward securing legislative action related to supervision and control of all schools for young children. Practically all states now provide for some authority vested either in the state or local officials to exercise some leadership function and to provide, in some instances, more or less limited supervision over nonpublic schools, either through directly expressed or implied legislative action.

Administering the programs for Early Childhood Education is either permissive or mandatory, depending on the type of legislative enactment. Legal authorization usually provides for some or all of the following: (1) registration and approval of schools; (2) authorization to develop rules and regulations for approval of nonpublic schools; (3) establishment of standards for schools; and (4) regulatory, administrative, supervisory, and leadership powers for each state's Department of Health, Education or Welfare.

Since the 1960s, as federal legislation relating to education of young children has been enacted, state legislation has followed in many areas. In addition, nonpublic funds have been made available for experimental and special programs.

Theories of learning

A look at the educational scene today must include not only an examination of programs for young children but also an analysis of the learning theories on which they are based. Education in America has been heavily influenced by stimulus–

---

[58] Davis, op. cit., pp. 1–15.

response (S–R) psychology. This behaviorist approach holds that the child is a purely reactive organism and reacts or responds rather than initiates; thus his or her behavior can be predicted from past experiences. Behaviorism as a psychological theory is represented by the well-known work of Ivan Pavlov, Edward Lee Thorndike, John B. Watson, Kenneth Spence, and Edwin Guthrie, among many others, and culminating in the work of B. F. Skinner.

In its simplest form, behaviorism teaches that all behavior is learned. The neurons automatically respond to incoming stimuli, and when such responses are strengthened by reward (reinforcement), learning takes place. However, without further reward or later reinforcement at certain intervals such responses are extinguished. In this manner, all responses (learning) can be shaped or modified by rewarding only predetermined desired responses. One of the strengths claimed by proponents of this approach is that "it works." The system is mechanistic and precise, and resulting behavior is highly predictable. Accordingly, in this view, one's behavior is molded by outside forces and measurable only by observable overt responses. Current behavioristic terminology places stress on "operant" conditioning and "behavior modification." For a description of a utopian society based on behavioristic principles, see the novel *Walden Two*.[59] Hence the need in programs for carefully planned structure and drill and for programmed materials of instruction reduced to small bits of information in order to assure success each step of the way. However, there have always been those who believe that children are capable of actively participating in and influencing their own behavior as they interact with the environment.

Most markedly opposed to behaviorism is a group of philosophies and theories that together are known as the humanistic approach to psychology. Proponents of humanism insist that the uniqueness of each individual is because of the fact that each human being has the inherent potential to become what he or she is actively and creatively, by behaving in ways that are consistent with his or her view of self. One behaves as a total, dynamic unity, accepting, rejecting, or acting upon external stimuli in keeping with one's own internalization of present and past events in terms of one's developed goals for self-realization. Thus the child has inner motivations (as compared to outer stimuli) that trigger response patterns. Under this view, learning environments are provided to enable the child to initiate and create rather than merely to respond to a fixed set of conditions.

A few of the many well-known leaders in the humanistic psychology movement include Gordon Allport, Arthur Combs, Abraham Maslow, Gardner Murphy, and Carl Rogers. The emerging school programs are largely based on one or the other or some variation of these opposing psychological viewpoints. When one is planning and executing programs, it is tempting to pick "the best" from each of the major theories—behaviorism and humanism. Educational research over a long period of time has indicated that most clearly defined learning theories produce good results

[59] B. F. Skinner, *Walden Two* (New York: Macmillan, 1948).

when applied consistently by a teacher who believes strongly in the theory and applies it uniformly to provide continuity.

The early work in child development as exemplified by the work of Gesell[60] would lead to the conclusion that behavior emerges in a fixed order or sequence according to a genetically determined timetable. Therefore, a child's development can be described in stages in relation to chronological time. The literature of the 1940s and 1950s described "typical two-year-olds," "typical five-year-olds," and so on. This approach led to the belief that innate forces peculiar to each child determined his or her "ability" to respond at any given time and that environmental experiences, though necessary, played a minor role in the child's behavior and learning. Instructional activities were designed to fit the stage of development for each child or for groups of "normal" children at each particular stage of development. Little attention was given to the possibility that response patterns could be changed or speeded up by intervention at some earlier point in time. Traditionally, schools have waited until the child displayed "readiness" for certain learnings or waited until a child fell behind the expected level of performance and then applied so-called remedial techniques in an effort to help the child "catch up." This is basically the approach of present-day "compensatory" programs.

It was not until the 1960s that the concept of intervention was used extensively to forestall expected deficiencies in learning. Placing major emphasis on intervention and compensatory techniques was the appropriately named Head Start program. It had been found that most children who didn't fit the expectations of the public school program were from lower-income families. Therefore, Head Start and similar programs were designed for children whose learning, physical, and social deficits were associated with problems faced by families with inadequate income. A new emphasis was also given to compensatory or remedial programs for children who were already behind in learning abilities when entering school. Both intervention and compensatory programs place more emphasis on environmental than on maturational influences than was previously true.

In recent years, the concept of critical periods in development has received much attention and has had a strong influence on programming experiences for young children. Biologists, who generally believe that the capacity to respond at any given time to specific aspects of the environment is genetically determined, were making breakthroughs of their own. Study of the genes, segments of the deoxyribonucleic acid (DNA) that fills the chromosomes in cell nuclei, suggested a master genetic code that provides a blueprint for life itself. Ribonucleic acid (RNA) is made in the nucleus of the cell by DNA and serves as the messenger to amino acids in the cell's cytoplasm, carrying out the genetic master plan. All the elements needed for any response an individual is capable of making are present in the DNA code at conception but do not go into operation until an appropriate environmental stimulus

---

[60] A. Gesell and Catherine S. Amatruda, *Developmental Diagnosis*, 2d ed. (New York: Harper, 1952).

triggers the response. While all the possibilities of growth, development, and learning are inherent, environment at all times plays an important role.

It is environment that must always fit the unfolding of the code. Consequently, throughout life there are critical periods during which the presence or absence of appropriate environmental stimuli results in following or altering DNA's master plan. A dramatic example of critical periods in development was the sharply increased incidence about a decade ago of babies being born with deformed or no arms and legs. The cause was traced to the fact that the mothers of these children had taken the tranquilizing drug thalidomide during the first seven weeks of gestation. The effects of maternal rubella (German measles) on the offspring during the prenatal period are well known. For a more detailed account of the biological bases of behavior and the importance of critical periods, see Beadle's lucid analysis.[61] There are also indications that chromosome aberrations may be directly responsible for certain behavioral characteristics. For example, in the case of Down's syndrome (mongolism) the child inherits three chromosomes of a given kind instead of the usual two.[62]

New discoveries of this type as well as findings in the fields of biochemistry and nutrition offer strong evidence that behavior described as "good" or "bad" by parents and teachers may well bear no relationship to the connotations thus implied and is not subject to change by known instructional strategies. Emerging schools are now often staffed with professionals from many disciplines who can detect and advise on procedures for those children who show early developmental or learning deviations. It would be all too easy to make the same error made by researchers and practitioners of the 1920s to the 1950s and assume that growth, development, and learning, though sequential through time, are fixed at conception and "unfold" according to each individual's timetable. Rather, what the newer evidence indicates is that, though growth, development, and learning are indeed sequential through time, the expression of the genetic potentialities is determined by environmental influences at any given time during the life of the individual. Although behaviors in the learning sphere are much more difficult to pinpoint than in the area of physical development, it can reasonably be said that a child who doesn't progress from random vocalizing of vowels to consonants to words within the first twenty-four months of life is likely to be severely handicapped in the use of language later.[63]

During the mid-1960s American education was badly in need of a panacea to remedy everything from poverty and unemployment to reaching the greatest potential of the gifted. There was an almost universal acceptance that early education could serve this purpose. Unanswerable questions arose immediately: How early should early education begin? Age five? Age four? Three or earlier? Who should

[61] Muriel Beadle, *A Child's Mind* (Garden City, N.Y.: Doubleday, 1970), pp. 11–24, 61–71.
[62] Ibid., p. 19.
[63] Ibid., p. 61.

receive early education? All children—or just those whose parents are poor and those who are "exceptional" in some way? What should be taught to young children? How should young children be taught and by whom? Which learning theory applies best to young children? Who should control schools for young children? The parents? The existing educational system? Or some other form of government or community organization? Because of these and similar questions, a wide variety of approaches and forms of control quickly emerged. They ranged from public or private Montessori schools to open classroom approaches and versions of the British Infant School.

As the nation approached the late 1970s, the evangelistic fervor of proponents of many varied schools of thought had somewhat abated. Fortunately, foundations and the federal and state governments insisted on research to validate or invalidate the effectiveness of sponsored innovations. The evidence is not all in, but certain trends are emerging. Among them are these:

1. Because of the uniqueness of each individual child, both genetically and experientially, no one approach is acceptable for all children.
2. Parents are important to the education of their young children, and parent involvement in the program can be an essential ingredient for success.
3. Specific content itself is not as important as the use that is made of the content to establish positive attitudes toward learning and toward self.
4. Young children, including very young infants, can and do learn. Because many authorities now feel that the first five years of life, including infancy, represent a critical period with regard to basic attitudes and values about self and others, the development of language, and the establishment of basic interpersonal relationships, programs for young children should not be entered into lightly and without careful planning and judicious use of qualified personnel.
5. Although aides, volunteers, and other paraprofessionals are now accepted as necessary and valuable personnel, adequately trained teachers and supervisory leaders are the most promising avenue to successful programs.
6. New and innovative practices in the preparation of teachers at both the pre-service and in-service levels are being developed.
7. As the age for starting education has moved downward from the traditional first-grade entrance at age six, there has been in each case mounting evidence that an earlier start was needed. Most prominent examples of programs designed to implement these findings are kindergartens for five-year-olds, Head Start, Home Start, a program to demonstrate alternate ways of providing Head Start type services for three-, four-, and five-year-old children where kindergartens were not available, and Parent-Child Centers for children from birth to three years of age. All represent efforts to enable large numbers of children to make use of learning opportunities provided by the nation's schools.
8. All recent programs place a new emphasis on the importance of early cognitive development, at the same time giving recognition to the profound influence of

good health and nutrition, healthy psychological and social development, and stable and accepting family relationships on successful learning.

9. Teachers and other staff personnel in these programs must be aware of the total needs of each child and be able to work with professionals in other fields to see that these needs are met. In fact, most programs now provide fully staffed components and consultative services in these areas to complement the educational process. Staffing of programs for young children is truly becoming interdisciplinary with differentiated but cooperative responsibilities.

10. The need for day care as mothers sought employment outside the home has brought about a reevaluation of many former programs for young and school age children. Without sacrificing quality care, innovative educational experiences are becoming an accepted component of full-day and year-round programs for infants and young children.

Types of programs for young children

Many types of children's programs are in operation today, and they vary as to purpose and program. Yet each type of program has a place in our society and has a contribution to make to the development of young children. Parents need help in selecting the best program for the child concerned.

Although the name of a center may not appear important, it should provide some guidance for selecting a school or center program. But the name is often misleading. This is because it is a common practice to select challenging and interesting names for programs even if the name selected is inconsistent with the purpose of a given program. In fact, the name may even convey the opposite impression of what the program really is. If you examine any local or state directory, such names will turn up as Finishing School for Tots, Kountry Klub for Kiddies, or Little Rascal's Heaven. Names such as Community Child Development Center or School for Young Children present a clearer indication of what one might expect to find.

Although most of today's programs for young children are not schools in the usual sense, still many parents and their children talk about "going to school," regardless of the type of program involved. As indicated, there is a vast array of services offered in the "world" of today's child. In any situation organized for children, learning takes place, whether desirable or undesirable. It is often difficult to distinguish a program designed primarily for the physical care of children from one that accepts the responsibility for a sound educational effort toward furthering the total development of each child involved.

It is little wonder that parents are confused and that Early Childhood Education specialists themselves often find themselves in disagreement about programs. In nearly every community we find "kindergartens" for three-, four-, and five-year-olds, Child Development Centers, nursery schools, comprehensive Family Day Care, Head Start centers, child-care centers, day care for exceptional children, schools for exceptional and handicapped preschool children, day care centers, co-operative child care, cooperative nursery schools, play schools, day and "drop-in" nurseries, child care programs for employees, babysitting services, and many more. For example, the Yellow Pages of the telephone directory of a city of 500,000 population lists 75 offerings under the heading Day Nurseries, 2 under Baby Sitters—Home Service, 91 under Schools—Nursery & Kindergarten (Academic), 6 Schools—Private, and 3 Child Development Centers. Of course, there are many duplications, which further adds to the confusion, and a large number are not even listed in the Yellow Pages. A brief definition of the most common types of preschool programs would appear useful to all concerned. The following descriptions are generally agreed upon by national organizations and authorities in the field of Early Childhood Education.

Nursery School. Nursery schools are often confused with day care centers, day nurseries, and nurseries. The nursery school is the first of a series of units making up an educational program. In public schools it usually is planned for four-year-olds; when operated under nonpublic school auspices, it generally includes children of three and four years of age. Because the emphasis is on an educational experience that includes socialization education, children under three years of age are seldom accepted except for children with special developmental deviations. The sessions are usually two and a half hours in length and may or may not take place five days a week, especially for the younger children.

In addition to the public and nonpublic nursery schools, there are many that may be classified according to the purposes they serve. These include cooperatives, those that serve as laboratories for research for an agency or institution, nursery schools sponsored by and for children of special groups, and nursery schools for children with special needs that cannot be provided for in the typical classroom. A large number of nursery schools serve as laboratories for observation of normal growth and development either by high school or college students.

Kindergarten. The school unit that enrolls five-year-olds, in some cases six-year-olds, on a regular basis for a year prior to first grade is designated as a kindergarten. This experience has usually been thought of as a transition from home to formal education or school. Today, however, most children have had a group experience away from home by the time they enter kindergarten. Consequently, much effort is being put forth to develop kindergarten curricula as a regular initial phase of the school's instructional program. In a few cases this was true in years past. Thus, kindergartens provide for a continuous educational experience under the guidance of a qualified teacher and in close cooperation with the parents. Many are a part of public school; others operate as church-related, privately owned, or sponsored special-purpose programs. Some, whether private or public, are full-day sessions, but many run half-day sessions. Though this is not recommended, it is common for one teacher to have two groups of children, one in the morning and one in the afternoon.

Child Development Center.   The designation of a comprehensive early childhood development program in the form of a Child Development Center was made popular by the Head Start program. The center is usually organized around activity rooms for various ages, from a few weeks after birth to age five or six, depending on the availability of kindergartens in the community. In addition, various amounts of space are available for play areas inside and out, facilities for food preparation and for conducting a health program, and provisions for parents to meet and to take part in instructional programs often of a home- and personal-improvement nature. As total development of the child in the context of the home and family is usually the major emphasis and though a key thrust is always a carefully planned educational experience, provision is made for a program for early diagnosis of problems not always recognized by parents, including dental, medical, and emotional problems. This type of program is both a concept and a community facility. It is a drawing together of all the resources in a community—both family and professional— that can contribute to the child's total development. The skills of professional workers in the fields of education, health, welfare, and related areas are utilized in building a program for each child. In the planning, it is recognized that both professionals and nonprofessionals can make a meaningful contribution; therefore, the family is emphasized as fundamental to the child's total development. The parents have an important role in developing policies and participating in the program. The concept of the child development center was used as a model for Head Start centers.

Unfortunately, there is a tendency on the part of many parents and paraprofessionals to feel that, when physical and safety needs have been met, all the child's needs have been met. As a result, some child development centers, often underfunded, are nothing more than depots for children of welfare parents. This of course, need not be the case, for the child development center concept is a sound one when adequately funded and operated by adequately qualified professional and paraprofessional personnel.

School for Exceptional Children.   The school for exceptional children is developed to meet the needs of an atypical child. Frequently, the entrance age is younger than three years, and special provisions are made for early diagnosis, treatment, and guidance of the atypical child. Teachers in these specialized schools require additional training, and clinical services are provided for teacher and parents as they work closely together in meeting specific mental, physical, or social needs of the child. Other provisions are discussed in Chapter 17.

Cooperative Nursery School and/or Kindergarten.   Cooperative nursery schools and kindergartens serve a real purpose in our present-day life. Through this program many children have opportunities to participate in an educational program within the limits of the family's income. Often these schools serve a twofold purpose, providing an intensive program of parent education as well as worthwhile educational experiences for the children. Some cooperatives are operated by parents under church sponsorship; others are neighborhood or community ventures sponsored by parents only. Most of these schools provide for a director qualified in Early Childhood Education who is assisted by the parents. As they work with the children, parents receive guidance and close supervision from the director. The term *cooperative* itself implies that each parent contributes services or time to the ongoing program.

Child Day Care Center and Day Nursery.   Child day care centers and day nurseries are planned to provide for the care of children whose mothers work. The length of time that the child remains at the center depends upon the mother's schedule of employment. Some offer an effective educational program whereas others place greater emphasis on custodial care. Some are organized specifically to provide for children from less privileged homes. At times the necessity to be self-sustaining or to provide an income or both, especially in the private sector, makes it difficult to provide a satisfactory arrangement that will benefit the child. However, the infusion of federal and, to a lesser extent, state funds into programs for children of the poor, which enables mothers of young children to engage in gainful employment, has brought attention to the problems of children in care services.

Family Day Care still provides care for more children in the United States than does any other type. Families provide care for a few children, often along with their own children, for remuneration. This service may be either purchased with public funds or paid for by the parents of the children served. Recognizing public responsibility for child care, Congress has passed legislation allowing sizable tax breaks when care is paid for by working parents. These provisions are constantly being studied and revised to help parents out as increasing numbers of women have become gainfully employed over the past several years.

Because of the large number of homes involved, Family Day Care programs range from inadequate babysitting services to those that provide the security and experiences very young children were usually provided in their own homes before so many mothers were not home during the day. In many ways, family day care has the potential of being better than that provided by often large and impersonal, but highly organized, publicly supported centers. This is especially true for infants and very young children when the continuity and security of the same caregiver or caregivers is so important to the forming of attachment bonds, self-identification, and later personality development.[64]

[64] J. Bowlby, *Attachment and Loss*, Vol. I (New York: Basic, 1969).

Play School.   Play school programs are usually operated under the sponsorship of a church, an organized group of parents, or a civic club; as part of a recreation program; or by a service set up for the care of underprivileged children. In many cases, play schools have expanded their facilities in order to incorporate activities formerly considered as those provided in a nursery school or kindergarten or both.[65] Closely related is a play program called a Drop-in Nursery, usually sponsored by a church, civic group, or shopping center. Children do not attend regularly but attend at the convenience of the parents, thus enabling the mother or father to have "some time off" or to do the shopping. Fees are usually on an hourly basis.

Innovative practices

Changes are taking place in the areas of curriculum, organization, and instruction, and experimentation is under way in the content areas as well as in reading and language development. Children in some situations have been encouraged to inquire on their own and to learn through discovery. Team teaching and multiage and multicultural groupings have become rather commonplace in programs for young children.

Interest, need, and research findings have translated into a great deal of expense and effort for the development of new materials, new methods, and model curricula for use with infants and preschool-age children. Delivery systems in operation range from computer-assisted individualized instruction in the home to elaborate and highly structured school or center arrangements. Perhaps this diversity represents one of the greatest strengths of Early Childhood Education, whether found in public schools or in private-for-profit offerings or as a service to employees of business or factory. Almost every community in the country has children's preschool child care centers operated by private individuals. In some cases, business firms provide child care programs for children of employees. It is significant that the private sector of society, including business and industry, is involved along with public agencies and the public schools.

Beginning in 1970, the U.S. Office of Child Development embarked on a program of involving nongovernment child development experts, day care and Early Childhood Education practitioners, and parents in a series of workshops, task forces, and related assignments culminating in a series of bulletins on day care. This series represents one of the best sources of information available. Because these bulletins are published by an agency of the federal government, they may be obtained from the Superintendent of Documents, U.S. Government Printing Office, Washington, D.C. 20402. Though the cost is always very modest, it is wise to write for current prices as they may change from time to time.

---

[65] Hazel F. Gabbard, "Status and Trends in Early Childhood Education," *Those First School Years*, Vol. 40 (Washington, D.C.: NEA, 1960) pp. 219–221.

Many of the programs have been motivated and influenced by the special problems and needs of children who come from environmental conditions thought to handicap them severely in their present development and later success in school. Goodlad and Klein point out, however, that the early education of all children, whether environmentally disadvantaged or not, should be guided by sound principles of learning and development.[66]

Some of the innovative practices based on particular points of view are briefly described here. No one innovation is the answer for all learners and all situations. Each must be carefully evaluated before being adopted.

Open Space Centers. Open space centers provide the setting for a new kind of learning experience planned in terms of the potentialities of children and the environment. The open space concept in teaching is, as much as anything, a state of mind.[67] It is the structuring of a living situation with a wide range of educational alternatives.[68] Facilities for such a center include large open spaces that can be used flexibly and in a number of ways. There are no separate, individual classrooms. The teacher does not work alone, but with an available team of adults, made up of teachers, aides, and volunteers.

Open education is considered by some as the legacy of the Progressive Education movement. Recalling the critics of progressive education, we should point out that open education is a carefully planned learning experience based on the observed needs of the children enrolled and is not a free-for-all, do-as-you-please smorgasbord as critics would have one believe.

British Infant School. The British Infant School, although English in origin, is thought by some to reflect many of the characteristics of Progressive Education in America.[69] The infant stage of British education includes children from four to seven years of age and utilizes vertical or family grouping. Children of varying ages are placed together in the same class as a deliberate educational policy.[70] Lavatelli points out that play is more explicitly used for cognitive growth than in the American child-centered schools.[71]

Rogers[72] lists the salient features of the British philosophy as follows:

[66] J. I. Goodlad, M. Frances Klein, and associates, *Behind the Classroom Door* (Worthington, Ohio: Jones, 1970), p. 7.

[67] AASA, *Open Space Schools* (Washington, D.C.: American Association of School Administrators, 1971), p. 20.

[68] J. Macdonald, "The Open School: Curriculum Concepts," *Open Education* (Washington, D.C., NAEYC, 1970), p. 26.

[69] B. Spodek, "Introduction," *Open Education* (Washington, D.C.: NAEYC, 1970), p. 7.

[70] Mary A. Mycock, "Vertical Grouping" in *Teaching in the British Primary School*, ed. by V. R. Rogers (New York: Macmillan, 1970), pp. 34–35.

[71] Celia S. Lavatelli, *Piaget's Theory Applied to an Early Childhood Curriculum* (Boston: American Science and Engineering, 1970), p. 23.

[72] V. R. Rogers, *Teaching in the British Primary School* (New York, Macmillan, 1970), p. 7.

Children should live fully and richly now. Education is life, not preparation for life.

The curriculum is a series of jumping off places and emerges through the mutual interests and explorations of children and teachers working together.

Studies are interrelated and cut across subject matter lines.

The teacher is "largely a stage setter," a stimulator who encourages and guides but who does not appear to direct.

Teachers are concerned with how the child learns, the significance of the process; the development of independence and responsibility in children. Teachers care deeply about children and respect children's ideas.

Piaget's Theories. Lavatelli describes Piaget's theory as a developmental one, pointing out that, according to this theory, the thinking of all children tends to go through the same stages and usually when they are about the same age.[73] Using what Piaget identified as the important cognitive developments for children, Lavatelli has planned a curriculum centered on classification, space and number, and seriation, based on step-by-step development in these areas. Short structured periods are utilized along with self-directed periods of play. Directed learning activities are conducted by a teacher with a small group of children. The concepts acquired are reinforced during play. The children's observations are directed to phenomena they might otherwise miss.

Other programs based on Piaget's theory have been developed, and each holds that the child learns by doing. The differences in the programs, however, stem from what is meant by doing, what is meant by experience, and how the child constructs knowledge.[74] Piaget's theories are also discussed in Chapters 9 and 11.

A Developmental–Interaction Point of View. The Bank Street Program is based on a theory developed by Biber et al.[75] to promote cognitive growth. It emphasizes the identifiable patterns of growth, the child's interaction with the environment (people as well as material objects), and the interaction between the cognitive and affective spheres of development. It is based on "a consistent philosophy of education comprising values, goals, and strategies congruent with a humanistic approach. Central to this philosophy are concepts of competence, interpersonal relatedness, individuality, and creativity."[76] Cognitive categories for use in analyzing teaching techniques have been developed and illustrated.

Cognitively Oriented Curriculum. The academically oriented centers are primarily interested in the cognitive development of children and in speeding up the acquisition of academic skills. Most controversial is the Bereiter and Engelmann

[73] Lavatelli, op. cit., p. 24–27.
[74] G. E. Forman and Catherine T. Fosnot, "The Use of Piaget's Constructivism in Early Childhood Education Programs," in B. Spodek (ed.), op. cit., pp. 185–203.
[75] Barbara Biber, et al., *Promoting Cognitive Growth: A Developmental Interaction Point of View* (Washington, D.C.: NAEYC, 1971).
[76] Ibid., p. 7.

program for disadvantaged children with the emphasis on preacademic skills in reading, language, and arithmetic. Weikart et al. developed a cognitively oriented program in which attention is not explicitly paid to the affective development of the child. Proponents feel that these needs are met through the style of classroom operation that the curriculum creates.[77]

Process Approach.   Berman[78] holds that any carefully designed conception of curriculum must be based on some fundamental assumptions about human beings, whom she considers to be "process-oriented beings." Curriculum is therefore concerned with process and process skills that include perceiving, communication, loving, decision making, knowing, organizing, creating, and valuing. Teachers at the University of Maryland Center for Young Children, using the process approach in developing a curriculum for young children, have focused on the process of "decision making." They developed suggestions for teacher statements, designed to focus the children's thinking on possibilities, outcomes, and awareness that choices have been made. Examples of the suggested statements follow.[79]

Thinking of possibilities: "Where do you think you could work?" "What other way could you have . . . ?"

Thinking of outcomes: "What else could you do to . . . avoid . . . ?" ". . . stop . . . ?" ". . . help . . . ?"

Technology and the young child

It is commonly held that television, computers, teaching machines, tape recorders, and a host of other electronic devices, games, and kits of programmed materials offer hope of breaking the age-old boring procedures used in many of the public schools. In effect, it is claimed that modern technology has the potential of bringing about a "revolution" in education. Almost all these devices offer the self-evaluation and immediate feedback features much sought by educators, parents, and taxpayers. Seizing an opportunity beginning in the early 1960s and late 1950s, huge commercial firms, often conglomerates, sought to provide the necessary hardware and often the "software" or programs for the emerging revolution in education.

As preschool programs gained priority, mainly because of federal and foundation funding, the availability of "complete" educational programs for young children greatly increased. Today preschool teachers and administrators can choose from an almost endless variety of kits, programmed and talking books, packaged learning materials, computer-assisted or computer-managed instructional materials, prepared television tapes, and the usual array of what were formerly known as audio-

---

[77] D. P. Weikart, *The Cognitively Oriented Curriculum* (Washington, D.C.: NAEYC, 1971).

[78] Louise M. Berman, *New Priorities in the Curriculum* (Columbus, Ohio: Merrill, 1968).

[79] Louise M. Berman (ed.), *Decision Making in Young Children: Part I, Monograph II* (College Park: University of Maryland, 1971), p. 48.

visual instructional materials. The list is almost endless. Yet after twenty years the impact has been visible only where programs have been heavily funded and researched; these programs often stopped when outside funds were no longer available. The most common research finding is that children in these programs achieve as well as they would under less costly conventional methods.

There are two commonly recognized problems with the use of educational technology—excessive cost and the fact that technology lends itself best to instructional programming based on behavioristic theory. Many educators, however—especially teachers—accept more readily procedures and materials based on humanistic approaches. This is especially true in relation to programs for young children. For a thought-provoking analysis of educational technology, see "The Myth of Educational Technology." [80]

Sesame Street. Although there are many programs for young children on commercial and educational television, none has captured the imagination of audiences (of all ages) to the extent that "Sesame Street" has. The multimillion-dollar program, funded by grants from the Carnegie Foundation, the Ford Foundation, the U.S. Office of Education, the Office of Economic Opportunity, and other federal agencies, went on the air on 163 public television stations on November 10, 1969. Its purpose was to determine whether television could teach preschool children via popular approaches used by commercial television. Berkman[81] suggests that "something just drastic" could happen to the generation of children, regardless of race or family income, who have watched "Sesame Street" regularly. He feels that schools, as they now exist, could "turn off" large numbers of children who are accustomed to "Sesame Street" exposure, necessitating a profound effect on early grade education. Edward L. Palmer,[82] vice-president and director of research at The Children's Television Workshop, which created and produced "Sesame Street," has described the careful planning and research involved in this best-known effort to teach young children by television.

To the authors of this text, "Sesame Street" represents a pioneer experiment in Early Childhood Education—an attempt to bring about social change as well as early cognitive learning. It is a well-known fact that children have different learning styles in keeping with their early family and cultural influences. There is evidence that certain children, especially children denied early exposure to cognitive experiences that best fit them for the demands made upon them when entering school, learn best when exposed to more structured, repetitive bits of information. "Sesame Street," with its deep roots in behaviorism, fits this requirement well. However, the authors feel that for most children real-life experiences strongly buttressed in

[80] D. Berkman, "The Myth of Educational Technology," *The Educational Forum*, **36**:14 (1972), pp. 451–460.

[81] Ibid., p. 460.

[82] E. L. Palmer, "Television Instruction and the Preschool Child," *International Journal of Early Education*, **4**:1 (OMEP, Dublin, Ireland: Irish U. P., 1972), pp. 11–17.

early sensory-motor experiences, as indicated in Piaget's theory,[83] are essential for later, more complex forms of *learning*.

Television.   Although television and other forms of technology are of immense importance in assisting learning, they should never be expected to replace the human element in the instructional process. Nor should behaviorally oriented programs exclude the values and creative initiative inherent in teaching strategies based on humanistic theory.

In a recent review of the effects of television viewing on preschool behavior, Moore[84] summarizes the effect from a review of the research. Children, at least over the short term, do learn prosocial behavior from such programs as "Mr. Roger's Neighborhood," changes in attitudes and behaviors from those like "Sesame Street," and behave in less prosocial behaviors after viewing certain other types of programs. The long-term effects have not yet been determined by research.

Postman, however, holds that the media (primarily television) are preventing children from being childlike by bombarding them with the adult "secrets" of sexuality and aggression. These secrets, he contends, were once available through the rite of passage called reading, which took time to learn. Television viewing, on the other hand, is a passive activity requiring no educational process; it is available to all persons from infancy.[85]

Microcomputers.   As microcomputers appropriate for young children become less expensive, questions arise as to productive ways in which they can be used. The computer can be used as a tool for teaching and can produce results in the development of basic skills. Another use of the computer is as a tool for thinking. Such use, according to its advocates, will help children to expand their cognitive and social worlds.[86]

In the fall of 1982 microcomputers were introduced into the classrooms at the Center for Young Children, University of Maryland, College Park. The Center staff consider the microcomputer as one of many teaching tools and are exploring its use in the areas of graphic art, science, language arts, math, and social studies. The child is helped to understand that the microcomputer is a machine programmed by people and to view himself or herself as the person in control. This is the beginning of a sound computer literacy program.[87]

[83] B. J. Wadsworth, *Piaget's Theory of Cognitive Development* (New York: McKay, 1971), p. 33.
[84] Shirley G. Moore, "The Effect of Television Viewing on the Prosocial Behavior of Young Children," *Young Children*, **32**:5 (July 1977), pp. 60–65.
[85] Neil Postman, *The Disappearance of Childhood* (New York: Delacorte, 1982).
[86] S. B. Silvern, "Opening the Door to the Microworld," *Child. Educ.*, **59**:4 (1983), pp. 219–221.
[87] Marilyn Church, "Microcomputers As A Creative Part of the Preschool Curriculum: A Computer Discovery Center Project Report," (mimeographed), presented at the National Educational Computing Conference, Baltimore, MD, June 5, 1983.

Change in perspective

Research conducted during the late 1950s and the early 1960s clearly demonstrated that at a very early age a child can master rather complex learnings, such as the abilities to read and to master complex mathematical concepts. Concurrently, emphasis on the necessity of a college education was increasing, and the demands for more and better education caused parents to become greatly concerned about the adequacy of their children's education. It was logical to assume that the more a child learned as early as possible, the better his or her chances would be to meet college entrance requirements. The proponents of a child-centered philosophy for nursery and kindergarten programs found themselves widely criticized by a new influx of researchers and scholars who held that the mastery of knowledge was not only possible and desirable at an early age, but necessary to later school success. It is small wonder that parents were worried if their children were not taught to read in kindergarten.

When this need for effective curriculum development and programming in Early Childhood Education arose, there was a paucity of thoroughly researched programs to provide guidance for the rapidly developing programs. As a result, large-scale federal and foundation funds, usually in the form of research and development grants, were made available to universities, schools, individuals, and consulting and technical assistance firms. Those conducting the programs were sometimes without previous training or experience in Early Childhood Education. The newly developing multimedia industry also quickly rose to the challenge. As a result, packaged programs complete with sponsors and consultative services were soon a part of the Early Childhood Education scene. Their goal was the development of exportable models and corresponding materials for sale or adoption by those conducting programs for young children.

The models and materials fall roughly into four categories: (1) those stressing basic learning skills through the use of behavioristic techniques, (2) those stressing the importance of parents on the instructional team, (3) those employing individualized instruction, and (4) those based on humanistic approaches. Some, of course, do not fall clearly into any one of these categories and are more eclectic in nature.

In actual practice there are only a few programs using exported models. Most programs for young children continue to stress the importance of children's needs. An effort is usually made to stress the importance of learning environment based on an understanding of child development. These programs usually have less structure than the models and permit children more freedom to explore their feelings and environment in imaginative and play-type activities. The teacher or caregiver serves as an observing guide, encouraging the children to participate in activities allowed by a prearranged environment. Such programs emphasize personal and social development with less emphasis on skills believed to be needed "later." Although difficult to evaluate because of the lack of specifics, to some extent all show more concern for preplanned activities to reach more specific objectives than was generally true of programs a decade ago.

Importance of cooperative effort

Many organizations are interested in the educational welfare of children at the local, state, regional, and national levels. Representatives from these organizations are working together closely to provide educational opportunities that allow children to reach their highest potential as they enter the continuous program of education from childhood through adulthood. Their cooperative efforts have greatly aided in securing better legislation, improved facilities and staff, and additional funds for programs for young children.

Through the years, this willingness of leaders to work together for the development of the programs of good schools for young children has been evident. This cooperative effort in searching for better ways to provide educational opportunities for the young child has resulted in the present-day recognition of the implications of these experiences for the continued education of the child. Through an analysis of the strengths and weaknesses of the present programs, a basis for improved educational opportunities can be established. America has faith in education and holds to the belief that all children should have access to the best possible educational opportunities according to each child's potential. This faith and belief should continue to give direction to the expansion of the present-day schools and to the development of new programs for young children in the world of today and tomorrow.

SUMMARY

The history, trends, and issues in preschool programs that have been presented include the following:

1. Extending public schools downward to include kindergarten, nursery school, child development centers, and programs for infants.
2. Developing pilot programs for infants and their families.
3. Changing patterns of school organization and adapting programs for specific purposes, such as those for the culturally different or for exceptional children.
4. Changing emphasis in day care programs to educational programs as well as day care.
5. Changing curriculum for preschool children by differentiating goals, activities, and materials to provide for individual differences within the group.
6. Changing the role of the teacher to that of a guide of child development as opposed to a director of activities.

7. Continuing need for church-related and private schools for preschool children.
8. Seeking an interdisciplinary influence in the training and experience of staff members and using volunteers and paraprofessionals with differentiated responsibilities extensively.
9. Expanding cooperative programs for preschool children.
10. Changing parent participation to parent involvement and replacing formal parent education with a cooperative teacher-parent team approach, which utilizes parents in the instructional programs of their children in both home and center.
11. Establishing longitudinal programs, such as Follow Through, for children aged three to nine, to study the effects of several well-defined and planned innovative approaches to the education of young children.

In an analysis of these trends, it will be noted that some are positive and good for children; others indicate situations that contradict all that is known about how children grow and learn. Shortened sessions and large groups of children are being accepted as emergency measures. Too frequently there has been a tendency to rationalize and accept these makeshift arrangements rather than to evaluate the services in terms of the effect on children. The present confusion regarding what is good for children must be cleared up and, in order to do this, there must be some guidelines by which to evaluate trends, a cooperative effort on the part of all those who are concerned with educational programs for young children.

Because of the high cost of Early Childhood Education, exportable models, programs using educational technology, and packaged instructional materials have been developed in an effort to make early learning experiences available to a greater number of young children. Changing social values and the rising numbers of mothers of young children in the labor market have created a need for more day care facilities. Public and professional demands have mandated an educational component in all such programs.

These developments have placed unprecedented demands on training programs, stressing the need for consultative services, in-service training, and on-the-job training. Most colleges and universities have responded with greatly expanded, innovative approaches of staff members, both professional and paraprofessional, including parents and volunteers.

Suggested Activities

1. Using the most recent census data, determine how many children in your home (or college) community are three through six years of age. Find out how many are in some kind of center for children. In what proportion of homes in your community does a need exist for nursery schools, kindergartens, or all-day care centers? Plan a discussion on the need for child care centers. Include members of the community other than teachers in this discussion.

2. Contact your state's Department of Education for statistics concerning the number of new kindergartens and other preschool programs established during the past five years. Chart or plot your findings. Explain the change.
3. View the film *The Preschool Experience: Four Programs* (New York: McGraw-Hill).
4. Make a survey of centers for children in your community. Trace the historical development of a selected number according to types. List requirements for admission, length of day, and types of services offered.
5. Compile a directory of these schools with an annotation showing services offered and so forth.
6. Compile a report of laws pertaining to schools and centers for young children in your state and in your community. Discuss the historical development of these laws and what provisions are made for enforcing them in your local community.
7. Have a panel discussion on present strengths and improvements needed in schools for young children in your area. Present statistical data to support this discussion.
8. Investigate the Head Start program, defining provisions made by the federal government and the relationship to state and local community. Describe programs in operation in your community, listing strengths and weaknesses.
9. Because of changing social and fiscal conditions, parents and those responsible for education are crying for results and achievement. Check with several programs in the community and report what each is doing about this concern.
10. Discuss pending legislation relative to schools for young children (at the national level, the state level, and the local level).
11. Visit three full day programs for children and describe the educational component of each. Find out what their objectives are, the methods used to attain them, and the evaluative procedures used.
12. Ask your librarian how to use the services of ERIC as a resource for your studies in Early Childhood Education.
13. Talk with several first-grade teachers and ask them what they would like children to be able to do when they enter first grade.
14. Consult the Yellow Pages of your local telephone directory to determine the types of schools for young children in your community. Visit at least three that appear to be different from the others, such as Montessori, academically oriented, or cooperative nursery schools. Evaluate each.
15. Ask your instructor to help you locate a research project (preschool) that you can correspond with by telephone or by letter or both, or perhaps that you can visit "on your own." Determine the "problem" being researched, the methods employed to find answers, and how the researchers view the project in relation to public policy.
16. View one of the following programs for young children for the microcomputer: Juggles Rainbow, Moptown, Bumble Games, or Gertrude's Secrets: The Learning Company, 4370 Alpine Road, Portola Valley, CA. 94023.

Related Readings

Almy, Millie. "Reoccurring Issues in Early Childhood Education." *The Early Childhood Educator at Work.* New York: McGraw-Hill, 1975.

ASCD. "Federal Funds to Assist or to Control?" *Educ. Leadership,* **24:**1 (1966).

Aties, Phillippe. *Centuries of Childhood.* New York: Vintage, 1965.

Baylor, Ruth M. *Elizabeth Palmer Peabody.* Philadelphia: U. of Pennsylvania, 1965.

Bennett, Neville S. "Time and Space: Curriculum Allocation and Pupil Involvement in British Open-Space Schools." *The Elementary School Journal,* **82** (Sept. 1981).

Biber, Barbara. "A Developmental Interaction Approach." in *The Preschool in Action.* Ed. by Mary Carol Day and R. K. Parker. Boston: Allyn, 1977.

Bissell, Joan S. *Implementation of Planned Variation in Head Start,* First Year Report, I, Review and Summary. Washington, D.C.: U.S. DHEW, OCD, 1971.

Castaneda, Alfreda, et al. *The Educational Needs of Minority Groups.* Lincoln, Neb.: Professional Educator's Publications, 1974.

"Children in the Age of Microcomputers." *Child. Educ.,* **59:**4 (1983), pp. 218–258.

Church, J. (ed.). *Three Babies.* New York: Random, 1966.

Concept of A Child Development Center, Relationship to Preschool and Day Care. Washington, D.C.: OEO, 1965.

Copple, Carol, Irving E. Sigel, and Ruth Saunders, *Educating the Young Thinker: Classroom Strategies for Cognition Growth.* New York: D. Van Nostrand, 1979.

Davis, G. *Childhood and History in America.* New York: Psychohistory Press, 1976.

Demause, L. *The History of Childhood.* New York: Psychohistory Press, 1974.

Dennis, Wayne. *Children of the Creche.* New York: Appleton, 1976.

Dittman, Laura L. "Project Head Start Becomes a Long-Distance Runner." *Young Children* **35:**6 (1980), pp. 4–9.

Divoky, Diane. "Early Childhood Education: Who's Doing What to Whom and Why?" M. Kaplan-Sanoff and R. Yablans-Magid (eds). *Exploring Early Childhood.* New York: Macmillan, 1981.

Frank, L. K. *On the Importance of Infancy.* New York: Random, 1966.

Gardner, J. E. *Paraprofessionals Work with Troubled Children.* New York: Wiley and Sons, 1975.

Gartner, A., et al. (eds.). *Paraprofessionals in Education.* New York: Human Sciences Press, 1976.

Harris, NiNi. "The Carondelet Historic Center and Susan Blow: Preserving Kindergarten History." *Child. Educ.* **59:**5 (1983), pp. 336–338.

Haskins, R. and J. J. Gallager (eds). *Care and Education of Young Children in America: Policy, Politics and Social Science.* Norwood, N.J.: Ablex, 1980.

Honig, A. S. "The Family Development Research Program with Emphasis on the Children's Center Curriculum." In *Compendium of Curricula for Toddlers and Infants.* Ed. by A. S. Bardwell. Columbus, Ohio: Ohio State U.P., 1973.

Katz, Lillian G. (ed.). *Current Topics in Early Childhood Education,* Vol. 1. Hillsdale, N.J.: Lawrence Erlbaum Assoc., 1977.

Katz, Lillian G. "Perspectives on Early Childhood Education." *The Educational Forum,* **37** (May 1973), pp. 393–398. Also in M. Kaplan-Sanoff and R. Yablans (eds). *Exploring Early Childhood.* New York: Macmillan, 1981, pp. 3–7.

Leidermann, H. P., et al. (eds.). *Culture and Infancy.* New York: Academic, 1977.

Levitt, Edith. "Views of Cognition in Children: 'Process' vs. Product Approach." *Young Children,* **23:**4 (1968), pp. 225–232.

Light, N. S., chm. *Early Childhood Education, Part II,* 46th Yearbook (NSSE) Bloomington, Ill.: Public School Publishing Co., 1929.

Lilliard, Paula Polk. *Montessori, a Modern Approach.* New York, Schocken Books, 1972.

Meek, Lois M., chm. *Pre-school and Parental Education, Part I, Organization and Development, and Part II, Research and Method,* 28th Yearbook (NSSE). Bloomington, Ill.: Public School Publishing Co., 1929.

Milhollan, F. *From Skinner to Rogers—Contrasting Approaches to Education.* Lincoln, Neb.: Professional Educator's Publications, 1972.

Osborn, D. Keith. *Early Childhood Education in Historical Perspective,* 2nd ed. Athens, Ga.: Education Associates, 1980.

Papert, S. *Mindstorms, Children, Computers and Powerful Ideas.* New York: Basic Books, Inc., 1980.

A Parent's Guide to Day Care. Washington, D.C.: U.S. Dept. of Health and Human Services, DHHS Publication No. (OHDS) 80-30254.

Rasmussen, Margaret (ed.). *Readings from Childhood Education.* Washington, D.C.: ACEI, 1966.

Snyder, Agnes, et al. *Dauntless Women in Childhood Education 1856–1931.* Washington, D.C. ACEI, 1972.

Spodek, Bernard (ed.). *Handbook of Research in Early Childhood Education.* New York: Free Press, 1982.

Suransky, Valerie P. *The Erosion of Childhood.* Chicago: U. of Chicago Press, 1982.

Vernon, Libby. "For Parents Particularly: Parents Consider Computers the Challenge of the '80's," *Child. Educ.,* **59**:4 (1983), pp. 267–270.

Verzaro-Lawrence, Marce. "Early Childhood Education: Issues For A New Decade," *Child. Educ.,* **57**:2 (1980), pp. 104–109.

Weber, Evelyn. *The Kindergarten: Its Encounter with Educational Thought in America,* New York: Teachers College, 1969.

Zigler, E. P. and E. W. Gordon (eds). *Day Care: Scientific and Social Policy Issues.* Boston: Auburn House, 1981.

CHAPTER 2

The Changing World of the Young Child

"When in recent memory has it been less a privilege to be young in America?" In answering this question, Scott Spencer calls attention to the closing of public schools and the slashing of domestic budgets.[1] It appears that social and educational programs will not be in the favor they once enjoyed. There have been and will continue to be changes. These changes will be both good and bad. It is important to consider what has happened and what is predicted for the 1980s.[2]

THE CHILD'S WORLD

Improvements in the means of travel and mobility associated with career opportunities have been such that many young children, long before their entrance to first grade, have traveled a great deal and have lived in many different and varied com-

---

[1] S. Spencer, "Childhood's End," in *Their Future Is Now . . . Today Is for Children*, ed. by Laura L. Dittmann and Marjorie E. Ramsey. (Washington, D.C.: ACEI, 1982), p. 20.
[2] D. K. Osborn, "Changes in the 1980's That will Affect Education," in *Today Is for Children*, ed. by Laura L. Dittman and Marjorie E. Ramsey. (Washington, D.C.: ACEI, 1982), pp. 10–15.

munities. Their eyes have thus been opened to a wider variety of experiences than that of many of the significant adults in their lives at the time of their entrance into preschool programs of whatever kind.

Although today the young child's world clearly offers more opportunities, it has a two-pronged effect, for it can equally be both confining and restricting, as well as frustrating and anxiety-producing. Today's child is influenced by many forces outside the home and family, some of which are social; some economic; some, political; and others, philosophical. The child's individual personality is molded by the pressures and decrees of society. In addition, the child's development is shaped by others in the life space—by parents, other adults, peers, and siblings. The behavior of those who bring up and instruct the child is also affected by the influences of society, and this enters the total equation in the way it is reflected in the child's development.

During their lifetime, the adults responsible for the young child's care and guidance have seen many changes in society, but they may not recognize that the present is the only world known to the young child. It is difficult for older adults, who so vividly remember their own childhood, to appreciate that young children, even young adults, cannot even relate to the recent past agrarian and village and small-city cultural society that was America when they were growing up. If children are to understand and connect with their rich heritage, the daily curricular offerings will have to provide opportunities for experiencing some of the activities in which their forebears engaged in the process of living. Visiting farms, forests, and blacksmith shops; making butter; and learning how to grow vegetables will give today's youngsters a taste of what life was like in days gone by. It will also bring them closer to older people who were brought up in that quite different world.

INFLUENCE OF TELEVISION

A prime example of an all-pervasive influence on children's lives is television. Most significant has been the universal availability of television from birth on. Estimates vary, but most authorities agree that, in terms of time involved, television eclipses all other categories of influences when time engaged is a major criterion. It is likely that TV is a contributing factor in how children learn to solve personal conflicts and problems. Force and violence, because they are necessary to produce "action," are the most commonly used means to find solutions.

Television has become a popular means of dissemination of research findings concerning children and families. Often such findings are reported somewhat informally on talk shows, the news, or documentaries long before they appear in print in professional and scientific journals. "Ninety-five per cent of American homes have at least one TV set."[3] A Neilsen study indicated that children under five years

[3] Helen A. Britton, *Television Violence and Youth Attitude Toward Law Enforcement: A Proposal for Critical Viewing Skills* (New York: American Bar Association, 1980), p. 146.

of age watch 23.5 hours of TV weekly.[4] The average preschooler spends 64 per cent of his time watching the tube.[5] This means about 3.5 hours a day that children watch television.[6] All too often TV serves as a babysitting device. William Glasser[7] points out that the "affluent television world" has created a new breed of children who feel self-important, have a need to be entertained, and are all too often passive recipients of the world around them. It should be noted, however, that despite certain handicaps, TV is a supervehicle for disseminating information for both children and adults. How children view their world is certainly strongly influenced by what they have seen on their TV sets. Parental guidance is needed in the choice and selection of programs viewed by children.

THE CHANGING FAMILY

Parents have traditionally worked in the fields, in the home, in the business "downstairs" beneath the family living quarters, or at a nearby place of employment. A major difference today is that the parents work where the children cannot see or contact them. Today's parents are dealing with temporary and frequent or regular periods of separation from their children. Consequently, much of the daily socialization that was formerly a natural part of family life is now provided by others.

The extended family, once the primary source of alternate caregivers, is virtually nonexistent. Only about 5 per cent of children with gainfully employed mothers have a "spare" adult in the family or household to care for them while their parents work.

A rapidly growing phenomenon in America is the one-parent family. Nearly 50 per cent of the children who were born in the late 1970s will spend part of their lives in single-parent homes before they are eighteen years old.[8] Since 1970 there has been a 79 per cent increase in single-parent families.[9] Accompanying this increase is the fact that children are bringing new problems to school. These problems affect their ability to achieve.

Divorce is most often responsible for single-parent homes. The provisional divorce rate was 5.3 per 1,000 population in 1981. This figure represents a 2 per cent increase since 1980.[10] If present predictions are accurate, the divorce rate will rise

[4] Ibid., p. 147.
[5] Nancy Larrick, *A Parent's Guide to Children's Reading*, 4th ed. (New York: Bantam Books, 1975), p. 1.
[6] John W. Santrock, *Adolescence* (Dubuque, Iowa: Brown, 1981), p. 343.
[7] William Glasser, quoted in B. F. Feingold, "Are Today's Kids Different Than Yesterday's?" *Instructor* 87:2 (Sept. 1977), Special Report.
[8] Pat Palker, "How to Deal with the Single-Parent Child in the Classroom," *Teacher*, 98:2 (Sept. 1980), p. 51.
[9] Ibid., p. 51.
[10] *The World Almanac and Book of Facts 1983*. (New York: Newspaper Enterprise Association, Inc., 1983), pp. 954–955.

to 50 per cent.[11] Divorce during the early years of a marriage means that the children affected are very young. The child becomes involed in emotional turmoil and needs help in coping with the changes in the family. Teachers can help and be supportive in the following ways:

> Talk with the parents and make sure that the child is told about the divorce.
> Ask parents to keep teachers informed about living and visitation plans.
> Encourage parents to help the child express all the feelings that he or she is experiencing.
> Keep communication between home and school open.
> Read to the child stories about children and divorce. (For example, Helen Spelman Rogers. *Morris and His Brave Lion.* New York: McGraw-Hill, 1976.)[12]

Another viable alternative is seen in the growing number of unmarried mothers, as society respects the right of mothers to keep their children. Economic conditions and the women's liberation movement have encouraged acceptance of gainful employment and career aspirations for mothers, whether single or married (Figure 2-1).

Each family unit, of necessity, arranges for the care of its children while the parent(s) work(s), usually involving a frequent change of caregivers. Will the lack of consistency of experiences rob children of the building blocks of self-esteem and personal security, as well as long-range attitudes, values, and orientation to others

[11] D. K. Osborn, "Changes in the 1980's That Will Affect Education," in Laura L. Dittman and Marjorie E. Ramsey (eds.), op. cit., p. 13.
[12] Nancy L. Schoyer, "Divorce and the Preschool Child," *Child. Educ,* **57**:1 (1980), pp. 3–7.

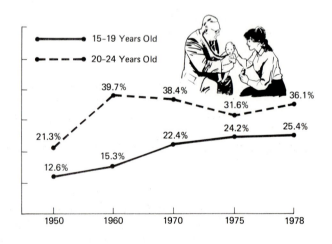

Percent of Out-of-Wedlock Births (per 1000 Live Births) to Women 15–19 Years Old

Figure 2-1
[U.S. Bureau of the Census, Current Population Reports, p-23, No. 114, Characteristics of American Children, and Youth: 1980, U.S. Government Printing Office, Washington, D.C., 1982, Table D, p. 7.]

and to life in general? The need for continuity of caregivers with values compatible with those of the parent(s) of the young children in their care cannot be stressed too much if the children are to continue as participants in their own rightful cultural and ethnic heritage.

Because of longevity there are more grandparents in the child's world today. The elderly population increased from 4.1 per cent of the total population in 1900 to 12.4 per cent in 1980. Some grandparents are in their early forties or fifties; hence more people are assuming grandparental roles than ever before. The role tends to be warm and indulgent with grandchildren because less direct responsibility is assumed.[13] A grandparent may give the children more possessions and more affection, which may be both important and meaningful to them, as well as detrimental.

A young boy, Eric, said, "Old people are valuable." He loves his grandparents' company and feels they enjoy his company too."[14] This is a positive way for a child to view growing old. He or she can see that when one gets old, one can still have fun.

Family relationships

The number of brothers and sisters as well as the ordinal position of each sibling should be taken into account in each individual family. Kavanaugh reported feelings expressed by an only child, an oldest child, and a middle child. The only child felt that a brother or sister might mean less attention but at least there would be someone to play with. An oldest child felt that one gets to do do many things and doesn't get treated like a baby. A middle child felt that if you do something to your sister or brother you get into trouble. If they do something to you, you still get in trouble.[15] Children really have these feelings, and it is important for a teacher and for parents to be familiar with such feelings.

Another factor is the effect of the parents' newness to the situation with the first child versus the parents' becoming more sure of themselves with each successive child. Parents who rear only boys or only girls within their familes have different ways of bringing up children. Some children may find themselves reared in a family in which they are more than wanted because their parents may be physically incapable of having other children; others may be unwanted. Still others are among the large number of exceptional children who are physically or mentally handicapped or who are superior or gifted.

Many families are not aware that children identify closely with parents and others in the home. How the parents act with each other and how they treat those within

---

[13] U.S. Department of Commerce, Bureau of the Census, *Statistical Abstract of the United States*, 102d ed. Supt. of Documents No.: C3.134:981 Washington, D.C., 1981, p. 12.

[14] Dorriet Kavanaugh, "Listen to Us," *Children's Express Report* (New York: Workman Publ., 1978), p. 55.

[15] Kavanaugh, op. cit., p. 51.

the family group constitute attitudes and values passed on to, and acquired by, the young child. Parents' reactions to various happenings locally or in the world and to the daily routines withim the home are all part of how children accept and begin to acquire their own ways of conduct with others. Since today's world for the young child is brought into the home by many media, children in turn are influenced by how parents verbalize their reactions to this information. Early impressions of adults' concerns over the constantly changing world will continue to play an important part in the children's own attitudes as the world affairs shift or change.

Parents today

The young child today may be reared in a home by parents who are both working or attending school. Young parents may be continuing their education, either in vocational school or college. These parents are likely to be in their early twenties. The present world in which they live with their offspring is very different from that known by many of the earlier child-development writers, researchers, or so called "experts." Many of these earlier writings are still used today either in the originals or by means of extensive quotes in some of the most recent materials. Much can be learned from these sources, and many of the findings are as true today as they were then. Nevertheless, many of the child-rearing practices prescribed as suitable for that day may, because of social and personal changes, be questionable for the world in which today's children find themselves.

Heavy emphasis on longitudinal family and child research in the 1920s and 1930s highlighted an approach to early education based on the maturational and developmental needs. Although this is certainly a valid approach and one approved by the authors of this text, children mature earlier today as a result of better nutrition, health, and general life-styles. In addition, the emphasis on infant and early childhood education as well as patterns of living documented elsewhere has produced children far ahead, in their cognitive and personal–social development, of children

Percent
of Children Under 6 Years
Living With Mother Only

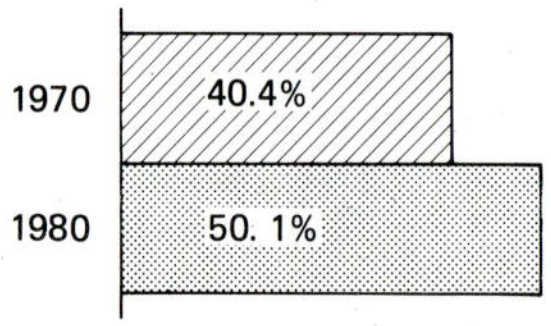

1970   40.4%

1980   50. 1%

Figure 2-2

[U.S. Bureau of the Census, Current Population Reports, p-23, No. 114, Characteristics of American Children, and Youth: 1980, U.S. Government Printing Office, Washington, D.C., 1982, Table 36, p. 38.]

reared in the 1920s and 1930s. A high quality of longitudinal research on children and their families in today's world is needed. The emphasis on early intervention education and the needs for immediate answers demanded by current accountability practices have made longitudinal research less appealing to those doing the research.

Contrary to tradition, the courts in divorce cases are increasingly awarding the custody of children to their fathers. Thus, the young child may be reared in a household without the presence of a mother, indeed without the presence of a regular female caregiver (Figure 2-2).

Children's clothing, games, and play equipment have become big business. Unfortunately, with the push for early academic achievement as documented throughout this text, educational materials, equipment, and systems of teaching have become highly commercialized. It becomes difficult for busy parents, teachers, and caregivers to know which of the magic formulas to invest in. A goal of parenting in terms of individual family needs should be established as a guide for decision making.

Parents today have a vast array of information and advice regarding children. So great is the amount of printed material, the frequency of radio and TV talk shows, and documentaries that it is easy to become confused by contradictory or conflicting points of view. Guidance is needed in distinguishing between advice based on sound research and theory and that proposed by biased persons or groups. Much advice and many valuable aids supplied by recognized and experienced professionals are available, a good example of which can be found in Mary B. Lane's work on education for parenting.[16] Research indicates that the best type of parenting is one of warmth and encouragement that gives the child independence with limits. Such parenting is important in increasing a child's autonomy.[17]

Mothers in gainful employment

There has been a steady rise in the number of working mothers. In 1980, 57.1 per cent of children enrolled in school had mothers who were in the labor force.[18] Of the 20 million children under the age of five years, about seven million have mothers who work. Adequate, licensed day care is available for only about 1.7 million children. In other words, there are over 5.5 million young children who do not have proper day care available for them.[19] Sager estimated that in 1974 70 per cent

[16] See Mary B. Lane, *Education for Parenting* (Washington, D.C.: NAEYC, 1975), for additional information.

[17] John W. Santrock, *Adolescence*, (Dubuque, Iowa: Brown, 1981), p. 213.

[18] U.S. Department of Commerce, Bureau of the Census, *Statistical Abstract of the U.S.*, op. cit., p. 140.

[19] D. K. Osborn, "Changes in the 1980's That Will Affect Education," in Laura L. Dittman and Marjorie M. Ramsey (eds.), op. cit., p. 13.

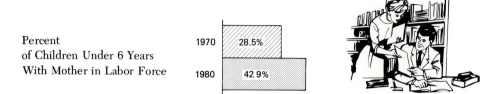

Percent
of Children Under 6 Years
With Mother in Labor Force

1970 | 28.5%
1980 | 42.9%

Figure 2-3

[U.S. Bureau of the Census, Current Population Reports, p-23, No. 114, Characteristics of American Children, and Youth: 1980, U.S. Government Printing Office, Washington, D.C., 1982, Table 36, p. 38.]

of young children needing day care were cared for either in their own homes or in family day care. Few of the family day care facilities are licensed.[20]

According to Bowlby's theory of attachment, child care involving daily separation from the mother places emotional strain on the very young child. However, factors such as familiarity with the caregiver and the surroundings also affect the child. There is need to identify aspects of the care environment which, when combined, make a difference for most children.[21] Economic need has been the primary reason that mothers work. However, with more education, women tend to work for other reasons—to achieve career goals or for personal satisfaction and freedom from being dependent on someone else. Whatever the effect on children when their mothers work (research is not at all definitive on this issue at this time), their days will be very different from those of children whose mothers are not gainfully employed outside the home (Figure 2-3).

Studies suggest that when work is a source of personal satisfaction for the mother, her role is positively affected. In other findings concerning maternal employment, daughters of working mothers saw women as "competent and effective," and the sons saw men as warm and expressive.[22]

POPULATION TRENDS

An important factor to consider is the effect of population trends on the child's environment. These population statistics will help one understand the child's world in relation to the people in the child's life space, particularly family size, family patterns, and alternatives to family care.

[20] Bettye M. Caldwell and Marjorie Freyer, "Day Care and Early Education," in Bernard Spodek, ed., op. cit., pp. 341–342.

[21] Greta Fein and Pamela M. Schwartz, "Developmental Theories in Early Education," in Bernard Spodek, ed., op. cit., pp. 86–89.

[22] Santrock, John W. *Adolescence* (Dubuque, Iowa: Brown Co. Publ.), 1981), pp. 131, 139.

The elderly population (sixty-five and over) has increased from 4.1 per cent of the nation's total population in 1900 to 12.4 per cent in 1980.[23] Those aged forty-five through sixty-four increased from 13.8 per cent in 1900 to 20.4 per cent in 1970. On the other hand, those in the high productive ages twenty-five through forty-four decreased from 28.1 per cent to 23.6 per cent during the same period of time. These shifts in proportions by age groups have important implications for planning for housing, schools, and social services. For example, experts predict that elementary school enrollments will continue to decrease through the mid-1980s, and high school enrollments will continue to fall by as much as 25 per cent until the period 1990–1991.[24]

During the 1980 school year, 8,133 children aged three to six, were enrolled in school. Of the three- and four-year-olds, 36.4 per cent were enrolled in school, and 95.7 per cent of the five- and six-year-olds were also enrolled.[25] Public school kindergarten enrollment has increased from 1965 to 1980 by 11.3 per cent.[26] The actual percentage of the population's three- through five-year-olds was 52.5 in 1980.[27] In 1975, 57.7 per cent of the population was in this age group.[28]

CHILD ABUSE

The incidence of child abuse is of great concern (Figure 2-4). Research indicates that over one million American children are suffering from abuse and neglect. One fourth of these injuries will be for life.[29] So serious did the problem of child abuse become that the Child Abuse and Treatment Act (P.L. 93-247) was signed into law January 31, 1974. This act established the National Center on Child Abuse and Neglect in the Children's Bureau within the Office of Child Development, now a

[23] U.S. Department of Commerce, Bureau of the Census. op. cit., p. 12.
[24] "House EL/SEC Panel Hears How Population Trends Affect Education," *Education Daily* (May 11, 1977), p. 3.
[25] U.S. Department of Commerce, Bureau of the Census, op cit., p. 139.
[26] Ibid., p. 140.
[27] Ibid., p. 139.
[28] Ibid., p. 139.
[29] California Department of Justice, *Sourcebook*, Criminal Justice Research Center, 1982, p. 15.

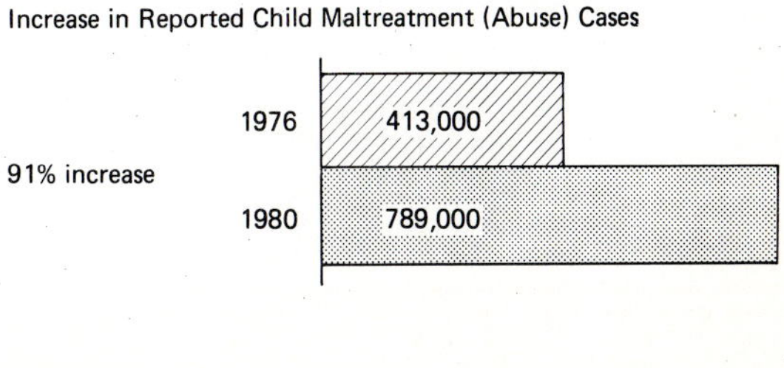

Increase in Reported Child Maltreatment (Abuse) Cases

Figure 2-4

[According to the American Humane Association in *U.S. News and World Report*, "Our Neglected Kids," August 8, 1982, p. 55.]

91% increase

1976   413,000

1980   789,000

part of the Administration of Children Youth and Families (CYF), Department of Human Services. Historically,

> Up to the twentieth century, children were considered the property of their parents in most cultures. Aristotle wrote that "the justice of a master or a father is a different thing from that of a citizen, for a son or slave is property. . . . In ancient Rome, a man could sell, abandon, or kill his child if he pleased. . . ."
>
> Infanticide has been practiced throughout history, often for economic reasons: to limit family size, to relieve the financial burden of the unwed mother, to assure crop growth by human sacrifice to the appropriate god or gods. Children have been slain, abandoned, and sold into slavery by parents unable to support them, by mid-wives and wet-nurses greedy for money, and by rulers fearing loss of their power. Other children, perhaps more fortunate than those murdered or exposed, were mutilated to increase their appeal as beggars or freak performers.
>
> Parents and schoolmasters, from the ancient philosophers to the American colonists, believed that sparing rods led to the spoiling of children. Whippings and floggings have been acceptable means of disciplining children in many cultures.
>
> The Massachusetts Stubborn Child Law, enacted in 1654, was reaffirmed in 1971 by the state's highest court, which ruled that children have no right of dissent against the reasonable and lawful commands of the parents or legal guardians. The law was finally repealed in 1973.
>
> Since the 1960's, all 50 states, the District of Columbia, the Virgin Islands, and Guam have enacted laws to protect children whose parents fail to meet minimal standards of care.[30]

Of the 649,690 reported victims of child abuse and neglect in a thirty-three-state case jurisdiction, 153,731 were aged seven and under.[31] As would be expected, abused children have learning, behavior, and habit disorders, and they themselves grow up to be abusers of their own children. Excellent and helpful material on this topic is available from the National Center on Child Abuse and Neglect referred to previously.

CHANGES IN LIVING STYLES

Today's children live in a "push-button age" surrounded by new gadgets and inventions represented to them as intricate plastic toys. Through the increasing influence of advertising, adults strive to make more money to purchase more goods to increase the ease of living and provide more leisure time. One can only surmise what

---

[30]*Child Abuse and Neglect—The Problem and Its Management,* vol. 1 (first of 3 vols.), DHEW Publication No. (OHD) 75-30073 (Washington, D.C.: Superintendent of Documents. U.S. Government Printing Office, 1975), p. 10.

[31]U.S. Department of Commerce, Bureau of the Census, op. cit., p. 15.

effect this continuous circle of striving will have on the growing child. Consideration is also given to the type of value system the child is developing in this fast-changing world. Easy acquisition of toys and other possessions may tend to develop irresponsibility for their care and use. With the increased emphasis on new commodities, we need to be aware of the effect of the adult's constantly shifting values on those of the child. This problem is accentuated as children move from place to place. What is acceptable to children in one region may only seem cheap or unacceptable to children in another area.

The fast-paced life-style of most modern families has meant drastic changes in their eating habits. There is no longer time to prepare and then leisurely enjoy good meals at home. The food industry has gone all out to meet this challenge and to make food preparation and serving as quick and as painless as possible. Fast-food restaurant chains are everywhere. In order to make these modern miracles possible, natural foods have been altered with quantities of additives, including preservatives, artificial colors and flavors, and excessive amounts of sugar. Many believe these additives have a profound influence on behavior patterns, including scholastic performance, especially of children. Even vandalism, truancy, and violence have been attributed to food alteration and nutritional problems.[32]

Affluence and an expanding economy have made it possible for just about everyone to have almost endless material possessions. The discipline and psychological rewards derived from planning for the future and from the conservation of material things were almost unheard of until recently for large numbers of young children. At the time of this writing children are participating more in concern for the environment.

With the increasing availability and use of television as a medium of communication, children have been affected by changing attitudes and concepts. Although children may be better informed, television has not been used as fully as it might as a result of commercialism. However, this medium has great potential in widening children's horizons.[33] There are many television programs designed especially for preschool children on both commercial and educational TV. Best known is "Sesame Street," which was developed to test the effectiveness of television as an instructional medium for preschool children, especially children living in the inner cities. "Sesame Street" has been criticized for placing too much emphasis on learning on the basis of rote. Meichenbaum states that such rote learning may cause problems later in developing and understanding of concepts.[34]

---

[32] B. F. Feingold, "Are Today's Kids Different than Yesterday's?" *Instructor* **87**:2 (Sept. 1977), Special Report.

[33] Wilbur Schramm, J. Lyle, and E. B. Parker, *Television in the Lives of Our Children* (Stanford, Calif.: Stanford University Press, 1961), p. 173.

[34] D. H. Meichenbaum and L. Turk, "Implications of Research on Disadvantaged Children and Cognitive-training Programs for Educational TV: Ways of Improving 'Sesame Street'," *Journal of Special Education* (1972), pp. 27–41.

MOBILITY OF POPULATION

Another important social change that is exerting pressure on the child is the increased mobility of our present population. It was reported in 1966 that in the nineteen annual surveys conducted since 1948, the proportion of movers has ranged from 18.6 to 21.0 per cent.[35] Between the years 1975–1980, 53 per cent of the population were classified as nonmovers. During the same period of time, however, 47 per cent of the population of the United States had moved at least once.[36]

This mobility factor causes persons interested in the child to ask, What does shifting from one place to another do to the children? Do children need the security that comes through establishing roots in one place, or are they able to adjust to continual change? Is it more advantageous for them to know more of the outside world than to have prolonged contacts with one neighborhood?

More divisions within the family have arisen as families move about; all family members develop their own friends, thus increasing the contacts they acquire as they shift from place to place. Widening and broadening of acquaintances may shift both the adult's and the child's perspective as individuals in society. The concern is this: Does the individual thus acquire greater understanding of human relations or broader knowledge of regional differences? Does the family remain intact? What are the effects of shifting population upon the family with growing children? To date, the specific answers are not known. It is only surmised that personalities do undergo change the more contacts people make.

Both mobility and travel tend to separate family members, at least for varying, and often irregular, periods of time. In view of "critical periods and attachment" research, the possible effects on children of such separations would depend on such factors as the age of the child and the length of time involved in the separation. For example, "attachment" research would tend to discourage total separations from known caregivers with whom the child has developed a feeling of security for more than twenty-four hours before the age of at least one year.[37]

EASE OF TRAVEL

Along with increased mobility and expanded means of communication, the world is known more easily and readily to children and adults through ease of travel, whether to nearby state parks or to faraway vacation spots. Families tend to take vacations; thus mobility in leisure-time activities has increased. Advertising has tended to lure families to see the parts of the world known only in earlier times through a geog-

---

[35] U.S. Bureau of the Census, *Population Characteristics*, Series P-20, No. 156 (Washington, D.C.: U.S. Government Printing Office, December 1966).

[36] U.S. Department of Commerce, Bureau of the Census, *Statistical Abstract of the United States 1982–83, 103rd ed.* Supt. of Documents no: C3.134:982, Washington, D.C., p. 14.

[37] J. Gewirtz (ed.), *Attachment and Dependency* (Washington D.C.: Winston, 1972).

raphy book. There has been an increased desire to become acquainted firsthand with other localities. State parks and camping facilities have expanded, and campers of all types are available for families. "Package" family trips are advertised to entice parents at any season of the year. Young children travel with their families by plane great distances in brief spaces of time. Thus the world is better known to children today than it was to a previous generation.

ADULTS IN THE CHILD'S WORLD

Traditionally, young children have been reared in the warmth and security of parental care. Most would agree that parents should, with a high degree of responsibility, administer care that is very personal and designed to produce an intense

Children need to have contact with older people—grandparents sometime serve as volunteers. Reading stories and playing games are favorite activities.

relationship that is mutually responsive and emotionally involved. This type of care is what Katz[38] calls "particularistic" relationships as opposed to "universalistic" relationships encouraged by teachers and caregivers. Both types of relationship involve warmth and affection, but in the latter case there is personal "distance," which desirably prevents intense personal involvement on the part of the adult as well as the children.[39]

Recognition is now given to the importance of health, nutrition, and physical care in the early years and a need for many adults in the program whose training and expertise differ from that of teachers. They form a significant part of the team of adults necessary for good Early Childhood Education programs. This does not depreciate the importance of the teacher, as learning is always taking place in the lives of children regardless of the purpose or type of program involved. Indeed, highly skilled and adequately prepared teachers are essential to all programs, all of which should include a carefully planned education component. Other adults, with the same potential for educational influence, may include caregivers, Child Development Associates, parents, parent liaison workers, volunteers, students, maintenance personnel, and others.

HOUSING

Housing is an important area to consider in relation to the activity of a child and available play space. The home may be crowded and small and have poor sanitation or safety hazards. It may be too large and overly clean and have no playmates accessible. There may be good sleeping arrangements and storage space for the child, or there may be noise, confusion, clutter, and no place the children can call their own for their possessions. Outdoor play areas may be adequate on a roof or in a yard, or they may be nonexistent.

Lemkau feels that "the house does not have a constant relationship to the household which lives in it, but that the relationship changes according to economic ideals and philosophic ideals." As a psychiatrist he feels that a house must offer a place in which children can lead a satisfactory existence. Crowded conditions and too many adults lead to lack of independence and poor control in guiding children.[40] Little research has been conducted on the effect of housing in rearing children. Concern has been expressed that families have adequate housing.

Of the new housing units started in 1981, 181,000 were condominiums; 145,000

---

[38] Lillian G. Katz, "Teachers in Preschools: Problems and Prospects," *Internatl. J. Early Childhood*, **9**:1 (1977), pp. 111–123.

[39] Ibid., p. 119.

[40] P. V. Lemkau, "A Psychiatrist's View of Housing," *Proceedings of Housing Conference*, Publication 180 (Philadelphia: Pennsylvania State University, College of Home Economics), p. 27. (Unpublished paper) n.d.

were multifamily units; and single family units numbered 36,000.[41] Condominiums and apartments have outnumbered single family units in the nation. In most cases, this type of home ownership is not the most appropriate housing for children, but these developments reflected attitudes toward children and the low birthrate of the times. In addition, the high cost of housing has priced the average family with children out of home ownership. "Proper balance between housing and income-supplementing programs will be important in achieving the goal of decent housing for every family. . . . The Department of Housing and Urban Development is intensifying its efforts to formulate and develop a balanced relationship between housing and income-supplementing programs."[42]

It seems clear that adequate housing for families is a prerequisite to adequate family life and learning experiences for young children. Schools and universities bulged with children and students during the 1950s and 1960s as a result of the World War II baby boom. The 1970s and 1980s found these same babies, now young adults, forming families of their own and facing acute housing problems. Mobile homes, apartments, and government-subsidized low-cost housing mushroomed because of the rapidly rising cost of new housing. Most of the new housing was not built where the need was the greatest. What importance housing plays in the life of a child is an area that needs and will continue to need increased and intensive exploration.

VARIATIONS IN CHILD REARING

The child is an important factor in the continuation of the culture, being the connecting link between the cultures of succeeding generations. How a parent rears a child is primarily dependent on the culture, the trends of the decade in which the parent is presently living, and the past experiences of the adult. Although psychologists, educators, and others have made much of the influences on children of culture and class differences, it seems apparent from recent research and thought on the subject that in the United States "the great power of the middle class has rendered differences into deficits because middle-class behavior is the yardstick of success,"[43] hence the term *culturally disadvantaged.* Pointing out that "cultural differences reside more in the situations to which cultural groups apply their skills than to differences in the skills possessed," Bruner casts doubt on the concept of "deficits" in minority and poverty groups.[44]

[41] *Statistical Abstract of the U.S.,* 1982–83, op. cit., p. 14.

[42] U.S. Department of Agriculture, *Family Economics Review,* ARS 62-5 (Washington, D.C., December 1966), p. 12.

[43] J. S. Bruner, *Beyond the Information Given* (New York: Norton, 1973), p. 464.

[44] Ibid., pp. 453, 464.

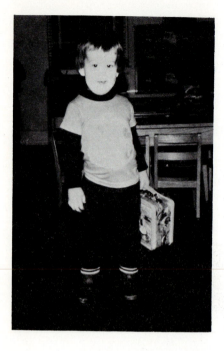

A three-year-old, whose mother works outside the home, arrives at Nursery School. "Here I am!"

More than three decades ago, Sears, Maccoby, and Levin conducted research in the area of child rearing with 379 mothers of five-year-old children, pretty much a classic work in the field. These workers found wide variations in the different methods measured—from mothers who never under any circumstances permitted certain forms of behavior to others who felt that specific behavior should be ignored. Some mothers were quite uncertain in the strength of their convictions. Some of the child-rearing practices reported placed emphasis on training children; others, on caretaking only; and others, on reactions of love, annoyance, pride, or concern. One of the most pervasive qualities measured was the warmth of the mother's feeling for her child.[45]

The present emphasis on Early Childhood Education and day care is clearly an indication that today there is a change from the traditional socializing influences of the family and school. Emphasis on the disadvantaged child has dominated the field of Early Childhood Education since the early 1960s, and most research since then has been concerned with that group of children and families. Studying the teaching styles of mothers from different social classes, Hess and Shipman found that mothers of one culturally different group controlled the child's behavior by imperatives.

[45] R. Sears, E. Maccoby, and H. Levin, *Patterns of Child Rearing* (Evanston, Ill.: Row Peterson, 1957), p. 482.

This method did not provide an opportunity for mediation of behavior by verbal cues or the use of language to bring meaning to the experience encountered.[46] Such a cognitive environment, they conclude, "produces a child who related to authority rather than to rationale . . . and for whom the consequences of an act are largely considered in terms of immediate punishment or reward rather than future effects and long-range goals."[47] This, of course, is in *direct contrast to the future-oriented long-range planning goals of middle-class American families*. As a consequence, schools of middle-class value orientation have not provided for the needs of children from lower-income families in such a way as to enable them to cope with the schools' expectations and demands.

Because of the time it takes to conduct research and to have it published and later interpreted for public consumption, there is a lag in adapting it to practice. Thus, if research finds it is "all right or better" to be less permissive in dealing with children, this concept may not be put into practice for seven or eight years. Therefore, we are likely to find some older parents still being very permissive in rearing children because of something they read earlier, whereas other parents who have attended a study group and discussed various ways of raising children may be recognizing individual differences and comparing these differences of their own children to new research findings.

SOCIAL CLASS

Regional and class differences are apparent in the literature and in the research on ways in which parents rear their children. Attitudes and values of families in lower, middle, and upper classes differ in regard to customs and aspirations; these differences are revealed in most communities.

Some researchers classify the social groups in American urban society as upper, upper-middle, lower-middle, working, and lower class. Classification of variables that characterize these classes is made on the basis of value orientations as they form, integrate, and symbolize a certain way of life.[48] There is a tendency for modern writers in the field of Early Childhood Education to ignore some of the potent forces that have a strong influence on the orientation to life of the young child, such as social class. They feel that there should be no "such distinctions" when the life of young children is concerned. We agree that there "should not" be such distinctions, but the cold facts of reality are that social classes do exist in America, and membership in certain classes either paves the way for, or strongly inhibits, the

[46] R. D. Hess and Virginia C. Shipman, "Maternal Influences upon Early Learning," in *Early Education*, ed. by R. D. Hess and Roberta M. Bear (Chicago: Aldine, 1968) p. 103.

[47] Ibid., p. 103.

[48] J. A. Kahl, *The American Class Structure* (New York: Holt, 1959).

Young children are influenced by many forces, especially by persons around them—parents, other adults, peers, and siblings.

opportunities to achieve and enjoy a role in important decision-making processes. Teachers and caregivers of young children "should" be aware of the influence of social class on how children are reared if they are to work effectively with children and parents of different social classes whatever their ethnic origins.

There is need to analyze carefully class influences that young children acquire from parents, teachers, and other adults. In the study by Sears, Maccoby, and Levin, the authors analyzed their data by socioeconomic status. Their cases were analyzed and divided into two groups, namely, "middle class" and "working class." There were marked differences in the practices and attitudes of these two classes of mothers. Working-class mothers were more punitive and restrictive. They were less permissive with respect to sex behavior, aggression, and dependency, and they placed high restrictions and demands on their children in all major respects. Many other findings with respect to differences in child rearing can be found in these research studies.[49]

Studies to date are limited with regard to subcultures of the very poor; however, Chilman has presented research findings that show differences in child-rearing patterns. These summarize studies on various aspects of child rearing according to middle-class versus very-low-income families. As schools are basically middle-class institutions, lower-class children have trouble achieving in such centers. For example, some of the studies revealed that low-income families use inconsistent, harsh discipline and ridicule; the discipline is based on whether the child's behavior does or does not annoy the parent. Middle-class parents on the other hand, used verbal, mild, reasoning and consistent discipline with more emphasis on rewarding good behavior.[50]

Such studies, though helpful, merely describe differences and seldom produce an understanding of the differences and why they exist. The following quotations from the 1970 White House Conference on Children report will help bridge the gap:

> Many children, effectively isolated from their cultural heritage by poverty, home environment, racial discrimination, and geography, do not develop pride in their heritages, and their feelings of identity remain vague and confused. These children need help in finding out who they are and where they came from.[51]

It would thus appear that social class and the influence of culture are powerful determinants of young children's behavior and must be taken into account when planning teaching and instructional strategies.

---

[49] Sears, Maccoby, and Levin, op. cit., p. 480.
[50] Catherine Chilman, "Child-Rearing and Family Relationship Patterns of the Very Poor," *Welfare in Review* (Washington, D.C.: U.S. Department of Health, Education, and Welfare, January 1965).
[51] *Report to the President*. White House Conference on Children 1970 (Washington D.C.: Superintendent of Documents, U.S. Government Printing Office) p. 48.

CHANGING SEX ROLES

There is a growing awareness by those interested in child development of the importance of the child's sex role. Many have suggested that sex-role labeling will affect children's performance on specific activities. Many variables moderate the effect of this type of labeling.[52] Kratz says that "sexism reinforces the stereotypes of male-female behaviors."[53] How the parents think of the feminine or masculine role plays an important part in how they rear the child. Questions relative to this include these: Are the father's and mother's concepts the same, or does each parent have a different way of looking at masculinity or femininity? Is the child's time spent mainly with the mother; if so, does the child have more awareness of the feminine role than the masculine? If the child is only seen and cared for by the father at brief intervals daily, is that enough for the child to identify with a masculine figure?

The recent emphasis on equal opportunity for women in education, the labor market, and the professions, along with public acceptance of one-parent (male or female) families and equality of the sexes, has brought about a need for a new look at the concept of sex roles. The women's liberation movement, too, has had its impact, creating the need for alternative forms of child rearing. As the sexes become less distinguishable from each other in these areas, it is reasonable to assume that sex-role differences will likewise tend to be less stereotyped or even eliminated.

At the time of this revision, we could find no tangible evidence that today's young children are learning "equality" of sex roles despite the fact that mothers engage in far fewer "feminine" activities at home and at work and fathers or other males in the household engage in far more "feminine" activities than formerly. Perhaps it is as Margolin[54] points out, "This [learning sex-linked traits] is a complicated issue. Whether they will begin to emulate certain males and accept their traits as their own will depend on how much they want to identify themselves with them." Today efforts are being made to eliminate sexism in children's (and adults') reading matter, illustrations, and everyday activities so that sex differences are becoming less clear cut. It will take many years to feel the full impact of these social changes.

A child learns early in life that boys and girls are treated differently, are dressed differently, and are expected to behave differently. Each culture defines the meaning of *male* or *female*, usually in terms of its social and economic needs. As these needs change, so do the roles of each sex change. Nevertheless, early in life all

---

[52] D. S. White, "Effects of Sex-Typed Labels and Their Source in the Imitative Performance of Young Children," *Child Development*, **49** (1978), pp. 1266–1269.

[53] M. Kratz, "Socializing Females for Reality," *The Social Studies*, **69** (1978), p. 122.

[54] Edythe Margolin, *Sociocultural Elements in Early Childhood Education* (New York: Macmillan, 1974), p. 62.

children must find their own sex role at home and in the ethnic group to which they belong if they are to be accepted members.

EDUCATIONAL THEORIES

Another factor in the child's world is the variety of theories relative to educating the child. Parents have been advised to have the child ready for school at age six, "ready for school" meaning to them ability to read, write one's name, to know certain facts. Others have advised the parent to leave the child alone, that the school's job is to teach the child everything he or she should know. Some children therefore arrive in first grade with certain taught skills; others, with none.

The push to educate very young children has had growing impetus since the Atomic Age intensified the need for further education in all lines of endeavor. Parents may pressure young children to "know certain facts" where other parents have a "let well enough alone" attitude. Those working with or teaching young children in organized groups also may feel they should prepare the five-year-old to read and write in order that the child be equipped to meet the standards of first grade. Pressure from society that all five- or six-year-olds should be able to measure up to certain prescribed standards may find school and parents in conflict.

Along with the variety of theories of child rearing and education, there are conflicting beliefs regarding the responsibilities of the home. Many young parents depend mainly on outside agencies—welfare organizations, family services, clinics, state and local societies—to handle their problems. One has yet to determine whether or not the agencies are so numerous that young parents are overaided and do not develop necessary self-sufficiency.

The recognition of the importance of the early years has given impetus to research in early learning. As a result, many different theories, methods, and types of instructional materials exist and have a direct impact on the type of educational opportunities available in the young child's world.

In an effort to note trends in any area of our rapidly changing life today, it appears significant to identify landmarks by which the degree of change can be measured. In an identification of trends in education for the young child, the following landmarks will indicate the changes that have developed both in beliefs and practice:

1. *The acceptance of the Froebelian philosophy and program for kindergartens.* For a time, the European philosophy of the kindergarten was transplanted with little change in relation to the needs of American life. The emphasis was on following Froebel and using his program and gifts for all children. Froebel's philosophy, rather than the child, was the center of study.
2. *The beginning of the child study movement.* Dewey and Hall found leaders in the kindergarten field eager to apply their findings and philosophy to the edu-

cation of young children. But it was not easy. For, only a century ago, the study of children was frowned upon by many. G. Stanley Hall has told how difficult it was in the middle of the last century to measure the height and weight of school-children because parents objected to the invasion of the child's rights.[55]

Studies today are far-reaching and have great implications for what happens to young children. For example, in the survey of "400 Famous People and How Their Childhood Affected Them," it was found that none of them had had an easy time in their home but that certain common elements were in the backgrounds of these leaders. As children, these famous people had had more opportunity for traveling, reading, thinking, and initiating and conducting original experiments. Many children do not have these opportunities at home; therefore, they need to have experiences provided under guidance to assist them in developing qualities of leadership and creativity. Such studies substantiate the value of, and give direction to, the content of desirable programs in Early Childhood Education.[56]

3. *Expansion of interest in child development and research to include children under six, soon after World War I.* The research during this period was concerned with establishing the value of the kindergarten in relation to later school adjustment and progress. In the 1930s and early 1940s there was concern for establishing tests and norms of development. In light of these research findings, kindergarten teachers have tried to better understand and meet the needs of individuals in their groups—to relate findings of child development to practice.

4. *Progressive Education.* Although the era of the Progressive Education Movement is usually associated with the years between 1896 and the late 1930s, extensions of the movement are found today in many programs, such as the British Infant Schools and other examples of open education for children, as well as in various alternative forms of schooling.

The common principles that Dewey felt existed in progressive schools included the following: expression and cultivation of individuality, free activity, learning through experience, acquiring meaningful and needed skills, making the most of each day of school because school is life, and developing acquaintances with the social and physical world. Progressive education combined the psychological principles of child growth with the moral principles of democracy.[57]

5. *Federal interest in early childhood centers.* The federal government has not only appropriated money for childhood centers, but it has developed materials, established supervisory programs, and assisted parents and entire communities in

[55] J. E. Anderson, "Principles of Child Development," in *Early Education* (Washington, D.C.: NEA, 1956), p. 14.

[56] Mildred G. Goertzel and V. Goertzel, *Cradles of Eminence* (New York: Little, Brown, 1962).

[57] James M. Squire (ed.), *A New Look at Progressive Education*, 1972 Yearbook (Washington, D.C.: ASCD, 1972), pp. 1–13.

developing a changed concept of early education. Many types of experimental programs have been established.

6. *The influence of Montessori.* The influence of Montessori may be found in special Montessori schools and to some extent in many preschools in the United States. The Montessori method provides for a personal space for each child, allowing children freedom to learn at a comfortable rate, but supervised by a teacher as they move about and talk. However, the first movement for exploration must come from the child. Each task is broken down into a series of smaller tasks. All the learning tasks, guided by the teacher, lead the child into the mastery of reading, writing, and mathematics as well as related skills. This program provides a variety of models for imitation as well as for older children to help and to teach younger children. The materials have been modernized, the use of equipment is more permissive, and the methods are used to insure greater academic achievement.[58]

7. *The influence of Piaget.* Piaget's theory is concerned with the development of thinking or intelligence from infancy to adulthood. The theory consists of three interdependent aspects, namely, structural, stage, and functional aspects.[59] Although Piaget's work has identified four major stages, two are especially important in early childhood: the sensorimotor period and the preoperational period. One of the preschool's basic functions is to facilitate the transition from one stage to another. By consolidating knowledge of objects, time, and space, the child builds a foundation upon which at a later date he or she can build other structures.

The rapid expansion of early education evident in the 1960s was even more apparent in the 1970s. With this expansion came some significant changes in points of emphasis. Among these are the following:

1. *Changes in philosophy and practice.* In this period changes of points of view or of greater emphasis are significant in the areas of interrelated learnings and learning by inference; the place and importance of expectancy in the learning process; greater emphasis on the child's learning from the peer group, especially in terms of hobbies and interests; the child's need for love from the teacher and his or her peers; the application of science to the child's development; and the positive interrelation between preschool attendance and behavior in adolescent years. In 1971 child development legislation was vetoed by the then President Nixon. This action signaled a change in federal policy and practice.

2. *Environmental influences.* The environment exerts a powerful influence on the preschool child. Children need space to play in large and small groups, to work, to discuss, to be alone, to listen, to think, and to create. They do need clean

---

[58] Evelyn Beyer et al. (eds.), *Montessori in Perspective* (Washington, D.C.: NAEYC, 1971), pp. 25–35.
[59] James M. Squire, op. cit., pp. 88–114.

air, freedom from excessive noise, and a well-planned attractive environment indoors and outdoors that has adequate space. The emotional climate should provide security, develop positive self-image, and encourage good health.

3. *Acceptance of individuals who are culturally or racially different.* To meet the objective of accepting into our society individuals who are culturally or racially different, teachers and caregivers must be sensitive to all children. Each child, rich, poor, or handicapped, racially or culturally different, makes his or her own contribution. Children need to learn to value other children for their own worth.

4. *The need for day care services.* Whether they are to serve the children of working mothers or the children of culturally different families, day care services for the preschool child should provide adequate care and educational guidance. Not all children needing preschool care are from indigent families; many families can provide financially for the care of their children.

As we move toward the mid-eighties, education is again in the news. The report of The National Commission on Excellence in Education, recently released, calls attention to the pressing problems facing the schools and makes recommendations for improvement.[60] The report focuses (primarily) on the high school, but Early Childhood Educators can use this opportunity to call attention to the importance of the early years of childhood and the relationship of early education to the total school program. The report states that our educational system must be reformed for the good of all—old and young alike, rich and poor, the majority as well as the mintority.[61] There is need to emphasize the importance of families, child welfare, child health, the need for day care, and for quality educational programs. The future of children in the United States will be affected by what is done during this decade.

SUMMARY

Because there are many new pressures and continuing forces that bear on each child growing up in today's world, the teacher or caregiver needs to consider what adults can do to help this growing individual. These adults need to consider the effects upon the child of such factors as mass media, family relationships, social patterns, and other forces discussed in this chapter. Adults must be aware that children will be continually changing individuals because of these many forces acting upon them. Human relations will become a greater force as today's children become adults. The teacher will need to recognize the importance of such factors as the child's mother working outside the home; whether the child is the oldest, middle, or youngest child; the community or region from which the child has come;

---

[60] American Association of School Administrators, Communications Department, *A Nation At Risk: The Excellence Report* (Arlington, Va.: AASA, 1983), pp. 1–16.

[61] Ibid., p. 4.

the age of the child's parents; whether the child has had a wide range of experiences; what attitudes or values the parents have in their rearing of this child. It is a challenge for a teacher or caregiver of young children to keep constantly in focus all the new literature, research, and materials that appear for possible use with the children she or he teaches.

Suggested Activities

1. Contact the child abuse center in your community and secure information regarding the incidence and treatment of abuse.
2. Make a list of values or attitudes you feel you have acquired from your own family. Analyze one of these in detail in terms of how it originated.
3. Study two preschool children, one who has been given every advantage and one who has had very few advantages. Contrast the two types of environments, and predict what types of children they are likely to become.
4. Watch and evaluate a preselected children's program on television. What changes would you recommend to the producers in the best interest of the children who view it? Why?
5. Design a brochure for an ideal day camp, summer playground program, or summer day care for young children. What information is crucial for parents?
6. Using the most recent census data, determine the divorce rate in your home (or college) community. Locate services for family counseling that are available. Discuss your findings with the class.
7. View one of the following films:
   Children of Divorce. Films Inc., 1144 Wilmette Ave., Wilmette, IL. 60091.
   A Time for Caring: The School's Response To The Sexually Abused Child. Lawren Productions, Inc., P.O. Box 666, Mendocino, CA. 95460.
   Whose Child Is This? Learning Corp. of America, 1350 Avenue of the Americas, New York, NY 10020.

Related Readings

ACEI. "The Child in the Community." *Childhood Education*, **59:**2 (1982), entire issue.
———. "Children in the Age of Microcomputers." *Childhood Education*, **59:**4 (1983), entire issue.
Antler, S. (Ed). *Child Abuse and Child Protection: Policy and Practice.* Silver Spring, Md.: National Association of Social Workers, Inc., 1982.
Borman, K. M. (Ed). *The Social Life of Children in a Changing Society.* Hillsdale, N.J.: Erlbaum, Lawrence, Assoc. Inc. 1982.
Capaldi, F. and Barbara McRae. *Step-Families: A Cooperative Responsibility.* New York: New Viewpoints/Vision Books, 1979.
Carlson, Nancy A., Alice Whiren, and Donna Howe. "After-Kindergarten Care: A Challenge to the Community." *Young Children* **36:**1 (1980), pp. 13–20.
Clarke-Stewart, Allison. *Day Care.* Cambridge: Harvard University Press, 1982.

Hill, S. and Barnes, B. J. (Eds). *Young Children and Their Families: Needs of the Nineties.* Washington, D.C.: Lexington Press, 1982.

Lamb, M.E. *Nontraditional Families: Parenting and Child Development.* Hillsdale, N.J.: L. Erlbaum Associates, 1982.

Langway, Lynn et al. "Bringing Up Superbaby." *Newsweek* (March 28, 1983), pp. 62–68.

Leavitt, J.E. "Helping Abused and Neglected Children," *Child Educ.,* **57**:5 (1981), pp. 262–266.

Lindsay, Jeanne W. *Do I Have A Daddy?* Buena Park, CA.: Morning Glory Press, 1982.

McNamee, Abigail Stahl. *Children and Stress.* Washington, D.C.: ACEI, 1982.

Moore, Shirley G. "The Effect of Television on the Prosocial Behavior of Young Children." *Young Children,* **32**:5 (1977), pp. 60–65.

Pitcher, E. G., and Schultz, L. H. *Boys and Girls at Play: The Development of Sex Roles.* New York: Praeger, 1982.

Polansky, N. A., Mary Ann Chalmers, Elizabeth Buttenweiser, and D. P. Williams. *Damaged Parents: An Anatomy of Child Neglect.* Chicago: U. of Chicago Press, 1981.

Polloway, Anne-Marie. *The Urban Nest.* Stroudsburg, Pa.,: Dowden, Hutchison, and Ross, 1977.

Postman, Neil. "The Disappearing Child." *Educ. Leadership,* **40**:6 (1983), pp. 10–17.

Quisenberry, James (Ed.). *Changing Family Lifestyles.* Washington, D.C.: ACEI, 1982.

Simmons, B. "Sex-role Expectations of Classroom Teachers." *Education,* **100** (1980), pp. 249–253.

Smith, R. E. ed. *The Subtle Revolution: Women at Work.* Washington, DC: The Urban Institute, 1979.

Suransky, Valerie P. "The Preschooling of Childhood." *Educ. Leadership,* **40**:6 (1983), pp. 27–29.

Westin, Jeane. *The Coming Parent Revolution.* New York: Rand McNally, 1981.

White, D. G. "Effects of Sex-Typed Labels and Their Source on the Imitative Performance of Young Children." *Child Development,* **49** (1978), pp. 1266–1269.

Winick, Marianne P. and Judith S. Wehrenberg. Children and TV II: Mediating the Medium." Washington, D.C.: ACEI, 1982.

Winn, Marie. *The Plug-in Drug: Television, Children, and the Family.* New York: Viking, 1977.

CHAPTER 3

The Young Child
As a Person

Children really want to find out who they are and what they are like, and to know how other people think of them.[1] Children need and seek interaction with others. As children grow, other people become increasingly important to them. Gradually, significant others help them to form a view of themselves.[2] Thus, the concept of self is formed. The way each child views himself or herself may not be the way others see them, or may even be far from objective reality. Nevertheless, the view each child holds is all-important in determining what that child will say, do, and think.

Current literature in child development tends to stress the importance of the way in which children view themselves.[3] This is another way of looking at child development. Some authorities hold that all growth and behavior are seen against

---

[1] Susan E. Warrell, *Helping Young Children Grow: A Humanistic Approach to Parenting and Teaching* (Englewood Cliffs, N.J.: Prentice-Hall, 1980), p. 39.

[2] Rosemary Althouse, *The Young Child—Understanding with Learning* (New York: Teachers College Press, 1981), p. 72.

[3] See Kaoru Yamamoto (ed), *The Child and His Image* (Boston: Houghton, 1972).

75

a backdrop of the child's search for identity and self-respect.[4] This is in contrast to most child development writings of a decade or two ago, which tended to be detailed descriptions of what the average child was like for a particular chronological age. These averages or norms had been obtained from observations of many children at each age level and were unrelated to the effects of particular teaching strategies, intervention techniques, or other than normal health care and family life patterns. It should not be inferred that information about normal growth and development is unnecessary for teachers and parents. On the contrary, it is the base from which slow or fast, normal or deviate, behavior can be detected and is an invaluable aid in planning learning strategies for any group of children.

Educators now regard the affective component of learning as complementary to the cognitive, believing that feelings, values, and attitudes are important in cognitive learning. It is now suggested by research that a holistic approach to education is needed, one that deals with schooling as an experience of the total person.[5] Many studies in recent years have focused on self-concepts as related to school performance. Research has suggested that a positive relationship exists between children's perceptions of themselves and how they perform in school.[6]

IMPORTANCE OF THE SELF-IMAGE

High self-esteem is the most crucial ingredient of mental health.[7] It comes from the quality of relationships that exist between the child and those "significant others." "Self-esteem is the mainspring that slates every child for success or failure as a human being."[8] Its importance cannot be overemphasized.

Mounting research shows that those people who are accomplished are very different from those who merely flounder their way through life. One difference lies in their attitude toward themselves, or their degree of self-esteem.[9] A person with high self-esteem has an inner security that radiates outwardly in his or her actions. These people have confidence, are eager to attempt new tasks, and take pride in a job well done. High self-esteem is the best guarantee that a child will make the most of his or her capacities and potential.

Young children with low self-esteem often feel that they are not capable of doing anything right and that nobody likes them. Usually, they have behavior problems. They often antagonize teachers and friends. Soon they become correct about nobody liking them. Unfortunately, the more a child misbehaves, is punished, and

---

[4] Dorothy Corkille Briggs, *Your Child's Self-Esteem* (Garden City, N.Y.: Doubleday, 1975), p. xiv.

[5] Jeanne C. Soule, R. J. Drummond, Walter G. McIntire, "Dimensions of Self-concept for K–2," *Psychological Reports*, **48** (1981), p. 83.

[6] Ibid.

[7] Briggs, op. cit., pp. 4–5.

[8] Ibid., p. 3.

[9] Ibid.

The importance of a healthy self-concept cannot be overemphasized. Children need to develop self-identity and view themselves as having competence and worth.

rejected, the greater the possibility of the child's being a "bad" person. Thus, a negative self-image is more firmly established. Both teachers and children lose dignity as human beings when rules are enforced with physical punishment.[10]

A person's self-esteem, or opinion about one's self, is formed early in life. It changes degrees constantly as the person is influenced by others.

Adults dealing with young children should bear in mind two important psychological needs of every child. First, a child needs to feel lovable for being himself or herself; and second, the child needs to feel competent in the environment.[11] Young children must be provided rich and varied environments in order to develop feelings of competence in the world in which they find themselves. The importance of

[10] Warrell, op. cit., p. 68.
[11] Briggs, op. cit., p. 4.

a healthy self-concept during the early years was recognized by the planners of Head Start programs for disadvantaged children. Included in the goals was: "To help children develop self-identity and a view of themselves as having competence and worth."[12]

The teacher's role

Teachers who are concerned with the development of fully functioning and independent thinking students must work on building more positive self-concepts. They are in a position to observe self-value, whether positive or negative, and to do something about it. How young children become self-confident and eagerly tackle new tasks or become "crippled with anxiety and fear of failure" may well be the most important question asked by adults who work with young children.[13]

Before successful learning can take place, children need to feel secure and good about themselves. Teachers can help children feel positive about themselves by creating a nurturing, supportive environment in which children feel loved, secure, and safe.

Focused attention is on one basic ingredient for an environment that provides psychological safety.[14] A teacher should show love and interest before a child asks for it. Teachers should "catch children being good" and praise them for it. Verbal encouragement is needed, along with touching, smiling, and sharing.

It may be more important to examine the quality of interactions with children than the number of contacts.[15] Some children require more contacts than others. All children, however, deserve focused attention, or quality contact with the teacher.

Evidence suggests that interactions with teachers exert powerful and long-lasting effects on the lives of students. For example, children who hear a high percentage of judgmental responses at school learn to depend on others to determine right and wrong, lose confidence in their ability to determine right and wrong, need more assurance from others, and become very comforming to the standards and expectations of others.[16] These consequences can be signs that pupils are losing the ability for internal evaluation—the most fundamental condition of creativity.[17] It is alarming to consider the effect on children of responses that are always judgmental.

Nonjudgment is, therefore, important in a supportive classroom environment. A

---

[12] Office of Economic Opportunity, *Project Head Start—Daily Program I* (Washington, D.C.: U.S. Government Printing Office, 1965), p. 11.

[13] Helen F. Robison, *Exploring Teaching in Early Childhood Education* (Boston: Allyn, 1977), p. 93.

[14] Briggs, op. cit., p. 312.

[15] W. Kyle Fordyce, "Coping With Dislike for a Child—A Worm in the Teacher's Apple," *Childhood Education,* **58:**5 (May–June 1982), p. 289.

[16] Selma Wasserman, "Interaction with Your Students, Learning to Hear Yourself," *Childhood Education,* **58:**5 (May–June 1982), p. 282.

[17] Ibid., p. 283.

teacher should be appropriately open about his or her own feelings. Children need teachers to be "human." Likewise, a teacher should recognize a child's humanness. A teacher should direct reactions to a child toward his or her behavior and not toward the child himself or herself. For example, a teacher should never call a boy or girl "bad" because he or she might have hit someone. Instead, the hitting could be labeled a bad way to express anger. There should be acceptable outlets of behavior for these feelings, such as verbal or artistic expressions. A child should never be seen as the same as his or her acts. Instead, he or she should be seen as a unique person with feelings all his or her own.

A child should be allowed to "own" these feelings without the disapproval of the teacher.[18] Expressions of feelings and emotions are normal and natural occurrences and should be accepted as such by the teacher. Children's reactions to planned activities should be respected also. Some children may enjoy finger painting, for example; others may not like the idea of messy fingers. Teachers should plan actively for differences among children, both in expectations and activities.

A teacher of young children should have empathy. An upset child needs this before any explanations, reasons, or reassurance.[19]

Trust is also important for psychological safety.[20] A child must be able to count on the teacher for friendly help with his or her needs. To develop a feeling of trust, a teacher must match words to his or her body language. Young children quickly pick up on nonverbal cues that communicate a teacher's attitude. Eye contact, physical caresses, facial expression, and body posture give cues that indicate a teacher's degree of interest. Tone of voice and pace of speech can communicate attitudes such as impatience, indifference, or anger.[21]

Respect is an important part of a supportive environment. Children need opportunities to know what the adults in their lives expect of them. Limits should be clearly established and enforced constantly. Democratic discipline, by which children and teachers establish mutually agreeable limits, fosters friendly feelings, respect, and independence.[22] A child should be given the chance to assume some responsibility.

Activities to develop positive self-images and self-esteem among children should be included in every early childhood curriculum.[23] Key concepts to consider follow.

1. *Every child is unique and special.* Activities may include body awareness exercises such as the use of photographs, songs, and activities employing children's names, self-portraits, tracing hands and feet, study of fingerprints, growth charts, recording of voices, and mirror activities.

[18] Briggs, op. cit., pp. 312–313.
[19] Ibid.
[20] Ibid.
[21] Fordyce, op. cit., p. 289.
[22] Briggs, op. cit., p. 312.
[23] Betty L. Broman, *The Early Years in Early Childhood Education* (Boston: Houghton, 1982), p. 221.

2. *Every child is like others in many ways.* Activities may include the use of a magnifying glass to compare hair or skin; and discussion of basic needs and also of home and family life.
3. *Each child is part of the group.* Activities may include many kinds of group charts, such as birthday charts and classroom helper charts.
4. *Every child needs friends.* Activities could include books, songs, and discussions about the meaning and importance of friendship.

EARLY DOCTRINES OF CHILD DEVELOPMENT

It is commonly proclaimed by present-day educators that a knowledge of the characteristics of children at any age or developmental level will enable the teacher to select and pace activities suitable for any given child at any age. This is the central concept in the value of the child study movement and in child development research. That this concept is not without precedent may be found in the more philosophical doctrines of earlier great educators. A few examples might be enlightening before presenting a brief summary of the physical, mental, and personal-social characteristics of young children as found by researchers in the field.

Hinting at the concept of natural changes, Plato in the *Laws* states, "Up to the age of three years, whether of boy or girl, if a person strictly carries out our previous regulations and makes them a principal aim, he will do much for the advantages of the young creatures. But at three, four, five, or even six years the childish nature will require sports. . . . Children of that age have certain natural modes of amusement which they find out for themselves when they meet. . . . The age of thirteen is the proper time for him to handle the lyre."[24]

Recognizing the need for education in keeping with the child's maturation and regardless of his or her economic status, Comenius wrote, "when boys are only six years old, it is too early to determine their vocation in life, or whether they are more suited for learning or for manual labor. At this age neither the mind nor the inclinations are sufficiently developed, while, later on, it will be easy to form a sound opinion of both. Nor should admission to the Latin School be reserved for the sons of rich men, nobles and magistrates, as if these were the only boys who would ever be able to fill similar positions. The wind blows where it will, and does not always begin to blow at a fixed time."[25]

An early proponent of child study, Locke, characteristic of modern thinking, stated in 1689, "Follow a child from its birth, and observe the alterations that time makes, and you shall find, as the mind by the senses comes more and more to be furnished with ideas, it comes to be more and more awake; thinks more, the more it has

---

[24] *The Dialogues of Plato*, vol. 2 trans. B. Jowett, (New York: Random House, 1937), p. 549.

[25] A. Comenius (Komensky), *The Great Didactic*, 1657, ch. 29; quoted in R. R. Rusk, *The Doctrines of Great Educators* (London: Macmillan, 1926), p. 101.

matter to think on. After some time, it begins to know the objects which, being most familiar with, have made lasting impressions."[26]

More explicitly, in regard to instruction, Pestalozzi states, "The elementary method limits itself to employ the impressions which nature puts at random before the child's senses, but extends the natural process along definite lines adapted to his capacities and requirements."[27] Foreshadowing modern readiness concepts, he wrote, "This principle [adapting the instruction to intellectual capacity and mental development] necessitated the subject matter being presented at the psychological moment in order, on the one hand, not to hold him back if ready, and on the other, not to load him and confuse him with anything for which he is not ready."[28]

Froebel also was aware of developmental processes, for he affirmed, "It is highly important that man's development should proceed continuously from one point, and that this continuous progress be seen and even guarded."[29] He further adds, "Human education needs a guide which I think I have found in a general law of development that rules both in nature and in the intellectual world. Without law-abiding guidance, there is no free development."[30]

In a more modern vein, Montessori asserted, "By education, must be understood the active help given to the normal expansion of the life of the child."[31] She goes on to state, "It is necessary then to offer those exercises which correspond to the need of development felt by an organism, and if the child's age has carried him past a certain need it is never possible to obtain, in its fullness, a development which missed its proper moment."[32] Although today considerable opposition can be found to the latter statement, Montessori implied the importance of pacing activities to psychological and developmental needs.

Montessori predated the modern critical or sensitive periods concept, which hypothesizes that there is a time when certain developmental events take place. Furthermore, the environmental impact or nurturance at that time is the most effective for better or for worse. This concept is basic to today's views of Early Childhood Education and is precisely why we have programs for young children. Such concepts as "readiness" and "teachable moment" are educational applications of this biological concept of critical periods in maturation. Kennedy[33] emphasizes the need for consideration of the "critical period" hypothesis in relation to the early development of children.

Early attempts at describing the characteristics of childhood, mostly biographical

---

[26] John Locke, *An Essay Concerning Human Understanding*, Book 4.
[27] J. A. Green (ed.), *Life and Work of Pestalozzi* (London: W. B. Clive, 1913); quoted in Rusk, op. cit., p. 179.
[28] J. H. Pestalozzi, *How Gertrude Teaches Her Children* (Syracuse, N.Y.: C. W. Bardeen, 1898), p. 26.
[29] Froebel, *Education of Man*; quoted in Rusk, op. cit., pp. 236–237.
[30] Baroness B. von Marenholz-Bülow, *Reminiscences of Frederick Froebel*, 1877; quoted in Rusk, op. cit., p. 238.
[31] Maria Montessori, *The Montessori Method* (New York: Frederick A. Stokes, 1912), p. 104.
[32] Ibid., p. 358.
[33] W. A. Kennedy, *Child Psychology* (Englewood Cliffs, N.J.: Prentice-Hall, 1971), p. 102.

in nature, were made by Galton,[34] Preyer,[35] Taine,[36] Tiedemann,[37] and Darwin.[38]

This type of observation led to later adaptations, such as the questionnaires of G. Stanley Hall[39] and the more recent extensive longitudinal observations as represented by the "ages and stages" development by Gesell and Ilg[40] and by many others.

Although many of the early writers projected their views from the standpoint of philosophy, they provided an excellent basis for extensive present-day research. The following statement by Olson is representative of present-day growth philosophy for education.[41]

> The general philosophy as applied to the growing child is a simple one. . . . Each child is to be assisted in growing according to his natural design, without deprivation or forcing, in an environment and by a process which also supply a social direction to his achievement. For the student of child development, education is a process by which children are assisted in growing; and the adequacy of administration, of the physical environment, of curriculum experiences, and of methods of teaching should be appraised in terms of the extent to which this function is realized.

There are infinite possibilities and challenges afforded adults who, as they work with young children, attempt to see each child for what he or she is, to see the influences of natural endowments and natural growth processes at work, and to discover and put into practice methods and use of materials that provide the best possible educational environment for the growing child.

LEFT AND RIGHT BRAIN FUNCTIONS

Findings of recent brain research indicate that the right and left cortical hemispheres of the brain have different functions. Although each part of the brain has specialized functions, each hemisphere also shares some functions.[42] Both the affective and psychomotor dimensions of learning are recognized. This new concept adds a psychophysiological perspective to the whole-child approach in early childhood education.[43]

---

[34] F. Galton, *Hereditary Genius*, 1869.

[35] W. Preyer, *Die Seele des Kindes*, 2 vols., 1888.

[36] H. Taine, "On the Acquisition of Language by Children," *Mind*, **2** (1877), pp. 252–259.

[37] C. Murchison and S. Langer, "Tiedemann's Observations on the Development of the Mental Faculties of Children," *J. Genet. Psychol.*, **34**:2, 1921), pp. 205–230.

[38] C. Darwin, "Biographical Sketch of an Infant," *Mind*, **2** (1877), pp. 285–294.

[39] G. S. Hall, "The Contents of Children's Minds," *Pedag. Sem.*, **1**:2 (1891), pp. 139–173.

[40] A. Gesell and Frances Ilg, *Child Development* (New York: Harper, 1949).

[41] W. C. Olson, *Child Development*, 2d ed. (Boston: Heath, 1959), p. 449.

[42] Margaret Hatcher, "Whole Brain Learning," *The School Administrator*, **40**:5 (1983), pp. 8–11.

[43] M. Languis, T. Sanders, and S. Tipps, *Brain and Learning: Directions in Early Childhood Education* (Washington, D.C.: NAEYC, 1980), p. 5.

Left brain activity deals with language, mathematics, symbols, and reason. Unfortunately, traditional education teaches almost exclusively to this side of the brain. The right brain helps humans comprehend through a nonverbal, intuitive mode. Right brain activity is holistic because it allows the individual to comprehend total contexts, to become aware of overall patterns.[44]

Some children use the left side of the brain predominantly to process information; others use the right. It is known that a left-brained child will be very accepting of the values of others. The left-brained child does not readily share his or her feelings. He or she sends messages in communication rather than receives. Such a child doesn't question or learn to make responsible decisions, but rather will be directed externally by the standards of others.[45]

The right-brained child is sensitive to others, shares feelings readily, is receptive to the ideas of others, but will question them. Thus, he or she develops the ability to make responsible decisions and will develop personal standards of conduct.[46]

A holistic education should be aimed at both hemispheres of the brain. The left hemisphere should be used to reinforce the right and vice versa.[47] Children should be provided alternative ways of knowing and expressing themselves.

In recent years, teachers have become more aware of the importance of selecting learning activities designed to enhance the right-brain mode of perception. Cultural education has made some difference. Each time a child sees an actor, dancer, or musician perform, he or she is getting practice in perceiving through the right brain.[48]

GROWTH, LEARNING, MATURATION, AND DEVELOPMENT

As adults work with preschool-age children and observe the numerous and varied movements, expressions, behavioral attitudes, and seemingly endless and often meaningless activities, they will have a better understanding of the needs of children if they are familiar with characteristics of growth, development, and maturation common to all children. For example, because movement and activity are essential to normal physical growth at this time, the prudent teacher avoids experiences that require long periods of quiet attention to the tasks at hand.

Likewise, all young children possess varying degrees of curiosity. Yet not all children confront new and novel situations with bubbling enthusiasm and excitement. Standing quietly and closely observing details by intently gazing at a new

---

[44]Thelma Palmer, "Why Our Kids Can Write or Running Slo's Through the Right Brain Equals the Morphology of Diddley Doos," *English Journal*, **69** (Sept. 1980), p. 49.

[45]Thomas Banville, "Responsibility: Which Side of the Gray?" *Early Years*, **11** (Aug.–Sept. 1980), p. 71.

[46]Ibid.

[47]Ibid.

[48]Palmer, op. cit., p. 49.

In no other area of growth and development are differences so obvious as in that of physical growth. These children all attend the same kindergarten. Their unique features and differences in height and body build illustrate the folly of the often-used description of "fiveness." Although a general description of a five-year-old may be helpful as a reference point, it is generally agreed that individual differences due to innate and experiential variations make the concept of "five" or "fiveness" misleading, and often suggest practices that do not enhance the opportunity for optimum development of each child.

object or event may be one child's way of expressing curiosity whereas another child in the same situation may jump up and down screaming joyously.

It is all too easy to speak of growth, learning, maturation, and development as a single concept although in reality each has a separate meaning that should be understood. Concepts of growth, borrowed from biology, deal basically with an increase of some dimension such as height, circumference of the head, and similar physical characteristics. Present-day educational literature sometimes uses the term to express change in function and includes such expressions as growth in vocabulary, growth in reading, or growth in social understanding. Often these and similar expressions are used in such a way as to imply development, a concept which will be dealt with presently.

Professional personnel working with the young child have long been concerned with the problem of physical growth and development, for they have observed that behavior of the moment is often related to the physical makeup of the child.

Physical growth has been so well charted that most events, like the eruption of a particular tooth, the start of walking, or a later growth spurt can be predicted with considerable accuracy. In fact, the helpless, uncoordinated, and unskilled infant is able to progress through a succession of predictable and orderly developmental tasks with advancing age. Of course, this progress assumes the prerequisite nurture supplied by the parent and the home.

The plan of physical growth is so well coordinated that the emergence of each stage seems to depend on the mastery of the previous one through activity and exercise. The result is a continuous orderly process. The motivation for this process is one of the marvels of life itself. There is a certain urgency about growth inherent in the child. The growing, developing child is the end product of meeting this urgency through interaction with the environment.

Physical disproportions at ages three and four, as compared to later years, dictate many of the expectancies adults should have for the three-year-old child. Eyes, for example, are a part of the body proportions that are "oversize." It is just so much easier for objects, such as sand, to get into them! Because of their peculiar shape and developmental status, farsightedness is the expectation. Young children may have difficulty copying simply because of immature eye development. Looking back and forth from something close to something farther away requires accommodation (ability of the lens to adjust for focusing). This maturing process may not be completed until seven or eight years of age.[49]

Large objects, long play runways, big sheets of paper, and lots of room for active play are essential partly because the eyes play an important role in eye-muscle coordination. Growth inconsistencies, improperly proportioned body parts, lack of fine control and of personal learning experiences add to the picture and account for many of the characteristics of the motor activities of the young child. The encouragement of formal reading instruction, work requiring fine muscle skills, or extended periods of concentration is wisely postponed until development catches up with the demands of these activities. However, children will seek to use these skills on their own as maturation occurs.

The teacher of young children should become familiar with what research has found to be true of the age group of children she or he is working with. Such books

---

[49] Valerie S. Kovitz, "For Btter Coppy Wrok," *Academic Therapy*, **18**:1 (Sept. 1982), p. 90.

as those by Breckenridge and Vincent,[50] Landreth,[51] Stone and Church,[52] Cantor,[53] Merry and Merry,[54] Smart and Smart,[55] and Garrison and Jones[56] will enable the teacher to acquire an excellent grasp of early research important to an understanding of the growth and development of the young child, as well as what to expect later.

It is helpful to think of maturation as a process, its characteristics and temporal patterns peculiar to the organism involved, that represents the innate forces producing growth and change in a fixed direction. When environmental forces such as the effects of food or exercise interact with the innate force responsible for maturation, development takes place. Development may then be thought of as the changing end product that results from the interaction of maturation and the environmental factors or nurture. Thus, there is the implication that development represents a "stage" that has been achieved at any particular point of time in the maturation process.

The expression *normal development*, when applied to an individual child, means that the nurture has been such that the child concerned has achieved whatever stage of development is under consideration at about the same time and with similar characteristics as has been achieved by most children his or her age. Developmental changes may be thought of as occurring because of the complex interaction of the forces of nature and nurture. The teacher and school have as a major purpose to provide many types of experiences that the child might not otherwise encounter but that are designed to assist nature in the child's developmental process.

Stages of development, as previously indicated, always follow in a particular sequence. Children do not stand before they sit, nor do they draw a square before they draw a circle. This orderly progression of events moves forward at different rates of speed, with some children growing and developing at a faster rate than others. In general, girls pass through these periods of maturity more rapidly than boys. But children as people are not just physical beings. While developing physically, their personal-social and mental development is moving forward at a pace that challenges the abilities of adults working with them. As an individual makes a transition from one developmental stage to another a *sensitive period* occurs. Such periods may be related to a child's readiness for certain types of learning. Propo-

[50] Marian E. Breckenridge and E. Lee Vincent, *Child Development*, 4th ed. (Philadelphia: Saunders, 1960).

[51] Catherine Landreth, *The Psychology of Early Childhood* (New York: Knopf, 1958).

[52] L. Joseph Stone and Joseph Church, *Childhood and Adolescence*, 2d ed. (New York: Random, 1968).

[53] Pamela Cantor, *Understanding a Child's World* (New York: McGraw-Hill, 1977).

[54] Frieda K. Merry and R. V. Merry, *The First Two Decades of Life*, 2d ed. (New York: Harper, 1958).

[55] Mollie S. Smart and Russell C. Smart, *Children: Development and Relationships*, 2d ed. (New York: Macmillan, 1972).

[56] Karl C. Garrison and Franklin R. Jones, *The Psychology of Human Development* (Scranton, Pa.: International Textbook Co., 1969).

nents of this theory attempt to integrate the biological, psychological, and social dimensions of the sensitive periods concept.[57]

A great deal has been written about learning. Psychologists devote much of their effort to research on the process. In this frame of reference, learning is usually thought of as any observable or inferred change in response behavior caused wholly or in part by experience. As a result, several theories of learning have been developed; much is known about the conditions of learning, but the process itself still remains a mystery. In the context of education, learning is assumed to have occurred when a person has acquired relatively permanent knowledges and skills. It is generally assumed that such knowledges and skills happen as a result of practice although learning certainly takes place as a result of single experiences. Because there is so much to learn, young children, unhampered by a large number of previous experiences, find the world a very fascinating place. As a result they learn easily and acquire knowledges and skills at a very rapid rate when their environment provides an opportunity for them to do so.

Psychologists speak of learning that goes on without specific intent to learn in keeping with the maturation process as autogenous learning. Much of the learning of preschool children falls within this category. Fortunately, young children are curious and eager to learn, and the rapidity with which they learn amazes adults. The important question for parents and teachers is, "What should be taught to children at each age level and why?" Choosing between required learning activities and the other essential activities of childhood can be a perplexing problem. Reported research has not been very helpful, for although complex and abstract concepts can be learned early, long-range effects have not been determined. It is doubtful that the time and effort expended on early reading or other academic pursuits make it a wise and efficient educational procedure.

Most preschool children are functioning either in what Piaget[58] describes as the sensorimotor stage or the intuitive phase of the preoperational stage of cognitive development. The sensorimotor stage (about the first eleven months) takes place prior to speech and thus lacks representation. This period, although it occurs before a child acquires language, is one of the more important periods in the sequence of development. The child changes from being capable of only reflex actions to an individual capable of internalizing thoughts.

The use of any one or of several sensory modalities simultaneously may be appropriate as children explore new experiences in ways that are unique to each. An observing adult soon learns and respects the mode of sensorimotor expression peculiar to each child in the group while at the same time encouraging new and different ways of discovering meaningful concepts. In each case, the child grows in

[57] Languis, Sanders, and Tipps, op. cit., pp. 29–30.
[58] Jean Piaget, *The Child and Reality: Problems of Genetic Psychology*, trans. Arnold Rosin (New York: Viking, 1974).

confidence as he or she learns more about the world by experiencing it through his or her available sensorimotor repertoire at any given point in time.

Piaget says young children learn as a result of tactile experiences with objects in their environment. They need to touch, feel, pour, taste, and manipulate the things around them. Information is obtained on the basis of this interaction with tangible objects. Gradually, they relate a new idea to information already known. Learning is not as meaningful or permanent when adults tell children answers as it is when they make their own discoveries from firsthand experiences.[59] Teachers can help children learn by providing materials and activities that invite self-discovery and manipulation.

Today the emphasis is on how children create meaning from experience. Individuals may generate different meanings from similar experiences. The concept of generative learning seems to have important relations as to how the child feels, thinks, values, loves, and plays.[60]

Even as early as three, sex roles are being learned. However, sex-role identification is at a minimum. Little boys and girls can play together, fight with each other, share the same toilet facilities, and are seemingly unaware of sex differences. Modesty plays no part whatever. However, using a picture-interview technique, Fauls and Smith found that five-year-olds had well-established sex-role perceptions in keeping with the expectations of the social group of which their parents were a part.[61] A recent study links reading achievement with degrees of sex-role stereotyping among boys. As degrees of sex-role stereotyping rose, reading achievement decreased. If boys attempt reading activities without perceiving them as suitable for men and boys, learning will be impeded.[62] Sensitive teachers can help by expecting both boys and girls to succeed and by planning activities that foster unbiased thinking.

The learning of language shows that a child is beginning to acquire symbolic thought and is in Piaget's preoperational stage. Between the ages of two and five, children learn to think in more sophisticated ways. They become able to substitute words and thoughts for actions. They become able to communicate what they think and feel.[63] The move from sensorimotor functioning to language functioning is one of the major transitions in development and probably is the most dramatic transition.

---

[59] Margery A. Kranyik, *Starting School: How to Help Your Three-to-Eight-Year-Old Make the Most of School.* (New York: Continuum, 1982), p. 4.

[60] Languis, Sanders, and Tipps, op.cit., p. 5.

[61] Lydia B. Fauls and W. D. Smith, "Sex-Role Learning of Five-Year-Olds," *J. Genet. Psychol.*, **89**:2 (1956), pp. 105–107.

[62] Charles Whitfield, "An Analysis of Sex-Role Stereotyping and Pupil Achievement," Ed.D. Diss., (Texas Tech University, 1980), p. 298.

[63] S. Cohen, and T. J. Comiskey, *Child Development—An Introduction*, 2d ed. (Boston: Houghton, 1981), p. 366.

The following observations depict activities and behavior common to children of normal development for the ages described. A range of individual differences is included, but these discussions are not intended to portray the characteristics of those who deviate widely from the expectancies of the respective age groups.

OBSERVATIONS IN A CHILD DEVELOPMENT CENTER

Three- and four-year-old children were observed in a child development center one morning in the fall of the year. In one particular group, there were four children. These children had been multiage grouped, so the differences between the younger and older ones were easily seen by the observer. A four-year-old boy was busily piecing together a puzzle, matching numbers with corresponding groups of pictures. This boy knew all number concepts up to twenty. He required a little help from time to time, and his vocabulary was advanced enough so that he could ask the teacher for assistance.

Two three-year-old children were having a great time splashing and playing with toys at a water table. The teacher encouraged them to use the proper words when asking for new toys to put in the water. Their vocabulary was not as advanced as the four-year-old's. A squabble broke out as these two grabbed the same toy. The teacher calmly explained that one of them was using it first and redirected the other's attention toward something else. These two seemed to enjoy playing beside each other although they were not actually playing together. They did some sharing, but still needed help with this from the teacher.

Another group of children, age three, were seated around a table. Their teacher had given each child a blob of "silly goo" (made from starch and glue) to manipulate. It was interesting to see what each child did with it and to hear what they had to say.

A three-year-old girl had divided her blob into five separate pieces. She carefully rolled each piece into a ball and put all five pieces in a row. This took quite a while, and she was very pleased with herself when she was finished.

Much about the normal development of young children was gleaned from this observation, which agreed with summary research findings about developmental characteristics of this age group. The teachers seemed well aware of developmental characteristics of particular age groups.

It is not within the scope of this book to present a detailed review of the voluminous research in child development on the characteristics of preschool-age children. The preceding observational report and discussion concerned itself with some of the major findings of importance to the teacher or caregiver of young children. A similar report of the findings of major importance to the kindergarten teacher follows.

OBSERVATIONS IN A KINDERGARTEN

Kindergarten students were observed during morning "center time" in the fall of the year. The children were given a choice of centers during the first half of the time period, and for the remainder of the time period they were assigned to a variety of centers. Although there were many activities going on at once, the children all seemed totally involved in what they were doing without being distracted by those in other centers. All children were observed in small groups. There was much social interaction within each group.

In the housekeeping center, there was a group of three boys. One had donned an evening gown. Another boy helped him to zip it up as they both laughed. The third boy was busy sweeping the floor. Clearly, these boys were having fun exploring grown-up roles and were very aware of sex differences in these roles. They were also able to cooperate and communicate well with each other. These boys had chosen this center for their free choice.

Another group of boys was observed in the block center. Each was wearing a red fire fighter's hat. The boys busily built something together; most likely it was a fire engine. They seemed very adept at stacking the large-and small-sized blocks and were very creative in their use of them.

Two girls had chosen the piano for their free time. The teacher had numbered the keys so that the kindergarteners could play songs. Song sheets had large numbers printed above the words to match the keys. The observer noted that these girls had enough eye-hand coordination to follow the numbers and play the song. Even though the song did not have the correct musical timing, it still showed much about the advanced skills of these children as compared to the skills of children just a year or two younger. Social skills were apparent during this observation. One girl waited patiently while the other played a song until it was her turn. There was no grabbing, pushing, or impatient actions, as there might have been with younger children.

At a small round table, a group of boys and girls were working on various seasonal activities with the guidance of a student teacher. As the children drew, colored, and wrote with pencils, it became obvious that they had progressed in their fine motor skills development. These children were able to color within the lines and draw straight lines to match like objects.

One boy was at the easel. He had painted a lovely rainbow, using five separate colors. The painting was another indication of fine motor control.

Outside there was another center where various activities were going on. Two girls had chosen to use tools to create something from wood. Three boys were busy going from a sandbox to a water-play tub. They all seemed to be playing separately although talking constantly to one another. Another girl was busy turning cartwheels. She was anxious to show off this new skill to the teacher aide who was supervising this center.

At no time did any child seem to miss mother or home. The morning produced

Interesting puzzles provide opportunities to recognize contrast, shape, form, and generalizations so important in the early phases of mental development. This child studies intently the remaining pieces of the puzzle as he tries to decide where they will go to complete the picture.

surprisingly few conflicts and squabbles, which were usually resolved quickly, often without the teacher's help.

In comparison to three-year-olds, most five-year-olds handle language well, using it to question, to answer, to suggest, and to get permission to do things. Both vocabulary and sentence structure have greatly improved. The five-year-old has become quite independent and responsible, able to run errands, follow directions, and carry out rather complicated tasks. The five-year-old's conscience seems to be developing rapidly, for the child quickly judges and reports the small deeds of others as right or wrong.[64]

Unfortunately, science has not been able to determine such orderly laws for the

[64] Gladys G. Jenkins, Helen Schacter, and W. W. Bauer, *These Are Your Children*, 3d ed. (Chicago: Scott, Foresman, 1966).

personal-social and mental areas of development as it has for physical development. It is likely that the unique personality characteristics so treasured by all account for the fact that personality descriptions tend to defy lawful prediction. However, great strides are being made in personality research.

EMOTIONAL DEVELOPMENT

Various studies of certain aspects of the emotional development of young children show that emotional control and generally more mature behavior gradually develop during the preschool years. For example, Goodenough's classic study of expressions of anger in young children showed a gradual decline with age of undirected general outbursts of anger and a corresponding increase in anger resulting from conflicts or situations that might be described as a reasonable excuse for anger. Of interest to teachers was the finding that there were more anger expressions just before meal-time, when the children were tired, were coming down with an illness, or when some atypical home condition, such as the presence of visitors, existed.[65]

Likewise, Jersild and Holmes found that most of the specific situations that evoked fear responses in two- and three-year-old children did not produce like responses from five-year-olds.[66] From ages two to five, children showed a decrease in fear of noise, strange objects, people, pain, falling, and sudden movement. The same children showed an increase in fear of the dark, animals, ridicule, and potentially dangerous situations, such as fire and deep water.[67] These developmental differences, like so many others, apparently are due to a combination of the effects of maturation and learning.

There is a key difference between fear and anxiety. Fear is usually a legitimate response to a tangible threat or danger. It appears rational to others. Anxiety involves inner conflicts that may appear irrational to others.[68] Fears can be dispelled if children learn to handle them. Anxiety, on the other hand, may persist even after knowledge and experience are gained. Confidence in ability to handle "inner" feelings through insight is needed.[69]

Possible causes of anxiety in two- to five-year-olds are fear of losing the love and protection of the mother, conflicts between desires and social codes and restrictions, concern about physical and psychological safety, lack of acceptance by others, and threats to self-esteem.[70]

[65] Florence L. Goodenough, "Anger in Young Children," *Univ. Minn. Inst. Child Welf. Monogr. Ser.*, 9 (1931).

[66] A. T. Jersild and Frances B. Holmes, "Children's Fears," *Child Develop. Monogr.*, 20 (1935).

[67] Cohen and Comiskey, op. cit., p. 353.

[68] Ibid.

[69] Ibid.

[70] Ibid., p. 359.

Anxiety may be minimized by providing support, satisfying needs, and encouraging independence. Everything possible should be done to help a child feel secure.

DEVELOPMENT OF MOTOR SKILLS

Large-muscle activity is the rule during the early years. Out of these large-muscle, aimless, and seemingly endless activities there gradually emerge patterns of coordination and control. Over a period of eight weeks, Hicks studied the learning skills of young children involved in throwing a ball at a moving target. One group practiced ten throws each week, whereas another group, which was matched with the experimental group on initial ball throwing ability, was not given the practice. When tested at the end of the experiment, both groups had made gains, but the experimental (practice) group did not make significantly better gains than the second (control) group. Apparently, children in the control group were practicing the same skills in the course of daily living.[71] Psychologists speak of learning that goes on without specific intent to learn in keeping with the maturation process as *autogenous learning.* Much of the learning of preschool children falls into this category.

Although the Hicks study is an earlier one, the findings still seem to be relevant as to the need for providing opportunities for physical activities for young children. The development and refinement of large motor skills increase a child's success in performing daily tasks. Much is learned about the environment by climbing, running, hopping, and jumping. The basis of meaning in early child language seems to be motor learning, as shown by the young child's gesturing while trying to tell about an experience.

As large motor coordination improves, small motor skills begin to develop, leading to improved readiness.[72] Before children can learn to write, they need to develop skills using the small muscles of the fingers and hand. Physical and mental activities appear to be closely related.

Learning activities that can contribute to the development of fine motor skills include the following: [73]

1. Manipulating finger puppets.
2. Stringing empty spools on a shoelace.
3. Screwing and unscrewing large nuts and bolts.
4. Punching holes with a paper punch.
5. Sewing designs on cardboard, using large needle and yarn.

[71] J. A. Hicks, "The Acquisition of Motor Skills in Young Children: A Study of the Effects of Practice in Throwing at a Moving Target," *Child Develop.*, **1**:2 (1930), pp. 90–105.
[72] Languis, Sanders, and Tipps, op. cit., p. 31.
[73] Kranyik, op. cit., p. 38.

6. Using crayons to connect dots.
7. Using puzzles.
8. Engaging in activities involving clay, finger paint, scissors, and paste.

Movement exploration is a relatively new program that stresses coordination and thinking. Children stretch their minds as well as their bodies.[74] This is in contrast to the physical education of previous years, which stressed task performance. There is no feeling of failure with movement exploration activities. All children participate without having to wait for their turn. They work in large and small groups, and nobody is singled out.

SUMMARY

Rather than listing a set of characteristics of the young child at various age levels, the authors have illustrated some of the principles this chapter has developed. Young children are not alike; each has unique qualities and features that become evident early in life. Beginning with innate differences, variations in growth and maturation processes interacting with the multiplicity of possible environmental differences, both physical and human, result in development that further differentiates, and thus accounts for the individuality of personality. An excellent example of this differentiation is found in the usually retarded language and achievement levels of children from culturally different homes. These basic components of individuality are well established during the preschool years. Because these processes take place very rapidly during the early years of life, major developmental differences occur during this period at shorter intervals than at any later period of life, which accounts for the dramatic and challenging changes observed in young children.

Today much emphasis is placed on the importance of how children view themselves, that is, on the development of the concept of self. There are those who would build a young child's learning experiences entirely around this concept. However, it is becoming increasingly clear that a healthy self-concept is dependent on how well a child's behavior fits social and environmental expectancies, for only such behavior receives the reinforcement provided by approval, praise, and acceptance. It would seem realistic, therefore, to view each child's self-concept in relation to all aspects of development, including cognitive development, rather than as an isolated concept.

Some insights from brain research are included here, along with suggestions as to their meaning for early childhood education. Students of child growth and development have found that development corresponds rather closely with maturational change and growth patterns. To the person who understands the processes of growth, maturation, and development, there are always small signs as to what

[74] Kranyik, op. cit., p. 39.

will occur later. For example, not long ago a mother called who was very concerned because the child was not walking when other children of the same age were. The child was observed during the interview. Certain signs were noticed, such as creeping and moving in a circular direction, attempting to pull himself up on every occasion, and a general effort to arrive in an upright position. These signs indicated that within a few weeks the child would be walking and that development was occurring as a result of maturation and growth. The mother was reassured, and she reported several weeks later that her child was walking. The important point here is that when one understands the developmental process and watches for the little signs that precede an actual act, anxieties can easily be relieved. It is also important to know that readiness is often primarily a biological function that cannot be hurried. Nevertheless, it is necessary to keep in mind that biological development does not proceed on its own without suitable environmental nurture. Unfortunately, lack of readiness has often been mistaken, in the past, for an inherent biological lack rather than a lack of adequate environmental stimulation to enable maturation to occur on schedule. However, when the stage or maturation point is arrived at and the act can be completed, the child will complete the act and do it with enthusiasm and with a high degree of motivation. Psychologists call this indigenous motivation, which means that when one is able to do something at the proper stage of maturation, one will do it, and with zest and vigor. Everyone has observed young children arriving at this stage.

Another important factor is that growth, although it occurs rather uniformly for an individual, may take place in one child at a speed or rate different from that of other children. So far as is known, this is an inherited characteristic. Each growing child possesses an individual pattern and rate of growth. When arriving at a certain place in this pattern, the child can "tune in" and achieve the goal just as a radio can be tuned in to get a program that was present all the time but was not coming in until it was tuned in to the proper wavelength. Similarly, certain activities and certain behavioral acts cannot be achieved until the proper "wavelength" represented by development can be tuned in to the circumstances provided in the environment. The teacher, caregiver, or parent can no more change this process than the color of one's hair can be changed. True, hair can be dyed, and temporarily it will appear different, but it will grow out to be the color it should be at a particular time; the change is only temporary. The same kind of thing often happens when youngsters are pushed and undue pressures put upon them or when remedial work is carried on for long periods of time. Always, the individual functions in keeping with his or her stage of development.

While a "stage" represents a point in development at a particular time, growth and maturation proceed as a somewhat erratic continuum. The concept of threes, fours, fives, and so forth merely represents specific points on the continuum from birth to maturity. This ongoingness of development is hard to describe primarily because developmental research on which such descriptions are based is developmental in name only, as it represents a succession of points rather than a true continuum.[75]

Perhaps the best way to summarize is to indicate that there are likely to be no "static," or discipline, problems when the wavelength is right and the activities are tuned in to the child's stage of development. It is important to realize further that all behavior is caused and that undesirable behavior results when the individual is not properly "tuned in" to activities that are consistent with his or her stage of development and, thus, the ability "to do."

Some three-year-olds may be able to do the tasks normally expected of five-year-olds, and some five-year-olds can perform only the tasks usually expected of three-year-olds. But in general, the expectancies adults have for each child should be in keeping with those suitable to his or her age group and particular stage of development. The concept of "threeness," "fiveness," and so on, so common in the literature, has served a useful purpose by pointing out the direction we can reasonably expect a child's development to take. However, educational programs for groups based on such concepts without provision for a wide range of individual differences in development would most surely fail to provide for the optimal development of each child as a person.

Suggested Activities

1. Prepare a detailed class report on the development of children on such topics as "a positive self image," "a typical five-year-old," "learning sex roles," "early speech development," and "motor development of four-year-olds." Use the references given in the text and any others that you can find on the topic.
2. Discuss and decide on a specific topic, such as "readiness for the first day of school," "teeth and the preschooler," "children's diseases," "socialization," "motor development and materials and equipment," "sibling relationships," "development of creativity," "crying," and so on. Prepare and report on one research study from the current periodicals related to the preceding topics. Discuss each report, and use the study as a basis for continuing discussion.
3. Arrange with a nursery school, day care or kindergarten teacher to observe for fifteen minutes a planned activity with a group of young children. Immediately afterward, write down what you learned about children and about yourself from the experience. If several members of the group do the same thing, such observations can provide the information for a lively class discussion.
4. Select a child to observe over a period of time. Evaluate his or her concept of self. Document with descriptive observations how you arrived at the conclusions of your evaluation.
5. Observe in a kindergarten during an activity period. Note activities designed to enhance the right brain mode of perception.

[75] R. B. McCall, "Challenge to a Science of Developmental Psychology," *Child Develop.*, **48**:2 (1977), pp. 333–344.

6. Examine sample observation tools included in textbooks that are listed in Related Readings. Use one with a young child.

Related Readings

Almy, Millie, and Celia Genish. *Ways of Studying Children: An Observation Manual for Childhood Teachers.* New York: Teachers College Press, 1979.

Biehler, Robert F. *Child Development, An Introduction.* 2d ed. Boston: Houghton, 1981.

Bloom, B. S., et al. *Compensatory Education for Cultural Deprivation.* New York: Holt, 1965.

Brockman, Lois M., and H. N. Riceluti. "Severe Protein-Calorie Malnutrition and Cognitive Development in Infancy and Early Childhood." *Develop. Psychol.,* **4:**3 (1971), pp. 312–319.

Cohen, Dorothy H. *Observing and Recording the Behavior of Young Children.* New York: Teachers College Press, 1978.

Copple, Carol E., R. DeLisa, and I. Sigel. "Cognitive Development" in *Handbook of Research in Early Childhood Education,* ed. by B. Spodek. New York: The Free Press, 1982, pp. 3–26.

Cratty, B. J. "Motor Development in Early Childhood: Critical Issues for Researchers in the 1980s," in *Handbook of Research in Early Childhood Education,* ed. by B. Spodek. New York: The Free Press, 1982, pp. 27–46.

Donaldson, M. *Children's Minds.* New York: Norton, 1978.

Earle, P. T., C. S. Rogers, and J. G. Wall. *Child Development: An Observation Manual.* Englewood Cliffs, N.J.: Prentice-Hall, 1982. (loose leaf).

Elkind, D. *Child Development and Education: A Piagetian Perspective.* New York: Oxford University Press, 1976.

Erikson, Erik H. *Toys and Reasons.* New York: Library of Human Behavior, 1977.

Field, T., and A. Fogel. *Emotions and Early Interactions.* Hillsdale, N.J.: Lawrence Erlbaum Assoc., 1982.

Flavell, J. H. *Cognitive Development.* Englewood Cliffs, N.J.: Prentice-Hall, 1977.

Fox, Marian N. "Creativity and Intelligence." *Child. Educ.* **57:**4 (1981), pp. 227–232.

Galin, D. "Educating Both Halves of the Brain." *Child. Educ.,* **53:**1 (1976), pp. 17–20.

Goodman, Kenneth. "Over the Editor's Desk." *Child. Educ.,* **57:**4 (1981), pp. 253–254.

Hetherington, E. M., and R. D. Parke. *Child Psychology: A Contemporary Viewpoint.* New York: McGraw-Hill, 1979.

Hunt, J. McV. "The Psychological Basis for Using Pre-School Enrichment as an Antidote for Cultural Deprivation." *Merrill-Palmer Quart.,* **10:**3 (1964), pp. 209–248.

Kallstrom, Christine. *Yellow Brick Road (Ages 5–6).* Austin, Texas: Learning Concepts, 1977.

Kaplan, A., and Joan Bean (eds.). *Beyond Sex-Role Stereotypes: Readings Toward a Psychology of Androgyny.* Boston: Little, Brown, 1976.

Langus, M., T. Sanders, and S. Tipps. *Brain and Learning: Directions in Early Childhood Education.* Washington, D.C.: NAEYC, 1980.

Lindberg, Lucile, and Rita Swedlow. *Early Childhood Education: A Guide for Observation and Participation.* Boston: Allyn, 1980.

Linskie, Rosella. *The Learning Process: Theory and Practice,* New York: Van Nostrand, 1977.

Mitzel, H. E., Editor in Chief, AERA. *Encyclopedia of Educational Research*, *5th ed.* New York: The Free Press, 1982.

Mussen, P. H., et al. *Child Development and Personality*, 5th ed. New York: Harper, 1974.

Oleron, P. *Language and Mental Development.* Trans. R. P. Lorion. Hillsdale, N.J.: Lawrence Erlbaum Assoc., 1977.

Phyfe-Perkins, E. *Effects of Teacher Behavior on Pre-school Children: A Review of Research* ERIC/EELE ED211 176 Arlington, Va.: Computer Microfilm International Corp., 1981.

Purkey, W. W. *Inviting School Success: A Self-Concept Approach to Teaching and Learning.* Belmont, CA.: Wadsworth, 1978.

Raman, Pattabi (ed.). *Nutrition in Human Development.* Stamford, Conn.: Greylock Publishers, 1977.

Ringness, Thomas A. *The Affective Domain in Education.* Boston: Little Brown, 1975.

Roedell, W. C. *Social Development in Young Children.* Washington, D.C.: DHEW, NIE, 1976.

Samuels, Shirley C. *Enhancing Self-Concept in Early Childhood.* New York: Human Sciences Press, 1977.

Smith, Charles A. *Promoting the Social Development of Young Children—Strategies and Activities.* Palo Alto, CA.: Mayfield, 1982.

Todd, Vivian E., and Helen Heffernan. *The Years Before School*, 3rd ed. New York: Macmillan, 1977.

Travers, J. F. *The Growing Child: An Introduction to Child Development.* New York: Wiley, 1977.

————. *The New Children: The First Six Years.* Stamford, Conn.: Greylock.

Vasta, R. *Strategies and Techniques of Child Study.* New York: Academic Press, 1982.

White, S. H., and A. W. Siegel. "Cognitive Development: The New Inquiry." *Young Children*, **31**:6 (1976), pp. 425–436.

CHAPTER 4

Research and the Young Child

Research in early childhood development and education has mushroomed over the past two decades. This chapter focuses on the significance of using children as research subjects to aid in determining public policy regarding programs for young children and their families. Such programs include education, health, and other social services. This chapter is not intended to be a review of research using children as subjects, nor is it intended to be a critique of research methodology. Throughout this book, relevant research is documented in the form of discussion, rather than in-depth analysis or critique.

RESEARCH AND PUBLIC POLICY

Perhaps the most significant development with respect to children and research during the 1970s was the consensus among members of the research community of the indispensability of the adequate and proper use of research findings in determining public policy for services and programs for children. Researchers were showing increasing concern for the individual obligation of each to see that their own research findings were properly interpreted and disseminated to the appropriate policymaking groups or individuals. Significant deliberations of the prestigious Society for Research in Child Development at the 1977 biennial meeting in New Orleans centered on the role of the society and its individual members in policy formation in relation to children.

In 1977, the Bush Foundation in St. Paul, Minnesota, established a Bush Institute of Child Development and Public Policy at Yale University. Three more institutes were begun the following year at the University of Michigan, the University of California at Los Angeles, and the University of North Carolina at Chapel Hill. The UNC-CH Bush Institute has a broadened scope that includes family as well as child policy. The primary charge to these institutes is to train doctoral and postdoctoral students of the social sciences in the analysis of policies dealing with children or children and families. The participants in these training programs come mainly from the fields of child development and education. Given the need for policy formulation, the Bush Foundation believes strongly that its training programs will better equip professionals to assess effectively the many options that are being and will be presented.

PUBLIC INTERVENTION

The changed child's world (see Chapter 2) clearly pointed to the need for public intervention in family life and child-rearing if the best interests of a large number of American children were to be served. These developments, as would be expected, had a profound effect on both the nature and purposes of the research being carried out. The then current need for early education and alternate parenting as more and more mothers of young children reentered the work force or continued pursuing their career objectives was reflected in the program of the Society for Research in Child Development meeting held in 1977. Of the 376 papers accepted for presentation, 91 were on infancy, 71 on socialization, 67 on cognition and memory, 55 on language and speech, 25 on perception, 16 on adolescence, 16 on biologic and genetic factors, 16 on socioeconomic and ethnic factors, 14 on clinical and intervention problems, and 6 on intellectual development.[1] At that time, researchers using children as subjects were assigning high priority to the social and developmental needs of infants and young children in order to assure more successful care and educational programs for three-, four-, and five-year-olds.

During the 1970s the Administration for Children, Youth, and Families funded a four-year study called the National Day Care Study (NDCS) involving 1,800 children in 64 centers in Seattle, Atlanta, and Detroit. Recognizing that the need for day care was definite, the study focused not on whether or not day care was benefi-

---

[1]*Report of the Program Committee*, SRCD Biennial meeting, New Orleans, March 17–20, 1977 (Topeka, Kansas: Menninger Foundation, *SRCD Newsletter*, Summer 1977), p. 12.

cial to children, but rather on what factors were instrumental in best serving the needs of day care children. The purpose of the study was to collect data that would aid the government in developing standards for day care. The major variables studied were staff education and training, staff-child ratio, and group size, all of which have implications for national social policy. Although results of the main studies have been published,[2] further analyses are still ongoing. Caldwell and Freyer point out the significance of this study by emphasizing that "experts in day care and child development, psychologists, economists, and a special minority task force regularly reviewed the study, scrutinizing its design, analyses, and findings to insure the objectivity and technical integrity. Such efforts, together with the technical quality control maintained by the research organizations that conducted the study, helped to ensure that the obtained information would be objective, reliable, and applicable to policy questions."[3]

PROTECTION OF HUMAN RIGHTS

There has been increasing concern for the protection of human rights. In 1972 the Society for Research in Child Development published a paper setting forth twenty-one principles that formed a core of ethics concerning research with children.[4] The right-to-privacy laws (Privacy Act of 1974) have been felt in educational circles as confidentiality of records, except under certain conditions, has been abolished by law. Concern for the protection of children participating in research projects has received much attention.

At the January 1977 meeting of the National Commission for the Protection of Human Subjects of Biomedical and Behavioral Research held in Bethesda, Maryland, it was decided that research including children is "important for the health and well being of children and can be conducted in an ethical manner."[5] The commission was established under the National Research Act of 1974 to identify ethical principles underlying research involving human subjects.

The panel of the commission, recommended at that time that the Secretary of Health, Education and Welfare support and conduct research with children within a broad framework, including approval of minimum-risk projects by institutional review boards, and that those posing greater than minimal risk be approved by a national ethical advisory board. It was suggested that appropriate consent from children and parents be secured and that participation be severely limited for children who had no parents.

[2] R. Ruopp et al., *Children at the Center: Final Report of the National Day Care Study*, Vol. 1 (Cambridge, Mass.: Abt, 1979).
[3] Bettye Caldwell and Marjorie Freyer, "Day Care and Early Education," in *Handbook of Research in Early Childhood Education*, ed. by B. Spodek (New York: Free Press, 1982), p. 361.
[4] Leon Yarrow, "Ethical Standards for Research with Children," *SRCD Newsletter* (Sept. 1972).
[5] Susan Lawrence, "Panel Takes up Children as Subjects," *APA Monitor* (Feb. 1977).

It is generally thought that research with children should protect the integrity of the family and the importance of parenting, as well as facilitate efforts that will involve both children and parents in decision making that affects their own lives. Since current emphasis in human research is on its usefulness to social policymaking, such involvement and restraints as discussed here are essential, for the lives of all Americans are affected by these decisions.

Behavioral scientists often use animals as subjects because custom and human values tend to discourage the use of human subjects in controlled experimentation. In many cases, the information obtained from such experimentation is likely to be as valid when interpreted in terms of human behavior; still, the question remains: Would humans react in the same way? College students provide a readily accessible source of subjects for research and have been used extensively as such. Preschool-age children as research subjects (except for hospital and institutional populations, such as orphans, seriously ill, and physically disabled children) have traditionally been much more difficult to secure.

Today, with thousands of young children in Child Development Centers, which usually require some participation on the part of parents, opportunities for research with children and their families are almost unlimited. It has been the experience of researchers in centers where parents participate that it is easier to secure their consent to have their children take part in research efforts. Such has not been the case where parents were only responsible for seeing that the children were delivered to the custody of the school or center. It enhances the self-concept of parents when they feel that they are actively participating in an effort that may produce new and better ways of providing a chance for their own children to have a richer, more rewarding life than they themselves have been able to enjoy.

CHILD RESEARCH IN PERSPECTIVE

Beginning in the 1920s, several universities established nursery schools and kindergartens to provide preschool-age children for research. This practice has continued, and many universities now have such laboratory groups of children. However, it was not until the advent of Head Start in 1965 that a large number of groups of preschool-age children became readily available for research purposes. Research sponsored by the Office of Economic Opportunity included provision for follow-up studies of Head Start children in the first three grades of the public schools in a program called Follow Through. This program provided funds for continuous evaluation and research, the results of which are continually being updated.

Research and evaluation of programs conducted by other government agencies and foundations during the 1970s are providing a wealth of information about how young children, particularly culturally different children, learn and also give clues to the improvement of educational practices for all youngsters. As would be expected, an all-out search for quick panaceas for the faults of the entire educational program took place at once, and often extravagant claims were made on the basis of short-term, sometimes poorly designed, and small-sample research.

There is no question that innovation and experimentation are to be encouraged, but the Early Childhood Education teacher should carefully weigh the evidence presented before making radical departures from accepted procedures that have in the past enabled most preschool children to make a successful transition to the more formal public school program.

Most such programs are conducted at a much greater cost than are regular programs. Consequently, more and better equipment and materials and usually more faculty and helpers are called into play. Often the teacher or experimenter is imbued with confidence and a missionary zeal. Without comparable conditions and support of existing programs, it is unfair to make comparisons and claim superior achievements.

Caldwell and Freyer point out the lack of feasibility of studies requiring clean-cut experimental-control designs. They assert that it is not possible to compare different patterns of day care services as to their effects on children when the use of these different patterns has been determined by existing differences such as

An observation booth with a one-way vision mirror lends itself to conducting research about children.

social class, education, and income level.[6] They suggest that more emphasis be placed on descriptions of actual events in child care facilities.

Many research programs have deliberately excluded the stimulation of areas of development other than the one being studied, usually the cognitive or intellectual area. It is not surprising that children learn specific facts or skills more rapidly when they are formally taught rather than when expected to learn them incidentally. The important question is whether these specific facts and skills are the "right" ones and whether they will truly be effective in the later school and personal life of the child involved. When areas of development, earlier shown to be necessary correlates to learning and personality development, have been purposefully omitted or relegated to roles of secondary importance, will the end product be in keeping with the goals of American education? Observations of the preschool programs in the early 1960s have indicated that the cognitive and intellectual development of young children, in some instances at least, have received less attention than have such areas as social, physical, and emotional development.[7] Calling attention to this lack can well serve a useful purpose in helping bring about a better balanced program of education for young children provided that other areas of development are not neglected. It is well known that the medical profession soon discovered that the quick acceptance and widespread use of antibiotics and other miracle drugs had made it harder to cure the very diseases the drugs were developed to cure because through overuse of these medications the organism tends to develop an immunity. Child development specialists caution that too intensive emphasis on academic learning, too early, might likewise make later learning more difficult to achieve.

Although it has been claimed that early research in child development neglected the cognitive areas, it can also be said that much of the research in the second half of the 1960s tended to ignore areas of development other than the cognitive area. The futility of an either-or approach was becoming evident as research merged into the 1970s. It was becoming accepted that whatever the research orientation or focus, the ultimate goal was the extension of knowledge that would enable children to have an opportunity for optimum personal development, assuring a "good" life for all.

Research, of necessity, cannot be global in nature. Rather, research must focus on specifics that can be defined and controlled but, at the same time, can be fitted into the larger stream of theory and ongoing practice. An example of such research is in the area of language.

---

[6] Caldwell and Freyer, op. cit., p. 369.

[7] F. M. Hechinger (ed.), *Pre-School Education Today* (Garden City, N.Y.: Doubleday, 1966). Also, C. Bereiter and S. Englemann, *Teaching Disadvantaged Children in the Preschool* (Englewood Cliffs, N.J.: Prentice-Hall, 1966).

RESEARCH REVIEWS

To expect the busy teacher or center worker to select helpful guidelines from thousands of research reports is asking the impossible. It is the responsibility of scholars and professional organizations to digest and integrate research findings into useful terms for research to serve its function and to justify its cost. Although large sample research using young children was not extensive prior to the 1950s, important reviews have been made. One such effort worthy of note is a volume edited by Hartup.[8]

Excellent analyses of research in all areas of development in young children can be found in *The Manual of Child Psychology*.[9] Descriptions and evaluations of the most common techniques and methods used in studying many aspects of child growth and behavior, as well as other valuable content, are included in the *Handbook of Research Methods in Child Development*.[10]

Prepared under the auspices of the Society for Research in Child Development, the *Review of Child Development Research* series provides the student with a reference to important research studies in child development as well as an excellent source of additional readings.[11]

Sears and Dowley have traced the effect of research on teaching and procedures used in the nursery school.[12] They draw attention to the fact that nursery education in the United States has had as its primary objective the welfare of persons other than the children, with a resulting lack of emphasis on the child as an individual. The *Handbook of Research in Early Childhood Education*[13] contains critical reviews of research in the areas of child development, developmental theories, classroom processes, public policy, and research methodology. Also valuable are both volumes of *Current Topics in Early Childhood Education*,[14] which review research covering a broad range of early childhood concerns.

[8] Willard W. Hartup (ed.), *The Young Child, Reviews of Research*, Vol. 2 (Washington, D.C.,: National Association for the Education of Young Children, 1972).

[9] Paul H. Mussen (ed.), *Carmichael's Manual of Child Psychology*, 4th ed., Vols. 1 and 2. (New York: Wiley, 1981).

[10] P. H. Mussen (ed.), (New York: Wiley, 1960).

[11] Editors of the respective volumes are:

Vols. 1 and 2, M. L. Hoffman and Lois Wladis Hoffman (New York: Russell Sage Foundation, 1964 and 1967).

Vol. 3, Bettye M. Caldwell and H. Riccuiti (Chicago: University of Chicago Press, 1973).

Vol. 4, Frances Degan Horowitz, E. M. Hetherington, Sandra Scarr-Salapetek, and G. M. Siegal (Chicago: University of Chicago Press, 1974).

Vol. 5, E. M. Hetherington, J. W. Hagan, R. Kron, and Aletha Hustin Stein (Chicago: University of Chicago Press, 1975).

Vol. 6, Willard Hartup (Chicago: University of Chicago Press, 1977).

[12] Pauline S. Sears and Edith M. Dowley, "Research on Teaching in the Nursery School," in *Handbook of Research on Teaching*, ed. by N. L. Gage (Chicago: Rand McNally, 1963), Ch. 15.

[13] Bernard Spodek (ed.), (New York: Free Press, 1982).

[14] Lilian Katz (ed.), Vol. 1 (Norwood, N.J.: Ablex, 1977); Vol. 2 (Norwood, N.J.: Ablex, 1979).

A plethora of information is contained in *Lasting Effects After Preschool: A Report of the Consortium for Longitudinal Studies.*[15] The consortium consists of twelve research groups conducting longitudinal studies on the outcomes of early education programs involving low-income infants and preschool children in the 1960s. At the time of the follow-up study reported here, the children ranged in age from nine through nineteen. Lasting effects were found in the following areas: fewer program children were assigned to special education classes; fewer children were retained in grade; the children scored higher on fourth-grade mathematics achievement tests and showed a trend in that direction on fourth-grade reading tests; they scored higher on the Stanford-Binet IQ test for up to three years after leaving the program though there were no treatment-control differences by age thirteen; program children tended to give more achievement-type reasons for being proud of themselves; and no differences were found between treatment and control families in their use of Title IV child welfare services.

Young Children Grow Up: The Effects of the Perry Preschool Program on Youths Through Age 15[16] gives updated information on one of the studies participating in the Consortium for Longitudinal Studies, the Perry Preschool Project. At the time of publication, data were being collected on the subjects at the age of nineteen.

For research relating to high-risk children and to special education, see *High-Risk Infants and Children: Adult and Peer Relations,*[17] *Research to Practice in Mental Retardation,*[18] *New Directions for Exceptional Children: The Ecology of Exceptional Children,*[19] and *Mainstreaming of Children in Schools: Research and Programmatic Issues.*[20] King describes actual classroom practices by teachers and aides;[21] Kohut[22] and Rosenshine[23] focus on reviews of studies concerning teacher effectiveness.

Use should also be made of such standard library resources as the *Annual Review of Psychology,* the *Encyclopedia of Educational Research, The Handbook of Research on Teaching, The Review of Educational Research, Child Development Abstracts and Bibliography, Psychological Abstracts,* and *Children and Youth Services*

[15] U.S. Department of Health, Education and Welfare: Office of Human Development Services, Administration for Children, Youth and Families, 1978. DHEW Publication No. (OHDS) 79-30178.

[16] L. J. Schweinhart and D. P. Weikart, Monographs of the High/Scope Educational Research Foundation, No. 7 (Ypsilanti, Mich.: High/Scope Press, 1980).

[17] T. M. Field et al. (eds.) (New York: Academic, 1980).

[18] P. Mittler (ed.), Vol. 1 (Baltimore, Md.: University Park, 1977).

[19] J. Gallagher (ed.), (San Francisco: Jossey-Bass, 1980).

[20] P. Strain and M. M. Kerr (eds.) (New York: Academic, 1981).

[21] R. King, *All Things Bright and Beautiful?* (New York: Wiley, 1978).

[22] S. Kohut, Jr., "Research and the Teacher: Teacher Effectiveness in Early Childhood Education," in *Aspects of Early Childhood Education: Theory to Research to Practice,* ed. by D. G. Range and J. R. Layton (New York: Academic, 1980).

[23] B. Rosenshine, "Content, Time and Direct Instruction," in *Research on Teaching: Concepts, Findings and Implications,* ed. by P. L. Peterson and H. J. Walberg (Berkeley, Calif.: McCutcheon, 1971).

Review. It is always wise to consult the current issues or volumes of these sources for the latest information available.

EFFECT OF RESEARCH ON PROGRAMS

The results of the several longitudinal studies of the 1920s and 1930s forced teachers to change their emphasis to concern for the growth and development of children. Following World War II, more concern for parent involvement developed, and the permissive, protective programs of small groups of children gave way to more structured programs of larger groups of children.

It was not until the late 1950s and 1960s that a genuine need for, and interest in, research on the early learning and development of cognitive skills took place. Landmarks in this area were the publication of Piaget's *The Origins of Intelligence in Children*,[24] Hunt's *Intelligence and Experience*,[25] Bruner's *The Process of Education*,[26] and Bloom's *Stability and Change in Human Characteristics*.[27] As a result of these and similar publications, researchers and programmers turned their attention to the early years of development. There were numerous experimental programs concerned almost wholly with the concept of learning as being the acquisition of specific material. Such acquisition was, and still is, widely lauded as superior to the kind of learning that grows out of meaningful experience and results from the interests and needs of children. Proponents of the acquisition concept point out that such early acquisition is necessary because the materials taught are the basic elements of what the child is expected to learn on entering a regular elementary school program.

Students of the history of education are not surprised by these developments, for history shows that educational programs have always been sensitive to contemporary social and cultural conditions. In a like manner, the accompanying research always has as its objective finding more efficient means of achieving the desired outcomes. The Space Age has brought about a need for highly structured areas of knowledge and public concern for the quality of education in the schools. The best development of each child as an individual thus became secondary to the aim of having children acquire as much specific knowledge as could be learned in the shortest possible time. Because research has discovered that young children learn rapidly and acquire vast amounts of specific knowledge quickly, much attention was directed to the education of preschool children in the mid-1960s.

Concurrent with the increased Space Age needs, poverty and its attendant educational problems increased at an alarming rate. Children of poverty-stricken fami-

[24] J. Piaget, *The Origins of Intelligence in Children* (New York: International Universities, 1952).
[25] J. McV. Hunt, *Intelligence and Experience* (New York: Ronald, 1960).
[26] J. S. Bruner, *The Process of Education* (Cambridge, Mass.: Harvard U.P., 1961).
[27] B. Bloom, *Stability and Change in Human Characteristics* (New York: Wiley, 1964).

Recording on task behavior and analyzing it in relation to a variety of learning centers is an important responsibility of the teacher. Such research is carried on in a naturalistic setting.

lies have always suffered an acute educational disadvantage. However, it was not until the affluent 1960s that the disparities between the poor and the rest of society became critical enough to cause national concern. Educators applauded when the federal government took measures to attack poverty with educational programs, especially programs for very young children. This mammoth effort required not only educational programs, but large-scale research to ensure the effectiveness and improvement of these programs.

After reviewing research concerning day care, Caldwell and Freyer cite the need for a theoretical underpinning to guide such research. With better theory, they posit, answers to important questions are more likely to be found. For example, no current theory can explain why the day care experience, which encompasses a significant portion of a child's early life, has as little effect as it does.[28]

[28] Caldwell and Freyer, op. cit., p. 370.

RESEARCH ON LANGUAGE ACQUISITION AND COMMUNICATION SKILLS

Crucial to all education is the acquisition of language and communication skills. Typical of the all-out attack on language acquisition is the work of Bereiter and Engelmann. They come to this conclusion: [29]

> Evidence was cited which suggests that lack of concrete learning has relatively little to do with the intellectual and academic deficiencies of disadvantaged children and that is the lack of verbal learning, in particular the lack of those kinds of learning that can only be transmitted from adults to children through language, that is mainly responsible for these deficiencies. Thus there is justification for treating cultural deprivation as synonymous with language deprivation.

Bereiter and Engelmann presented evidence that the exclusion of every possible opportunity to experience other than the specifics being taught results in a much greater rate of learning than is normally experienced by children. It is their thesis that by teaching the essential and fundamental content for school achievement the culturally different children will quickly catch up with their more privileged peers and, thus, be able to compete favorably with them in regular school. The experienced educator, though impressed with the valuable contributions of this work, will view with caution the authoritarian evangelism with which the authors present their program.

Because highly developed speech and language distinguish humans from all other living organisms, the importance of these faculties has long held the attention of scholars and research workers. As both faculties are highly developed before American children are required to enter school, a knowledge of research findings in these areas can be of great value to the preschool teacher.

Language is not only a symbolic representation of objectives and ideas; it is also a means of expressing feelings and thoughts, including facial expression and gestures. Piaget early believed that thought precedes language but that as language competency develops, language directs thinking.[30] The earliest and most frequent use of language by very young children is essentially emotional in nature and is used to express desires and feelings.[31] The use of words and symbols for objects or events comes later. Thus, it would appear that teaching letters of the alphabet, parts of words representing sounds and sound combinations, and written symbols before meaningful experiences that result in feelings and thoughts on the part of the child would not be the most efficient means of promoting language success.

[29] C. Bereiter and S. Engelmann, *Teaching Disadvantaged Children in the Preschool* (Englewood Cliffs, N.J.: Prentice-Hall, 1966), p. 42.
[30] J. Piaget, *Language and Thought of the Child* (New York: Humanities, 1951).
[31] Dorothea McCarthy, "Language Development in Children," in *Manual of Child Psychology*, 2d ed., ed. by L. Carmichael (New York: Wiley, 1954).

Language development is indeed an exceedingly complex problem, and much research attention is being given to it by psychologists, linguists, learning theorists, and grammarians. Reacting to papers presented at a conference on the acquisition of language, Deese comments thus:[32]

> The human being is able to transcend the effects of a reinforcement schedule through his ability to store and internalize environment behavior and intrabehavioral relations through the mediation of language; therefore, it is that aspect of language which makes it different from elements of behavior simply and entirely under the control of reinforcement contingencies, which makes language unique and worth studying in its own right.

Interesting theories regarding the origin, structure, and modification of language have been provided by linguists in recent years and have generated testable hypotheses for research. Notable in this respect has been the work of Brown.[33]

Bernstein[34] believes that language shapes both thought and social class initiating and reinforcing behavior appropriate to each specific class. Lower-class children use what he calls restricted codes whereas middle-class children use elaborated codes that correspond roughly to the English expected by the schools. Thus, children outside the mainstream group experience difficulty with the language used in the classroom. Recent efforts to treat Standard English as a second language for language-different groups is an example of the aplication of these findings.

Brown found that children begin using two-word sentences at 18 to 24 months of age. Most significant is the fact that almost universally from the very start, the child expresses the basic grammatical relationships among subject, predicate, and object of the verb, even though words have been left out. Programs that stress language development accept simple, incomplete, but grammatically accurate, expressions on the part of the children. Thus, the young child may say, "Where book?" for "Where is my book?" or "Leo run?" for "Will Leo run?" or perhaps meaning "Can Leo run?" No one knows for sure why language usage develops in this way, but research does show that early language development is an orderly process governed by rules present in the language modeled by the adults in the child's immediate environment. These rules vary from class to class and from culture to culture. Current theory has it that no one set of standards is superior to another, as long as the language used serves its purpose of meaningful communication. For those who wish to investigate the applications of theory and research presented here, help will be

[32] James Deese, "Comments and Conclusions," in *The Acquisition of Language*, ed. by U. Bellugi and R. Brown, *Mongr. Soc. Res. Child Develop.*, 29:1 (1964), p. 180.

[33] R. Brown, *A First Language* (Cambridge, Mass.: Harvard U.P., 1973).

[34] B. A. Bernstein, "A Sociolinguistic Approach to Socialization: With Some Reference to Educability," in *Language and Poverty: Perspectives on a Theme*, ed. by F. Williams (Chiago: Markham, 1970, pp. 25–61).

found in the work of N. Chomsky,[35] Oleron,[36] Tough,[37] deVilliers and de Villiers,[38] and Danks and Glucksberg,[39] and the general references at the end of this chapter.

PARENT INVOLVEMENT IN EARLY CHILDHOOD EDUCATION

Henderson[40] and Leler[41] have reviewed programs that involve parent participation. All the studies reviewed by Henderson and 83 per cent of the 40 studies reviewed by Leler report positive results concerning the relationship between child achievement and parent participation. Publications emanating from the Parent Education Follow Through Program (PEFTP), developed by Gordon and his associates and established in ten communities across the country, also point to the positive effects of parent involvement.[42] Begun in 1969 and still continuing in eight communities, the program focuses on families with children in kindergarten through the third grade. The main aspects of the program include the following:[43]

1. Home visits made by program parents employed as paid paraprofessionals who spend one half of their time working as classroom instruction personnel and one half of their time visiting the homes of children in the classroom.
2. Six parental participation roles, including teacher of own child, paid paraprofessional, decision maker through policy advisory committees, adult learner, audience, and classroom volunteer.
3. Comprehensive services for participating families including social, psychological, and health services.

Between 1969 and 1981, approximately 8,000 per year were served. Since 1981, approximately half that number are being served. Despite the positive results com-

---

[35] Noam Chomsky, *The Logical Structure of Linguistic Theory* (New York: Plenum, 1975).

[36] Pierre Oleron, *Language and Mental Development*, trans. Raymond P. Lorion (Hillsdale, N.J.: Lawrence Erlbaum Assoc., 1977).

[37] Joan Tough, *Listening to Children Talking: A Guide to the Appraisal of Children's Use of Language* (London: Ward, Lock, 1976).

[38] J. deVilliers and P. deVilliers, *Language Acquisition* (Cambridge, Mass.: Harvard U.P., 1978).

[39] J. H. Danks and S. Glucksberg, "Experimental Psycholinguistics," in *Annual Review of Psychology*, ed. by M. Rosensweig and L. Porter, Vol. 31 (Palo Alto, Calif.: Annual Reviews, Inc., 1980).

[40] A. Henderson, ed., *Parent Participation—Student Achievement: The Evidence Grows* (Columbia, Md.: National Committee for Citizens in Education, 1981).

[41] H. Leler, "Parent Education and Involvement in Relation to the Schools and to Parents of School-aged Children," in *Parent Education and Public Policy*, ed. by R. Haskins (Norwood, N.J.: Ablex, in press).

[42] P. P. Olmsted and R. I. Rubin, "Linking Parent Behaviors to Child Achievement: Four Evaluation Studies From the Parent Education Follow-Through Program," *Studies in Educational Evaluation* 8 (1983), pp. 317–325.

[43] Ibid.

ing from these studies and those reviewed by Henderson and Leler, federal education programs are putting less emphasis on parent involvement.[44] See also Chapter 15 for a fuller discussion of parent involvement.

OTHER APPLICATIONS OF RESEARCH

The coming of Head Start in the mid-1960s had a strong impact on educational research. The favorite effort was to "raise the IQ," often losing sight of the important gains made by Head Start children in areas other than cognitive development. For example, the "Kirschner Report"[45] on the impact of Head Start was optimistic that fundamental changes in educational and health institutions had taken place in the short period of less than five years. In both instances the traditional "middle-class" orientation had become more responsive to "the needs and desires of the poor."[46]

Cognition, or the process of knowing, has long been a subject for theory and research, especially by European scientists. Because cognition embraces thought and concept formation or meaningful understanding, an increasing number of American researchers and theorists have turned to studies of cognition in young children in an effort to determine more effective educational procedures. Although the age-old battle concerning the effects of heredity and environment on intelligence and learning ability is far from resolved, much emphasis today is placed on environmental effects. The Russian scientist, Zaporozhets, summarizes thus:[47]

> At the beginning, a new way of becoming acquainted with an object is usually carried into practice by organs that are capable of performing both practical and cognitive functions, such as the hands' touching and manipulating an object or by the muscle apparatus of the larynx. . . . In reality, as we have tried to show in our paper, a given form of perception is the product of a continuous development that goes on in the child under the influences of practical experiences and learning.

Flavell,[48] an American exponent of Piaget, Ojemann and Pritchett,[49] and Deutsch,[50] among others, have presented evidence to show that cognitive devel-

[44] Phi Delta Kappa, "Parent Involvement in Education," *Practical Applications of Research* (Dec. 1981), pp. 1–4.

[45] *A National Survey of the Impact of Head Start Centers on Community Institutions* (Washington, D.C.: prepared for the Office of Child Development, HEW, by Kirschner Associates, 1970).

[46] Ibid., p. 19.

[47] A. V. Zaporozhets, "The Development of Perception in the Preschool Child," in *European Research in Cognitive Development, Monogr. Soc. Res. Child Develop.*, **30**:2 (1965), pp. 98, 100.

[48] J. H. Flavell, *The Developmental Psychology of Jean Piaget* (New York: Van Nostrand Reinhold, 1964).

[49] R. Ojemann and K. Pritchett, "Piaget and the Role of Guided Experience in Human Development," *Perceptual and Motor Skills*, **17** (1963).

[50] M. Deutsch, "Facilitating Development in the Pre-School Child: Social and Psychological Perspectives," *Merrill-Palmer Quart.*, **10**:3 (1964), pp. 249–263.

opment can be modified and accelerated by manipulating the child's environment in specific ways. As a result, many preschool programs are becoming more structured than in the past. Considered modifications of the more permissive, relatively unstructured programs of the past, placing more emphasis on learning and intellectual development, do result in better educational experiences for young children. It is only when undue stress is placed on learning or on a single component of development that the quality of a good school program is endangered. The early childhood teacher must have preparation to enable him or her to understand and interpret research so as to provide the best possible educational experiences for young children.

To say that interest in the importance of early education to the child's later development had waned would be a gross misstatement. The National Society for the Study of Education devoted its Seventy-first Yearbook to Early Childhood Education.[51] While reading the yearbook, one cannot help but be impressed by the documented dependence on research for the viewpoints expressed by the various contributors. It would be highly premature to say that a theory of Early Childhood Education had emerged at the time of the publication of this text. Indeed, it would be more accurate to say that the research of the 1960s and 1970s, though clearly building on and adding to earlier findings, was only a beginning, albeit a fruitful and encouraging one. The yearbook's chapter on research and evaluation[52] points the way toward more fruitful research strategies and methodology to provide information enabling the development of innovative and functional education programs for young children.

By the late 1970s, Early Childhood Education had become firmly entrenched. A new dimension had been added as well: the handicapped. Titles like *Instructional Materials for the Handicapped: Birth Through Early Childhood*[53] appeared. In addition, research was providing more reports of successful programs.[54]

One example of such a program is The Frank Porter Graham Child Development Center of the University of North Carolina at Chapel Hill, which conducts basic and applied research on factors affecting the development of socially disadvantaged children. Two longitudinal and multidisciplinary research projects form the core of the research program. Both projects are concerned with understanding and preventing retarded development.[55]

[51] Ira J. Gordon (ed.), *Early Childhood Education*, The Seventy-first Yearbook of the National Society for the Study of Education, Part II (Chicago: U. of Chicago, 1972).

[52] Ibid., pp. 261–290.

[53] A. R. Thorum et al., *Instructional Materials for the Handicapped: Birth Through Early Childhood* (Salt Lake City: Olympus Publishing Co., 1976).

[54] *Educational Programs That Work*, 3d ed. (San Francisco: Far West Laboratory for Educational Research and Development, 1977).

[55] Craig T. Ramey, David MacPhee, and Keith O. Yeates, "Preventing Developmental Retardation: A General Systems Model," in *Facilitating Infant and Early Childhood Development*, ed. by L. A. Bond and J. M. Jofee (Hanover and London: U.P. of New England, 1982), p. 367.

The oldest program (begun in 1971 and known as the Carolina Abecedarian Project) involves a longitudinal comparison of high-risk infants assigned randomly at birth to either an intensive educational day care program or to a condition in which no educational day care but some family services are provided. Experiences for the children are planned to foster language development and to promote appropriate and adaptive social behavior.

Children may begin attending the center as young as six weeks of age. After they reach three years of age, the educational curriculum continues to promote active child participation and independence and to provide a good deal of variety while giving the children a systematic exposure to areas such as science, math, and music. Upon entry to public school kindergarten, one half of each preschool group receives special family education services for the first three years of public school. This design allows researchers to pursue the issues of timing and consequences of special education services.

The second project, begun in 1977 and known as Project CARE (Carolina Approach to Responsive Education), is a comparison of two different intensities of preschool preventive educational programs begun at birth. One condition contains a family education component, and the other condition combines the same family education component with educational day care for the child. Both experimental groups are compared to a randomly constituted control group.

Researchers and educators from both projects have generated a variety of theoretical and practical insights, empirical findings, and professional opinions about how they can contribute to preventing or lessening the impact of social disadvantage.

EDUCATIONAL ASSESSMENT AND EVALUATION

Perhaps the concept *educational assessment* is more fitting than research per se in determining the effectiveness of specific educational and teaching strategies when dealing with programs for young children. This should in no way detract from the value of basic research as a means of providing assumptions and hypotheses for making decisions for change. However, assessment rather than research may well provide the most valuable data on which to make decisions to continue, discontinue, or modify existing procedures and programs. For an elaboration of educational assessment, see the ASCD publication edited by Beatty[56] and the *Handbook for Measurement and Evaluation in Early Childhood Education.*[57] In addition, Western States Technical Assistance Resource (WESTAR) has produced two pub-

[56] Walcott H. Beatty (ed.), *Improving Educational Assessment and an Inventory of Measures of Affective Behavior* (Alexandria, Va.: Association for Supervision and Curriculum Development, 1969).
[57] W. L. Goodwin and L. A. Driscoll, *Handbook for Measurement and Evaluation in Early Childhood Education* (San Francisco: Jossey-Bass, 1980.)

lications of particular interest: *Evaluation Case Studies* [58] and *Ongoing Data Collection for Measuring Child Progress.* [59] See also *Handbook of Research in Early Childhood Education.* [60]

As program accountability has become so much a part of early childhood education, evaluation has become increasingly important. Programs in health, human services, and education that are federally funded now require evaluation reports. The Head Start Performance Standards, 1975, is an example of such reports. [61]

SUMMARY

The technological, economic, and social developments of recent decades have brought about a reevaluation of the effectiveness of the American educational program. This has led to general acceptance of the importance of education during the early childhood years. However, there is little accord as to the best methods and curriculum to be used.

Influenced by an abundance of sponsored research, many innovative and experimental schools for young children have come into being. Recent research has pointed particularly to the importance of language and cognitive development during the early years. Much of this effort has been aimed at enabling children who have been deprived of normal early experiences to catch up with, or compensate for, the lack of learning competencies thus brought about.

Research on the early years of life is long overdue and should be welcomed and encouraged. However, as is true of all research, findings should be implemented only as they apply to conditions under which the research was conducted; they should not be generalized. Educators should not view all research efforts with alarm. Rather, with the present improved research technology and support, early childhood educators should view these developments as the frontier movement in education today and point the way to innovation and improvement in the entire educational system.

We are long past the point of abandoning research efforts solely to raise the IQ in favor of recording sophisticated observable change resulting from the implementation of early stated objectives whether they be in the physical, affective, or cognitive domain. We believe that any program that ignores major areas of the growth and developmental needs of the child will not succeed in producing individuals who can function intelligently in a democratic society.

How are research findings used to (1) determine public policy in regard to the

[58] Ruth Pelz (ed.), *Evaluation Case Studies*, WESTAR Series Paper No. 16 (Monmouth, Oreg.: Western States Technical Assistance Resource, 1982).

[59] Meave Stevens-Dominguez and Kathleen Stremel-Campbell (eds.), *Ongoing Data Collection for Measuring Child Progress* (Monmouth, Oreg.: Western States Technical Assistance Resource, 1982).

[60] *Handbook of Research in Early Childhood Education*, op. cit., pp. 523–652.

[61] *Ibid.*, p. 618.

rights of children and (2) to implement and design programs for specific purposes? These concerns have had an impact on the type of research that is being conducted.

Suggested Activities

1. Invite child psychologists and research personnel to discuss with the class the latest research findings in relation to Early Childhood Education.
2. Have various members of the class report on research findings published in current journals. Discuss the findings.
3. Organize a discussion or debate on the pros and cons of the more structured programs for young children. Use research findings to support each view.
4. Select one instrument for assessing a teaching strategy. Use it with children and evaluate its effectiveness.
5. Why have researchers become concerned about "public policy" and their part in its formulation? Invite a member of the state legislature or a member of Congress or a member of the local school board or a combination to meet with your class. Ask them to discuss the basis on which they make their decisions on public policy matters when the education of preschool children is concerned.
6. Write the Children's Defense Fund, 1520 New Hampshire Ave., N.W., Washington, D.C. 20036. Ask the director how educators can influence public policy decisions about early childhood education.

Related Readings

Bloom, B. S., G. F. Madaus, and J. T. Hastings. *Evaluation to Improve Learning.* New York: McGraw-Hill, 1981.

Chomsky, N. *The Logical Structure of Linguistic Theory.* New York: Plenum, 1975.

Crittendan, Alan. *Language in Infancy and Childhood: A Linguistic Introduction to Language Acquisition.* New York: St. Martin's, 1979.

Dare, P. *A Four-Year Longitudinal Study of Follow Through Children.* San Francisco: Far West Laboratory for Educational Research and Development, 1973.

Educational Programs That Work, 3d ed. San Francisco: Far West Laboratory for Educational Research and Development, 1977.

Educational Research: Limits and Opportunities. Washington, D.C.: U.S. DHEW, NIE, 1977.

Gage, N. L. (ed.). *Handbook of Research on Teaching.* Chicago: Rand McNally, 1963. Ch. 15.

Harris, C. W. (ed.) *Encyclopedia of Educational Research,* 3d ed. New York: Macmillan, 1960.

Hoffman, M. L., and Lois W. Hoffman (eds.). *Review of Child Development Research,* 2 vols. New York: Russell Sage, 1964, 1967.

Jencks, C. et al. *Inequality: A Measurement of the Effect of Family and Schooling in America.* New York: Basic, 1972.

Kamerman, S. B. "Child Care and Family Benefits: Policies of Six Industrialized Countries." *Monthly Labor Review*, Nov. 1980, pp. 23–28.

Kaplan-Sanoff, Margot, and Renee Yablans-Magid. *Exploring Early Childhood: Readings in Theory and Practice.* New York: Macmillan, 1981, pp. 246–300.

Karnes, Merle B. "Evaluation and Implications of Research with Young Handicapped Children," *Compensatory Education for Children, Ages 2–8, Recent Studies of Educational Intervention: Proceedings.* Ed. by J. C. Stanley. Baltimore: Johns Hopkins, 1973.

Lindfors, Judith. *Children's Language and Learning.* Englewood Cliffs, N.J.: Prentice-Hall, 1980.

Mann, A. J. "A Review of Head Start Research Since 1969 and an Annotated Bibliography." U.S. HEW, Publication no. (OHDS) 77-31102, 1977.

Renner, J. W. et al. *Research, Teaching, and Learning with the Piaget Model.* Norman: U. of Okla., 1976.

Review of Child Development Research, Vols. 1–6. Chicago: U. Chicago (Society for Research in Child Development Series).

Ryan, Sally (ed.). *A Report on Longitudinal Evaluations of Preschool Programs*, Vol. 1. Washington, D.C.: U.S. DHEW, OCD, 1975.

Stein, A. H., and L. K. Friedrich. "Impact of Television on Children and Youth," in *Review of Child Development Research*, Vol. 5, ed. by E. M. Hetherington. Chicago: U. Chicago: 1975.

CHAPTER 5

Play and the Young Child

Play is an essential part of early childhood. Researchers have been investigating the relationship of play to cognitive, language, social, and gross motor development.[1] Play and learning activities are interrelated and certain types of play seem to facilitate certain types of learning. Through environmental adjustments it has been found that the quality and quantity of play can be manipulated.[2]

Play continues to be included, almost without exception, in all early childhood programs. But, says Butler, "there are vast differences in what is meant by play and what is believed to be its relative value."[3]

There are teachers who feel that free play has little merit and should be replaced with educational play. In the direct-instruction type of program, play usually involves use of equipment to teach specific concepts and teacher-directed games to

---

[1] Doris Sponseller, "Play and Early Education," in B. Spodek, ed. *Handbook of Research in Early Childhood Education.* (New York: The Free Press, 1982), p. 232.

[2] Ibid., p. 231–232.

[3] Annie L. Butler, *Current Research in Early Childhood Education: A Compilation and Analysis for Program Planners* (Washington, D.C.: American Association of Elementary-Kindergarten-Nursery Educators, N.E.A., (1970), p. 13.

stimulate language and thought. Play is directed by the nature of the equipment. Spontaneous play is usually limited to short periods of outdoor activity, which are not considered to make any significant contribution to learning. In what are termed the *more open* centers, "self-initiated play is the major vehicle for learning."[4]

Almy says that psychoanalytic theory has long regarded spontaneous play as a reflection not only of the child's emotional needs but also of developing intellectual competence.[5] There are teachers, however, who are so preoccupied with the emotional aspects of play that they neglect its intellectual connotations. Utilizing the cognitive values of spontaneous play does not necessarily mean pushing or pressuring the child but rather nurturing basic abilities as they develop. The teacher needs to diagnose cognitive functioning as revealed in play. By observing and evaluating the child's curiosity and interest in investigation, problem solving, and mastery, the teacher can give guidance in play and in other curricular areas.

The several points of view regarding the value of play are related to differences in what is considered good education for the young—whether the emphasis should be on cognitive learning or on a more broadly based curriculum. Another cause of the confusion regarding the value of play, says Frank, "arises from the old distinction between work and play, with the feeling that, while work is good, play is somewhat questionable, if not bad or sinful."[6] Baker says that often play is considered as an alternative to work. But he reminds us that a four-year-old is working physically hard as he or she carries buckets of sand from one place to another in play. The leisure/labor, play/work dichotomy, according to Baker, must be prevented from rising too early in the child's life. This can be done, he suggests, by adults identifying with children in their play and treating them as adults and helpers and by avoiding giving the impression that play is "time out."[7]

THE YOUNG CHILD'S PLAY

Froebel, the father of the kindergarten, recognized the importance of play in learning. His ideas were of practical value. However, his conception of play did little to explain the nature of a child's play. In order to clarify the meaning of play, one should examine the research and theories regarding its nature and function. Some of the earlier theories may be helpful.

1. The *recapitulation* theory states that the individual in his or her play development passes through stages that are typical of those through which the race has

[4]Ibid., p. 14.

[5]Millie Almy, "Spontaneous Play: An Avenue for Intellectual Development," *Young Children*, **22**:5 (1967), pp. 265–277.

[6]L. K. Frank, "Introduction," in Ruth E. Hartley and R. M. Goldenson, *The Complete Book of Children's Play* (New York: Crowell, 1957), p. viii.

[7]D. Baker, "Worlds of Play," *Child. Educ.*, **53**:15 (1977), pp. 247–248.

Children of different ages play together. "It's your turn next—"

passed. When applied on the playground, this theory resulted in somewhat arbitrary division of ages and the experiences appropriate for them. Investigations, however, have shown that children of a given age differ widely in the development of their play interests and that there is much overlapping between age groups. According to another theory, not all the energy produced by the child is needed for growth, and play is the result of an accumulation of *surplus energy.*

2. The *recreation* theory maintains that through play, tensions may be released and relaxed.

3. The *anticipatory* or *preparatory* theory "considers play as primarily a preparation for future life and work; in make-believe, children are practicing for future roles."[8]

Each theory presents an aspect of the truth regarding play. Hurlock reported earlier experimental studies of children's play by Bott, Arlitt, Van Alstyne, Parten, and others.[9] A brief summary of the review follows.

The child at three usually enjoys an activity as an end in itself, but by five shows interest in the end result. Imaginative play reaches its peak between five and eight

[8] W. C. Olson, *Child Development,* 2d ed. (Boston: Heath, 1959), p. 94. See also Susanna Millar, *The Psychology of Play* (New York: Jason Aronson, 1974), pp. 13–22.

[9] Elizabeth B. Hurlock, "Experimental Investigations of Children's Play," in *Child's Play,* ed. by R. E. Herron and B. Sutton-Smith (New York: Wiley, 1971), pp. 51–70.

years of age. The dramatic play of four-year-olds centers around living conditions, animals, and family relations.

Play that involves skilled muscular movement is very popular during childhood. The young child likes to test the powers of muscular control by such activities as hopping on one foot or walking along the edge of a curb.

An important element in children's play is construction and building. The young child begins to save and collect things.

The average attention span for the eight most popular play materials was 7.0 minutes for two years, 8.9 for three, 12.3 for four, and 13.6 for five.

No definite preference was shown for playmates of the same or the opposite sex. Apparent sex differences in play are due to training.

Among three- and four-year-old children, raw materials such as sand and blocks were ranked as first choice. Dolls representing children were favored by the five-year-old children.

Frank expresses the point of view held by many of those who work with young children: "Play is the way the child learns what none can teach him. It is the way he explores and orients himself to the actual world of space and time, of things, animals, structures and people. . . . Play is the child's work."[10] Play can be satisfying and pleasurable and these are good values for young children.

From his observation of children, Piaget states that games (synonymous with play) "reproduce what has struck the child or evoke what has pleased him or enabled him to be more fully part of his environment."[11] Piaget's theory of play is closely related to his theory of the growth of intelligence. Play begins in the sensorimotor period. Symbolic or make-believe play is characteristic of the age from two to seven years.[12] Such play is influenced by the play materials available and is enhanced by realistic materials and toys.[13]

Vygotsky points out that play is the leading source of development in the preschool years. At this age special needs and incentives arise, which are important to the child's whole development. Incentives and motives should not be disregarded. The child has a great number of tendencies and desires that cannot be realized immediately. When such tendencies appear in development, according to the viewpoint from the affective sphere, play is invented. If needs that cannot be realized immediately did not develop in the preschool years there would be no play.[14]

Play, says Vygotsky, is wish fulfillment—not as isolated wishes, but in terms of generalized effects. A child plays without realizing the motives of the play activity in which he or she is engaging. An imaginary situation is created by the child.

---

[10] Frank, op. cit., pp. vii, viii.

[11] J. Piaget, *Play, Dreams and Imitation in Childhood*, trans. Gattengo and Hodgson (New York: Norton, 1962), p. 155.

[12] Millar, op. cit., pp. 53–54.

[13] Greta G. Fein, "Pretend Play: New Perspectives," in Janet F. Brown, ed. *Curriculum Planning for Young Children* (Washington, D.C.: NAEYC, 1982), p. 23.

[14] L. S. Vygotsky, "Play and Its Role in the Mental Development of the Child," in *Play—Its Role in Development and Evolution*, ed. by J. S. Bruner et al. (New York: Basic, 1976), pp. 537–538.

Vygotsky holds that rules for play grow out of the imaginary situation. A child playing the role of Mother follows rules of maternal behavior.[15] Play, for the child, is purposeful activity.[16]

Jersild identifies characteristics and purposes of a child's play. Apart from being a self-chosen activity, any new play experience often involves an element of risk.[17] This is true when a child seeks to climb, build, ride a bicycle, use a hammer or saw, or even paint on an easel. One five-year-old expressed it this way: "I don't know how, but I guess I can try."

Repetition is also an important aspect of children's play. Through repetition the child can consolidate skills and, as he or she becomes more expert, can begin to experiment on his or her own. The child learns to ride a tricycle and is content to ride it up and down the sidewalk or porch, repeating the skill already learned. Soon, however, the child experiments as he or she backs up, turns around, rides fast and slow. In a short time the tricycle becomes a part of dramatic play. A traffic sign and a police officer are added.

HOW PLAY HELPS THE CHILD

Play may serve as a means of helping the child solve a problem. A child may select a toy that represents an object he or she fears or one toward which there is resentment. Play serves as a means of self-assertion through which a child can declare his or her needs. If the child wants affection, he or she can be the "baby" in the dramatic play. In this role the child can receive attention and affection as he or she is fed, rocked, or put to bed.

Closely related to this is the role of play in self-revealment. Observing a child at play, one may note the joys, fears, or hopes revealed. Although this is the basis for play therapy, even the teacher who is not a trained therapist can learn much from watching the child as she or he plays.

There appears to be a connection between play and creativity.[18] Others have found that creativity and inventiveness in the child's play are associated with later facility in divergent thinking.[19]

Through play children learn many things. They are helped to develop social relationships and skills. They learn to use play materials and equipment with others; to take turns; to lead and to follow; to ask for what they want or need; to understand

[15] Ibid., pp. 539–51.

[16] Ibid., p. 552.

[17] A. T. Jersild, *Child Psychology*, 5th ed. (Englewood Cliffs, N.J.: Prentice-Hall, 1960), pp. 424–425.

[18] J. L. Dansky and I. W. Silverman, "Effects of Play on Associative Fluency in Pre-School Children," in *Play—Its Role in Development and Evolution*, ed. by J. S. Bruner et al. (New York: Basic, 1976), p. 650.

[19] Corrine Hutt and Reena Bhavnani, "Predictions from Play," in *Play—Its Role in Development and Evolution*, ed. by J. S. Bruner et al. (New York: Basic, 1976), pp. 216–219.

Play may serve as a means of helping the child solve a problem.

the role of mother, baby, father, or the doctor. As children climb, walk, skip, and jump, they are exercising muscles and gaining in physical fitness. Contact with other children and the need to communicate with them help to stimulate language growth. The following incidents illustrate some of the values of play:

> Dan opened the door of the storage room and rolled the wagon in. Quickly he loaded it with blocks, just as many as he could pile on the wagon. As he pulled the wagon through the door, blocks fell in every direction. Without annoyance or concern he pushed the wagon in again and repeated the process. But this time, with an empty wagon, he stopped and looked. He rolled the empty wagon in and out the door. No difficulty. Then he rolled the wagon back in again and loaded it carefully. Not one block extended beyond the edge of the wagon. He pulled the wagon safely out into the yard without losing a single block. Dan had encountered a problem and worked out a solution, all in play.

> An elaborate train had been built from blocks and Jane, Pete, Joe, and Charles were ready to "play train." Roles were assigned and the conductor and passengers took their places. The engineer, however, went to the back of the train. As the teacher watched, the train was ready to pull out of the station. She said to Joe, "You are the engineer. What is your job?" Joe replied, "Oh, I'm just the engineer." Pete added, "He drives the train." Teacher, "If the engineer drives the train, where does he need to be?" The light dawned. Joe crawled onto the engine.

Observation of these children at play helped the teacher see that Joe and perhaps Jane and Charles did not know the role of the engineer. This evaluation of their knowledge of trains indicated to the teacher the need for pictures, stories, and perhaps a field trip in order to clarify their understanding. Interest and curiosity are aroused and questions raised that result in increasing vocabulary and clarification of concepts. Play can serve as a means of helping the teacher to evaluate the learning, attitudes, and understandings of the child.

Bruner emphasizes the connection between play and human culture. Play, he says, reflects the culture or the subcultural condition, such as poverty, in which it takes place.[20] Rubin and colleagues conclude that the level of the child's social play may be related to socioeconomic factors.[21] Smilansky notes that the levels of sociodramatic play were of lower quantity and quality in lower socioeconomic groups.[22]

Herron and Sutton-Smith report that children in Head Start Programs do not always evidence the same kind of capacity in make-believe as do some children in other middle-class centers. Neither do they seem to show as much interest in make-believe stories or show the same capacity for thinking about things that are remote in time and place.[23] They raise the question as to whether the middle-class parent, by playing with the children, reading and talking to them, and providing play equipment, is actually encouraging the development of representative capacity and critical thinking.

Often inner city children have inadequate space or materials at home for physical movement and play activities. It is especially important that these childen have opportunities for play.[24]

THE DEVELOPMENTAL SEQUENCES OF PLAY ACTIVITIES

In summarizing findings on play, Sponseller concludes that the development in a child's play ability and in all developmental areas are parallel.[25] The teacher can gain insight to a child's overall development by observing his or her play. Jersild says, "Generally speaking, the younger the child is, the more will the things he chooses to do give an indication of what he can do or can learn to like to do in the selection of equipment, materials, and supplies."[26] The teacher then needs to know the developmental sequences of play activities and how to use the information in the selection of activities and equipment. Strang says that "the play life of a child

---

[20] J. S. Bruner, Alison Jolly, and Kathy Sylva, *Play—Its Role in Development and Evolution* (New York: Basic, 1976), p. 21.

[21] Sponseller, op. cit., p. 218.

[22] Ibid.

[23] R. E. Herron and B. Sutton-Smith, *Child's Play* (New York: Wiley, 1971), p. 2.

[24] Dorothy J. Skeel, *Children of the Street: Teaching in the Inner City* (Pacific Palisades, Calif.: Goodyear, 1971), pp. 80–81.

[25] Sponseller, op. cit., p. 232.

[26] Jersild, op. cit., p. 424.

is an index of his social maturity and reveals his personality more clearly than any activity."[27] This is illustrated in the following incident:

> On a warm, sunny fall day, the four-year-olds were busy in the nursery school yard. Three had climbed up into the tree house. Others were at the jungle gym and the tire swing. Some were running around on the grass and some were building with blocks. A student observer remarked, "I'm going to teach four-year-olds." When asked the reason for her choice, she replied, "Oh, they are so easy to work with. Just look. Everybody is busy and happy." The instructor sitting beside her asked, "What do you think would happen if the teacher suddenly called the children together to play a game of baseball?" In amazement the student replied, "Why, she wouldn't do that!" "But if she did? Would they be playing as happily or contentedly?" For a moment she was puzzled, but then she smiled slowly as she asked the instructor, "Are you saying to me that the four-year-olds are playing this way because the teacher has structured the situation and planned it according to what the children can do?" The student answered her own question. "That's it," she said, "Fours aren't just naturally good. They are playing this way because of the way the teacher plans for and guides their play."

And so it is! The teacher needs to know the developmental sequence of play and to recognize the variations in maturity and interests that will be found among individual children.

Parten classified children's play behavior into six categories: unoccupied, solitary, onlooker, parallel, associative, and cooperative. The sequence includes ages three through five years.[28] Although ages are identified in relation to the developmental sequence of play, the teacher who understands children knows that each child progresses at his or her own rate. Some fives are not ready for cooperative play, and some fours cooperate easily and well.

More recently, Millar has described a sequence in the development of social play. This classification begins with solitary activity and is followed in order by parallel, associative, and finally by cooperative play.[29]

At first children usually play alone and engage in solitary play. As an "onlooker" the child watches as the others play. In parallel play the child plays alongside another child but is primarily interested in his or her own activity. Associative play is characterized by an increased interest in playing with other children. Two or three may play together in a group, but both the group and activity change constantly. Dramatization and imagination are beginning to enter into play. The child is willing to wait a turn and, with supervision, will put toys away. The block play is concerned largely with manipulation, rather than building any one thing.

As children continue to grow and play, they may choose a friend of the same sex for a specific play activity. A marked increase is noted in the constructive use of

---

[27] Ruth Strang, *An Introduction to Child Study* (New York: Macmillan, 1951), p. 495.
[28] Mildred Parten, "Social Participation Among Pre-School Children," *J. Abnorm. and Soc. Psychol.*, **27**:3 (1932), pp. 243–269.
[29] Millar, op. cit., p. 178.

The outdoor environment offers many opportunities for physical activity. Outdoor play can help to lessen pressures on children. Physical activity and physical growth are major concerns in centers for children.

materials. The child uses blocks to build something. In the dramatization of play, one likes to dress up and finds props such as a cowboy hat, nurse's cap, or doctor's bag important. One may suggest turns but is often bossy in directing others. Such a child is not yet ready to make the social adjustment necessary for participation in group games.

The five-year-old usually can engage in cooperative play, the size of the group ranging from two to five children. Piaget believes that really cooperative play does not develop until after the age of seven or eight.[30] There is a definite interest in finishing an undertaking even though it may need to be carried over from one day to the next. The request, "May I leave my block house and fort up? I haven't finished. Do I have to put the blocks away now?" is familiar to the kindergarten teacher. Dramatic play can be creative, both in actions and costumes that may be created from materials at hand. By this age there is usually fairly good control of body movement. The five-year-olds like climbing and other activities involving the large muscles. As a rule they are not ready for organized group games.

The first dramatic play of the young child usually centers around the situation most familiar and important to him or her, but the situation may vary according to the background of the child. For many children the situation will be the home. From this, the child branches out to individuals important to her or his immediate world—the doctor, the grocer, and the police officer. Other roles are added as experiences with books, stories, and television reveal cowhands, spaceships, boats, and airplanes. The characteristics of play that have been described can be used by the teacher as guides in the selection of equipment, materials, and activities.

Hartley, Frank, and Goldenson report, from records of children three to five-and-a-half years old, eight functions that dramatic play serves in usual group situations of preschool centers. Through dramatic play the child has the opportunity:[31]

"(1) to imitate adults; (2) to play out real life roles in an intense way; (3) to reflect relationships and experiences; (4) to express passing needs; (5) to release unacceptable impulses; (6) to reverse roles usually taken; (7) to mirror growth; and (8) to work out problems and experiment with solutions."

Matterson describes three categories of children's play.[32] *Creative play* is encouraged by providing raw materials of all kinds such as sand, paint, and scraps. In *imaginative play* a child can create situations for himself or herself and work out reactions and solutions. Dress-up clothes encourage this type of play. *Adventure play* involves overcoming obstacles, gaining new skills through exercising, and us-

---

[30] Ibid.

[31] Ruth Hartley, L. K. Frank, and R. M. Goldenson, *Understanding Children's Play*, (New York: Columbia U. P., 1952), pp. 27–28.

[32] E. M. Matterson, *Play and Playthings for the Preschool Child* (Baltimore, Md.: Penguin, 1967), pp. 5–8.

ing the coordination that exists. Garvey identified five areas of play as motion, objects, language, social materials, and games with rules.[33]

In order to use the findings of research in practice, teachers need to decide on the types of play they want to facilitate and the developmental and/or learning processes they hope to influence.[34]

SUMMARY

The importance of play in early childhood has been stressed in this chapter. The relationship of play to cognitive, language, social, and motor development has been examined. Characteristics of the child's play and the developmental sequences of play activities have been described. The selection of play equipment and materials is included in Chapter 19, "Physical Facilities, Equipment, and Materials."

Suggested Activities

1. Discuss in class the values of play for young children. Observe young children at play, and note the values that you think they may be gaining.
2. Visit a center for young children, and observe the children at play. Note examples of basic intellectual skills being used, such as investigation or classification. Share your findings with the class. Note factors in the situation that you think may influence the achievement of cognitive values of play. Describe the teacher's role.
3. Visit a program for young children. Observe and describe situations that are examples of parallel play and cooperative play.
4. Observe young children involved in block play. Note shapes of blocks and accessories used. Note teacher's role. Describe and give examples of learning that the children seem to be achieving.
5. View the following films: *Blocks—A Medium for Perceptual Learnings;* and *Concept Development in Outdoor Play,* Campus Films, 2 Overhill Road, Scarsdale, N.Y. 10583.
6. See the film *Children's Play,* from CRM McGraw-Hill Films, 1011 Camino De Mar, Del Mar, Calif., 92104.

Related Readings

Almy, Millie. "Spontaneous Play—An Avenue of Intellectual Development." *Bulletin of the Institute of Child Study,* **28:**2 (1966).

Anker, Dorothy, Jackie Foster, Joan McLane, Joyce Sobel, and Bernice Weissbourd. "Teaching Children as They Play." *Young Children,* **29:**4 (1974), pp. 203–213.

[33] Phi Delta Kappa's Center on Evaluation, Development, and Research. "Play" in *Practical-Applications of Research.* **5:**2 (Bloomington, IN.: Phi Delta Kappa, 1982), p. 2.

[34] Sponseller, op. cit., p. 231.

Baker, D. "Worlds of Play." *Child. Educ.*, **53**:5 (1977), pp. 245–249.

Baker, Katherine Read. *Let's Play Outdoors.* Washington: NAEYC, 1966.

Bruner, Jerome S., Alison Jolly, and Kathy Sylva. *Play—Its Role in Development and Evolution.* New York: Basic Books, 1976.

Butler, A. L., E. E. Gotts, and N. J. Quisenberry. *Play as Development.* Columbus, Ohio: Merrill, 1978.

Caplan, F., and Theresa Caplan. *The Powers of Play.* Garden City, N.Y.: Anchor Press/Doubleday, 1973.

Carini, Patricia. "Building a Curriculum for Young Children from an Experiential Base." *Young Children*, **32**:3 (1977), pp. 14–18.

Cartwright, Sally. "Blocks and Learning." *Young Children*, **29**:3 (1974), pp. 141–146.

Cherry, C. *Creative Play for the Developing Child: Early Lifehood Education Through Play.* Belmont, Calif.: Fearon, 1976.

Dennis, L. "Play in Dewey's Theory of Education." *Young Children*, **25**:4 (1970), pp. 230–235.

Dimondstein, Geraldine. *Children Dance in the Classroom.* New York: Macmillan, 1972.

Flood, J., and Diane Lapp. "Understanding Play; the Work of the Child," in *Language/Reading Instruction for the Young Child* (New York: Macmillan, 1981), pp. 69–106.

Friedberg, M. P. *Playgrounds for City Children.* Washington: D.C.: ACEI, 1969.

Frost, J. L. (coordinator). *Developing Programs for Infants and Toddlers.* Washington, D.C.: ACEI, 1977.

Frost, Joe L., and Barry L. Klein. *Play and Playgrounds.* Boston: Allyn, 1979.

Garvey, Catherine. *Play.* Cambridge, Mass.: Harvard U.P., 1977.

Hill, Dorothy M. *Mud, Sand, and Water.* Washington, D.C.: NAEYC, 1977.

Hirsch, Elisabeth S. (ed.). *The Block Book.* Washington, D.C.: NAEYC, 1977.

Hurlock, Elizabeth B. "Experimental Investigations of Childhood Play." *Mental Hygiene*, **52**:3 (1968).

Inhelder, B., and J. Piaget. *The Early Growth of Logic in the Child.* New York: Harper, 1969.

Isenberg, J., and J. Jacobs. *Playthings as Learning Tools: A Parents Guide.* New York: John Wiley, 1982.

———— and Evelyn Jacob, "Literacy and Symbolic Play: A Review of the Literature," *Child. Educ.* **59**:4 (1983), pp. 272–274.

Jameson, K., and Pat Kidd. *Pre-School Play.* New York: Van Nostrand Reinhold, 1974.

Lieberman, J. N. *Playfulness: Its Relationship to Imagination and Creativity.* New York: Academic Press, 1977.

Maxwell, W. "Games Children Play." *Educ. Leadership* **40**:6 (1983), pp. 38–41.

Moffitt, Mary W. "Play as a Medium for Learning," in Margot Kaplan-Sanoff and Renée Yablans-Magid, eds. *Exploring Early Childhood: Readings in Theory and Practice.* New York: Macmillan, 1981, pp. 126–132.

Pellegrini, A., and L. Galda. "The Effects of Thematic-Fantasy Play Training on the Development of Children's Story Comprehension." *American Educational Research Journal* **19**:3 (1982).

Pelz, Ruth (ed.) *Developmental and Clinical Aspects of Young Children's Play.* WESTAR Series Paper #17. Monmouth, Oreg.: Western States Technical Assistance Resource, 1982.

Rubin, K. H. "Play Behaviors of Young Children." *Young Children,* **32**:6 (1977), pp. 16–24.

Smilansky, S. *The Effects of Sociodramatic Play on Disadvantaged Pre-school Children.* New York: Wiley, 1968.

Stone, Jeannette G. *Play and Play Grounds.* Washington, D.C.: NAEYC, 1970.

Strom, R. D. "The Merits of Solitary Play." *Child. Educ.,* **52**:3 (1976), pp. 149–152.

Sutton-Smith, B. "The Role of Play in Cognitive Development." In *The Young Child: Reviews of Research.* Ed. by W. W. Hartup and Nancy L. Smothergill. Washington, D.C.: NAEYC, 1967. Pp. 96–108.

Tyler, Bonnie. "Play," in *Curriculum for the Preschool—Primary Child—A Review of the Research.* Ed. by Carol Seefeldt. Columbus, Ohio: Merrill, 1976. Pp. 225–246.

Wolfgang, C. *Helping Aggressive and Passive Preschoolers Through Play.* Columbus, Ohio: Merrill, 1977.

Yawkey, T. D. "More on Play as Intelligence in Children." *Journal of Creative Behavior* **13**:4, 1980.

PART TWO

Curriculum and Young Children

CHAPTER 6

Planning for Learning

One important purpose for bringing children together in any school is to plan, to arrange, and to maintain the quality of the learning environment. Each center for young children is unique, whether it is a nursery school, a kindergarten, Head Start, or a day care program. The type of program and the schedule planned for various activities depend on such factors as the educational philosophy of the staff, the amount of time the children spend in school, the special needs of the children enrolled, the physical facilities available, and the location in terms of climate. However, all centers aim to provide a happy place with opportunities for worthwhile play and work experiences so that children will grow and learn under the guidance of well-qualified teachers.

Each day is important, and the children can live the day only once; therefore, the teacher is acutely conscious of the fact that how *this day* is lived helps determine how capable the child will be to direct his or her energies as one day slips into the next and on and on into adulthood. The teacher asks such questions as how to plan so that this child can acquire skills and work habits, yet be flexible enough to live in a rapidly changing society with ever-changing occupations. How to plan for a child who will live in this world with the expanded community concept? How to plan so that a pattern of work and play will be developed that will guide the child in knowing how to work, how to use leisure time, and how to relax and rest?

In order for children to have such opportunities, the teacher utilizes knowledge about each child, the level of the developmental tasks the child faces, and the sequence of skills within the various subject areas in selecting learning activities and materials to be used. It is in the selection and guidance of activities for young children that the teacher's education and skill are evident.

As planning begins, a teacher of a group of five-year-olds looks at the notes on each child. These notes are a part of the information that has been assembled from parent conferences, observation of the child, and anecdotal records.

Here are examples of what might be read: Gloria needs help in group situations; Karen and Kirsten, the twins, have limited language development; Jennie needs to develop muscular control; and so on until the needs of each child in the group have been considered. The teacher studies these notes and ponders such questions as these: What is the role of the teacher in working with these children? What shall be the teaching tasks, the children's activities? What materials will be needed? Which materials should be prepared or assembled in advance of the arrival of the group, and which materials should be selected and collected by the children under teacher guidance? How can the teacher tell if the children are developing according to their potential as they participate in the planned and the incidental activities?

Using the long-range goals already developed, the teacher must analyze each child's achievement and discover his or her needs, plan a daily schedule, and select learning opportunities and activities. Suggestions for the teacher in each of these areas follow.

ASSESSING LEARNING AND DEVELOPMENT

The teacher's concern in analyzing the child's present level of development or achievement is in securing information to be used as the basis for curricular planning for each child. Observation of children in a variety of situations can yield valuable information. The following questions may be helpful:

What is the relation of the child to others in the situation? Does the child engage in solitary play, parallel play, cooperative play, share toys, take turns?

How does the child use materials? Does the child show evidence of good coordination, a willingness to experiment with new media? Does he or she organize well?

What is indicated about the experiential background of the child? Are there limited experiences, good vocabulary, secure home relationships?

What concepts need to be clarified?

If the opportunities for learning are paced for each child, enthusiasm for learning can be developed through participation in many, yet diverse, activities. Within each curricular field and in the areas of physical, mental, and social growth there is a developmental sequence that can serve as a guide for the teacher. The teacher can identify the child's present level and when the child is ready for the next step the adult is ready to help. There is a need for instruments to help the teacher in analyzing the child's achievement. An analysis of each child can help the teacher in utilizing experiences and activities to facilitate learning. For example, if the teacher finds that Melissa does not recognize a dime or a quarter, she can be included when planning for a committee to buy bird food at the pet store so that she will have opportunities to become acquainted with and use money. This information—that Melissa does not recognize certain coins—can be shared at a parent conference, and parents can be encouraged to provide similar meaningful opportunities.

An analysis of the entire class may reveal that only 10 per cent recognize a dime and a quarter. Is this to be expected? In answering this question, the teacher can consult research and authorities in this area and then set goals. If such competency is to be expected for children at this age, the teacher will need to consider appropriate learning opportunities for the group as well as for individuals within the group. Thus, plans can be made for each child in terms of achievement. Results of periodic evaluation may be also used by the teacher to determine a child's achievement over a given period of time.

The following Achievement Checklist is planned to help in making an analysis of each child. It is not a test. No attempt was made to establish norms for different age groups. It consists of a list of items for assessing achievement that were selected from the literature and have been reviewed by specialists as being appropriate for the early childhood years. The checklist is intended to help the teacher gain a picture of the child's status that will serve as a basis for planning and guidance and as a means of assessing a child's progress. Other items relating to the curriculum can be added to the checklist.

The teacher studies carefully the data secured through the use of the checklist. Activities that will provide continued practice as well as introduce opportunities for new learnings are planned. The progress of the children is assessed periodically to assist in further planning. However, the teacher is constantly aware that, in order to achieve, all children need to feel secure and loved, to be free from fear, and to have some recognition and success as they participate in a variety of learning opportunities.

RECORDING THE DEVELOPMENT OF CHILDREN

With the present emphasis on accountability and preplanning in terms of assessed needs, it is imperative that Early Childhood Education personnel be skilled in record keeping, especially in being objective as to what is recorded. The Freedom of Information Act requires that all school records be available to the individual or families on request unless this right is waived in writing. This makes it desirable that record keeping be a joint venture, with the parents of each child always being

Child's Name _____ Date _____

Achievement Checklist for Young Children

Directions for Using: Below is a list of items which may be achieved by some three-, four-, and five-year-old children. Put a check (✔) in the appropriate column to indicate how frequently, in your experience with this child, he or she has achieved in each item.

Section I	Always	Sometimes	Never	Does Not Apply
Eats with spoon				
Eats with fork				
Holds silver correctly				
Holds cup with one hand				
Spills food or drink only once during meal				
Spills food or drink more than once during meal				
Goes to toilet without help with clothing				
Flushes toilet				
Hangs clothing in locker				
Puts on sweater that opens down front alone				
Puts on coat alone				
Buttons sweater				
Buttons coat				
Puts on slip-on sweater alone				
Manages zipper				
Ties shoe laces				
Climbs jungle gym				
Jumps from 12-inch height				
Skips				
Catches ball				

Achievement Checklist for Young Children

Section I	Always	Sometimes	Never	Does Not Apply
Pedals tricycle				
Climbs steps with alternate feet				
Puts three-piece puzzle together				
Puts puzzle of five or more pieces together				
Holds scissors correctly				
Cuts on a line				
Knows full name				
Writes given name				
Section II				
Follows simple directions				
Sits and listens to story for at least 5 minutes				
Sits and listens to story for at least 10 minutes				
Puts away blocks or toys when finished				
Responds to own name				
Recognizes locker				
Leaves mother after one "good-bye"				
Rides to school in car with someone other than parent				
Chooses to look at picture books				
Looks at books from front to back				
Looks at page from top to bottom				
Recognizes name				
Recognizes name of at least one other child				

Achievement Checklist for Young Children

Section II	Always	Sometimes	Never	Does Not Apply
Contributes to experience story				
Reads experience story with group				
Identifies words in experience story				
Can identify rhyming words				
Can match beginning consonant sounds				
Counts by rote 1–5				
Counts by rote 1–10				
Counts rationally 1–5				
Counts rationally 1–10				
Uses ordinal numbers first through third				
Recognizes money—penny, nickel, dime				
Recognizes geometric shapes—circle, square, triangle, rectangle				
Solves problem without number				
Uses number in problem solving				
Writes numerals 1–5				
Speaks without baby talk				
Uses personal pronouns				
Speaks in sentences (uses sentences of at least five words)				
Tells events or story in sequence				
Engages in conversation with other children				
Engages in conversation with adults				
Speaks in group situation				

Achievement Checklist for Young Children

Section III	Always	Sometimes	Never	Does Not Apply
Sings alone				
Sings songs of at least two phrases				
Recognizes songs sung or played by others				
Manipulates and experiments with instruments				
Uses instrument as accompaniment to movements (beats drums as marches, but not necessarily in time with the steps)				
Knows names of at least two better-known musical instruments				
Listens and identifies sounds of different instruments				
Matches tones				
Draws or paints lines and circles				
Draws or paints squares				
Shows ground line in painting or drawing				
Names paintings or drawings				
Names (or recognizes) primary colors				
Names at least five colors				
Adjusts bodily movements to accompaniment of regular beat (can keep time to music)				
Adjusts bodily movements to accompaniment that involves contrasts (slow–fast, light–heavy)				

Directions for Scoring: Note items in which the pupil has achieved, the items that need continued practice, and those that need to be introduced. Plan learning opportunities in terms of analysis of achievement items. Ignore those items which do not apply.

informed or consulted whenever permanent entries are made. Parents should always be a part of deciding what is to be recorded and why.

The best possible time to obtain accurate information, not only concerning a child but also regarding the child's family background, is during the preschool years. Teacher or other personnel and parents feel a closer bond of responsibility for the young child at that time. Never again will the parents express personal feelings, family problems, and other concerns so freely. A careful record, not in scores or numbers alone, but also in accurate, descriptive anecdotes and accounts of actual happenings and of what is being observed or said will provide the basis later for each child's cumulative school file. Such records have proved of inestimable value to the child's teachers and other school personnel during later school years. All personnel concerned with young children should be skilled in record keeping and in the ability to share the child's strengths, weaknesses, and needs with parents and other professionals working with the child.

What should be recorded

Consistent with changing points of view, what is considered as the most important information to know about a child's development has changed drastically during the past decade. Not only has new terminology come into the picture, but new concepts of evaluation have evolved. The use of tests and direct measurement continues, and searches for more meaningful ways of determining behavioral and growth changes are emerging. The search goes on because the traditional IQ and achievement test scores, although valuable, inadequately furnish information needed to justify the cost of intervention or early start programs. As in all phases of business and industry, such concepts as cost analysis and accountability have found their way into the educational world. With early education a high priority area of education, early childhood education has not escaped the demands of lawmakers and parents for accountability. Early attempts using test results have failed to meet the criteria for success needed for continued support of early education programs. After a review of commonly accepted educational rationale for record keeping, the above concepts and their implementation will be treated in more detail later.

Many feel that permanent records should not be kept, especially if behavior of a personal nature is recorded. They argue that anyone reading these records later will likely be biased by them and thus actual harm to the child involved might result. Yet no one argues in this manner when physicians record events of a personal nature. The medical profession has long recognized the value of the developmental medical record. Child development specialists, too, know their value. The crux of the matter is that teachers who are truly professional know the importance of the past behavioral development of the children they teach. A child with special problems, even if these are no longer present, may need certain kinds of treatment if the problems are not to recur. Sound curriculum development is always based on the variation present in the needs of each group of children involved. Without a record of what has taken place in the past, the teacher is at a distinct disadvantage. The necessity of accuracy in recording thus becomes evident.

Because development and developmental changes occur so rapidly during the early childhood years, a carefully kept developmental record is essential in planning and providing the best possible activities, learning experiences, and opportunities for the health, safety, and well-being of each child. A teacher or caregiver, knowing that a child walked a little later or learned to talk somewhat slower than most children, will not have as high expectations in activities involving fine muscular control or language fluency as she or he will have for certain other children. In discussing problems of this type with parents, the teacher probably will learn of the parent's concern and be able to suggest ways in which the parent can be more accepting, thus reducing obstacles to the child's healthy personal or self-development.

Information for parents

The importance of parent-teacher conferences has been recognized. However, the value of a written record of the conference is often overlooked. Although teachers find it difficult at times, it is desirable to send to the parents by first-class mail a summary report of periodic parent-teacher conferences. Such letters may, of necessity, omit certain confidential information. Parents find this procedure very helpful, and the school copy becomes a valuable part of the child's record.[1] Copies of these letters; health reports including immunization, illnesses, and annual physical examination results; family background file; and the informal type of observations mentioned earlier provide the best possible type of record keeping during the early childhood years. Formal or uniform printed report cards, though often used, probably have little or no place in the preschool program.

The Space Age has already had its impact on early childhood education. There are those who believe that education, particularly reading, should be formalized as early as two or three years of age, and expediency sometimes takes priority. Only a careful evaluation of each child's abilities and developmental status can provide an adequate basis on which the teacher can judge when children possess a sufficient readiness for specific experiences such as beginning reading. The harmful effects, from a mental health point of view, of forcing learning experiences too early have long been known. Because readiness is related to maturation and development rather than chronological age, some children can benefit from certain experiences long before the majority of children of the same age. Guidance, based on observed facts,

---

[1] LaMittice Pearson, "Reaction of Teachers and Parents to the Letter-Summary Method Used for Reporting Parent-Teacher Conferences at the Florida State University Nursery School," Seminar Study, The Florida State University Institute of Human Development, Tallahassee, 1956.

is as important during the early years as later; thus, evaluation based on careful study and records of such evaluation becomes an important responsibility of those guiding young children. Program personnel must now become aware, more than ever before, of the importance of child study as a branch of science and the contributions that have and can be made.

Studying young children

Present-day educational philosophy and practice stress the importance of providing a curriculum, not only in keeping with the goals and purposes of the school, but also in keeping with the ability, growth, and development of the children involved. This implies that the teacher must, at all times, know a great deal about, and understand the motivations of the children taught. This is particularly true of teachers of young children, for important changes occur rapidly at this age. Following the work of Freud, "the present century has witnessed a shift to intensive investigations of early childhood from many theoretical points of view because of a realization of the importance of this period to later development and behavior."[2]

Colleges and universities were quick to see the value of having organized educational programs with young children for research purposes as well as for teacher education purposes. These laboratory and research programs necessitated extensive record keeping, often burdening teachers and students with the task of recording "everything observable."

Today records are kept for specific purposes. The teacher in a nonresearch school must ask, "What is it that should be known about each child and why? What should be known about a child's family, neighborhood, health history, personal characteristics, or playmates?" Such questions must be answered and interpreted in terms of the program's purposes and goals. When this procedure is followed, it is likely that no two schools will keep identical records. Although records of young children will have much in common, more extensive recording will be required for some children than for others. A school may wish to use a standard form for common information about all its children, but it must also provide the necessary flexibility in record keeping to enable planning for maximum opportunities for each individual child. Overstandardization of records is probably as undesirable as standard reporting forms in Early Childhood Education programs. In no way should this "be construed as an effort to depreciate the value of good records and reports. In fact, it may necessitate a new look at how and what to record."[3]

Murphy and research collaborators at Sarah Lawrence College presented a detailed study of one child as a sample of normal childhood.[4] This is an excellent

[2] R. L. Witherspoon, "Studying Young Children," *Nursery School Portfolio*, Leaflet 9 (Washington, D.C.: ACEI, 1961), p. 1.
[3] Ibid.
[4] Lois Barclay Murphy, *Personality in Young Children*, Vol. II (New York: Basic, 1956).

example of the difficulty and complexity of the task of assessing and understanding personality development. Study of such materials will enable one to appreciate not only the importance of, but also the care that should be exercised, in gathering and recording information that will be of value in understanding children. A conscientious and continuous effort on the part of the teacher to learn more about each child in the group is essential to a good educational program for young children. Because memory cannot always be relied on to produce accurate recall of important events or the recurrence of significant behavioral incidents, a recording system is necessary. As previously pointed out, such a system must have flexibility to be effective.

How to record

Obviously, everything that happens cannot be recorded. What is recorded, in addition to basic identification information and objective data such as height, weight, health immunizations, and similar materials, will be determined largely by the purpose of the school. Each item recorded should include the date, time, and place, and the name of the person recording. If the program is one of the usual university or college laboratory schools, the information will be organized in keeping with the needs of observing and participating students. The teacher should plan with the students' instructors so that the records will serve a useful purpose in the college classes as well as assist the teacher in an understanding of each child and his or her needs.

If the program serves as a research laboratory, the records will be kept to satisfy the demands of the particular research being undertaken at the time. Witherspoon indicates the following:[5]

> An understanding of approaches used will make the research process more intelligent and provide better results. . . . An experiment may seek only a single, often minute, clue which when fitted into existing or proposed theories may set off a chain reaction of efforts needed in understanding children. A teacher or parent cannot usually be expected to do research, but cooperation with those who are trained to and whose work it is to do research can benefit all concerned.

Summarizing observations of children playing with miniature life toys, Hartley, Frank, and Goldenson have concluded this:[6]

> These detailed records have unique value for studying the child at leisure, for checking impressionistic opinions against factual data, and for focusing several minds on a single problem without subjecting the child to intolerable scrutiny.

[5] Witherspoon, op. cit., p. 3.
[6] Ruth E. Hartley, L. K. Frank, and R. M. Goldenson, *New Play Experiences for Children* (New York: Columbia U.P., 1952), p. 49.

Many approaches to studying children have been proposed, each demanding different information and different types of records. Witherspoon states the present trend as follows:[7]

> Many students and teachers are finding a problem approach to child study more challenging and profitable than the traditional directed observation, case studies, cumulative records and testing "programs." New insights into individual children and individual parent or teacher motivations will be discovered when a group of teachers undertakes, for example, a study of the development of responsibility in children. When teachers and parents respond to a questionnaire prepared cooperatively and dealing with what they expect of children, they may be surprised to find that they are not in agreement. When children are asked to answer the same questions in relation to the expectations of home and school, more surprises may be expected. Such evidence provides excellent information for individual teacher-parent conferences, parent group discussions, and individual stock-taking by teachers. Getting ready to read, eating patterns, using free time, learning to be friends, what school life is like, leadership and later underachieving, and homework are only a few problems which make interesting "springboards" for studying young children.

The instructional process in the various areas of the curriculum is facilitated by a continuous record of the activities each child engages in. In order to insure a balance among the activities in which each child participates, the teacher keeps a record of his or her choices. A duplicated summary form containing the names of children and activities usually available provides a simple procedure for checking each child's participation. Samples of each child's paintings, crayon drawings, and so on, and teacher-made sketches of the results of participation in construction activities, along with dates and teacher comments, become a valuable part of the child's cumulative file.

Management by objectives

In the early 1970s, the national Head Start Office mandated that all Head Start programs be implemented by a system of operation known as Management by Objectives. Thus, a behavioral model of methods common to business and industry was adapted to child development programs for young children on a large scale in compensatory, intervention, pilot, and research situations. Many other educational programs are, and have been, based on the same model, which places considerable stress on the prior development of behavioral objectives. This simply means that if the teacher or the research staff is to be able to assess the effectiveness of the program efforts, the teacher must know prior to instruction what the end result of that instruction is expected to be. She or he must be able to observe, or otherwise be able to show, the degree to which each objective has been achieved. For ex-

---

[7] Witherspoon, op. cit., p. 2.

ample, if the stated objective is for each child to be able to recognize his or her name in print by the middle of the kindergarten year, the teacher (or test examiner) can arrange situations at midyear that will indicate whether each child recognizes his or her name.

Starting with a set of generalized goals such as ability to classify objects by size, color, and form, the teacher then determines which specific concepts—like big, little, red, blue, round, square, and so on—the child must know in order to achieve the larger goal. Once these specific objectives are spelled out and placed in order of difficulty, teaching strategies and materials are devised to enable the child to experience and thus learn each of the specific concepts necessary to the achievement of the larger goal.

Formative and Summative Evaluation. It is necessary, at any point in time during the aforementioned process, to assess where each child is if instruction is to be meaningful and efficient. As the rate of achievement will vary from child to child, it is essential that daily records be kept. If the objectives have been clearly defined, arranged in a sequence to fit the planned strategies, and available in multiple copies (one for each child), record-keeping is greatly simplified. All the teacher has to do is enter the date after each item when it is achieved by each particular child. This is a type of "formative" evaluation and eventually becomes a record of "summative" evaluation. Formative evaluation takes place "while the course or instructional program is in progress, whereas 'summative' evaluation occurs at . . . the end of the instructional program."[8]

Of course, it is impossible to foresee all events and their expected end results. Nevertheless, it is invaluable both from the standpoint of accountability and for planning teaching and learning situations to have an attainable plan for the group and for each individual child. The latter is essential to the success of an individually prescribed instruction program. Fitting expectancies to attained levels of development has long been a goal of education. Careful, accurate, continuous records for each child go a long way toward making this goal attainable.

Recording planned observations

Most authorities agree that planned observation for a specific purpose and a more or less informal type of recording best serve the purposes for which most teachers and caregivers of young children need records. It is desirable to begin records as early as possible: "Young children are honest and frank; they usually express their feelings freely in action and word. Teachers and parents let a golden opportunity pass when they learn to ignore the continuous activities, imaginations, and antics

---

[8] Daniel Tanner, *Using Behavioral Objectives in the Classroom* (New York: Macmillan, 1972), p. 5.

of the children in their presence. They tend to arrive at this conclusion: 'I just don't understand Mary. I guess she never will grow up and get out of my hair.' "[9]

However, although the preceding is essential for obtaining and maintaining an ongoing global picture of each child's stream of development, such records are insufficient to meet today's accountability standards. Such concepts as cognitive stimulation, intervention, and compensatory education all imply that something is being interjected into the path that the child's development is taking to change its course. School lunch programs have been developed to ensure proper nutrition for the growing child. Infant stimulation programs for babies and young children from deprived homes are designed to head off the cumulative learning deficit so commonly found among children from such homes. Remedial reading, for example, strives to help the child make up for missed experiences to enable reading on a level with more fortunate peers. It is no longer sufficient to assume that these and similar programs will produce the desired results or that IQ changes and test scores are the relevant criteria of measurement.

The first rule of good record keeping is to know what it is that should be recorded and why. Short-term and long-term goals defined in attainable and observable objectives enable the teacher "to know" which behaviors and achievements to look for as a result of instructional activities. Take time to stop, look, and listen. Be perceptive of the child's feelings whether they be those of elation or those of fear and insecurity. Once the teacher learns how to be observant and to share in understanding in the child's reactions at all times, it becomes easier "to accept a child for what he is and to include in his record significant events and signs of progress or retardation in his developmental pattern."[10]

A second rule is to recognize the importance of making and recording observations over a period of time. Young children grow and change rapidly, and this pattern of change or lack of change should be clearly evident in the record. Many teachers have a pencil and pad handy at all times in order to note briefly situations or events that are expanded into a full account at the close of the day. Anecdotal records and behavior journals provide a convenient method of systematizing records.[11]

Recording of any kind requires objectivity. However, sensitivity to the meaning of what is observed is necessary if a desirable course of action is to be pursued. In the words of Lee and Lee,[12]

> We must try as well as we can to "see" through his [the child's] perceptions—first, the situation he is in and, second, what his present actions may accomplish for him. We must put aside for the moment the situation as it is and try only to see it as he feels it. We must not consider the actions that he really might take in it, but rather

[9] Witherspoon, op. cit., p. 2.
[10] Witherspoon, op. cit., p. 2.
[11] For a detailed manual for use of the behavior journal, see W. C. Olson, *Child Development*, 2d ed. (Boston: Heath, 1959), pp. 467–473.
[12] J. M. Lee and Doris M. Lee, *The Child and His Development* (New York: Appleton, 1958), p. 291.

we must only consider the actions that he, for many reasons, sees himself as able to make.

Many forms, record books, and manuals for recording the behavior of children have been published. Suchman has prepared one of the most extensive guides.[13] A more recent comprehensive guide has been prepared by Lindberg and Swedlow.[14]

The Case Study. Perhaps the most frequently used technique for studying children is the case study, which serves as a means of bringing together in an organized fashion all the information that can be learned about an individual child. Case studies probably serve their purpose best when made for particular children who do not seem to be getting along well academically or socially. The careful collection of accurate information about such a child will usually enable the teacher to evaluate the difficulty. Witherspoon points out the following:[15]

> If the child is to be helped, the teacher must know his unique characteristics and needs and have some knowledge of underlying developmental trends and an understanding of their causes. Because the case study entails a history of what has occurred, it can be very helpful in providing useful insights and at the same time point the way for future development. The case study should not be considered as merely a diagnostic tool but should spell out the direction of events and provide useful suggestions and recommendations for the future.

Most teachers have had adequate training that enables them to experiment with the use of case materials. At first, teachers tend to put emphasis on academic matters, and their case studies tend to be heavily weighted with this type of information. Unfortunately, few school records contain even the most elementary knowledge of the home and family situations from which the children come. Undesirable behavior may be noted without reference to personal or social factors that may be the cause of the behavior described. It is easy for the teacher to interpret findings superficially on the basis of incomplete information and thus confirm earlier suspicions, preconceptions, and prejudices. The writing of objective records requires skill and an open mind in order to see the deeper underlying emotional stresses and conflicts. At times it is desirable to call in the school psychologist or other specialist to assist with interpretation. Yet "despite these shortcomings, the case study approach offers the teacher a challenging opportunity to study objectively certain youngsters and certain problems encountered."[16]

Case studies usually include detailed information organized under such broad categories as developmental history of the child, family characteristics and history,

[13] J. Richard Suchman, *Observation and Analysis in Child Development: A Laboratory Manual* (New York: Harcourt, 1959).
[14] Lucile Lindberg and Rita Swedlow, *Early Childhood Education: A Guide for Observation and Participation*, Boston: Allyn, 1976 (loose-leaf).
[15] Witherspoon, op. cit., p. 3.
[16] Ibid., p. 4.

socioeconomic status and community relationships, behavior descriptions, and appraisal and recommendations. A manual providing a guide for the preparation of case studies was prepared by Garrison, Kingston, and Dekle.[17]

The Behavior Journal.   Many teachers find the behavior journal a convenient and valuable way to keep a continuous developmental record of children. Uses of the behavior journal as summarized by Olson are characteristic of the practical value of other observational techniques. His summary follows:[18]

1. In schools where the report to the parents is of the letter type, the recorded incidents furnish a useful basis for the behavioral aspects of the letter.
2. The journal reveals points of strength and weakness in the public relations program.
3. The recurring problems indicate points at which parent education is needed.
4. The records reveal gaps in curriculum planning.
5. Specific entries provide useful supplementary data for personal, educational, and vocational counseling.
6. The incidents may be used in instruction to illustrate principles of child development.
7. The making of the record stimulates teachers to the consideration of the problems of individual children.
8. The accumulation and persistence of unusual behavior items assists in locating children who require special diagnostic study and treatment.
9. The journal gives the specialist to whom the child is referred additional data for diagnostic purposes.
10. The record points to the incipience and development of special talents.
11. The journal furnishes material for appraisal and research. It may assist in locating significant research issues and in setting the conditions for objective and controlled studies.

Tests.   In an educational world where precision and objective measurement are held in high esteem, it is only natural that an effort would be made to apply the same procedures to young children. Consistent with the testing movement in general, early efforts were made to develop tests to measure the intelligence of infants and young children. Typical of these efforts were the *Minnesota Scale*,[19] *Cattell Intelligence Scale for Young Children*,[20] *Merrill-Palmer Scale*,[21] and *The California*

---

[17] K. C. Garrison, A. Kingston, and O. T. Dekle, *Students' Workbook for the Psychology of Childhood* (New York: Scribner, 1967).

[18] Olson, *op. cit.*, p. 471.

[19] Florence L. Goodenough and M. J. Van Wagenen; *Minnesota Preschool Scales—Forms A and B*; rev. ed. (Minneapolis: Educational Test Bureau, 1940).

[20] Psyche Cattell, *The Measurement of Intelligence of Infants and Young Children* (New York: Psychological Corporation, 1940).

[21] Rachel Stutsman, *Mental Measurement of Preschool Children with a Guide for the Administration of the Merrill-Palmer Scale of Mental Tests* (Yonkers, N.Y.: World Book, 1931).

First Year and Preschool Scales.[22] The pioneering work of Gesell has provided a wealth of information about the growth and development of children.[23]

Currently, because of the need to measure results of programs for disadvantaged children, many new preschool tests are being developed although long-range values have not yet been established. It is likely that many valuable tests will emerge as a result of the Head Start research program. (Tests being widely used are the *Peabody Vocabulary Test, The Illinois Test of Psycholinguistic Abilities* (ITPA), *The Revised Stanford-Binet, the Bayley Scales of Infant Development,* and the *Lexington Developmental Scales.*) Test results used in the context of the purpose for which the test was intended can be invaluable to the teacher in her or his day-to-day planning as well as providing an index of progress over time. However, using tests to predict later aptitudes can be very hazardous. Preschool tests of intelligence, for example, have been repeatedly shown to be poor predictors of later intelligence test scores.[24] Preschool tests require special training and skills not commonly acquired in testing courses. Tests should not be administered to preschool children unless the examiner is thoroughly familiar with the characteristics of the age of the child being tested if the results are to be valid and useful.

PLANNING LEARNING OPPORTUNITIES

As the teacher plans opportunities for experiences and activities for and with the children, the teacher takes into consideration their individual and group goals, likes, needs, and abilities, as well as the child's home life and experiential background. With these factors in mind, the teacher will plan so that the children may:

1. Plan together—for the day, for the period, and for special events.
2. Make decisions—as to work, play, rest, and behavior.
3. Learn new skills—as an individual child and as a group.
4. Expand interests—in special areas or in new areas.
5. Have balance—between active and quiet activities and between indoor and outdoor play.
6. Have opportunities—to laugh together, to console one another, to help one another.
7. Have opportunities to work alone—to browse among materials or to think and muse quietly.
8. Visit places—within the school, at home, an interesting place in the community, or have a person from outside the school visit them.
9. Establish routines—of physical habits, work habits, discipline, or self-direction and self-control.

[22] Nancy Bayley, "On the Growth of Intelligence," *Amer. Psychol.,* **10**:12 (1955), pp. 805–818.
[23] Arnold Gesell and C. S. Amatruda, *Development Diagnosis,* 2d ed. (New York: Hoeber, 1947).
[24] Ibid.

10. Develop social values—following through with an activity and receiving group acceptance, developing a balance between independence or initiation and consideration or aggression, developing pride in ownership yet willingness to share, acquiring a feeling of security for self but also a sense of responsibility to the group.
11. Develop readiness—in reading, speech, mathematics, writing, according to child's maturity.
12. Grow—through creative self-expression in music, rhythm, dramatic play, art activities, games.
13. Explore natural environment—through observing, investigating, experimenting, experiencing.

As the teacher considers these points, she or he knows that emphasis will not be placed on all of them each day, yet all are so interrelated that many of them will appear daily in some form. Certainly a group would not take a trip each day nor would someone from outside the school visit the group very often.

APPROACHES TO TEACHING

How, then, does the teacher plan and teach in order to achieve the desired results? What are some of the strategies that may be used? Descriptions of a few teaching strategies follow. These are applicable to any subject area. Examples of use in various subject fields, such as social studies and science, are included in chapters dealing with the subject areas.

Reinforcing, Clarifying, Explaining, and Discussing Incidents That Affect Children During the School Day. Often opportunities for reinforcing, clarifying, explaining, and discussing incidents that affect children during the school day are lost. However, a comment by the teacher at the right moment can be most effective in utilizing both in- and out-of-school experiences that children mention in their conversation. In the following example, two four-year-olds complain to Miss D., "We don't like Steve. He knocks our blocks down."

> Miss D.: Why do you think he knocks them down?
> Hal: He's just mean.
> Joe (thoughtfully): He doesn't know how to play with other children.
> Miss D.: Why do you think he doesn't know how?
> Joe: He just came to nursery school.
> Miss D.: How could we help him?

In response to the question, two suggestions were made.

1. "We could say, 'Please don't knock down the blocks. We don't do that at nursery school.'"
2. "We could ask him to play with us."

These four-year-olds were being taught to understand that rules can help us live happily together.

With five-year-olds a typical example might be this: "Mrs. K., Janet said that I can't play with them."

> Mrs. K.: Janet, Susie seems to be feeling very sad because she feels that you do not want her to play with you. Can you help me to understand why she feels this way?
>
> Janet: I didn't say that she couldn't play.
>
> Mrs. K.: Why do you think she feels that you do not want her then?
>
> Linda: But she always wants to be the mother and tell us what to do.
>
> Mrs. K.: Susie, what do you think you could be instead of the mother?
>
> Susie: I don't know.
>
> Linda: She could be the little sister.
>
> Mrs. K.: Susie, would you like to be the little sister today, or would you rather choose another center?

These children are learning that belonging to a group means sharing decision making with other members of the group.

Cooperative Planning.   Cooperative planning means that the teacher and children plan together, examine alternatives, and make decisions appropriate for consideration by the child. They can participate in planning for many different activities such as field trips, cooking, a visit by a resource person, or what to do in the classroom. For example, the teacher says, "This is a rainy day. We can't go out on the playground. What could we do inside?" The teacher and children discuss the possibilities available, make choices, and plan for their use.

Cooking.   Cooking is a good foundation activity for language growth among children.[25] Such experiences provide opportunities for developing basic concepts such as size, shape, number, color, measurement, weight, smell, taste, sound, and temperature change.[26]

The classroom is an appropriate place to introduce the child to foods that are not only appealing but also nutritious. Recipes should be carefully chosen. The foods to be prepared should be those that promote good health. The recipes should have only a few steps that the children can follow easily from illustrations on laminated task cards.

In guiding cooking activities, the teacher should keep in mind the following suggestions:

Use simple recipes that children can follow from pictures.
Maintain constant, alert, adult supervision.

[25] Barbara Johnson and Betty Plemmons, "Individual Child-Portion Picture Recipes," in *Cup Cooking* (Lake Alfred, Fla.: Early Educators, 1980), p. 5.
[26] C. F. Eliason and L. T. Jenkins, *A Practical Guide to Early Childhood Curriculum*, 2d ed. (St. Louis, Mo.: Mosby, 1981), p. 205.

Cooking activities provide opportunities for exploring the physical world, discussing and planning, taking turns, following directions, learning quantitative measurement, using desirable health habits, developing scientific concepts, and beginning reading experiences.

Exercise care in the use of the stove and hot liquids.

Discuss the safety rules.

Practice desirable health habits. Be sure that hands are washed and utensils are clean.

Relate cooking to various phases of the school program, such as health, science, social studies, and holiday celebrations.

Picture the ingredients to be used on a chart as a reference for the children.

Experiment with using various measures, such as one tablespoon or one-half cup, before the cooking activity.

Keep the project simple enough so that the children will have a successful and happy experience.

Allow time for children to do the work.

The entire group need not "cook" at the same time.

A cooking activity can contribute to learning in the various areas of the curriculum.[27] For example:

1. Language Arts
   a. Discussing plans.
   b. Listening to and following directions.
   c. Learning new words.
   d. Reading plans and recipes.
2. Social Studies
   a. Learning about home activities.
   b. Working as a member of a group.
   c. Learning where foods come from and how they are transported.
   d. Understanding about division of labor.
3. Science
   a. Learning how foods grow.
   b. Understanding how matter changes form.
4. Mathematics
   a. Measuring ingredients.
   b. Understanding quantities.
   c. Learning how foods are sold; measuring; weighing.
5. Health and Safety
   a. Developing the concept that many foods help us grow strong.
   b. Practicing reasonable cautions—"cooking can be done safely."
   c. Practicing desirable health habits, such as handwashing.
   d. Helping improve self-image because child is really doing something worthwhile.

Field Trips. Visits may be made to spots within walking distance of the school, or sites farther away that necessitate transportation. In either case, one should use the following checklist in preparing for the trip:

1. Formulate purpose of trip. Too many trips are taken merely because they are novel or unusual and provide an activity for the group. Trips should be made only after the teacher has clearly in mind reasons for taking the trip and feels that the trip offers the most effective method of helping the children to develop certain understandings and appreciations and to acquire certain knowledge and facts. In deciding whether the trip is the most effective method to use, the teacher will find it important to consider such factors as the following:
   a. Length of time required for transportation and the visit. Considering the age of the children, is it too long? Will they become too tired? Will it interfere with the routines for eating and resting?

---

[27] Tricia Godshall, "Discover Cooking with Preschoolers," mimeographed, Project Florida Head Start, University of Miami, Coral Gables, n.d.

b. Complexity of the concepts and difficulty of the facts to be gained. Are they appropriate for the maturity of the children? Could they be acquired more effectively when the child is older?

c. Experience background of the children. Have the children had, or are they likely to have, this experience with their parents?

d. Security of the child. Is the security of the child threatened by leaving school with "a stranger," an adult who is helping with the trip?

2. Obtain administrative permission. Investigate school policies covering field trips, and observe these in planning for the trip.

3. Obtain written permission of the parents. The following is a sample form that may be used and covers trips for the entire school year:

_____ has my permission to go on
(Child's Name)

excursions away from Nursery School. I understand that these excursions will be planned and adequately supervised.

_____

(Parent's Signature)

It is important, however, to notify parents of each trip away from school. Such notice helps parents to understand the value of the trip and to know the details involved that may influence the clothing the child wears that day and also the schedule for bringing and picking up the child.

4. Visit site before taking children. This is essential in order to determine whether or not the site is appropriate and can fulfill the purposes of the trip. Safety hazards should be noted. Talk with adults who will serve as guides and talk with the children.

5. Arrange transportation. When private cars are used, be sure that the parent has adequate liability insurance. Two adults should be in the car, one in the back seat. The number of children per car should be limited so that there is room for each child to sit down. If the group is walking, the number of adults will vary with the age of the children. With three-year-olds there should be at least one adult for every two children. For four- or five-year-olds, there should be at least two adults for every five or six children.

6. Invite parents to assist. Select parents whose presence in the school situation does not overstimulate their own child. In order to help the adult "keep up" with the children assigned to her, each child might have a name tag, the color of the children's tags matching the color of the tag worn by the adult. Discuss with the parents the purposes of the trip. To provide consistent guidance, talk with them regarding the standards of behavior that have been developed for the trip.

7. Plan with the children. Talk about what we hope to see, to observe, to learn. Be sure that they know why they are taking the trip. Discuss reasons for standards of behavior, such as listen to the adult who is with you; sit down in the

car; and when you get out of the car, wait for the group and the adult. Count the children before leaving school and frequently during the trip.

8. Evaluate the experience. Variety is needed here. Too often the group only discusses the trip or paints pictures about it. On one field trip a child was overheard to say, "Don't look 'cause when we get back, we'll have to read and write." Although preschool children do not read or write about the trip, the comment reflects the child's reaction to the exclusive use of one type of evaluation. Children's comments, conversation, and dramatic play all can be used to determine whether or not the purposes of the trip have been fulfilled.

Organization and Use of Centers of Interest and Learning Centers.   The terms *learning center* or *station* are often used, and the question arises as to the difference between them and the term *centers of interest* as used in programs for young children. A center of interest is just what the name implies—a place in the nursery, kindergarten, or Child Development Center in which the child can engage in activities related to one of many interests. These centers provide interrelated experiences that may be adapted to the child's interests, maturity, and experiential background. Through such experiences the child can grow in appreciation of his or her world, relationships, and roles. In such a center the children can manipulate objects, build, and engage in conversation and role-playing and can learn at their

Learning centers aid in individualizing instruction.

own level. The use of blocks may range from manipulation by some children to the building of a structure related to a topic of interest. One child may rock the doll as she or he plays alone whereas three others may engage in cooperative play and role-playing. Opportunities for practicing physical and social skills as well as cognitive development are available. Some children, however, do not utilize them.

The learning center has evolved as an attempt to individualize instruction for more effective education of children. The learning center emphasizes cognitive growth and provides for self-evaluation.[28] There are certain tasks to be performed, such as: "Find four blocks that are just alike." Self-evaluation can take place as the child puts the blocks in a frame or storage shelf to test for size.

In the use of centers with young children, whether called *interest* or *learning*, it is important that the intellectual growth of the child not be affected adversely—activities should not be boring and dull on the one hand or too structured and demanding on the other.[29]

The role of the teacher in planning for and supervising the centers is an important one. Suggestions for the teacher in planning and organizing centers follow:

1. Select centers that are appropriate to the child's level of development and interests, and vary these from time to time. Be sure that the centers are attractive, inviting, uncluttered, and safe. Enough equipment should be available so that the child does not have to wait too long for a turn. Some centers, such as block building and the doll corner, are available each day. Variety may be provided by the addition of different materials on certain days. For example, toys related to transportation—trucks, trains, and airplanes—may be placed in the block-building area. Conversation may be encouraged by including toy telephones in the doll corner. Specific learning tasks may be added. The materials and tasks selected will vary with the emphasis that the teacher considers to be important at the time.

   Other centers of interest may be set up for a few days only. Such centers may relate to a holiday or to the unit of study that is in progress at the time.

2. Set up centers around the room in order to utilize space and minimize conflicts. Related centers should be near each other. Maintain a balance between quiet and noisy centers and between those that accommodate a group or an individual.

3. Maintain a classroom atmosphere that is conducive to effective use of the centers and one in which the child is free to move from one activity to another. Sufficient time is needed for the child to engage in the activity and to move around without being hurried or pushed. In supervising the centers of interest, the teacher observes the responses of children in the situation. This information can be of great help in analyzing pupil achievement.

[28] D. E. Day and D. W. Allen, "Organization for Individual Work," *Learning Centers: Children on Their Own* (Washington, D.C.: ACEI, 1970), p. 31.
[29] Ibid., p. 32.

4. Guide the children's activities so that the experience may be satisfying and valuable. For example, the teacher may help each child find some activity, help a child get into a group, help in quarrel situations, raise questions that may clarify the situation, assist in problem-solving situations, and clarify use of materials.
5. Watch for indications of leads into future activities.
6. Arrange for several learning centers to be available and to be set up before the child arrives at school. The child's attention span is short, and he or she may participate in several centers of interest during the morning. A wide variety of activities should be available. The following list of centers suggests the types that the teacher might make available.

Housekeeping Center.   This center is available every day. A partition or shelves to separate it from the rest of the classroom encourages language development. Activities relate to the home, kinds of homes, members of the family. A learning task may be planned to involve classification. For example, "Hang the clothing here. Put the cooking utensils on the table." Vary the tasks from time to time.

Block Center.   The block center offers opportunities for construction of houses, trains, identification of community helpers who work on the train. Provide caps for conductor and engineer.

The housekeeping center provides many opportunities for dramatic play.

Puzzle and Game Center. Puzzles and games should be color-coded according to level of difficulty, so that children can be directed to a choice that can be successfully completed. By shape-coding them for skills, the teacher can direct the student to the activities that are most needed. Games should include commercially made favorites as well as teacher-made games that are suitable to the class interests at that time and are of appropriate level of difficulty.

Book Center. This center should be located in a part of the room that has little traffic. Book shelves should display the covers of the books. Books displayed for the day may relate to the unit that is under way. Carpets or rugs and soft chairs or pillows placed in an environment that includes attractive paintings and flowers attract children to this area.

Mathematics Center. Counting rods, geoboards, containers for measurement, and felt figures for comparing may be utilized. A suggested task might be, "How many nuts balance one apple? Write the number."

Science Center. The possibility to observe and care for a pet should be a part of every early childhood classroom. Games for classifying or categorizing objects from the natural environment, such as seeds, seashells, leaves, insects, or tastes, can be provided.

Sand and Water Centers. These centers are appropriate for outside, but can be used inside if a table is placed in an area where the floor is of appropriate material.

Listening Center. Commercial and teacher-made tapes of stories and songs encourage children to listen and interact with what they hear.

Sound and Music Center. Color-coded piano or xylophone keys may be matched with color-coded notes on large sheet music so that the child can play a melody on an instrument. Other materials, such as sand blocks, drums, or bells, can also help the child develop an appreciation for sounds and rhythm.

Art Center. An easel, large table, paints, paper, clay, and ample storage space are basic. Children need easy access to materials and should be able to put them away independently.

Carpentry Center. A heavy wooden table, 8- to 10-oz hammers, hand drill, miter box, backsaw, "C" clamps, soft wood, and nails are the basics for this center. This center should be located where it can be supervised at all times.

Puppet Center. A simple stage and numerous commercial, teacher- and child-made puppets provide an opportunity for creativity and language development.

Physical Education Center. A balance beam, hopscotch, Hula-Hoops, jump ropes, romper stompers, beanbag games and balls are equipment that can be used inside or outside if a patio area is available.

Cooking Center. Provide a low table where children can follow task cards and prepare nutritious foods. (See earlier suggestions.)

PLANNING FOR TEACHING

Very few teachers can plan and teach exactly as they might wish. In most situations, planning and teaching are influenced to some degree by regulations of the state, the county, Head Start, the parent cooperative, or the private school. There is usually a "handbook" and a curriculum guide. The teacher should become familiar with these, not to be followed slavishly, but as a framework of learnings to be taught.[30]

Neither is the choice of a topic for teaching based exclusively on the interests of the child, nor is it entirely dependent upon the occurrence of some incident. The teacher utilizes both the child's interest and incidents within the framework of learnings to be taught.

Often the question is asked, "What can the children do tomorrow?" and the reply is in terms of activities in which the children may participate. The most important question for the teacher to ask, however, is, "What am I trying to help the children learn, to understand, to experience?" When this has been answered, activities can be planned, and incidents utilized.

The teacher should be more concerned about justifying some of the topics routinely used. He or she should ask frequently: What contribution will the study of this topic make toward helping this child become more competent for living in this modern world? Is this worthwhile? Why? What difference will this make in the life of the child? Honest answers to such questions can help make the content and learnings more meaningful.

Once the learnings and the concepts have been selected, the teacher will do further planning. The educational long-range goals have already been developed. These are reviewed frequently to see how each lesson fits into and furthers the achievement of the goals.

Good planning is based on goals the teacher hopes to achieve. Plans may take a variety of forms. Some teachers make lesson plans from day to day with little thought for continuity or reinforcement of learning. Others choose a more integrated approach, which helps avoid a fragmented program. The latter approach includes

---

[30] J. Jarolimek, *Social Studies in Elementary Education,* 5th ed. (New York: Macmillan, 1977), pp. 25–27.

long-range planning as well as daily lesson or teaching plans. A description of this type of planning follows.

A Plan for Developing Units.   A plan for developing key concepts is a means of organizing materials for instructional purposes.[31] Such a plan, traditionally thought of as a *unit*, is usually a collection of teaching materials and suggested activities organized around a topic such as "Our Homes," "Money Is Used for Many Things," or "Many People Help Us." These plans (or units) may be developed well in advance by the teacher or committee of teachers as is done in some school systems. Such plans or units do not necessarily limit the teacher because from these resources the teacher is free to select and work out a lesson or teaching plan with a specific group of children.

The Lesson or Teaching Plan.   The lesson or teaching plan may be developed from the materials related to the key concept (or unit plan). The teacher selects certain phases to emphasize for a period of time and provides opportunities through which learning can take place.

A plan of work may be for a part of a day, one day, or for several days, depending on the maturity and interest of the group. Whatever the length of time involved, whether it be a unit or a teaching or lesson plan, good planning includes (1) objectives or purposes, (2) activities or opportunities for learning experiences through which these objectives may be realized, (3) materials needed, and (4) plans for evaluating to determine whether or not the purposes have been achieved. Examples of units are included in Chapters 10 and 12.

Classroom management

To accomplish the objectives that have been chosen, a well-organized classroom management plan is essential. The centers that have been described earlier will provide the setting in which each child will be given the opportunity to meet the objectives that have been set for him or her. "The teacher no longer teaches just by telling but instead facilitates or guides learning by providing an interesting and meaningful environment."[32] If the management of learning in the centers is not guided with extreme care, it is very easy for children to appear busy and yet not be advancing in their cognitive, physical, emotional, and social skills.

The contract approach can help the teacher and child develop a feeling of success as they work through the day. The child and teacher plan together for the work that the child is to do.[33] The work will vary according to the maturity, needs, and

[31] Ibid.

[32] Barbara Day, *Open Learning in Early Childhood* (New York: Macmillan, 1975), p. 6.

[33] Robert M. Wilson and Linda B. Gambrell, "Contracting—One Way to Individualize," *Elementary English*, **50** (March 1973), p. 427.

interests of the child. For one child the contract may be that of completing a simple puzzle. Another child may plan to work in the Math center, doing a matching number game. The child works at his or her own pace within the time limits agreed upon. The teacher and child evaluate the work when it has been completed.

A simple contract such as the following can help the child to plan his or her activities and yet give the teacher an opportunity to provide direction to ensure that different skills are met by everyone in the class.[34]

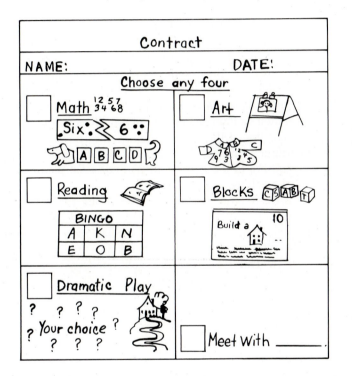

INSTRUCTIONAL RESOURCES

The use of instructional technology in children's centers has greatly increased in recent years. Educational media may be used to help children visualize and understand ideas more clearly.

Models, Collections, and Museums. The resources of models, collections, and museums may be used for instructional purposes. Models and collections may belong to one of the parents, one of the children, or someone in the community. A file of

[34] Day, op. cit., p. 182.

such resources, identifying possible uses and values, can be most helpful. Expensive and rare collections that may be easily broken or damaged should not be brought to the nursery school or kindergarten. Museums, especially those for children, will often plan a special exhibit. Others have collections that may be borrowed by the teacher for use at school. For example, one Junior Museum has "Treasure Chests" for loan to schools, and some are appropriate for the young child. The chests include pictures, books, filmstrips, and objects related to a special topic.

Films, Slides, Filmstrips, and Television Programs. Films, slides, filmstrips, and television programs can contribute to children's understandings when used for specific purposes. In using them, the teacher will find the following suggestions helpful: Always preview films, slides, and filmstrips, and listen to recordings before using them with children. Judge their value and appropriateness in terms of length, difficulty, and number of concepts presented, vocabulary used, voice of the narrator, and relation to the teacher's purpose. Slides and filmstrips make questions and comments possible at the time each picture is shown. To use a film that shows only one scene directly related to the purpose and that contains many other concepts may be confusing to the child. One slide or a flat picture might be a better choice for effective teaching.

Clarify with the children the purpose or the reason for viewing the film, slide, or filmstrip. Relate the visual material to the problem or question with which children are concerned. Use the visual materials more than once if possible. The second viewing often answers questions and clears up misunderstandings. Observe the behavior of the children, their attention, questions, and comments as indications of the value of the experience to them.

It is important that the teacher go with the child to books to "find out." The teacher may say, "I think I know where to find this." The teacher and child look at pictures together.

Bulletin Boards. "Typically used for display purposes," says Jefferson, "the bulletin board's seasonal pictures and flat objects 'cutely' arranged prove meaningless to young children." The most effective use occurs when the bulletin board reflects current interests of the group and when children are engaged in the activity. Such boards are called *involvement bulletin boards.*[35] Jefferson suggests the following as appropriate uses for the bulletin board with young children.[36]

1. Preparation for and summary of field trips.
2. Learning about current events and happenings.
3. Helping children learn colors and distinguish shapes.
4. Special projects.

---

[35] Ruth Jefferson, "Bulletin Boards for Young Children," *Involvement Bulletin Boards* (Washington, D.C.: ACEI, 1970), p. 60.
[36] Ibid.

Resource Persons.   Resource persons may be invited to talk with the children, to show pictures, materials or other items, or to share a skill, such as singing, playing a musical instrument, or cooking. Such persons may be the parents or family members of a child in the group, some person in the community, or another teacher. If the person is to talk with the children, the teacher needs to be sure that he or she can talk with them in a manner they can understand. Don't ask someone to come and talk about a general topic, such as "rocks." Before the visit, be sure your guest speaker understands the questions raised by the children and the length of time in which to talk.

Packaged Materials.   Commercially prepared materials are now available in many areas, such as concept development, auditory and visual perception, and language. The *package*, however, is different from such materials. The package is a full program, and the primary purpose is to create a curriculum along with the necessary accessories,[37] a system of instructional media and materials along with a plan for their use. Some plans are very flexible whereas others are quite restrictive.

The packages have usually been field-tested before general distribution. If a teacher is considering the use of packaged materials, it may be well to examine the objectives and how these are to be accomplished; the background research; opportunities for active participation by the children and creative use by the children and teacher; initial cost and cost of replacement of parts; necessity for teacher training; and the relationship to other courses and activities in the school or center.[38]

In summary, the words of Murphy are appropriate:[39]

> Gimmicks for learning are a dime a dozen and there is a new bandwagon every year! . . . Not that all old methods are bad or that all new methods are good. Rather, we need to choose carefully and combine wisely the methods that will help children to become intelligent members of a democracy. To do this, we need to learn what each approach can offer and what are its hazards.

PLANNING THE DAY

Planning the day's schedule is important as it assists the teacher in developing an effective educational program. The day's schedule, though it may vary in length, is much the same in a school or a day care center because each is based on what is

---

[37] Carolyn Wakefield, "Evaluation of Packaged Materials for Young Children," unpublished graduate paper, University of Maryland, College Park, 1971.

[38] Ibid., pp. 6–7. Detailed criteria for the selection of packaged instructional materials may be found in the following publication: *Selecting Educational Equipment and Materials for Home and School* (Washington, D.C.: ACEI, 1976), p. 29.

[39] Lois B. Murphy, "Multiple Factors in Learning in the Day Care Center," *Child. Educ.*, **45**:6 (1969), p. 311.

good for children. There are conditions, however, that affect the teacher's plans. These include the following:[40]

> The chronological age, developmental level, and experiential backgrounds of the children.
> The length of the allotted school day.
> Weather conditions.
> Bus schedules, car pools, transportation variations.
> Space and physical facilities, location of bathroom and playground.
> Class enrollment.
> The ratio of adult leadership to the number of children.

A good day begins with a friendly informal exchange of greetings followed by some activity that has concern for the health of the child. Some schools require that the parent wait until this has been given the necessary attention before leaving the child at school. The daily school period varies according to the situation and purpose. The length of the day is not significant provided there is proper balance between rest and play, with attention to indoor-outdoor play and active and quiet activities. The general plan may vary from day to day; however, some orderly planning is important to the security of the child and the teacher. The schedule should not be so inflexible that special events and unexpected happenings cannot be a part of the program.

An example of a plan that includes blocks of time follows:

1. Arrival. (Approximately 15 minutes.)
2. A period in which the children decide what they want to do and move freely from one activity to another. (For many children, toileting should be the first activity; this is especially true for the very young child. Others may need food.) The teacher plans and prepares for this period in advance. Many and varied activities and materials are used. Block building, painting at the easel, dramatic play, drawing with large crayons and chalk, looking at books on the library table, working with clay, and many other indoor or outdoor activities are planned for each day and varied from day to day. (Approximately 60 minutes.)
3. A period for routines of toileting, eating, and resting or relaxing. The rest period may be a story hour, or there may be quiet music. Some children may go to sleep during this period. Freedom from glare and bright lights is important. The teacher is alert to notice that the lights appear different at his or her eye level and checks light in terms of the child's eye level. The teacher should remain quiet and as a rule seated during this period. After relaxing, the child may get up quietly and prepare for the next activity. Rest should be pleasant and happy and not regarded as punishment. (Approximately 20 minutes.)
4. A period of total group activity that may involve singing, experimenting with rhythm instruments, listening to records or a story (if not used in item 2), or dramatization of a story read. (Approximately 15 minutes.)

[40]*A Guide: Early Childhood Education in Florida Schools*, Bull. 76 (Tallahassee: Florida State Department of Education, 1969), p. 41.

5. Outdoor play (if not in first period and weather permits). Activities with large-muscle equipment, wheel toys, construction, balls, and ropes. All the work-play periods are closely supervised, and the activities are guided by the teacher. (Approximately 60 minutes.)

6. Evaluating and planning for the next day. Through these activities the teacher receives suggestions for the next steps, and the children leave with a feeling of accomplishment and anticipation for returning the next day, which holds new challenges for them. They get ready to go home. (Approximately 20 minutes.)

7. Dismissal.

Some teachers find it desirable to develop a form to be used in planning and recording the activities for the day and for the week. Whatever the form used, it should allow space for specific notes to serve as reminders as the day develops and to record points to remember in future planning. The example given of a planning form was developed for use in planning, with all persons involved in the daily activities, including the teacher, parents, and aides. Plans for *arrival* are given here. Plans may be developed for each activity or for part of the day.

When? Date and Time	What? Activity-Purpose	Where? Location(s)	How? Methods-Techniques	What? Materials Equipment	Who? Is Responsible	For Future Use*
Monday-9-6-79 9:00-9:15	Arrival of children — Each child: (1) is greeted in a pleasant manner and helped to feel "wanted":	Gate	Greets child and parent (or adult). Makes informal health check Comments on something child is wearing. Asks Sue about new baby brother		Teacher	Call Mrs. Narvo. Tell her Paul used tools today. Get caps for conductors on block train. Puzzles 1 and 5 have pieces missing.
	(2) puts away wrap. (3) finds and begins an activity.	Inside – near classroom door	Greets each child. Remind child to remove and hang up wrap. Talks with child about possible activity.	Blocks Puzzles Clay Easel Paint	Aide	Cheryl painted today-first time.

*Be sure to include these notes in planning for tomorrow.

Adapted from ACTIVITY PLANNING FORM distributed by Head Start Regional Training Officer, Nancy Goldsmith, University of Maryland, College Park, Md. (Mimeographed).

Teachers in centers that operate either a morning session or an afternoon session or both find that they can adapt this schedule to suit the local situation. In schools that operate on a full day, the schedule will need to be adapted to include a 30- to 45-minute lunch period at school. This period will be followed by an afternoon session that includes a nap period of approximately 1½ hours and a period of outdoor play of approximately the same length.

Two examples of a suggested daily schedule and plan follow. One schedule, for a center that operates all day, can be adjusted for sessions of varying lengths (note suggested dismissal times) and may be adapted and used in daycare centers, Head Start programs, kindergarten, or nursery groups. The second schedule is for a group of three-year-old children in a half-day program.

Table 6-1
Daily Schedule

8:30–9:00	Children enter center. Informal health check. Free play with materials such as puzzles, table toys, crayons, blocks. Outdoor play if weather permits. This is a good time to give special attention to individual children.
9:00–9:15	Clean up. Put materials in order for later morning work time. (Some materials might be left so that play can resume after breakfast or juice time.) Each day a few children with one adult help set up for breakfast or juice.
9:15–9:30	Breakfast or juice and crackers. Clean up.
9:30–9:45	Short discussion of day's plans, what was done the previous day, or other topics of interest to children. Include some music and physical activities.
9:45–10:30 indoors and/or outdoors	Work time. Housekeeping and dramatic play, carpentry and woodworking, water play, table games and toys, sharing and caring for pets, blocks, art activities, such as finger painting, easel painting, wood, collage, crayons, clay, play dough.
10:30–10:50	Clean up. Adults work with children.
10:50–11:00	Bathroom. If center set-up permits, children go to bathroom on their own as the need arises. If children must go at a specific time with adult supervision, it is possible to go in small groups.
11:00–11:30	Outdoor activities. If adults are available, stagger coming inside so that not all children arrive indoors at one time.
11:30–12:00	Clean up and getting ready for lunch. Quiet activity—story or rest. Getting ready for dismissal for those leaving before lunch.
12:00–12:45	Lunch. If possible, children should be able to leave table when they are finished. They may participate in a quiet activity until the bus or car arrives or begin rest time if the program continues into the afternoon.
12:45–1:00	Getting ready for dismissal for those leaving at this point. Getting hats, coats, and art work. Listening to story or records.
12:45–2:00	Rest time. Children should *not have* to go to sleep. They should rest on mats or cots quietly. If possible, they should rest in small groups, or the room should be divided so that there are just a few children in each area. Provision should be made both for those children who wake up early and for those who sleep longer. An adult can take those waking early outside or to another area for quiet activities. Another adult should stay with the sleepers.
2:00–2:15	Afternoon snack.

Table 6–1
Daily Schedule (continued)

2:15–2:45	This time can be used in a very flexible way. Be sure to provide for individual needs. Some children need physical activity; others need quiet kinds of involvement.
	Outdoor time if weather permits: Activities such as water play, hiking, digging, science activities.
For indoors:	Table activities, manipulative materials, science activities, music, rhythms, stories, filmstrips, movies.
2:45–3:00	Dismissal for those leaving at this point.
	Some changes will be necessary if there is more than one class per center. Plans need to be made for the staggered use of the bathroom and playground so that facilities are used by only one class at a time.

Adapted from Sample Schedule distributed by the Head Start Regional Training Officer, Nancy Goldsmith, University of Maryland, College Park, 1980 (mimeographed).

Alternate Afternoon Plan For Children Remaining at the Center Until 5:30 or 6:00 P.M.

2:00–2:30	Toileting, dressing, looking at books, playing with puzzles until all resters are awake.
2:30–2:50	Afternoon snack, table conversation, clean up.
2:50–3:20	Music, rhythms, singing, playing instruments, dancing, listening to records.
3:20	Outdoor play or special activity such as cooking, digging, and planting gardens, experimentation with science aspects of the environment.
4:20	Story, filmstrips, movies, slides. Quiet games, review of the day, plans for next day.
5:00	Dismissal for some.
5:15	Light evening snack. Quiet games, songs, individual time with the teacher until picked up to go home.

Half-Day (Three-year-old children)

9:00–9:45	Dramatic play, blockbuilding, easel painting, science (feeding fish, turtle, etc.), puppets, stories, singing.
9:45–10:00	Clean up, handwashing, toileting.
10:00–10:15	Snack or juice.
10:15–10:40	Rest on mats.
10:40–11:00	Put away mats, story, singing, rhythms.
11:00–12:00	Outside play, short trips.

From *A Guide: Early Childhood Education in Florida Schools*, Bull. 76 (Tallahassee: Florida State Department of Education, 1969), pp. 45 and 44, respectively.

EVALUATING DAILY PLANNING

The teacher uses the following questions to check activities and to determine how effective the plans were as developed and used with the children:

	Yes	No	Comments
1. Was there a balance of activities as to type and place? Were these activities planned in terms of weather, space, length of session, and maturity of each member in the group?	___	___	_____
2. Was provision made for each child to have time of his or her own to do as he or she chose? Were the periods kept short where the child was expected to sit in one place?	___	___	_____
3. Was there a balance between large group, small group, and individual work-play?	___	___	_____
4. Were there new materials, new activities, and new situations for learning provided for each child according to his or her interest and growth pattern? Were these paced to his or her need?	___	___	_____
5. Was enough of the familiar included in the day in terms of routine, activity, and learnings to give the child security?	___	___	_____
6. Did the children have freedom to create, to explore, to experiment? If so, what happened—how did each child use this time?	___	___	_____
7. Were the activities and experiences goal-centered and so planned that the attitudes and feelings, the skills and information were satisfactorily developed? Were the desired results obtained or were the activities a form of busy work?	___	___	_____
8. Was time provided for necessary routines so that no child became tense or frustrated?	___	___	_____
9. Was special consideration given to planning for certain children with special needs?	___	___	_____

A plan for the next day should include an evaluation of the day's work in terms of the activities of each child. The teacher may list needs that have been observed in the space for "comments" (see preceding chart).

PLANNING FOR THE CHILD'S FIRST DAY

As a child leaves home and enters an organized group for the first time, whether it be a first experience of this nature or entry into a new school group, the teacher is concerned as to what will be expected of the child in the daily program. He or she considers what can be done to assist the child in making the transition with security, yet with anticipation, curiosity, and challenge from the unknown, the untried, the inexperienced.

Most schools find it better to induct the children on a staggered basis; that is, some on Monday and Wednesday, others on Tuesday and Thursday, and all on Friday. Other schools take two weeks to induct all the children. In one kindergarten the following schedule was used:

Monday	—Group 1 (12 children)	9:00–11:00 A.M.
Tuesday	—Group 2 (13 children)	9:00–11:00 A.M.
Wednesday	—Group 1	8:30–12:00 noon
Thursday	—Group 2	8:30–12:00 noon
Friday	—Total Group	8:30–12:30 P.M.

Children need to be a part of a group, but what happens to them as they enter the group for the first time has significance for their sense of belongingness. It is the responsibility of the teacher to plan for this induction into the group so that the child comes to feel a part of a happy working situation. Children can learn this only if they experience it to be true.

Even though the daily planning is flexible throughout the year, the first day of the school (and also the first day for the child who enters later) demands even greater flexibility in planning. It is important that this day be a happy one for the child, the parent, and the teacher so that they may continue to "live and learn together" happily. On the first day, the regular routine can be observed, but much more time and individualized attention will need to be given in greeting the children and parents, for helping children to place their wraps and possessions in lockers, and for gaining security in the setting. Even though each child and parent have visited the school previously, this time and attention are important on the first day. Name tags for children, parents, and teacher help to give security and assist the teacher in getting acquainted. An inspection tour of the room will orient and interest the child. Outdoor orientation will include instruction and guidance for the children in use of equipment.

After routines of toileting and handwashing, the children have a brief period of outdoor play. The bathroom routines will need guidance as to place and procedure. However, no child should be coerced to use the bathroom. Children will develop proper habits as they gain security in the new environment. The same is true of outdoor play. It may be that the children will feel more secure in the room. If so, all should remain unless there are two people to supervise, one indoors and the other outside.

Following the getting-acquainted period for each child, the children will need time to look, to handle, and to explore interesting materials and equipment. Provision should be made for centers of interest that will encourage manipulating, creating, building, exploring, and experimenting. Some will begin free play; others will move from activity to activity. This freedom of movement is important for release of tension and gaining security. After most of the children are actively interested in some center, the teacher will call them together by striking a gong, triangle, or a note on a piano or by singing a quiet call to come and sit down together. This then becomes a period for talking, sharing, listening, finger plays, singing, or storytelling. As a rule, midmorning lunch and rest are omitted the first day as the children are too excited to make these events practical. Therefore, the quiet period needs to be a time for relaxation.

The dismissal should be a happy time with discussion of plans for tomorrow, such as feeding the fish, building a train, or riding a tricycle. Care should be taken that each child leaves with a parent or with the person designated in writing by the parent. Kindergarten children who live in the immediate vicinity can go home on their own provided the school is in an uncongested traffic area and parents have given their permission.

By allowing the child's day to be increased gradually in length, time is granted for the young boy or girl to become adjusted to the new environment and to the change in the pattern of living that results from attending school.

WORKING POLICIES AND PLANS

Much of the planning for the year takes place before the school opens. Although the teacher may not have been involved in some of the planning, it is important to become familiar with the policies and plans of the center. Current practice usually provides time for continuous planning throughout the year. Plans for the physical facilities, the necessary equipment, and basic supplies are related to the broader plans involving policies related to the number and type of children to be accepted. Policies will need to be developed and plans made regarding the following:

1. Registration—procedures, amount, and plan for payment of fees, scholarships, insurance and medical costs, and refund, if necessary, of fees paid.
2. Composition of Group—balance between boys and girls, limiting size of group to facilities and personnel, age range of group as related to staff and space.
3. Operation—the school day (hours and days), vacations, holidays, opening and closing dates, induction of children, provision for children who arrive early and for those who leave later, getting acquainted with children before entering school, lunch (if provided), and midmorning snack. The staggered entrance schedule can be a factor in helping the child make a satisfactory adjustment to school; this plan provides for the teacher to have a smaller number of children to orient to the new situation, and, more important, the child has a smaller group to which he or she must adjust. Parent contacts and visits help the child and the teacher as well as the parents to plan for the child's adjustment in the school situation.
4. Health and Safety—health examination and inoculations before entering school, securing child's health history, daily health inspection and teacher observation

of health, provision for isolation or transportation home if needed, and information relative to contacting parents and preferred physician if needed.

5. Transportation of Pupils—how provided, cost, regulations, provision for safe drivers, insurance coverage, and plans for emergencies.

6. Working with Parents—initial interview, parents' stay at school during orientation and induction, mutual agreements and acceptance of responsibility between parents and teachers, reports to be made to and from school, scheduled parent conferences and informal contacts, parent observation and participation, follow-up at home of school activities, contact and work with parents who cannot or do not visit school, and provision for parent meetings and study groups.

7. Cooperation—with other schools in community, with community agencies, and institutions; coordination of school calendar and records with community calendar; provision for satisfactory transfer or transition to another school.

8. Interpreting the School Program—to parents, to general public, to other school groups.

9. Staff Responsibilities—working hours, provision for health examination and insurance, sick leave, substitutes.

10. Consultant Service—for child problems, for staff problems, for professional growth of staff.

SUMMARY

Good planning provides opportunities for desirable learning experiences that are educationally significant. It provides for continuity and balance day by day, but it also provides for relating the experiences so that the teaching objectives, the ideas, the teaching procedures or activities, the materials and resources are so organized that the insight and understanding of the child are continually deepened and broadened. For some children, the depth and breadth may be less deep and narrow; for others it will be deep and broad; and for others, deeper and broader. To plan and to guide the learning opportunities so that this will occur are the challenges of teaching.

Suggested Activities

1. Observe groups of three-, four-, and five-year-olds. How do their interests and maturity levels differ? What are the implications of these differences for planning for different age groups?

2. Observe the same groups and identify differing interests and maturity levels among the children of the same age groups. What does this imply to the teacher in terms of planning?

3. Plan a day's tentative activities for three-, four-, and five-year-olds. Include goals. List materials needed and teacher preparation required.
4. Indicate how the plan might be modified for a full-day program.
5. Assess achievement of at least two children using the Achievement Checklist given in this chapter. Make plans for each child in terms of the data secured.
6. Select one teaching strategy. Plan for and use it with a group of three-, four-, or five-year-olds. Evaluate the effectiveness of your teaching. Make follow-up plans.
7. Examine a daily schedule in a center for young children. Evaluate the schedule in terms of the criteria listed in Table 6–1. Are there differences? What might be possible reasons for the differences?
8. View the films *Organizing Free Play* and *Organizing the School Day*, Modern Talking Picture, 2323 New Hyde Park Rd., New Hyde Park, N.Y. 11040. (Available in Spanish.)
9. View the film *Setting the Stage for Learning*, Churchill Films, 622 North Robertson Blvd., Los Angeles, Calif. 90069. Discuss.
10. Visit the centers or schools for young children in your community, and determine the methods used in each for reporting to parents. Summarize your findings, and make recommendations for changes or improvement in these practices.
11. Write to public schools having kindergartens, and ask for an explanation of the methods used for reporting pupil progress to parents. Request samples if formal report cards or printed evaluation forms are used. Evaluate your findings in light of the material in this chapter.
12. While visiting schools for young children in your community, ask about the type and number of records kept. Are these records sent to the school when the child enters first grade? Do they become a part of the school's cumulative record for each child?
13. Ask first-grade teachers what information they would like to have on each entering child. From these suggestions, formulate a possible record plan for obtaining the necessary information.
14. Discuss the pros and cons of using formal report cards in nursery schools and kindergartens.
15. Review several recent research reports to find out what tests and techniques are currently being used with young children.
16. Find a program that uses a need or problem approach for the basis of records kept. Evaluate this approach. If such a program cannot be easily located, find a research project, and determine how the project influences the records kept.

Related Readings

Almy, Millie. *The Early Childhood Educator at Work*. New York: McGraw-Hill, 1975. Pp. 55–77, 109–142.

Almy, Millie, and Celia Genish. *Ways of Studying Children: an Observation Manual for Childhood Teachers*. New York: Teachers College, 1979.

Ames, Louise B. *Your Five Year Old*. New York: Delacorte Press, 1979.

Association for Childhood Education International. *Migrant Children: Their Education*. Washington, D.C.: ACEI, 1971.

Barbard, Marilyn R., and R. C. Endsley, "How Can Teachers Develop Young Children's Curiosity?" *Young Children* **35**:5 (1980), pp. 21–32.

Bayley, Nancy. "On the Growth of Intelligence." *Amer. Psychol.*, **10**:12 (1955), pp. 805–818.

Berk, Laura E. "How Well Do Classroom Practices Reflect Teacher's Goals?" *Young Children*, **32**:1 (1976), pp. 64–81.

Bronfenbrenner, U. "Reality and Research in the Ecology of Human Development." *Proceedings of the American Philosophical Association*, **119** (1976), pp. 433–469.

Butler, Annie L., "How to Evaluate and Report Individual Progress," in *Exploring Early Childhood: Readings in Theory and Practice*, Margot Kaplan-Sanoff and Renée Yablans-Magid, eds. New York: Macmillan, 1981, pp. 493–498.

Cannon, Gwendolyn M. "Kindergarten Class Size—A Study," *Child. Educ.*, **42**:1 (1966), pp. 9–13.

Cohen, Dorothy H. *Observing and Recording the Behavior of Young Children*. New York: Teachers College, 1978.

Dodge, Diane. *House Corner: A Creative Curriculum for Early Childhood*. Washington, D.C.: Creative Assoc. Inc., 1979.

Firlik, R. J. "Display as a Teaching Strategy." *Child. Educ.* **57**:1 (1980), pp. 26–32.

Frazier, A. *Adventuring, Mastering, Associating: New Strategies for Teaching Children*. Alexandria, Va.: ASCD, 1976.

Galen, Harlene. "Cooking in the Curricula." *Young Children*, **32**:2 (1977), pp. 59–69.

Goff, Regina. "Mind-Content and School Readiness with Special Reference to Low-Income Children." *Child. Educ.*, **51**:5 (1975), pp. 290–294.

Goodwin, William L., and Laura Driscoll. *Handbook for Measurement and Evaluation in Early Childhood Education*. San Francisco: Jossey-Bass, 1980.

Hatcher, Barbara, and Velma Schmidt, "Half-Day vs. Full-Day Kindergarten Programs." *Child. Educ.* **59**:5 (1983), pp. 342–349.

Hayne, W. E. *Advances in Child Development and Behavior*. Vol. II. New York: Academic, 1976.

Jackson, Nancy E., et al. *Cognitive Development in Young Children*. Monterey, Calif.: Brooks/Cole, 1977.

Johnson, Barbara, and Betty Plemmons. *Individual Child Portion Cooking*. Rainier, Md.: Gryphon House, 1980.

Katz, Lilian G. "Children and Teachers in Two Types of Head Start Classes." *Young Children*, **24**:6 (1969), pp. 342–349.

———. "What Is Basic for Young Children?" *Child. Educ.* **54**:1 (1977), pp. 16–19.

Keliher, Alice V. "Effective Learning and Teacher-Pupil Ratio." *Child. Educ.*, **43**:1 (1966), pp. 3–6.

Lemlech, Johanna Kasin. *Classroom Management*. New York: Harper, 1979.

Linder, R. "Learning to Identify Children's Interests." *Child. Educ.* **52**:6 (1976), pp. 296–299.

Madden, P. "Experiencing Joy in Teaching." *Child Educ.* **54**:1 (1977), pp. 12–15.

MacCraken, Mary. *Lovely: A Very Special Child*. Philadelphia: Lippincott, 1976.

MacKinnon, D. W. "Parents and Teachers as Play Observers." *Child. Educ.*, **51**:3 (1975), pp. 139–141.

Mcaffee, Oralie, Evelyn W. Haines, and Barbara B. Young. *Cooking and Eating with Children—A Way to Learn*. Washington, D.C.: ACEI, 1974.

Moore, Shirley. "Research in Review: The Effects of Head Start Programs with Different Curricula and Teaching Strategies." *Young Children*, **32**:6 (1977), pp. 54–61.

Mugge, Dorothy J. "Taking the Routine Out of Routines." *Young Children*, **31**:3 (1976), pp. 209–217.

Oelerich, Marjorie L. *Kindergarten: All Day Every Day?* Ed 179 282. Arlington, Va.: Computer Microfilm International Corporation, 1979.

Papert, Seymour. *Mindstorms*. New York: Harvester, 1980.

Raskin, L. M., W. J. Taylor, and Florence G. Kerckhoff. "The Teacher as Observer for Assessment: A Guideline." *Young Children*, **30**:5 (1975), pp. 339–344.

Thompson, David. *Easy Woodstuff for Kids*, Rainier, Md.: Gryphon House, 1981.

Tough, Joan. *Listening to Children Talking: A Guide to the Appraisal of Children's Use of Language*. London: Ward, Lock, 1976.

Zeitlin, Shirley. *Kindergarten Screening—Early Identification of Potential High-Risk Learners*. Springfield, Ill.: Thomas, 1976.

Ziajka, A. "Microcomputers in Early Childhood Education? A First Look." *Young Children* **38**:5 (1983), pp. 61–67.

CHAPTER 7

Curriculum and Young Children

Deciding what young children will do during their day in kindergarten, nursery school, day care, or any other program is by far the most important decision faced by Early Childhood teachers.

After the ferment, experimentation, and innovations that took place in Early Childhood Education during the 1960s a reordering of priorities appears to be under way. Attention in curriculum planning is beginning to focus on the child and the totality of his or her experience.

Frazier says:

> The whole child seems to be newly before us today. Over the past 15 or 20 years, we may be thought to have let our historic commitment to rounded development go by the board. Immersed as we were in trying to understand and do better by cognitive functioning, we may have forgotten the rest of the child. What we found, of course, is that when it comes to behavior, the child insists on putting himself or herself back together again. Detached from the hand or the heart, mind does not function very well.
>
> . . . Competence is based on control of mind, body, and feeling. And when we neglect any of these, or overlook their interrelationships, we find ourselves in trouble.[1]

[1] A. Frazier, *Adventuring, Mastering, Associating: New Strategies for Teaching Children* (Alexandria, Va.: ASCD, 1976), p. 127.

177

What a curriculum is, how it is developed, and what factors influence curriculum development are treated in this chapter. Various approaches to teaching young children are discussed as well.

The term *curriculum* encompasses more than the academic subjects. Curriculum includes all opportunities for experiences that may take place in the school but may often extend beyond the classroom into the home and the community. Planning for the curriculum or the program involves both the school and the parents.[2] The word *program* is used interchangeably with, or in place of, curriculum.

CURRICULUM DEVELOPMENT

Curriculum development is neither simple nor quick. Curriculum planners are deciding what the children will be experiencing and are, in fact, shaping the growth and development of those children. These decisions are made on many levels: within a classroom, a school, a school system, and on the state level.[3] Those involved in such planning must define the broad goals of the program and provide for a variety of developmental evaluation techniques.

Developing the goals

The first step in developing a curriculum is to decide what the goals are.[4] The goals represent the broad aims of the program. There are many concerns, among them being the totality of the child's development, humane education, the processes and skills involved in living, multicultural education, and mainstreaming of the handicapped. Incorporating such concerns into curriculum planning is indeed a complex operation. The possible interrelationships are many. Experiencing the curriculum should help all children to feel worthy, respected, capable, and competent as well as giving them the opportunity to gain desirable skills.

The following is an example of broad goals that might be developed for a program:

Provide a setting in which

- The child's interests and background are used as a basis for activities.
- Opportunities are provided for the child to learn academic skills through day-to-day activities.
- Provision is made for the individual needs and interests of children.

[2] Millie Almy, *The Early Childhood Educator at Work* (New York: McGraw-Hill Book Co., 1975), pp. 55–56.
[3] Peter F. Oliva, *Developing the Curriculum* (Boston: Little, Brown, 1982), p. 10.
[4] Michael Langenbach and Teanna West Neskora, *Day Care: Curriculum Considerations* (Columbus, Ohio: Merrill, 1977), pp. 36–41.

- Each child has opportunities to solve problems, develop problem-solving abilities, make decisions, and raise questions.
- Each child is helped to develop an awareness of the world around him or her.
- Opportunities are provided for children to make discoveries and use these as a basis for learning.
- Opportunities are provided for each child to be creative.

Provide an atmosphere in which

- Each child enjoys school.
- Each child is helped to feel good about himself or herself.
- Adults and children relate to one another in a sincere and honest manner.
- Each child develops a love of learning.
- Children learn to evaluate their world and their activities.
- Children learn to cooperate and to help others.
- Provision is made for healthy interaction among the children.
- Children develop self-reliance and independence.[5]

It is also important to consider how the teacher develops goals for and with children and their parents. Teaching objectives are related to broad educational goals and are planned for both the group and the individual. The teacher may be concerned with helping the group set standards for behavior as she or he and the children plan together for using the new tools. In helping an individual achieve the same goal, the teacher may plan to support attempts to make a particular decision, and to carry it out. For example, Emmie was having trouble in sawing the wood and started to leave. The teacher offered to hold the board, and with this help Emmie was able to finish the job.

The teacher has the responsibility of helping the child become aware of the goal currently being developed. For example, the teacher may be trying to help the child gain confidence in his or her ability. When the child says, "I can't do this," the teacher may reply, "Do it your own way. What can you do first?"

In selecting a goal for emphasis, the teacher might choose a focus because of the interest and readiness of the children or because there has been little opportunity to work toward achieving this objective. Attainment of goals may often involve teacher support and clarification as well as participation in selected activities.

The behavior of the child may tend to obscure a teacher's goals, but the wise teacher understands. Kim picked up Jane's mitten and ran to the jungle gym. Jane told the teacher. The teacher said, "She was trying to play with you. I think she wanted to be your friend." The role of the adult in working with children involves observing, supporting, clarifying, enhancing, and sharing.[6]

[5]*North Carolina Public Kindergartens in the Eighties.* (Raleigh, N.C.: Department of Public Instruction, 1982), p. 2.

[6]Sandra B. Horowitz, *From Theory to Practice: A Personal Diary of a Teacher of Young Children* (College Park, Md.: U. of Maryland, 1971), pp. 19–22.

Parents and teachers usually share the same goals for children though they may have different methods of attaining them. They are mutually dependent. Parents and teachers must work together in order to understand the role of each and to reinforce important learnings that come from the experiences that each provides.

The goal of good schools for young children is to provide a succession of situations, of activities, whereby children may have the opportunity to develop at their own rate and in their own way in personal affective skills and values, academic learnings and cognitive skills, group values, and parental relationships. The following examples will illustrate behavior that can be observed and that seems to indicate progress in the realization of particular goals.

PERSONAL VALUES, SKILLS, AND AFFECTIVE RELATIONSHIPS

Learning to like and trust others.
　For example,
　　In the housekeeping center Lynn said, "I made a cake like yours. You make good things to eat."
Expanding the concept of what it means to be human.
Gaining a positive image of self.
Accepting children of differing ethnic and cultural traits.
Learning to manage feelings.
　For example,
　　Ron was building an elaborate structure with blocks. Roy ran up and knocked down one of the walls. Ron turned as if to give chase. He seemed to be angry. Suddenly he stopped short, paused a moment, and said, "And I was making it for you."
Developing the ability to organize, to plan, and to follow through on simple tasks.
Increasing in ability to make wise choices and decisions in a consistent manner.
Developing a sense of the importance of and relationship between independence and dependence.
Developing the ability to set standards for personal behavior and to live by them.
Establishing routines and patterns of living.
Developing spiritual values.
Developing physical adequacy and mental health.
Finding both satisfactions and limitations in the field of make-believe.
Expecting and accepting failures as well as successes.

GROUP VALUES AND RELATIONSHIPS

Feeling wanted, valued, and cared for by peers and the adults in one's life.
Making voluntary contacts with other children without regard to sex, race, or class.
Understanding that a cultural trait that is different is not inferior or nonhuman.
　For example:
　　Harry took one of Gale's blocks. Gale asked, "Why doesn't he know how to play?"
　　The teacher replied, "He is learning to speak English. He comes from another country. He may not know how to ask for the block."

Developing a willingness to share privilege with groups differing from themselves.
  For example,
    Gloria said, "They *are* boys, but let's let them use the wagon."
Becoming a social person; developing ability to interact with age mates.
Developing the attitude toward and the ability for being a part of a social group.
Knowing what is acceptable socially and having the desire to apply this knowledge consistently in functional situations.
Learning to distinguish between private or personal property and what belongs to the group.
Learning the necessity of sharing and cooperating with others.
  For example,
    Debbie, wanting to play with the bear that Lisa was using, said, "Lisa, will you let me have the bear when you're finished?" Lisa said, "I'm not ever going to finish today." Debbie said, "Lisa, you're supposed to say yes when I ask you like that." Lisa smiled and said, "Let's build a house for this bear."
Participating in the group while preserving one's own distinct ethnic and cultural traits.
Developing positive contact with peers.

ACADEMIC LEARNINGS

Satisfying natural curiosity, which results in creative learnings.
Pursuing an interest wholeheartedly to greater depth and breadth.
Developing new interests and building upon recent ones.
Bringing into consciousness those things in the child's environment that he or she does not perceive (physical and biological).
Developing the beginnings of good work-study habits; learning successes are earned through repeated effort.
Learning to think; learning how things are done.
Developing meaningful vocabularies basic to thinking; developing language as a satisfactory means of communication.
Applying mathematical and scientific information to the solution of a problem.
Expanding knowledge through exploration, investigation, assimilation, and reflection.
Building new or expanding concepts and correcting misconceptions.
  For example,
    Sally, while examining the seed experiments, remarked that the formica tabletop was soft. Hearing her comment, the teacher asked her to tap the table with her fist and then to tap the cotton used in the experiments. Sally tapped both the table and the cotton. She replied, "Oh, the cotton is soft; the table is hard." The teacher asked her what word could be used to tell how the table felt when she slid her hand across it. Sally slid her hand over it, thought for a moment, and said, "Smooth. The table is hard and smooth." She then proceeded to touch and tap other materials and objects. She explained that the jar was hard and smooth, the wall was hard and rough. The egg carton was rough, but not as hard as the jar.
Having experiences with many types of media and using them wisely.
Becoming interested in and appreciating books.

PARTNERSHIP WITH PARENTS

Learning to relate self to family and close associates.

Selecting clothing, toys, and activities (books, television, and radio programs) appropriate to the child's developmental level.

Developing an understanding of changes in oneself while progressing through the normal developmental sequence.

Participating in educational experiences that cannot be offered through the home situation; extending these experiences through cooperative planning involving teacher, parent, and child.

Beginning to recognize one's sex role through identification with family members and other age mates.

For example,

Mitchell rode up on his tricycle and said, "Well, good-bye. I have to go downtown to work. I'll see you tonight." Away he went on his tricycle. In a few minutes he was back. He got off his tricycle, dropped on a bench, and said, "Boy, I'm tired. That garage work is mighty hard. Yeh, man, it sure is hard."

Although goals have been identified in the areas of personal and affective skills, cognitive and academic learnings, group values and parental relationships, this does not mean that each child must develop the same values, learnings, and skills in the same way or at the same time. One child may have feelings of fear, whereas another may have feelings of impatience and anger. For example, the teacher observed that both Louise and Lester need help in managing their feelings. Lester seems to feel afraid of making a mistake or doing anything wrong. Every day he sits quietly looking at a book or builds carefully with blocks, activities in which he feels safe and in which he can succeed. He is not yet able to try new activities. Louise wants her turn to ride the tricycle and pushes Laney off the saddle. Although the goal for both children is in the area of personal skills, the skill needed by each child is different.

The goals for each child are based on belief in (1) the worth, value, and dignity of each individual and (2) the recognition that group interaction and understanding are fundamental needs basic to American society. Translated into practical application, this means that each child needs to develop in keeping with his or her potential so that each can, through critical and creative thinking (1) select and set worthwhile goals, (2) arrive at purposes that will give direction to behavior, and (3) plan and carry out the necessary actions to realize these goals in terms of his or her own purposes. Accepting these objectives for children, the goal of the teacher then becomes one of determining:

1. How does the child feel about himself/herself? What is happening to this child? What kind of picture of self is he or she building—self-confidence and respect or defeatism and failure?
2. How can opportunities for experience be provided so that the child will learn to set realistic goals and select appropriate means for arriving at them?
3. How can an atmosphere of mutual trust be developed so that each child retains

the right to be different as he or she thinks, discusses, and plans for experiences at the level of his or her ability and within clearly established limits?

4. How can a climate of increasing freedom coupled with an acceptance of increasing responsibility be established?

5. How can a stable environment be built by means of consistent patterns of freedom to do and to explore the new? How does one avoid overstimulation? How does one adapt the program to the child's needs?

6. How can the habit of placing value on accomplishments be developed in each child? How can each child be helped to value personal achievement according to standards and criteria appropriate for the purpose at this time but which will eventually lead to broader purposes and higher standards and criteria for achievements?

7. How can the teacher find new and better ways to work with each child?

8. How can opportunities be provided and experiences interpreted so that the child achieves the desired goals of personal values and skills, academic learnings, group values and relationships, and partnership with parents?

The program developed in schools for young children provides for activities that will contribute to the physical, mental, and social development of children. The objectives both for the program and for the activities are the changes expected to take place within each child through new experiences. Provision is made for continuous growth in social and emotional development through a balanced program that will meet the developmental needs of the preschool-age child. But because all children do not develop at the same rate, do not come from the same backgrounds, do not have the same needs and aspirations, the program is flexible and varied. The learning environment is made up of many people and many factors. Every environment is a learning environment. As has been said, "No environment in itself is good or bad. It is good or bad, effective or ineffective, only in terms of response to it."[7] It is important, then, to examine the people, places, and things that surround the child in terms of his or her reactions to them.

Selecting learning opportunities

Although developing goals is the first step in planning a curriculum, simply stating what one would like to have happen is not enough. The curriculum must answer the question of how the goals are to be realized. Learning opportunities must be planned on a variety of developmental levels. Activities can be used in the development of skills that the children will learn in order to achieve a goal or goals. For instance, a curriculum may include social skills, communication and academic skills, gross and fine motor development, perceptual skills, and assumption of responsi-

[7] R. R. Leeper (ed.), *Creating a Good Environment for Learning*, 1954 Yearbook, ASCD (Alexandria, Va.: ASCD, 1954), p. 5.

bility. Suggestions for learning activities are needed for each category. These suggested activities may be a separate file or "bank" and need not be limited or finite.[8] The curriculum is the planned guide of opportunities for experiences for the children and should not be carved in stone, or remain the same forever.

Evaluating the curriculum

The curriculum must include an evaluative scheme. There must be open avenues for improvement and change. Evaluation may be informal and conducted at various intervals of time or may be an ongoing, continuous process. The program should be flexible and recognize changes in the child population, the children's needs, or the community's expectations. Teachers and parents, as well as program administrators, should be actively involved.[9] Because the curriculum encompasses what the children in the program will receive in terms of instruction, activities, and opportunities for experiences, it is vital that the curriculum be flexible. It should be the ongoing concern that the program is achieving what the curriculum purports to do.

FACTORS INFLUENCING THE CURRICULUM

In the development of the curriculum, there is no one formula or method that the teacher can use to plan an effective program. This task calls for intelligence and understanding, imagination, and flexibility rather than formulas. There is need for knowledge of research and the factors that influence children's learning. These include (1) what the children are like and how they learn, (2) what the culture expects, and (3) academic content and skills. The first two factors are discussed in this chapter.

What the children are like

The children are the most significant consideration in planning the curriculum. The teacher will find it important to remember how young children learn, not just what they need to learn. Young children are on the go constantly. They are energetic and do not by nature sit for long periods of time.[10] Their physical growth dictates the need for big body movements. It is also the time for discovery of little muscles,

[8] Langenbach, op. cit., pp. 36–41.
[9] Eugenia Hepworth Berger, *Parents as Partners in Education: The School and Home Working Together* (St. Louis: Mosby, 1981), p. 85.
[10] James L. Hymes, Jr., *Teaching the Child Under Six* (Columbus, Ohio: Merrill, 1974), p. 37.

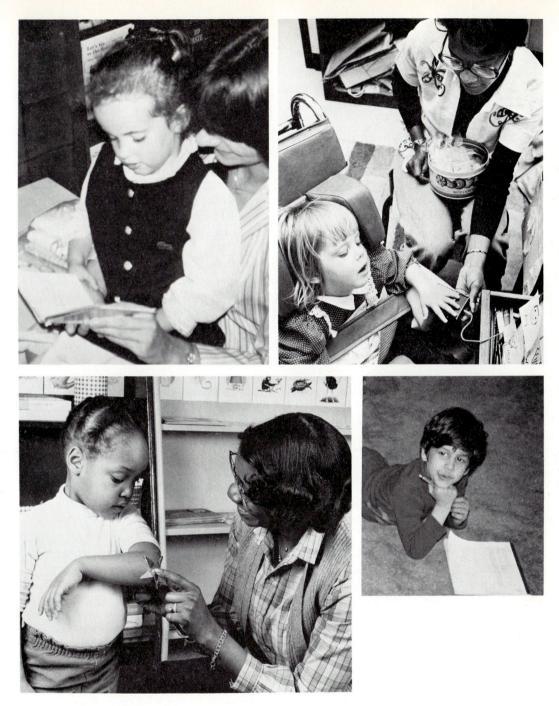

The children are the most significant consideration in planning the curriculum.

especially hands and fingers.[11] Coordination needs to be nurtured and developed. Language and speech are relatively new to them, and the opportunities, formal or informal, to develop those skills are essential.

Most important, children learn by doing. Young children have yet to develop skills of abstract thought. To them, intangibles beyond their immediate world are vague and unreal. Young children are sensory-dependent, needing to see and touch, to hear or feel. They learn by directly interacting with their world. A lecture or a story about a fire station holds little interest for a young child when compared with seeing the large trucks or trying on a fire fighter's hat. A broad base of diverse experiences will enable the child later to learn abstractly of things beyond his or her immediate world.

The curriculum must be shaped around these basic needs. But one must also consider characteristics specific to the group of children. Background and home environment can enhance or hamper a child's progress. It is important to keep in mind the potential range of individual differences within a group. For example: the teacher opens the top file drawer in which the records of a group are kept. She or he examines the first folder—a boy, age: four years, six months; height: 42 inches; weight: 38 pounds. The next folder is also a boy's—age: four years, five months; height: 41 inches; weight: $39\frac{3}{4}$ pounds. Now for a girl's record—age: four years, six months; height: 43 inches; weight: 44 pounds. The folders reveal that among sixteen children there is variation in height, weight, and age. In Table 7–1 the range in heights, weights, and ages of four groups of children is given. These groups include children in a nursery school, a child development center, and a kindergarten. Note the overlap in height and weight among the groups and the variation within each group.

What do these heights, weights, and chronological ages mean in terms of equipment, activities, and materials? Important as these factors are, there are still others to be considered. A close examination of several folders reveals the following:

> Karen and Kirsten are twins, five years old. They live in a six-room house with their parents and a sister who is three years older. The father attended college for two years, has no church affiliation, and is engaged in a business of his own—upholstering. The mother was born in Denmark and lived there until she married. She has no church affiliation and feels that for her civic and social activities can wait until the children are older. She speaks both English and Danish to the children.
>
> In the testing situation both girls showed good discrimination in objects and forms and performed best on items requiring nonverbal responses. Test results, probably influenced by language, indicate that the girls are of low average intelligence. They are among the oldest children in the group and are above average in height and weight. Karen enjoys mealtime whereas Kirsten often refuses food. The girls have had few trips in the community but spent last summer in Denmark with their grandparents.

[11] David L. Lillie, *Early Childhood Education: An Individual Approach to Developmental Instruction* (Chicago: Sci. Res. Assoc., 1975), pp. 55–57, 109.

Table 7–1

Variations in Four Groups

Group	Age Range	Height Variation	Weight Variation
Threes	2 years, 9 months	$36\frac{3}{4}$ inches	33 pounds
	3 years, 8 months	$39\frac{1}{2}$ inches	$45\frac{1}{2}$ pounds
Fours	3 years, 9 months	$36\frac{3}{4}$ inches	32 pounds
	4 years, 7 months	45 inches	48 pounds
Fours	4 years, 1 months	39 inches	35 pounds
	5 years, 1 month	47 inches	60 pounds
Fives	4 years, 11 months	$37\frac{1}{2}$ inches	35 pounds
	6 years, 1 month	48 inches	55 pounds

The teacher notes these facts: twins, mother of foreign background, limited language development, good muscular control, limited experiences in community.

Lisa, now four, is the older of two children. The walk to and from school each day with her mother serves as exercise for her mother, who is expecting another baby soon. Once home, Lisa must remain in the apartment because her mother is not able to take her to a playground. Her father, a day laborer, is proud of Lisa, but has little time to spend with the children except during inclement weather when he can't work. Lisa is a bit larger than the other children in her group. She often takes leadership roles in small group activities and participates eagerly in school activities.

The teacher notes the following: mother pregnant, father can't work in bad weather, limited outdoor activity, assumes leadership roles, few experiences in the community.

Shaw knows that he is an adopted child. He lives with his foster parents and an older brother (also adopted) in a comfortable seven-room house. His father is a very successful businessperson. Both father and mother are active in civic and church activities. Shaw accompanies his parents on trips to the beach and mountains. He is his father's hunting companion. He expresses himself well, enjoys books, likes school. Results of an individual intelligence test indicate that he is a gifted child. His height and weight are average, but he is one of the youngest in the group. In situations that seem difficult, Shaw continues to try. His mother says, "He does not get hot and bothered. He has the patience of Job."

The teacher notes these facts: adopted, gifted child, meets difficult situations confidently, good language facility, rich experience in immediate environment.

Gloria's oldest sister, a first-grader, is responsible for bringing her and another sister, who is in kindergarten, to the center each day. Before the parents leave for work at 7:30 A.M. the mother gets the children up, dresses, and feeds them. The girls stay in the apartment alone until a neighbor tells them that it is time to go to school. In the afternoon they are alone until the parents come in from work. The mother gives them money for candy and gum because they are left alone so much of the time. Gloria is a superior child and learns easily. She has difficulty in joining a group activity. At story time she sits on the lap of the adult assistant.

The teacher notes the following: both parents work, often left alone without an adult, given money as compensation, seeks adult attention, superior child, difficulty in group situations.

Jennie's father and mother are both students. The mother arranges her classes around the father's schedule so that one parent is free to care for the children, Jennie and a younger sister. The family lives in a small, dirty, cluttered apartment. The mother worked until the week before Jennie was born. Jennie is not permitted to cry at home. The father says, "Carsons do not cry." At school Jennie cries often and is afraid of children. An offer of friendship is greeted by, "He's bothering me." When she first entered the group, she became so excited by the children that she had a fever for several days. Her muscular coordination appears jerky. She tires easily. Mental test results indicate that she is a child of high average ability.

The teacher notes as follows: preoccupation of both parents in their work—little time for children, cramped living space, normal emotional outlets denied, ill at ease with children, poor muscular coordination.

And there are others: Bob, whose father deserted the family; June, whose father is unemployed—only the "welfare" money is available to feed and clothe six children; Roger, whose father makes a great deal of money—there is plenty of money to buy things but little time for shared family experiences; Jan, who seldom stops talking and is at home in any group; and Pete, who seldom utters a word—occasionally, there is a faint smile of communication.

These children face common developmental tasks, yet because of various factors in their own lives, they will achieve them in different ways. Wise is the teacher who understands this and is able to plan a program to provide for experiences that meet common needs of the group as well as individual needs.

Cultural expectations

Those planning a curriculum must also take into account the culture's expectations. A child growing up in American society is confronted with certain "tasks" to be mastered if he or she is to make normal progress. These "developmental tasks are those major common tasks that face all individuals within a given society."[12] Within the society there is a variety of groups that differ from the majority of the population. Children from these groups face the same developmental tasks as do other children. In helping these children achieve these tasks, the teacher must show respect for the children and their backgrounds.

Each task has certain stages of development appropriate to different age groups—

[12] Caroline Tryon and J. W. Lilienthal, "Developmental Tasks: The Concept and Its Importance," *Fostering Mental Health in Our Schools*, 1950 Yearbook (Alexandria, Va.: ASCD), p. 77.

infancy, early childhood, adolescence, adulthood, and old age. If one is successful in achieving the earlier tasks, one is likely to be happy and successful in achieving later tasks. Failure in achieving these earlier tasks usually leads to unhappiness and difficulty with later ones.

These developmental tasks are set by both inner and outer forces, namely the expectancies and pressures of society, the changes that take place in the physical organism through the process of maturation, and the individual's values and aspirations.[13] An active learner who is interacting with the social environment is meeting an individual need as well as a demand of society.[14] Havighurst includes such developmental tasks as learning to walk, to take solid foods, to talk, to control the elimination of body wastes; forming concepts and learning language to describe social and physical reality; getting ready to read; learning to distinguish right from wrong; and beginning to develop a conscience as characteristic of infancy and early childhood.[15]

Among the developmental tasks noted by Tryon and Lilienthal the following have been selected. The stages of development appropriate to early childhood are summarized, and suggestions are made for helping the child achieve them.[16] The tasks described would influence curriculum goals and the suggestions for meeting the goal.

1. The task—achieving an appropriate dependence-independence pattern. The child needs to adjust to less private attention and to become more independent. This means that physically while learning to be independent in dressing, eating, and toileting, the child is also learning to share the teacher's attention with others in the group. In order to help the child in this respect, the school needs to:
   a. Maintain a warm, accepting atmosphere in the group. The child cannot adjust to less personal attention unless he or she is secure and receives much private attention. The group must be small enough for the teacher to give this attention to each child.
   b. Provide facilities that enable the child to become independent. For example, child-size bathroom fixtures, accessible lockers for hanging clothing, table and eating implements of appropriate size.
   c. Provide time in the program and facilities suitable for the child to put away materials or to hang up clothing. Explain to parents how important it is for the clothing to be such that the child can manage it independently.
2. The task—achieving an appropriate giving-receiving pattern of affection. The child needs to achieve an appropriate pattern of giving and receiving affection. At this stage, children learn to give as much love as they receive and to form friendships with other children of their own age. In order to help the child in this respect, the school program should:

---

[13] R. J. Havighurst, *Developmental Tasks and Education*, 3d ed. (New York: McKay, 1972), pp. 1–18.
[14] Ibid., p. vi.
[15] Ibid., pp. 8–17.
[16] Tryon and Lilienthal, op. cit., pp. 77–128.

    a. Provide opportunities for children to show affection for others in desirable ways—greetings, sharing toys, playing together.

    b. Avoid unfavorable comparison of one child with another. It is difficult for a child to share affection or love unless the child feels secure and loved.

3. The task—relating to changing social groups. It is important that the child develop the ability to relate to changing social groups. At this stage of development he or she is learning to feel a part of the school group, beginning to interact with age-mates, and to adjust to the expectations of the group. In order to help with this task, the school program should:

    a. Provide opportunities for the child to be a part of the group in planning and sharing, such as news and possessions.

    b. Stress cooperative and voluntary effort rather than domination and force.

    c. Provide opportunities for learning to give and to receive helpful suggestions and criticisms.

4. The task—developing a conscience. In early childhood this task involves developing the ability to take directions, to be obedient in the presence of authority, and gradually becoming able to be obedient in the absence of parents or teachers when conscience substitutes for authority. This is usually the period in which, as the child identifies with adults, he or she identifies with their values and standards of behavior. In order to help with this task, the school should:

    a. Offer explanations of or reasons for actions in simple, direct terms which can be understood by the child.

    b. Avoid moralizing.

    c. Provide opportunities for choices within limits.

    d. Provide opportunities to respond to signals and directions, and to learn respect for authority.

5. The task—learning one's psycho-socio-biological sex role. In early childhood the child is learning to identify with adult male and female roles. As children enter this stage, at the age of two, three, or four years, boys and girls exchange roles freely. During this stage, however, a change usually commences. The boys usually begin to identify with their fathers, then with men in general, while the girls begin to identify with their mothers and then with other women in general. In order to help with the task, the school program should:

    a. Provide opportunities for dramatic play.

    b. Provide opportunities for the child to find out about the work that mothers and fathers do. Visit some parents at work, or invite them to visit the school.

    c. Avoid the use of sex stereotypes.

6. The task—accepting and adjusting to a changing body. Still another task includes managing a growing body and learning new motor patterns. The child needs to develop muscular control and skill in coordinating movements. At school, space, equipment and opportunities are needed for climbing, running, sawing, painting, cutting as well as opportunities for dressing, using buttons, and tying shoelaces.

7. The task—developing an appropriate symbol system and conceptual abilities. At this stage of development, children are increasing their vocabulary and improving sentence structure and pronunciation, so basic to the ability to communicate and to read. They are gaining concepts, not only of values but of ideas and things. At school, help in achieving these specific tasks can be provided by experiences gained

through trips, stories, books, and opportunities for conversation and speaking in the group.

In planning a program, the teacher, then, becomes familiar with various factors involved in the lives of the children in the group and the expectations of the culture in which they live. The teacher reviews the research pertinent to these factors and determines the implications of these findings for the children he or she teaches. Within this framework of the child, the culture, and research findings, the teacher selects, plans, and organizes activities for the children in a particular group.

EXPERIENCE APPROACH TO ACADEMICS

In this discussion of the curriculum for young children, the importance of formulating goals and meeting the needs of both the children and the culture has been stressed. Program developers now must choose among the varying viewpoints as to the approach to use in educating young children.

According to one approach, the focus of the curriculum can be academically oriented. In the academic approach, the work is more formal. Readiness for first grade is the key. Kindergarten and other Early Childhood Education programs are seen as "prefirst grade," looking only at what the child will be doing later.[17] A more formal curriculum is designed, using workbooks, drills, and defined subject areas. This viewpoint contends that the overall goal of Early Childhood Education is preparation for the formalized instruction of later grades.

A differing viewpoint contends that learning occurs naturally and should be allowed to do so. Such a program would be child-directed, allowing the child to choose activities. Without any structure, the child is allowed to do whatever he or she desires to do at any time.[18] Such a program does not necessarily support and nurture the young child.

Children need opportunities for experiences that will help them learn, but not through the formal methods of later school years. A good program utilizes the experiences of children and attempts to meet their needs as three-, four-, and five-year-olds. The program does not ignore so-called academics. On the contrary, it provides opportunities for experiences that build foundations for later learnings in these fields. Cognitive development is important. The issue is not whether academic subject matter should be taught but how it is taught. In the early years, all learning should be a hands-on, doing activity: a "laboratory, field study approach."[19]

A good program is not totally organized into a rigid schedule with separate periods for language arts, number activities, and science. Neither are certain activities

[17] Hymes, op. cit., pp. 21–23.
[18] Lillie, op. cit., p. 4.
[19] Hymes, op. cit., p. 85.

labeled as appropriate for four-year-olds and some for five-year-olds. For example, while playing in the housekeeping center, the child may use a variety of skills, such as language arts—conversation, asking questions, talking on the telephone, and listening; or mathematics—cooking, measuring a cup, quart, teaspoon, and reading numerals on radio or TV dials.

Table 7–2, based on a study of trees, emphasizes some of the conceptual learnings a child might acquire in a given subject area while participating in a variety of activities. Opportunities for the practice of some of the basic skills are also indicated. However, not all of the subject areas or the skills have been included.

Piagetian theories show that children develop the mental acts of abstract reasoning through concrete learning activities. Deductive reasoning is possible around the age of six, but the starting point for thought is always concrete and real.[20] What this means in the reality of a classroom is that young children cannot be expected to learn abstractly via books, lectures, and films until they have had a chance to develop thought processes through experiences in the real environment. The real learning of preschool years is accomplished by the child's active participation.

According to Hymes, schools for young children are for the development of the whole child.[21]

To foster such development, the curriculum provides for academic learning and the development of skills such as decision making, categorizing, and reasoning. It also allows for motor skill development, both gross and fine motor skills. Language development, communication skills, and group socialization are encouraged, allowing children to experiment, to touch, to watch, to hear, and to be a part of the

Table 7–2
Conceptual Learnings—Trees

Conceptual Understandings	Experience, Activity, and Play Possibilities
1. There are many kinds and sizes of trees. 1,2,3,4,5.	1. Identifying and classifying local trees. 2,3,5. A,B,C.
2. There are many colors, shapes, and sizes of leaves on the trees. 1,2,3,5.	2. Collecting leaves, acorns, nuts on a nature walk for use in making collages and in other activities. 1,3,5. A,B,C.
3. Trees have many uses.	3. Making a poster showing foods that come from trees. 1,3,4,5. A,B,C,D.
4. Trees live in many different localities. 4,5.	4. Plant a tree. 1,3,5,A,B.

Key: Subject Area		Skills	
Music and the Arts	1	Communicating	A
Mathematics	2	Decision Making	B
Science	3	Patterning	C
Social Studies	4	Creating	D
Language	5		

event. And the curriculum allows the children to play. For children, play is an activity to which they give active thought and in which they are completely absorbed. In play, children are thinking, solving problems, using memory skills, planning, organizing, making decisions; it is learning.[22]

The children need music and art, as well as drama. If the "product" is to be a well-rounded, thinking, caring human being, then the curriculum must reflect such diversity.

"At the very heart of curriculum planning," says Weber, "stands the problem designated by Hunt as the 'problem of the match.' "[23] The perfect match may mean boredom and little development. Differences that are too great may mean distress or negative motivation. Teachers must seek the match that will challenge the child to learn without undue stress.

> Young children have to have a balance between vigorous motor activities and quieter moments. They require individual and small-group situations. They depend upon significant adults working together—parents, teachers, aides, pediatricians. They need an expanse of space indoors and outdoors with adequate equipment and materials to challenge them and keep curiosity alive. They must have spontaneous and planned experiences which utilize their deep motivation to understand their world. They require a program that fosters intellectual growth. The need for integrating intellectual and affective growth is readily apparent.[24]

The authors of this text maintain their belief in the theories of child growth and development. The need for cognitive or intellectual development is recognized, but emphasis is also placed on socialization, physical development, creativity, and the processes of learning.

The new challenge in curriculum planning, according to Frazier, is the recognition that all children have a right to learn what is taught; to learn whatever is necessary to keep options open to further learning; to learn that which will enlarge or enrich human experience. He speaks of an "equal rights curriculum" for all children—all children have an equal right to profit fully from a broadly based program. By "all children" Frazier includes minority children and children from the majority, those who live in the city and those in the suburbs, poor and affluent children, children from working-class and professional families, less able learners and the eager, able learners—all children.[25]

Some children have a richer, more relevant experience than others. Some are not taught things they need to be taught. All children have a right to learn about

---

[20] Ellis D. Evans, *Contemporary Influences in Early Childhood Education* (New York: Holt, 1975), p. 199.

[21] Hymes, op. cit., p. 5.

[22] Ibid., pp. 101–102.

[23] Evelyn Weber, *Early Childhood Education: Perspectives on Change* (Worthington, Ohio: Charles A. Jones Publishing Co., 1970), p. 179.

[24] Ibid.

[25] Frazier, op. cit., pp. 3–12.

the environment, the full range of the arts, love and friendship, media and the marketplace, play and playfulness, political action, self-understanding, value clarification, the world of work, and a world view.[26]

MULTICULTURAL EDUCATION

Multicultural education must begin with the very young if ethnic, racial, and cultural attitudes of children are to be influenced. Teachers and parents need to be aware of their own attitude because stereotypes seem to be learned early in a child's life. Multicultural education is important for all children, even though there may be no minority children in the group.[27] For many American children the school culture is highly consistent with their own culture. This is not true, however, for many children of distinct ethnic groups who often find the school culture alien, hostile, and self-defeating.[28] Earlier, these children were considered culturally disadvantaged. This concept implied deficits in their cultural background. More recently these children are recognized as culturally different.

Because of cultural and value differences, as well as different child-rearing practives, culturally different children often experience failure when entering the mainstream of child life at the primary school level. Because of this fact, experiences at the preschool level are particularly important for this group. During this period children explore their physical world, become sensitive to the environment, have opportunities for action responses, reproduce and symbolize experiences, and learn to use language to develop and understand concepts. The child who is culturally different from the majority of children may not have had an opportunity to communicate in Standard English or to share and have close relationships with others from different backgrounds. The educational program will have to make certain adjustments to accommodate the uniquely different needs of these children. The problems faced by these children are varied and complex.

The migrant child

Providing preschool experiences for the children of migrant families presents difficulties because of the pattern of work—moving from place to place as the need for labor arises. Many migrant children are language handicapped and frequently are unable to speak fluently or comprehend Standard English. In addition, the migrant families have their own values in terms of speech, honesty, and love. They give their children a sense of belonging to the family but not to the larger group.

---

[26] Ibid., pp. 12–13.

[27] Patricia G. Ramsey, "Multicultural Education in Early Childhood," in *Curriculum Planning for Young Children*, Janet F. Brown, ed. (Washington, D.C.: NAEYC), 1982, pp. 131–141.

[28] J. A. Banks, "Cultural Pluralism and the Schools," *Educ. Leadership*, **32**:3 (1974), p. 164.

There are, however, significant developments in migrant education that include aide training, use of consultants, continuous progress plans, demonstration schools, evaluation, health and nutrition, home and family education, interagency involvement, interstate cooperation, instructional packages, migrant centers, mobile units, parent involvement, preschool programs, six-month extended day programs, programs for Spanish-speaking children, student and volunteer involvement, teacher education, uniform migrant transfer record forms. There are also plans for computerized services.[29,30] Florida, Idaho, New York, and Oregon have developed educational programs for migrant children. The programs involve the use of teacher aides and volunteer services. Special teacher education projects and in-service education programs have also been developed. Except during school hours, no law protects the children, and facilities vary from community to community.

The culturally different approach recognizes the dignity of the child's culture and seems to be a positive response to the needs of children of distinct ethnic groups.[31] The school in our society has a difficult task—the task of helping all children develop "cultural literacy," to learn of and respect the many cultures in the United States, and in so doing to help them recognize and value the pluralistic nature of our country. Children must be helped to gain skills needed to function effectively within their ethnic culture as well as in the dominant culture.[32] Although the school values and reflects cultural diversity, there is also the "responsibility to teach a commitment to and a respect for the core values" of our democracy, which include justice, equality, and human dignity.[33]

In response to this need, culturally pluralistic education or multicultural education has developed. This type of education encourages people to accept and respect their own cultural heritage as well as that of people of different backgrounds.[34] For such education, a curriculum that responds to the diverse needs of a pluralistic society is essential. The curriculum plays an important role in influencing children's attitudes and must, therefore, respect the dignity of all children.[35]

In planning programs for culturally different children it is helpful to consider what changes and additional provisions are required and how they may be achieved. Recognition of their problems has rapidly led to the establishment of preschool programs inasmuch as the deprivation effects build barriers to later achievement.

[29] Sylvia Sunderlin (ed.) *Migrant Children: Their Education* (Washington, D.C.: ACEI, 1971), pp. 3–6, 35–61.

[30] H. A. Curtis and J. A. Klock, "Florida Prekindergarten Migrant Compensatory Program: An Evaluation." Florida State University, Tallahassee, Florida, 1972 (mimeographed).

[31] D. J. Puglisi, "Two Approaches to Minority Education," *Educ. Leadership*, **32:** (1974), pp. 173–175.

[32] Banks, op. cit., p. 165.

[33] Ibid., p. 166.

[34] Donna Gollnick, F. H. Klassen, and J. Yff, *Multicultural Education and Ethnic Studies in the United States: An Analysis and Annotated Bibliography of Selected ERIC Documents* (Washington, D.C.: American Association of Colleges of Teacher Education and ERIC, 1976), p. 10.

[35] Gloria W. Grant, "Criteria for Cultural Pluralism in the Classroom," *Educ. Leadership*, **32:**3 (1974), p. 190.

Such lack of commonly expected early experiences progressively limits children as they attempt to fit into schools with children who have had different care, parental teaching, and value development. Their program must provide a balance between order and freedom in a steady routine, but permit freedom to explore, to ask questions, and to expect and receive answers from adults. This type of program needs to be continued without interruption. The parents of these children should be actively involved in the program to provide for this continuity in the child's home environment. Because the development of the child's self concept takes place along with the development of language it is important that the program for these children begin at an early age.

Instructional plans are based on the recognition that culturally different children are not dull children. Every effort should be made to include activities and experiences that assure an enriched environment; provision for helping the child master language related to specific situations; opportunities for helping mothers develop the cognitive facilities needed by their children; provision for differentiated instruction; utilization of informal language; and gradual development of a more formal mode of communication.

The basic principles for curriculum development apply to the development of a multicultural or culturally pluralistic curriculum. There are, however, suggestions that can be helpful in developing a curriculum or in modifying an existing one. One important way to begin is to emphasize similarities rather than differences in young children. For example, children can be helped to understand such concepts as:

> *Children everywhere play games.* Begin with learning about games played by children in the group and then learning about games played by other children. Rather than emphasizing the different games, the fact that all children play games is stressed.
>
> The same procedure may be used with other concepts: *Children everywhere celebrate holidays, All children eat food, Most children live in some type of family.*[36]

Be sure that the books, pictures, and other instructional materials are accurate and free of stereotypes.

Another way to begin is to evaluate the current curriculum. Grant has developed criteria for such an evaluation. She says that a culturally pluralistic curriculum should do the following:[37]

1. Reflect the pluralistic nature of our society, both past and present.
2. Present diversity of culture, ethnicity, and custom as a strong positive feature of our nation's heritage.
3. Present the cultural, sexual, and racial groups in our society in a manner that will build mutual respect and understanding.
4. Portray people—boys and girls, men and women—whatever their culture, as dis-

---

[36] Joan E. Moyer and Guillermina Engelbrecht, "Multicultural Education: Where Do We Begin?" *Child. Educ.*, **53**:5 (1977), pp. 241–244.
[37] Gloria Grant, op. cit., p. 192.

playing various human emotions, both negative and positive. Individuals of different cultural groups should be described working and playing together.

5. Provide a balanced representation of cultural groups.
6. Present members of various cultural groups in positions of authority.
....
9. Show that every cultural group has many individuals, such as educators, scientists, artists, writers, architects, and others, who have made important contributions to society.
10. Portray cultures other than from a "special occasion" point-of-view. For example: Is there usually a "piñata" when studying Mexico? Are native Americans presented mostly around Thanksgiving? Is the study of Blacks confined to Black History Week? Are Asian Americans usually studied around the Chinese New Year?
....
14. Provide opportunities for experiences that will help build positive attitudes toward and respect for a child's own cultural group and acceptance of other cultural groups.
15. Use words and phrases that are complimentary and honest for the culture. Avoid stereotypes.
16. Make certain that cultures are not presented separate or in isolation from each other. A pluralistic curriculum should provide experiences that show how people of one culture have adopted food, clothing, and language from other cultures.

It is necessary to evaluate existing curricula to determine if the program meets the needs of a multicultural society, the needs of cultural development, and the needs of the children. These factors will influence the goals and purposes of the curriculum and will be reflected in the planning process.

SUMMARY

A good program provides many opportunities for developing social, cognitive, and physical skills; develops from the immediate environment of the children; allows time and opportunities for children to express themselves freely through many media; and involves parents as well as children. Certain curriculum principles are important in planning the program. These principles apply to programs for all children. For example, although the immediate environment of the children is different, a good program develops from the environment, whether it is slum or suburb.

There is no one formula or method that the teacher can use to plan an effective program. This task calls for intelligence and understanding, imagination, and flexibility rather than formulas. There is need for knowledge of research and the factors that influence the learning of children, an appreciation for the whole child, and an understanding of an experience-based approach to learning. The curriculum is determined by (1) what the culture expects, (2) what the children are like and how they learn, and (3) academic content and skills. The first two factors were discussed in this chapter. The third factor is treated in subsequent chapters.

Suggested Activities

1. Visit a center for young children, and evaluate the program in terms of the criteria presented in this chapter. Discuss observations with the class. Note similarities and differences among programs observed by class members. Discuss possible reasons for these.
2. Visit a center in which culturally different children are enrolled. Compare the principles of learning and development and teaching strategies used in working with these children. How are individual needs met? How are children helped to participate in group activities?
3. Select one developmental task characteristic of early childhood. Observe a group of children, and note evidences in their behavior that indicate attempts to meet the task selected. Share observations in class discussion.
4. Visit a center that has developed an innovative program. Note the curriculum, organization, and teaching strategies used. Discuss observations with the class.
5. Observe in an Early Childhood Education program and in a later grade classroom. Compare and contrast the activities and methods of teaching.
6. Formulate activities appropriate for one of the goals listed at the beginning of this chapter.

Related Readings

Bartolome, P. I. "The Changing Family and Early Childhood Education." *Child. Educ.* **57**:5 (1981), pp. 262–266.

Biber, Barbara. "Thinking and Feeling." *Young Children* **35**: (1979), pp. 4–16.

Bushell, D., Jr. "The Behavior Analysis Model for Early Education." In *Handbook of Research in Early Childhood Education*, ed. by B. Spodek. New York: The Free Press, 1982, pp. 156–184.

Combs, A. W. *Educational Accountability: Beyond Behavioral Objectives.* Alexandria, Va.: ASCD, 1972.

Delgado, M. "Providing Child Care for Hispanic Families." *Young Children* **35**:6 (1980), pp. 26–32.

Dittmann, Laura L. "Migrant Children in an Early Learning Program." *Young Children,* **31**:3 (1976), pp. 218–228.

Eliason, Claudia F., and Lou Thomson Jenkins. *A Practical Guide to Early Childhood Curriculum,* 2nd ed. St. Louis: Mosby, 1981.

Elkind, D. "Humanizing the Curriculum." *Child. Educ.*, **53**:4 (1977), pp. 179–182.

———— "Piaget and Montessori." In *Handbook of Research in Early Childhood Education,* ed. by B. Spodek. New York: The Free Press, 1982, pp. 65–73.

———— "Child Development and Early Childhood Education: Where Do We Stand Today?" In *Curriculum Planning for Young Children,* ed. by Janet F. Brown. Washington, D.C.: NAEYC, 1982, pp. 4–11.

Evans, E. D. "Curriculum Models in Early Childhood Education." In *Handbook of Research in Early Childhood Education,* ed. by B. Spodek. New York: The Free Press, 1982, pp. 107–134.

Forman, G. E., and Catherine T. Fosnot. "The Use of Piaget's Constructivism in Early

Childhood Education Programs." In *Handbook of Research in Early Childhood Education*, ed. by B. Spodek. New York: The Free Press, 1982, pp. 185–214.

Harvey, J. "Special Program Needs of the Culturally Diverse Child." *Early Childhood Education for Exceptional Children*. Reston, Va.: The Council for Exceptional Children, 1977. Pp. 158–181.

Lagenbach, M., and Teanna West. *Day Care Curriculum Consideration*. Columbus, Ohio: Merrill, 1977.

Leeper, Sarah H. "Reflections—Directions." *Child. Educ.*, **53**:1 (1976), pp. 5–8.

Macey, Joan Mary. "The Family Way—1980." *Child. Educ.*, **57**:2 (1980), pp. 101–102.

McAfee, Oralie. "Planning the Preschool Program." In *Curriculum Planning for Young Children,* Janet F. Brown, ed. Washington, D.C.: NAEYC, 1982, pp. 367–378.

Moore, Shirley G. "The Effects of Head Start Programs with Different Curricula and Teaching Strategies." *Young Children*, **32**:6 (1977), pp. 54–61.

Ornstein, A. C. "What Are We Teaching in the 1980s?" *Young Children* **38**:1 (1982), pp. 12–17.

Parnell, Kaye. "Young and Old Together: A Literature Review." *Child. Educ.* **56**: (1980), pp. 184–188.

Pasternak, Michael. *Helping Kids Learn Multicultural Concepts*. Champaign, Ill.: Research, 1979.

Ramsey, Patricia G. "Multicultural Education in Early Childhood." In *Curriculum Planning for Young Children*, Janet F. Brown, ed. Washington, D.C.: NAEYC, 1982, pp. 131–142.

Sims, Rudine. "What Has Happened to the 'All-White' World of Children's Books?" *Phi Delta Kappan* **64**:9 (1983), pp. 650–653.

Stewart, Ida Santos. "The Larger Question: Bilingual Education, Family, and Society." *Child. Educ.*, **57**:3, (1981), pp. 138—143.

Verzaro-Lawrence, Marce. "Early Childhood Education: Issues for A New Decade." *Child. Educ.*, **57**:2 (1980), pp. 104–109.

Wassermann, Selma. "Teachers As Curriculum Makers." Leaflet 4, *Success-in-Teaching Series*. Washington, D.C.: ACEI, 1979.

White, B. L., and others. *Experience and Environment: Major Influences on the Development of the Young Child*, Vol. 2. Englewood Cliffs, N.J.: Prentice-Hall, Inc., 1978.

CHAPTER 8

Communication: The Language Arts

As children participate in a variety of activities and have opportunities for a variety of experiences at home and at school, they develop skill in the language arts—listening, speaking, reading, and writing. As a result of technological advances in the nonprint media such as film, television, computers, photography, and filmstrips, some would add viewing as one of the language arts. These areas of the language arts are interrelated, and one area reinforces other areas.

The strands of listening, speaking, reading, and writing are so interwoven that they are almost inseparable except when special attention is given to one specific area.[1] Each aspect of the language arts, however, is discussed separately in this chapter in order to identify the trends, research, and development of skills in each area. In the second part of the chapter, the activities involving children are included to illustrate the contribution of the activity to the development of language skills.

---

[1] Paul C. Burns and Betty L. Broman, *The Language Arts in Childhood Education*, 4th ed. (Chicago: Rand McNally, 1979), p. 3.

SPEAKING—LANGUAGE DEVELOPMENT

A great deal of money has been spent to support research and federal programs for children from low-income families. The language used by these children has received much attention because language skills are considered a prerequisite for school success. Today this focus on language has been broadened to include children of minorities and culturally different groups. From infancy the child hears language almost continuously, but the language that is learned and applied is that used in the speech of persons who are significant in the child's world.[2]

Before they go to school, children have much practice with spoken language. The child has developed much of the skill in speaking before he or she receives any formal instruction. By the time the child arrives at school age, he or she has already learned to speak with whatever sound system, grammar, and vocabulary heard most often at home or in the neighborhood.[3] Other studies by Strickland[4] confirm the fact that the language patterns of children are largely set by the time they enter school.

Young children bring their language to school from a variety of backgrounds. How the teacher or caregiver accepts and treats the child's initial language influences the child's concept of self and family and the child's progress in school.

The pace at which children acquire language varies greatly, but considerable evidence indicates that the pattern of development is similar for all.[5]

It has been shown that different children approach the complex system of language in different ways. Some begin by emphasizing nouns; others emphasize phrases. These different approaches to mastery can tell us important things about learning, language, and the developmental process.

Piaget believes that language development is reflective of cognitive development. There is support for Piaget's view that thought precedes language even though many linguists disagree.[6] It is probably more realistic to point out that language and other forms of learning develop together than it is to argue whether language is a product of learning or that learning results from language development. Whatever the genesis, it is generally agreed that language plays an essential role in the rapid acquisition of knowledge, attitudes, and other ways of responding during the early preschool years.

[2] Courtney B. Cazden, *Child Language and Education* (New York: Holt, 1972), pp. 2–3.

[3] Doris I. Noel, "A Comparative Study of the Relationship Between the Quality of a Child's Language Usage and the Quality and Types of Language Used in the Home," *J. Educ. Res.*, **47**:3 (1953), pp. 161–167.

[4] Ruth G. Strickland, *The Language of Elementary School Children: Its Relationship to the Language of Reading Textbooks and the Quality of Reading of Selected Children* (Bloomington: School of Education, Indiana University, 1962).

[5] L. G. Butler, "Language Acquisition of Young Children: Major Theories and Sequence," *Elementary English*, **51**:8 (1974), pp. 1120–1123.

[6] Katherine Nelson, "Individual Differences in Language Development: Implications for Development and Language," *Developmental Psychology*, **17**:2 (1981), p. 183.

It is theorized that a continuous use of words is the young child's way of testing his or her newfound power—the ability to communicate. The rapid learning of language and its ability to make possible the control of environment are two of the most challenging and important aspects of development during the preschool years. At this stage, language is, at least partly, an imitative process. The adults present must avoid baby talk and be conscious of the fact that their enunciation and pronunciation are the model that the child is following.

The mere repetition of sounds or words on the part of younger children represents the beginnings of verbal communication. The child soon learns that speech is useful in bringing approval or disapproval. In this way language is a strong force in the socialization process. At the same-time it is directly functional, for through it the child is learning to communicate first with and about himself or herself and then with and to others. Many studies refer to these patterns of speech as the egocentric and socialized functions of language. There seems to be a gradual replacement of the egocentric expressions so prevalent in the early stages of language development by those of a socialized nature so that egocentric speech practically disappears by the time the child is seven or eight years of age.[7]

From the birth cry to mature language, verbal development follows a definite pattern, but the rate of verbal development varies with each child. According to Lenneberg, "it is only under conditions of intellectual or environmental deprivation that this pattern varies."[8]

Children discover rules and how the language works and learn grammar gradually on their own. They use content words such as nouns, verbs, and adjectives before they use function words such as prepositions and conjunctions. While learning to form noun and verb endings at a certain period of their development, children may say, "Foots" instead of feet and "Goed" instead of went. These apparent errors should be seen as evidence that the child is beginning to understand the form of language. Correct usage of the exceptions to the rules will come later.[9] Nursery school children often substitute -ed for irregular forms of the past tense, for example, *growed* or *throwed*.[10]

During the early years, children's language development reflects their mental processes, interests, and relationships with the world. The use of the pronoun *I*, which begins at about two years of age, reflects interest in one's self. As the child advances in age, there is an increase in the number of other pronouns used, such as *he, we, you,* and *they,* and a trend toward more socialized speech in which children speak and respond to one another.

[7] R. I. Watson, *Psychology of the Child* (New York: Wiley, 1959).

[8] E. L. Robbins, "Language Development Research," *Interpreting Language Arts Research for the Teacher* (Alexandria, Va.: ASCD, 1970), p. 5.

[9] Courtney B. Cazden (ed.), *Language in Early Childhood Education* (Washington, D.C.: NAEYC, 1972), p. 4.

[10] Dora V. Smith, "Developmental Language Patterns of Children," in *Effective Language Arts Practices in the Elementary School: Selected Readings,* ed. by H. Newman (New York: Wiley, 1972), p. 9.

At about age five or six the language abilities have developed so that children can usually handle language situations in an almost adult manner.[11] However, as the five-year-old encounters new experiences in kindergarten and makes the necessary adjustments, pressures may be reflected in his or her speech. The child may temporarily revert to patterns of speech practiced at an earlier age.

By the age of three a child's articulation improves and becomes fairly clear. There is a sequence in the child's ability to pronounce the consonant sounds, and an understanding of this may be of help to parents and teachers, not as a basis for pressuring the child but rather for guiding him or her. Ages at which 75 per cent of the subjects correctly produced specific consonant sounds in the Templin study are listed."[12]

3 years: m, n, ng, p, f, h, w
3.5 years: y
4 years: k, b, d, g, r
4.5 years: s, sh, ch
6 years: t, th, v, l
7 years: z, zh, j

Cramer describes the stages in language development.[13] These stages should not be considered as being precise. They can be helpful, however, in observing a child's language development. Age limits are not given, only the sequence. They can be outlined as follows:

Stage 1. This stage is the babbling stage. During this prelinguistic stage, children produce all the sounds relevant to their native language, as well as sounds in languages other than their own.

Stage 2. Children at this stage begin the development of recognizable language behavior. The child begins to be capable of expressing needs, responds to verbal language, and the clearly recognizable and meaningful vocabulary increases.

Stage 3. At this stage, the beginning of the expansion of speech occurs, so that it sounds more like adult speech. The previous one word utterances develop into two and three word utterances. Speech becomes more precise, enabling the child to express himself or herself more coherently. Children's language is governed by rules and contains elements of mature language.

Stage 4. This stage is marked by the development of grammatical structure in the language. Pflaum states that these changes are manifested in increasing length of sentences and the use of negative sentences, questions, and verb forms such as *ed, ing,* and transformations.[14]

[11] A. T. Jersild, *Child Psychology,* 6th ed. (Englewood Cliffs, N.J.: Prentice-Hall, 1968), pp. 424–425.
[12] Mildred C. Templin, *Certain Language Skills in Children,* Institute Child Welf. Monograph Series 26 (Minneapolis: U. of Minnesota, 1957), p. 53.
[13] Ronald L. Cramer, *Children's Writing and Language Growth* (Ohio: Merrill, 1978), pp. 13–14.
[14] Susan W. Pflaum, *The Development of Language and Reading in the Young Child* (Columbus, Ohio: Merrill, 1974).

Stage 5. When a child has reached this stage, the grammar of the native language has been internalized. The child has extensive control of his or her language, but it should be remembered that further development occurs as children mature.

Growth in vocabulary

Growth in the vocabulary of the young child has been studied by a number of investigators. The reports are of interest in noting the changes that have occurred.

One of the early vocabulary studies was done by Madorah Smith in 1926. Her estimates of the size of the vocabulary of young children have been widely used. She found the vocabulary to consist of 896 words at three years, 1,540 at four, 2,072 at five, and 2,562 at six.[15] In the late 1950s, Loban found that at kindergarten level, subjects varied in vocabulary from 180 to about 5,000 words with 3,000 words as the average.[16] Since Smith's study, changes may have occurred in the speech of young children as a result of increased TV viewing, number of experiences, and changes in child-rearing practices.

An extensive study of language skills in children was completed by Mildred Templin in 1957. In comparing her work with earlier studies, she reports, "In the areas of articulation and vocabulary, one is impressed with the stability of results over a period of time among studies using comparable methods, but carried on with different samples and by different investigators. . . . Differences occur, however, in the increased loquacity of children in child–adult situations and in a tendency for children of the same age to use more mature language than they did twenty-five years ago."[17] More mature speech is interpreted as the use of fewer one-word remarks and simple and incomplete sentences and the use of more complex sentences and adverbial clauses.

More recently, however, concern for the size of the child's vocabulary has not been important. Studies seem to focus on how the child acquires and uses language, and on the language of minority and culturally different children.

Factors that influence language development

Robbins reports many studies supporting the notion that there are influences in the child's environment that interfere with language development. Research done by Hess and Shipman, Jensen, May, Olem, and Reissman indicates "a direct relation-

---

[15] Madorah E. Smith, "An Investigation of the Development of the Sentence and the Extent of Vocabulary in Young Children," *University Iowa Studies Child Welf.*, 3:5 (1926), p. 54.

[16] W. Loban, *The Language of Elementary School Children* (Champaign, Ill.: NCTE, 1963), p. 37.

[17] Templin, op. cit., p. 150.

"A comb and brush go together." The size of the child's vocabulary is not so important as the fact that the child acquires and uses language.

ship between the quality of the child's environmental circumstances and his language facility."[18]

It has been found that the speech patterns of the child from the less-favored economic or culturally different environment are different from and often conflict with the language used in the school. Crosby says, "the child's natural language, often dynamic, descriptive and forceful is frequently not the language of acceptability in the school. Aware of the rejection of his natural language, the child is nevertheless unskilled and inexperienced in using the standard, informal English of the school."[19]

Recent studies have compared the language abilities of children from upper and lower socioeconomic levels on elements other than those found in standard English. Robbins says, "Their findings support the view that there are no significant differences between the language abilities of low and high socioeconomic children when nonstandard language criteria are used."[20] The problem, then, becomes one of *different* language usage and is treated in much the same manner as teaching another language to a young child.

The quality and type of the teacher's interaction with the child are very important. Lillian Katz, after studying children and teachers in two types of Head Start classes, concluded that perhaps teacher style was a more important factor than the method. She observed that the teachers in this study did not follow through on the

[18] Robbins, op. cit., p. 11.
[19] Muriel Crosby, "Identifying Oral Language Relationships," *Children and Oral Language* (Alexandria, Va.: ASCD, 1964), p. 5.
[20] Robbins, op. cit., p. 11.

specified teacher behavior. They tended to neglect the praise and supportive aspects of their role and the behaviors that seemed to interfere with the learning of children were increased.[21]

The skill with which children use oral language will vary from child to child. Certain environmental factors as well as the child's mental and physical abilities have an influence on language development. Some of these factors are discussed here.

Family.   The child's family is an important consideration. An only child or a singleton seems to have the advantage, probably because of the greater opportunity for association with adults. The number of children in the family affects the growth of vocabulary. At five and one-half years of age, the singleton uses 94 words; the twin, 89 words; and the only child, 104 words in 50 remarks.[22]

Considerable evidence in the literature cited earlier tends to indicate that there exists a marked relationship between socioeconomic status of family and the child's linguistic development. Children from more favored environments use more words meaningfully at earlier ages. Templin found consistent differences in the language performance of children from upper and lower socioeconomic levels. Differences in the linguistic environment provided by homes of the two levels were recognized.[23]

If children hear very little speech or if the speech of the significant persons in their lives is limited and restricted, they are likely to have a language deficit when compared with others from a more favorable environment. A language deficit does not necessarily mean that the child is limited in the ability to learn language. The deficit may indicate the inadequacy of the environment in which the learning took place.[24]

The research of Milner regarding patterns of parent–child interaction seems important here.[25] Striking differences were found in the patterns of family life between first-grade children scoring high and low on language tests. Families of "high scorers" usually had breakfast together and engaged in conversation with the children at mealtime and before school. These children also received more overt affection from significant adults in the home. Milner's study points up the fact that parental attitudes toward children and habits of family life are the really significant factors for language development and they may vary with socioeconomic status.

In an effort to describe how mothers influence language development, Hess and

[21] Annie L. Butler, *Current Research in Early Childhood Education: A Compilation and Analysis for Program Planners* (Washington, D.C.: EKNE, 1970), p. 39.

[22] Edith A. Davis, *The Development of Linguistic Skill in Twins, Singletons with Siblings, and Only Children from Age Five to Ten Years*, Institute Child Welf. Monograph Series 14 (Minneapolis: U. Minnesota, 1937), p. 114.

[23] Templin, op. cit., p. 147.

[24] R. D. Hess and Doreen J. Croft, *Teachers of Young Children* (Boston: Houghton, 1972), p. 178.

[25] Esther Milner, "A Study of the Relationships Between Reading Readiness in Grade One School Children and Patterns of Parent-Child Interaction," *Child Develop.*, **22**:2 (1951), pp. 95–112.

Shipman studied parent teaching styles and found social class differences.[26] The affective elements of the mother's interaction with their children differed little. The main differences were in the verbal and cognitive environments that the mothers presented. Among working-class mothers and their children there was a tendency to act without taking time for reflection and planning.

What can the school do for children who lack the intimate parent–child interaction growing out of shared experiences? Certainly the school cannot and should not replace the home. The teacher can, however, provide opportunities for these children to talk with him or her, and for the teacher to show an interest in their conversation. The teacher must help each child feel important as an individual and that he or she can make a contribution to the group. The task includes helping children to appreciate the speech of others, and providing opportunities to handle materials, to talk about them, to listen to the comments of other children, to ask questions, and to express feelings—all a part of learning.

Another Language—Bilingualism. Americans are becoming increasingly aware of the importance of languages in communication and understanding among nations in the world today. Recognition of these facts has resulted in a heightened interest in teaching foreign languages to young children. To achieve this end, an English-speaking child is given instruction in a foreign language for short periods of time spaced throughout the school week.

As concern for multicultural education has increased, new appreciation has been given to the language minority groups in the United States. Recent concern has been focused on the child who comes to school from a home in which the language spoken is one other than English. Often these children are Mexican Americans, Puerto Ricans, American Indians, Haitians, or Vietnamese.[27] Children from homes in which nonstandard English is spoken may face problems similar to the non-English-speaking child. A number of language-related factors have been identified as reasons for the school difficulties experienced by these children. The young child who does not speak English is unable to understand the language of the teacher or to express his or her feelings in a strange language. The child's reaction may be one of frustration, fear, aggression, or a feeling of inferiority. The child, eager to learn, may find it necessary to stop to learn English words for everything that has been taught in another language.[28]

The non-English-speaking child has often been forced to learn the second language immediately upon entering school before the first language is well established. When the second language is introduced before the child has developed

---

[26] R. D. Hess and Virginia C. Shipman, "Early Experiences and the Socialization of Cognitive Modes in Children," in Margot Kaplan-Sanoff/Renée Yablans-Magid, eds. *Exploring Early Childhood* (New York: Macmillan, 1981), p. 267.

[27] Judith Socolov (general ed.), *Early Childhood Education Project* (New York: Modern Language Association of America, 1971), p. 1.

[28] Ibid., pp. 164–165.

adequate cognitive skills in the native language, both the native and second language usually develop in limited ways and may lead to intellectual and academic retardation.[29] The time, then, at which the second language is introduced is very important.

Other research suggests that the way in which the two languages have been learned helps determine whether bilingualism becomes a handicap and, if so, the extent of the handicap. The socioeconomic and cultural background of the non-English-speaking child is just as important as it is for the English-speaking child.[30]

In summary, when the second language is introduced, how it is introduced and to whom it is introduced are factors that affect the speech of the non-English-speaking child.

Suggestions for teaching an English-speaking child a second language are also applicable to teaching the non-English-speaking child English just as they are to teaching the child who needs help in learning standard English.

There are those who recommend patterned drill as the most effective procedure for helping bilingual children. Others favor the "natural" method and hold that young children can acquire the structure of the language with sufficient exposure to a rich vocabulary and interactions with adults that include a complex syntactical model. Lavatelli recommends that a model for language training should incorporate the following features.[31]

1. Provision should be made for some language training in small group sessions in order to facilitate two-way communication between teacher and child.
2. The speech of the teacher should serve as a model in the sessions. Children should be encouraged to use the sentence structures that the teacher is modeling.
3. The process of modeling should be carried on in a "natural conversational manner" during free play activities as well as in small group sessions.
4. The teacher should keep in mind the child's level of linguistic development as well as "the possible contribution of the structure to logical thinking."
5. The environment should be warm, friendly, and supportive.

Penfield recommends "the mother's method," the direct method of teaching language that is employed in the home. There, language for the child is only a means to an end, not an end in itself. "When he learns about words he is learning about life, learning to get what he wants, learning to share his own exciting ideas with others, learning to understand wonderful fairy tales and exciting facts about trains and trucks and animals and dolls."[32]

According to this point of view, then, there should be no question of teaching

---

[29] Ibid., p. 171.
[30] Ibid., p. 173.
[31] Celia S. Lavatelli, *Piaget's Theory Applied to an Early Childhood Curriculum* (Boston: American Science and Engineering, 1970), pp. 77–78.
[32] W. Penfield and L. Roberts, *Speech and Brain-Mechanisms* (Princeton, N.J.: Princeton U.P., 1959), p. 254.

the child of this age to read or write in another language. Children first learn a second language orally as they do their own language.[33]

Some suggestions for teaching a second language to young children include the following:

1. The language experiences should be those which can be used in daily living. Translate as much as possible of the new language into action. Greetings, dramatizations, songs, nursery rhymes, role playing, and games may all be used effectively. The use of familiar experiences and everyday activities for games and dramatizations help to make them more meaningful. Avoid having children answer questions or recite in chorus because it is difficult to hear whether or not individual children are pronouncing words correctly.
2. Keep vocabulary of a second language in relation to the spoken English of the child. A word should not be introduced in the second language until it is first a part of the child's vocabulary.
3. Create visual impressions of how the person who speaks another language acts or behaves. Suggestions include the following:
   a. Invite a native speaker to visit class.
   b. Visit a home or center where the language is spoken natively.
   c. Use films.
4. Create a "climate of sound" in which the child hears words of the second language spoken correctly. It is important that children use their learnings throughout the day, in greetings, responses, listening to tapes or recordings, and talking with a native speaker.

Travel Experiences.   The development of concepts to which symbols of communication can be attached is important in the language development of young children. For them, this development of concepts is largely one of direct, personal experience. Bean reported that travel and events that broaden the child's experiences are accompanied or followed by increases in vocabulary.[34] Although the kindergarten teacher cannot force the growth of language, he or she can provide experiences and events through which the children can increase their vocabularies. The trips around the neighborhood, to the train, to the fire station, and to the farm; picture books for the child and storybooks to be read; films, filmstrips and recordings can be provided. For example, if we refer to the children in Chapter 7, Shaw has frequent trips to the beach and mountains and hunts and fishes with his father. The twins, Karen and Kirsten, as well as Lisa and Gloria, have few trips in the community.

Olson and Larson report field trips as the most frequently used activity in an

---

[33] O. E. Perez, *Spanish in Florida Elementary Schools* (Tallahassee: Florida State Department of Education, 1960), pp. i–iii.
[34] C. H. Bean, "An Unusual Opportunity to Investigate the Psychology of Language," *J. Genet. Psychol.*, **40**:2 (1932), pp. 181–202.

experimental curriculum for culturally different kindergarten children. "Trips were assumed to be valuable in eliciting linguistic responses from children; language output could not be expected without provision for input. The planning and evaluation experiences relating to field trips provided opportunities for the growth of language facility."[35]

Personal Factors.   In addition to the environmental factors, there are personal factors that have an influence on the child's language development.

INTELLIGENCE.   Differences in language development are closely related to the differences that exist in intellectual development, and there is the possibility of a wide variation in speech development in a group of children.

It is important to remember the limitations regarding intellectual measurement. Growth in language depends upon other factors in addition to those discussed in this chapter. Children from different backgrounds may not have had the opportunities for developing their intellectual potential. According to Almy, these children may have had perceptual experiences but lacked verbal labels to apply to them.[36]

Studies have shown that intelligence tests may not accurately reveal the potential of the highly creative individual. Getzels and Jackson suggest that the term *giftedness* should be used to include other potentially creative groups besides the children of high IQ.[37]

SEX.   In nearly all aspects of language development that have been studied, there seems to be a slight difference in favor of girls. Olson, in comparing the growth curves in language for boys and girls from the same family, found that, age for age, the girls regularly exceeded the boys. He further states that many of the differences may be due to maturity rather than sex.[38] Boys at a given age attain achievements and behavior at about the same rate as somewhat younger girls. Young found sex differences in language development more marked among children of lower socioeconomic levels than among those from superior homes.[39] Templin found differences between the sexes less pronounced.[40] Many believe today that the differences are not due to sex or maturity but to environmental influences.

[35] J. L. Olson and R. G. Larson, "An Experimental Curriculum for Culturally Deprived Kindergarten Children," *Educ. Leadership*, **22**:7 (1965), pp. 557.

[36] Millie Almy, "New Views on Intellectual Development in Early Childhood Education," *Intellectual Development: Another Look* (Alexandria, Va.: ASCD, 1964), p. 21.

[37] J. W. Getzels and P. W. Jackson, "Giftedness and Creativity," *Newsletter* (Chicago: U. of Chicago, November 1960), pp. 5–6.

[38] W. C. Olson, *Child Development*, 2d ed. (Boston: Heath, 1959), p. 155.

[39] F. M. Young, "An Analysis of Certain Variables in a Developmental Study of Language," *Genet. Psychol. Monogr.*, **23**:1 (1941), pp. 3–141.

[40] Templin, op. cit., p. 147.

HEALTH. Loban found a low but positive correlation between health and language proficiency. He pointed out that the health measures that he used were crude and that the correlation might well be higher.[41]

Educational Factors. If educational influences can help make the child's association with language pleasant, he or she will be more likely to have a positive attitude toward language.

EFFECTS OF SITUATION. It was found by Van Alstyne that over half the time preschool children tended not to talk to other children while using certain play materials.[42] Some materials seemed to be more conducive to conversation than others. Play with dolls, blocks, crayons, and clay was accompanied by conversation for a high percentage of the time; painting, using scissors, and looking at books were low in conversation value. McCarthy in reporting this study comments:[43]

> It is interesting, in view of the sex differences previously shown, that the doll-corner activities and dishes, which are typical girl activities, were among the highest in conversation value. It might be concluded that certain differences in language are due to the situation, but it must also be remembered that certain situations may attract children of different levels of language development.

Crowe recorded the conversation of kindergarten children in nine activities.[44] She found that housekeeping play and group discussion held the greatest potential for language use, in both the amount and maturity of speech. Block play, dancing, and woodworking held least. Crowe suggests that adult participation, a concrete topic of conversation, physical arrangements, and noise seem to influence speech.

The Language Program. Some of the characteristics of the spoken language of young children and the factors that influence it have been identified. With an awareness of these, the program can be planned to facilitate the language growth of children. Important elements include the teacher, the climate, and the goals.

Hess and Croft report that children seem to acquire vocabulary and pronunciation of words by imitation and repetition whereas the grammar seems to be acquired on their own as they learn to speak.[45] It is important, then, to provide opportunities for children to have much verbal interaction, with one another and

---

[41] Loban, op. cit., p. 87.

[42] Dorothy Van Alstyne, *Play Behavior and Choice of Play Materials of Preschool Children* (Chicago: U. of Chicago Press, 1932).

[43] Dorothea McCarthy, "Language Development in Children," *Manual of Child Psychology*, 2d ed. (New York: Wiley, 1954), p. 595.

[44] E. G. Crowe, "A Study of Kindergarten Activities for Language Development," and C. B. Cazden, "The Neglected Situation in Child Language Research and Education," in *Language and Poverty*, ed. by F. Williams (Chicago: Markham, 1970).

[45] Hess and Croft, op. cit., pp. 182–184.

with adults on a one-to-one basis. Teachers can provide such opportunities as they elaborate and qualify their answers to children's questions; read aloud from a variety of materials; and make tapes, records, books, and pictures available. It is important, however, that the teacher provide time for the children to talk about what they hear and see.

THE TEACHER.   It is important that the teacher take time to listen to the child. If preparations for the day have been made in advance, the teacher can be free to greet each child as he or she arrives. Here is an opportunity to practice the social courtesies of greeting, such as, "Good morning" or "Hello." The child, fresh from home, often has news to share. It can be fun for the child to talk to the teacher. It can be frustrating, too, trying to tell the teacher something very important while he or she is stirring paint, or cutting paper without even a glance in the child's direction and making only a noncommittal, uninterested reply, such as, "Yes" or "Oh." Perhaps the teacher is busy and doesn't have time at that moment to listen. If so, then she or he may say to the child, "I am busy, but I will talk with you as soon as I have finished." And she or he must be very sure to remember the promise and not keep the child waiting too long.

Speech instruction, according to Anderson, begins with the teacher's voice. The tone of voice, the manner of speaking, and the vocabulary she or he uses all have an influence on the quality of instruction.[46] A voice can invite conversation, or discourage it. A harsh, loud voice can irritate and embarrass whereas a soft, well-modulated voice can help one to be relaxed and comfortable.

The teacher's speech should set a good example in enunciation and pronunciation. It is easy to fall into habits of slovenly speech. Teachers should use the tape recorder and listen to their own speech.

THE CLIMATE.   The atmosphere of the kindergarten, nursery school, or child development center reflects the attitude of the teacher. The atmosphere should be supportive, one in which a child is free to converse, to enjoy experiences, to use language, to make mistakes, and to correct them.

Lavatelli says that "the child should hear directed at him a wide variety of well formed utterances to which he must make a response."[47] She also suggests that for children from different backgrounds there should be some time during the day when a child can be part of a small group under the guidance of the teacher and have an opportunity to listen, to respond, and to be responded to.[48]

As the teacher works in a relaxed, happy school atmosphere, she or he keeps in mind certain objectives of the language program for children.

[46] P. S. Anderson, *Language Skills in Elementary Education*, 2d ed. (New York: Macmillan, 1972), p. 83.
[47] Butler, op. cit., p. 133.
[48] Ibid.

THE GOALS.   As the teacher works with children, she or he will help each child to accomplish the following:[49]

1. Develop fluency and naturalness in expression. Opportunities for many experiences will introduce new words and provide the child with something to talk about. These, together with the stimulation of an understanding teacher, can help the child gain desired fluency and spontaneity and build a functional vocabulary.

2. Develop the ability to speak distinctly in a pleasant voice with good control both as to volume and tone—a voice free of baby talk and incomplete enunciation, not too high, too loud, or too soft. The teacher may give guidance by such comments as, "I'm sorry, I didn't hear what you said. Tell me again and speak just a little louder, please." Such guidance helps the child realize that "too soft" voices can't be understood, and the child is helped to feel adequate and secure enough to speak louder.

3. Form habits of correct usage. Constant criticism can interfere with the fluency and spontaneity of expression. Constructive helpfulness, gauged to the needs of the individual child, is essential. For example, a child may say, "Jim comed to my house." The teacher may smile and repeat, "Jim came to my house."

   Children learn grammar gradually. They usually learn irregular verb forms first because words like *went* and *came* are among the most common verbs in the English language. As children reach the stage of discovering the rule for the past tense, they may overgeneralize and say *goed* and *comed*. Finally the mature pattern is achieved. Identification with particular models of speech is very important. The child uses the language that is heard as examples from which to learn, not as examples to learn in themselves.[50]

4. Use language as a social tool. The teacher needs to help each child learn to talk freely and easily, to listen courteously, and to use socially accepted phrases such as "thank you" and "excuse me."[51] The school in which children are helped to develop an awareness of and concern for others offers opportunities for practice. If the teacher sincerely uses the accepted terms in his or her speech and actions, the children in this environment will use them also. Use of such words without an appreciation of their meaning is futile. The teacher may also use comments such as, "Voices that are too loud bother others. There are voices for the playground and voices for the kindergarten room. We are inside now."

5. Develop the ability to name, describe, and classify objects common in the environment. The teacher may talk with one child alone and give an opportunity to name what he or she sees, feels, hears, or smells. Different children may be asked to categorize objects on one, two, or three dimensions: for example, find two green objects, two green circles, two large green circles.[52]

---

[49] H. A. Greene and W. T. Petty, *Developing Language Skills in the Elementary School*, 5th ed. (Boston: Allyn, 1975), pp. 90–94.

[50] Cazden, op. cit., pp. 5–6.

[51] Greene and Petty, op. cit., p. 92.

[52] Louise M. Berman (ed.), *Toward New Programs for Young Children* (College Park: U. of Maryland, 1970), pp. 16–17.

6. Develop the ability to communicate with others. This skill involves not only expressing one's ideas, but understanding what has been said; being able to repeat in one's own words what another has said and being able to respond appropriately to the meaning of another person's statement. The teacher may give directions such as, "Lucy, please put the cups on the table."[53] Children may also be helped in this regard by having the opportunity for retelling a story in their own words after they have heard it read. Conversation allows children the opportunity to share their ideas and feelings.

7. Organize ideas in expression. Often, the child's mind races ahead while speaking, and the result is a disorganized comment or story. For example, listen as Joe was telling about a hunting trip: "We got up early. We ate breakfast—and, oh! We got dressed in our hunting clothes—and, oh! My mother bought me a new rain coat and boots." At this point the teaching may say, "You were telling us about your hunting trip," helping him get back on the track, to organize his ideas, and to relate his experiences in proper sequence.

8. Learn about the language. Strickland has identified elements in the field of linguistics that appear highly valuable for younger children. She proposes that development of concepts about language begin in kindergarten. Though the concepts may seem formal and meaningless for the kindergarten child, the examples indicate many opportunities for learning in relation to daily activities. Some of the concepts and examples, as adapted, follow: [54]

Language is a system of sounds.

The patterns of sound convey meaning to those who know the language.

(Learning familiar words in another language—e.g., "Thank you.")

Pitch, stress, and juncture are a part of the sound system of the language and help to convey meaning.

(Use same words to convey different messages—e.g., *When* do you expect him? When do you expect *him?*)

The sounds convey meaning only when put together in patterns of words and sentences.

(Help child speak in sentences. Note how meaning and emphasis are influenced by position of words in sentence—e.g., The boy in the yard ate his lunch. The boy ate his lunch in the yard.)

A language changes; old words may be given new meanings and new uses.

Likewise, old words are dropped and new words are coined of old parts to represent new meanings or modifications of old ones.

(Note old words in Mother Goose Rhymes—"*fetch* a pail of water."

What does it mean today?

Note new words; *telstar, supersonic.*

Note new meanings for old words; *capsule.*)

---

[53] Ibid., pp. 17–20.

[54] Ruth G. Strickland, *The Contribution of Structural Linguistics to the Teaching of Reading, Writing, and Grammar in the Elementary School* (Bloomington: School of Education, Indiana University, 1963), pp. 7–9.

LISTENING

Listening, as a means of learning, is an important facet of the language arts. It has been referred to as the primary language skill. Chronologically speaking, listening is the first language skill to appear. Children listen before they speak, speak before they read, and read before they write.

When children go to school for the first time, they generally have had four or five years' experience in listening, but the range in ability varies greatly. Jennie, described in Chapter 7, is inclined to "tune out" sounds and ignore them because much of the talk at home has been impatient and nagging, such as "Be quiet, I must study." Many children who live in the inner city have also learned to "tune out" sounds, because their environment may be noisy. There are many street sounds as well as those from neighboring apartments. When a large family lives in cramped space there is likely to be much talking and voices are raised in order to be heard above the confusion. A child from such an atmosphere may have had little opportunity for "peace and quiet" and listening. Children hear many sounds. Just hearing, however, does not guarantee listening. Listening involves recognizing sounds, giving them meaning from one's experience, reacting to or interpreting them, and integrating them with one's knowledge and experiences. It is a major means of learning. Dawson says, "It is through listening, then, that the young child gains much of his vocabulary, most of his sentence patterns, and nearly all of his imitatively acquired ways of enunciating and inflecting. Listening, of course, also contributes to his constantly growing stock of ideas."[55]

Types of listening include the following:

1. Informational listening is involved in situations when the child listens to directions or announcements, to note main ideas, to remember details, to anticipate conclusions or inferences.
2. Appreciative listening is involved when the child enjoys a story, a poem, or a recording, and senses images and moods.
3. Critical (analytical) listening occurs when the child analyzes what he hears in terms of his own experience. One may hear the child pondering, "I wonder why."[56]

The listening skills

Listening skills are related to the child's purpose for listening—perception or comprehension. The perceptual skills follow:[57]

[55] Mildred Dawson, *Learning to Listen*, Language Arts Notes, No. 3 (Yonkers, N.Y.: World Book, n.d.), p. 1.
[56] Burns and Broman, op. cit., p. 135.
[57] W. T. Petty, Dorothy C. Petty, and Marjorie F. Becking, *Experiences in Language: Tools and Techniques for Language Arts Methods* (Boston: Allyn, 1981), pp. 151–152.

Perception of language sounds and discrimination among them. Each speech sound must be heard, identified, and recognized as different from every other speech sound.

Identification of a group of sounds as a symbol—a word—to which meaning is attached and identification of a group of words—a combination of words, a phrase, or a sentence—to which meaning is attached.

Deduction of the meanings of unknown words and phrases through context. Because in listening (as in reading) not every word is familiar, it is often necessary to get the meaning from the general understanding of the context in which it is said.

The skills for getting the meaning of the total communication follow:

Comprehending what has been heard by:
Noting details and fitting them together.
Determining the main idea and subordinate ideas.
Finding the order or sequence of the communication.
Recognizing emotional appeal or propaganda or both.
Noting clues to the speaker's thoughts or opinions.

In relating what was heard to previous learning in order to build new understandings, the child is making use of what has been received. This means going beyond merely understanding and calls for inferences and drawing conclusions.[58]

Teaching listening

Listening makes up 45 per cent of a child's school day.[59] Much of a child's day at school is spent in listening to directions, stories, music, and human interaction through communication. All these require that a child acquire mastery of the listening skills.

To grow as an accurate and critical listener, children must be taught how to listen and how to use the results of listening. Some suggestions for teaching this type of listening are

1. Remember that young children are easily distracted. Because they have a short attention span, the teacher tries to adjust to this and at the same time to help the child grow in ability to attend, without undue pressure.
   a. Plan brief periods of any one activity. The length of stories, recordings, music periods should be within the child's attention span.
   b. Vary methods of presentation with attractive materials. Pictures, bright colors, interesting objects, help to gain attention.

[58] Ibid.
[59] Ibid., p. 150.

c. Accept wiggling and twisting. Monroe suggests that trying to hold his or her body still takes conscious effort on the part of a little child and may therefore be distracting.[60] Rather than insisting that "we sit up straight, feet on the floor, hands in our laps," the teacher may suggest that each child sit comfortably. The teacher may use a finger play, such as

> Open, shut them, open, shut them
> Give a little clap
> Open, shut them, open, shut them
> Fold them in your lap[61]

and immediately begin the story or activity.

d. Arrange the physical environment so that children are comfortable and that outside noises and interferences are at a minimum.

2. Help the children understand that listening is important. For example, don't repeat explanations, directions, or announcements over and over.
   a. If children know that the teacher will repeat for them whenever they are ready, why should they stop to listen with the group?
   b. Make activities so interesting that children will want to listen and will miss something if they don't.
3. Teach the children to listen.
   a. Speak in a voice that is adequate, but low enough to require listening if the child is to hear what is being said. Don't try to talk above the noise of the children nor speak so softly that you cannot be heard.
   b. Talk only when there is something meaningful to say. The voice that goes on and on becomes monotonous and the children tend to "tune it out."
   c. Allow time for the child to get ready to listen. After saying, "Children," or "Boys and girls," allow a moment or two for the child to put down the block or crayon. Often the announcement is made while the child's effort is expended in balancing the block rather than listening.
   d. Give explanations simply and in well-organized sequence.
4. Set a good example of attention. A teacher who is preoccupied with personal problems, such as writing a note or getting a drink of water while a recording is being played, does not emphasize the importance of listening. "A teacher who looks attentively into the face of the child who is talking, listens closely to what he is saying, tries to understand his exact meaning, however poorly phrased, and gives him the most thoughtful reply she is capable of, will hold that child's attention better than any device than can be suggested."[62]
5. Create a relaxed, happy atmosphere and relaxation among the children and be-

---

[60] Marion Monroe, *Growing into Reading* (Chicago: Scott, Foresman, 1951), p. 177.

[61] For other finger plays, see Margaret A. Stant, *The Young Child: His Activities and Materials* (Englewood Cliffs, N.J.: Prentice-Hall, 1972), pp. 125–129.

[62] Monroe, op. cit., p. 178.

tween them and yourself. A child who is relaxed and free from emotional strain can listen more easily than the child who is uneasy, hostile, or afraid.

6. Help the child develop an awareness of sounds, the sounds they hear every day. The teacher may begin by calling attention to types of sounds, such as those of nature, or the traffic, or human sounds. One approach is to say to the children, "Close your eyes. Listen carefully and tell me what you hear." They may identify the sounds and describe them as loud, soft, close, far away, sharp, and so on.

7. Provide many opportunities for a wide variety of meaningful listening experiences. There should be listening for pleasure, appreciation, and information. The teacher may use stories, poetry, records, directions, tapes, musical instruments, television, radio, and conversation with adults and other children.

8. Arrange opportunities for children to listen for certain purposes, such as answering questions, solving riddles, completing rhymes, putting ideas in sequence, identifying words which do not rhyme, and detecting irrelevant sentences.[63]

READING AND THE YOUNG CHILD

Changes in the type and amount of reading instruction in the kindergarten have occurred over the last several years.

As the importance of early learning opportunities to a child's development were recognized, interest in early reading has become apparent. In 1964 the U.S. Office of Education held a Conference on Teaching Young Children to Read. Although reports indicated that approximately one fourth of the school systems maintaining kindergarten offered reading instruction, there was a lively controversy regarding the practice.[64] Despite the controversy, an increasing number of programs are attempting to teach reading to prefirst-grade children.

Nila B. Smith said that there is no question in regard to whether or not young children *can* read; the main consideration is whether they should be *taught* to read at an early age.[65] Smith affirmed that young children in kindergarten who want to read and are ready to read should be given the help they request. This procedure is quite different from introducing formal reading instruction to all kindergarten children.

As the result of a six-year study of children who had an opportunity to learn to read in a language arts program at the age of four, Durkin reports no negative

---

[63] P. C. Burns, Betty L. Broman, and Alberta L. Lowe, *The Language Arts in Childhood Education*, 2d ed. (Chicago: Rand McNally, 1971), pp. 71–73.

[64] Mary C. Austin, "Current Reading Practices," *Teaching Young Children to Read* (U.S. Office of Education, Washington, D.C.: U.S. Government Printing Office, 1964), pp. 16–20.

[65] Nila B. Smith, "Trends in Beginning Reading Since 1900," *Teaching Young Children to Read* (U.S. Office of Education) (Washington, D.C.: U.S. Government Printing Office, 1964), pp. 14–15.

effects on later achievement in reading. She believes that future achievement depends on the type of instruction offered in the later grades.[66]

Other issues involved in the controversy relate to the nature of reading readiness, the question of when to begin the teaching of reading, and how reading is taught.

Reading readiness

An examination of what is meant by the term *reading readiness* may help the reader understand the term as used in this text. A child is ready for reading when his or her capacities are mature or adequate in relation to the requirements of a specific learning situation.

"Readiness," as Krogman explains, "implies a best-time for initiating a specific task situation."[67] Readiness for reading, then, has to do with the "best time" for beginning reading instruction. Reading instruction, however, involves many tasks or learning situations of varying difficulty. The focus, then, is upon the relationship between the child's particular abilities and the learning opportunities available. The opportunities for learning to read are influenced by the teacher and the teaching method used. The child may have the opportunity to acquire certain visual skills, such as looking at the page from left to right, top to bottom. As children use books, listen to stories, and help to dictate stories to the teacher, they may have opportunities for processing information, learning that printed words have meaning, that words say something; for attaching the label of reading to the experiences. Some children may relate these experiences to those of having mother read aloud. A concept of reading is being formed.

This explanation implies that readiness for reading depends on nature and nurture, maturity and training. Olson uses the equation, "Maturation × Nurture = Development," which may well be applied to readiness for reading.[68]

Some factors involved in readiness are wholly dependent on maturation. The teacher cannot say to a child, "Focus your eyes" or "Coordinate your muscles" and expect such a response. Such development depends on maturity. When this has been achieved, appropriate experiences may be supplied and the child learns happily and successfully. Olson states, "Synchronization between maturity and opportunity seems to be the safest guide to educational practice."

Durkin reports that the child's capacity at any given time is the product of nature and nurture.[69]

[66] Dolores Durkin, "A Six-Year Study of Children Who Learned to Read at the Age of Four," *Reading Research Quarterly*, **X**:1 (1974–1975), pp. 9–61.
[67] W. M. Krogman, "Physical Growth as a Factor in the Behavioral Development of the Child," *New Dimensions in Learning* (Alexandria, Va.: ASCD, 1963), pp. 15, 21.
[68] W. C. Olson, op. cit., pp. 14, 17.
[69] Dolores Durkin, *Teaching Them to Read* 3d ed. (Boston: Allyn, 1978), p. 162.

The environmental factors in a child's life have become especially significant as the importance of early learning opportunities have been recognized. Learning to read involves the ability to associate meaning with symbols and to interpret what is read. Such skill requires the intellectual capacity and the mental maturity necessary to reason, to form meaningful associations, and to remember word forms. In one of the earlier studies, Morphett and Washburne found that among the first-grade children studied, those with mental ages between 6.5 and 7.0 years profited most from the initial reading instruction.[70]

Research has shown, however, that a child's mental age is only one of many factors related to success in reading. The degree of mental maturity required for success in beginning reading depends to some extent on the way in which beginning reading is taught, the materials used, and the child's interest in learning to read. Gates and Bond report a low correlation of mental age with reading achievement. They conclude that the optimum time for beginning reading depends not entirely on the child, but also on the reading instruction he or she receives. They

[70] Mabel V. Morphett and C. Washburne, "When Should Children Begin to Read?" *Elem. Sch. J.*, **31**:7 (1931), pp. 496–503.

Handling, using, and loving books can help the child become interested in learning to read and to know that reading can be fun.

indicate that the general and social returns to the child from learning to read are important also.[71]

Durkin points out that different types of instruction in reading make different demands of the child.[72] She views reading readiness instruction as reading instruction in its earliest stages. The teacher then, chooses the type of reading instruction appropriate to the child's abilities and needs.

It is difficult, if not impossible, to isolate single factors involved in readiness because of their interrelationship. Such physical factors as age, vision, hearing, eye-hand coordination, and general health are considered important. Likewise, a child's concept of his or her ability to learn to read and his or her interest in reading affect the progress that will be made. The mental and intellectual factors involved have been discussed. The quality of instruction that the child receives is also very important. Durkin emphasizes the importance of a child's capacity in relation to the instruction that will be available. Some abilities are necessary for one reading program whereas different abilities are required for another program.[73] A look at these factors seems important here even though the combination of factors and their interrelationship will vary with each child.

Age. Chronological age has not been found to be a realistic index to readiness. Some children will begin reading at about six years of age. Some children, however, will be ready earlier; some not until later. Durkin reminds us that beginning reading in the first grade, at the age of six, is a product of convention, not of evidence that six years of age is an especially good time to begin reading.

Vision. The young child is usually farsighted, and only gradually will the eyes mature sufficiently for him or her to maintain them in focus at the distance required for reading. The child may be able to see distant objects clearly, but the same object becomes blurred when examined closely at near vision. A child may look at a picture in a book on the table, seeing it clearly, and still have difficulty in looking at the small letters involved in a word.

According to Gesell, a child of five may have trouble in adapting to the blackboard and in making adjustments from far to near and near to far.[74]

Park and Burri found that the percentage of children with vision below 20–20 declined from approximately 50 per cent in the prereading stages to 20–35 per cent in the early elementary and junior high school period.[75] Good fusion, stereop-

[71] A. I. Gates and G. L. Bond, "Reading Readiness: A Study of Factors Determining Success and Failure in Beginning Reading," *Teach. Coll. Rec.*, 37:8 (1936), pp. 679–685.

[72] Durkin, *Teaching Young Children to Read*, 3d ed. (Boston: Allyn, 1980), pp. 72–73.

[73] Durkin, *Teaching Young Children to Read*. 3rd ed. (Allyn, 1980), p. 64.

[74] A. Gesell, Frances Ilg, and G. E. Bullis, *Vision: Its Development in Infant and Child* (New York: Paul B. Hoeber, 1948), p. 289.

[75] G. E. Park and Clara Burri, "Eye Maturation and Reading Difficulties," *J. Educ. Psychol.*, 34:9 (1943), pp. 535–546.

Working with puzzles, manipulating clay, painting, and hammering nails into wood offer opportunities for visual discrimination, training in visual perception, and the development of eye-hand coordination—all important skills in learning to read.

sis, and the power to maintain binocular single vision also improve during this period.

One concern in relation to preschool reading has been the harmful effect upon a child's vision. Durkin points out, however, that these early concerns were not supported by research data and were not stated by medical personnel. And the lack of adequate research is still evident. Durkin recommends that until research on this question is available, caution should be exercised. She says that young children who show an interest in reading are probably visually ready for reading. When young children are not interested in reading, one "ought to keep in mind the dearth of facts about the effect of early reading on vision and be cautious."[76]

Early childhood programs offer many opportunities for experiences that provide visual discrimination and training. Many such activities are used daily, but the teacher is often unaware of their value. The children's responses to these activities suggest their readiness for more complex situations or their need for some less

[76] Durkin, *Teaching Them to Read* (Boston: Allyn, 1970), pp. 50–51.

difficult. The teacher who is alert to the child's needs can select materials for learning encounters appropriate for each child.

Activities involving letters and words may begin with showing the child his or her name on a locker or painting and later matching it with his or her name on an experience chart; or noting words that begin alike in the recipe for making apple sauce. The teacher may use a question such as: "Look and see what else we need to make the cookies," thus providing opportunity for visual recall.

Working with puzzles; rolling, throwing, catching balls; manipulating clay; painting; and hammering nails into wood offer opportunities in developing eye-hand coordination. The child can be helped to acquire other visual skills, such as looking at the picture book from front to back and top to bottom and the pictures from left to right across the page. Such skills can be acquired most effectively as the child examines picture books and observes the book as stories are read. Experience charts, records of trips, lists of committee responsibilities all may be used in developing the left to right eye-movement.

One child in first grade had developed the habit of looking at words from right to left. This was observed in the following situation: The sentence—"Here is the dog"—was on the board. The teacher gave the pointer to Herb and asked him to read it. He moved the pointer from *dog* to *Here* as he read the sentence. When asked to find the word *dog*, he pointed to *Here;* and to *dog* when asked to find *Here*. Visual examinations by competent specialists failed to reveal any difficulty. The doctors reported that the child had learned to look from right to left. A parent conference revealed that in kindergarten Herb had done many exercises for visual discrimination. Evidently these had not been closely supervised, and he had found the picture that was different by beginning at the right side of the page. Well-meaning teachers who use formal readiness material without proper supervision may be encouraging the development of harmful habits.

Hearing. As children live the first five years of their lives, they hear many sounds about them, but by the time they enter nursery school or kindergarten, there are wide differences in their experiences with sounds and their awareness of sounds. Some children have listened to frogs croak, cows moo, sheep bleat, and dogs bark; others recognize the sounds of planes, trains, and trucks. For some there have been poetry, stories, and music. Others have had no one to share with them the fun of hearing different sounds or noises.

Some children are handicapped by faulty hearing; others have normal hearing acuity but have not learned to discriminate differences in sounds. In either case, this deficiency in auditory acuity can be responsible for continued baby talk or faulty pronunciation. If a child does not hear the difference between two words, it will be difficult for him or her to distinguish between their printed symbols. The teacher should be alert to detect hearing difficulties, make adjustments for the child, and recommend correction to the parents.

Before learning to read, the majority of children will profit from learning about sounds with special reference to language. This should not be interpreted to mean formal phonetic drill but rather opportunities for experiences by which children become aware of sounds and the ways in which sounds differ and are alike. Children need to become able to discriminate, identify, and match sounds. Such experiences can offer beginning contact with phonics. For example:

Sounds can be loud or soft—"Turn up the record player so that the record will be a little louder. I can't hear it." Or, "How do you feel when you hear this music?" "It is very soft and slow. I feel sleepy." Or, "Talk softly. The baby [doll] is asleep."

Sounds can be high or low. Match tones in music. The teacher strikes a note on the piano. She says to the child, "Find a sound that is low," or vice versa. In singing, call attention to the way in which the song goes up and down.

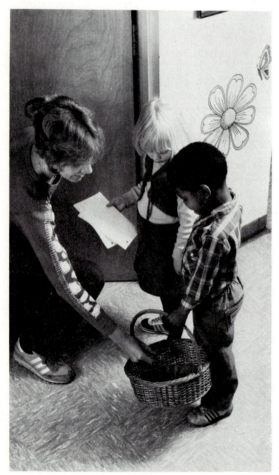

"On our treasure hunt we found things that start with the sound of 'P.' "

Sounds can be made by people, animals, and things. Ask the children to close their eyes, listen, and name the sounds they hear. Make a recording of the children's voices. Ask them to listen and identify the voices. Make a recording of sounds heard on the playground. Ask children to identify a sound and decide if it was made by a person, animal, or thing. Show pictures of animals and ask children to make a sound appropriate for each. Ask children to find a person, animal, or thing in the classroom that can make a sound. Listen to the sounds of each.

Sounds can be the same. Use stories with initial consonant sounds, such as *choo choo, chug chug*. The teacher may say, "milk," and ask the child, "Can you think of a word that begins with the same sound as milk?" Begin with short words and their initial sounds.[77] It is important that children understand the meaning of words used in discussing sounds such as alike, same, different.

Other Physical Factors. The general health and nutritional status influence the child's energy level. A child who has frequent colds and is absent often must continually make adjustments to school. He or she may get settled and begin to feel comfortable with the group, then be ill and out of school for four days. Upon returning, the child finds that the group is not as familiar as it was last week. Two days after the return, he or she feels secure again. This happy state lasts only a few days, and the child is out again, and the process must be repeated.

Muscular control and development affects what the child can do. Jennie, you recall, has "jerky" muscular movements and is afraid to climb the jungle gym. This inability to climb successfully further limits her social contacts with other children.

Emotional-Social Factors. It is easier for a child who is emotionally secure in the school situation to learn to read. He or she is free to devote attention to the job at hand. Jean, a six-year-old, returning home from her first day in first grade, expressed this truth. Bounding through the front door, she called, "Mommie, a little girl cried at school today." For Jean, who had been so eager to go to school, the little girl's tears had evidently been quite a surprise. Her mother asked, "Why did the little girl cry?" Jean thought for a moment, then replied, "I guess she hadn't been to kindergarten. She didn't know her mother would come at 12 o'clock and everything would be all right."

Programs for young children can make a great contribution to the social and emotional adjustment of children. They can learn to feel secure in a situation away from home with adults other than their parents. Children can learn that the teacher is friendly, that everything is all right. The child can learn that groups can be friendly, too—the child can be a member and speak, sing, listen, or sit in the group. Children can begin to direct their own behavior, to follow directions, to select and use materials, to assume responsibility for jobs in the room.

[77] Durkin, *Teaching Young Children to Read*, 3rd ed., op. cit., p. 171.

Experiential Background. An important factor influencing a child's readiness to read is his or her experiential background.[78]

A variety of experiences, when accompanied by a good language environment, will contribute to the expansion of a child's listening and speaking vocabularies, which will help a child decode unfamiliar words when reading. In order to understand a story, a child needs to have some knowledge of the situation. For example, if a child had never had a pet, he or she could not understand the feelings the character in the story was experiencing in the loss of a pet dog.

Children who have trips and visits in the community, associations with people, and knowledge of things around them will probably have more words in their vocabulary and more things to talk about. Almy found a significant, positive relationship between success in beginning reading and the child's experiences in kindergarten, in play, and with adults, which involved being read to and looking at books, papers, and magazines.[79]

McCormick reviewed research and concluded that reading aloud to children significantly improved their vocabulary, knowledge, and reading comprehension.[80]

Children's capacity for learning to read is also influenced by their own concept of their ability, which is influenced by previous experiences. Some present views of intellectual development assume that the position a child has reached indicates the intellectual progress already made, but the prediction of future development depends on knowledge of the experiences in store for the child.[81]

Attention Span. In learning to read, the child needs to to be able to focus attention on the specific instructional task. For example, in recording an anecdotal record, one student wrote, "tension span" instead of "attention span." Perhaps in reality this was not an error. Tensions do build up, and the span indicates the length of time before they interfere with the child's ability to attend. The attention span indicates the length of time for which a child can focus thoughts on, listen to, or concentrate on a given topic.

Olson states that it has been difficult to determine the attention span of children at different ages, but there is rather general agreement that the attention span of children for toys and play materials increases with age. A range of 7 to 20 minutes has been identified for the preschool period. Individual differences are great and the time seems to vary with the appropriateness of the material for the age.[82] Durkin says that the attention span of the same child varies in length and depth according

---

[78] Wayne Otto, Robert Rude, and Dixie Lee Spiegel, *How to Teach Reading* (Reading, Mass.: Addison-Wesley, 1979), pp. 81–82.

[79] Millie C. Almy, *Children's Experiences Prior to First Grade and Success in Beginning Reading* (New York: Teachers College, 1949).

[80] Sandra McCormick, "Should You Read Aloud to Your Children?" *Language Arts,* **54**:2 (1977), pp. 130–143.

[81] Almy, *Intellectual Development: Another Look,* op. cit., p. 13.

[82] W. C. Olson, op. cit., p. 95.

Peter is matching postcards to pictures in travel folders.

to the activity in which the child is engaged.[83] A report of an observation made by Otto and colleagues in a kindergarten showed that girls had longer attention spans for tasks than boys.[84]

Summary. The following statements regarding readiness are important to its understanding.

1. Readiness refers to a combination of abilities, understanding, and opportunities. Readiness does not consist only of specific abilities in specified quantities.
2. Readiness is the product of nature and maturation as well as nurture and the environmental factors in the child's life.
3. Readiness is concerned with the relationship between the child's capacity and the type of reading instruction available.[85]

[83] Durkin, *Teaching Young Children to Read*, 3rd ed., op. cit., pp. 14–15.
[84] Otto et al., op. cit., pp. 80–81.
[85] Durkin, *Teaching Young Children to Read* 3rd ed., op. cit., pp. 72–73.

Assessment of Reading Readiness.   In order to provide reading instruction appropriate to the developmental level of each child, each child's readiness for reading must be assessed. Commercial readiness tests are usually administered to small groups of children. These tests are primarily concerned with the child's vocabulary and visual and auditory discrimination. Total scores are the basis for deciding if children are ready for reading. Subtest scores may be used in diagnosing strengths and weaknesses of a child.

If tests are used, results should be supplemented by teacher judgment, often more reliable than test scores in predicting success in reading. In an informal manner the teacher can observe areas included in the test as well as the child's interest in stories and reading. After studying the results of tests and observations and after talking with the parents, the teacher can make an intelligent decision as to the type of instruction appropriate for an individual child.[86]

Durkin believes, however, that the use of total scores on readiness tests does not take into account the different understandings required for different types of instruction and how the instruction is carried out. She recommends an alternative method of assessment using learning opportunities. Her proposal may be summarized as follows:[87]

[86] Elizabeth M. Goetz, "Early Reading: A Developmental Approach," in *Curriculum Planning for Young Children*, Janet F. Brown, ed. (Washington, D.C.: NAEYC, 1982), pp. 79–82.
[87] Durkin, *Teaching Young Children to Read*, 3rd ed., op. cit., pp. 64–70.

Reading aloud to children can help to develop their interest in reading, improve their vocabulary, and increase their general knowledge. Young children never tire of having stories read to them once they discover the magic contained between the covers of a book.

1. Provide a variety of opportunities for children to begin to read. For example, an easel painting may be used to provide a reason for kindergarten children to learn to write their names, to dictate captions, and later to write and read the captions. These activities give the teacher the opportunity to note children who have difficulty with the motor skill of writing, who have difficulty dictating the caption, or who remember whole words easily.
2. Use results of observation in both readiness and reading instruction. For the child who has difficulty in writing, the teacher may provide clay, fingerpaint, chalk, crayons, and pencils for scribbling that can later be channeled into drawing and writing. The child who had difficulty composing captions for the picture may need opportunities for increasing his or her vocabulary and for experiences that will provide something to talk about. The child who composes captions easily may also be able to read words in the caption.
3. Remember that the results of any learning opportunities depend upon the child's abilities. Each child is ready for some instruction. For some, this may be readiness; for others, reading.

Teaching reading

One of the questions often raised in regard to teaching reading is *when* to begin the instruction. Durkin points out that instruction should begin when the child is ready to succeed with a particular kind of instruction.[88] The problem becomes one of assessing readiness and synchronizing instructional opportunities with the capacities and interests of the children to be taught.

MacGinitie states that before the teacher can determine when reading instruction should begin, he or she must define what is meant by teaching beginning reading. Individual differences must be taken into consideration when beginning reading instruction. According to MacGinitie, every four- or five-year-old is ready to learn something about reading as long as it is adapted to the child's background. It is not appropriate simply to transfer what is currently being taught in the first grade to the four- and five-year-old programs. These programs should be less oriented toward formal, complex rules. Such programs should present the child with opportunities to practice, become acquainted with letters and words, and develop reading objectives.[89]

The term *reading instruction* does not necessarily mean formal instruction—a situation in which all the children are taught the same prescribed material at the same time and at the same rate. Such procedure is not appropriate for the kindergarten or any grade level.

How does one teach young children to read? There are many ways of teaching children to read. The methods vary from an informal approach for children who are

---

[88] Durkin, *Teaching Them to Read*, 3rd ed., op. cit., p. 169.
[89] Walter H. MacGinitie, "When Should We Begin to Teach Reading?" *Language Arts*, **53**:8 (Nov.–Dec. 1976), pp. 878–882.

ready to read, to others that favor a highly structured beginning reading program for all kindergarten children.[90] Hymes suggests that reading be taught to fit the child. There are many differences among children of the same chronological age and these must be considered in planning for reading instruction. Children can't be lumped together. Each child remains an individual. The teacher teaches as much as each child can comfortably, naturally, and easily learn.

When reading instruction was begun first with the fives and later with the fours, little attention had been given to adapting the reading process to the very young— to fitting it to the child. First-grade procedures were usually used. The books, methods, and materials formerly used for the six- and seven-year-old children were moved down to the kindergarten. Today, however, there is a growing awareness that reading for the prefirst-grade child is different. The program can be one of trips, jobs and activities, pets, visitors, creative experiences, and play. The program needn't be one in which children are sitting quietly rather than being active. It can grow out of the children's activities and experiences relevant to them.[91]

The practice of drilling on letters and sounds before the child learns what reading and learning to read are all about ignores the relation of reading to the other language arts. When this practice is used in beginning instruction, the relation of spoken and written language is bypassed and some children do not know what the sounding of the letters is all about.[92]

Language Experience Approach (LEA)

The Language Experience Approach, a method of reading instruction that capitalizes on what children already know, offers an alternative to more traditional methods and seems very appropriate for the young child. Such an approach integrates listening, speaking, writing, and reading. The children's oral language and experiences are used as the basis for developing reading materials. Children learn to read in conjunction with talking, listening, and writing. One of the important types of reading material used in the language experience approach is the experience story.

The experience story, or chart, (plans, news, stories) may be developed individually or in a group situation, with the children's ideas being recorded by the teacher. The content of the stories should be familiar, growing out of the experiences of the children.[93]

[90] L. O. Ollila, *Handbook for Administrators and Teachers: Reading in the Kindergarten* (Newark, Delaware: International Reading Assoc., 1980), pp. V and 68.

[91] J. L. Hymes, Jr., "Teaching Reading to the Under-Six Age: A Child Development Point of View," in *Claremont Reading Conference 34th Yearbook* (Claremont, Calif. 91771: Claremont Graduate School 1970), pp. 79–83.

[92] Durkin, *Teaching Them to Read*, 3rd ed., op. cit., p. 84.

[93] Mary Anne Hall, *Teaching Reading as a Language Experience* 2d ed. (Columbus, Ohio: Merrill, 1976).

Susan's Birthday Plans
Banana Birthday Cake
White and Pink frosting
Apple Juice
Make "Bugs on a Log" Snack
Listen to "Annie" Record
Read Madeline In Paris
Role Play Madeline With Puppet
Sing and Dance "Hokey Pokey"
Tea Party Outside

Children learn to read in conjunction with talking, reading, and writing. The experience story is one of the important types of materials used. The experience story often includes plans, recipes, and news. The teacher recorded the birthday plans for Susan.

The Language Experience Approach has been found by many teachers to be an effective method for teaching young children to read. Jensen and Hanson state[94] that this approach is effective because the child's language and experiences are the basis for reading; it is a flexible technique that is easily adapted to the various needs and abilities of each child and can easily be used along with most reading programs.

The basic ingredient of this approach is dictation or experience-charting, which draws upon children's reactions to and ideas about a particular individual or shared experience. As the children verbalize their ideas, the teacher records these on a chart without altering or correcting the children's expressions. In this manner, the child is helped to realize that one's thoughts, when verbalized, can be written and read. Teachers must involve the children in order to encourage responses during the dictation.[95] The Language Experience Approach includes five major components:

1. Prepare for dictation.
2. Take dictation.

[94] Mary A. Jensen and Bette A. Hanson, "Research in Review: Helping Young Children Learn to Read: What Research Says to Teachers," *Young Children*, 36:1 (November 1980), pp. 61–71.
[95] Dorothy Grant Hennings and Barbara Moll Grant, *Written Expression in the Language Arts: Ideas and Skills* (New York: Teachers College, 1981), p. 78.

3. Read the story.
4. Conduct immediate follow-up activities.
5. Develop basic skills.[96]

The experience story may be used in a variety of ways depending on the maturity and interests of the children. The teacher refers to the needs of the individual child and the group. For one child, participation in expressing ideas for the teacher to record is enough. Another child can illustrate ideas expressed in the story as a follow-up activity. Others may be learning that written words have meaning, that words express ideas that have been recorded; beginning the development of the skills of reading, such as focusing on print, reading from top to bottom and left to right, and making the return sweep across the page; and having practice in matching and letter recognition. Still others are developing a sight vocabulary and learning to identify words. One child may be able to name letters of the alphabet but not recognize them or how they function. The teacher may write, call attention to, and name the letters in the child's name. Other words from the story that have some of the same letters may be used.

In writing an experience story, the teacher may find the following suggestions helpful.[97]

1. Use manuscript writing.
2. Leave a margin of at least three inches between the title of the story and top of page and between the title and the first line of the story.
3. If a sentence is too long for one line, divide the sentence between phrases.
4. Place large pictures near the top center of the chart.
5. Leave a margin of one and one half or two inches on the left side of the story.
6. Place smaller pictures along right margin or at bottom of the chart.
7. Children may become restless while waiting for the teacher to write the story carefully on the chart. If so, record the comments quickly and transfer them to the chart later.

Suggestions for language arts activities that can contribute to reading are included later in this chapter. Art and music activities can make a contribution as well as activities in social studies, science, mathematics, health and safety, and play.

Learning centers may be utilized. Suggestions for developing comprehension by using tapes or recordings in a center follow:[98]

Children listen to riddles and identify the appropriate pictures.
Children listen to a story and arrange pictures of the story in proper sequence.

[96] Denise D. Nessel and Margaret B. Jones, *The Language Experience Approach to Reading* (New York: Teachers College, 1981), p. 4.
[97] V. E. Herrick and Marcella Nerbovig, *Using Experience Charts with Children* (Columbus, Ohio: Merrill, 1964).
[98] "Some Suggestions for the Development of Sensory and Language Skills at the Kindergarten and Primary Level" (Rockville, Md.: Montgomery County Public Schools, 1970), p. 71 (mimeographed).

Children listen to a story and respond to questions that may be answered by the selection of an appropriate picture.

Summary.   A prefirst-grade reading program that provides instruction appropriate to the abilities and interests of children may be described as follows.

Abundant exposure to language would be a central goal of such a program. Situations in which children will talk spontaneously are planned. The teacher reads to the children as well as writes down what they say. As children gain in language competence, they approach the time when they are able to learn to read words and comprehend what they have read. Children reach this point at different times. Some are even ready when they first come to school. For this reason a school program offers a spectrum of activities ranging from concrete experiences to adventures in reading to accommodate the different levels of development of its children.[99]

WRITING

A nursery school teacher exclaimed in shocked tones, "Writing! Why the nursery school has nothing to do with writing!" Perhaps she was thinking in terms of formal instruction in writing, or perhaps she did not recognize the opportunities available for developing an awareness of writing and its values.

Before a discussion of how writing begins and the opportunities for beginning, it is important to emphasize the why of writing. The purpose of writing is to communicate or to express an idea. This purpose is so often lost in the beginning stages of practice. Handwriting is a tool, a means to an end. With this purpose in mind, one may examine the beginnings of writing, which occur long before the child takes pencil in hand to write.

The child scribbles and draws pictures. The child can deliver or receive simple notes, invitations, or letters; dictate individually or participate as the group dictates and the teacher writes captions for pictures, experience charts, plans, invitations, thank-you notes, charts about pets, experiments, or some other phase of group interest.

At home the child has had the fun of receiving a letter. In reply he or she has scribbled a note to Grandmother, often talking as he or she writes. The teacher offered to write the name for four-year-old Mary on her letter. The child replied, "You don't need to write it. I can do it. Here it is." (She pointed to a penciled scribble.) That signature sufficed for a while, but there came a time in nursery school when the scribble wasn't sufficient—another child claimed Mary's picture, the one she had painted at the easel. The teacher said, "Next time, I'll write your name on the picture. Then we will know it is yours." Writing was important now— to communicate her name to others.

[99]*Prereading, Bulletin 246* (Rockville, Md.: Montgomery County Public Schools, 1974), p. 101.

For a time, Mary made no attempt to write her own name, but each time she asked the teacher to do it for her. She became aware that her name was written in other places too—her locker, her books, her sweater—and that there were other names that belonged to other children. *Such awareness also contributed to readiness for reading.* She learned that when the teacher wanted to tell Mother about a trip or something else at nursery school, sometimes she used the telephone, but sometimes she wrote her a note either by hand or on the typewriter. The teacher said, "This is a message I have written to your mother."

Along with the experiences that helped establish a need for writing, the child used clay, finger paint, easel paints and brushes, blocks, crayons, hammers and nails, puzzles, paste, and many other media. Through these experiences she was doing exercises that involved arm and finger movement, eye–hand coordination, and muscular control, all of which are essential to learning to write. Mary had these experiences in nursery school. For some children, these experiences with writing do not come in the nursery school or Head Start program but are delayed until kindergarten or even first grade.

Anderson has identified three kinds of experiences that contribute to writing readiness.[100]

1. Manipulative experiences are planned to strengthen the muscles used in writing and to gain control over the writing tools.
2. Many activities are planned to increase the child's vocabulary.
3. Practice activities are related to the basic movements of writing, usually beginning at the chalkboard.

The amount of actual writing will depend on the child's experiences and interest as well as intellectual, physical, and emotional maturity. Actual writing begins with attempts at writing letters, usually the letters in the child's name. The letters written with pencil, crayon, chalk, or paint will probably be of varying size, scattered over the page with little evidence of fine motor control. As this control develops, the child can use smaller spaces and letters. Young children should not be expected to copy letters or words from a large chart or the chalkboard. Eye-hand coordination usually is not fully developed, and it is difficult for the child to look up at the copy and down again at the paper. A copy of the child's name or the needed word should be available at the table.

Formal writing instruction is not included in nursery school and is not usually undertaken in kindergarten. Individual guidance is given the children at the time they ask and are ready for it. Their purposes will suggest the content.

The following questions can be helpful in evaluating a child's readiness for beginning handwriting instruction.

[100] Anderson, op. cit., p. 178–79.

Manuscript writing is recommended for use with young children. Individual guidance in writing is given the child at the time he or she asks and is ready for it. The amount of actual writing will depend upon the child's experiences and interest, his or her intellectual, physical, and emotional maturity.

1. Has the child developed a hand preference?
2. Does the child show dexterity in finger and wrist movement when using scissors and show development of small muscles in manipulative activities?
3. Does the child follow a left-to-right direction when looking at pictures or when writing?
4. In art and building activities does the child show awareness of size, shape, and spatial relationships?
5. Does the child use words that will be needed in handwriting instruction, such as large, small, short, straight, round, and middle?
6. Does the child hold the writing tool properly and in a relaxed manner?
7. Does the child recognize his or her own name?
8. Is the child aware of uses for writing, such as a thank-you note or a message to be taken home?[101]

Stauffer adds that the fundamental aspect of learning the skill of writing is that of a favorable attitude toward writing. He states that in order to achieve this attitude, the first step in handwriting should be to establish a purpose, for example, to place one's name on one's own work.[102] Following are some suggestions for guiding children who indicate readiness.

The first writing instruction should be done on a chalkboard where the child has the space to make use of the large muscles, which are better controlled than some

---

[101] Petty et al., op. cit., p. 244.
[102] Russell G. Stauffer, *The Language-Experience Approach to the Teaching of Reading,* 2d edition (New York: Harper, 1980), p. 127.

small ones. Corrections can be made easily. The first writing should be on unlined paper, such as newsprint (preferably 18 inches by 24 inches). The children may write with crayons, a felt-tip marker, chalk, or pencil. If pencils are used, it is easier for most children to use pencils with large, soft leads. As a child shows evidence of maturity and increased muscular control, fold the paper once in the middle for a crease; then smooth it out. Children may write their name on the top and the bottom. Later, they may use the crease as the line on which to write the letters. After a child manages this easily, the paper may be folded into quarters.

Children should continue to use unlined paper until they are able to meet the following standards reasonably well.

1. Use the correct direction for strokes. (Check method used in the school system.)
2. Observe the size of the letters.
3. Write letters so that they will approximately fill the spaces between folds.
4. Hold the crayon or pencil easily and correctly and move the hand freely.
5. Achieve a degree of body relaxation.[103]
6. Be sure that the child holds the writing tool properly. The tool should be held loosely with the finger above the point, about an inch from the tip.[104]

The first lined paper should have lines spaced one inch apart. Later, paper with narrower lines (one-half inch apart) can be introduced.[105]

Type of writing

Manuscript writing (sometimes called print-script)[106] is recommended for use with young children because

1. Letter forms are based largely on circles and straight lines, which require only simple strokes. This makes writing easier for the child who is just gaining skill in the use of the small finger muscles and who is soon able to use writing for communicative purposes.
2. Letter forms more closely resemble printed forms than do the cursive script letters. The writing helps encourage and reinforce beginning reading, and the child is not confused by two types of writing.

Manuscript writing should be distinguished from the other types of writing in use. It is often referred to as printing. Though some of the letter forms are the same as printing, others are different. Following are listed samples of writing. Note differences in a, g, t, y.

[103] Petty et al., op. cit., pp. 244–245.
[104] Lamme, Linda L., "Handwriting In an Early Childhood Curriculum," in Janet F. Brown, ed., *Curriculum Planning for Young Children* (Washington, D.C.: NAEYC, 1982), pp. 111–112.
[105] Petty et al., op. cit., p. 246.
[106] Anderson, op. cit., p. 176.

Manuscript	and get yes
Print	and get yes
All capitals	AND GET YES
Cursive script	and get yes

In the writing of children's names, capital letters are used by many kindergarten teachers because they are all one size, as **TOM**. The child does not have to make the adjustment in writing between upper- and lower-case letters. First grade teachers sometimes complain because children coming from kindergarten use the capital letters only, and it is necessary for them to change to the manuscript forms. One teacher tried using the manuscript forms with kindergarten children. Lockers and other labels were done in manuscript. When a child asked for help with his or her name or a word, it was written in manuscript. The teacher used upper- and lower-case letters, but no attempt was made to have the child use them. Some children were able to use "tall and small letters," such as the name **Jack**. On the other hand, a child might write **JαCK**, making no difference in the height of the letters, but using the manuscript forms. As the child gained in muscular control, he or she began to use both sizes of letters and gradually reduced their sizes.

Sometimes there was the comment, "That's not the way my mother writes my name." The teacher replied, "There are different ways to write. This is the writing we use in kindergarten." Some children, however, had not been taught to write with only capital letters, and for them to begin with the manuscript forms eliminated one type of writing.

Explain to parents the writing forms being used. It may be a good idea to provide a manuscript alphabet for them. If letter samples are displayed for reference by the children, they should be placed conveniently in the room at the child's eye level.

Reversals

As the young child writes, one often notices that letters or numbers are reversed, as **Ƨ** or **S**. The letters in a word may be written correctly, but in reverse sequence, such as **nhoJ** for **John**. Such errors are common and are often indicative of inexperience in writing from left to right, limited visual memory as to how the number, letter, or word should look, and lack of mature eye-hand coordination. Watch the child as he or she writes. The right-handed child who has not yet learned to begin at the left side of the paper may put his or her pencil down at the extreme right side of the paper. There is no room to go to the right, so the child writes to the left and, as a result, **nhoJ**. This is not strange, nor necessarily indicative of visual difficulty. It does indicate, however, that this child needs guidance in establishing the left-to-right sequence.

As children practice and use writing, with proper guidance, such reversals usually disappear. If they persist, it may be advisable for the child to be referred for a visual examination.

Handedness

Theories regarding handedness appear to be conflicting. This confusion is reflected in practice. One theory holds that handedness is determined by cerebral dominance inherent in the child whereas another takes the position that the child is born with no preference but learns to favor one hand over the other. If one accepts the first theory, then the teacher would not interfere with the child's hand preference. According to the second theory, the child can be taught to use his or her right hand without strain but this should be done before habits are formed that must be broken at a later time.

Olson states that "Perhaps the teaching profession has been oversold through an earlier literature which, often painted the dire effects of handedness on speech and emotion."[107] Consequently, the child has been allowed to select the hand of preference. According to present thinking, this is probably wise.

The teacher, however, may sometimes permit the child to become left-handed accidentally. Some children, upon entering nursery school or kindergarten have not yet developed a hand preference, and as they begin to work with materials, may inadvertently use the left hand. The teacher can suggest, "Try using the scissors in your right hand." If the child makes the transfer easily, well and good. If the child persists in using the left hand, it is probably wise not to insist on changing.

When left-handed writers are allowed to retain their hand preference, they require special instruction in handwriting. Goodson has recommended the following procedures when working with left-handed writers:

1. Have children assume positions that are the opposite of those used by right-handed children, one that is most comfortable to them.
2. The position of the paper is reversed for the left-handed writer. However it may be less slanted and more toward a straight up-and-down position. The direction of the felt-tip marker, chalk, crayon, or pencil is reversed also. The grip is basically the same as that for right-handed students.
3. Seat left-handed children so that the light comes over their left shoulder.
4. Provide many opportunities for writing on the chalkboard.
5. Furnish left-handed children with pencils that have slightly harder lead that will not smear as easily, thus giving less reason for twisting the wrist into the upside-down position.
6. Encourage left-handed children to grasp their writing instrument at least an inch-and-a-half from the point. At this distance, the child can see over or around

[107] Olson, op. cit., p. 88.

his or her hand. A rubber band around the pencil at the point helps the child know where to grasp it.

7. Encourage left-handed children to develop a writing slant that is natural and "feels" good.

8. Avoid any attention that may cause the child to be self-conscious.[108]

By writing the child's name in the left-hand corner of the paper instead of the right, the teacher can give the child a clue as to where to begin to write. Such procedure can also help the child in developing the "left to right" skill needed in reading.

Most children, by the end of kindergarten, will regard writing as a means of communication and will be able to write their names.[109] In addition, the child can also develop visual discrimination, learn letter names, become aware that words are made up of letters and that letters stand for sounds, and gain some knowledge of letter-sound associations.[110] There will be wide variations, however, as with all skills, because of the quality of the program and the teacher, as well as the child and his or her background.

VIEWING

Most teachers of language arts spend much of their time on books and other forms of written expression. However, most of the children spend much time outside of school on television and other nonprint media. Thus, with the growing technology of nonprint media, educators must learn to incorporate these nonprint media into the language arts as well as other content areas of the curriculum. These new media can offer teachers fresh strategies for encouraging creativity, knowledge, and self-expression. If used properly, these new media may aid teachers' goals of teaching literacy. The term *literacy* as used here refers to the ability to communicate through speaking and writing.

Nonprint media should not compete with printed media; they should complement each other. The visual mode should not replace the verbal mode; they should both be used simultaneously to give teachers the full advantage of what both modes have to offer.

Benefits of Nonprint Media in Language Arts.   Nonprint media may be beneficial in the teaching of the language arts in the following ways.

1. A child's ability to read may be enhanced by allowing him or her to follow a printed story while listening to a record or a cassette.

---

[108] Adapted from Roger A. Goodson, *Handwriting* (Alexandria, Va.: Alexandria City Public Schools, 1968).

[109] Anderson, op. cit., pp. 173–174.

[110] Durkin, *Teaching Young Children to Read*, 3rd. ed., op. cit., pp. 165–166.

2. A literature film aids visual interpretation of a book, stimulates interest in reading the story, encourages oral discussion, and stimulates children's imagination.
3. Art films stimulate oral, dramatic, and art expression.[111]

Children enjoy the nonprint media, which have too often been ignored in the learning process.[112] Nonprint media can offer teachers supplemental resources for stories, plays, or skills that are being taught, such as rhyming words. However, teachers should use these nonprint media appropriately. Nonprint media may be used as supplementary activities; they should not be used to replace the teacher. Today computers play an important part in the development of communication skills.

LANGUAGE ACTIVITIES

Suggestions labeled here as "Language Activities" can be used in many different learning situations. One activity can contribute to growth in several of the arts, and, for that reason, activities have not been labeled as appropriate for reading, speaking, listening, or writing. Rather, the activities of storytelling, using poetry, sharing, and dramatizing are discussed, and the ways in which each contributes to growth in the language arts are noted. Certain activities have not been labeled for child development center, day care, nursery school, or kindergarten because of the wide range of individual differences from group to group. Using information pertaining to development and experience of the children in the class, the teacher can select and adapt the activity most appropriate for them.

In working with children from culturally different backgrounds, the teacher will find the language arts activities essential. It is especially important, however, that the teacher utilize the information pertaining to the maturity and experiential background of the children in the selection of the story, poem, book, or materials for dramatic play.

Although activities discussed in this chapter are labeled language arts activities, it is emphasized that these activities are applicable and usable in many different learning situations. Poetry may be read and stories told that relate to social studies, mathematics, and other subject areas. Books with science content may be read to the children. Role-playing and dramatization are techniques useful in a variety of learning situations.

STORYTELLING

Young children today enjoy a good story just as children always have. Although the content of the story may vary from generation to generation, the use of storytelling

[111] Iris Tiedt, "Input, Media Special," *Language Arts*, **53** (Feb. 1976), p. 119.
[112] James R. Squire, *The Teaching of English* (Chicago: U. of Chicago, 1977), pp. 104–105.

to entertain, to teach, and to develop appreciation of literature continues to be an important art.

Although many other values are recognized, the discussion in this part of the chapter will relate primarily to storytelling as an activity that offers opportunities for developing skills in the language arts. Specifically, the child may learn to listen and have experience in speaking while talking about the story or telling original stories. The child may learn to keep in mind a sequence of ideas, increase vocabulary, and enlarge the background of experiences. These points are emphasized, not to limit the creative possibilities of storytelling or formalize the art, but rather to indicate ways in which this creative activity can make a contribution—a fact often overlooked.

Teachers without training in speech or dramatics may hesitate to undertake telling stories to children. Others have questions regarding the selection and use of stories. Rather than use a general discussion for guidance, we have identified questions that are often asked in regard to storytelling and discussed suggested procedures.

Selecting an Appropriate Story for Young Children.   A checklist that may be used by the teacher in the selection of stories includes the following criteria:

1. A simple, well-developed plot, centered in one main sequence of events, structured so that a child can anticipate to some degree the outcome of events, with action predominant. A slight surprise element which makes the children wonder what will happen next can add much to the story.
2. A large amount of direct conversation.
3. Use of repetition, rhyme, and catch phrases that the child memorizes quickly and easily.
4. Use of carefully chosen, colorful language.
5. Situations involving familiar happenings. The new, unusual, and different may be included, but there must be enough of the familiar with which the child can identify. The "familiar happenings" will not be the same for all children. Children from culturally different homes have often had different experiences. In selecting stories for them, the teacher should consider their experiential background.
6. Simple and satisfying climax.
7. One main character with whom the child can easily identify. Too many characters can be confusing.
8. A variety of ethnic, cultural, and racial backgrounds. Such stories should present realistic pictures, not ridiculous stereotypes of racial or ethnic groups.

Children's books are often a source of stories to be told. Criteria listed for selecting a story are also applicable to the contents of a book. In addition, the following questions may be helpful.[113]

1. Does the book help the child gain some insight into his or her own personal life or the lives of other people?

[113] Mary Hill Arbuthnot, *Children and Books*, 3d ed. (Glenview, Ill.: Scott, Foresman, 1964), p. 19.

2. Does the plot or action of the story hold the child's interest?
3. Does the content add to the child's joy in living and a feeling that life is good?
4. Are the characters honest, well described, unforgettable?
5. Does the story include humor, dramatic elements, and beauty of language appropriate for the child and the story?
6. Is the information accurate? Will the information help expand the child's experiential background?

These questions should be considered as generalizations and not applied too rigidly. There may be books or stories which do not measure up in every detail, yet may be good for a special child or occasion.

Deciding whether to tell or to read a story

The question is often asked as to whether a story should be read or told to the child. As we examine the values involved, there appears to be a place for both telling and reading. Telling the story enables the teacher to establish and maintain eye contact with the children and thus encourage listening. Because no script is involved, the teacher can easily make explanations or adaptations in length or vocabulary for the children. The story that is told seems more direct, informal, and intimate than one that is read.

Reading the story aloud, however, does have its advantages, especially when the style is an intrinsic part of the story.[114] Reading aloud also has the advantage of the example of the teacher reading from the book, helping the child to recognize that reading can be fun and to associate pleasure with reading. It is important that the teacher set a good example in holding the book and turning the pages, seated so that the book is at the eye level of the children. The teacher should be familiar enough with the story to be able to read it well and with proper expression. Reading should not, however, be a crutch to avoid the effort of learning to tell the story.

Preparing and telling a story

Some teachers say that it is hard for them to learn to tell a story. Storytellers do not agree on a fixed method of learning a story, but memorization is not always necessary. In memorizing the exact wording of a story, the teller does not lose any of the original meaning, but often memorization results in recitation.[115] The following suggestions for preparing and telling a story may be helpful:

1. Picture the story to yourself because the story should be learned as a series of pictures. Read the story slowly, forming a picture in your mind of each character

[114] Ramon Ross, *Storyteller*, 2d ed. (Columbus, Ohio: Merrill, 1980), p. 200.
[115] Ibid., p. 44.

and event. Close the book, and think through the story in terms of the pictures you have made. Read the story again for language. The words fit themselves to the pictures and the story takes form.[116]

2. Use direct quotations when a character speaks.

3. Plan a good beginning to gain the attention of the audience. Avoid unnecessary descriptions and explanations.

4. Use a conversational tone of voice, speaking slowly and distinctly. Avoid excessive use of *and, er*. Avoid a sing-song, uneven tone and a voice pitch that is too high. Too many gestures tend to detract from the story. Avoid exaggerated facial expressions.

5. Look directly at the children. Include all members of the group, not just those directly in front of you.

6. Sit on a low chair.

7. Use timing effectively; vary the tempo. As action increases and things begin to happen, hurry the tempo. Before a moment of question, surprise, or awe, a pause can be most effective.

8. Keep the story or the listening period within the limits of the child's attention span. A range of 7 to 20 minutes has been identified for the preschool period.

9. Following the story, the children may have a few questions or comments. Take time for these, but do not force discussion by use of questions. This procedure often detracts from the child's enjoyment of the story. If, during the story, a child interrupts to relate an incident, one should encourage him or her to keep it until the story is finished. Occasionally, such a contribution is valuable and should be allowed, but many such interruptions can spoil the story.

Helping children listen to the story

Often children want to crowd around the teacher to see the pictures as the story is read or told. The teacher is concerned with getting them to sit down and listen. Before beginning the story, arrange for the children to sit in comfortable positions, in a group or in a semicircle, in front of the storyteller. Be sure they can hear and see easily. They may be seated either on the floor, on a rug, or in chairs.

Give the children an opportunity to see and enjoy the illustrations as the story is being told. This may be done in several ways. In telling a story, the teacher can hold the book in front and slightly to the side, always at the eye-level of the children. Using the book in this way enables the child to see the pictures while the story is being told and helps to hold attention.

The teacher may not find it necessary to show the pictures throughout the story. She can show the picture and say, "See the picture. Now I will tell you the story," or, "Just as soon as I tell you a part of the story, I will show you the picture." The

[116] Ruth Sawyer, *The Way of the Storyteller* (New York: Viking, 1962), pp. 131–148.

teacher then pauses briefly at the appropriate time to share the picture. The teacher who forgets to show the picture invites trouble. The child who crowds up may be reminded quietly to sit down so that everyone can see.

When reading the story, the teacher may also hold the book to the side to show the pictures to the children. If this practice is followed, the teacher will need to group the children so that all may see and so that it will not be necessary to turn the face and voice away from them. As the children become able to listen to the longer story with more plot, the teacher may not find it necessary to show the picture while reading.

Using aids in storytelling

Aids can be used to make the story more effective and to offer variety. Perhaps the most effective of all the visual aids is the flannel board if it is used correctly. With an enthusiastic, well-prepared storyteller, the children seem unaware of the constant hand movement and become absorbed in the story being told. Flannel symbols provide the foreground for exciting visual adventures as the child uses his or her imagination to create wholeness. Figures cut from felt or flannel can be used on the board. Pictures made or cut out by an adult or the children can be prepared by gluing strips of sandpaper to the back of the picture.[117] Be careful not to overdo, keeping in mind that children can create whatever is not there.

Puppets are another aid to storytelling. Puppets are effective when the storyteller moves them and speaks their lines in full view. The children will come to ignore the presence of the teller just as they ignored the hands in the flannel board presentation if the storyteller is well-prepared and enthusiastic.[118] Various materials can be used in making puppets, but perhaps the easiest is the tennis-ball puppet. Punch a hole in the ball for a finger, and decorate the rest of the ball like the head of the character desired. The flannel board and the puppets can be left out for the children to use in retelling or creating stories.

Using fairy stories or tales

The fairy tale, according to Bettelheim, is a unique form of art. Children can be entertained by the fairy tale, helped to understand themselves and develop their personalities, and encouraged to learn the advantages of moral behavior.[119]

Bettelheim says that we cannot know the age at which one child may be interested in a particular fairy tale. Usually the parents, teacher, or other adults begin

[117] Ross, op. cit., pp. 107–110.
[118] Ibid., pp. 140–143.
[119] Bruno Bettelheim, *The Uses of Enchantment—The Meaning and Importance of Fairy Tales* (New York: Knopf, 1976), pp. 12–13.

Using the earphones these children listen to the story while looking at the illustrations in the book.

by reading or telling to children a tale that was their favorite. This tale, however, may not be appropriate for a particular child or group of children. The reactions of the children should be noted, especially those of younger children.[120]

As a rule, the traditional fairy tales with cruel witches and stepmothers, kings, and queens are not used with young children. The child at this age usually is not yet able to distinguish easily between fact and fancy, and the gruesome details, easily accepted later as "make-believe," often trouble the young child.

This does not mean, however, that fanciful tales are to be omitted. Some stories relate imaginative experiences of children. In many children's favorites, animals are elevated to the human level in much the same way that children elevate their stuffed animals and pets. Imaginative experiences of children abound in fanciful tales. Fables, however, are rarely suitable for young children. In some instances, if the moralizing is omitted, the storytelling value is high.

[120]Ibid., pp. 17–18.

USE OF BOOKS

Not by accident does a child develop a love for books, a feeling that books can be friends and companions, an awareness of the fun and enjoyment that can come from books, an appreciation of good literature, the knowledge that books can be sources of information, and an interest in caring for books. All these attitudes, which it is hoped the young child will develop, evolve as the child has many pleasurable experiences with books both at home and at school.

Opportunities for the children to listen to and enjoy stories, read and told, and also to handle, use, and love books can help them to learn that reading can be fun and to become interested in learning to read. In the selection of a book, the contents, illustrations, and physical makeup are important items to be considered.

Types and content of books

Young children should be introduced to a variety of types of literature. These types include picture books, Mother Goose rhymes, books of poetry and counting, concept, and alphabet books. Also, children should have books that are informative, humorous, and inspirational. There should be books about animals, everyday experiences and those that stimulate creative expression.

Illustrations

Children look for illustrations that interpret the story. The content, mood, and the feeling of the illustrations should be relevant and should match the plot and tone of the story. Children also prefer the text and picture to be synchronized. Action shots are almost always enjoyable, as are brightly colored pictures. Black-and-white and muted-color illustrations should not be excluded, however, and details should never be minimized. Children notice virtually every aspect of an illustration and frequently read their books by means of pictures.[121]

Format

Children need sturdy, firmly stitched bindings for their books. The covers should be attractive in order to encourage the child to care for them. A binding that comes off the book at the first careless handling can be most discouraging for the child. It is well to talk with children about how books should be cared for and where they are kept.

[121] Zena Sutherland and May Hill Arbuthnot, *Children and Books*, 5th ed. (Glenview, Ill.: Scott, Foresman, 1977), pp. 113, 114.

Among the collection of books are those for holidays and special occasions that will not be used as often as some of the others. These books may be purchased in the less expensive editions, but the same criteria for content and illustrations apply. For the favorites that are used day in and day out, a good binding is an economy. The pages should be of strong, heavy paper to prevent their tearing easily as the child turns them. The size of type and spacing of words are important.

Most of the books should be light enough and of a size that is easy for the child to handle. Some large books may be included for occasional use and enjoyment on the rug or the table.

Using book collections

The well-selected collection of books is not enough. For it to be effective in the lives of children, it must be well used. All of the books need not be displayed all the time. Change the books on the library table and in the library corner often. Unless this is done, the child may become so accustomed to seeing the book that it becomes a fixture rather than an exciting adventure. Display books attractively on a table or on a low shelf. Flowers, a plant, or cutouts of characters in the story may be used to advantage.

Manipulative objects and figures representing various characters may be placed on or near the book display. Use of these materials can allow children to become more involved with the characters and the plot line by giving them direct hands-on experiences.

Plan ahead so that the time spent in looking at or using books becomes important. Avoid using books when there is nothing else to do or just to "fill in." For example, the child may say to the teacher, "I've finished. I don't know what to do." Too often, an indifferent reply is made, "Go and get a book," and the child responds in the same indifferent manner.

Arrange for children to borrow a favorite book to take home and share with their families. In one kindergarten, choosing a book is part of getting ready to go home. If the child wants a book, she or he brings it to the teacher, and together they write the name on the book list. The list is posted, and when the book is returned, the child checks his or her name off the list. Such a procedure helps children to develop responsibility in using and caring for books. Children may be encouraged to bring books from home to share with the group. A visit to the library can help to develop an interest in books and an understanding of how books are cared for. The teacher can provide suggested book lists for parents. The books may be purchased or secured from the local or school library.

Bulletin boards may be used to display children's paintings, drawings, or other art products of their favorite book. Jackets of favorite books may be used in the display.

The teacher, then, must not only select a good collection of books but must use them effectively with children. Personal interest in and knowledge of the classics as well as current books, skill in using books with and reading them to children, and a true appreciation and enjoyment of books determine in large measure the extent to which children gain the values that may be derived from books. In selecting books for the collection, the teacher may consult several sources:

1. Published book lists and catalogs. One that is inexpensive and revised frequently is *A Bibliography of Books for Children.*[122] The American Association of School Librarians and the Association for Childhood Education International have published *Excellent Paperbacks for Children.* The list is revised frequently.[123] The Children's Book Council publishes a Book Calendar each year with current titles and literary reviews.[124] R. R. Bowker and Company publishes a list annually of the 4,000 best books for preschool through grade 7.[125]

2. Reviews of books for children published in professional periodicals. The teacher may supplement the nursery school or kindergarten collection by borrowing books reviewed from a library. In some cities a teacher may borrow as many as twenty books for a two-week period. When these are returned, others can be selected.

Movement and children's literature

Huck suggests that basic rhythmic movements may be introduced through Mother Goose rhymes. "Jack and Jill" may be used for children to walk to, "Ride a Cock Horse" for galloping, "Jack Be Nimble" for jumping, and "Wee Willie Winkie" for running.[126] Actions and exercises can be created to accompany other poems also.

POETRY

Experiences with poetry can be happy and spontaneous ones for children. They enjoy the sounds around them; create sounds; laugh at unusual combinations of words; sense the rhythm of running, skipping, and speaking. The spontaneous language of children is often poetic in nature. Dorothy, telling about the little bird that had fallen out of the nest, said, "The little bird was shivering with scaredness."

[122] *A Bibliography of Books for Children* (Washington, D.C.: Association for Childhood Education International, 3615 Wisconsin Ave., NW, 20016, 1980).

[123] *Excellent Paperbacks for Children* (Washington, D.C.: Association for Childhood Education International, 3615 Wisconsin Ave., NW, 20016, 1978).

[124] *Children's Book Council Calendar* (New York: Children's Book Council, Inc., 67 Irving Place, 10003, 1982).

[125] *Best Books for Children* (New York: R. R. Bowker and Co., 1180 Avenue of the Americas, 10036, 1982).

[126] Charlotte S. Huck, *Children's Literature in the Elementary School* 3d ed. (New York: Holt, 1979), p. 664.

Poetry, if well selected and correctly used, can help the child to listen carefully, to learn new words and ways of expressing one's feelings, to develop increased auditory awareness or acuity, to improve the quality of one's own voice, and to feel secure in the group as one participates in saying poetry with the group. Poetry can bring laughter and happiness to the child.

The success of the teacher in presenting poetry to children depends on several factors: (1) the selection of verses that are appropriate for the age of the child and for use in a wide variety of situations, (2) the teacher's own appreciation of poetry and the manner in which she shares poetry with the children, and (3) the extent to which poetry is used.

Selecting poetry for use with children

Children enjoy a wide variety of poems, including those about the here and now; situations familiar to the children—playmates, clothing, and pets; poems about nature—the seasons, the wind, the falling leaves or signs of spring; poems that are fanciful and imaginative; holiday poems; humorous verses, and those filled with the repetition of unusual sounds with a singing quality. One should use poems related to the experience at hand, but it is undesirable to force correlations that do not fit.

The content of the poem should be sufficiently related to the child's experiences that he or she can understand something of the meaning expressed by the words.[127] How many children today are likely to understand Stevenson's likening the sound of the wind to the passing of "ladies skirts across the grass"?

Jacobs says:

Children enjoy good poetry that
Gives them an exhilarating sense of melodious movement.
Makes the everyday experiences of life vibrant.
Tells wonderful stories.
Releases health-giving laughter.
Carries them into extravagant or fanciful situations.
Extends their appreciation of their natural world.
Creates memorable personages or characters.
Sings its way into their minds and memories.[128]

Sharing poetry with children

First of all, if children are to appreciate and enjoy poetry, it is imperative that the teacher appreciate poetry and share his or her enjoyment in presenting the poems

---

[127] Arbuthnot, op. cit., p. 195.
[128] L. B. Jacobs, "Enjoying Poetry with Children," in *Literature with Children* (Washington, D.C.: ACEI, 1972), pp. 33–34.

to them. Arbuthnot suggests that in exploring a new poem, the teacher read it aloud first in order to become familiar with the words, mood, and tempo.[129] Unless this is done, the teacher may not find the sound pattern or rhythm of the poem and as a result the reading will be dull and meaningless.

The poem may either be read or shared from memory. The teacher who knows a number of poems can share them informally with a small group or even with one child on the playground, while taking a walk, observing a pet, or whenever there is an opportunity. But no one teacher can memorize all the poems that will be needed. Familiarity with children's poetry and knowing where to find it will mean being able to share the poem at a later time, merely recalling the incident or mood to which it refers. However, not all poetry should be related to some thing or incident. Sometimes it is shared just for fun or pleasure.

Memorizing poetry

Children have often been turned away from poetry when forced to memorize poems. A teacher who reads well-selected poetry to children in a simple, natural, and appreciative manner will soon find that the children will "say" the poem while it is being read. Many children will learn poems in this manner without the pressure to memorize.

Choral speaking (or a verse choir) for young children is largely speaking poetry in unison. Children may experiment with different ways of saying a verse once it has been learned in the manner suggested earlier. For instance, the boys may say the verse; then the girls. Use questions such as, "How does it sound?" If questions or conversation are used, as in the verse "Sing-Song" by Christina Rossetti, try having one child speak those lines and the entire group the remaining lines. Some poems may be broken up and each child say a line or two. Mother Goose rhymes such as "Pease Porridge Hot" or "This Little Pig" are examples.

SHARING TIME AND GROUP DISCUSSION

The word *sharing* is often used in nursery school and kindergarten with reference to the use of toys and materials. It implies the willingness to "take turns" or to "let Jane have some clay." Sharing may also refer to communicating—between children or between teacher and child. For the child who is beginning nursery school, this communication may involve only a few words accompanied by a facial expression that emphasizes the thought. On the first cool morning, Mary arrived dressed in a new blue sweater. "Look," she said as she displayed the sweater, her eyes sparkling and her face alight with an expression of joy and well-being. As this informal com-

---

[129] Arbuthnot, op. cit., p. 205.

municating and sharing continues, the child uses more words to express her thoughts. As children become more secure in a group situation, they want and need to talk together, and a time in the school day for planning and sharing may be designated. This activity is usually considered appropriate for kindergarten groups although some more mature nursery classes may begin such a period. The time for beginning such a group activity, however, will depend on the children involved—their interests, attention span, and readiness to participate in a group situation.

This period for sharing often goes by the name "Show and Tell," which, as such, has been somewhat discredited. Such a name implies an activity in which the child shows some object and tells about it. There are those who claim that this is an artificial situation and becomes a monotonous routine, thus losing its language value. The activity, however, allows the child to express himself or herself and to exercise the cognitive ability to organize his or her thought processes.

Sharing time implies communication. Objects may be shown and talked about, but plans, incidents, and news may be discussed too by the teacher as well as by the children. Discussion time requires teacher planning and evaluation. It is problem-centered. Plans may be made for a trip or a special project for the morning. The choice of activities may be discussed. This type of sharing time and discussion can be rich in opportunities for developing skills in the language arts. The child can learn to

1. Speak distinctly and clearly.
2. Speak in front of a group.
3. Tell an incident in sequence.
4. Listen politely.
5. Take turns in speaking.
6. Speak in complete sentences.

Encouraging children to participate

Some children never speak in the group, and the question is often asked, "How may they be encouraged to participate?"

First, it is important to determine why the child does not participate. Is he or she afraid of a group situation? Could it be that the child has nothing to share? Is the child bored, uninterested? Not knowing the other children well, might she or he feel no need to communicate with them? The answers will depend on the reason.

Only gradually does a child come to feel secure in a group situation. Both Jennie and Gloria seemed to remain on the fringes. Fear of the group will not be overcome by forcing participation. Rather, the teacher may encourage sharing with them at times other than the organized period. Such flexibility is better for the children because it is important for every child to share during the day, at different times, and in different ways. One-to-one and small group interaction is much more effective for the children, and wait time is not wasted. Gradually, one or two children may be included by comments such as, "That is a beautiful book. Let's show it to Joe," or "Such good news! Tell Bob." The number of individuals may be expanded to form small groups, gradually increasing the size. One must remember that sharing does not always mean speaking. First attempts may involve showing a book or toy without a comment. With maturity and security, speaking will come later.

For a child who has nothing to share, the teacher may be alert during the day to help the child identify something worthy of sharing with the group. For example, as the child arrives in the morning, he or she tells the teacher that on the way to school there was a squirrel scampering up a tree. A few questions, such as, "What was it carrying in its mouth?" may help the child clarify and identify the details of the incident. The teacher may say, "That is a very interesting story. Please tell the other children at sharing time."

A child may become bored or lose interest because he or she does not have an opportunity to speak. This can happen when a few children are permitted to dominate the situation, speaking loudly and often. The teacher can help these children learn to take turns. A reminder, "You had a turn, Joe," may help. Consistently, the teacher must remind the children of those who have shared and those who still need a turn. A child with several items to share may need to be reminded, "You have told us about one thing. The other children need a turn before you tell us more."

Encouraging good habits of listening

The teacher may refer to the suggestions given earlier in this chapter regarding listening. In addition, it is important to help children learn what is involved in good listening. The teacher may say to the child who is ready to share, "Look around the circle. See if everyone is ready to listen before you begin to speak."

DRAMATIZATION

The word *creativity* is often used only in connection with the arts. The discussions on using books, poetry, storytelling, and the creative arts present creativity as related to these areas. Many activities considered simple and unimaginative may offer opportunities for creative expression. If language expression is to be creative, it must be based on thoughts and ideas that are the child's own. The child should therefore be given opportunities for experiences to develop many ideas and thoughts. In the language arts, the creative expression of the child may take many forms. Some children may express their feelings in pantomime whereas others may use puppets. Dramatization can offer many activities through which creativity in oral language may be encouraged.[130]

Dramatization may include dramatic play, creative dramatics, and using puppets. Though there is no clear-cut distinction, each has a unique characteristic. The relationships and differences are discussed in the following sections.

Dramatic play

Dramatic play is spontaneous and free of teacher direction. As McCaslin points out, it is fragmentary and momentary.[131] This type of play is one in which the child may try living life as an adult; find out how it feels to have certain responsibilities, such as feeding the baby or cooking dinner; clarify concepts regarding the role of mother, the fire fighter, or the doctor; and practice certain basic language skills, such as speaking, using conversation, listening, learning new words, clarifying the meaning

[130] H. A. Greene and W. T. Petty, *Developing Language Skills in the Elementary Schools*, 5th ed. (Boston: Allyn, 1975), pp. 179–183.

[131] Nellie McCaslin, *Creative Drama in the Classroom*, 3d ed. (New York: Longman, 1980), p. 6.

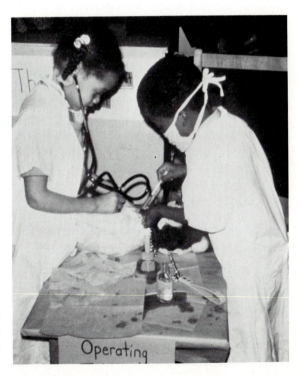

In dramatic play children may try living as adults and find out how it feels to have certain responsibilities. In this instance, Portia is the doctor.

of words; and social amenities. Dramatic play offers opportunities for children to come to understand their world and the people in it. In this section, the focus is on the aspects of dramatic play as they relate to the language arts.

The teacher's responsibility includes providing many interesting opportunities for the children because the child's creative efforts are limited to experience—trips, contacts with various people, recordings, books, pictures, and films—and providing space, materials, and time for the activity. Once this has been done, usually nothing more is required. If a child does not participate readily, the teacher may help the child enter the group by suggesting some role the child can assume. Conversation between the teacher and child can yield leads to dramatic play and to more talking among the children.

The teacher does not direct the activity. The children do this. The teacher seeks to guide the dramatic play so that the experience is satisfying to the children. This means that the teacher may need to help in the settlement of a dispute and solving problems that arise. Timing of teacher help is very important lest the play become disrupted and the children discouraged. The teacher also observes possible leads for further study and notes concepts that may need to be clarified.

John, Lisa, and Myron, who were building a train of large blocks, were engaged in a heated argument as to the location of the engine. John, the engineer, insisted that it was first, but Myron and Lisa were certain that it should be after the coaches. In talking with the children, it became evident that they did not know the purpose or the names of the various cars on the train or the people who work on the train. Here was a lead. A trip, a film, pictures, stories, models were all used to clarify the concept.

Puppets

Puppets are often used by children in dramatic play or dramatizations. The child who hesitates to speak with others or before the group may speak freely through a puppet. With young children, the puppets are generally used informally without screens or stories. Usually, the conversation is supplied by the individual child or perhaps two children. Puppets are made available, and the child chooses to use them as he or she wishes or needs to do so.

Puppets for the young are kept simple. Pictures of people or animals glued on sticks, sacks filled with air and with ends twisted to make a handle, or commercial hand puppets are all useful.

Creative dramatics

In this group activity, an experience is acted out by the children as they are guided in thinking, feeling, and creating their own dialogue and action. There are no lines to be memorized, no formal audience, no costumes, or technical aids. The dramatization may be original as to the idea or it may be based on a poem or story written by someone else. Creative dramatics for young children has four major objectives: artistic exposure, social awareness, expressive development, and enjoyment.[132] Creative drama can encourage children to develop the ability to use the language arts skills of speaking, listening, and making auditory discriminations. Activities such as pantomime, acting out plays or stories, puppetry, and storytelling may be introduced.[133]

As children play out appropriate stories and verses, they enjoy and learn to appreciate good literature. Lease and Siks offer suggestions for introducing creative dramatics to young children.[134] They suggest that the teacher begin with

1. Rhythmic movement. Create the mood by several statements before asking the question. "Let's pretend that we are going outside to pick up nuts. Let's see how many nuts we can find. What is one way you can look for the nuts?" Some may crawl on hands and knees; others walk slowly, looking down on the ground; some skip; others run.

   The children may also do characterizations in rhythmic movements. For instance, they may characterize animals by the way they walk and sound, the weather, the wind blowing, rain falling.

2. Songs. Many children's songs suggest action, pantomime, or characterizations. The teacher may sing while the children do the actions. The teacher may use a recording to which the children respond or let one group of children sing while the remainder pantomime. Singing games offer opportunities for beginning experiences in this area also.

3. Finger plays. As children participate in finger plays, vivid pictures may be formed in their minds, and they may be guided to feel and act as characters felt in the finger play.

4. Dramatic play.

5. Pantomime poetry or verse. Nursery rhymes, Mother Goose, and other poems that are short, the characterizations limited and the action direct, are appropriate.

   After children have had considerable experience in the activities already described, they are ready to play the role of an individual character. The teacher selects a verse already familiar to the group, for instance, "The Caterpillar," and says it to the children.

> Fuzzy wuzzy, creepy crawly
> Caterpillar funny,
> You will be a butterfly
> When the days are sunny

---

[132] Nellie McCaslin, *Children and Drama*, 2d ed. (New York: Longman, 1981), p. 16.

[133] Donna E. Norton, *The Effective Teaching of Language Arts* (Columbus, Ohio: Merrill, 1980), pp. 57–83.

[134] Ruth G. Lease and Geraldine B. Siks, *Creative Dramatics in Home, School, and Community* (New York: Harper, 1952), p. 37.

> Winging, flinging, dancing, springing
> Butterfly so yellow,
> You were once a caterpillar,
> Wiggly, wiggly fellow.[135]

Then the teacher may say something like this: "Here is some nice green grass. Let's all be caterpillars crawling on the grass." After the children have enjoyed being caterpillars, the teacher may say, "What creepy, crawly caterpillars. Now you have become a butterfly. How do you think the butterfly feels? Let's all be butterflies here on the grass." The questions will lead to lively discussion and creative thinking. It is important, however, that the teacher not spend too long in talking and planning with very young children. They are eager to *do*, to play the role. The teacher in talking about the characters, will do well to discuss how the butterfly feels rather than what it says or does. As Lease and Siks say, "When children are thinking and feeling in character, the action will be spontaneous."[136]

Following group partcipation in the roles of the different characters, one child will be chosen to be the butterfly and one to be the caterpillar. This may be repeated several times with different children playing the different characters. Some children may pantomime a Mother Goose rhyme, for example, "Little Miss Muffett," while others try to guess what it is.

6. Dramatize or play a story. Folk tales provide stories that are short and in which the actions and feelings of the characters are easily identified. Suggestions pertaining to pantomime are relevant here. Once the children are familiar with the story, the teacher may plan briefly with the children for one scene of the story. Do not try to plan for the entire story at one time. Characters are identified and children asked to play the different roles. They may be helped to assume roles of the different characters by questions directed to the entire group. For instance, if the story were *Three Billy Goats Gruff*, comments such as the following might be used. "What kind of goat was the first billy goat? How did he feel when he heard the Old Troll? Tell us about the Old Troll. What kind of creature was he?"

Emphasis is not placed on remembering what the character says. Once the child has a feeling for the character and senses how the character feels, then the child's speech as well as actions will be spontaneous. The child may easily forget *what* to say if taught only the words. If one is playing the *role*, then there are several different ways, however, to express the character's feelings. The child is seldom at a loss for words.

TEACHER INVENTORY

The confident teacher of young children possesses certain information important to the child's development in the language arts. Anderson has developed a self-evaluation form for language teachers, a partial inventory that may be used in di-

---

[135] Lillian Schulz, "The Caterpillar," in ACEI, *Sung Under the Silver Umbrella* (New York: Macmillan, 1962), p. 77.
[136] Lease and Siks, op. cit., p. 39.

recting efforts toward improving one's understanding, knowledge, and skills. An adaptation of the form follows.[137]

Do I know

how children master language before coming to school?
how language instruction fits into the school day?
books that should be read to children?
how to share a picture book with little children?
how to direct children in a simple verse choir?
how to help a left-handed child learn to write well?
why I teach handwriting as I do?
why it is important to listen to children?

Can I

select and purchase books intelligently for a center for young children?
hold children's attention as I read or tell a story?
involve children in dramatic play and creative dramatics?
teach a finger play to a child and explain its importance to the parents?
read poetry well?
use manuscript (print-script) writing?
write legibly so as not to be embarrassed when writing a note to a parent?

If some of your answers are "No," you should devote special attention to the discussion and practice the suggestions found in this text.

SUMMARY

Teachers who have used activities such as stories, poetry, and dramatic play without analyzing, understanding, and noting ways in which they contribute to growth in the language arts may not be articulate in resisting questionable practices. Table 8–1 summarizes the contributions of each activity included in the chapter, not to prove the academic value of the activities described, but to emphasize the fact that creative, spontaneous language experiences can also contribute to foundation learnings.

Suggested Activities

1. Listen to and record the speech of three four-year-old children for a period of fifteen minutes each. Compare as to the total number of words spoken, the number of different words spoken, the length of the sentences used, the interests revealed, and consonant sounds that were mispronounced. Identify possible reasons for similarities or differences.

---

[137] Anderson, op. cit., pp. 8–9.

Table 8–1
Contributions of Language Arts Activities

	Reading Readiness	Listening	Speaking	Writing
1. Dramatization	Visual and auditory discrimination, enriched vocabulary; clarification of concepts; interest in books and reading.	Appreciation and enjoyment of good literature; listening while others speak.	Discussion and planning, speaking in front of group, taking turns in speaking; feeling secure and a member of the group.	Recognition of value of writing; list of characters on chart.
2. Poetry	Auditory acuity; hear likenesses and differences in sounds.	Appreciation and enjoyment of poetry.	Encourages distinct speech; encourages speaking before the group; choral reading may help the child feel a part of the group.	Use of writing to record one's ideas.
3. Storytelling	Experience in listening; enriched vocabulary; clarification of concepts; interest in books and reading.	Appreciation and enjoyment of good literature.	Conversation about the story.	Recognizing that a story is recorded for others to share at a later date.
4. Sharing	Enriches vocabulary; clarifies concepts; encourages listening and keeping in mind a sequence of ideas.	Experience in listening to other children.	Takes turns in speaking; speaks distinctly and clearly; tells an incident in sequence; speaks in front of group; speaks in complete sentences; develops a sentence sense; takes part in group planning; asks questions.	Awareness of importance of writing through dictating plans or invitations.

2. On the basis of your observation of the children's speech, plan a language learning activity for one of the children. Use the activity with the child. Evaluate.

3. Observe in a center. Record incidents in which the teacher elaborated on a child's comment in order to increase the child's vocabulary.

4. Observe in a kindergarten. Note activities and experiences used to help the child understand that "writing is communicating."

5. Observe a kindergarten teacher, and note the ways by which he or she gained the attention of the group of children.

6. Select, prepare, and tell a story appropriate for a four- or five-year-old group of children. Evaluate your performance in terms of the criteria in this chapter. Select another story and prepare figures for use on a flannel board to accompany it.

7. Begin to keep a poetry file. Choose three topics appropriate for the young child, such as Play, Bed-Time, Holidays, Minorities. For each topic, select and record several poems.

8. Examine a collection of books for young children. Select and evaluate three each of picture books and books that deal with concept development, holidays, and minority groups, in terms of criteria presented in this chapter.

9. Visit a center for young children, and become acquainted with several of the children. For the group, select a story, and read it to them. On another occasion, select a poem, and say or share it with the group. Evaluate.

10. Observe young children engaged in dramatic play. Note the roles that the children seem to be assuming and the topics for play. Compare your observations with those of others in your class. Discuss differences observed. Note the teacher's role. Note materials provided for dramatic play.

11. Visit a materials center or a distributor's display. Examine current kits and packaged materials for young children in reading, writing, speaking, and language development. Evaluate in terms of the goals of your center.

12. View the film *Dramatic Play, An Integrative Process* (Campus Films, 20 East 46th Street, New York, N.Y. 10017, 1972). Compare with own observations.

13. Observe a total group situation in the kindergarten. Identify children who had difficulty in listening. Discuss possible causes of the difficulty.

14. Practice manuscript writing. Write a note to a friend using this type of writing.

15. Record an experience story dictated by a child. Transfer the story to chart paper.

16. View the film, *Foundations of Reading and Writing.* Campus Films, 2 Overhill Road, Scarsdale, N.Y. 10583. Compare with your observations.

17. Make several different kinds of puppets for children's use.

18. View the following: *The Great Big Enormous Turnip* by Alexei Tolstoy, Weston Woods Studios Sound-Filmstrip 140 and *Where The Wild Things Are* by Maurice Sendak, Weston Woods Sound-Filmstrip 84, Weston Wood Studios, Weston Woods, Conn. (nd) Evaluate and use one with a group of young children.

19. View the film *Reading: A Language Experience Approach* by Robert J. Canady (Birminghan: Promethean Films South, 1980).

20. Listen to Children's Book Council. *Prelude Series of Tapes: Think-Seminars on Using Books Creatively.* 1981 Cassette Tapes. Select a book and use it with a small group of children, as suggested on one of the tapes. Evaluate your performance.

Related Readings

Anderson, P. S. "Rediscovering Children's Literature." *Language Skills in Elementary Education*, 2d ed. New York: Macmillan, 1972. Pp. 121–168.

———. "Speech and Listening." *Language Skills in Elementary Education*, 2d ed. New York: Macmillan, 1972. Pp. 57–118.

Baker, D. *Functions of Folk and Fairy Tales.* Washington, D.C.: ACEI, 1981.

Ballenger, M. "Reading in the Kindergarten: Comment." *Child. Educ.* **59**:3 (1983), pp. 186–187.

Bissex, Glenda L. *GNYS AT WORK: A Child Learns to Read and Write.* Cambridge, Mass: Harvard U. Press, 1980.

Bussis, Anne M. "Burn It At The Casket: Research, Reading Instruction, and Children's Learning of the First R." *Phi Delta Kappan* **64**:4 (1982), pp. 237–241.

Cazden, Courtney B. (ed.). *Language in Early Childhood Education.* Washington, D.C.: NAEYC, 1972.

———. "Studies of Early Language Acquisition," *Child. Educ.*, **46**:3 (1969), pp. 127–131.

Ching, Doris C. *Reading and the Bilingual Child.* Newark, Del.: International Reading Association, 1976.

Chomsky, Carol. "Write Now, Read Later." In *Language in Early Childhood Education.* Ed. by Courtney B. Cazden. Washington, D.C.: NAEYC, 1972. Pp. 1–2.

———. "Stages in Language Development and Reading Exposure." *Harvard Educational Review*, **42**:1 (1972), pp. 1–33.

Clay, Marie. "Exploring With A Pencil." *Theory into Practice*, **16** (December, 1977), pp. 334–341.

Day, Barbara, et al. "Reading and Pre-First Grade—A Joint Statement of Concerns About Present Practices." *Educ. Leadership*, **34**:5 (1977), p. 325.

Davis, Hazel G. "Reading Pressures in the Kindergarten." *Child. Educ.* **57**:2 (1980), pp. 76–79.

Eisenson, Jon, and Mardel Ogilvie. *Speech Correction in the Schools*, 5th ed. New York: Macmillan, 1983.

Flood, J. and Diane Lapp. *Language/Reading Instruction for the Young Child.* New York: Macmillan, 1981.

Gold, Yvonne. "Teaching Attentive Listening." *Reading Improvement*, **18** (Winter 1981), pp. 319–320.

Griffith, J. N., and C. H. Frey. *Classics of Children's Literature.* New York: Macmillan, 1981.

Hall, Mary Anne. *Teaching Reading as a Language Experience.* 2nd ed. Columbus, Ohio: Merrill, 1976.

Herrick, V. E., and Marcella Nervobig. *Using Experience Charts with Children.* Columbus, Ohio: Merrill, 1964.

Hickman, Janet. "Children's Response to Literature: What Happens in the Classroom." *Language Arts*, **57**:5 (1980), pp. 524–529.

Honig, Alice S. Research in Review: "Language Environments for Young Children." *Young Children* **38**:1 (1982), pp. 56–67.

Huck, Charlotte S. *Children's Literature in the Elementary School*, 3d ed. New York: Holt, 1979.

Jensen, Mary A., and Bette A. Hanson. "Research in Review: Helping Young Children Begin to Read: What Research Says to the Teacher." *Young Children* **36**:1 (1980), pp. 61–71.

Jersild, A. T. "Handedness." *Child Psychology*, 6th ed. Englewood Cliffs, N.J.: Prentice-Hall, 1968. pp. 156–160.

———. "Language Development, Perceptual Development." *Child Psychology*, 6th ed. Englewood Cliffs, N.J.: Prentice-Hall, 1968. Pp. 414–442.

King, Martha L. and Victor Rentel. "Toward a Theory of Early Writing Development," *Research in the Teaching of English*, **13**:3 (1979), pp. 243–253.

Language Arts **58**:4 (1981). The entire issue is devoted to Children's Literature.

Mason, Jana M. "When Do Children Begin to Read: An Exploration of Four-Year-Old Children's Letter and Word Reading Competencies." *Reading Research Quarterly*, **15**:2 (1980), pp. 203–227.

McCaslin, Nellie. *Children and Drama*, 2d ed. New York: Longman, 1981.

———. *Creative Drama in the Classroom*, 3d ed. New York: Longman, 1980.

Monson, Dianne L., and Bette J. Peltola (compilers). *Research in Children's Literature*. Newark, Del.: International Reading Association, 1976.

Nessel, Denise D., and Margaret B. Jones. *The Language Experience Approach to Reading*, New York: Teachers College, 1981.

Ollila, L. O. (ed.). *The Kindergarten Child and Reading*. Newark, Del.: International Reading Association, 1977.

Resnick, Loren and Phyllis Weaver (eds.). *Theory and Practice of Early Reading*, Volumes 1–3. Hillsdale, N.J.: Erlbaum Associates, 1979.

Rogers, V. R. "What Research Tells Us About The Three R's." *Phi Delta Kappan* **64**:4 (1982), p. 236.

Ross, Ramon. *Storyteller*, 2d ed. Columbus, Ohio: Merrill, 1980.

Sadker, Myra D., and D. M. Sadker. *Now upon a Time: A Contemporary View of Children's Literature*. New York: Harper, 1977.

Schickedanz, Judith A. "Hey! This Book's Not Working Right." In *Curriculum Planning for Young Children*, Janet F. Brown, ed., Washington, D.C.: NAEYC (1982), pp. 69–78.

———. "The Acquisition of Written Language in Young Children." In *Handbook of Research in Early Childhood Education*, ed. by B. Spodek. New York: The Free Press, 1982, pp. 242–263.

Siks, Geraldine B. *Drama with Children*. New York: Harper, 1977.

Simmons, Barbara, and Paula Smith Lawrence. "Beginning Reading: Welcome Parents." *Child. Educ.*, **57**:3 (1981), pp. 156–160.

Smith, C. A. "Puppetry and Problem Solving Skills." In *Curriculum Planning for Young Children*, ed. by Janet F. Brown. Washington, D.C.: NAEYC (1982), pp. 213–227.

Smith, J. A., and Dorothy M. Park. *Word Music and Word Magic: Children's Literature Methods*. Boston: Allyn, 1977.

Stewart, Ida Santos. "The Larger Question: Bilingual Education, Family and Society." *Child. Educ.* **57**:3 (1981), pp. 138–143.

Tanyzer, H., and Jean Karl (eds.) *Reading, Children's Books, and our Pluralistic Society*. Newark, Del.: International Reading Association, 1972.

Temple, C. A., Ruth G. Nathan, and Nancy A. Burris. *The Beginnings of Writing*. Boston: Allyn and Bacon, Inc., 1982.

Tway, Eileen. "When Will My Child Write?" *Child. Educ.* **59**:5 (1983), pp. 332–335.

Urzus, Carole. "A Language–Learning Environment for All Children," *Language Arts*, **57**:1 (1980), pp. 38–44. (Includes second language acquisition.)

Vukelich, Carol, and Joanne Golden. "The Development of Writing in Young Children: A Review of the Literature." *Child. Educ.* **57**:3 (1981), pp. 167–170.

Veatch, J. *Key Words to Reading: The Language Experience Approach*. Columbus: Merrill, 1979.

Williamson, P. M. "Literature Goals and Activities for Young Children." In *Curriculum Planning for Young Children*, Janet F. Brown, ed. Washington, D.C.: NAEYC (1982), pp. 102–108.

White, Doris (compiler). *Multi-ethnic Books for Head Start Children, Part I: Black and Integrated Literature*. Urbana, Ill.: ERIC Clearinghouse on Early Childhood Education and National Laboratory on Early Childhood Education, 1969.

CHAPTER 9

Mathematics: Quantitative Living

Mathematics permeates the daily life of everyone. Infants discover relationships and become aware of quantity in their world. Preschoolers use physical realities, then symbols to represent these realities as they construct mathematical concepts. From birth throughout adulthood mathematical processes are taking place.

THE MATHEMATICS CURRICULUM

Mathematics programs for young children vary greatly. In some programs proficiency in counting, writing numerals, and other mathematical skills is the primary objective. In others, the almost exclusive use of the incidental activities in which the child participates each day becomes the basis for whatever mathematical skills may be developed. A mathematics curriculum organized primarily around one of these positions tends to ignore the possible interrelationships of various phases of development and the questions relating to content, teaching, and learning. A balanced program can be planned in such a way as to provide for an intellectual orientation as well as a recognition of the broader aspects of the child's development.

The balanced program should:[1]

Emphasize the thinking processes and concept development.

Emphasize language acquisition and use of oral language in relation to the child's real-life activities—not as rote verbalizations.

Introduce new language and written symbols slowly.

Build a child's self-confidence in perception and the ability to find information and to draw conclusions from it.

Encourage the child to perceive, describe, and extend patterns.

Provide for balanced emphasis on concepts, skills, and abilities.

Provide opportunities for the child to explore, manipulate, make decisions, and experiment.

In order to provide for a balanced program, the teacher needs a knowledge and understanding of the children to be taught, a knowledge of the instructional process and of mathematical content. Teachers need to be acutely aware of the children with whom they work, gearing their teaching to each child's style and level of learning so that the child will not be bored or confused but rather stimulated and interested.

There are many theories concerning children's development and many implications of such theories for math education. Since the 1950s there has been a revival of interest in the work of Piaget. His theories have helped produce programs that emphasize the development of broad intellectual powers rather than the mastery of narrow academic skills. Piaget's research, based on observing children as they solved tasks, demonstrated the difference between adults' and children's thinking. He identified certain stages of development in sequence, each one rising out of a previous stage and building on it. Each has approximate chronological age boundaries even though, because of individual differences, some children will enter a stage earlier whereas others may not leave the stage until later. Only the preoperational stage that includes the ages covered in this text is discussed here.

The preoperational stage begins at about age one or two and lasts until approximately age seven. This is the stage of representation and symbolism. The preoperational child is egocentric and assumes that everyone thinks as he or she does. The child's thoughts are governed by perceptual comparison and sensorial experiences. Symbols and representations of the world are manipulated; play involves imagination and make-believe; words often represent things, too. Children in the preoperational stage function intuitively rather than logically. Things are what they seem to be. If an object seems bigger, the child assumes it is bigger and has difficulty with conservation. If objects are rearranged, the child is unsure of whether they represent "more," "less," or the "same" number of objects. Liquid poured into different sizes or shapes of containers seems to change volume.

---

[1] Glenadine Gibb and Alberta M. Castaneda, "Experiences for Young Children," in J. N. Payne (ed.), *Mathematics Learning in Early Childhood* (Reston, Va.: National Council of Teachers of Mathematics, 1975), p. 124.

Piaget makes a distinction between the acquisition of two kinds of knowledge related to mathematical development: physical knowledge and logico-mathematical knowledge. Physical knowledge is sensory, external knowledge gained in direct interaction with the environment. Logico-mathematical knowledge comes from relationships and theories created by actions performed on objects and, therefore, is internal or reflective. Logico-mathematical knowledge must be constructed by each child through his or her activities, assimilating reality into mental concepts. It is through reason or logic that children learn to reject or overcome sensory impressions and form abstractions.

In order to reach coherent generalizations, the child needs opportunities for many experiences with manipulative activities and concrete materials, those in the natural environment as well as those especially designed to meet each child's needs. Many opportunities are necessary for the child to act on objects, to manipulate, explore, make choices, and decisions. Developing thinking processes, not just learning correct answers, is vital as the child experiments, tests, discovers. Gradually, and over a period of time, the child moves into the next stage.

Such information about the child can be of value to the teacher in serving as a guide for expectations, for diagnosing a child's situation, and in individualizing instruction. Too often there is concern for moving the child faster and faster through the stages of development and accelerating learning. Piaget, however, holds that maximum efforts to accelerate the development of logical thinking are not desirable.[2]

HOW TO TEACH MATHEMATICS

Effective learning occurs as the child fulfills a real need. Passing out materials to each child in the group, setting the table, selecting "just enough" blocks to complete the structure, counting apples, or comparing lengths of pretzel sticks at snack time can help to make each child mathematically aware. The activity in and of itself can contribute little to the child's mathematical understandings, but the interaction of the child, the teacher, and the activity is significant. As the child passes out napkins for lunch, does the teacher say that one napkin is given to each child? Is there an opportunity to give one to Mary, one to Tony, and so on, thus working out a one-to-one correspondence? Or is the child merely told to count five napkins and give them to the children without having the opportunity to think through the process and gain knowledge of the one-to-one correspondence?

The teacher provides opportunities for a wide range of mathematical experiences within an environment that is appropriate, comfortable, flexible and in which the child has many opportunities to interact with objects and people, to have many

---

[2] Richard W. Copeland. *How Children Learn Mathematics: Teaching Implications of Piaget's Research* (New York: Macmillan, 1979), pp. 38–42.

experiences, to reflect upon his or her discoveries, and to develop ideas and concepts.

Emphasis on the child's learning through his or her own activities does not mean that the teacher does not plan for mathematics. The teacher plans and organizes so that the learning is developed through incidental and not accidental activities that provide opportunities for learning. A child may manipulate and observe materials without understanding their mathematical significance. Interaction between teacher and child is essential. The child may play with a rectangular block and not know the word "rectangle," unless he or she hears this word and uses it in context.

To avoid gaps in certain areas of number experiences, it is essential that the teacher give attention to the conditions of learning as related to mathematics, de-

Quantative words are used correctly in school situations. "My hand is smaller than yours."

velopmental sequence of mathematical concepts and skills, and to questions related to planning for and organizing activities.

Only through listing the attitudes, skills, and understandings desired can a teacher select and plan wisely for the continuous development of number concepts. He or she must plan in terms of the development of individuals and small groups of children as well as for the larger group. The teacher may give help individually, in small groups, or by working with a larger group in which each child contributes according to maturity. Accurate records are important. The teacher keeps records of skill and concept development and of how each child uses what is taught in the course of participating in other activities and in free play.

Some mathematical opportunities that build on and extend previous experiences are often a repetition of earlier activities, though in a different setting. The child counts spoons, children, and chairs. This change in the setting is important so that the concept, and not the setting, can be learned. Therefore, the skillful teacher utilizes all the natural settings that occur in the daily life of the school and uses the quantitative words correctly in situations. For example, the teacher says: "It is ten o'clock—time for our lunch," or "It is twelve o'clock—the time your mother will meet you," or "In ten minutes your father will come."

When outside or on a field trip, the teacher may use a compass with the children to guide their directions or to determine the direction an airplane is flying. The teacher is careful to use such words as *high, low, higher than, lower than, slow, fast, faster, far away, near.* On a trip children observe street signs pointing directions and listing distances. As the children play, they estimate, then measure, and compare distances that they jump or run.

Often the large thermometer in the room is read and records made on a calendar as the changes in weather are noted or the date is discussed. Countdown for games and division of materials for work and play become opportunities for developing number learnings if the teacher is alert and plans the activities in terms of the readiness of the children. Selected songs, games, and finger plays develop interest in, and provide for, motivated repetition of concepts presented.

Concepts of quantity and of contrasting sizes and shapes are introduced and used informally. Guided observations and discussions assist the children to know many quantitative words and to apply them in meaningful situations.

The classroom offers many opportunities for measuring. The clock, the calendar, and the weather are constantly changing. Children are interested in various measurements of their own bodies as well as other objects in their environment. Games often offer opportunities for measuring activities.

As activities are planned, the teacher records and analyzes the types of home and school experiences that have contributed to the child's number readiness. The teacher builds on and supplements these experiences and plans with the parents so that additional opportunities may be provided in the home for the child to apply and to reuse what has been learned at school.

In one kindergarten, a list of five names written under the word *thermometer* was observed on the teacher's desk. Upon inquiry, the teacher explained that as the result of a recent activity, she had found that these five children did not know how to measure the temperature in the classroom. She had listed these children as those who would need special activities and guidance in the use of the thermometer.

In the same room was another list of children's names written under the figure "25¢." Explanation of this list indicated that these children should be included in activities related to the trip to the store and that guided experiences should be provided for them to use 25¢ in *real* money (as a quarter, five nickels, or two dimes and a nickel) in functional situations.

All planning for experiences should be flexible, yet should make provision for situations that will require use of mathematics and quantitative thinking in a comprehensive yet balanced program.

WHAT TO TEACH: MATHEMATICAL CONCEPTS, PROCESSES, UNDERSTANDINGS, AND SKILLS

The teacher, familiar with developmental skills and the curriculum, takes advantage of each experience as it occurs. In addition, the teacher projects and develops many creative situations through which the desired mathematical learnings are functionally introduced, used, reused, and evaluated. These meaningful experiences offer opportunities to develop simple understandings that later unfold as the child meets more and more difficult situations. Therefore, the teacher needs to make a careful listing of abilities, the skills, teaching suggestions, and activities, plans for parent cooperation at school and at home, and ways of evaluating the progress for each child and for groups of children.

Classification for young children involves simple classification used to decide if objects belong together, classification of objects in disjointed sets, and multiple classification that involves the use of two or more attributes as the basis for classifying objects.[3]

Copeland reports that children usually sort first by shape, then by color, and last of all by size.[4] The young child's first experiences with classifying should involve only one difference such as things that float and things that sink, toys with wheels and toys without wheels, blocks that are red and blocks that are blue. As the child begins to recognize attributes easily, the level of complexity can be increased by moving to more or more difficult concepts. Gibb and Castaneda say that when children are able to classify objects and see the collections thus formed as entities, they can then classify sets of objects as equivalent or nonequivalent.[5]

[3]L. I. Richardson, K. L. Goodman, N. N. Hartman, and H. LePique, *A Mathematics Activity Curriculum for Early Childhood and Special Education* (New York: Macmillan, 1980), p. 180.
[4]Copeland, op. cit., p. 64.
[5]Gibb and Castaneda, op. cit., p. 98.

Underlying the concept of number are classifying, comparing, and ordering. These fundamental processes are related to and involve counting, fractions, shape and space, measurement, and organizing and presenting data and patterns. Experiences in these processes provide necessary background for the higher degree of abstraction required later.[6] Emphasis should be placed upon simple beginnings and expansion of these skills and understandings according to the developmental pace of each child. The developmental pace and level of each child are different. A three-year-old child may have acquired a skill not yet mastered by a five-year-old. Hence, no designation is made as to specific experiences for nursery school, Head Start, Day Care Center, or kindergarten for three-, four-, or five-year-old children.

A discussion and a list of the concepts, abilities, and understandings to be used as a frame of reference for planning, and for analyzing the present development and progress of young children may be found in the following chart.

Classifying

Young children participate in classifying as they name objects, such as a shoe or a box, put together things that are alike, and engage in a variety of sorting activities. But in order to be able to classify, the child must understand the meaning of the words used by the adult in giving instructions, such as *alike, put together, go together*. Concepts and words for attributes, purposes, positions, locations are necessary. The development of concepts and vocabulary is an essential part of early mathematics learning. Language related to sets is seldom a part of the child's everyday conversation. Classifying, however, can be used to help the child develop concepts and language related to sets. Blocks, a tea set, a pair of shoes may not be thought of as sets, but are considered as single entities.

Abilities	Teaching Suggestions and Activities
To understand the meaning of such words as alike, put together, go together, use, set.	Use activities to develop meaning for words and phrases used in the classifying process, such as *alike, put together, belong together, combine*.
To make a collection of objects that are alike in some way.	Talk about how objects such as toys, fruit, and clothes are alike and how they are different. Include not only words of size, shape, and color, but also words that relate to use, location, and position.
	Have collected objects, such as buttons, seeds, nails, blocks, felt shapes, and checkers available in boxes. Using one or two sets of objects, ask children to find two objects that are the same. Talk about how objects are the same. Pick out one object. Ask children to find another object that is the same. Discuss.

[6] Gibb and Castaneda, op. cit., p. 98.

Abilities	Teaching Suggestions and Activities
To classify objects according to one attribute, such as use, color, shape, size.	Make a collection of felt cutouts using a variety of shapes and colors. Ask children to put together the felt cutouts that are alike in some way or are the same. Discuss. Repeat, using other objects that can be sorted such as buttons, washers, caps, nails, various toys, cups, spoons.
To classify objects according to two attributes, such as round and blue. Arrange a collection of objects into a set.	Ask child to select two toys that are in some way the same. Ask other children to guess how the two toys are "the same." Repeat, using dolls, children, books.
	Classify fabrics by color, checks, stripes; objects in the classroom by function (sit on, write with); objects by material (wood, metal).
	Show several dolls. Use the word *set*. "This is a set of dolls." Repeat, using children, books, crayons.
	Make a collection of magnetic and nonmagnetic materials. Classify as to whether or not a magnet can pick them up.
To identify a way or ways in which objects are alike.	Classify children in a class as to boy or girl, eye or hair color, height or weight (maintaining awareness of the children's self-concept), food eaten for breakfast, type of shoes worn.
	Sort items on an overhead projector. Let children state how (color, size, shape) sorting was done.

Comparing

In the process of comparing, the child explores and establishes a relationship between two objects, using a specific attribute as a basis. For example, when a child says that one crayon is longer than another, the relation, "is longer than," is established. It is essential in comparing that the child have an understanding of the attributes and vocabulary used, such as longer, shorter, taller, smaller, or heavier than. The comparing process serves as a foundation or base for ordering and measuring.

Abilities	Teaching Suggestions and Activities
To acquire and use vocabulary related to size, shape, distance, weight such as bigger, shorter deeper, ruler, scales.	Select two objects, such as dolls or blocks, that differ only in height. Ask the children which doll is taller or shorter. Talk about what they had to do to be sure.
To compare two sizes of objects and tell which is smaller and larger.	Have two sizes of several objects such as apples, pie tins, pine cones, buttons. Let the children compare and put the objects into large and small categories. Discuss how decisions were made.

Abilities	Teaching Suggestions and Activities
To arrange a group of objects in categories, for example, large and small.	Use stories such as "The Three Bears" or "The Three Billy Goats Gruff." Make flannel board or puppet characters to use for size comparison. Discuss vocabulary.
Compare objects according to one attribute.	Compare which of two ice cubes melts first, which of two candles burns more slowly, which rock is heavier, and how much longer one's leg is than one's arm.
To compare objects according to more than one attribute, for example shape and color.	Ask the children to complete open-ended sentences such as "This spoon is longer than a _____." "Your foot is the same length as a _____." "A mouse is smaller than a _____." "Your pencil is shorter than a _____."
To identify a way or ways that objects are alike.	Eat pretzel or carrot sticks. Have two children compare after one, two, or several bites. Whose pretzel stick is longer? Shorter?

Ordering

Ordering by the young child means arranging objects or sets of objects so as to have an origin and a direction and to reflect some rule. A child may be asked to order five pencils of different lengths from the longest to the shortest. The rule would be that each pencil after the first must be shorter than the pencil it follows.

Children should be asked to order objects only on the basis of attributes they understand and can compare. The child can order the pencils from the longest to the shortest only if the meanings of shortest and longest are understood. It is suggested that in beginning activities no more than five objects should be used.

Learning the position of objects in a set, the ordinal sense of numbers, precedes understanding the number of objects in a set, the cardinal sense of numbers. Children need many opportunities for comparison before number concepts develop.

Abilities	Teaching Suggestions and Activities
To acquire and use vocabulary related to ordering, such as first, last, middle.	Show a child a set of objects arranged in some order. Give a duplicate set, and ask that it be arranged in the same order as the one you showed first.
	Select three spools. Paint each a different color. Thread the spools on string, tying a knot between each to prevent slipping. Put the spools inside an empty cardboard tube, and pull the spools through the tube. Ask children to watch and tell which spool comes first, and so on. Repeat with spools in different order.

Abilities	Teaching Suggestions and Activities
	Ask a child to order a set of objects according to a specified relation, for example, "longest to shortest."
To order a set of objects according to a specified relation, for example, "largest to smallest."	Show five cardboard cylinders that have been ordered according to height. Show five more objects. Arrange first, third, and fifth object according to height. Ask children to put in the two remaining objects so that the set is ordered like the first set. Order children according to height.
To tell how the order of the objects was decided, for example, "Which was tallest?"	Show three objects of differing height. Indicate the object of medium height. Ask a child to choose one of the two remaining objects, compare it to the medium one, describe the comparison, and place the object to one side of the medium object. Ask another child to repeat this activity for the remaining object.
	After children can copy the order of sets of objects, have them reverse the order, extend the order (as in patterning), put in missing parts or gaps in the order, or even use objects to create an order of objects.

Patterning

The ability to recognize patterns is important to a child's mathematical development. The child should be helped to discover the pattern rule and follow the rule in completing the pattern. Such an activity helps to develop visual and auditory discrimination.[7]

The recognition and awareness of patterns may be developed through the use of real objects, pictures, designs in weaving, symbols, and drawings. Give the child practice in seeing, describing, completing, and repeating patterns.

Abilities	Teaching Suggestions and Activities
To understand and use vocabulary such as pattern, repeat.	Make a pattern of objects, such as one red, one white, one blue plastic spoon. Ask a child to make a pattern just like the one shown directly below it. Use blocks, beads, pipe cleaners, anything of distinctive shape, color, or other attribute.
To identify the pattern rule followed with objects, shapes, colors. To identify auditory patterns and patterns of actions.[8]	Make a necklace of wooden beads or colored macaroni in a two- or three-colored pattern (blue, yellow, green, blue, yellow, green). Ask the child to make a pattern just like the one in the necklace. Let him or her wear it.

[7] Richardson, et al., op. cit., p. 385.
[8] Ibid., pp. 432–344.

Abilities	Teaching Suggestions and Activities
To reproduce a pattern of objects. To reproduce a pattern of action.	Clap hands, slap legs, and snap fingers in a pattern. Have the children join in as they recognize the pattern.
To create a pattern of objects.	Look for patterns in cloth or wallpaper (stripes, paids, checks).
To create an auditory and movement pattern.	Make a pattern of children standing, sitting, standing, sitting or front, back, front, back.
	Ask one child to make a pattern from collected objects. Ask another child to copy the pattern.
	Let the children form patterns using parquetry blocks, tiles, cubes, wooden classroom blocks.

Counting

Counting is one of the first number ideas taught to children but, according to Copeland,[9] the numbers that children recite may have little meaning for them. The first counting is often a rote activity. When the child understands and uses number

[9] Copeland, op. cit., p. 119.

Sinae carefully observes Wanda place numbers "between," "before," and "after."

ideas, such as one-to-one correspondence or matching, he or she is counting ration-ally. The child should be asked to count only with number names that are mean-ingful, and the process should follow the establishment of meaning for one, two, three, four, and five. Usually cardinal number is what is meant. Children at this (preoperational) level usually have difficulty in grasping the relationship between cardinal and ordinal number.[10]

Gibb and Castaneda say that a premature effort to teach counting may result in the undesired effect of teaching the child to associate number names with single objects rather than sets of a certain number. The child may count, "one, two blocks." Later, when asked to bring two books to the table, the child may count, "one, two" and bring only the second book.[11] Activities involving matching or one-to-one cor-respondence first utilize people and/or concrete objects, such as napkins to spoons, children to chairs. After children can match objects to objects in pictures, they can begin learning to match number names or numerals to objects.[12] Children may not realize that the last number counted can refer to the whole collection.[13]

Abilities	Teaching Suggestions and Activities
To establish one-to-one relationship.	Count by rote, but do not mistake counting by rote as evidence of readiness to work with numerals.
To recognize small groups without counting, such as groups of two, groups of three, groups of four.	Use nursery rhymes, rhyming words, finger plays, singing games such as, "One two, buckle my shoe," "This Little Piggie," "Ten Little Indians."
To develop feelings of oneness, twoness, three-ness, fourness.	Identify pairs, twos as in shoes, mittens, bicycles. Extend to threes as in tricycle or in games.
To extend counting through use of ordinals and acquiring additional vocabulary such as first, sec-ond, next, last, pair, partner.	Have the child touch each object; count only with number names meaningful to child. Repeat this in various settings until this need to touch or to point to objects is no longer necessary.
To recognize the printed symbol of numbers (this will interest the more mature child).	
To observe figures and develop readiness for writing.	Provide many manipulative counting situations with beads, but-tons, cookies, napkins, children, chairs. Match beads to boxes, children to chairs.
To compare through noting changes in size and form.	Determine the number of places, quantity of milk, silverware, napkins, and so on, needed at the table. Match milk to napkins, and so on.
To extend counting concept to "how many," "how many more," and later to "how many less" or "how many fewer" through six as it appears in the environment; the more mature children may extend these concepts through ten.	Read and use numbers. Identify numbers on television. Observe figures on a page. Dial telephone numbers. Play with number cutouts. Write home address. Look for numbers on signs.

[10] Copeland, op. cit., p. 99.

[11] Gibb and Castaneda, op. cit., p. 113.

[12] Copeland, op. cit., pp. 93–94.

[13] G. Mascho, "Familiarity with Measurement," in *Mathematics Learning in Early Childhood*, ed. by J. N. Payne, op. cit., p. 61.

Abilities	Teaching Suggestions and Activities
	Play games involving "more" or "less."
	Read stories containing numbers. See the listing of books later in this chapter.
	Use the words "One for you and one for me and one for you . . ." or "One for Sally, one for Jim . . ." when passing out materials.
	Look for opportunities during the day to use one-to-one correspondence. "Are there enough swings for those who wish to swing?"
	Make certain no pressure is exerted on the child to attempt to write figures before his or her small muscles are coordinated and he or she can perceive relationships. Call figures by name; do not refer to them as numbers.
	Play games such as Musical Chairs.
	Arrange games using different configurations of dots to represent numbers. Have children match "three dots to three dots."
	Use sandpaper numbers and felt cutouts for playing.

Shape and space

Children begin to explore space and shape very early in life. Shape and spatial concepts are formed informally as children move, build, compare, pour, and observe. They crawl around and through objects and up and down stairs, roll balls, finger the edge of a low table while walking around it; they play with blocks, dishes, and wheel toys—all motor activities important in helping to develop an awareness of likenesses and differences in the shape of objects.

Preoperational children can recognize open and closed figures but cannot necessarily name or reproduce the most common shapes. The first activities should be planned to help the child develop a general concept of shape, later to talk about likenesses and differences in shapes, and finally to learn the names for the most common shapes. Too often the naming of shapes is one of the first activities.

Abilities	Teaching Suggestions and Activities
To understand and note shape and size of objects and places in environment, especially circle, square, triangle.	Discuss shapes in the child's environment. Use blocks, puzzles, boxes, wheels, clocks, containers, toys, doors, scrap lumber.
To understand and use vocabulary to express size and shape such as *big, little, middle-sized, tall, thin, fat, tiny, wee.*	Find shapes on material or wallpaper samples. Paste shapes onto a large paper that is cut into the same shape.

Abilities	Teaching Suggestions and Activities
To understand and use relationship words such as *large—small, full—empty, short—long, near—far, round—square.*	Give the children each a paper shape. Ask the children to find "the same shape" somewhere in the classroom. Take a walk and repeat the procedure, finding "the same shape" outdoors.
To recognize that certain shapes are useful for a given purpose and that types of containers have different capacities.	Discuss shapes and sizes of blocks and toys during building or cleanup time.
To acquire such vocabulary as *quart, pint, cup, empty, full.*	Cut shapes into two parts. Let the child fit the shape back together.
To recognize and understand size and shapes as related to construction.	Examine other, noncommon, shapes: tire treads, seashells, snowflakes.
	Show the child a shape. Ask the child to use rubber bands or pegs to form the shape on the geoboard or pegboard.

Measurement

Young children are often taught measurement, but their understandings are usually superficial. Piaget points out that as long as the child's conception is egocentric, measurement is not possible.[14] Young children differ greatly in their experiences with and their ideas of time, money, and linear and liquid measure with little mastery evident. As age, socioeconomic level, or mental ability increased, so did the child's familiarity with measurement.[15] The teacher, therefore, needs to study the composition of the group in relation to the factors mentioned when planning activities involving measurement.

In early measuring activities the child makes a visual estimate. Joe was sawing legs for a table. When offered the yardstick to help him get the legs the same length he replied, "I can just look and tell they are the same." Not until after the legs were attached to the table and the table wobbled did he ask for "that stick." The child at this stage uses measuring instruments but may not use them correctly. Later, after experimentation the child can begin to use measuring instruments more effectively. Joe reached the stage at which he carefully measured the table legs.

After the gelatin didn't jell, the fives were very careful to measure exactly one cup of water. The teacher should not hurry the children. Rather, time and opportunities are provided for children to build concepts related to measurement.

Young children cannot and should not be expected to use money in a meaningful

---

[14] J. Piaget, quoted in Richard W. Copeland, *Diagnostic and Learning Activities in Mathematics for Children* (New York: Macmillan, 1974), p. 55.

[15] G. Mascho, "Familiarity with Measurement," in *Mathematics Learning in Early Childhood*, edited by J. N. Payne, op. cit., p. 61.

Pretzel People
1 pkg. yeast.
1½ c. warm water. ⟩ Mix
Let stand 3 minutes.
Add 1 t. sugar.
3-4 c. flour.
Knead. Make Pretzel People shapes.
Beat 1 egg and brush on top.
Salt lightly.
Bake 425° 12-15".

The recipe for "Pretzel People" is available for reference as the children work. This activity can involve use of measurement, simple fractions, counting, and reading.

sense. They should, however, begin to recognize and understand the relative value of coins and their use. Vocabulary related to money such as *buy, sell, money, cent, nickel, five cents, dime, quarter, dollar, coin, change, pay, cost* should be included in daily experiences. As the children mature, money experiences will become more purposeful. Instruction in systematic measurement should not be introduced before the latter part of the third grade.[16] Direct measurement of length, weight, volume, area, and money uses concrete quantities and, therefore, should precede indirect abstract measurement of time and temperature.

Abilities	Teaching Suggestions and Activities
Space: To acquire and use vocabulary related to shape, size, capacity, and distance, such as *measure, big, fat, wee, tiny, short, wide, deep, low, high, hole, pound, ruler, teaspoon, tablespoon, cup, quart, pint, speedometer, round, circle, square, cube, cone, triangle*. To extend concept of round to circle, circle from round to round and flat, and then to round and flat and with a center.	Develop and use vocabulary related to weight, temperature, time, money, size, capacity, and distance, such as *measure, big, fat, wee, tiny, short, wide, deep, low, high, hole, pound, ruler, teaspoon, tablespoon, cup, quart, pint, speedometer, round, circle, square, cube, cone, triangle, thermometer, clock, hour, minute, buy, sell, penny, nickel, dollar, scales*. (Note: Do not confuse the group by introducing both standard weights and measures and their metric equivalent at the same time.) Ask questions about size. Discuss paper, pencils, rulers, yardsticks, and so on, in terms of shape, size, and purpose.

[16] Richard W. Copeland, *How Children Learn Mathematics: Teaching Implications of Piaget's Research* (New York: Macmillan, 1979), p. 315.

Abilities	Teaching Suggestions and Activities
To understand and use vocabulary related to distance, direction, and location, such as: *indoors, outdoors, front, back, top, bottom, beside.*	Cut paper to fit the sides of boxes. Have children match each paper to the box side with the same area. Discuss shape.
	Use geoboards and rubber bands for measuring area.
	Pour liquids into different sizes and shapes of containers. Experiment by filling containers with liquids and nonliquids. Discuss.
Money:	Use real or play money in classroom activities.
To understand and use vocabulary related to money as a measure of value and as a means of use, such as: *buy, sell, trade, money, nickel, five cents, penny, dime, quarter, dollar, coin, change, pay, cost.*	Let the children buy food at a local grocery store, items in a class "store."
	Use change for sorting into piles of pennies, nickels, dimes, quarters. Count pennies.
To recognize and begin to understand relative value of coins and their use.	Use much water play and many sand activities involving weighing and measuring capacity.
These money experiences are provided as they become functional according to the child's maturity and purpose.	Use cooking activities for measurements of all types: length, area, volume and capacity, weight and mass, time, temperature.
	Use nonstandard units (feet, hands, popsicle sticks, pencils) for measuring.
Time:	Measure distance a child runs, jumps, or throws ball. Measure a plant's growth on a stick or string.
To begin to understand duration of time and time sequence.	Respond to different rhythmic time patterns.
To acquire and use vocabulary related to time such as: *now, soon, night, day, week, days of week, hour, minute, sometime.*	Call attention to the clock in relation to jobs as discussed. Ask questions requiring clock—use words *hour, minute,* and so on. Raise questions such as these: What time for lunch? To go swimming? How long until lunch?
To begin in understanding and using clock as a means of measuring time.	Read and discuss books such as *All Kinds of Time* by Harry Behn or *Mike Mulligan and His Steam Shovel* by Virginia Lee Burton. However, this discussion should not destroy the child's enjoyment of the story by overemphasizing the number words and concepts.
To begin to understand calendar for measuring and recording time.	Post an attractive calendar. Fill in days and dates on calendar on the bulletin board. Discuss days, dates, and special events. Note special days for celebrations.
Temperature:	Use sand or kitchen timers.
To begin development of understanding and awareness of variations in temperature and adjustments made accordingly.	Post a large thermometer and call the children's attention to it.
To acquire and use vocabulary related to temperature such as: *hot, cool, cold, warm, freeze, summer, spring, fall, winter, thermometer.*	Check temperature and record on calendar periodically, but not necessarily daily. Summarize findings.
	Discuss various ways of telling temperature. Observe and discuss habits of people, animals, trees, and so on, according to changes in temperature. Feel two objects. Note differences in temperatures. Observe school nurse taking temperature. Post pictures of cool things and warm things, and discuss.

Abilities	Teaching Suggestions and Activities
Weight:	
To begin to develop concept of weight.	Have scales available for weighing. Weigh children. Graph the results.
Simple understandings related to balancing objects (like or unlike weights).	Lift different objects. Discuss why some are heavier than others although smaller. Weigh on scales, balancing scales. Read labels giving weight.
To begin to understand use of lever.	Use wheel or slanted board to raise objects.
To acquire and use vocabulary related to weight such as *pounds, ounces, scales, balance, lift, float, heavier, even, light, weigh, weight.*	

Fractions

The idea that a fraction is a bit, a piece, or a part of something is essential. This concept can be acquired by children at an early age—a part of an apple, a part of a banana. In order to develop the correct concept of a fraction, the teacher helps the child to describe the whole object, to decide how many pieces are in that whole object, to decide how many pieces one wants from the whole object, and whether or not the pieces are the same in size or weight.[17]

The number of pieces in the whole can give the child the name for a part of the fraction. For example, an apple divided into four pieces leads to the name *fourths.* Ordinal names help in learning the names of fractions. Pieces of the whole should be equal. Young children cannot correctly divide units into equal pieces. They need time, many opportunities for practice, and much help in recognizing equal size parts, and in dividing the whole into equal parts.

Abilities	Teaching Suggestions and Activities
To begin knowledge of simple fractions usually at about six years of age.	Use vocabulary to express parts of a whole, such as $\frac{1}{2}$, $\frac{1}{2}$ cup, cup; both, quarter, half, divide, piece, middle, double, alike.
To extend whole concept into use of parts and acquisition of vocabulary suited to this concept.	Provide for sharing in terms of "half an apple," "half a sandwich," "a whole carrot."

[17] A. Coxford and L. Ellerbach, "Fractional Numbers," in *Mathematics Learning in Early Childhood,* ed. by J. N. Payne, op. cit., pp. 192–193.

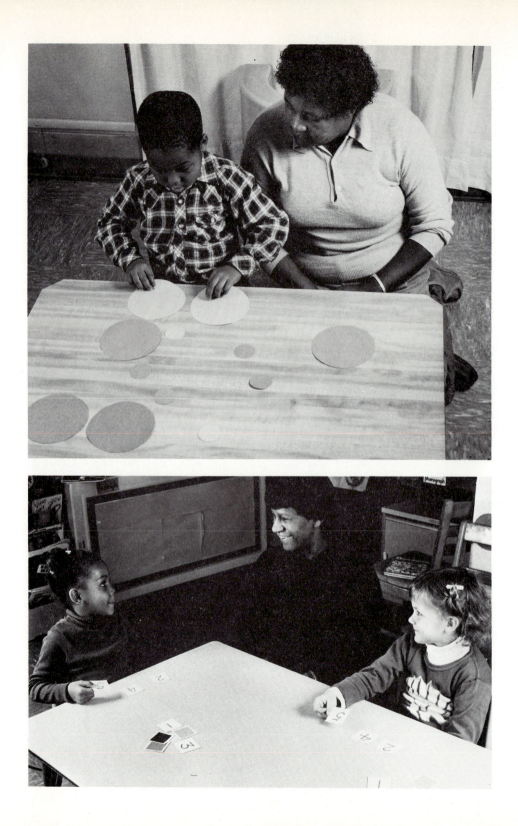

"In the math center we can do many things: We can match by size, shape, and color; we can match numbers; we can fold our papers into four equal squares; we can put all parts together and have a circle.

Abilities	Teaching Suggestions and Activities
To understand and use vocabulary to express parts of a whole, such as: $\frac{1}{4}$, $\frac{1}{2}$ *cup, cup; both, divide, piece, middle, double, alike.*	Plan situations requiring use of half a sheet of paper.
	Use unit blocks for comparison and fractional concepts.
	Use playdough for dividing, cutting into parts, and rolling together again as a whole.
	Prepare pizza, vegetable dip, or applesauce, using measuring spoons and cups.

Vocabulary

A beginner's math program emphasizes the development of concepts and the acquisition of oral language. Appropriate words are needed for expressing number ideas. It is important, then, for the teacher to remember that the young children he or she teaches are still in the process of learning language and may not be able to verbalize how a problem was solved. Many opportunities are needed for the child to acquire a mathematical vocabulary. Activities should be interesting as well as challenging to the children, offering several levels of solution. A positive attitude toward any and all suggestions made by the children is vital both for the young child's self-concept as well as development of vocabulary.

Suggestions for vocabulary development are found in Chapter 8.

Abilities	Teaching Suggestions and Activities
To use number words that at first have no numerical significance.	Place emphasis upon experiences that will demand number judgments in routines such as resting, toileting, cleaning up, convening into a group, planning for better ways of work, engaging in dramatic play or block building, playing store, measuring height and weight.
To understand and use meaningful vocabulary with reference to numbers.	
To acquire vocabulary of number names: understand and use such quantitative words as *all, big, bunch, group, many, more, most, once, small, together, heavy, light, tall, short.*	

Numerical operations

Too often young children are presented with addition or subtraction problems before they can comprehend them. Children must be able to count objects in one set before they are able to consider or count objects in two sets simultaneously. They

"We are learning about pairs—a pair of boots, a pair of shoes, and a pair of socks."

must be able to see sets combined, separated, recombined (reversibility of thought) before addition and subtraction have meaning. With most children, these abilities are not acquired until seven or eight years of age. Prior to that, children need opportunities with manipulative objects—making sets, joining sets, counting sets, dividing sets. With age and experience comes understanding.

EVALUATING MATHEMATICAL LEARNINGS

Evaluation is an essential part of any school program, but it becomes increasingly important in a program based largely on incidental teaching. Because the experiences are a part of the child's life, it is necessary to check to see whether he or she is making progress in all the areas of the number program. Evaluation helps the teacher understand the progress of each individual child, alleviates problems that may have arisen, and provides guidelines for the curriculum. The teacher will do a better job of guiding mathematical learnings if he or she makes the following evaluations:

The program

1. Has provision been made for activities involving all abilities, understandings, and concepts in the areas of counting, measurements, and so on? It is easy to have had many experiences in one area and comparatively few or even none in another area.
2. Is teaching in terms of the readiness of the children? No two children will be at the same level of readiness; even if two appear to give the same response, one may have a more complete understanding.
3. Has there been practice in the repetition of a skill in a functional setting? Have the children been able to work out practical procedures for using their understandings?
4. Is there a variety of materials and methods designed to develop the desired number concepts? Consider, for example, the use of rhymes or finger plays in counting.

Progress of the individual child

1. Is the communication between the teacher and child positive? Is the vocabulary appropriate and familiar? Is the child allowed to arrive at concrete responses, encouraged to explain both correct and incorrect conclusions?
2. Has the child acquired mathematical skills and understandings in the areas of vocabulary, fractions, and so on, appropriate to his or her developmental level?

As the teacher evaluates, findings are summarized and recorded in order to aid in planning for and working with the child. The record may be in the form of a checklist, which can make individualization of instruction more effective. A checklist may be developed for each area of the math program. Different colored pens for different dates of evaluation can aid in determining needs and accomplishments.

CHECK LIST FOR COUNTING

Date _____

	counts 1-5 by rote	counts 1-10 rationally	child touches each object as counting	child matches objects using one-to-one correspondence
Julie	X	X	X	X
Jan	X	—	—	—
Marcus	X	X	—	X
Marguerita	X	X	—	X

X = accomplished

— = needs continued experience

USING TEACHING MATERIALS AND RESOURCES

Teaching materials can be used by children in exploratory activities, in collecting information, in pursuing interests, and in developing and using a mathematical idea and concept. Activities that involve the use of materials can contribute to mathematics learnings, but an intelligent and balanced use is necessary. Trafton says, however, that they are not "cure-alls." The real experiences of the children as well as manipulative and audiovisual materials may be effectively used.[18]

Manipulative materials

Manipulative materials found within the home can be collected and used in the classroom—egg cartons, empty berry containers, bottle tops, small and large boxes, buttons, and empty spools. Children's socks, shoes, gloves also provide valuable resources. Here is a list of other manipulative materials that should be readily available in the classroom:

Empty spools, perhaps enameled in red, blue, or green.
Straws and toothpicks of various colors.
Balls of several sizes.
Large wooden beads of many colors.

[18] P. Trafton, "The Curriculum" in J. N. Payne, ed. *Mathematics Learning in Early Childhood*, op. cit., p. 39.

Blocks of varied size and shape; signs with numbers and shapes.
Empty milk or fruit cartons in quarts, pints, half pints.
Measuring cups marked into thirds, fourths, and halves.
Separate measuring cups holding $\frac{1}{3}$, $\frac{1}{2}$, and $\frac{1}{4}$ cups.
Measuring spoons.
Bottle caps, aluminium washers, colored plastic clothespins, buttons.
Play money in coins and paper dollars.
Scraps of cloth of varied sizes, colors, shapes, and materials.
Simple tools as hammer, saws.
Scraps of lumber.
Nails of several sizes.
Paper bags of many sizes.
Cardboard clock.
Stopwatch.
Clock with alarm.
Clock with second hand.
Timers for stove and for egg.
Sundial.
Scales of several types—balance, kitchen, bathroom, postal.
Cubes of soap.
Cake pans of various sizes and shapes, and muffin tins.
Pegboards, flannel boards with figures.
Magnetic board, magnetic figures.
Toy telephones, cash registers, adding machines.
Various types of dials—TV, washing machine, and radio.
Calculators and computers.
Ribbon, string.
Mirrors.
Food coloring.
Pitchers, funnels.
Puzzles with geometric designs.
Calendar.
Thermometer.

The mathematical materials provided and distributed by publishers of professional materials may be added if funds are available.

Pictorial materials have a place, and a carefully selected picture file is of great value in illustrating the use of arithmetic in daily life. A collection of books, stories, finger plays, and poems that expand arithmetical concepts is a valuable resource for the teacher to read and for the children to look at or to take home to be shared. Such materials need to be selected carefully as to relationship with and treatment of the concepts to be developed as well as to the maturity of the child. This material

Manipulative materials can provide opportunities for counting, matching numbers and shapes.

should be artistic both in content and in the method of presentation. The mathematical problem should be involved in the story, and the content and use should be essential to the solution of the problem in the story. Through use of these materials the child acquires facility in use of vocabulary and builds understanding for use in more complex situations.

Books

Teachers have found children's books to be of value in developing mathematical concepts. Here are a few good examples.

Cole, William. *What's Good for a Three Year Old?* Holt, 1974.

SHAPES AND SIZE

Carle, Eric. *My Very First Book of Shapes.* Crowell, 1974.
Feltser, Eleanor B. *The Sesame Street Book of Shapes.* Little, Brown, 1970.
Kohn, Bernice. *Everything Has a Shape.* Prentice-Hall, 1964.
———. *Everything Has a Size.* Prentice-Hall, 1964.

COMPARING

Asbjornsen, B. C., and J. E. Moe. *The Three Billy Goats Gruff.* Harcourt, 1957.
Froman, Robert. *Bigger and Smaller.* Crowell, 1971.

COUNTING

Hoban, Tana. *Count and See.* Macmillan, 1972.
Wohl, John, and Stacey. *I Can Count the Petals of a Flower.* National Council of
  Teachers of Mathematics, 1975.
LeSeig, Theo. *Ten Apples Up On Top.* Random House, 1961.
Lathan, Jean L., and Bee Lewi. *The Cuckoo That Couldn't Count.* Macmillan, 1961.

FRACTIONS

Dennis, J. Richard. *Fractions Are Parts of Things.* Crowell, 1971.

METRIC SYSTEM

The United States is the only major country that has not completely converted to the metric system of measurement. As the metric system becomes more widely used in our country, eventually children will need to learn to use metric units of measure. The basic units of the system include the meter (length), the liter (capacity), the gram (weight), and the degree Celsius (temperature).

The basic mathematical concepts, abilities, and understandings apply to the metric system as they do to the English system still commonly used in the United States. One word of caution is needed, however. The two systems should not be introduced simultaneously. If, for example, the teacher begins with the English system, this system should be used until the child has achieved beginning understandings. Concepts related to the metric system may then be introduced but without reference to, or comparison with, the English system. As the child works with the two separately, through the process of discovery he or she will come to see that one meter is a little longer than one yard, that one liter is a little more than one quart, and that one kilogram is a little heavier than two pounds.

Young children should not be taught to convert from one system to another. Children may hear the weather report refer to the temperature at 23° Celsius. Such an incident may be used as the basis for discussing the two systems of measuring temperature. Children may find food items that are labeled with metric units. They can look for signs using metric length. This discussion is not intended to suggest that young children be taught to convert from one system to another.[19]

ELECTRONIC DEVICES

At one time there was fear that using hand-held calculators would prevent children from learning basic mathematical facts. Results of recent studies, however, show no adverse effects resulting from calculator use.[20] The extent of the potential contribution calculators can make to mathematical programs has yet to be determined, and comprehensive longitudinal studies are needed.

Computers

An electronic device receiving much attention is the computer. As the cost for computers drops, they are being introduced into schools and homes. Educational publishers are developing courseware for the various computers, and teachers are being urged to become computer literate. Use of computers has been largely directed to elementary children and older youth. One example of an exploratory study of use with young children follows.

In the fall of 1982 microcomputers were introduced in the Center for Young Children (ages three, four, and five), University of Maryland, College Park. Programs for the microcomputer are selected to relate to the overall curriculum. The staff is exploring the use of the microcomputer as a teaching tool in mathematics as well as language arts, social studies, and the graphic arts.[21]

The National Council of Teachers of Mathematics (NCTM) in 1980 made recommendations concerning calculators and computers.[22] Those appropriate for young children follow.

> All students should have access to calculators and increasingly to computers.
> Use of electronic tools should be integrated into the mathematics curriculum.
> Calculators should be available for appropriate use in all mathematics classrooms, and instructional objectives should include the ability to determine sensible and appropriate uses.

[19] Edith Robinson, M. Mahaffey, and D. Nelson. "Measurement" in *Mathematics Learning in Early Childhood*, edited by J. N. Payne, op. cit., pp. 249–259.

[20] Elizabeth Fennema (ed.), *Mathematics Education Research: Implications for the 80's* (Alexandria, Va., Association for Supervision and Curriculum Development, 1981), p. 157.

[21] Marilyn Church, "Microcomputers As A Creative Part of the Preschool Curriculum: A Computer Discovery Center Project Report," Presented at the National Educational Computing Conference, June 5–8, 1983, Baltimore, Md.

[22] Fennema (ed.), op. cit., p. 166.

They should be used in imaginative ways for exploring, discovering, and developing mathematical concepts, and not only for drill and practice.

Suggested Activities

1. Contact a group of children in the neighborhood, in the home, and/or in an organized group. Talk with them informally, and jot down examples of number vocabulary used. Note their ability to match, to count, and to recognize common coins. Note differences among three-, four-, five-, and six-year-olds and differences among children of the same age group.
2. Observe a group of three-, four-, and five-year-olds. List the vocabulary used by the group in terms of shape, size, weight, distance, time, and temperature.
3. List or develop some suggested activities suitable for three- or four-year-old children at varying stages in the development of mathematical concepts.
4. Discuss the differences among the relative values of the incidental, the social, the drill, and the meaningful approach in the development of mathematical concepts, abilities, and understandings. Justify your statements as to the relative values of these approaches.
5. Observe in a center for three-, four-, or five-year-olds or a combination. List materials available for the children and how these materials were utilized in the development of mathematical abilities and understandings, such as classifying, patterning, ordering, comparing, measurement, and problem solving. Describe the method and organization used by the teacher to guide the children in their selection and use of these materials. What did the teacher do to enhance the children's learnings?
6. Observe children engaged in activities such as block building, dramatic play, and painting. Discuss the opportunities available in these activities for classifying, counting, ordering, patterning, using fractions, comparing, building vocabulary, and using shapes.
7. View the film, *Foundations of Mathematics*. Campus Films, 2 Overhill Road, Scarsdale, N.Y. 10583. Compare your observations with the film.
8. Examine a school supply catalog for appropriate manipulative materials for young children.
9. Examine some teaching activities texts for prenumber teaching materials and activities.

Related Readings

Ball, Marion J., and Sylvia Charp. *Be a Computer Literate*. Morristown, N.J.: Creative Computing, 1977.

Benham, Nancy B., Alice Hosticka, Joe D. Payne, and Catherine Yeotis. "Making Concepts in Science and Mathematics Visible and Viable in the Early Childhood Curriculum." *School Science and Math*, **82**:1 (1982), pp. 45–56.

Burton, Grace M. "Patterning: Powerful Play." *School Science and Math*, **82**:1 (1982), pp. 39–44.

Castaneda, Alberta M., E. Glenadine Gibb, and Sharon A. McDermit. "Young Children and Mathematical Problem-solving." *School Science and Math*, **82**:1 (1982), pp. 22–28.

Copeland, Richard W. *How Children Learn Mathematics: Teaching Implications of Piaget's Research*, 3d ed. New York: Macmillan, 1979.

Cruishank, D. E., D. L. Fitzgerald, and Linda R. Jensen. *Young Children Learning Mathematics*. Boston: Allyn and Bacon, 1980.

Fennell, Francis (Skip). "Early Childhood and Mathematical Concerns Regarding Teacher Preparation." *School Science and Math*, **82**:1 (1982), pp. 11–21.

Follis, Helen D., and Gerald D. Krockover. "Selecting Activities in Science and Math for Gifted Young Children." *School Science and Math*, **82**:1 (1982), pp. 57–64.

Hirsch, Elisabeth S. (ed.). *The Block Book*. Washington, D.C.: NAEYC, 1974.

Hollis, Loye Y., and B. Dell Felder. "Recreational Mathematics for Young Children." *School Science and Math*, **82**:1 (1982), pp. 71–75.

Hughes, Rowland. "The Mathematical Knowledge of the Entering School Child." In *Early Childhood Education*. Ed. by Leonard H. Golubchick and Barry Persky. Wayne, N.J.: Avery, 1977. Pp. 176–179.

Johnson, Martin L., and John W. Wilson. "Mathematics." In *Curriculum for the Preschool-Primary Child: A Review of the Research*. Ed. by Carol Seefeldt. Columbus, Ohio: Merrill, 1976. Pp. 152–174.

Kamii, Constance. *Number in Preschool and Kindergarten: Educational Implications of Piaget's Theory*. Washington, D.C.: NCAEYC, 1982.

————. "Piaget, Children, and Number." In *Exploring Early Childhood: Readings in Theory and Practice*. Ed. by Margot Kaplan-Sanoff and Renee Yablans-Magid. New York: Macmillan, 1981.

————, and Rheta De Vries. *Physical Knowledge in Preschool Education: Implications of Piaget's Theory*. Englewood Cliffs, N.J.: Prentice-Hall, 1978.

Kleiman, Glenn, and Mary Humphrey. "Learning with Computers." *Compute*, **23**:4 (1982), p. 80.

Labinowicz, Ed. *The Piaget Primer: Thinking, Learning, Teaching*. Menlo Park, Calif.: Addison-Wesley, 1980.

May, Lola. "The Focus of Math: Problem-Solving." *Early Years*, **13**:2 (1982), pp. 50–53.

National Council of Teachers of Mathematics. *An Agenda for Action: Recommendations for School Mathematics of the 1980's*. Reston, Va.: National Council of Teachers of Mathematics, 1980.

Piaget, Jean. "How Children Form Mathematical Concepts." *Scientific American* (Nov. 1953), pp. 202–206.

Price, G. C. "Cognitive Learning in Early Childhood Education: Mathematics, Science, and Social Studies." In *Handbook of Research in Early Childhood Education* ed. by B. Spodek. New York: The Free Press, 1982, pp. 264–273.

Richardson, L. I., Kathy L. Goodman, Nancy N. Hartman, and H. C. LePique. *A Mathematics Activity Curriculum for Early Childhood and Special Education*. New York: Macmillan, 1980.

Silverman, Helen. "Beyond the Workbook: Mathematics and the Young Child." In *Early Childhood Education*. Ed. by Leonard H. Golubchick and Barry Persky. Wayne, N.J.: Avery, 1977. Pp. 180–182.

Thompson, Charles S., and John Van de Waler. "Let's Do It: Paper Plate Dots Give Numbers Meaning." *Arithmetic Teacher* **28**:1 (1980), pp. 3–7.

CHAPTER 10

The Social Studies: Interaction and Environment

An important goal of early childhood education is to help young children grow beyond concern for themselves alone toward a concern for others and a knowledge of the social world in which they live. The years of early childhood are those in which the child is forming basic personal and social concepts and feelings.[1]

Education for realizing this goal cannot be delayed until the children are older. The early years are very important, and instruction must begin during these years. Hess and Easton attempted to discover the concepts, attitudes, and values held by children about the political world. Data collected seem to indicate that the child's political world begins to take shape before he or she enters elementary school and is subject to rapid change. Many basic political attitudes and values are firmly established by the end of elementary school.[2]

Lambert and Klineberg reported views that children hold of their own and foreign peoples. Such findings seem to imply the necessity of early concern for the

[1] H. M. Walsh, *Introducing the Young Child to the Social World* (New York: Macmillan, 1980), pp. vi–vii.

[2] R. Hess and D. Easton, "The Role of the Elementary School in Political Socialization," *The School Review,* **70**:3 (1962), pp. 257–265.

development of international views and attitudes essential to intercultural and international understanding. For example, by age six children stressed differences rather than similarities of people from other countries.[3] Goodman reported that the onset of bigotry and racially related value systems is to be found in children as young as four years.[4] Findings such as these should influence both the content and the techniques of social studies for young children and emphasize the importance of social studies in the day care center, child development center, the nursery school, and the kindergarten. Jarolimek says,

> Learning about people, how and where they live, how they form and structure societies, how they govern themselves and provide for their material and psychological needs, how and why they hate each other, how they use and misuse the resources of the planet that is their home—all this is what social studies education is really about.[5]

WHY TEACH SOCIAL STUDIES?

Through content and experiences, the social studies are designed to develop intelligent, responsible, self-directing people who can function as members of groups—family, community, world—with which they become identified. The goals of the social studies program can be stated as follows.[6]

1. To help children understand more about people and their relationships to each other and to their environment.
2. To foster the development of human dignity and a respect for human life with an appreciation for the rights of others, personal property, honesty, and courtesy.
3. To provide knowledge and skills necessary for the survival of individuals, groups, democratic ideas, and life itself. Stress the interdependence of children and adults at school, at home, in the neighborhood, and in the community.
4. To help children make choices relevant for them about important economic, political, and social issues, focusing on here-and-now interests of the home, school, and neighborhood.
5. To help children lead richer, more satisfying, and more personally fulfilling lives. Provide opportunities for the child to play and work with others of various nationalities, races, and religions. Include understandings relating to children in other parts of the world.

Social studies are concerned, then, with behavior, goals, values, skills, and knowledge. The objectives may be classified in three categories: understandings,

---

[3] W. E. Lambert and O. Klineberg, *Children's Views of Foreign Peoples* (New York: Appleton, 1967).
[4] Mary Ellen Goodman, *Race Awareness in Young Children*, rev. ed. (New York: Macmillan, 1964).
[5] J. Jarolimek, *Social Studies in Elementary Education*, 5th ed. (New York: Macmillan, 1977), p. 4.
[6] Elliot Seif, *Teaching Significant Social Studies in the Elementary School* (Chicago: Rand McNally, 1977), p. 46.

which deal with knowledge and knowing; attitudes, which deal with values, appreciations, ideals, and feelings; and skills that must be related to the social skills of living and working together, skills that make for civic competence.[7] Concepts, skills, and behavior are all interrelated. In guiding behavior, teachers must consider the feelings and needs as well as the ideas, attitudes, and skills of the child. As Ojemann pointed out, if a child is in a position where his or her security, self-respect, or activity is seriously threatened, it will be difficult for the child to cooperate with others.[8]

In setting up learning situations and planning teaching strategies, the teacher must make sure that each child has opportunities to gain some measure of self-respect, satisfaction, assurance, and emotional security through the desired behavior. In working to realize the goals, however, certain concepts are important for teachers to remember.

1. Children are easily influenced.

    Research in this area supports the belief that the values and attitudes of children reflect those of parents, teachers, and other adults in the community. What a child comes to recognize as important often depends on the values of the adults in his or her life.

    One who teaches young children needs to be reminded of the implications of the old saying, "What you are speaks so loud I can't hear what you say." The school situation must be planned so as to help children to observe and practice behavior consistent with the beliefs and values that it is hoped they will choose.

2. All children are different.

    Backgrounds of children vary widely and they are not all at the same stage of maturity. Lacey found that the differences in concept development within a grade group seemed to be of more importance than the differences between grades.[9] Harrison used fifty common terms relating to time and found that children of high intelligence in the kindergarten scored almost as many correct responses as children of lower intelligence in the third grade.[10]

3. Children use labels or words without understanding the meaning of the word or concept.

    Because there is no inevitable connection between the meaning of a concept and the word that stands for it, it is quite possible for a child to use the word with little understanding of the meaning or even the wrong meaning. For example, a *train-bearer* to a four-year-old meant a little boy carrying a "choo-choo" train rather than a member of a wedding party. One group of five-year-olds

---

[7] Jarolimek, op. cit., pp. 7–8.

[8] R. Ojemann, "Social Studies in Light of Knowledge About Children," *Social Studies in the Elementary School*, 56th Yearbook NSSE (Chicago: U. of Chicago, 1957), p. 78.

[9] Joy M. Lacey, *Social Studies Concepts of Children in the First Three Grades* (New York: Teachers College, 1932).

[10] M. Lucile Harrison, "The Nature and Development of Concepts of Time Among Young Children," *Elem. Sch. J.*, **34**:7 (1934), pp. 507–514.

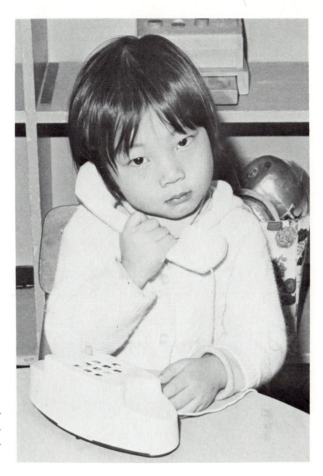

Early contact with children from other countries can contribute to the development of multicultural and international understandings.

talked about being kind to one another. That they did not understand the meaning of kindness was evidenced by the fact that immediately following the discussion, these same children forced another child out of the playhouse, without a turn to play.

4. Children and adults hold different values.

Just because the child knows the desired response does not mean he/she will behave in that way. Children often answer the way they think adults want them to answer. Fite and Jersild found that during an interview a three- or four-year-old may say that fighting is bad, yet actually engage in fighting.[11] Combs says that "our greatest failures are those connected with the problem of helping peo-

[11] M. D. Fite and A. T. Jersild, "Aggressive Behavior in Young Children and Children's Attitudes Toward Aggression," *Genet. Psychol. Monogr.*, **22**:2 (1940), pp. 151–319.

ple to behave differently as a result of the information we have provided them."[12]

Children need opportunities to discover the personal value and usefulness of the concept. Until children find that they can solve problems satisfactorily, get a turn at the slide, or use the blocks without fighting, they will probably continue to hit, grab, and push. The child needs help in finding different ways of solving a problem and of evaluating the various methods.

To plan effectively for learning situations through which the objectives of the social studies may be realized, teachers must observe the following basic principles:

1. Children must have an opportunity to clarify what they say and to relate this to what they do; to live what they learn; to experience and to practice kindness, courtesy, sharing; and to make choices. Verbalization alone is not adequate.
2. Meaningful experiences closely related to the activities of the child and behavioral goals are essential. The child must find in the desired behavior some satisfaction, some enhancement of self-respect, security, and personal worth.
3. Standards, teaching strategies, and learning activities must be adapted to the differences prevalent in the group. Each child needs the opportunity to participate in challenging activities, to make choices, and assume responsibilities suited to his or her background.

WHAT TO TEACH: CONTENT

This area of the early childhood curriculum combines the social sciences of anthropology, economics, geography, history, environmental education-ecology, political science, and sociology. These social sciences share the same subject matter: the behavior of human beings.[13] Each of the social sciences views humans from a different vantage point. The curriculum area that focuses on the activities of human beings is social studies.[14] The various ways in which people interact with each other and with the various environments in which they find themselves are the foundations of the social studies.[15]

Social studies for young children focus on the immediate environment and experiences of the child, and there should be a provision for many firsthand experiences. The content, then, at any grade level is negotiable so long as the major focus is on human interactions. Usually, content for younger learners emphasizes family and community structures.

The traditional social studies programs are built on the "widening horizons the-

---

[12] A. W. Combs, "Personality Theory and Its Implications for Curriculum Development," *Learning More About Learning* (Alexandria, Va.: ASCD, 1959), p. 9.

[13] Arthur K. Ellis, *Teaching and Learning Elementary Social Studies* (Boston: Allyn, 1977), p. 13.

[14] Dorothy J. Skeel, *The Challenge of Teaching Social Studies in the Elementary School* 3d ed. (Santa Monica: Goodyear, 1979), p. 17.

[15] Ellis, op. cit., p. 14.

ory."[16] According to this philosophy, certain topics are more relevant to the experiences and development of children at certain ages. The typical social studies curriculum provides for younger children to study about themselves, their families, and their communities whereas older children will study about cities, states, and countries. Unfortunately, these assumptions limit a teacher to teaching certain types of content regardless of the experiences, development, and interests of the children.

It is necessary to learn as much about the children as possible. Teachers must take into account the interests, needs, developmental levels, and experiences of children before selecting content. The determination of content can be done in a number of ways: through observation of students, allowing children to choose content, or a joint decision by teacher and children.

The traditional organization of content is based on earlier research related to the development of the child's concept of time and experiential background. Dunfee, however, reports that

> A review of the studies of time concepts seems to indicate that children may be able to understand time and chronology concepts at an earlier age than previously predicted and that many children are receptive to planned instruction in these relationships.[17]

It is impossible, however, to limit the child's learnings to those of the home and school. Many children, by the age of five, have lived in other countries or have some member of their family living abroad. By means of television the child becomes aware of holidays and hears something of their historical significance. Few, if any, children move sequentially from home to school, to community, state, nation, and the world in their experiences.

The store of information young children have today, their continual quest for knowledge, and their struggle to organize information into a meaningful conceptual framework have significant implications for school programs. It is apparent that teachers of young children must support their efforts to acquire information and to organize it.

In view of the changing experiences and concepts of children, it appears wise to enlarge the scope of the social studies for young children to include understandings from all the major areas of social studies and provide for the growth of children through constantly enlarging experiences. Simple ideas introduced in the early years will lay a foundation for understanding more complex ones in later grades. Such a "spiral approach" introduces concepts to the young child and provides for reteaching these concepts in a more complex situation at a later date. According to Bruner, in the spiral curriculum "ideas are first presented in a form and language, honest

---

[16] Skeel, op. cit., p. 39.
[17] Maxine Dunfee, *Elementary Social Studies: A Guide to Current Research* (Alexandria, Va.: ASCD, 1970), p. 29.

These children helped to reseed their playground in the spring. When they came back to the Center in the fall, they looked at the seeds on the grass.

though imprecise, which can be grasped by the child, ideas which can be revisited later with greater precision and power until finally, the student has received the reward of mastery."[18]

As an example of this approach, certain areas of the social studies are listed. The name associated with the area (for example, history or anthropology) is used in order to indicate that the concepts or beginnings may be developed with young children. The study of history or anthropology is appropriate for young children, but the concepts selected for study and the procedures used are not the same as those used for older children. For each area, some of the appropriate concepts are listed, along with suggested opportunities for experiences that can contribute to the development of concepts, understandings, values, and skills.

The possible interrelationships among the areas should be noted. While the teacher is developing the concept that each person has worth and dignity in the

[18]J. S. Bruner, *On Knowing* (Cambridge, Mass.: Harvard U.P., 1962), p. 62.

Table 10–1
Learnings in Social Studies

Area	Examples of Concepts To Be Learned	Some Learning Activities That Can Contribute to Concept Development
1. Moral education.	Each person has worth and dignity. We are not all alike.	Introduce each child in class. Talk about how children are alike and yet different. Use books, songs, pictures, discussion, snapshots.
2. Civics.	Rules can help us live happily together (respect for rules and regulations.)	Participate in discussion of "limits" or "rules" for the slide. Make plans for taking a walk. Note "how we cross the street," "why we walk on the sidewalk." Accept "limits" set by group.
3. Conservation.	Money is used to buy food, clothing, and school supplies. These items can be used freely but without waste (respect for personal and public property). Water has many uses. Water can be conserved.	Take care of one's own possessions. Hang coat in locker; wear apron while painting. Use paper towels as needed. Help clean up after work period. Turn off water faucets.
4. Economics.	People do different types of work (appreciation of contribution of others). People live in different types of homes (understanding of how others live). Money is used to buy what we need.	Learn about the work that parents do; use stories, pictures, trips, visitors, and discussion. Learn about homes in which the children live: trailer, apartment, one-story houses. Make use of pictures, art products, trips, stories, discussion.
5. History— American heritage.	Understanding that great men and women had great ideas. They were honest, brave, kind (historical understanding). An event is a part of a chronological series. Simple time relationships exist. Our society changes.	Celebrate holidays. Emphasize historic significance. Use stories, films, trips, role-playing, music, bulletin-board displays. Discuss and clarify meaning of honest, brave, kind. Learn how time is measured. Use clock and calendar. Discuss important events in lives of the children. Observe changes in neighborhood or town. Discuss reasons for change.
6. Geography— where we live. Relationship of scientific and social change.	People travel in different ways. Messages are sent in different ways. Weather affects the way we dress and where we play (readiness for geography).	Learn about the ways people travel. Take a bus or train ride. Visit the airport. Send messages— use telephone; mail a letter. Observe evidence of seasonal changes.

Table 10-1 (continued)

Area	Examples of Concepts To Be Learned	Some Learning Activities That Can Contribute to Concept Development
7. International understandings.	People live in other countries. Children live and play in other countries. (Recognition that people are different—not necessarily that one is better than another.)	Learn games and songs of children in other lands. Compare them with games and songs of the kindergarten children. Invite persons from other lands to talk with children.
8. Anthropology.	People live according to certain values, skills, and traditions.	Talk about how each family celebrates birthdays. Role-play social skills. Make choices and examine alternatives. Consider what each child values most. Examine behavior of group.
9. Sociology.	The family is the basic social unit in our society. All families are not alike.	Learn about members of the family. Play roles of family members. Use pictures, books, and songs.
10. Environmental education— ecology.	Water and air can be polluted. Many familiar sounds cause noise pollution. Waste disposal is a severe problem.	Observe effects of air pollution on one's eyes and breathing. Note effects of water pollution on where children can swim. Identify sounds that contribute to noise pollution. Plan to reduce noise at school and home. Plan for cleaning room. Observe disposal of school waste.

area of moral education, there are also possible learnings in anthropology and sociology as well.

Through content there is the development of concepts, processes, and values. There is now less emphasis on facts and more on concepts and generalizations.[19]

PLANNING AND TEACHING

A teacher will find many opportunities for helping the child develop desirable habits, attitudes, and skills and to gain useful information. Suggested strategies for planning and teaching are discussed in Chapter 6, and the reader is urged to refer to this section for a more detailed treatment. Certain strategies are illustrated here with examples from the social studies.

[19] Seif, op. cit., pp. 45-46.

1. Reinforcing, Clarifying, Explaining, and Discussing Incidents that Affect Children During the School Day.   For example, one Monday morning the kindergarten children were telling about what they had done over the weekend.

> Jack: "I went to Sunday School. I go to the Presbyterian Sunday School."
> Joseph: "I don't. We go to the Episcopal Church."
> Several children joined in, identifying the church that they attended. Then Edith spoke. "I don't go to Sunday School. My mother doesn't take me." The teacher replied, "On Sunday, Jack and Joseph went to church with their parents. Edith stayed at home. We can do that because we live in our country, the United States. In our country, mothers and fathers can choose whether or not they want to go to church. They can choose the church, too."

While children at this age do not understand the term "religious freedom," a discussion such as this can provide the experience on which generalizations can be developed later.

2. Instructional Resources.   Make maximum use of direct experiences, where possible, but when opportunities for direct experiences do not exist, the teacher can use vicarious experiences, such as films, models, or pictures.

3. Cooperative Planning.   Cooperative planning involves the teacher and children planning together to provide for varied learning activities. This helps the children develop understandings of cooperative group living and an appreciation for the rights of others. An example of cooperative planning follows: The kindergarten children had been given a collie puppy. It was their very own puppy, and it must have a name. The teacher and children sat down together.

> Teacher: Several of you have already suggested names for the puppy. Hugh wants "Candy." Glen wants "Collie." Joan wants "Spot." How shall we decide?
> Glenn: We could vote.
> Teacher: Yes, we can vote. That means I will write down each name: Candy, Collie, and Spot. Then I will ask each of you to tell me the name you like best. We will count to see how many children like each name. The name that most of you like will be the name of our puppy. Do you want to do it that way?
> Children: Yes.
> Teacher: Think for a moment about the names: Candy, Collie, and Spot. Decide on the one you want.
> Each name was written on a piece of newsprint. As each child's name was called, the teacher made a mark by the choice. Together they counted the marks:

Candy—20.
Spot—3.
Collie—2.

> Teacher: Candy has twenty votes. That is more votes than for the other two. So Candy will be our puppy's name.

Glenn, who wanted "Collie," angrily stamped his foot and said, "Why vote, if you can't get what you want?"

Teacher: Glenn, we vote to give everyone a chance to say what one wants. You didn't get your choice this time. We will vote again some other time on another idea. Maybe you will win then.

4. Field Trips.   Field trips may be made in connection with the study of a variety of topics in the community. Trips may be made to centers such as the library, the fire station, or the post office; sources of food supply, such as the farm, the orchard or grove, the dairy, the supermarket; transportation to locations such as the airport, the railroad terminal, bus station, a street or highway; the home, which could include a look at the various types of homes and the actual construction of a building.

5. Resource People.   Parents, members of the family, or community persons might serve as resource persons. For example, the teacher said, "Stephen's grandfather is visiting us today. He doesn't speak English but he will play his violin for us."

At another time she said, "Mrs. Olson is Swedish and in her family they make a gingerbread house every year at Christmas time. She is here today to help us make one." The group could also visit the resource person at his or her home, office, or other locations.

6. Learning Centers.   The use of learning centers offers opportunities for children to gain important values related to social studies. Learning centers should allow students to (a) obtain basic information, (b) practice a skill, (c) follow up on class activities, and (d) enrich and extend basic instruction.[20]

Units may be referred to as plans for developing key concepts. In the selection of the topic for study, a balance among various areas of the social studies is desirable. It is possible for an undue proportion of time to be spent in activities that contribute most directly to one area. For example, geographic understandings may be emphasized to the extent that the child may have few learning opportunities in other areas of social studies. Children need contact with history and anthropology too.

Examining the background of the children can give leads to topics. McAulay found in interviewing seventy second-graders that sixty-three of the children could name at least two duties of the police officer and sixty-five at least one duty of the fire fighter. Units had been planned on both topics.[21] The same situation exists in many children's programs today.

The teacher should not be upset by the fact that children already have some information about a topic selected for study. The teacher needs to find out what the children already know and to make plans for the educational needs of each.

[20] John Jarolimek, *Social Studies in Elementary Education*, 6th ed. (New York: Macmillan, 1982), p. 122.
[21] J. D. McAulay, "Social Studies in the Primary Grades," *Social Educ.*, **18**:8 (1954), pp. 357–358.

There is so much to learn and know that children should not be bored with the repetition of information already familiar to them. This type of organization offers flexibility and makes possible a variety of learning opportunities that can be adapted to individual needs and interests.

There are two types of units: the *resource unit* and the *teaching unit*. A *resource unit* pulls together all pertinent resources for a unit of study. All possible activites for the unit are listed and explained. Also included are films, filmstrips, study prints, books (for both teacher and student use), records, and any other materials available that relate to the proposed unit of study. The activities for the resource unit should integrate various curriculum areas. Three types of activites should be included: (1) initiating activites to begin the unit, (2) middle activities that are used to develop the concepts, and (3) culminating activities that will draw the unit to a close. The list of activities in the resource unit will probably be more than can be used in the teaching unit. Also included in the resource unit should be a plan of evaluation to determine if the stated purposes of the unit have been met.

The *teaching unit* is what is actually taught. Selections from the resource unit will vary depending on the needs of the group of children. A teaching unit includes daily lesson plans for the unit of study. Objectives for each lesson are established and activities are selected. The materials needed and the methods used are described. An evaluation of the lesson is included.

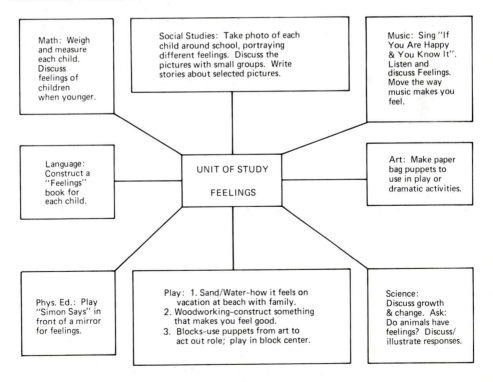

Math: Weigh and measure each child. Discuss feelings of children when younger.

Social Studies: Take photo of each child around school, portraying different feelings. Discuss the pictures with small groups. Write stories about selected pictures.

Music: Sing "If You Are Happy & You Know It". Listen and discuss Feelings. Move the way music makes you feel.

Language: Construct a "Feelings" book for each child.

UNIT OF STUDY

FEELINGS

Art: Make paper bag puppets to use in play or dramatic activities.

Phys. Ed.: Play "Simon Says" in front of a mirror for feelings.

Play: 1. Sand/Water-how it feels on vacation at beach with family.
2. Woodworking-construct something that makes you feel good.
3. Blocks-use puppets from art to act out role; play in block center.

Science: Discuss growth & change. Ask: Do animals have feelings? Discuss/illustrate responses.

A PLAN FOR DEVELOPING A UNIT (KEY CONCEPTS)

| | Topic—Feelings: How Do I Feel?
How Do Others Feel?[22]
For Four- or Five-Year-Olds—
Early in the Year |
Outline for Planning	
1. *Purposes:* These give direction to planning. Here the expected outcomes are stated. Simply state the purpose or task. "What am I trying to do? What do I hope to accomplish?"	a. *Purposes:* To help the child achieve beginnings of self-understanding, to develop the ability to identify and express one's feelings or emotions, to become aware of the feelings of others, and to begin to understand how feelings influence behavior.
	b. *Concepts To Be Developed.* I have feelings. I can be happy, thankful, angry, afraid. Other children have feelings too. They can be happy, and so forth. The way we feel affects how we act. If I am happy I may be kind. If I am angry I may cry, hit, snatch. The way I treat other children affects how they feel.
2. *Initiating the Plan:* Plan to initiate the study in such a way as to arouse the curiosity and interest of the children. Regardless of the plan for beginning, children should be involved in the planning. Several means of initiating a plan are listed:	
a. Teacher Suggestion. The teacher may propose certain questions about the topic, leave questions unanswered, provoke some discussion, and then say that the answers to the questions will be found during the study of the topic.	When the children come together for a group session, the teacher can introduce each child individually. She might ask, "What were you like when you were a baby?" "How much have you grown since you were born?" "What does it mean to grow?" "How do you feel now that you are five years old?" "How did you feel when you came to school?" The teacher may use a story, such as *The Growing Story*, following it with questions such as the preceding ones. Questions such as "How do you feel?" may need to be followed by words such as *afraid? happy? lonely?* Thus the teacher can help the child find the meaning for these terms and also for his or her feelings.

---

[22] Suggestions for parts of the unit adapted from C. K. Ducolon, "Loving: A Process Approach," unpublished graduate paper, University of Maryland, College Park, May 1971.

	Topic—Feelings: How Do I Feel? How Do Others Feel?[22]
Outline for Planning	For Four- or Five-Year-Olds— Early in the Year

b. Incidents. Some incident or happening in the life of a child or in the local community, state, nation, or world might be the means of creating interest in a particular topic. For example, a good time to have a unit on the circus is when the circus comes to town. Holidays, festivals, and seasons of the year also offer leads.

    The incident—It is the first day the children are together. As the teacher greets each child, she pins on a name tag and says, "This is your name." She may ask, "What do you like about your name?"

c. Audiovisual Materials. Use of any of the following: motion pictures, filmstrips, slides, flat pictures, recordings, radio, field trips, TV, or resource persons.

    In small groups, view a portion of a filmstrip that presents a problem of dealing with feelings. Role-play possible solutions to the problem.

d. Ongoing Experience. A preceding topic may lead directly into a second one. If interest in the preceding topic was high, it should be sufficient to carry over.

e. Arranged Environment. Arrange a display of some type in which books, objects, pictures draw attention to a particular topic. For example, if the topic to be studied is on "Our Homes," the teacher would arrange books, pictures, and models of different types of homes on a table or bulletin board. The arrangement should be set up the day before and children should be permitted some time to view the display, to talk freely about the things they see. They may identify the specific questions and topics to be considered.

    Polaroid pictures could be taken of each child and mounted on the bulletin board. Actions in pictures could be labeled in connection with teacher questions such as "What were you doing there?" "How did you feel doing that?"

3. *Learning Opportunities:* There must be a relationship between the learning opportunities and the purposes. It is through the activities that the purposes are attained. Learning activities should be numerous and varied so that individual differences can be met. The following is a list of possible activities. They are not listed in order of importance. One plan may not include all of them. Activities are classified according to subject areas to illustrate how a topic such as *Feelings* can offer opportunities for academic learnings in the various subject areas. It is important to remember that one activity can contribute to learnings in several areas.

	Topic—Feelings: How Do I Feel? How Do Others Feel?[22]
Outline for Planning	For Four- or Five-Year-Olds— Early in the Year
a. Language Activities. Discussion, dramatization, conversation, telling stories, listening to stories and poems, and writing letters and stories (dictated to the teacher), looking at books.	Make a tape recording of children's voices. Ask children to listen and to identify their own voice. The teacher may ask, "How did you feel when you heard your voice? How did your voice sound?" Listen to stories, poems, recordings about a child or children. Look at books about a child or children. Books such as *What Mary Jo Wanted* and *Will I Have a Friend?* could provide identity figures for the children and encourage them to express their feelings about characters in the stories and their own personal wants and attitudes. Possible teacher questions might include "Why do you think Mary Jo wanted a puppy?" "What does it mean to share?" "What is a friend?" "How do we make friends?" "How do friends feel about each other?" Role-playing could emphasize the feelings of children and how these feelings influence their behavior. Pictures can provide a good beginning. Possible questions include "What do you think is happening here?" "How do you think the children feel?" "Why?" "What do you think the children might do next?" "Show us." The *Let's Start Collection* can be helpful. *Feelie Boxes* can be fun. Objects of different shapes are included. The child is asked to reach into the box and respond to the questions "How does it feel?" "What shape do you think it is?" "Is it a happy shape?" "How do you know?" Make picture books using titles such as "How I Feel Today," or "My Friends." Pictures may come from magazines or they may be drawn or painted. Create poems or stories (dictated to teacher). Note children's names under photographs. Play games: Identify child by his or her voice. "Who am I?"

Outline for Planning	Topic—Feelings: How Do I Feel? How Do Others Feel?[22] For Four- or Five-Year-Olds— Early in the Year
	Practice use of courteous terms such as "Thank you" and "Excuse me." Discuss meanings of terms and relate them to how one feels.
	Develop meanings for vocabulary words such as happy, thankful, angry, lonely, friend, enemy, afraid, hope.
	Act out the meanings while others identify the feelings.
b. Community Resources. Field trips to places of interest such as city hall, library, post office, airport, bakery, grocery, and farm. The immediate school environment is a laboratory in itself. Many individuals in the community can be brought into the classroom as resource persons. Don't overlook parents as resource people; they have much to offer.	Take field trips around the school and in the community. Take pictures on the trip. Dictate stories to go with pictures. Make picture books using titles such as "People at the Airport."
c. Audiovisual Experiences. Films, filmstrips, slides, radio, recordings, television, models, charts, graphs, flat pictures, dioramas, wall murals.	View films and filmstrips. *The Joy of Being You* and *All Kinds of Feelings* are filmstrips that can be used to introduce children to their own feelings, how they may be expressed, and the meaning of feelings such as joy or loneliness. Listen to and respond to recordings. The song *Growing* (album by Hap Palmer) encourages children to feel what it is like to grow.
d. Handicrafts and Arts. Painting, clay modeling, paper maché modeling, and construction out of paper or wood.	Paint and draw pictures of self and others. Draw a picture of self while looking into a mirror. Have each child describe the color of his or her eyes and hair. Draw a sad face. Draw a happy face. Draw a surprised face. Draw or paint a "loving picture." Discuss feeling of love. Children can trace around each other on large sheets of paper placed on the floor. Details may be filled in later. Teacher questions might include "Is your face happy?" "How do you think your friend feels in his picture?"

Outline for Planning	Topic—Feelings: How Do I Feel? How Do Others Feel?[22] For Four- or Five-Year-Olds— Early in the Year
	Use finger paint. Questions that may be asked include "How does the paint feel on your hands?"
	View reproductions of famous paintings. Ask questions that relate to how the painter might have felt when painting the picture and how the people in the picture feel.
	Make paper-bag puppets. Faces could be happy, sad, or lonely.
	Make a picture time line of growth from babyhood to the age of five years.
	Make a silhouette of each child, play a game identifying each silhouette, and then label with child's name.
e. Music and Physical Activities. Songs, rhythms, games, listening to records, playing instruments.	Play musical selections on piano or record player. Ask children to listen to and respond to questions such as "How does the music make you feel?" "Sleepy?" "Lazy?" "Happy?" "If you feel like that music how would you act? Show us."
	Sing songs about self and other children. Songs such as "If You're Happy and You Know It" can be used for encouraging responses. Feelings such as *sleepy* or *hungry* can also be used.
	Use an adaptation of the game "Simon Says." Ask a small group of children to face a mirror and to make facial expressions to match certain feelings. For example, "Simon says to make a happy face (or to make a frown or to be afraid)."
	Do a movement activity. Use music with varied tempos for moving in different ways such as running, hopping, jumping, skipping. Discuss with the children how these movements made them feel.
f. Mathematics Activities. Opportunities for counting, measuring, weighing, development of concepts and vocabulary.	Weigh and measure children. Chart differences over time period. Involve children. Make a time line, using pictures of the children from birth to time of school entrance.
	Make cookies for someone to make him or her happy.

Outline for Planning	Topic—Feelings: How Do I Feel? How Do Others Feel? [22] For Four- or Five-Year-Olds— Early in the Year
g. Growth in Social Skills and Attitudes. Opportunities for leadership, cooperation, a dramatization, a film, or a discussion period may be used.	Make choices. Share materials and equipment. Take turns. Discuss how one feels when one shares or takes turns and how the other child feels. Avoid moralizing. Cooperate in clean-up. Learn other children's names. Practice courtesy in asking for and receiving materials, turns, and so on. Relate to feelings. Read *Ask Mr. Bear* and *Play With Me* to begin discussion. 1. Tell what your mother does to make you "happy." 2. your friend, 3. your dad, and 4. your teacher. Read *Frederick, Swimmy, Tico, and the Golden Wings.* Act out the following situations: (1) how people feel when you smile, (2) how people feel when you wait, (3) how people feel when you take turns with them, and (4) how people feel when you help them learn something new. Discuss feelings in the following situations: (1) when hungry, (2) when tired, (3) when left out, (4) when hurt, (5) when lost, (6) when one does not get his or her own way, and (7) when there is a new baby brother or sister.
4. *Culminating Activities:*	Make a mural of the class with varied feelings portrayed. Develop a class drama about feelings. Invite parents and friends to the presentation.
5. *Evaluation:* Ask the question "How can I know whether or not the purposes stated in the beginning have been realized?"	Observe dramatic play. Note conversations and comments of children for indications of self and others that have developed. Observe children's behavior for evidences of planning, sharing, assuming responsibility, using courteous forms of speech.

	Topic—Feelings: How Do I Feel? How Do Others Feel?[22] For Four- or Five-Year-Olds— Early in the Year
Outline for Planning	

Observe children's art products. See Chapter 14.

Use anecdotal records. See Chapter 6.

6. *List of Materials:* List the materials needed to teach the unit. The materials should be accessible and ready to use when needed.

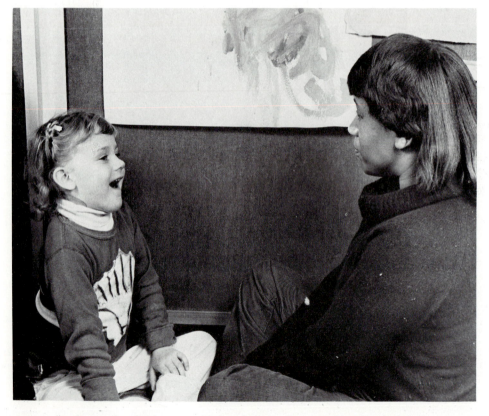

Amy is developing the ability to express her feelings. "I can make a happy face."

Unit resources

BOOKS

Anglund, Joan W. *A Friend Is Someone Who Likes You*. New York: Harcourt, 1958.

Balian, Lorna. *I Love You, Mary Jane*. Nashville, Tenn.: Abingdon, 1967.

Beim, Jerrold, and Lorraine Beim. *Two Is a Team*. New York: Harcourt, 1945.

Bromhall, Winifred. *Peter's Three Friends*. New York: Knopf, 1964.

Bryant, Bernice. *Let's Be Friends*. Chicago; Children's Press, 1954.

Cohen, Miriam. *Will I Have a Friend?* New York: Macmillan, 1967.

Cole, William. *Frances Face-Maker*. New York: World, 1963.

Ets, Marie H. *Just Me*. New York: Viking, 1965.

———. *Play With Me*. New York: Viking, 1955.

Evans, Eva K. *People Are Important*. New York: Capitol, 1957.

Flack, Majorie. *Ask Mr. Bear*. New York: Macmillan, 1958.

Green, Mary M. *Is It Hard? Is It Easy?* Reading, Mass.: Addison-Wesley, 1960.

Guilfoile, Elizabeth. *Nobody Listens to Andrew*. Chicago: Follett, 1957.

Iwasaki, Chihiro. *Will You Be My Friend?* New York: McGraw-Hill, 1974.

Keats, E. J. *The Snowy Day*. New York: Viking, 1962.

———. *Whistle for Willie*. New York: Viking, 1964.

Keesler, L., and Ethel Keesler. *Kim and Me*. New York: Doubleday, 1960.

Krauss, Ruth. *The Growing Story*. New York: Harper, 1947.

Kushin, Karla. *Just Like Everybody Else*. New York: Harper, 1959.

Lionni, Leo. *Frederick*. New York: Pantheon, 1966.

———. *Swimmy*. New York: Pantheon, 1963.

———. *Tico and the Golden Wings*. New York: Pantheon, 1964.

Ness, Evaline. *Exactly Alike*. New York: Scribner, 1964.

Orbach, Ruth. *I'm Dan*. New York: Scribner, 1970.

Udry, Janice May. *Let's Be Enemies*. New York: Harper, 1961.

———. *What Mary Jo Shared*. Chicago: Whitman, 1966.

———. *What Mary Jo Wanted*. Chicago: Whitman, 1968.

Vreeken, Elizabeth. *The Little Boy Who Would Not Say His Name*. Chicago: Follett, 1959.

Yashima, Taro. *Youngest One*. New York: Viking, 1959.

FILMSTRIPS

The Joy of Being You. (6970), Scholastic Kindle Filmstrips, 902 Sylvan Avenue, Englewood Cliffs, N.J. 07632.

All Kinds of Feelings. (6968), Scholastic Kindle Filmstrips, 902 Sylvan Avenue, Englewood Cliffs, N.J. 07632.

RECORDS

Learning Basic Skills Through Music. Vol. I, Educational Activities, Inc., Box 392, Freeport, N.Y. 11520.

POETRY

Aldis, Dorothy. *All Together*. New York: Putnam, 1952.

Frank, Josetts (ed.). *Poems to Read to the Very Young*. New York: Random, 1961.

Hopkins, Lee Bennett (ed.). *Me: A Book of Poems*. New York: Seabury, 1970.
Jacobs, Leland B. *Alphabet for Girls*. New York: Holt, 1969.
Livingston, Myra C. *Whispers and Other Poems*. New York: Harcourt, 1957.
Untermeyer, Louis (ed.). *The Golden Treasury of Poetry*. New York: Holden, 1959.

PICTURE SETS

Let's Start Picture Collection: School Experiences. Scholastic Magazine, 902 Sylvan
Avenue, Englewood Cliffs, N.J. 07632, 1968.
Let's Start Picture Collection: Urban Environment. Scholastic Magazine, 902 Sylvan
Avenue, Englewood Cliffs, N.J. 07632, 1969.
Role Playing Photo-Problems for Young Children. Holt, New York.

SONGS

McCall, Adeline. *This Is Music*. Boston: Allyn, 1966.
Nelson, Mary J., and Gladys Tipton. *Music for Early Childhood*. New York: Silver
Burdett, 1952.
Pitts, Lilla Belle, et al. *The Kindergarten Book*. Boston: Ginn, 1949.
Seeger, Ruth Crawford. *American Folk Songs for Children*. New York: Doubleday,
1948.
Winn, Marie (ed.). *Children's Songs*. New York: Simon & Schuster, 1966.
Zetlin, Patty. *Castle in My City—Songs for Young Children*. San Carlos, Calif.: Golden
Gate Junior Books, 1966.

The *teaching plan* may be developed after the teacher becomes acquainted with
the children. Looking at the plan, "Feelings," the teacher may decide to use the
concepts "I have feelings," "Other children have feelings." Selections that are appropriate may be chosen from the unit. The *teaching plan* is developed from the
overall plan and includes detailed plans for the day. For example, Albert enters
kindergarten a few days after the other children. The teacher decides to use this
incident in developing beginning understandings of the concept, "I have feelings.
Other children have feelings too." The plan for this part of the day might include
the following:

1. Purposes: To help each child achieve beginning understandings of his or her
   feelings and feelings of the other children, as evidenced by such statements as
   "I didn't know anybody when I came to kindergarten. I was lonesome. Now
   I am glad."
   "Albert has some friends now. He likes to play with me."
2. Initiating the plan: When Albert came to kindergarten he was introduced individually to the children. Later in the morning as the children come together for
   a group session the teacher might say.
   "Albert came to kindergarten today for the first time. How did you feel when
   you came to school? Happy? Afraid? Lonely? How do you think Albert felt?
   Why?"
3. Learning Opportunities: Discuss questions. Discuss ways to help children feel

happy at kindergarten. Jot down children's comments. Make into experience charts later. Summarize suggestions. Read story *Will I Have A Friend?*

4. Materials:

Book: Cohen, Miriam. *Will I Have a Friend?* New York: Macmillan, 1967. Paper and marker for experience chart.

5. Evaluation: Observe children's behavior for evidences of concern for the feelings of others. Note conversations and comments of children.

At other times, on other days, the teacher may continue to provide opportunities for experiences through which the children may learn about feelings. The teacher may select other concepts and provide appropriate learning opportunities. Little by little, experience by experience, the understandings, attitudes, and skills are learned. As one teacher was told, "Just keep on keeping on."

Suggested Activities

1. Select one concept to be developed with young children from the areas listed earlier in this chapter. Make a unit for teaching the key concepts using the suggested outline. Indicate the age level for which the plan or unit is intended. Select another concept. Plan a series of learning encounters for developing this concept.

2. Observe in a children's center. Describe ways in which the teacher is helping the children or a child develop an understanding and acceptance of others, how they live and feel.

3. Note the ways in which the backgrounds of children in a group that you visited differ. Describe ways in which the teacher is making provision for and utilizing these multicultural backgrounds.

4. Discuss in class the time concepts of young children. Observe a group of young children, and note the words used in relation to time. Were the words used accurately? Note instances of how the teacher helped develop an awareness of time with the children.

5. Select a site that you consider to be appropriate for a field trip for young children. Visit the site and evaluate it in terms of the checklist in Chapter 6. What learnings might the children gain from the trip?

6. View the film *Sugar and Spice*. (Odeon Films, Inc., 51 West 86th St., New York, N.Y. 10024). Discuss how you feel about this film in helping children understand and assume sex roles.

7. Invite someone from another country to come and teach a group of young children a game from that country.

8. Invite the mother of a child from a different ethnic background to come to the center. Perhaps she could cook some food or serve some food appropriate to her background.

9. Read stories to children about children in other countries, the games they play, their homes, their food.

10. View the film *Head Start to Confidence* (U.S. National Audiovisual Center, General Services Adm., Washington, D.C. 20409).

11. Discuss a children's book that depicts life in another country. Evaluate the selection for social studies teaching.

12. Select several children's books that could be a stimulus for interest in a new social studies unit.

Related Readings

Banks, J. A. *Teaching Strategies for Ethnic Studies.* Boston: Allyn, 1975.

Clark, Kenneth B. *Prejudice and Your Child.* Boston: Beacon, 1963.

Cooper, T. T., and M. Ratner. *Many Hands Cooking: An International Cookbook for Girls and Boys.* New York: Crowell and UNICEF, 1974.

Danilov, V. J. "Museums as Educational Partners." *Child. Educ.*, **52**:6 (1976), pp. 306–311.

Goodman, Mary Ellen. *The Culture of Childhood.* New York: Teachers College, 1970.

Hatcher, Barbara. "Putting Young Cartographers 'on the Map'." *Child. Educ.* **59**:5 (1983), pp. 311–315.

Hoopes, David S. *Intercultural Education.* Bloomington: Phi Delta Kappa, 1980.

Ickis, M. *The Book of Religious Holidays and Celebrations.* New York: Dodd, 1966.

Jalongo, Mary R. "Using Crisis-Oriented Books with Young Children." *Young Children* **38**:5 (1983), pp. 29–36.

Jantz, R. K. "Social Studies." In *Curriculum for the Preschool-Primary Child, A Review of Research*, ed. by Carol Seefeldt. Columbus, Ohio: Merrill, 1976. pp. 83–123.

Koeller, Sally. "Economics Education Applied to Early Childhood." *Child. Educ.* **57**:5 (1981), pp. 293–296.

Morris, D. N. "Rallying Around the Children of the World." *Child. Educ.*, **53**:5 (1977), pp. 235–240.

Oliner, Pearl M. *Teaching Elementary Social Studies.* New York: Harcourt, 1976.

Price, G. G. "Cognitive Learning in Early Childhood Education: Mathematics, Science, and Social Studies." In *Handbook of Research in Early Childhood Education*, ed. by B. Spodek. New York: The Free Press, 1982, pp. 275–283.

Rohrer, Georgia K. "Racial and Ethnic Identification and Preference in Young Children." *Young Children*, **32**:4 (1977), pp. 24–33.

Schmidt, Velma E., and Earldene McNeill. *Cultural Awareness: A Resource Bibliography.* Washington, D.C.: NAEYC, 1978.

Seefeldt, Carol. *Social Studies for the Preschool–Primary Child.* Columbus, Ohio: Merrill, 1977.

Skeen, Patsy, and P. C. McHenry. "The Teacher's Role in Facilitating a Child's Adjustment to Divorce." In *Curriculum Planning for Young Children*, ed. by Janet F. Brown Washington, D.C.: NAEYC, 1982, pp. 228–239.

Slobodzian, K. A., and Sally E. Antes. "Dealing with Death." *Child. Educ.* **57**:3 (1981), pp. 289–292.

Van Camp, Sarah S. "Social Studies for 5-Year-Olds." *Child. Educ.*, **57**:3 (1981), pp. 144–147.

Walsh, H. M. *Introducing the Young Child to the Social World.* New York: Macmillan, 1980.

CHAPTER 11

Children and Values: Moral Education

Moral education has historically been one of the school's major concerns. However, over a span of years public schools have given less direct attention to developing certain values and to helping children to think about such values. Events of recent years and societal trends have reawakened a sense of urgency in relation to the need for moral education. Moral education, as defined by Purpel and Ryan, is the intervention by the school, direct and indirect, that affects the moral behavior and the capacity of the child to think about issues of right and wrong.[1]

Educating for values is no simple task. The responsibility for value development is shared by the school, the home, organized religion, and various agencies of the community. This does not, however, lessen the task of the school, for value development is an integral part of the learning process.[2] Values and the valuing process are related to the moral development of children.

Moral education in the schools is, according to Fraenkel, *unavoidable*. A teach-

---

[1] D. Purpel and K. Ryan, *"What Is It and Where Are We?"* in D. Purpel and K. Ryan, eds., *Moral Education . . . It Comes With The Territory* (Berkeley, CA.: McCutchan Pub. Corp., 1976), pp. 3–5.
[2] ASCD, *Toward Better Teaching*, 1949 Yearbook (Alexandria, Va.: ASCD, 1949), pp. 154–155.

er's actions, sayings, and choice of activities suggest that he or she believes that certain ideas, individuals, events, or other phenomena are more important than others.[3]

A Gallup poll in 1976 demonstrated that parents were very concerned about moral education. Forty-five per cent of the parents noted the need to emphasize moral development. Seventy-nine per cent of the parents said that schools *should* assume a share of the responsibility.[4] Such learning, however, is complicated by the very nature of American society. There are groups differing as to race, national origin, religious beliefs, and social and economic levels.

Many persons believe that the family plays a crucial role for children in the development of values and awareness. Raths points out, however, that the changes in the family are dramatic, if not frightening. The consequence, he says, has been a growing confusion and conflict in relation to values.[5]

There are both general and personal values. General values reflect the basic orientation of our society which is democratic. Personal values are those that have to do with making choices and decisions in our personal lives. Children can be helped to think about their choices in terms of a "values framework."[6]

WHAT ARE VALUES?

Values form the basis for inner direction by the individual. They have been defined by many authorities in many ways. Several definitions follow.

> Values are concepts. They are standards of conduct, beauty, efficiency, or worth that a person endorses and tries to live up to or maintain.[7]
> A value is the comparative weight, esteem, or price attached by the individual to a given idea, person, or object.[8]
> Our values show what we tend to do with our limited time and energy.[9]

Values, says Raths, are based on the three processes of choosing, prizing, and acting. He has identified criteria, all of which must be met if something is to be

---

[3] J. R. Fraenkel, *Helping Students Think and Value: Strategies for Teaching the Social Studies,* 2nd ed. (Englewood Cliffs, N.J.: Prentice-Hall, 1980), p. 211.

[4] R. H. Hersh, D. P. Paolitto, and J. Reimer, *Promoting Moral Growth: From Piaget to Kohlberg* (New York and London: Longman, 1979), p. 7.

[5] L. E. Raths, M. Harmin, and S. B. Simon, *Values and Teaching: Working with Values in the Classroom* (Columbus, Ohio: Merrill, 1966), pp. 15–20.

[6] J. Jarolimek, *Social Studies in Elementary Education,* 5th ed. (New York: Macmillan, 1977), pp. 67–69.

[7] Fraenkel, op. cit., p. 215.

[8] ASCD, op. cit., p. 154.

[9] Raths, et al., op. cit., p. 27.

called a value. One must choose freely from alternatives after considering the consequences of each alternative. One cherishes values and is willing to affirm them publicly. One acts upon values and repeats them. They are incorporated into one's behavior and tend to persist. The following guidelines can be helpful to the teacher in understanding how children develop values.[10]

Values Grow Out of and Change with Experience. For children, values build up as the result of their many experiences both in and out of school. For example:

> It was May. Jane was sharing with the teacher some feelings about nursery school. She said, "You know, when I first came to nursery school, I didn't hang up my sweater. I didn't play with the other children. I hit them. Now I put things in my locker, and I like to play with Mary and Brenda." The teacher replied, "You have learned many things in nursery school. You have learned to care for your belongings. You have learned to play with Mary, Brenda, and the others."

The Importance of an Experience in Relation to Value Building Varies According to the Individual Child, His or Her Maturity, Family, Friends, and Background of Experiences. A situation may be helpful to one child in formulating values, but it may not have the same results for another child. For example:

> One morning the five-year-olds were moving with music. Maria skipped gracefully, and Rose said, "Maria can skip. She's good. Look at Albert. He's so funny." This situation, including Rose's remark, offered Maria an opportunity for building a positive self-concept while for Albert the effect was probably negative.

Some of the Values an Individual Holds and Exhibits May Conflict with One Another. The child may value friendship and want very much to play with other children. The child, however, may not recognize that aggressive behavior patterns stand in the way. For example:

> Ted wanted to play with Robert and Juan, two five-year-old boys who were using the blocks. Ted picked up a ball and threw it at the block structure. When talking with the teacher, he asked, "What else could I do? I wanted to play with them."

In considering values one should remember that "the formative school years present a challenge to the educator to contribute to the development of values desirable in a democracy. This whole area of appreciations, interests and goals, character and morality, social and spiritual values is basic to the entire educational process."[11]

---

[10] Raths, et al., ibid., p. 28–30.
[11] ASCD, op. cit., p. 9.

SELECTING VALUES

"In a pluralistic society, diversity is an important value that our educational institutions should express," says Fantini.[12] But Fantini's statement describes the dilemma faced by the teachers of young children. When values are divergent and in conflict, what can the teacher do? The following quotations offer criteria for the selection of values to be taught.

> For a pluralistic society to survive, certain common values must be accepted, such as *mutual respect and concern for the welfare of others.* These common values take precedence over the freedom to be different. Pluralism is not a justification for polarization and estrangement.[13]

> In this society with its many values, some confused and conflicting, two values are basic: *a belief in the potential worth of each individual, and reliance upon the method of individual and group intelligence in the solution of problems.* When either of these basic values is challenged, democracy is threatened. The teacher, as the agent of a democratic state, has a responsibility to help students develop attitudes and beliefs that are consistent with these fundamentals of democracy.[14]

Pressure to have the teacher of young children work for acceptance of values held by the majority violates one of the democratic values—reliance on intelligence, which involves examining different points of view and evolving one's own values.

Recent efforts on the part of some persons interested in respecting a diversity of values have apparently gone to the extreme of accepting any behavior that is different by reason of racial, class, or ethnic origin as "good." Prejudice or violence or aggressive behavior, for example, may be strong in certain situations. In relation to this, however, it is important to consider the following statement.[15]

> Any manifestation of pluralism, cultural identity, or individuality becomes invalid when it contradicts or conflicts with the "inalienable rights" and "privileges of others." This basic American understanding is crucial to any consideration of values and must be a fundamental lesson in value learning for every American child.

To help children develop their values, the adult must first examine his or her own value system and attitudes toward others. For example, there has been a tendency to consider middle-class values as those of children in suburbia and lower-class values as belonging to children of the inner city. Such a tendency not only overlooks migrant and rural children but those of differing social, ethnic, and minority groups as well. The tendency implies a stereotype, assuming that all persons

---

[12] M. D. Fantini, "Public Schools of Choice and the Plurality of Publics," *Educ. Leadership*, **28**:6 (1971), p. 585.

[13] *Report to the President*, White House Conference, op. cit., p. 64.

[14] ASCD, op. cit., p. 155.

[15] *Report to the President*, White House Conference, op. cit., p. 64.

of the same class have the same values. To the contrary, values that are held by the family and that affect the child may differ greatly from the stereotype. Families in the inner city as well as those in suburbia and rural areas may value cleanliness and good health for their children. Families in the inner city may not have the resources necessary to maintain cleanliness and good health, but that does not mean that these qualities are not valued.

Beliefs and feelings about what children should be and do differ widely. The teacher needs to know the behavior patterns expected of each child and the cultural beliefs about what the child should do and be. Such knowledge can help the teacher in dealing with value conflicts between the home and the school.

As the teacher placed a hand on Jimmy's shoulder, he yelled, "Take your hand off my shoulder." The teacher's gesture of affection was interpreted by the child as an aggressive act.

Aggressive behavior may be valued in each of two homes, yet the value may be

Susan understands that Kyla is unhappy because she did not have time to complete a wood-working project. She is gaining some insight into the behavior of others.

expressed in different behavior patterns. In one home the child shows aggression verbally, talks loudly, and perhaps ignores others who want a chance to speak. In another home the child may be encouraged to hit and fight in order to "get along." The difference may be in the behavior manifestations rather than in the value itself.

The teacher must begin with the children where they are and must use the resources of each child and his or her cultural background in order to help identify and clarify values.

The values common in our democracy need to be considered because these are the values that the schools hope to develop. "These values are a part of our political and religious heritages."[16] One list of these values has been used in developing a statement appropriate for young children.[17] The terms such as *moral responsibility* and *devotion to truth* are adult terms, expressed in adult language. However, these have been used to suggest that the foundations of such concepts have their beginnings in the very early years. The adult terms for the values and teacher goals are used, but the behaviors, attitudes, and comments are those of children.

It is important not only that the values be known, but that the teacher recognize behavior, comments, and attitudes of children that are conducive to the realization of the values. A statement of values, including teacher goals expressed in terms of children's behavior, attitudes, and comments, follows.

HUMAN PERSONALITY

Teacher's goal: Help each child—
1. To have a sense of personal worth and to know that
    "My Daddy and Mother love me.
    My teacher loves me too.
    I can climb high on the jungle gym.
    I am Ann's friend."
2. To feel secure in the nursery or kindergarten and to feel that
    "I belong to this group.
    The children like to play with me.
    The children miss me when I am not here.
    The teacher misses me when I am absent.
    The children are glad to see me when I come in the morning.
    Ann is my friend."
3. To develop self-understanding as expressed through
    "I like to play with Sue.
    Sometimes, when children won't let me play with their toys, I get mad and hit them.
    I can talk with Jim, instead of hitting him.
    Children don't like for me to hit them."

[16] Jarolimek, op. cit., p. 67.
[17] National Education Association and American Association of School Administrators, Educational Policies Commission, *Moral and Spiritual Values in Public Schools* (Washington, D.C., 1951).

4. To gain insight into the behavior of others and to understand that
"Jim can't fix the block house. It is going to fall. I will help him.
Tom is crying. He fell and cut his foot.
Joe hasn't been to school before. He doesn't know how we play."

MORAL RESPONSIBILITY

Teacher's goal: Help each child—

1. To develop a willingness to try new activities and experiences as evidenced by such statements as
"I don't know how to paint on the easel, but I can try.
I haven't been to the airport. I might be afraid. But Miss Jones will go with us—mother, too. I can have fun."
2. To recognize ownership and understand that
"Some things belong to me. Some things belong to others. Some things are for all of us to use.
I will share only the things that belong to me or that are for all of us to use.
I will ask if I may use something that belongs to somebody else.
I will use materials carefully."
3. To develop consideration for the welfare and convenience of others. For example,
"Miss Jones is reading a story. The children want to hear. I will not play the record player now.
It is lunch time. I will come to the table. I will not keep the other children waiting."
4. To develop a willingness to let others have turns and practice such behavior as evidenced in
"Here is a ball. You can play with it.
Jim, you can ride the tractor now."
5. To gain an understanding of what it means to do a job. For example
"I will get the things I need to work with. I'm going to paint. I need an apron.
I will finish my job.
I will put materials away."

INSTITUTIONS AS THE SERVANTS OF PEOPLE

Teacher's goal: Help each child—

1. To develop an understanding that each person has a job to do. For example,
"There are many jobs to be done at school.
The teachers teach children. They read stories to us. They watch us when we play.
The custodian cleans our room. The custodian sweeps the floor. The custodian washes the windows."
2. To understand that some jobs help all of us. For example,
"The police officer helps us cross the street. He or she reminds the cars to drive slowly in front of our school.
Mrs. Brown cooks the food for our lunch at school."

COMMON CONSENT

Teacher's goal: Help each child—
1. To develop the willingness to talk things over. For example,
   "If I talk to somebody, I don't have to hit or to snatch the toy."
2. To gain an appreciation of the value of planning together. For example,
   "We all have good ideas.
   Now we all know what we are going to do."
3. To develop an understanding of how we plan together. For example,
   "We can talk about what we want to do. We can ask questions.
   We talk about what we can do.
   We decide what we will do.
   There are different ways to do things."
4. To gain an understanding of the individual's responsibility for following a plan. For example,
   "We made a plan. I helped.
   I will do what we decided.
   Jim forgot. He came down the slide 'head first.' What did we decide to do?"

DEVOTION TO TRUTH

Teacher's goal: Help each child—
1. To learn that some things are true and some things are not true, and to understand that
   "Some children tease just for fun.
   Some stories are make-believe, and I enjoy them.
   Sometimes I can pretend or make-believe.
   Sometimes children do not understand what their mother said and tell something that is not true.
   Sometimes children 'make up' a story just to get others to listen.
   Sometimes children are afraid to tell what really happened."
2. To learn how we can find out the truth. For example,
   "We can go and see for ourselves.
   We can look at pictures.
   We can look at movies.
   We can ask grown-ups.
   We can listen while grown-ups read to us."
3. To develop understanding of what it means to be honest. For example,
   "I will try to remember what happened.
   I won't blame Jim when he hit me. I will remember that I was angry and I pushed Jim.
   Jane didn't make me fall and skin my knee. I wasn't looking where I was going. I tripped and fell.
   I will try to find right answers.
   When I am asked a question, I will tell the truth.
   I can ask myself if this is the best I can do."

RESPECT FOR EXCELLENCE

Teacher's goal: Help each child—

1. To learn to do one thing well, such as walk straight, rest comfortably, drive a nail all the way into the board.
2. To come to recognize his or her best effort, as evidenced by such statements as
   "I can do it better now. Watch me.
   I will try.
   I don't like this picture. I tore it.
   I'm tired now. I'll make another boat tomorrow."
3. To appreciate the achievements of others, as evidenced by the following statements:
   "Jan built a big block house.
   Look, Joe can skip.
   I like your picture. That's good."
4. To set standards for himself or herself. For example,
   "I want to tie my shoe. Please help me."
5. To enjoy learning, as evidenced by such statements as
   "It is fun to say new words.
   I have learned a poem. I can say it."

BROTHERHOOD

Teacher's goal: Help each child—

1. To develop an understanding that children are different, yet alike. For example,
   "We are different in the way we talk, look, dress, worship, the food we eat, the games we play, and the homes we live in.
   But we do talk, eat, wear clothing, worship, play, and live in homes.
   I live in a brick house. Joe lives in an apartment. I am happy in my home.
   He is happy in his.
   Jane's hair is curly and blond. Tina's hair is straight and black."
2. To develop a willingness to treat other children as one wants to be treated. For example,
   "I will take turns.
   I will share my toys."

SPIRITUAL ENRICHMENT

Teacher's goal: Help each child—

1. To develop sensitivity to and appreciation for beauty. For example,
   "The bird is hopping on the grass.
   The sun is so gold and shiny.
   Oh, look. See the little new leaf."
2. To engage in creative activities, with resulting comments such as
   "I know what we can do. I thought about it. [creative thinking]
   The little bird was shivering with scaredness. [creative language]
   The music makes me want to dance and dance." [creative movement]
3. To experience successful achievement. For example,

"You were a good helper, Joe. You put the blocks away.
I did it! I did it! I did it! I painted a house."

4. To develop an understanding that there is law and order in our natural world, which we can regard with reverence and wonder. For example,
"There are seasons. It is spring. The flowers are blooming.
The sun sets in the evening. The sun rises in the morning."

5. To develop an appreciation of kindness, friendliness, cooperation, and loyalty in others. For example,
"When I was lonesome, Pam played with me.
Miss Helms helped me fix my truck.
Sam let me look at his book. He was kind to me."

6. To learn that God is very great. He created beauty for us to enjoy. One child said:
"See the little new moon. God made it. I wish the sky was full of little new moons."

Many early childhood experiences can build spiritual values if the teacher is consciously working toward that end. The teacher's role is an important one.

HELPING CHILDREN DEVELOP VALUES

The child learns moral character in various ways and at various levels of complexity. The form, however, that children's moral education should take and the values to be taught are controversial.[18] This concern for the development of moral values, beliefs, and character among the young is not new. Through the years various methods have been used in teaching morals. Children have been admonished, preached at, punished, and praised. They have been required to memorize passages from the Bible and other religious materials. Their textbooks have been filled with moral precepts and examples of moral conduct. And they have participated in activities designed to build character.

According to Fraenkel, however, a variety of research suggests that these kinds of value education alone have seemed to have little effect on the development of moral individuals.[19] The Character Education Inquiry, begun in 1924, raised questions regarding the methods of character education which were then in use. Hartshorne and May reported that "the main attention of educators should be placed not so much on devices for teaching honesty or any other 'trait' as on the reconstruction of school practices in such a way as to provide not occasional but consistent and regular opportunities for the successful use by both teachers and pupils of such forms of conduct as make for the common good."[20] Kohlberg says that the findings of recent research support these conclusions.[21]

[18] S. R. Stengel, "Moral Education for Young Children," *Young Children*, 37:6 (1982), p. 23.
[19] Fraenkel, op. cit., p. 270.
[20] H. Hartshorne and M. A. May, *Studies in Deceit* (New York: Macmillan, 1928), p. 414.
[21] L. Kohlberg, "Development of Moral Character and Ideology," in *Review of Child Development Research*, Vol. 1, edited by M. L. Hoffman and Lois W. Hoffman (New York: Russell Sage Foundation, 1964), p. 426.

Some have advocated teaching children good reasons for moral actions and re-warding them for behaving in accordance with those reasons. Stengel questions this method.[22] He points out that parents and teachers can not continue to control rewards. As children begin to interact with other children, they also respond to rewards outside of the home and family. . . . If adult reward is the only method used, children may change their behavior as soon as the reward is no longer present.

One of the forums of the 1960 White House Conference on Children and Youth considered the topic, Beliefs—religions, spiritual and secular beliefs, and personal codes of conduct that affect the development of the young.

> The Forum affirmed "the importance of personal faith in God, the strengthening of moral and religious values, and the necessity for a continuing re-examination of personal conduct in order that the Nation's children may realize their full potential for a creative life in freedom and dignity." The ethical principles to be set before our young people "have as their ultimate source the belief that man is created by God and is therefore possessed of dignity as an individual." Churches, synagogues, character-building agencies, and all citizens were called upon to cooperate in encouraging moral and religious training, values, and beliefs among our children and youth.[23]

Throughout the years along with the concern for the development of moral and spiritual values, there has been the concern for the role of the public school in this area of instruction. Schools for young children are operated under various auspices. Some are public schools whereas others are private or church-related. Still others are sponsored by an organization or community agency. Centers supported by public funds, in keeping with the ideas that have been expressed, avoid sectarian emphasis. The church-related and private centers, however, may present spiritual and moral values from their denominational point of view. Regardless, however, of the sponsorship of the school, certain principles are basic to the development of these values in young children.

Jones points out that the capacity to grow spiritually must be nourished just as the capacity to grow physically. The nourishment, however, must be provided in terms of the needs and capacities of a child of a given age. "Overstimulation may be as detrimental to the child's development as is malnutrition."[24] It is important then to provide the needed spiritual nourishment to each child at each stage in his or her growth.

By the age of four the child is becoming assertive. The child has a lively mind and asks many questions, some of which relate to God, the universe, and who made it. Gesell says that "the vast intangible creative force called God is often grasped

---

[22] Stengel, op. cit., p. 25.

[23] *Conference Proceedings* (Washington, D.C.: The Golden Anniversary White House Conference on Children and Youth, Inc., 1960), p. 192.

[24] Mary Alice Jones, *Guiding Children in Christian Growth* (Nashville, Tenn.: Abingdon, 1949), p. 11.

rather well by the mind of the four-year-old."[25] The child is beginning to understand relationships and needs help in comprehending the difference between the activity of God and the work of man. Children, for example, are told that "God gives us food." They should, however, be helped to see that man, using the sun, rain, and soil provided by God, can grow plants or fruit that can be used as food. Man may work with God.

At this age the child often shows a marked interest in death but has little understanding of its meaning. Comments, however, may sound plausible because the child's vocabulary exceeds his or her experiences. The finality of death is not yet understood. By five years of age, the child has the tendency to bring God within the scope of the everyday world. The age of six is described as the peak period of the child's interest in a creative power to which he or she can relate. The child thinks of God in terms of creation. Prayers are becoming important.[26]

Some children think of God as kind and loving whereas others think of Him as stern, terrifying, and awe-inspiring. Jersild points out that a child's concept of God as father will be influenced by experience with one's own father or others in a paternal role. Concepts of sin and forgiveness will be influenced by the ways the child has been treated after misbehaving.[27]

Harms reported that, regardless of different backgrounds and experiences, children show a similar pattern of development in their religious concepts.[28] "The growth in understanding right and wrong is a slow process, dependent upon a growing ability to think, to reason, to make comparisons, to foresee consequences."[29] By the age of three, the child usually knows that some behavior is considered good and some bad by adults he or she knows. At five years the child is able to make some generalizations when the situations are similar. The child up to seven or eight years of age usually accepts, almost entirely, the values of his or her parents and family. Young children coming from different homes bring with them the values of their parents.

There are several approaches to the moral development of children. A discussion of each follows. Two terms frequently used in the various approaches, *cognitive* and *affective*, are defined by Krathwohl. *Cognitive* approaches vary from simple recall of material learned to highly original and creative ways of combining and synthesizing new ideas and materials; *affective* approaches emphasize a feeling tone, an emotion, or a degree of acceptance or rejection.[30]

---

[25] A. Gesell and Frances Ilg, *Child Development, II* (New York: Harper, 1949), p. 86.

[26] Ibid., I, p. 128.

[27] A. T. Jersild, *Child Psychology*, 6th ed. (Englewood Cliffs, N.J.: Prentice-Hall, 1968), p. 520.

[28] E. Harms, "The Development of Religious Experience in Children," *Am. J. Sociol.*, **50**:2 (1944), pp. 112–122.

[29] Jones, op. cit., p. 29.

[30] D. R. Krathwohl, B. S. Bloom, and B. B. Masia, *Taxonomy of Educational Objectives, Handbook II: Affective Domain* (New York: McKay, 1964), pp. 6–7.

Cognitive-Developmental Approach. Both Piaget and Kohlberg are exponents of the cognitive-developmental approach to moral development. This approach involves analysis of the thought structures that underlie the moral concepts of persons at different age levels. Such analysis is used to define a general development.[31] Piaget has evolved two broad stages of moral development, which include the following:[32]

1. "Moral realism, morality of constraint or heteronomous morality." In this stage the child feels that he must comply with rules because they are "sacred and unalterable." Behaviors are viewed by the child as totally right or wrong and he thinks that others view them the same way. The rightness or wrongness of an act is judged on the basis of the consequence or punishment. For example, severe punishment may be interpreted to mean that the deed was very wrong. Violations of rules are followed by accidents or misfortunes.

2. "Autonomous morality, morality of cooperation or reciprocity." In this stage rules are not viewed as unchangeable but as established and maintained through mutual agreement and thus subject to modification in response to the situation. In determining right or wrong, one considers the role of "intention." "Did he mean to do it? or was it an accident?" Now the child is more likely to consider the welfare of others and considers punishment as related to a consequence of an act. For example, an act that causes much damage may deserve more punishment. In making the transition from one stage to the next, Piaget holds that both maturation and experience are involved.[33]

Kohlberg has developed a theory of moral development based on three hierarchical levels. In Level I, "Premoral," one is sensitive to rules and external evaluations and functions in terms of consequences of behavior and the power of those making the rules. In Level II, "Conventional Role Conformity," one wants to do what is expected of him or her. In Level III, "Self-Accepted Moral Principles," one attempts "to define moral values and principles apart from the supporting authority."[34]

Kohlberg's theory, however, deals only with the basis upon which a person evaluates behavior as right or wrong. There are those who believe that this approach is not sufficient. The child's emotional development is also important. The cognitive and emotional development are interdependent. Beck suggests that an interactive approach that involves both intellectual and emotional development is needed.[35]

The interrelationship between the affective and cognitive domains is one of the

[31] M. L. Hoffman, "Moral Development," in *Carmichael's Manual of Child Psychology*, 3d ed., ed. by P. H. Mussen (New York: Wiley, 1970), p. 264.
[32] Ibid., pp. 256–266.
[33] Ibid., p. 266.
[34] D. Graham, *Moral Learning and Development* (New York: Wiley, 1972), p. 228.
[35] J. R. Fraenkel, "The Kohlberg Bandwagon: Some Reservations," *Social Education*, **40**:4 (1976), pp. 221–222.

most frequently cited justifications for affective education. The affective domain may influence the degree to which what is learned is used.[36] The child's receptivity to learning may also be influenced by his or her self-esteem.[37] Heath believes that helping children to understand their own feelings and those of others helps them to keep their feelings under control.[38] Exploring the affective sphere can also help children to understand differing viewpoints, gain skill in integrating their abilities, and develop more "stability and personal autonomy."[39]

Clarifying Strategies.   Raths identifies four basic approaches to the development of values used in schools: the lecture method, use of peer group pressure, finding or setting examples for children to respect and emulate, and a reward and punishment rationale. Raths contends that these methods are rather ineffective "partially because they are based on the assumption that the knowledge of moral and ethical choices necessarily leads to ethical conduct."[40] Such an assumption, he holds, seems to have little basis in fact. Raths recommends the use of clarification procedures by which the teacher strives to (a) establish a climate of psychological safety, and (b) apply clarifying strategies.[41] In establishing a climate of psychological safety, the following procedures are suggested:

1. Express nonjudgmental attitudes. In order to provide an atmosphere in which children are free to express themselves without threat of disapproval, or ridicule, teachers should refrain from using expressions such as "That's poor." "Can't you do better than that?" "That's good." Rather use comments such as "You've finished the picture." "You climbed on the jungle gym."
2. Manifest concerns. The teacher should be concerned with the ideas the child expresses. This may be done by listening to the child and remembering what was said. If the teacher shows no interest in listening, the child is not likely to be interested in sharing thoughts.
3. Provide opportunities for the sharing of ideas. Children need to be able to express their opinions, feelings, beliefs about moral issues significant to the young child. Such issues might include "taking care of our things" or "taking turns."

Two clarifying strategies, with examples pertinent to young children, follow:

1. Asking questions. The teacher may try to clarify the ideas or feelings expressed by the children by asking questions. For example, Leroy was feeding the rabbit. Douglas pushed him away and stuck the carrot into the hutch. Leroy yelled, "I hate you." "I hate the rabbit." "I hate nursery school." The teacher, using the clarifying strategy, might say, "You don't like Douglas to take the carrot away from you and feed

[36]T. A. Ringness, *The Affective Domain in Education* (Boston: Little, Brown, 1975).
[37]E. Levine, "Affective Education: Lessons in Ego Development," *Psychology in the Schools*, **10** (1973), pp. 147–150.
[38]D. H. Heath, "Affective Education: Aesthetics and Discipline," *The School Review*, **80** (1972), p. 366.
[39]Ibid., p. 369.
[40]J. D. Raths, "A Strategy for Developing Values," *Educ. Leadership*, **21**:8 (1964), pp. 509–514.
[41]Ibid., p. 512–514.

the rabbit. Is that what you mean?" or "You don't like to come to nursery school. Is that what you mean?"

The five-year-olds were planning a trip to the apple orchard. Sandra exclaims, "I have a good idea. We can get the school bus to take us." The teacher may say, "In what way is that a good idea?"

2. Acceptance without judgment. The purpose of an exchange of ideas between teacher and child is to clarify children's ideas. It is important that the teacher find a way to accept these ideas without communicating agreement or praise of them except in cases where the health or safety of the group is involved. For example, Nancy, with her sandy hair cut very short, was gently stroking Mary's long dark hair. She said, "It's so soft. It's so long. I wish I had long hair like Mary's." The teacher might reply, "I can see how you would feel that way."

Instant changes and miracles are not likely, according to Raths. He says, "It may take a long sustained effort to help children develop serious purposes and aspirations through the clarifying process. For a free society, opportunities to clarify and to choose must be created again and again.[42]

Process Skills. "Loving" has been identified by Berman as one of the process skills that should help the young child handle himself or herself and the world more effectively and to gain a better understanding of others.[43]

If teachers want children to become loving individuals, opportunities must be provided for them to learn what it means to love and be loved. Leiserson has developed suggestions for creating a loving environment for young children.[44] These suggestions may be familiar. They are used in this context, however, to indicate how the creating of a loving environment can be related to guiding children in the development of values or in any phase of the curriculum. An adaptation of her suggestions follows:

In a loving environment the teacher

1. Looks at each child as a unique person and gives the child opportunities to develop a positive self-concept. One may say, for example, "Erik's feeling very grown-up. His new shirt is size 5."[45]
2. Helps each child feel accepted and that he or she belongs to the group. One learns the children's names quickly, is courteous, and shows the children that she or he is happy to see them. For example, one may say, "I'm glad that you are feeling better. We missed you yesterday."[46]
3. Gives support and assurance to the child and lets him or her know the expectations

[42] Ibid., p. 514.
[43] Louise M. Berman, *New Priorities in the Curriculum* (Columbus, Ohio: Charles E. Merrill Publishers, 1968), p. 173.
[44] Marion L. Leiserson, *Creating a "Loving" Environment for Young Children* (College Park, Md.: University of Maryland, 1971), pp. 3–12.
[45] Ibid., p. 3.
[46] Ibid., p. 5.

"It's easy when we help each other . . .

in regard to the school environment. For example, one may say, "It isn't safe to climb on top of the brick wall. There's concrete below if you should fall."[47]

4. Lets children learn by experience, sometimes through mistakes and at other times through successes. The child may say, "My caterpillar crawled out because I did not have the top on the jar."[48]

5. Helps child understand that he or she creates his or her own emotional environment; helps him or her see the effect of actions on others. The teacher said, "She was knocked down when you bumped her. Is there something you could do to make her feel better?"[49]

6. Listens to children. What the child has to say is important, and the comments indicate concepts that have been developed. After the child tore the paper cover of a book, the teacher explained, "After the story you can help me mend the cover."
   Child: "What does *mend* mean?"
   Teacher: "It means to fix or repair it."

[47] Ibid.
[48] Ibid.
[49] Ibid., p. 8.

Child: "OK, but can I sit on your lap now and hear the story? Then I can be quiet." [50]

7. Helps the children to assume responsibilities. One may say, "Do you remember what our plants need to grow? Could you take care of them today?" [51]

8. Appears relaxed, pleasant, and in control of the classroom. Lets the children know that she is available if help is needed. The teacher might say, "Sometimes boots are tight. I'm here if you need help with them." [52]

SCHOOL PRACTICES

As one consciously works to build values, questions often arise regarding practices. Practices in public schools must be in accordance with the legal interpretation regarding religious instruction. If certain practices are contrary, they should be omitted. Some of thse questions are identified and discussed here:

1. Shall we say "Grace" at mealtime if there are children of different faiths in the group?

   Grace at mealtime is one way of helping children develop a spirit of appreciation and thankfulness. If Grace is used, however, it is important that the teacher keep in mind the following:

   a. Grace, if it is to develop the value of appreciation, should be said happily and reverently. Take time for the children to be seated, relaxed, and ready. Avoid statements such as "Hurry and be quiet so we can say Grace and you can have your juice." Such comments emphasize not the purpose of the Grace, but characterize it as something "to get through with" in order to be able to eat.

   b. If the Grace is to be said by all the children, select a form that is acceptable to all faiths. To thank God is usually acceptable to both Christian and Jewish parents. If there are children in the group who come from homes without affiliation or other beliefs, it may be well to use a statement such as, "We are thankful for our food" or "We are glad that we have food to eat."

   c. Grace is only one way of expressing appreciation. There are many other opportunities throughout the day.

      The children may learn a poem to use as a prayer or sing a song that expresses thanks. On other days, each child may say, "Thank you," whispered quietly, or a child may volunteer to say Grace for the group, expressing thanks in the child's own words.

2. Should a special time each day be set aside for a "devotional" or "worship" period in church-related programs?

   Heinz has said that "worship has a very special place in the kindergarten. . . . Worship can come from a fleeting moment of wonder, as when it was discovered that a moth had emerged from the cocoon." [53]

   There are times, however, when a teacher makes definite plans for guiding chil-

---

[50] Ibid., p. 9.

[51] Ibid., p. 10.

[52] Ibid., p. 11.

[53] Mamie W. Heinz, *Growing and Learning in the Kindergarten* (Richmond, Va.: John Knox, 1959), p. 122.

dren into worship. When such plans are made, it is well to remember that worship cannot be forced. Music, pictures, stories, poetry, and Bible selections can be used as aids in creating an atmosphere and helping children worship. The suggestions made in regard to planning other group situations and the selection of materials are appropriate here.

3. How may selections from the Bible be used with young children in church-related programs?

Much of the language in the Bible is difficult for the children to understand. For choosing selections from the Bible to be used with young children, Heinz formulated questions that may be of help to the teacher. Does the selection—

a. Help the child to grow in appreciation and understanding of God?

b. Add to a feeling of security and love, or does it promote fear?

c. Create a feeling of wonder and beauty for the child?[54]

Jones suggests the following verses from the Bible as appropriate for the young child:[55]

> He has made everything beautiful in its time.
> A child is known by his doings.
> God is Love.
> Love one another.

The way in which these verses are used is very important. They may be used many times, not for memorization, but as they relate to the experience that the children are having. A verse thus used can help a child express thoughts of God.

4. How can differences in the religious backgrounds of children be respected in celebrating religious holidays such as Christmas?

Celebration of religious holidays should be planned in such a way as to respect the worth and dignity of each child and not to threaten one's security or place in the group. If children have been helped to become aware of the differences among the children in the group and to know that they are all accepted, this awareness can be used as an approach to understanding different religious beliefs and the way in which people in other lands celebrate Christmas. If children from Christian and Jewish homes are in the group, both may have an opportunity to share their beliefs. A Jewish child and parent can tell the others about Hanukkah, and another child and parent may share a crèche and tell of the birth of Jesus. In both celebrations, gifts are given even though the origin of the gift giving is different. It is suggested that the interpretation of a religious belief be given by a person of that faith in order that the interpretation be accurate. In this way, each child can accept his or her own religious beliefs and yet understand those of others, thus furthering intercultural understanding among young children.

Mary, relating her Christian activities, said, "I mailed Christmas cards to everybody in my kindergarten but three." The adult to whom she was talking asked, "Why didn't you mail cards to the three children?" Mary replied, "They are Jewish. They don't believe in Christmas as we do. They have Hanukkah. I didn't want to hurt their feelings."

[54]Ibid., p. 128.
[55]Jones, op. cit., p. 100.

These children learn that working together makes a task easier.

Programs have been developed that attempt to increase a teacher's communication skills. One such program is Gordon's *Teacher Effectiveness Training*.[56] Gordon advised using various listening techniques, particularly *active listening*. For example,

> When it is time for the class to go outside, Jamie balks and says he wants to stay in the room. A typical response might be this: "Come on, Jamie. You know we always go out together. You can't stay in here by yourself."
>
> The active listening exchange, however, might go like this:
>
> Teacher: You don't want to go outside right now.
>
> Jamie: No, I want to finish my picture.
>
> Teacher: You really like the picture you have been drawing.
>
> Jamie: Yes, and I'm not finished yet.
>
> Teacher: It's hard to stop working on something you really like.
>
> Jamie: Yes. I want to finish it when we come back inside.

As a teacher listens "actively," respect is shown for a child and a willingness to hear his or her point of view is demonstrated. Active listening on the part of the teacher provides a model for children to use.[57]

Active listening avoids putting children and teacher in an adversarial position.

[56] T. Gordon, *T.E.T. Teacher Effectiveness Training* (New York: Wyden, 1974).

[57] Stengel, op. cit., p. 28.

Instead, the technique helps to develop empathy and respect and increases the children's awareness of their own and another's point of view.[58]

Glasser suggests another approach that teachers can use to help students to develop responsibility.[59] He defines responsibility as the ability to fulfill one's needs in such a way as not to deprive others of an opportunity to fulfill their needs. The needs that Glasser mentions are the need to give and receive love and the need to be respected by others and oneself.

SUMMARY

Values form the basis for inner-direction by the individual. It is in the early years that the foundation for moral and spiritual values is laid. "So far as we can tell," say Sears, Maccoby, and Levin, "there is a learning of internal control that goes on mainly in the years before puberty, perhaps chiefly in the first six to ten years, determining the extent to which conscience will operate throughout the rest of life."[60]

According to Dewey, "A child's moral upbringing has an effect upon him which will remain largely untouched by anything that happens to him thereafter. If he has had a stable upbringing, whether on good principles or on bad ones, it will be extremely difficult for him to abandon those principles in later life—difficult but not impossible."[61]

The challenge to equip children with the skills to think independently and to weigh judiciously the social and moral conflicts that will confront them throughout their lives is great. Stengel points out that schools already teach moral values "with every action, every rule, and every activity." Teachers should plan for moral education just as they plan for other areas of the curriculum.[62]

Suggested Activities

1. Reread the description of the broad stages of moral development evolved by Piaget and Kohlberg. Visit a center for young children, and describe situations in which a child's or children's behavior illustrate the first stage.
2. Arrange for a panel to discuss in class the role of the public school in developing values and moral conduct.

[58] Ibid., p. 29.

[59] W. Glasser, "The Effect of School Failure on the Life of a Child," Pt. 2, *National Elementary Principal*, 49 (1969), p. 13.

[60] R. R. Sears, E. E. Maccoby, and H. Levin, *Patterns of Child Rearing* (Evanston, Ill.: Row Peterson, 1957), pp. 367–368.

[61] R. E. Dewey, F. W. Gramlich, and D. Loftsgordon, *Problems of Ethics* (New York: Macmillan, 1961), p. 480.

[62] Stengel, op. cit., p. 31.

3. Visit a center for young children. Look for situations in which the teacher uses a clarifying strategy, as described by Raths, in developing values. Share your observations with the class.

4. Conduct a class discussion on the topic, "Which Values to Teach Young Children."

5. Identify values that you have chosen, cherish, and affirm. What do you believe to be the source of these values?

6. Visit a center for young children. Observe how the teacher tries to create a "loving" environment. How do his or her techniques compare with those described in this chapter?

7. Discussions about decisions to be made offer opportunities for children to talk about what they think is important. Observe such a situation. What did the children identify as being important?

8. Two formalized approaches to affective education for young children are the DUSO[63] and Human Development programs.[64] Examine and evaluate.

9. Reread the statement of values common in our democracy. Select one of the values, such as *moral responsibility*. Plan opportunities to help children grow in accepting moral responsibility.

Related Readings

Barcus, F. E., and Rachel Wolkin. *Children's Television: An Analysis of Programming and Advertising*. New York: Praeger, 1977.

Baskin, E. J., and R. D. Hess. "Does Affective Education Work? A Review of Seven Programs." *The Journal of School Psychology*, **18** (1980), pp. 40–50.

Cochrane, D., and D. Williams (guest eds.). "Moral Education and the Social Studies." *The History and Social Science Teacher*, **13**:1 (1977). Entire issue.

Combs, A. W. (chm.). "Convictions, Beliefs and Values." *Perceiving, Behaving, Becoming*. Alexandria, Va.: ASCD, 1962. Pp. 198–212.

Costa, A. L. "Affective Education: The State of the Art." *Educational Leadership*, **34**, (1977), pp. 260–263.

Damon, W. *The Social World of the Child*. San Francisco: Jossey-Bass, 1977.

Day, B., and R. Brice. "Academic Achievement, Self-Concept Development, and Behavior Patterns of Six-Year-Old Children in Open Classrooms." *The Elementary School Journal*, **78**, (1977), pp. 133–139.

Duska, R., and M. Whelan. *Moral Development: A Guide to Piaget and Kohlberg*. New York: Paulist Press, 1975.

Frankel, J. R. *How to Teach About Values: An Analytic Approach*. Englewood Cliffs, N.J.: Prentice-Hall, 1977.

Hersh, R., Diana Paolitto, and J. Raimer. *Promoting Moral Growth: From Piaget to Kohlberg*. New York: Longman, 1979.

---

[63] D. Dinkmeyer, *Developing Understanding of Self and Others: Manual DUSO D-1* (Circle Pines, Minn.: American Guidance Service, 1970).

[64] Described by E. Levine, "Affective Education: Lessons in Ego Development," *Psychology in the Schools*, **10** (1973), pp. 147–150.

Jacobs, L. B., Barbara Biber, and L. E. Raths. "Value-Outcomes of the Curious Mind: A Symposium." *Child Educ.*, **51**:5 (1975), pp. 245–248.

Jarolimek, J. *Social Studies in Elementary Education*, 5th ed. New York: Macmillan, 1977. Pp. 66–71.

Jersild, A. T. "Moral Development and Religion." In *Child Psychology*, 6th ed. Englewood Cliffs, N.J.: Prentice-Hall, 1968. Pp. 506–524.

Jones, Jessie Orton. *Small Rain*. New York: Viking, 1943.

———. *This Is the Way*. New York: Viking, 1951.

Katz, Joseph. "Bridging Values. *Child. Educ.*, **57**:3 (1981), pp. 130–137.

Kohlberg, L. "Moral Education in the Schools: A Developmental View." In *Exploring Early Childhood: Readings in Theory and Practice*, Margot Kaplan-Sanoff and Renée Yablans-Magid, eds. New York: Macmillan, 1981, pp. 188–208.

———. *Philosophy of Moral Development*. New York: Harper, 1981

Leeper, R. R. (ed.). "Values: The Challenge, The Dilemma." In *Curricular Concerns in a Revolutionary Era*. Alexandria, Va.: ASCD, 1971. Pp. 2–26.

Lerner, M. *Values in Education*. Bloomington, Ind.: Phi Delta Kappa Foundation, 1976.

McQuoid, Barbara C. "What Does It Mean to Be a Church-Related Preschool?" *Young Children* **38**:5 (1983), p. 21.

Osborn, D. K., and Janie D. Osborn. "Television Violence Revisited." *Child Educ.*, **53**:6 (1977), pp. 309–311.

Piaget, J. *The Moral Judgment of the Child*. New York: Free Press, 1965.

Purpel, D. and K. Ryan, eds. *Moral Education: It Comes with the Territory*. Berkeley, CA.: McCutchan, 1976.

Raths, L. E., M. Harmin, and S. B. Simon. *Values and Teaching*. Columbus, Ohio: Merrill, 1966.

Scherer, D. *Personal Values and Environmental Issues*. New York: Hart, 1978.

Stengel, Susan B. "Moral Education for Young Children." *Young Children* **37**:6 (1982), pp. 23–31.

Superka, D. P., et al. *Values Education Sourcebook*. Boulder: Social Science Education Consortium, 1976.

Walsh, H. M. *Introducing the Young Child to the Social World*. New York: Macmillan, 1980, pp. 35–47.

CHAPTER 12

Science: Investigating and Discovering

As young children watch, wonder, study, investigate, discover, and question, they are experiencing science as a part of everyday living. The young child and science seem to go together. The child is active, curious, and likes to manipulate and experiment with objects. Children ask many questions about how, why, where, and when. Children possess those characteristics that are important to the study of science.

Have you observed a young child watching intently as the squirrel nibbles the acorn held tightly in its paws, or as the jet streaks across the sky? Have you heard a young child ask, "Why does it rain? How does it work?" Have you listened as a child shouts, when he or she steps on a hot sidewalk without shoes, "Wow! The sun is hot. I'm getting in the shade." Such experiences can help children to gain an appreciation of the world around them; to keep alive the sense of wonder; to understand the orderliness of the universe; to develop a method of thinking and finding answers to questions.

In science education today the processes of learning are emphasized. The "process approach" offers opportunities for the child to participate in the processes of science as inquiry, as exploration, and as discovery, and to begin development of

Kindergarten provides exploration and experiences upon which later school learning is built.

skills in observation, description, problem solving, classification, comparison, veri-
fying, creating, hypothesizing, seeing relationships, logical reasoning, and inferring.
Each child should progress, at his or her own rate, from concrete learnings (facts)
through conceptual images (concepts) to more abstract generalizations. For example, a child experiences daily changes in the weather, in night and day, in plants
and animals. Temperatures can be recorded, and variations noted. From such concrete facts develops a concept of change. This concept can serve as a basis for future
understanding of the generalization that living things and the environment change
all the time.[1]

In the teaching of children who live in the inner city it is especially important
that the science program be based on the child's environment. Skeel reminds the
teacher that the environment of the inner city is not one of "butterflies and fishes."

[1] Ruth L. Roche, *The Child and Science—Wondering, Exploring, Growing* (Washington, D.C.: ACEI,
1977), p. 2.

These may become a part of it but are not the most effective topics for beginning. Begin with questions important to the child, such as, "What happens to the garbage?" or "Where does our drinking water come from?" From these topics the child's environment may be extended in many of the ways discussed in this chapter.[2]

Both Piaget and Robert Gagné have influenced the teaching of science. Based on his analysis of the cognitive stages of children, Piaget's approach includes the provision of a free, unstructured, highly enriched learning environment. In contrast, Gagné's is a behavioral approach and suggests a curriculum based on structured "learning hierarchies." The learning environment would be arranged beginning with simple learning tasks graduating into harder subtasks, which would eventually lead to the more complex tasks. The process skills, according to Gagné, such as communicating, measuring, and observing, are necessary in science and can be taught with structured exercises.[3]

Parents and teachers have the responsibility of helping and encouraging children to explore and find out about their environment. In rural areas there are farms and forests; in cities there are museums and a wide variety of exhibits and displays. Everywhere there are human resources to be tapped. The teacher's responsibility, however, is not only to help and support the child but to help in providing concrete materials and planning for experiments and investigation, all of which foster the child's intellectual development.[4]

Too many children, however, seem to lose much of this curiosity as they grow older. This curiosity should be nourished. Children do not acquire the ability to think scientifically through maturation. This ability must be nurtured from the early years on.[5]

GOALS IN TEACHING SCIENCE

Blough holds that the major objectives for teaching science are essentially the same at every level of learning. "They vary only to the degree that they are attainable at a given level."[6] The teacher needs to be aware of them even though he or she may make only a small step toward achieving them. The teacher must understand the ultimate purpose if he or she is to make an effective beginning.

[2] Dorothy J. Skeel, *Children of the Street, Teaching in the Inner-City* (Pacific Palisades, Calif.: Goodyear, 1971), pp. 71–72.

[3] Louis I. Kuslan and A. Harris Stone, *Teaching Children Science* (Belmont, Calif.: Wadsworth, 1972).

[4] Willard J. Jacobson and Abby B. Bergman, *Science for Children, A Book for Teachers* (Englewood Cliffs, N.J.: Prentice-Hall, 1980), p. 4.

[5] Bernard Spodek, *Science in the Early Years* (Englewood Cliffs, N.J.: Prentice-Hall, 1972), p. 114.

[6] G. O. Blough, "Content and Process in the Kindergarten," address to New England Kindergarten Conference, November 1966 (mimeographed).

Four generally recognized goals are presented in the following outline, with suggestions for realizing them.[7]

1. To develop in children the ability to solve problems through the use of methods of science. To help children begin to become problem solvers and achieve these skills the teacher may do the following:
   a. Make as much use as possible of the natural curiosity of children and of their many questions.
   b. Help children say exactly what they want to find out. The statement of the questions or problems is important.
   c. Help children grow in suggesting ways to find out. Call these ways by names: looking, experimenting (or trying out), and listening.
   d. Keep trying things together. For example: "Remember what we did the other day to find out? Could we try it again?"
   e. Label these experiences *science*.
   f. Remember that the process of discovery is as important as what is discovered.
   g. Guide discovery by suggesting processes without telling the answer.
2. To develop in children an attitude—commonly called a scientific attitude. Elements of such an attitude are these: Don't jump to conclusions; look at a matter from all sides; evaluate sources of information; be open-minded, don't be superstitious. To help the very young to take the beginning step in the direction of developing this attitude, the teacher may use comments and questions such as the following:
   a. "Do you think that was a true story?"
   b. "Let's measure and find out."
   c. "Shall we try it *again* and see what happens?"
   d. "Let's *look at more* pictures and books."
   e. "Let's each take a turn at looking and see if we all see the same thing." (Observe carefully and often.)
   f. "How much does it weigh?"
   g. "What can we find out by looking?"
   h. "What can we do to be sure?"
   i. "Wonder who said that."
   j. "Let's see who wrote the book?"
3. To help children gain scientific knowledge and information. Subject matter can be overemphasized, but it can also be neglected. It should be selected from the environment of the children. Because process and content are so closely related, the following suggestions are similar to those for problem solving.
   a. Keep the learning of information at the children's level, but *don't underestimate* children's abilities and interests.
   b. *Intend* to have children begin to learn some science ideas.
   c. Help children put ideas together. Recall related information, and help children go as far as they can in seeing relationships.
   d. Keep a record of some of the things children have learned. They can't read it. They don't need to, but they can listen to it.

[7]Ibid.

4. To develop in children an interest and appreciation in the science around them. To help in developing this interest and appreciation, suggestions for the teacher follow:
   a. Keep the interest children have, add to it, and broaden it.
   b. Try for satisfying experiences so that interest will grow.
   c. Urge children to show and discuss, to listen and to think, to manipulate, and to wonder.
   d. Present materials and problems that will open new interests children have not thought about.
   e. Remember you cannot help another person get interested in or have an appreciation for science unless you yourself are interested.

CHARACTERISTICS OF AN ADEQUATE SCIENCE PROGRAM

Evidences of science can be found in almost every center for young children. This does not mean, however, that one can find a well-balanced science program in all schools for young children. Science to many teachers has sometimes meant only a haphazard approach to nature study. This approach has been based on the incidental method and has utilized the casual consideration of some object: a leaf, a pet, or a rock brought into school by one of the children. This procedure is often justified because the child brings to school what is of interest to him and the child's interests form a reliable basis for the science curriculum. The incidental interests of children can provide excellent teaching and learning opportunities if they are used to improve children's observational skills and if they can provide significant learnings. However, dependence on children's interests for the total program often results in gaps in content. Some areas receive overemphasis whereas others are untouched. Furthermore, children's interests are limited by experience. Children may not bring a certain object to kindergarten or discuss a specific topic when they know nothing about it. They might, however, become very interested if they had the opportunity to become acquainted with the topic. A good science program includes incidental teaching and a flexible, general framework as well.[8]

How, then, can teachers utilize the incidents and yet provide a well-balanced science program that is flexible and adaptable to the needs and interests of children? It is important first to consider the requirements for an adequate science program for young children. These include:

1. *Planning that is both definite and flexible.* It is important that planning be both definite and flexible. This does not mean a detailed outline of specific learnings to be followed rigidly. Rather, there is a framework that is flexible enough for children and teachers to plan cooperatively for experiences that meet their par-

[8] G. O. Blough and J. Schwartz, *Elementary School Science and How to Teach It*, 5th ed. (New York: Holt, 1974), pp. 71–72.

ticular needs. Such a framework often helps the teacher to utilize incidents more effectively because he or she sees in the situation possibilities for developing certain concepts. Without such planning many incidents may not be utilized or too many incidents of a similar nature may be emphasized; thereby the science program may tend to be limited in scope.

2. *Understandings from all major areas of science.* These understandings include all major areas of science, the earth and universe, living things and their activities, human beings and their environment, and matter and energy. Children are interested in all of these areas. Simple ideas that are introduced in a children's center lay a foundation for understanding more complex ones later as children grow through constantly enlarging experiences. At one time the belief that science for children should deal primarily with biological concepts was prevalent. Investigators have found that children are also interested in the physical sciences.[9] They have found, too, that young children are able to generalize to some extent. This skill does not appear suddenly but is one that develops steadily with maturation and experience.[10]

Some of the areas and some generalizations or concepts appropriate for young children are listed. Some suggested activities through which the learnings may be achieved are also included. For each activity the teacher will develop goals, concepts, and vocabulary to be utilized for the children with whom he or she is working.

Area	Examples of Facts and Concepts to Be Learned	Some Activities and Learning Encounters That Can Contribute to Concept Development
Matter and Energy (Physics)	Air is around us. Air fills space. Wind moves many things. Heat changes some things. We breathe air. Fire needs air to burn. Air has water in it. Substances can change form (water is found in more than one form). Electricity makes light. A magnet will pull some things but will not pull other things.	Blow up toy balloons. Observe things that are being moved by the wind. Visit windmill. Churn milk. Make butter. Cook different foods and observe changes. Make ice cream. Observe ice or snow melt. Experiment with magnets. Visit a building under construction. Collect pictures of machines used to help people.

[9] H. Mutsfeld, "Science Experiences Afford Opportunity for Experimentation," *Child. Educ.*, **29**:2 (1952), p. 81.

[10] J. G. Navarra, *The Development of Scientific Concepts in a Young Child* (New York: Teachers College, 1955).

Area	Examples of Facts and Concepts to Be Learned	Some Activities and Learning Encounters That Can Contribute to Concept Development
	Sounds travel a long distance. Many things make sound. Machines do work for us. Some machines burn fuel; some use electricity; some are run by the wind. Water evaporates. Some objects float in water.	Find simple machines at school. Use a pulley to lift a heavy object, such as a chair. Compare to lifting by hand. Make an inclined plane using a walking board. Experiment with musical instruments. Note differences in sounds. Listen and identify sounds. Do water painting. Observe what happens to picture. Collect pictures of how electricity is used at home. Discuss ways to conserve electricity.
Living Things and Their Activities (Biology)	Living things need air, water, warmth, and food. Animals eat different foods. Animals move about in different ways. Some plants grow on land; some plants grow in water. Some plants grow from seeds; some plants grow from bulbs. Some trees lose their leaves in winter; some do not. Animals and plants make adaptations to changes in seasons. All animals have young animals. Some young animals need care; some do not. Some animals migrate in winter.	Hatch chicken eggs. Visit a zoo and observe different animals. Plant a garden. Care for plants. Construct a bird feeder. Observe birds. Collect different seeds. Dramatize and compare ways in which various animals move. Collect examples of homes of various animals. Visit farm or zoo and see young animals. Care for pet at school. Keep aquarium in classroom.
Our Earth and the Universe (Astronomy)	The moon, sun, and other stars are in the sky. People have put satellites in orbit around the earth. People have traveled in rockets into outer space. Stars move in the sky. The sun gives light and heat. The earth is composed of water and soil. Air is around the earth. There are different kinds of soils.	Observe and measure shadows at different times of the day. Engage in shadow plays. Compare objects in sun and shade. Talk about how they feel.

Area	Examples of Facts and Concepts to Be Learned	Some Activities and Learning Encounters That Can Contribute to Concept Development
Humans and Our Environment (Ecology)	Humans use plants and animals for food, clothing, and shelter. Animals help us work. We use animals for pleasure. We can travel in many ways. We use and control light. We use and control heat. Living things are dependent on one another. We can help keep the earth clean. Litter pollutes the environment.	Collect samples of different soils. Make a trip to the store. Note vegetables (plants) used for food. Note meats (animals) used for food. Pick up and put away toys on the playground. Clean up the classroom. Visit a farm. Observe and note foods grown. Talk about how to save energy. Collect pictures of where heat comes from. Place trash cans on the playground. Wage an antilitter campaign. Collect pictures of ways water is used in the home; how homes are lighted and heated.

3. *Integration of science learnings with other experiences of the young child.* In the study of "living things and their activities," the science learnings may be closely related to health and social studies. With the change in weather, living things make adaptations to the cold or heat. Children may discuss the relation of proper clothing to health status. The ways in which clothing is secured relate to social learnings. Experiences are needed that help the child see how science is related to his or her own life; for example, electricity for light, cooking, cooling, and heating. The social implications of science in relation to community activities help children to understand why transportation is important and why the city provides water.

4. *Variety and balance in the activities in which children participate.* Field trips, experiments, instructional media, observations, learning centers, and resource people afford opportunities for a wide variety of science experiences. This does not mean that every science experience will include a field trip or an experiment. The teacher will choose carefully the activities most appropriate for developing the basic generalization under study.

TEACHING SCIENCE TO YOUNG CHILDREN: METHODS AND RESOURCES

A variety of teaching strategies are described in Chapter 6. Refer to these in planning learning for science. Examples of some of these strategies as applied to science follow.

1. The science center is a part of the room that reflects what children are doing in science. The pets or animals may be kept here. There may be an aquarium or a terrarium. Books with pictures that answer children's questions can be displayed. A corner of the room may be used for experimentation and reinforcement of concepts discussed during a unit study. It may also be used for scientific discovery when children have access to a range of science materials.
   a. A magnet with magnetic and nonmagnetic materials, and a tuning fork.
   b. A magnifying glass, objects to observe.
   c. Scales and objects to weigh and compare.
   d. Materials for making models: wind vane, or a pinwheel.
   e. Activities for a science learning center may include matching seeds, types of food, animals and their homes, mother animals and their babies.[11]
2. Clarifying, explaining, reinforcing, and discussing comments made by children and sharing ideas and things brought to school by them are valuable techniques. Jane entered the kindergarten wearing a new red jacket. She greeted the teacher and said, "I wore my coat because it is cold. It is very cold—almost to freezing." The teacher said, "Yes, it is cold. How do you know it is freezing outside?"
   Jane: "The weatherman said so on TV."
   Teacher: "How does the weatherman know it is freezing?"
   Jane: "Because he is a weatherman."
   Teacher: "He reads the thermometer and finds out how cold it is. There is a thermometer in our room. Let's put it outside and see what happens." The teacher and Jane cross the room together.
3. Experimentation, as in germinating seeds or testing with different kinds of soil and with little or no sunlight, can be successful. Experiments are planned to test, to try out ideas, and to help the child to come to accurate conclusions. They are not arranged to provide a display of magic and arouse fears and doubts in the child's mind. If there is a problem to be solved, children may be helped to use an experiment in finding the solution. The following steps may be used:
   a. State the problem of the experiment in order that children know what they are trying to find out.
   b. Decide on what is to be done to solve the problem or answer the question.
   c. Get the materials needed.
   d. Do the activities agreed upon.
   e. Observe carefully what happens.
   f. Answer the question.
   The following example is used to illustrate these steps. With young children, the problem of the experiment often grows out of their questions. Instead of answering the question with a pat "Yes" or "No," the teacher sees in the question an opportunity for experimentation and problem solving. For example:

---

[11] Barbara Day, *Open Learning in Early Childhood* (New York: Macmillan, 1975), pp. 106–108.

This sink and float center provides many opportunities for classifying, observing, and categorizing. "Test these items—which ones sink and which ones float."

Jim is showing Sam how his magnet will attract and pull nails to it. He comments, "My magnet will pull anything."

Sam replies, "Oh no, it won't. I know."

"Miss W., will this magnet pull anything?"

Miss W. answers, "Let's see. Will a magnet pull iron nails?"

"Yes," the boys reply.

"Iron tacks?" "Yes."

"A pencil?" Sam is not sure, though Jim is confident.

Miss W. asks, "How can we find out if a magnet will pull a pencil?"

"We can try it and see," said Sam.

"Yes," said Miss W. "Are there other things you would like to try?"

"Oh yes." Looking around the room the boys name blocks, iron screws, chalk, crayons, and scissors. "Let's see if the magnet pulls them."

The boys take the magnet from one object to another and test the pull. Miss W. asked, "Did the magnet pull the blocks?" "No."

"The iron screws?" "Yes." "Chalk?" "No." "Crayons?" "No." "Scissors?" "Yes."

"Your magnet won't pull everything. It won't pull chalk, crayons, or blocks," concluded Sam.

Jim looked down at the floor, crestfallen that his magnet had let him down. Miss W. said, "That's right, the magnet won't pull everything. But, Jim, your magnet will pull some things. What kind of things will it pull?"

Jim's face brightened as he said, "My magnet won't pull everything, but it will pull some things. It will pull iron and steel things."

The teacher should encourage the child to tell what he or she finds out. The teacher also encourages the child to speak in sentences and explain his or her findings clearly. For example, "Can you explain it better?" "Begin, 'I found out. . . .'"

4. Observations may be closely related to any of the activities for science experiences that have been described. Observations, however, may be planned as an activity for the nursery school or kindergarten room. Children will watch birds, fish, bees, ants, rabbits, turtles, or rats intently, sometimes talking to one another, but often looking and musing alone.

Listen to three-year-old Ann as she watches the white rats:

"Long tails, long tails, long tails!"

Questions may be used to sharpen or focus the observation. For example: "How does the animal eat its food? How does it move? What does it eat? Where does it sleep in the cage?"

5. Caring for living things affords opportunities for children to broaden the experiential learnings they have developed regarding both plants and animals. Animals and plants can be compared; differences and likenesses, noted. An awareness of the many kinds of plants and animals and an understanding of what is involved in the care of living things can be fostered through observing, using books, looking at pictures and discussing.

Caterpillars, guinea pigs, hamsters, birds, dogs, chickens, mice, fish, tad-

Caroline is developing skills of observation and description. Her task is to draw and color.

poles, cats, and even goats have been cared for at school, either in the classroom or outside near the building. It is important that cages be kept clean and proper food and water be provided. Arrangements for care over the weekend should be made. Often arrangements can be made with parents for a child to take one of the pets home.

When using animals with young children, the teacher may need to be responsible for their handling, encouraging but not forcing the children to observe and to "pet" them. A child, not knowing how to handle the pet, usually squeezes it, causing the animal to react by biting or scratching. Then the child may become frightened or hurt, and as a result the desired learnings are not accomplished. Also, the animal may be injured.

6. Resource persons who are invited to talk with the children about some aspect of science may be parents of a child in the group, another teacher, or some other person in the community. Before the visit, be sure that the guest understands the questions raised by the children and the length of time to talk.

7. Commercial programs available for use include:[12]

   a. SAPA (Science—A Process Approach).

   b. SCIS (Science Curriculum Improvement Study). Both of these programs are based on the hierarchical skills developed by Gagné. The assumption that children must master simpler skills before moving on to more sophisticated behaviors is considered throughout these programs.

[12] Bernard Spodek, *Teaching in the Early Years* (Englewood Cliffs, N.J.: Prentice-Hall, 1972), pp. 128–29.

    c. ESS (Elementary Science Study). In this program the children are encouraged to do what they want with the materials and, through their excitement, formulate questions and make discoveries.

8. Field trips offer opportunities for children to observe natural phenomena and activities that cannot be brought into the classroom.

9. Capitalize on guessing. Guessing leads to observing and testing. Telling and sharing through demonstrating, acting, drawing, or constructing help the child remember his or her findings. Creating an atmosphere for questioning enhances the guessing process. The goal of science for the child as well as the scientist is to make better guesses.[13]

10. Cooking activities afford opportunities for learning how foods are prepared and understanding how matter changes form. For example, water freezes and there is ice; apples are cooked and can become apple sauce.

11. Relate science activities to other areas of the curriculum. Mathematics is used in almost all the sciences. Modern science would be impossible without mathematics. Mathematical skills can be developed through science experiences. Some examples of the interrelationship of scientific processes and mathematics follow.[14] In science, children can compare fruits and vegetables. To communicate the results of these observations, they must use units of measurement. They can classify seeds by shape or size and count the number in each set. Data relating to the weather can be presented in the form of a bar graph.

12. The unit (a plan for developing key concepts) may also be used as a means of organizing science materials. As an example, a unit related to ecology is presented in this chapter. One value of the unit plan for organizing is that materials and activities are included to provide for a range in ability, maturity, and interests appropriate for a group of children whether they be three, four, or five years of age or whether they live in the city, the suburb, or the country.

A PLAN FOR DEVELOPING A UNIT (KEY CONCEPTS)

Generalizations from the area *humans and their environment* have been developed into the following unit. One concept may be selected and developed in a learning activity or a series of encounters.

ENCOUNTERS WITH THE ENVIRONMENT

1. *Purposes:* To help the children begin to
    a. Develop an awareness of, and an appreciation for the environment as evidenced by statements such as

---

[13] Steve Tipps, "Making Better Guesses: A Goal in Early Childhood Science," *School Science and Mathematics*, **82**:1 (1982), pp. 29–37.

[14] Willard J. Jacobson and Abby B. Bergman, *Science for Children—A Book for Teachers* (Englewood Cliffs, N.J.: Prentice-Hall, 1980), Ch. 7.

Through meaningful encounters with the environment children are introduced to an important area of science—living things and their activities. What fun to watch the animals! What opportunities for language!

"See the tiny green leaves. Spring must be here."

"This yard is a mess. There is paper all over it."

  b. Know that living things and the environment change all the time. Some changes are caused by nature, some by man. For example,

"Look at the crack in the walk. It is getting bigger."

"The rain washed the sand out of the box."

  c. Understand that living things depend upon one another and upon their environment. For example,

"The plant grows toward the sun."

"We picked oranges from the tree."

  d. Conserve resources in our environment. For example,

"Turn off the faucet. The water is dripping."

"You didn't eat all your apple. Don't throw it away."

2. *Initiating the plan:* Leads into *Encounters with the Environment* may come from

  a. Incidents. For example, a child's comment. "There is so much junk here I can't work." The teacher may say, "You can't work at the table. Why?" During the conversation, other children may be involved; and questions, raised. "Where do the books belong? Where are the puzzles kept? How can we have space to work and play?" Follow with discussion and planning. Another child may announce to the teacher, "My Daddy rides to work on the bus (car pool, train). Gas costs too much." Follow with discussion and planning.

  b. Teacher suggestion. Arrange for a walk. Questions may be raised: "What happened to the sand in the box? Why did the leaves fall from the tree? Why did the sidewalk crack? What changes have people made?" Follow with discussion and planning.

3. *Learning opportunities:* Take a walk or a field trip. On various trips ask children to observe (1) evidences of change on the playground, (2) evidences of beauty in the environment, (3) things that make them feel happy, and (4) evidences that living things depend on one another and their environment.

  a. Develop meanings for such words as *environment, living things, waste, change, depend.*

  b. Rake leaves. Make a compost heap, or observe what happens to leaves left in the gutter or a corner of the yard.

  c. Plant a garden. If possible, pick and cook vegetables.

  d. Visit an orchard. Pick apples. See how many ways the children can use the apples.

  e. Visit a farm. Pick vegetables. Gather eggs. Watch as cows are milked.

  f. Pull up a weed by the roots. Observe how it looks next day.

  g. Ask children to identify natural things by touch: grass, water, leaf, peach, each other.

     by smell: flower, grass, soil, leaf, apple.

     by taste: apple, orange, banana.[15]

  h. Record natural sounds such as a bird singing or fussing, wind blowing, cricket chirping, leaves rustling. Play recording. Listen carefully, and identify sounds.[16]

[15] R. Caras, "Time to Join the World," *Early Years,* **2:**9 (1972), p. 36.

[16] Ibid.

   i. Make gifts for parents using "recoverables from the recycling heap." Examples: Make paper weights. Children collect smooth, clean rocks and decorate with poster paint. Make wall plaques (piece of plywood and shellac) or a pencil holder (tin-can base). Children collect scraps of string, yarn, cord. Cover wood or can with glue. Pull, wind, twist pieces of string, and so forth into design.[17]

   j. Make miniature trash receptacles. Decorate milk cartons, coffee cans, paper bags. Use at home, at school, or in the car. Involve parents.

   k. Collect samples of soil from different places (around the building if possible). Compare as to color, moisture, temperature. "How do they feel? How are they different?" Spread out samples of soil on the paper. Pick out animals (earthworms, crickets), and put them in a jar. Ask questions such as "How many different kinds of animals did you find? Were there the same number in each kind of soil?"[18]

   l. Take a trip to the zoo. Focus on foods of animals. Find out the native foods of animals and the food given them in the zoo. Ask where the zoo foods come from. Ask children to name foods that they give their pets. Ask them to find out where the foods come from.[19]

   m. If changes are taking place near the children's center (buildings being torn down, highways being built, construction), ask children to observe changes. Take photographs.[20] Ask questions such as "Are there as many homes now? Stores? Plants? Trees? Animals?" Observe how tools and power help people work.

   n. Observe birds, and try to find out what they are eating. "Are they eating seeds? Insects? Berries?"

   o. Collect leaves that have been damaged by insects. "Why did the insect damage the leaf?"[21]

   p. Dig up a plant from hard, dry soil. Plant it in loose, fertile soil, and keep it watered. Observe what happens. Discuss reasons.[22]

   q. Turn the hose on the playground on hard soil and again on soft, loose soil. Observe the running water and the materials it carries away. Discuss meaning of *erosion*. After a rain, collect muddy water from the street or yard. Observe sediment that settles to the bottom. "What is it? Where did it come from?"

   r. Observe that the praying mantis eats a grasshopper. "What did the grasshopper eat? How can you find out?"[23]

   s. Plant bean seeds. Expose some seedlings to more light than others. "What are the differences? Why?"

   t. Discuss water conservation. Keep records of ways in which water was conserved.

---

[17] Maija Kaljo, "Love, Nature and the Recycling Heap," *Early Years*, **2**:9 (1972), pp. 38–39.

[18] Beth Schultz, "Your Town: A Biotic Community with People," in *Environmental Education in the Elementary School* (Washington, D.C.: NSTA, 1972), p. 35.

[19] Ibid.

[20] Ibid., p. 34.

[21] Ibid., p. 35.

[22] Ibid., p. 36.

[23] Beth Schultz, "Ecology for the Child," in *Environmental Education in the Elementary School* (Washington, D.C.: NSTA, 1972), p. 14.

Learning about zoo animals is fun, especially if you can build cages and put the animals in them.

4. *Evaluation:* Observe dramatic play. Note comments and conversations of children for awareness of interdependence, environment, change.

Observe children's behavior for evidences of assuming responsibility, caring for materials.

Observe children's art products.

5. *List of Materials:*

BOOKS

Alexander, Anne. *Noise in the Night.* Chicago: Rand McNally, 1966.

Atwood, Ann. *The Wild Young Desert.* New York: Scribner, 1970.

Borten, Helen. *Do You Hear What I Hear?* Eau Claire, Wisc.: E. M. Hale, 1966.

Busch, Phyllis S. *Puddles and Ponds: Living Things in Watery Places.* New York: World, 1969.

————. *At Home in Its Habitat: Animal Neighborhoods*. New York: World, 1970.

————. *Swamp Spring*. New York: Macmillan, 1969.

Darling, Lois, and Louis Darling. *Worms*. New York: Morrow, 1972.

Dayton, Mona. *Earth and Sky*. New York: Harper, 1969.

Hawes, Judy. *What I Like About Toads*. New York: Crowell, 1969.

Hazen, Barbara S. *Where Do Bears Sleep?* Reading, Mass.: Addison-Wesley, 1970.

Hurs, Edith Thacher. *Wilson's World*. New York: Harper, 1971.

May, J. *Alligator Hole*. Chicago: Follet, 1969.

————. *Blue River*. New York: Holiday House, 1971.

Merz, R. *The Mockingbird Book*. New York: Harper, 1962.

Miles, Miska. *Apricot ABC*. Boston: Little, Brown, 1969.

Peet, B. *The Wump World*. Boston: Houghton, 1970.

Pelgreen, J. *Backyard Safari*. New York: Doubleday, 1971.

Podendorf, Illa. *Food Is for Eating*. Chicago: Children's Press, 1970.

————. *Every Day Is Earth Day*. Chicago: Children's Press, 1971.

Pringle, Laurence P. (ed.). *Discovering the Outdoors*. Garden City, N.Y.: Natural History Press, 1969.

Pringle, Laurence P. *From Field to Forest: How Plants and Animals Change the Land*. New York: World, 1970.

Seuss, Dr. *The Lorax*. New York: Random, 1971.

Showers, Paul. *Listening Walk*. New York: Macmillan, 1961.

Shulevitz, Uri. *Rain Rain Rivers*. New York: Farrar, 1969.

Simmons, Diane. *Gardening Is Easy When You Know How*. New York, Arco, 1974.

Tresslet, Alvin. *The Beaver Pond*. New York: Lothrop, 1970.

————. *It's Time Now!* New York: Lothrop, 1969.

Van Leeuwen, Jean. *One Day in Summer*. New York: Random, 1969.

FILMSTRIPS

Plant and Animal Relationships: The Forest, The Pond, The Desert, The Swamp, The Seashore, The Grasslands. Encyclopedia Britannica Films, Inc., 1150 Wilmette Ave., Wilmette, Ill.

Discovering Life Around Us Series: A Visit to the: Seashore, Farm, Garden, Weeds, Pond. Encyclopedia Britannica Films, Inc., 1150 Wilmette Avenue, Wilmette, Ill.

POETRY

Association for Childhood Education International. *Sung Under the Silver Umbrella*. New York: Macmillan, 1952.

Arbuthnot, May Hill (ed.). *Time for Poetry*. Chicago: Scott, Foresman, 1961.

Behn, Harry (trans.) *Cricket Songs*. New York: Harcourt, 1964.

Bramblett, Ella. *Sheets of Green*. New York: Crowell, 1968.

Fischer, Aileen. *In the Middle of the Night*. New York: Crowell, 1965.

————. *In the Woods, in the Meadow, in the Sky*. New York: Scribner, 1965.

Ferris, Helen (ed.). *Favorite Poems Old and New*. New York: Doubleday, 1957.

Stevenson, R. L. *A Child's Garden of Verses*. New York: Watts, 1966.

Songs

McCall, Adeline. *This Is Music.* Boston: Allyn, 1966.

Nelson, Mary J., and Gladys Tipton. *Music for Early Childhood.* New York: Silver Burdett, 1952.

Pitts, Lilla Belle, et al. *The Kindergarten Book.* Boston: Ginn, 1949.

Winn, Marie (ed.). *Children's Songs.* New York: Simon & Schuster, 1966.

Zeitlin, Patty. *Castle in My City—Songs for Young Children.* San Carlos, Calif.: Golden Gate Junior Books, 1966.

Suggested Activities

1. Select one generalization to be developed with young children from the areas listed in this chapter. Develop a plan (unit) for teaching the key concepts related to this generalization.

2. Select a site that you think might possibly be appropriate for a field trip by a four-year-old group. Visit the site and evaluate it. Share your conclusions with the class. What possible learnings might children gain from this trip?

3. Visit a center. Observe and list evidences of science activities. Identify the areas to which the activities contribute. Note the generalizations that are being developed. Share your findings with the class.

4. In your class, conduct an experiment that you consider to be appropriate for young children, using the steps listed in this chapter.

5. Select a learning opportunity listed in the unit in this chapter. Plan and develop it with young children. Evaluate.

6. Listen to and evaluate five recordings with science content for use with young children.

7. Visit a library or a center with a collection of children's books. Select and evaluate five books with science content for use with young children. Indicate the areas of science in which the books may be used.

8. View and evaluate filmstrips for use with children. Describe how you might use the filmstrips.

9. Make a collection of flat pictures for use in science with the young child.

10. Visit a children's center, and note ways in which a child or the group is encouraged to observe, classify, engage in problem solving, and then hypothesize.

11. View the film *Foundation of Sciences* (Campus Films, 2 Overhill Rd., Scarsdale, N.Y. 10583). Discuss.

12. View the film *Water Play for Teaching Young Children* (N.Y. Univ. Film LIbrary, 26 Washington Place, New York, N.Y. 10003).

13. Discuss how early mathematics learnings can be integrated with science teaching.

Related Readings

ACEI. "The World's Bounty." *Child. Educ.*, **40**:8 (1964). Entire issue.

———. "Outdoor Education." *Child. Educ.*, **44**:2 (1967). Entire issue.

————. "The Living World." *Child. Educ.*, **47**:4 (1971). Entire issue.

Althouse, Rosemary, and Cecil J. Main. *Science Experiences for Young Children*. New York: Teachers College, 1976.

————. "The Science Learning Center: Hub of Science Activities." *Child. Educ.*, **50**:4 (1974), pp. 222–226.

Bennett, L. M., and Gloria Bassett. "Games and Things for Preschool Science." *Science and Children*, **9**:5 (1972), pp. 25–27.

Blough, Glenn, and Julius Schwartz. *Elementary School Science and How to Teach It*, 5th ed. New York: Holt, 1974.

Cadwaller, Sharon. *Cooking Adventures for Kids*. Boston: Houghton, 1974.

David, A. R. "Science for Fives." *Child. Educ.*, **53**:4 (1977), pp. 206–207.

Day, Barbara. *Open Learning in Early Childhood*. New York: Macmillan, 1975, pp. 85–115.

Durgin, H. J. "From Curiosity to Concepts: From Concepts to Curiosity—Science Experiences in the Preschool." *Young Children*, **30**:4 (1975), pp. 249–256.

Fraenkel, Jack R. *Helping Students Think and Value—Strategies for Teaching the Social Studies*, 2d ed. Englewood Cliffs, N.J.: Prentice-Hall, 1980.

Gega, D. C. "Directions—Elementary School Science." *Teacher*, **94**:3 (1976).

Good, R. G. *How Children Learn Science: Conceptual Development and Implications for Teaching*. New York: Macmillan, 1977.

Gratz, Pauline. "Maintaining a Supportive Physical Environment for Man." *Educ. Leadership*, **27**:2 (1969), pp. 173–175. Also in *Curricular Concerns in a Revolutionary Era*. Alexandria, Va.: ASCD, 1971, pp. 261–263.

Grossman, Shelley, and Mary Louise Grossman. *The How and Why Wonder Books of Ecology*. New York: Grosset, 1971.

Harbech, Mary B. "Opinion: Is Science Basic? You Bet It Is." *Teacher*, **94**:3 (1976), pp. 22–26, 30.

Harlan, J. D. *Science Experiences for the Early Childhood Years*. Columbus, Ohio: Merrill, 1977.

Holt, Bess-Gene. *Science with Young Children*. Washington, D.C.: NAEYC, 1977.

Jacobson, W. J., and Abby B. Bergman. *Science for Children*. Englewood Cliffs, N.J.: Prentice-Hall, Inc., 1980.

Kamii, Constance, and Lucinda Lee Katz. "Physics in Preschool Education: A Piagetian Approach," in *Curriculum Planning for Young Children*, ed. by Janet F. Brown. Washington, D.C.: NAEYC, 1982, pp. 171–176.

Lindberg, Lucile, and Rita Swedlow. *Early Childhood Education*. Boston: Allyn, 1976, pp. 218–239.

Moffitt, Mary W. "Children Learn About Science Through Block Building." In *The Block Book*. Washington, D.C.: NAEYC, 1974, pp. 25–32.

Newman, D. "Sciencing for Young Children." In *Exploring Early Childhood: Readings in Theory and Practice*, ed. by Margot Kaplan-Sanoff and Renée Yablans-Magid. New York: Macmillan, 1981, pp. 317–328.

Riechard, D. E. "A Decade of Preschool Science: Promises, Problems, and Perspectives." *Science Education*, **57**:4 (1973), pp. 437–451.

Rigden, J. S. "The Art of Great Science." *Phi Delta Kappan* **64**:9 (1983), pp. 613–617.

Russell, H. R. *Ten-minute Field Trips: A Teacher's Guide Using the School Grounds for Environmental Studies*. Chicago: J. G. Ferguson, 1973.

Shephardson, R. D. "Simple Inquiry Games." *Science and Children*, **15**:2 (1977), pp. 34–36.

Shymansky, James A. "Mum's The Word—More About Science and Silence." *Science and Children*, **14**:1 (1976), pp. 26–27.

Smith, R. F. "Early Childhood Science: A Piagetian Approach." In *Curriculum Planning for Young Children*, ed. by Janet F. Brown. Washington, D.C.: NAEYC, 1982, pp. 143–150.

Strongin, Herb. *Science on a Shoe String*. Menlo Park, Calif.: Addison-Wesley, 1976.

Victor, Edward. *Science for the Elementary School*, 3d ed. New York: Macmillan, 1975.

Williams, D. C. "On Science for Young Children." *Science and Children*, **13**:2 (1975), pp. 34–35.

CHAPTER 13

Health and Safety

Health and safety education in any center for young children is most effective if it is incorporated into all the activities of the center. Health education cannot be limited to such activities as "daily inspections," "handwashing," "special demonstrations," and "play in the out-of-doors." Safety education should not be limited to learning safety slogans or singing safety songs. These aspects may be included but the program should also emphasize the importance of a healthful and safe environment that offers opportunities to practice and acquire desirable information, habits, and attitudes and to participate in activities that contribute to healthful and safe living. These are broad, inclusive terms that must be analyzed and the implications for teachers of young children noted. Health and safety are considered together because of the interrelationships involved.

This chapter focuses on health and safety in the school environment and within the community. It is important for the teacher to know the rules and practices of good health and safety. In today's society the child often spends at least half of his or her day in school. The teacher becomes the prime caretaker. Willgoose points out that the problems, diseases, and inadequacies of present day adults did not suddenly appear but emerged gradually, having their roots in the early years.[1]

Transportation has become a major consideration. Many children ride to school. It is important that the teacher help children to develop responsibility and exercise caution en route to and from school.

Nutrition is also discussed. The child's appearance, vigor, and enthusiasm for school activities are influenced by his or her nutritional status.

A HEALTHFUL ENVIRONMENT

The environment determines to a considerable extent the quality of healthful living possible in the situation. The effects of group care on the health of young children are raising questions for parents, the public, and professionals in the field of child care. A review of the literature on this topic by Kendall emphasizes the importance of a carefully planned and monitored environment and program.[2] Programs should include preventive health care services such as health education, not only for children, but also for parents and teachers; training of the staff in the detection and referral of problems, and in emergency and safety procedures; and follow-up by health professionals.[3]

Too often emphasis has been placed upon the physical aspects of the environment, assuming that adequate space, toilet facilities, and appropriate equipment assured healthful living. There is increased recognition, however, that the best physical environment can be wasted unless the teacher is alert to its utilization and opportunities for learning. The sunshine may be glorious, but if the teacher plans no time in the out-of-doors the children cannot experience its values. Playground equipment that offers opportunities for exercise and muscular growth will be useless if the children are kept inside. Well-planned bathrooms with wash basins and toilets, exactly the right size, may not contribute to the development of desirable habits and attitudes if they are not kept clean and pleasant.

The recognition of each child and his or her parents as persons of worth, the provision for each child of an educational program appropriate to his or her developmental level, and the maintenance of a warm and accepting human environment all contribute to the positive mental health of each child. The total program of an adequate center for children can be considered as a mental health service and a significant part of a healthful environment.[4]

---

[1] Carl E. Willgoose, *Health Education in the Elementary School,* 5th ed. (Philadelphia: Saunders, 1979), p. 33.
[2] Earline D. Kendall, "Child Care and Disease: What Is the Link?" *Young Children* **38**:5 (1983), pp. 68–75.
[3] Ibid., p. 74.
[4] *Project Head Start, Health Services—A Guide for Project Directors and Health Personnel* (Washington, D.C.: U.S. Government Printing Office, 1969), p. 48.

Effective use of an adequate environment can benefit the young child greatly. It is essential that attention be given not alone to the adequacy of the environment but to the effective use of it in developing physical, mental, and social health. This concept of a healthful environment maintains that children will learn when they are involved in situations concerning health and safety and are then helped to practice consistently what they have learned. The effectiveness of this approach depends on such factors as the school personnel, the emotional tone of the situation, physical facilities, policies, practices, and program.

PERSONNEL

Children learn from people in their environment. What a child considers important usually depends upon the values placed on the event by the people with whom he or she comes in contact. All adults in the school situation are important to children. Personnel includes all persons who have any responsibility for any part of the program. Their responsibilities include maintaining and utilizing a healthful environment as well as good personal health.

The teacher or caregiver, however, is the key person in the situation. It is essential that he or she be in good physical health. Energy and vigor are prerequisites for alert, active, yet intelligent, patient, and sympathetic guidance of children. Regular physical examinations, an adequate diet, sufficient rest, appropriate recreation, and comfortable clothing are as important for the adults as for the child. Yet these alone are not enough. Mental health is most important.

Witherspoon has formulated the following questions that may be used by the teacher or other adults for self-examination.[5]

> Do I see children as they really are? Or are my concepts clouded by my own experiences as a child?
>
> Can I show kindness and affection toward others? Or do I feel that this is unnecessary?
>
> Do my actions and deeds reflect confidence and integrity? Or are they merely an attempt to "save face" in order to protect me from myself?
>
> Recognizing that how I feel about my life and my environment is the only frame of reference that enables me to evaluate my actions, am I happy with my lot in life? Or do I feel that this life has been unkind to me?
>
> Do I view myself as physically healthy, ambitious, and enthusiastic? Or do I see myself as tired all the time even though I am healthy in the physical sense?
>
> Do I usually finish each day with a feeling of pride of accomplishment? Or do I go home merely feeling that I have done my duty whether anything was accomplished or not?
>
> Is working with young children what I most like to do? Or do I see teaching as a job?
>
> Am I sure that others think of me as their friend? Or do I feel that I am not quite sure whether I have any friends at all?

[5] R. L. Witherspoon, "Teacher, Know Thyself," *Child. Educ.*, **35**:2 (1958), p. 56.

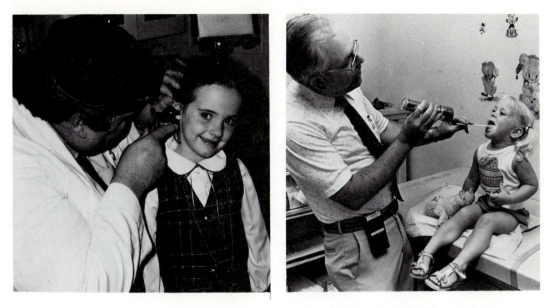

The early school years are fraught with health and safety hazards. Thorough examinations are important in the early detection of illness and existing health defects.

Do I face crises calmly and confidently so that I can face reality whatever it may be? Or do serious "accidents" always happen to me?

Do I recognize when I need help? Or am I afraid of what others will think of me if I seek assistance?

If one can answer yes to the first part of these questions, children in the classroom have a person who can help them to become confident, alert, and imaginative. If one truthfully has to answer yes to some (or all) of the last parts of these questions, there is need for self-evaluation and resolve to improve. The self-concept of the teacher or caregiver is as important as that of each child in the program.

The teacher's knowledge of the growth and development of children influences expectations of them. What the teacher expects has a great effect on the mental health of the child and the emotional tone of the classroom. Expressing undue concern when a three-year-old has an accident and wets his or her pants, insisting upon the use of "good adult manners" by the four-year-olds, or expecting each five-year-old to cut out an object evenly and smoothly along a line can result in anxieties and negative attitudes, none of which are conducive to positive mental health. Adults who understand threes, fours and fives do not indulge them, but pace expectations and activities to their developmental level.

Alert supervision by the teacher is imperative in order to safeguard the health and safety of the children. This means careful observation of the child for signs of illness such as flushed face, paleness, listlessness, irritability, coughing, sneezing, running nose; adjusting wraps to changes of temperature or activity; closing or opening windows to prevent drafts or improve ventilation; raising or lowering shades for proper lighting; seeing that cups, spoons, and other eating utensils are not used in common; removing safety hazards; paying close attention to children who are climbing in high places or to children using such tools as hammers, saws, hoes, or shovels. The teacher must always be alert and watchful.

Attitudes can greatly facilitate or hinder the team approach to health. Such an approach makes it possible to utilize the contributions of the parents, the physician, the nurse, and the psychologist, as well as the teacher or caregiver or both. No one person can do the job adequately alone. Persons working with young children need to know the resources available within the community and understand how these may be used for children. It is recognized that one cannot do everything alone and that it is a sign of strength, not weakness, to ask for help. Through this approach, common understandings regarding the goals of the health program and the role of each member of the team can be developed.

PHYSICAL FACILITIES

Physical facilities, equipment, materials, and grounds are discussed in Chapter 19. In this section the emphasis is placed on the use of the facilities to promote health and safety.

Facilities for rest

All centers should make some provision for relaxation or rest periods. Facilities for resting in all-day schools include cots, sheets, blankets, and storage space. Spacing of the cots is important (approximately three feet apart) so that children will not lie with faces too close together. Shades should be drawn to facilitate rest. Quiet music is sometimes played during the rest period. The cots may range in size from 27 by 48 inches for four-year-olds, 27 by 52 inches for four- to five-year-olds, to 27 by 54 inches for children of five to seven years of age.

In schools not operating an all-day program, rugs and towels are often used for a midmorning rest. Such practice may be questioned on two important points:

1. If the floor is not warm and free from drafts, the rug or towel may not provide adequate protection for the child. Pads, from ½ to 1 inch thick, are now being used in some schools. These are not as expensive as cots and yet provide more adequate protection from the cold floor. The pads may be made of foam rubber or cotton, with a washable cover. A plastic cover can be easily cleaned whereas a cotton slip must be laundered frequently.

2. If rugs or towels are stacked together, the side of the rug next to the floor may be placed in contact with the "face" side of the next rug. This hazard can be minimized by having the floor side clearly marked, folded to the outside, and stored in each individual's locker. In order to prevent the "head part" from being folded to the "foot part," teach the child to fold the rug lengthwise first. If mats are used, the floor side should be marked also. Sheets can be used and stored in each child's locker. Children should be involved in the process of getting out and storing cots or mats.

Drinking fountains

Drinking fountains, if used, should be low enough for the child to reach easily. It is important that the child be taught to drink so as not to put his or her mouth on the fountain. This is not easy for the child, and supervision is necessary. For these reasons, individual paper cups are used in some schools.

Lockers

It is recommended that each child have a locker in which to keep clothing and supplies. Individual lockers are of value in helping the child establish proper habits of caring for clothing and supplies. Moreover, there is less danger of spreading contagious diseases when children's wraps are kept separate in individual lockers. It is often desirable to provide some lockers or storage cabinets on casters for use in partitioning off areas and for increased flexibility of activities in the room.

Furniture

Furniture should be of appropriate size for each child. This means that not all furniture within the classroom will be the same size. As children differ in height, so should the tables and chairs. It is important that tables and chairs be matched and that a high chair not be used at a low table. Help the child to decide whether or not he or she has the right chair by using such questions as

1. Can your feet reach the floor?
2. Is there room for your knees under the table?
3. Are you comfortable?

Play equipment

Play equipment and toys that are sources of danger should be repaired or removed. Broken toys with sharp edges and protruding nails, unsteady ladders, splintery boards and blocks are examples. Loose gravel, sticks, or stones on the playground as well as roots, stumps, and holes can be safety hazards. Constant vigilance is essential.

Temperature, ventilation, and lighting

Temperature, ventilation, and lighting are important factors to consider in helping the child acquire desirable habits and attitudes. Although maintaining proper temperature, lighting, and ventilation is the responsibility of the teacher, it is important that opportunities for learning by the children be utilized. Comments and the activities that follow illustrate the teaching opportunities. For example, the comment "John, I feel too warm—let's check the thermometer" helps John learn the following:

1. The thermometer is used to measure temperature.
2. The correct temperature for the room.
3. To become aware of feeling uncomfortable when one is too warm.
4. Some things to do when one is too warm.

In schools where the temperature is regulated by an engineer at a central control, the teacher assumes responsibility for reporting undesirable temperatures.

Another example involves Jane, who is looking at a book in the bright sunlight. The teacher may adjust the shade while the child is unaware of what he or she has done. Or the teacher may say, "Jane, your book is in the sunshine. The glare makes you squint your eyes. Let's fix the shade," or, "Move your chair over here out of the sun." This situation can help Jane learn the following:

1. Looking at or reading books in direct sunlight is not a desirable health practice.
2. Why she squints and how the eyes feel in such a situation.
3. Some things to do to correct the situation.

POLICIES

Policies relating to health and safety should be formulated, made available to parents and all personnel involved, and consistently enforced. Policies are needed in the following areas:

Physical Examinations for Children, Teachers, Aides, and Other School Personnel. Such examinations should be made within one month prior to the date the child enters school or the adult begins work at the school. Forms for recording the results of the examination may be secured from the local health authority or developed by the school. Records should be filed so as to be easily accessible.

Immunizations. Those required should be specified by a health authority. Records of immunizations should be kept up to date.

Communicable Diseases. Policies should cover procedure when a child or adult has been exposed, the length of time a child should stay out of school when he or she has a communicable disease, and on what authority he or she is readmitted to school. Usually, it is wise to follow the policies set by the local health authority.

Accidents and Sudden Illness at School. Such policies should include the procedure for contacting parents or a person designated by the parents (if they cannot be reached) and for contacting the child's physician or providing the authority to use another physician if the child's cannot be reached. The extent of the school's liability and insurance coverage in such situations should be clearly defined and made known to the parents.

Health Information. Policies are needed regarding procedures for informing parents of defects observed by the teacher or the nurse, results of screening tests, information regarding height and weight, and of the incidence of a contagious disease in the group.

Morning Inspection. The routine for morning inspection needs to be understood by parents and children. Such a policy will probably state that the parent or adult bringing the child must wait until the child has been checked and admitted to the group. Inspection is usually done in such a way as not to embarrass the child. The adult may make a quick check while greeting the child.

Transportation. If transportation is provided, then a policy is needed as to the number of children transported in each car, the responsibility of the driver for the conduct of the children, the conduct expected of the children in the car, and the procedure for having a child delivered to someone or at someplace other than home. If parents and their cars are used for field trips, policies are needed to ascertain the amount of liability insurance the driver of the car should carry, the number of children and adults per car, and the conduct expected of the children.

SCHOOL SAFETY

The original thrusts of the safety program were largely the protection of the child. However, it has now become clear that safety needs and instruction must extend beyond protecting and sheltering the child. Safety education should include accident prevention and the elimination of hazards. Individual and group safety consciousness should be developed as well as wholesome attitudes and practices related to safety. The importance of safe conduct in normal activities and the relationship of safety practices to a healthful environment should be emphasized. This can be done as children engage in activities such as cooking, woodworking, or using play equipment.

"This sign says stop."

In spite of the teacher's attempts to teach safety and to keep the school and its surroundings safe, accidents may occur. Some will be minor and others may be more serious. Teachers need an understanding of more common accidents, the emergency care for them, and first-aid practices. When accidents occur, the teacher should not panic. Common sense and basic first-aid knowledge are the best medicine. The injured child needs to be comforted and helped to feel secure.

For safety learnings to be effective there must be opportunities for guided experiences in and reinforcement of safety practices. Merely telling a child to be careful does not ensure the exercise of care by the child. He or she must be helped and supervised in this regard.

Ross and Seefeldt recommend four basic safety measures that children can learn through experience.[6] These are important for all children, but they are especially important for children who walk to school.

> The child should stop before entering any street, driveway, or area that is used by cars, trucks, or other vehicles.
> The child should listen and look before crossing the street or area.
> He or she should cross intersections safely.
> The child should look at and interpret traffic lights.

Some children, especially those attending public kindergarten, ride the bus to school. Whitmer recommends that such children learn the following rules.[7] Children should

> Wait at the bus stop for the bus.
> Get on and off the bus in an orderly manner.
> Stay in the seats, seated properly.
> Cross the street in front of the bus only.
> Look in both directions before crossing the street.

It is important that the child learn safety rules that apply when he or she is a passenger in a car. The child should observe the following behavior: Sit quietly on the seat, because wrestling, standing, or loud shouting may distract the driver; use the seat belt; keep arms and hands out of the windows and inside the car. Children who have bicycles should learn and practice safety rules.

NUTRITION: LUNCHES AND SNACKS

Children's centers can offer many opportunities for developing knowledge of and habits of good nutrition. Some centers serve only a snack in the morning or afternoon. In addition to snacks, however, some all-day centers may serve breakfast as well as lunch, whereas others serve only lunch. Whatever food is served, whether a snack or a meal, the menus should be well planned and nutritionally balanced, the food tastefully and carefully prepared, and served attractively in comfortable, pleasant surroundings. Children are more likely to eat nutritious food if the food is colorful and interesting; if the table, utensils, and the room are clean, quiet, and attractive; if the food is clean and the people around them are clean; and if they are comfortable and have clean hands and faces.[8]

The schedule for snacks and meals should take into account the child's home

---

[6] Sylvia P. Ross and Carol Seefeldt, "Young Children in Traffic: How Can They Cope?" *Young Children* 33:4 (1978), pp. 69–70.

[7] Daniel G. Witmer, "Teaching Children Bus Safety," *The Education Digest* (May 1980), p. 82.

[8] Maryland State Department of Education, Division of Vocational-Technical Education, *Preschool Nutrition Education Program For A Child Development Curriculum* (Baltimore, 1980), p. 70.

Young children learn to value each other's feelings by waiting for a small group to be served: Steven has poured his juice; he is waiting for Susan to pour hers and then for Wright to pour his.

routine. The teacher or caregiver needs to talk with parents regarding such routines. Children who have had a good breakfast are usually ready for a light snack about ten o'clock in the morning. Children who have had no breakfast will need a heftier snack when they arrive at school.[9] (Suggestions for routines related to eating are included in Chapter 16.) Suggestions for snack or mealtime include these:

1. Adults should set good examples.
2. Maintain a relaxed, pleasant atmosphere.
3. Encourage child to try new foods—at least a bite.
4. Involve children in planning and preparing foods.
5. Encourage children, as they can, to assist in serving—for example, pouring milk or juice.
6. Use eating utensils appropriate to the size of children.

Nutrition education is a vital part of the curriculum. Teachers can help children to learn good food habits and to learn about nutrition by providing opportunities

[9]Margaret McWilliams, *Nutrition for the Growing Years*, 2nd ed. (New York: John Wiley and Sons, 1975), p. 236.

for them to be involved in concrete experiences with foods. Nutrition concepts can be learned as children are learning concepts in other curriculum areas such as social studies and science. Food and nutrition concepts appropriate for young children are included in this chapter in the section, "Practices and Program."

Results of nutrition research have indicated a possible relation between adequate nutrition and a young child's behavior, the ability to learn, and healthier adult years.[10] A Nutrition Research Project was conducted at the Center for Young Children, University of Maryland.[11] Goals for the nutrition program included these: to help the child to know about a variety of foods; to be able to classify foods into the food groups of fruits, vegetables, milk, meat, bread, and cereal; to recognize that some foods are needed for growth and health; to know the sources of some foods, and foods prepared in different ways. Parents and caregivers received attention as well as the children. The nutrition program was planned to involve children with foods in a variety of ways on a concrete level. Results of the study indicate that it is possible for young children to learn some basic concepts about nutrition.

Planning for snacks and meals, and preparing and cooking foods afford opportunities for teaching children about health and nutrition.[12] Healthful snacks can replace the cookies, cakes, or other foods that children often take turns bringing to school each day. Parents can be encouraged to send only fresh fruit and vegetable snacks.

SEX EDUCATION

More questions related to sex are asked by young children than by those of any other age group.[13] Responding to these questions can be an important part of sex education for the young child. In planning for such education it is very important that parents be involved. If the sharing of information between teacher and parent is encouraged, the development of similar ways for teaching the young child about sex at home and school will be facilitated.

Suggestions for teaching sex education to young children include the following:[14]

> Find out how much the child already knows. The teacher can ask the child a question when answering one. "How do you think it happens?" This response helps the teacher to learn if the child's information is correct and to clear up misinformation.

[10] Judith Herr and Winifred Morse, "Food for Thought: Nutrition Education for Young Children," in *Curriculum Planning for Young Children*, ed. by Janet F. Brown (Washington, D.C.: NAEYC, 1982), p. 158.

[11] Marilyn Church, "Nutrition: A Vital Part of the Curriculum," *Young Children* **35**:1 (1979), pp. 61–65.

[12] Rosalie Blau et al., *Activities For School-Age Children* (Washington, D.C.: National Association for the Education of Young Children, 1980), p. 65.

[13] Sally Koblinsky, Jean Atkinson, and Shari Davis, "Sex Education with Young Children," in *Curriculum Planning for Young Children*, ed. by Janet F. Brown (Washington, D.C.: NAEYC, 1982), p. 160.

[14] Ibid., pp. 161–168.

Use correct vocabulary when talking with the child about body differences between boys and girls.

Give accurate information about birth and reproduction. A child from a family expecting a new baby often shows curiosity about reproduction.

Avoid negative responses such as frowning, shaking one's head, or saying, "That's not nice." Such responses may result in feelings of guilt in the child.

Show warmth, affection, and support for others as a model to the child for interpersonal behavior.

Koblinsky and colleagues have developed a *Bibliography of Recommended Sex Education Books for Preschoolers*.[15] Such a list can be of help to both teachers and parents. These books should be left on the shelf along with the child's other books.

PRACTICES AND PROGRAM

Direct instruction in health is not usually undertaken with very young children. Rather, teaching is done in connection with the daily school activities and routines.

This does not mean that all teaching is incidental and that no planning is necessary. To illustrate how goals in health and safety can be identified and opportunities used to achieve these goals, instructional areas are suggested.[16]

For each of the areas, there are listed basic concepts, beginning understandings, and learnings that it is hoped the child will achieve. Activities and learning encounters through which these may be realized are also listed. The lists are suggestive only. From these concepts and activities the teacher can select those that are appropriate for the group of children being taught. At regular intervals the teacher should review the activities in which the children have participated, note areas in which there has been little or no activity, evaluate progress toward goals, and plan for additional activities and learning encounters in needed areas.

Area	Examples of Concepts to Be Learned	Some Learning Activities That Can Contribute to Concept Development
Personal Health and Fitness	The eyes and the nose can be injured by pencils, scissors, fingers, and other objects. Skin, hair, and nails need care.	Blindfold a child for a few minutes. Ask the child to tell how it feels when unable to see. Arrange for children to participate in vision and auditory screening. Show pictures of children with clean faces, hair, and nails. Discuss.

[15] Ibid., pp. 169–170.

[16] D. B. Stone, L. B. O'reilly, J. D. Brown, *Elementary School Health Education: Ecological Perspectives* (Dubuque, Iowa: Wm. C. Brown Co. Publishers, 1976), pp. 282–370.

Washing hands before snack time and lunch and after "blowing noses" is emphasized by the adults in this child development center. Child-size facilities are important.

Area	Examples of Concepts to Be Learned	Some Learning Activities That Can Contribute to Concept Development
	Children grow at different rates. The nose is an organ for breathing and smelling.	Ask children at what time they go to bed. Weigh and measure children. Discuss sizes of children in group. Talk about different sizes in plants and animals. Identify some things by smell. Talk about keeping objects out of the nose.

Area	Examples of Concepts to Be Learned	Some Learning Activities That Can Contribute to Concept Development
Dental Health	The food we eat is important for good teeth. Candy and sweets can cause teeth to decay. The dentist helps in the care of our teeth. Brushing and flossing the teeth help to care for our teeth.	Make a poster showing foods that may cause tooth decay. Make a trip to a dentist's office. Have a dentist visit the classroom. Demonstrate proper way to brush and floss teeth. Arrange practice sessions.
Food and Nutrition	Good foods help children grow. We eat food for health, growth, energy, and enjoyment. Foods come from plants and animals.	Plant a vegetable garden. Prepare, serve, and eat a variety of foods and beverages, such as fruit, fruit juices, and raw vegetables. Visit a farm, a dairy, a grocery store, or supermarket. Arrange snack trays according to colors. For "green" include green foods with a variety of flavors—green grapes, apples, peppers. For "yellow" include yellow apples, grapefruit, pineapple, and cheese.[17]
Family Life Education	Families are different in size, ages of the members, and in their customs. Families live in different kinds of homes. Growth and reproduction are common to all living things.	Talk about how birthdays and other holidays are celebrated in each child's family. Make family pictures. Invite family members to visit the school or center. Show pictures of mothers and babies. Show pictures of mother animals and their babies. Learn names for mother animals and their babies.
Sex Education	Boys and girls are made differently.[18] The baby comes from the mother.[19]	Answer children's questions, using correct names for body parts and giving accurate information. Talk with parents about the use of anatomically correct dolls and puzzles. Consult with parents about recommended books for children on sex education.

[17] McWilliams, op. cit., pp. 243–247.
[18] Koblinsky et al., op. cit., p. 161.
[19] Ibid., p. 163.

Area	Examples of Concepts to Be Learned	Some Learning Activities That Can Contribute to Concept Development
Drug Education	The use of some drugs can be dangerous. The doctor should prescribe medicine that children take. Smoking is hazardous to health.	Talk about why children take medicine. Collect pictures to show ways to rest and relax when you are tired. Discuss possible effects of playing with drugs.
Communicable Diseases	Children should stay at home when they are ill. Some diseases spread from one person to another.	Show pictures of a child who is ill. Talk about how we can tell the child is ill. List some of the symptoms of a cold.
Environmental and Community Health	Children can help keep the community clean. There are doctors, nurses, and dentists who help us keep well. Hospitals are built to care for people who need special care.	Engage in cooperative planning by teacher and children for care of center, playground, and equipment. Engage in dramatic play. Arrange for a visit by a public health nurse. Visit the school clinic.
Safety	Getting in and out of a car safely helps to prevent accidents. One must not tease pets or play with strange animals.	Dramatize getting in and out of cars safely. Care for pets.
Mental Health and Human Relations	Each child is alike and different from all other children. Kindness, thoughtfulness, and courtesy help us live together happily. Young children, as well as adults, have responsibilities.	Talk about ways in which children are alike and different. Share toys and materials. Demonstrate courtesy to classmates. Send letters, dictated to the teacher, of thanks and appreciation. List jobs to be done in relation to a certain activity. Choose jobs to do.

Areas of concern for the health and safety of young children in the various types of centers include the school environment, personnel, physical facilities, practices, and the program, all of which are interrelated. As children experience a healthful school environment, use desirable health and safety practices, and participate in a school program appropriate to their needs and maturity, they have opportunities to develop into individuals who experience physical, mental, and social well-being.

"We are learning the parts of our body. I have a star on my knee."

Suggested Activities

1. Visit the local health unit. Secure a copy of regulations and policies pertaining to communicable diseases. Discuss in class.
2. Identify agencies or organizations in the community that may serve as health resources; for example, the county or city health unit, the speech and hearing clinic, mental health clinic. For each one determine the services available, the cost, and referral procedures.
3. Find out the requirements of your state for the health and safety curriculum. Share with the class.
4. Obtain from several different school or city departments copies of health manuals or written instructions to teachers pertaining to health observation and practices in the school system.
5. Visit a playground for young children. Identify any possible safety hazards. Note provisions made for children's safety.

6. Select one concept to be developed from the areas of the health program listed in this chapter. Plan a learning activity appropriate for developing this concept and utilize your plan with a group of young children. Evaluate the activity.

7. Reread the material relating to policies. Visit a center for children, and talk with the teacher regarding the center's policies on the topics listed in this chapter.

8. Observe in a center for young children. Note provisions made for handwashing, toileting, developing a positive attitude toward health practices, snacks, or lunch and for sick children. What was the role of the teacher?

9. Observe the role of the teacher or aide in providing for the safety of the children.

10. Prepare a list of books, filmstrips, and other teaching aids useful in teaching the various areas of health and safety.

11. View the following films:

    Jenny Is A Good Thing (Modern Talking Pictures, 2323 New Hyde Park Rd., New Hyde Park, N.Y. 11040). Available in Spanish also.

    Play in the Hospital (Campus Films, 2 Overhill Rd., Scarsdale, N.Y. 10583).

    To Prepare a Child and *A Hospital Visit with Clipper* (Children's Hospital, Washington, D.C., National Medical Center).

    Patterns for Health (Modern Talking Pictures, 2323 New Hyde Park Rd., New Hyde Park, N.Y. 11040).

Related Readings

Aaron, J. E., F. Bridges, and D. O. Ritzel. *First Aid and Emergency Care*. New York: Macmillan, 1972.

Althouse, Rosemary, and C. Main. "Food." In *Science Experiences for Young Children*. New York: Teachers College, 1975.

Bell, J. E., and Elisabeth A. Bell, "Family Participation in Hospital Care for Children." *Children*, **17**:4 (1970), pp. 154–157.

Bryer, Judith E. "Handle With Care: 10 Common School Accidents." *Teacher* (March 1978), pp. 60–61.

Calderone, M. S. "Sex Education and the Very Young Child." *PTA Magazine*, **61**:2 (1966), pp. 16–18.

Cohen, M. D. (ed.). *Children and Drugs*. Washington, D.C.: ACEI, 1972.

Collins, Ruth H. "Planning for Fire Safety." *Young Children*, **32**:5 (1977), pp. 28–32.

Dayton, D. H. "Early Malnutrition and Human Development." *Children*, **16**:6 (1969), pp. 210–217.

Denk-Glass, Rita, Susan S. Laber, and Kathryn Brewer. "Middle Ear Disease in Young Children." *Young Children* **37**:6 (1982), pp. 51–53.

Fassler, D. "The Young Child in the Hospital." *Young Children* **35**:6 (1980), pp. 18–25.

Furman, Erna. "Helping Children Cope with Death." *Young Children* **33**:4 (1978), pp. 25–32.

Harms, Thelma. "Evaluating Settings for Learning." In Margot Kaplan-Sanoff and Renée Yablans-Migid eds., *Exploring Early Childhood: Readings in Theory and Practice*. New York: Macmillan, 1981, pp. 488–492.

Herr, Judith, and Winifred Morse. "Food for Thought: Nutrition Education for Young Children." *Young Children* **38**:1 (1982), pp. 3–11.

Highberger, Ruth, and Linda Carothers. "Modification of Eating Behavior in a Day Care Setting." *Home Economics Research Journal,* **6**:1 (1977), pp. 48–52.

Hildebrand, Verna. *Guiding Young Children.* New York: Macmillan, 1975, pp. 149–167.

Johnson, Beverely H. "Before Hospitalization: A Preparation Program for the Child and His Family." *Children Today,* **3**:6 (1974), pp. 18–21.

Klieber, D. A., and Lynn A. Barnett. "Leisure in Childhood." *Young Children* **35**:5 (1980), pp. 47–53.

Lindberg, Lucile, and Rita Swedlow. *Early Childhood Education—A Guide for Observation and Participation.* Boston: Allyn, pp. 111–119, 268–269.

McNamee, Abigail S. (ed.). *Children and Stress: Helping Children Cope.* Washington, D.C.: ACEI, 1982.

Nutrition and Intellectual Growth in Children. Washington, D.C.: ACEI, 1968.

Regele-Sinclair, Linda. "Providing Food Services." In Margot Kaplan-Sanoff and Renée Yablans-Magid, eds. *Exploring Early Childhood: Readings in Theory and Practice.* New York: Macmillan, 1981, pp. 463–470.

Skeen, Patsy, and P. C. McKenry. "The Teacher's Role in Facilitating a Child's Adjustment to Divorce." *Young Children* **35**:5 (1980), pp. 3–12.

Truesdell, William, and Carol Wicks. "Bike Education for Teachers and Kids." *Instructor* (Aug.–Sept. 1976), pp. 68–70.

Waetjen, W. B., and R. R. Leeper (eds.). *Learning and Mental Health in the School.* Alexandria, VA.: ASCD, 1966.

West, Anne, R. "Bringing the Hospital to Preschoolers: Teaching Young Children About Hospitals and Health Care." *Children Today,* **5**:2 (1976), pp. 16–19.

CHAPTER **14**

Creative Expression: Art, Music, and Movement

Too often creativity is considered to be solely in the province of the fine arts. Findings in creativity, however, indicate that many aspects of the school program can be learned more effectively in creative ways.[1] Although creativity is discussed in connection with art and music, this is not intended to imply that the creative process is limited to these two areas of the curriculum.

CREATIVE LEARNING

Creativity is a complex process that usually involves a range of qualities including awareness, originality, fluency, flexibility, commitment, and complexity.[2] The creative product may be something tangible, such as a poem; or it may be intangible, such as a new way of attacking problems.[3]

---

[1] E. P. Torrance, "Adventuring in Creativity," *Child. Educ.*, **40:**2 (1963), p. 79.
[2] Louise M. Berman (ed.). *Toward New Programs for Young Children* (College Park: University of Maryland, 1970), pp. 45–52.
[3] Louise M. Berman, *New Priorities in the Curriculum* (Columbus, Ohio: Merrill, 1968), pp. 139–140.

From the best research evidence available and the observations of many investigators, creative imagination during early childhood seems to reach a peak between four- and four-and-a-half years, and is followed by a drop at about age five when the child enters school for the first time. This drop has generally been regarded as the inevitable phenomenon in nature. There are now indications, however, that this drop in five-year-olds is a man-made rather than a natural phenomenon.[4]

It seems urgent, then, that school experiences and opportunities of young children be examined. What happens to discourage creativity? Hendrickson and Torrance have identified several cultural obstacles to creative thinking. These and some of the authors' examples follow:[5]

Peer Pressures for Conformity. Children exert a powerful influence on one another, even at an early age. This influence may affect choice of activity, clothing, or actions. One four-year-old wore cowboy boots to nursery school and soon "everybody" was wearing boots—even though they were hot and unsuitable for climbing and rhythmic activities. Parents reported pressure at home from their child to buy the boots and to wear them. Not until the teacher worked with the parents was it possible to relieve this pressure.

Pressures Against Questioning and Exploration. Even though the questioning stage is a phase of the young child's development, attempts are often made to squelch the asking of "What, why, and when." Rather, the emphasis is all too often on listening to and following directions. Have you heard an adult say, "Don't ask me why. Just do as I say"? Listening to and following directions are important skills, but so is questioning. Instead of discouraging the child from asking questions, the teacher should help the child learn how to ask the right questions. Closely allied with this obstacle is the tendency to equate questioning with misbehavior. The child who asks the question is often considered impudent or impolite.

Emphasis on Sex-Role Differences. In our culture certain traits and activities have been associated with masculinity or femininity. Comments such as "The girls may play in the doll house. The boys may use the blocks" tend to limit opportunities for exploration and discovery. Some children have sacrificed their creativity in order to maintain expected sex roles. Teachers must be careful not to perpetuate the old stereotypes.

A Success-Oriented Culture That Makes Errors Fatal and Makes Children Afraid to Take a Chance on Trying a New Approach. One five-year-old had encountered this obstacle early. Each day he chose to play with blocks but consistently avoided

---

[4] Torrance, op. cit., p. 83.

[5] P. R. Hendrickson and E. P. Torrance, "Some Implications for Art Education from the Minnesota Studies of Creative Thinking," in *Creativity and Art Education,* ed. by W. Lambert Brittain (Washington, D.C.: National Art Education Association, 1963), pp. 20–25.

the easel. After much encouragement to Joel to try the easel, the teacher said to him, "Today you are going to paint on the easel." In dismay Joel replied, "I can't. I don't know how. I might make a mistake." The teacher reassured him, "It's all right if you make a mistake. Go ahead and try." With relief in his voice, Joel said, "Okay. I don't know how, but I guess I can learn." Joel had older brothers who adored him but who teased him when he made a mistake. Joel soon learned to avoid the teasing by doing the things he could do well and without a mistake. Pressures for conformity and adult standards may also cause children to be afraid to try.

Work-Play Dichotomy. In an austere, no-fun, all-business atmosphere, there is evidence that creative thinking abilities are usually least used. The philosophy of the old adage, "Work while you work and play while you play," seems to prevail still with many persons rather than a recognition that play can be the child's work.

Integrating the arts into all subject areas leads to new and exciting ways to learn. Each curriculum area can be enriched by adding creative activities. By enriched subjects, each child's background can be enhanced. It is sad to think that many children go through school with little or no exposure to the creative arts. The arts provide a way for children to express themselves. This could be especially helpful to those with language problems. The multisensory learning brought about by making lessons creative involves the child more and leads to more self-discovery.[6] Creativity in the language arts is presented in Chapter 8. A look at creativity and the principles underlying its development indicates that whatever the curriculum area there is opportunity for creative teaching and learning.

PLANNING FOR CREATIVITY

The teacher is the first concern. To foster creativity in children, the teacher must be an adequate, fully functioning person. According to Combs, such persons have the following characteristics: "(a) a positive view of self, (b) identification with others, (c) openness to experience and acceptance, and (d) a rich and available perceptual field."[7] Acquiring these characteristics requires that "we all do more efficiently and effectively what some of us now do only sometimes and haphazardly."[8]

Carlson suggests that the teacher can develop inner resources through[9]

1. Eliminating negative, hostile thoughts, fears, and feelings.
2. Building more positive satisfactions through undertaking new experiences.

---

[6] Lynne K. List, *Music, Art and Drama Experiences for the Elementary Curriculum* (New York: Teachers College, 1982), pp. 7–9.

[7] A. W. Combs, "A Perceptual View of the Adequate Personality," *Perceiving, Behaving, Becoming,* 1962 Yearbook (Alexandria, Va.: ASCD, 1962), p. 51.

[8] Ibid., p. 62.

[9] Ruth K. Carlson, "Emergence of Creative Personality," *Child. Educ.,* **36**:9 (1960), p. 404.

3. Participating in original thinking processes.
4. Developing a more active *awareness* of environmental learning experiences.
5. Discovering new dimensions of learning.

Next, the methods of the teacher, the ways of working with children, and the program should be examined. Suggestions for change follow:[10]

1. Discard regimented routines, such as following directions for drawing, using patterns or models to be imitated, or ditto outlines.
2. Identify points in one's practice that are examples of stereotyped, habit-bound teaching performance. Project an alternative that is less rigid, more flexible.
3. Be attentive to the unusual questions children ask.
4. Respect the unusual ideas of children.
5. Show children that their ideas have value.
6. Give credit for self-initiated learning.
7. Provide chances for learning and discovery without threats of immediate evaluation.
8. Encourage aspects of behavior often attributed to the creative process. An adaptation from *Toward New Programs for Young Children* follows.[11]

   Awareness—of the five senses, detail, perceptions, alternatives. Suggestions follow.

   Provide a wide range of environmental stimuli such as trips, walks, and opportunities for touching, smelling, hearing, tasting, and seeing. Show a "surprise box" that contains an object. Ask questions such as "Can you tell what is in the box? How can you tell without looking?" Use questions about materials that children are using, such as "How does it feel? How does it taste?" Sensitize child to feelings of others. Use comments such as "Mary fell down. How do you think she feels?"

   Originality—in manipulating constructive materials, in questioning and wondering, in using new and novel responses. Suggestions follow.

   Make a collage tray available. Include materials such as leather, styrofoam, feathers, fabrics, cotton, and wood scraps. The teacher may say, "The materials are for you to use. See what you can make."

   Fluency—in the production of ideas and possible solutions to a problem. Suggestions follow.

   Give the child a box of objects and say, "What can you do with these?" Observe number of ideas and time required for expression. Encourage verbalization of problem for clarification. The teacher may say, "Tell me what the trouble is. Why do you think the bridge fell?"

   Flexibility—in using information in a variety of ways, developing and using a flexible schedule. Suggestions follow.

   Provide opportunities for the child to experiment with many types of materials to see how many ways he or she can use one material. Help the child expand

[10] E. P. Torrance, "Conditions for Creative Learning," *Child. Educ.*, **39**:8 (1963), pp. 369–370; Laura Zirbes, "What Creative Teaching Means," *Child. Educ.*, **33**:2 (1956), pp. 53–54; and Carlson, op. cit., p. 403.

[11] Berman, *Toward New Programs for Young Children*, op. cit., pp. 43–50.

verbally his or her experiences by comments such as "Why were you surprised?" "What else did it remind you of?"

Involve the child in planning a change of schedule.

9. Release the child's fears, hostilities, aggressions, and substitute a feeling of confidence, security, and satisfaction with his or her school activities.

The creative being does not emerge suddenly. The creative person develops gradually and grows by meeting problems and situations, recognizing them, and being able to solve or face them successfully. Experiences in art, music, movement, and other activities in children's centers can contribute to the development of a creative person.

ART ACTIVITIES

There are evidences of art activities, of clay, paints, and crayons in almost every child development center, nursery school, and kindergarten. In some situations one can see children working individually or in small groups, moving about freely, engaging in a variety of creative activities, such as painting, pasting and using scraps, cutting, tearing, or working with chalk. In other rooms, however, one can find all the children seated, quietly engaged in the same activity, coloring pictures, all very much alike. These two extremes indicate that even though there are art activities in almost every program, children are having quite different experiences and are acquiring quite different values and attitudes.

Art activities are considered an important part of any program for young children. Most children enjoy art activities, but there are also other reasons for including them.

Values of art activities

Art for young children is more than an amusing pastime.[12] Brittain holds that art activities provide one of the most effective ways for a young child to understand, organize, and use concepts.[13] Art is used to express what children do, see, feel, think, and talk about. Art activities provide opportunities to explore and experiment, to express ideas and feelings about themselves and the world around them. They strengthen ability to imagine and to observe and increase sensitiveness to self and to others. As the child works with materials, he or she assumes responsibility for choosing and shaping them, uses judgment and control, and gains success experiences that aid in establishing a self-concept of worth as an individual.

Art experiences have therapeutic values and may serve as an outlet for emotions.

[12] W. L. Brittain, *Creativity, Art, and the Young Child* (New York: Macmillan, 1979), p. 203.
[13] Ibid., p. 183.

Through art materials the child can express feelings that are otherwise unacceptable and can learn to handle such feelings in an acceptable manner. Because the young child's speech is limited, strong feelings can often be expressed through art experiences that involve psychomotor activity. Materials such as clay for pounding, paper for tearing, and nails for hammering offer opportunities for handling negative feelings through positive action.

John, who pounds the clay with such vehemence, has learned that this is an acceptable way to work off the anger he feels toward the child who has the train he wanted to run. As he pounds and squeezes, he drains off his angry feelings to make them more manageable.

Helping a child to turn feelings into creative channels gives an outlet that can be used throughout life. To offer patterns or models could block this means of expression and prevent future growth; asking what has been drawn or telling how to do it might be just as detrimental. By leaving the child free to use materials in his or her own way, the teacher can sometimes gain insight into a child's private world by observing how such materials are used, the results obtained, and the feelings about the results.

Children grow socially through art experiences. As they participate in self-chosen activities, groups form easily from common interests. They learn to share materials, tools, and ideas, to make decisions; and to experience the give-and-take of group living. They learn to respect the rights, property, opinions, and feelings of others. As individuals interact with each other, group leadership qualities develop, and children become aware of the importance of cooperation and self-control. These values are derived when children are free to choose materials and use them in their own way.

Intellectual growth takes place through art activities as the child invents new ways of using materials and refines methods previously used. As Jonathan, for example, becomes absorbed in work, he finds a need for more mature speech in order to talk about it, to explain, or to inquire. Concepts are developed as the child explores the properties of materials such as clay or paint and learns such terms as *slick*, *pliable*, *soft*, and *hard*. The child can develop an art vocabulary, using words such as *artist*, *texture*, *color*, and *space*. The greater the variety of materials with which Daniel works, the greater his confidence in his ability to express himself. As he grows in ability to define problems and seek solutions, he grows in creative ability. A child's drawings are used as indicators of the child's intellectual development.[14]

Opportunities for physical growth, exercise, eye–hand coordination, and motor coordination are also available. As children use fingers in painting or drawing with crayons and in manipulating clay, they are developing muscular control that will be used later in handwriting. Selecting shapes, choosing colors, and determining sizes offer opportunities for visual discrimination.

[14] Ibid., pp. 129–132.

Environment for growth

The role of the teacher in art activities is to create an environment that fosters optimum growth, a setting that is challenging and stimulating and that gives opportunities for the beginnings of aesthetic appreciation. Following are suggestions for the teacher in creating such an environment.

Individual Attention. Children grow in depth and quality of ideas, in spontaneity and clarity of expression when they are accepted as individuals. The teacher helps each child to experience some success every day, to develop a healthy attitude toward mistakes, and gradually to assume responsibilities in the care of materials. The teacher guides, supports, and extends the child's thinking. The teacher must create a feeling of security that leaves the child free to think, imagine, select, and make decisions.

The teacher offers help when needed, raises questions to stimulate thought, and gives wholehearted approval of the child's honest attempts. Through wise guidance, the child is increasingly able to take part in planning activities and in assuming more and more responsibility for maintaining the orderliness and attractiveness of the room. This requires time and planning so that the child will know where materials are kept, can take these out as needed, and can return them when finished. This also requires a teacher who is friendly, sincere, and understanding. Suggestions for becoming a more creative teacher are found earlier in this chapter.

Provision of Adequate Space, Time, and Materials. Space is needed to enable children to move freely, to work alone or in small groups, at tables, easels, or on the floor, inside and out-of-doors; to permit children to obtain, arrange, and care for equipment and materials easily. Water should be available for mixing paint and for cleaning up. Adequate light is needed. The teacher must provide time for unhurried, satisfying explorations, time to make and carry out plans, time for each child to work at his or her own rate, and to clean up when he or she has finished. The teacher must also provide a variety of materials from which the child may choose. The materials are discussed later in this chapter.[15] The care and use of art supplies should be discussed with the children.

To meet the needs of all the children, the teacher makes allowance for their short attention span by offering them a choice of several activities. The teacher provides the class with large sheets of paper, paint brushes in a variety of sizes, chalk, and wax crayons and generous amounts of clay and dough, scissors, and woodworking and scrap materials.[16] Because taste and touch are so important to young children, the materials used are safe and washable. The teacher provides many opportunities

---

[15] For a detailed list of suggested materials, see *Selecting Educational Equipment and Materials for Home and School* (Washington, D.C.: ACEI, 1976), pp. 53, 62–64.
[16] Brittain, op. cit., pp. 215–223.

for kinesthetic experiences with ample provision to indulge in tactile operations where the child uses hands for a tool. Because supervision is necessary, the teacher offers one "messy" or new medium requiring close supervision along with several familiar media that the children can handle largely by themselves.

In making a selection of the types of materials for the day's use, the teacher may choose the scrap material and puzzles because they are familiar to the children and can be handled by them with few requests for help. The teacher can give time and attention to finger painting, which does require supervision. The introduction of new material could have been handled in the same manner. The housekeeping center, blocks, and easel painting are available every day.

The children are permitted to move freely from one activity to the other, which encourages them to make choices and to assume the responsibility of finding something to do.

Creative Expression.   Children need rich experiences to stimulate creative expression. This should begin with their everyday living and their love of play. Through discussions of what they have seen or felt or by talking with them about their play, the teacher can help them to vividly recall happenings they had only vaguely noticed before. They should be encouraged to talk about themselves and their feelings toward others and to dramatize these feelings. Through bodily action, children often are stimulated to express themselves in other media. By providing a variety of materials, the teacher enables them to select the media best suited to their individual need.

Planned trips are another means of stimulating creative expression. The teacher must not only plan these excursions, but later help the children to relive and recall them more fully through discussions and questions. The wise teacher does not necessarily expect to see these experiences depicted in the child's art. The child has been given ideas for creative thinking. Juliette must have freedom to choose what she wishes to express. As the children work following a trip, the teacher observes their behavior and seeks ways of helping them change habits and attitudes and to deepen their awareness of their environment. The teacher can call attention to flowers, trees, birds, asking, "Are the two the same shape, color? Tell me how they are different." Children's creations indicate their frustrations and problems as well as their ideas of themselves and their surroundings.

Parental Attitudes Toward the Child's Creative Expression.   The teacher must also act as interpreter of the child's work to parents. Often adults mistakenly stifle creative growth through imposing mature standards and ideas. The understanding teacher helps parents to appreciate the art qualities of children's drawings and to be familiar with the developmental stages the child goes through. In this way they may savor and enjoy each succeeding phase as well as provide a home atmosphere conducive to such wholesome growth.

The teacher can suggest suitable materials and ways of presenting them to the child at home. A suggestion that space be provided for the child to display artistic endeavors often opens new avenues of enjoyment for both parent and child. One parent of a nursery school child kept the paintings on the kitchen bulletin board where all might enjoy and discuss them.

Some inner-city parents, as well as some in suburbia, show little, if any, appreciation of their children's art, and often little, if any, space is made available for displaying what the child brings home. Consequently, many children are not encouraged by the home and may become downhearted and uninterested. Display and appreciation of art products at school for such children become very important.

Parents should be encouraged to take children on trips around the neighborhood or community. These experiences will be reflected in the artwork.

As parents become involved in school activities, serving as aides or attending meetings at school, the teacher has the opportunity to show them their children's art. Appreciation of the child's work can be encouraged and an explanation given of how the child is expressing growth and ideas. In talking with parents, the teacher may suggest comments and questions that might be used with the child. The importance of conversation as a means of language development should be emphasized. A decorated folder may be given to the parent for keeping samples of the child's work.

The teacher should talk with parents about the use of coloring books. Parents sometimes need help in seeing the poor art qualities present in coloring books as well as the physical inability of the small child to stay within lines. They need to realize that patterns may rob the child of self-confidence and deaden imagination and spontaneity so important to all learning. Models made by teachers or adults can sometimes rob the children of the opportunity for self-expression. Telling children how to paint can keep them from using their own ideas and initiative.

Comparing the artwork of one child with that of a sister or brother can make for negative feelings and attitudes.

Consideration of Developmental Level. The teacher should know the characteristic stages of growth in children's art and the developmental levels through which such growth evolves. It is important that the teacher know and use the findings of research related to children and art. It has been found, for example, that middle-class children, when using finger paints, evidence more anxiety about getting dirty than do lower-class children.[17] Such findings can give clues to the teacher for working more effectively and understandingly with children of differing home backgrounds.

There is a pattern of developmental levels through which a child's artistic expression evolves. These levels of maturation determine the selection of media, the size

[17]Thelma G. Alper, H. T. Blane, and Barbara K. Abrams, "Reaction of Middle and Lower Class Children to Fingerpaints as a Function of Class Differences in Child-Training Practices," *J. Abnorm. and Soc. Psychol.*, **51**:3 (1955), pp. 439–448.

of paper and tools, and the kinds of experiences that will prove most effective for stimulating future growth.

Lowenfeld identified these stages as scribbling, presymbolic, and symbolic. Later the stages were known as scribbling, preschematic, and schematic.[18] He emphasized that exceptions with regard to the period over which any stage is extended are quite frequent.

The stages, as identified by Lowenfeld, are described here in order to picture the sequence of development. Although each child progresses through these stages, he or she does so at his or her own rate. In a group, ages three to five years, there are likely to be children in all three stages of development. Activities geared to only one of these would limit children who happen to be in other stages. The same child may not develop in all media at the same rate, owing to experience with and interest in the media. It is important for the teacher not only to understand the general stages of growth in art but also the development levels in each medium.

Brittain describes developmental stages in the scribbling process. *Random* scribbling begins at about one year and lasts until about two or two and a half. This stage appears to be the first for all children. *Controlled* scribbling comes next and lasts about a year. Children begin to name their scribblings at about the age of three and a half or four years.[19]

The scribbling stage begins when the child is first introduced to pencil, crayons, clay, or other media and usually extends to about the fourth year. The first efforts of the child are exploratory and largely muscular activity. Sarah is interested in the tool or material and what it can do. If using a crayon, she swings her arm and watches the resulting marks on the paper and soon becomes aware that she can control them by lifting the crayon up or repeatedly drawing lines consciously up and down and across the paper. Tasting is as important as feeling at this stage, so precautions must be taken to see that the materials are safe.

From uncontrolled muscular activity the child gradually develops the ability to make circular patterns. The development of motor control and muscular coordination is the major growth at this age level. To be able to hold a tool and make it go in the direction desired is a step in development. Until this level is reached, the child is not ready or able to perform other tasks requiring coordination such as eating and dressing. When the child begins to name scribbles or tell stories about them, he or she has taken still another step in development. The child is no longer thinking in terms of physical action but in terms of images and symbols. These symbols hold meaning for the child if not for the adult, so confidence and encouragement must be given. A simple "Tell me about your picture" gives the child a feeling of pride in the work and encourages him or her to imagine and to verbalize.

Between the ages of four and seven, a different mode of painting begins in which the child consciously creates forms. The child continuously tries out new concepts

[18] V. Lowenfeld and W. L. Brittain, *Creative and Mental Growth* 6th ed. (New York: Macmillan, 1975).
[19] Brittain, op. cit., pp. 23–32.

in an effort to establish his or her own individual pattern or symbol. This stage, known as the preschematic, is characterized by flexibility, by the child's constantly changing symbols. This preschematic stage begins as the child strives for a relationship with reality in drawings. A circle for a head with lines representing arms or legs gives a resemblance to a man. As Jerry becomes more aware of his relationship to the environment, he feels a need to enrich his new-found symbol and produces a large variety of symbols for the same object. This shows flexibility and ability to adjust. Because the child is most flexible at this time, it is important that the teacher stimulate and increase his or her awareness through individual experiences. When children see themselves as part of the environment, they place everything on the baseline.

Development is also reflected in the child's clay products. At the age of two he beats, pounds, and pulls the clay. At three the child makes balls and long snake-like rolls. By four the child uses the balls and rolls of clay to make more complex forms. The child of five may tell what he or she is going to make and then make the object.[20]

Bloomer[21] points out that in the sensorimotor stage (ages two or three), the child scribbles. In the perceptual motor stage (three to four years), the child perceives that his or her scribbles can be made into shapes and designs. In the cognitive motor stage (ages four and five), the child begins making specific designs to represent certain things like a house or tree. The concrete operations stage includes ages five through eight years. The baseline is the main achievement in this stage. Bloomer reminds the teacher that all children do not pass through these stages at the same time.

McFee holds that the time at which a stage begins or ends depends on the opportunities the children have. She quotes Dubin's study, which indicates that young children can change their level of graphic representation by being encouraged to conceptualize about what they are doing.[22] McFee also says that a teacher should consider the individual and environmental influences on the child, as well as physical and psychological growth.[23]

Providing opportunities in art

Authorities advocate the use of a creative approach as the most appropriate method for working with young children. The teacher who uses a creative approach encourages children to choose their art activity, the way in which they will express or do it, and the way in which they will organize ideas or materials. This does not

---

[20] Brittain, ibid., pp. 42–45.
[21] Carolyn Bloomer, Professor of Art, University of North Carolina at Chapel Hill, Fall 1982.
[22] June King McFee, *Preparation for Art*, 2d ed. (Belmont, Calif.: Wadsworth, 1970), pp. 240–241.
[23] Ibid., p. 220.

"We can make our own finger paint." These children are experiencing the kinesthetic and tactual sensations of finger painting.

mean that children proceed without guidance; it does mean that they will make decisions and choices.

There should be many art activity areas available to children each day. These should be changed frequently, taking into account the weather, season, curriculum, and the moods of the children and the teacher. Occasionally, changing places where the child finds art activities may encourage new ideas and ways of doing things. However, some things remain in the same place—some things are left unchanged in order to help the child feel secure.[24]

[24]Clare Cherry, *Creative Art for the Developing Child* (Belmont, Calif.: Lear Siegler/Fearon, 1972), p. 3.

There are times when it may seem wise for all the children to use the same topic, which may be selected by either the children or the teacher. This may sound rather formal; however, each child is free to choose how he or she will develop and organize the topic. As time for the Easter egg hunt approached, the children needed baskets for their eggs. They made their baskets, but what a variety of baskets! Some were very intricate, made by cutting and folding paper. Others were oatmeal boxes, gay with fingerpainting papers glued on. Other oatmeal boxes were painted with tempera paints. Berry baskets were painted and handles attached. Each child made a basket according to the level of his or her ability and perception. How did the teacher manage this with so many children and only one adult to help?

The teacher and the children talked about the many possibilities for making baskets. The materials were secured and arranged in areas around the room. One table had scissors, colored sheets of construction paper, rulers, and paste. On another table there were boxes, paint, heavy cord for handles, scissors, colored paper, finger paintings, magazine pictures, and paste. Berry baskets, paint, cord, and scissors were in another work area. The teacher also set up blocks, puzzles, and easels. These activities were familiar to the children and required a minimum amount of supervision.

Not every child could work on baskets at the same time because space and teacher help were not sufficient for this. The teacher and children discussed the materials available, and the children went to work in the area where the materials they needed were available. Some worked on baskets. As one child finished a basket another child took his or her place. A part of the group worked with blocks, puzzles, and at the easel. After experimenting, each child was free to move to another center if he or she wished. The teacher observed and was available as needed.

Contrast this situation with a directed lesson in which every child not only made a basket but made the same kind. The teacher gave directions, step by step. When each child finished the step, he or she had to wait until directions were given for the next step. Sue and Jim finished quickly and found it difficult to wait while the teacher helped Jerry. Jerry knew that "he was holding everybody up" and felt inept and embarrassed.

In both situations the children had experience in following directions and using art media. The creative situation, in addition, offered an opportunity for choices and decision-making, working at one's own pace, expressing one's own ideas, assuming responsibility, and building confidence in one's self.

There are those who reject the creative method for such reasons as these: "The child must learn to follow directions." "The child must learn to color within the lines." "With only one teacher it is impossible to let children do whatever they choose. One teacher can't supervise all of them." "Parents expect their child to make what the other children make." Such statements indicate a mistaken concept of the creative approach as being one of "confused pandemonium."

Two mothers were observing in a kindergarten as the children were preparing for the work period, or, as some call it, "the art activity period." The teacher and children talked together about activities available for the day. The teacher turned to John and asked, "What do you plan to do?" To another child she said, "What do you want to do?" Then she said, "Those who have made a choice may go to work. If you have not decided, wait just a minute, and I will help you."

The mothers were aghast. "Does she let them do whatever they want to do?" "No," was the reply. "The child chooses within the limits of the activities available. The teacher has selected those appropriate for the day. But the child does make a choice, and the ability to make a decision is an important skill. Note that all children have not yet acquired this skill. The teacher must help them."

As the mothers watched, they saw children assume responsibility for getting the materials they needed, using them, and putting them away. As a child finished one job, he or she was free to move to another. Jim finished a picture at the easel and went to play with three other boys in the block corner. Children shared materials and took turns. Some had to wait for their turns at the finger-painting table or wait to use the dry cell batteries in the electricity center. The teacher moved quietly among the children, reminding a child to put on an apron before painting and talking with another about some work.

Types of activities

All art activity must be tailored to the mental and physical capacities of the child. A program that is not fitted to the developmental level of the child is meaningless. Brittain found that changing materials seemed to have no advantage in developing concepts. New or different materials do not seem to speed up development.[25] Different materials do provide variety that the child may enjoy.

Some art activities are labeled as noncreative by Brittain.[26] These tasks were planned and directed by the teacher. During such activities it was observed that children talked less about what they were doing than when they enjoyed their own work; spent less time with the activity; and were easily distracted. These activities, Brittain feels, do not truly involve the child except for the physical movement.

Through a variety of well-planned activities in an environment where the child is free to explore and experiment, one progressively becomes aware of the environment and is better able to communicate this awareness to others. Moving at one's own pace, a child develops and refines the large muscles, strengthens the smaller ones, increases eye–hand coordination, and gains shape and color concepts that build toward reading readiness. The child develops socially through sharing materials, taking turns, assuming increasing responsibilities for using these materials and cleaning up afterward. Three-year-old Jane at the dough table showed this social

[25] Brittain, op. cit., pp. 214–215.
[26] Ibid., pp. 18–19.

growth when she said, "I want to share with you." Tom, in the block corner also evidenced it when he told the teacher, "Look at my house. It has room for some more people." As a child works and plays with paints, clay, blocks, and tools, he or she is building perceptual and thinking abilities as a basis for further learning. As one gains skill in using materials, one grows in self-confidence.

Materials for art activities are unlimited. A creative teacher can provide for art activities even with a limited budget. There are possibilities in materials such as cloth, straw, boxes, gift wrappings, and feathers. It is important to help children see beauty and value in the world around them—in seedpods, leaves, grasses, and sand. Such materials may be called "junk" by some but to the creative teacher they offer opportunities for enriching experiences for boys and girls. The use of such materials is limited only by the vision of the teacher. The creative teacher experiments with new ways of presenting them and evaluates their true worth to the children using them.

There was no doubt in the teacher's mind about the feeling of achievement Jerry experienced when he confronted the powdered tempera in small dishes with a jar of water and brushes nearby. He wet his brush, dipped it into the dry paint, and then applied it to the paper. With shining eyes he exclaimed, "I made paint." She also shared Judy's delight in the kinesthetic sensation of finger paint that equaled her enchantment with the color as she sang, "Purple hands, purple hands. Look at my purple hands."

Art experiences for the young child are basic to developing a happy, wholesome, and creative personality. Through these early experiences in art children develop the ability to imagine, feel, explore, and express ideas. They learn to share materials, to cooperate, to assume responsibility, and to grow in awareness of themselves as individuals and of their relationship to those around them. They become involved in making choices, judging outcomes, and solving problems. Working with materials a child may become sensitive to one's own needs and the needs of others. Gaining skill in using materials, a child attains feelings of success that help establish a self-concept of worth as an individual and as a member of the group. Finished creations reflect one's unique personality and insights.

The following chart gives some of the basic materials for optimum creative growth. The chart also presents types of activities and attempts to suggest developmental levels in each type of media. It also lists the important values of each activity and suggests some of the responsibilities of the teacher in making the art experiences meaningful to the child. Following the chart are recipes for some of the materials that are suggested for use with the young child. It is hoped that these will encourage the teacher to experiment with ways of using these and other materials.

Modeling (Clay, Dough, Sawdust and Wheat Paste, Salt Ceramic)

Characteristics of Work	Values Derived	Teacher Techniques
The Child: Beats and pounds; later breaks and rolls material to make forms. Names product. Begins to pull out or add on details such as nose, ears, arms, legs. Product has meaning for adult.	Develops large and small muscles and eye-hand coordination. Provides direct sensory experiences deeply satisfying to children. Stimulates different kind of thinking, builds concepts of form, allows changing of these concepts. Provides another outlet for emotional release and aggressive impulses.	Provide frequent opportunities to explore material. Encourage feeling, handling, and verbalizing. Do not model or show how to make something. Keep materials soft and pliable by storing properly.

Pasting, Using Scraps, and Styrofoam

Characteristics of Work	Values Derived	Teacher Techniques
The Child: Feels, manipulates, and explores. Uses paste lavishly showing little interest in its purpose. Uses with other materials such as scraps and sand.	Provides tactile experience and opportunities for manipulation and coordination. Offers emotional release and opportunity to acquire motor skill.	Furnish enough to allow child freedom to explore its uses and experiment. Help child find its use as a tool for creative expression. Show curiosity about materials. Use with scraps, sand, paper, crayons, cotton, cloth, styrofoam, and feathers.

Cutting and Tearing

Characteristics of Work	Values Derived	Teacher Techniques
The Child: Cuts and tears aimlessly exploring possibilities of material. Practices for skill trying to control scissors and direction of tearing.	Builds muscle control, eye-hand coordination. Provides another means of self-expression.	Provide scissors when child can handle them; be sure they will cut. Teach the child proper safety rules.

Characteristics of Work	Values Derived	Teacher Techniques
The Child: Names the forms. Forms have meaning for adults. Combines colors and textures.	Offers opportunities to grow creatively and in awareness of form concepts. Provides another means for release of tension.	Help child to discover the possibilities of tearing. Provide variety of colors and textures of paper, fabrics, and materials.

Finger Painting

Characteristics of Work	Values Derived	Teacher Techniques
The Child: Feels and experiments with paints. Uses fingers, hands, and arms, overlays and mixes all colors. Exploration is long, accompanied by smearing and finally frenzied smearing. Experiments with patterns. Develops an appreciation for form and color.	Allows release from home pressures to keep clean by offering an acceptable means just to mess. Frees inhibited children for greater spontaneity. Provides social growth and openness to contact. It provides kinesthetic and tactual sensation and opportunity for large muscle activity. It encourages creative expression through its direct contact between child and product and a chance for self-discovery.	Provide free choice of paper, paint on formica-top table, or oilcloth. Allow child freedom to experiment. Encourage this freedom by painting to music, talking about swing of body. Allow time to continue as long as interest is sustained. Allow child to mix the paints. Provide several choices of colors. Encourage children to clean up themselves. Make hand- or footprints on paper. Vary paints.

Painting (Working with Paint, String, Soap, Sand, Chalk, Crayon)

Characteristics of Work	Values Derived	Teacher Techniques
The Child: Uses it to explore, to spread and overlay. Makes lines and circles, then form, using squares and blocks of color.	Allows the child opportunity to work alone. Offers opportunity to experiment, explore, and express feelings that the young child finds difficult to put into words.	Furnish large sheets of paper, large brushes, and a choice of rich bright colors including red, yellow, and blue. Easel of suitable height, away from traffic, should be available at all times so that children can paint satisfying experiences or frustrations as they feel the need.

Painting (Working with Paint, String, Soap, Sand, Chalk, Crayon) (cont.)

Characteristics of Work	Values Derived	Teacher Techniques
The Child: Names the painting; the adult sees meaning. Shows evidence of relating objects.	Provides a means for motor expression. Helps the withdrawn child to give form to feelings and accept help. Permits messing in a controlled form and helps the too-neat child ease into finger paint and clay.	Locate activity in area that cannot be harmed by paint. Use linoleum or plastic on floor. Provide opportunities for painting on tables, the floor, and outdoors. Include variations such as *spatter painting* (hold wire screen over paper; dip toothbrush in paint and rub over screen); *straw painting* (put blob of paint on paper; blow through straw on the paint to create design); *string painting* (dip string into paint; drop string on paper; pull around to make design); *printing* (use objects such as paper cups, pencil erasers, cut vegetables, ends of tubes or straws, cookie cutters; dip into paint and print on paper; add a few drops of glycerin or oil of wintergreen to paint mixture to keep it from becoming smelly).

Using Blocks

Characteristics of Work	Values Derived	Teacher Techniques
The Child: Plays with single blocks. Stacks them. Creates a building and then names it. States kind of building and then builds it.	Their flexibility and ease of handling make an excellent first medium for the child. Their cleanness and sturdiness are nonthreatening to children from homes with parents' admonitions against dirt and breaking.	Provide ample space and materials. Allow opportunity to leave structure up when desired. Warn children ahead of time to clean up. Watch for ways of helping timid child to participate.

Characteristics of Work	Values Derived	Teacher Techniques
The Child: Uses knowledge gained in dramatic play.[27]	They offer opportunities for playing alone, parallel to, or in cooperation with others. Offer sense of achievement and power to cope with physical world. Offer emotional release through tearing down or dramatic play. Offer physical release through lifting, carrying, and piling. Cultivate creative expression and a sense of design. Offer opportunities for problem solving, growth in number concepts, and language.	Offer help when needed to prevent frustration. Avoid setting patterns. Listen to and observe child while building to gain insights into behavior and growth.

Using Tools (Hammers, Saws, Nails)

Characteristics of Work	Values Derived	Teacher Techniques
The Child: Handles and manipulates tools. Uses tools in hammering, nailing, sawing. Concerned with activity—simply hammering nails in wood or sawing wood. Tries to make something. Object may not be recognizable. Makes recognizable object.	Offers opportunities to develop eye-hand coordination and muscle control. Provides another outlet for emotional release. Stimulates thinking and problem solving. Builds concepts of size and form.	Arrange for ample space. Provide for real tools, not toys.[28] Provide scraps of soft wood—flat and in a variety of shapes. Help boys and girls enjoy working with tools. Provide nails in a variety of sizes. Accept product that satisfies child. Don't strive for perfection in end product. Supervise activity at all times. Use tools only in woodworking area.

[27] Frances M. Guanella, "Block Building Activities of Young Children," *Arch. Psychol.* **26**:174 (1934), p. 92, cited by D. H. Russell, *Children's Thinking* (Boston: Ginn, 1956).

[28] For a detailed list of tools for woodworking, see ACEI, op. cit., pp. 52, 64.

Recipes

Fixative

For chalk:
1. Glue thinned with water to the consistency of milk.
2. One part shellac. Two parts denatured alcohol.

For chalk, pastello, and charcoal:
1. Gum arabic, thin with water until consistency of thin mucilage. Spray—repeat twice.
2. Spray powdered milk mixed with water.

Colored Dough

---

3 cups flour
¾ cup salt
dry paint or 2 tsp. food coloring
½ cup water

Sift flour and salt together into a pan. Mix coloring with water, and add gradually to flour and salt mixture. Knead as you would bread dough until the mixture is smooth and easy to handle. The more the mixture is kneaded, the smoother it becomes. If mixture becomes sticky, add more flour. When not in use, place in plastic bag and keep in a cool place. (Should last at least two weeks.) Children can make this recipe.

Play Dough (Cooked)

---

2 cups flour
1 cup salt
4 teaspoons cream of tartar
2 tablespoons oil
2 cups water (substitute 2 teaspoons of water with 2 teaspoons of peppermint or wintergreen flavoring for scented dough)
food coloring

Heat all ingredients in a pan over moderate heat. Stir frequently until mixture pulls away from pan. The mixture looks very lumpy before it pulls away, but it smooths out again. Knead until smooth. Will keep in airtight container and does not require refrigeration.

Sawdust	Wheat-paste Mixture
4 cups sawdust	2 cups wheat flour
2 cups wheat flour	3½ cups cold water
1 cup water	

Produces a very pliable media—used like dough but not as firm a consistency. (Liquid starch—mixed with sawdust and powdered paint or with tissue paper.)

Paste

---

1 tbsp. powdered alum
1 cup flour
1½ pts. boiling water
Few drops oil of cloves

Mix flour and alum in cold water. Add boiling water, and cook for two minutes. Add a few drops of oil of cloves.

Finger Paint

½ cup dry starch
1⅓ cups boiling water
½ cup soap flakes
Vegetable coloring, show card or poster paint
1 tbsp. glycerin

Mix the starch with enough cold water to make a smooth paste. Add boiling water, and cook the paste until glossy. Stir in the dry soap flakes while the mixture is still warm. Cool. Add glycerin, and pour the mixture into jars. The mixture can be kept for a week if it is covered with a damp cloth or a tight lid. Add color later.

Two or three tablespoons of liquid starch may be poured on the wet paper and one-half teaspoon powdered paint added and mixed as the child paints with it. Color may also be added to wheat paste, paste, or liquid soap.

Sand Painting

Add ¼ part paint powder to 1 part sand and combine in large shakers. Use extra container to empty excess sand. Children shake on paper they have covered with paste. This is also excellent outside on the bare ground.

Soap Painting

Fill small dishes with soap powder. Add a little powdered paint and water. Mix thoroughly until it has a medium texture (not too stiff nor too soft). Children apply to various kinds of paper with fingers or brushes.

Evaluation

To know if the children are achieving the values and skills it is hoped they will derive through art activities, the teacher has to collect evidence for the purpose of evaluation. Techniques that may be used follow:

Samples of Children's Work.　Samples of work can be used to observe progress as the child moves through the developmental sequence from scribbling to forms that one consciously creates. A folder of the child's paintings and drawings and samples of other work, such as clay and wood, may be used for this purpose. It is important to date each product. Such samples may be helpful to the teacher in talking with parents.

Conversation.　Brittain says that a child needs someone to talk to. He found that the amount of time spent in drawing and other art activities increases as the child talks about what he or she is doing. Rather than merely providing interesting materials, teachers can help children become more involved by raising questions about what the child likes best and by making comments.[29] Informal conversation gives clues as to the child's ideas and feelings about one's self, one's work, and others. For example:

> One of the children stops painting long enough to ask for more red paint. The teacher puts a spoonful on the paper, and the child moves the red paint into a yellow area. Martha looks up with a smile of wonder and pride and says, "Did you know I could make orange? I put red and yellow together and made orange."

There may be other conversation between the teacher and the child regarding the child's work. Questions such as "What is it?" may be asking the child to identify an object when there was no object in mind. Perhaps the child was only manipulating and using materials. Comments such as "I like your car" may indicate to the child that the teacher has not recognized the object just made. Use comments that do not put the child in an embarrassing position. "Tell me about your picture" or "You have used such pretty, bright colors—I like the red," are much more appropriate for the young child.

Jefferson points out that it is not necessary to discuss everything that children produce in art. Children may be apprehensive if they know everything they produce will be discussed.[30] Negative comments during a discussion may be embarrassing for a child. He or she may lose feelings of confidence as well as an enjoyment of art.

In considering a discussion of art products, the teacher will do well to remember that the young child may not appreciate pictures made by other children. According to Munro, research and experience indicate that though children make schematic pictures, they tend to prefer more realistic ones. This means that they do not prefer to look at the type of pictures they make themselves.[31]

Anecdotal Records. Children's reactions during art experiences constitute a significant part of the child's behavior at school and serve as a source for understanding the young child. Anecdotal records of this behavior can be helpful. Record keeping is discussed in Chapter 6.

Records of Work Choices. A record of choices of activities that the children make from day to day can help identify the child who uses only one or a limited number of media; the child who skips from one material to another, not following through with the selected task; the child who uses a variety of materials freely and wisely. Such evidence can be used in helping the child. An example is shown in Table 14–1. List activities for the day across the top of the sheet. Write the child's name under one or more activities in which the child participates.

[29] Brittain, op. cit., pp. 224–225.
[30] Blanche Jefferson, *Teaching Art to Children* (Boston: Allyn, 1959), pp. 88–89.
[31] T. Munro, "Children's Art Abilities: Studies at the Cleveland Museum of Art," in *Readings in Art Education,* ed. by E. W. Eisner and D. W. Ecker (Waltham, Mass.: Blaisdell, 1966), pp. 179–180.

Table 14-1
Work Choices

Date	Blocks	Easel	Puzzles	Clay	Tools
5-9-78	Tom Ruth Bill	Ruth Jane Hal	Ruth Jane	Jane Hal	Tom Ruth Joe

Teacher's Evaluation. A weekly summary for each child can include the teacher's reactions to the child and his or her art activities, such as "Free in movement. Restricted in movement. Dependent. Experimental."

Interpretation of Children's Art Products. The psychological interpretation of children's paintings or drawings is wisely referred to the psychologist. There are, however, studies and scales that may be used to help the teacher gain greater insight into the children's products.[32]

MUSIC ACTIVITIES

The child's world is filled with music. On the TV children hear the musical accompaniment for the commercials. The country singer plays a guitar or picks a banjo and sings. Rock and pop music fill the air. On the radio one record after another is played. Some children have their own record players and a collection of recordings. Even with so much music of varying types in the lives of children, Smith says that their musical tastes are not fixed and definite when they come to school.[33] It becomes increasingly important to consider the role of music in all centers for young children.

[32] Florence L. Goodenough, *Children's Drawings: A Handbook of Child Psychology* (Worcester, Mass.: Clark U.P., 1931); D. B. Harris, *Children's Drawings as Measures of Intellectual Maturity (A Revision and Extension of Goodenough Draw-A-Man Test)* (New York: Harcourt, 1963); Rhoda Kellogg, *What Children Scribble and Why* (San Francisco: San Francisco Golden Gate Nursery, 1955); Rhoda Kellogg, *Analyzing Children's Art* (Palo Alto, CA.: National Press Books, 1969); and Beatrice Lantz, *Easel Age Scale* (Los Angeles: California Test Bureau, 1955).

[33] R. B. Smith, *Music in the Child's Education* (New York: Ronald, 1970), p. 4.

Shelley says that "An imaginative and balanced music program in which a young child learns how to 'play with music' can contribute to the child becoming an active learner."[34] Musical activities, chanting, singing, playing instruments, moving, listening, creating and recreating music, and the materials available should be such that the child is actively involved in making music. As children have the opportunity to interact with an enriched musical environment, they can learn to listen, expand the power of concentration, improve speech, develop language, and acquire tonal and rhythmic repertoire—all prerequisites for developing a musical child.

Shelley suggests the following guidelines for creating an environment for musical growth.

1. Have a flexible schedule so that music may be enjoyed when the need or occasion arises. Begin the day by singing songs that create good feelings.
2. Let music be informal. Welcome the child's ideas.
3. Work at a comfortable pace allowing for repetition. Children enjoy repetition.
4. Work with individuals, small groups, large groups.
5. Show appreciation of every effort a child makes to participate and contribute to the group. Do not force a child to participate. Appreciate the child's point of view.
6. Accept the child at his/her level, but encourage and challenge.
7. Encourage creative response in all music activities. Use questions such as "Is there another way you could do that?" "What would happen if . . . ?"
8. Provide for many and varied sensory experiences that will stimulate the child to use higher levels of thinking. Encourage the child to identify, discriminate, analyze, recall, synthesize, and make value judgments.
9. Help the child use nonverbal skills, such as movement. Help the child create simple orchestrations to reveal understanding of the mood, style, and structure of music.
10. Allow time for free exploration and manipulation of materials and equipment. Have instruments available so that children can touch, manipulate, play, and discover on their own.

Music helped Matt to grow socially. He was a very aggressive five-year-old, eager for attention regardless of how it was gained. He swaggered up to Miss S., who was standing near the piano. "I'll bet you don't know 'Ten Little Indians,' " he boasted. The teacher smiled, sat down, and played the song. "Is that the song you mean?" Matt nodded. She replied, "Sing it with me." Together they sang several songs. Matt not only enjoyed singing but found in singing an acceptable form of recognition.

Shull states, "Many educators are apparently unaware of vocal music by many distinguished composers written especially for children to sing."[35] Shull found a considerable body of songs and music of distinguished composers appropriate for

[34] Shirley Shelley, "Music and the Whole Child—Implications for Curriculum Planning" (mimeographed), EDEL 640, University of Maryland, November 17, 1977.

[35] C. N. Shull, "A Study of Children's Vocal Literature Written by Selected Distinguished Composers," unpublished dissertation, Florida State University, Tallahassee, June 1961.

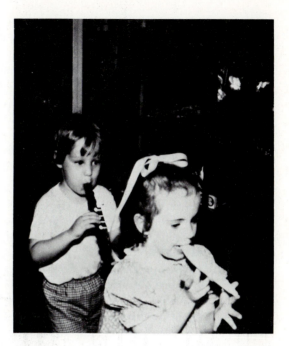

These three-year-olds are making spontaneous music. Could it be a circus parade or march of the toy solider?

use with young children. Listening to classical music may also be enjoyed by young children.[36]

The first responses of young children to music may appear awkward and uncertain, but as they grow physically and socially as well as in the enjoyment and understanding of music, their responses are gradually refined. A variety of free and pleasurable experiences in music invite participation by the child. To provide a balance, activities should include singing, creating, listening, and experiences with rhythms, movement, and instruments. For each activity there is a sequence of development from the first simple responses to those that are more complicated and refined. Knowledge and understanding of this sequence can enable the teacher to pace opportunities for experiences to the level of the child's development.

For example, because the child is not ready to participate in one activity, the teacher may decide he or she should not be forced and leave him or her alone. True, one should not be forced, but activities can be paced to development, and the child can be helped to take the next step. "Not forcing" does not necessarily mean leaving the child alone, unchallenged, and untouched for weeks or months. For example, a four-year-old, unable to skip, should not be subjected to drill in the practice of skipping each day. It does not mean, however, that nothing is done.

[36] Eunice Bailey, *Discovering Music With Young Children* (New York: Philosophical Library, 1958), pp. 39–42.

Rather, the teacher who understands the growth and development of the child, as well as the stages of development of the skill of skipping, can arrange many worthwhile experiences. There will be opportunities to climb, run, and jump, all of which can help the child gain control of the large muscles. As children experiment with bodily movements, they will set their own tempo, which the teacher can emphasize. The child listens to music, responds, and the rhythmic response is accepted. Gradually, in keeping with the child's rate of maturity, he or she reaches the point where skipping is possible.

Nye and Nye make suggestions for helping children from a culturally different background musically.[37] In reality, the suggestions are applicable to all children.

1. Examine and analyze a child's background. Involve the child in planning and exploring songs he or she would like to sing or know; instruments and rhythmic movements the child might use with a song.
2. Provide opportunities for the child to use divergent and creative ways of interpretation.
3. Find out and understand conditions in which the child may live. There may be complete indifference to musical values and experiences.
4. Involve parents in music activities at school. Help them to find out about musical programs and experiences available to them in the community and about appropriate programs for viewing on TV.
5. Encourage the child in self-evaluation. Evaluate the child's progress in order to meet his or her needs.

Developmental sequence of music activities

The description of the developmental sequence presented here attempts to give a picture of the stages through which each child passes at his or her own rate, and to help identify the next step that he or she is able to take. Such a sequence can prove helpful in making plans for a variety of individuals and situations. Wide differences among the group should not lead the teacher to the conclusion that some children can benefit from musical activities and others not. Smith says, "all young children have musical capacities, and all should have the opportunity to develop this potential."[38] Guidance and the introduction of new ideas at the appropriate time are necessary to help the child move to the next level.[39]

---

[37] R. E. Nye and Vernice T. Nye, *Music in the Elementary School*, 3d ed. (Englewood Cliffs, N.J.: Prentice-Hall, 1970), pp. 558–571.
[38] Smith, op. cit., p. 9.
[39] Barbara L. Andress, et al., *Music in Early Childhood* (Reston, Va: Music Educators National Conference, 1973), p. 24.

Singing

Developmental Sequence	Suggestions to the Teacher
The Child:	1. Children are at differing levels in the developmental sequence. Don't expect same response of all children. Give each child opportunity to participate at own level.
1. Plays with sound of own voice. Changes sound and pitch of voice. Repeats sounds.[40]	
2. Sings egocentric phrases about self, parents, toys.	a. Join in with a child who is singing. Add an idea to child's song. Don't make child feel his or her song is inferior.
3. Enjoys listening to song sung by another; sings spontaneously as one plays.	b. Sit with one or two children. Show picture. Sing, for example, "See the red _____". Encourage child to sing response, "apple."[41]
4. Responds with actions to song sung by another.	
5. Joins in with an occasional word or phrase as another sings.	c. Record some of child's chants or songs. Play for child to hear own voice.
6. Sings with an adult or group but not always in time with them (may be a measure behind and may not use the same words).	d. Some will listen as they are in block corner whereas others come to piano for a song. Accept child in doll corner at his or her level, but don't leave the child there all year. Work to help the child take the next step and the next. Perhaps sing a song (lullaby or one appropriate to the activity) for the child in the doll corner. He or she can rock the doll as you sing.
7. Sings along with adult or group, able to match tones.	
8. Sings alone.	
9. Selects and requests favorite songs.	
10. Recognizes songs sung or played by others.	
11. The child's voice range centers around G above middle C, but the voice he or she uses often varies with the activity and the purpose for singing.[42] The lower pitches, however, are sung more easily.[43] Smith reports a range from middle C to G above.[44]	e. Some learn words easily and sing with teacher; accept this along with the response of an occasional word and a happy, eager expression. Avoid such statements as "Now let's *all* sing." "Jane knows *all* the words. Jane, sing them for us. Now listen so you can learn the words too." Jane can sing alone for the group, yes— but not as a model that may discourage others.
12. Acquires a repertoire of songs.	
13. Sings tunefully. Reproduces a melody accurately within a given tonality.[45]	2. Include songs of varying length, tonal range, and content.

[40] Ibid., p. 42.

[41] Ibid., p. 44.

[42] A. T. Jersild and Sylvia F. Beinstock, "A Study of the Development of Children's Ability to Sing," *J. Educ. Physchol.*, **25:**10 (1939), p. 491.

[43] Dorothy T. McDonald with J. H. Ramsey, "Awakening the Artist: Music for Young Children," in *Curriculum Planning for Young Children*, ed. by (Washington, D.C.: NAEYC, 1982), p. 189.

[44] Smith, op. cit., p. 17.

[45] McDonald, op. cit., p. 189.

Singing

Developmental Sequence	Suggestions to the Teacher
	3. Provide many opportunities for singing throughout the day. Avoid "sing-song-ing" every comment to the child, but chanting some comments offers opportunities for individual and group responses.

"Mary has a new doll.
Who gave it to you?"

—

   —

     —

    —

      —

       —

Mary   —
   has a
      new doll.
Who
   gave
    it
     to
      you?

4. Limit length of group musical experiences, taking into account the attention span of the group. A few songs, well selected, sung happily, and enjoyed can be of much more value than a longer period in which children may lose interest.

5. Select songs within the expected voice range of the young child. Many songs are written too high for the majority of children. The range within the song should not extend beyond three or four adjacent notes. Songs that are a little more difficult vary in total range, but a limited-range pattern should be repeated several times.[46]

6. Include songs
   a. of a variety of types—patriotic songs; ethnic songs; religious songs, and hymns, songs about holidays, the here and now, everyday experiences, counting, folk songs, familiar songs.
   b. of a pleasing melody and musical appeal.

[46] Smith, op. cit., p. 18.

Singing

Developmental Sequence	Suggestions to the Teacher
	c. that are brief and simple and repeat certain phrases. d. containing words that are easily sung. 7. Teach songs using voice rather than piano.[47]

Listening

Developmental Sequence	Suggestions to the Teacher

The Child:
1. Is engrossed in one activity but listens just enough to be aware of what is being sung or played.
2. Enjoys a short song, a recording, or an instrument, alone or with an adult (range of attention span varies from 2 to 20 minutes).
3. Enjoys a short song, recording, or an instrument along with a few other children—gradually the size of the group expands to include the entire nursery or kindergarten group.
4. Listens and analyzes what is heard. Can distinguish between loud and soft or happy and sad music. Can listen for details and for answers to questions. Can listen to his or her own singing and playing in order to correct or to match tones. Can listen to accompaniment for rhythmic responses.
	1. Include a variety of musical listening experiences.
	  a. Different purposes:
	    Mood—fast, slow, happy, sad, rhythmic response.
	    Stories in music.
	    Sounds of contrasting timbre, such as metal, wood, paper.
	  b. Different types:
	    Recordings—vocal and instrumental.
	    Include a variety—chants, patriotic, ethnic, folk songs, and some examples of rock music.
	    Instruments—teacher plays piano; a father plays a horn; another child plays with a rhythm stick.
	    Singing—teacher sings; mother sings; another child sings.
	  c. Individual and in a group.
	  d. Resource people—sing or play an instrument.
	  e. Identify instruments in the music.[48]
	
	2. Provide record player and records that children can use.
	3. Watch child who spends too much time listening. The child may be using this as an escape from group adjustment—may need help getting into the group.
	
	The suggestions listed for language arts (Chapter 8) are applicable in listening to music.

[47] McDonald, op. cit., p. 190.
[48] Ibid., p. 191.

Rhythmic Experiences

Developmental Sequence	Suggestions to the Teacher
The child expresses rhythm through:	
1. Making random movements, using large muscles.	1. Provide space and opportunity for movement.
2. Moving rhythmically in one's own way for short periods of time.	2. Observe child's movements and tempo. Accompany the child with piano, percussion instrument or by clapping in his or her own tempo. The child sets the pace. Avoid accompaniments that include melodic and harmonic elements.[49]
3. Moving rhythmically in own way, the child responds when teacher emphasizes his or her movement with an accompaniment.	3. Help child with transition from moving rhythmically in his or her own tempo to moving to an accompaniment. For example, the teacher might say,
4. Moving at fast tempo before conforming to slower tempos.	"Tim, I've been beating the drum as you walk. I will do it again and beat every time you take a step. Then I am going to beat differently—maybe faster or maybe slower. Listen and see if you can walk when I beat the drum."
5. Adjusting bodily movements to accompaniment of regular beat. Can "keep time."	4. Provide accompaniments in faster tempos, using those that invite the slower, more deliberate movements at a later time. Vary soft and loud tones.
6. Listening before participating.	5. Use even foot patterns such as walking, marching, running before the uneven patterns like galloping and skipping.[50]
7. Adjusting bodily movements to accompaniment which involves contrasts (slow and fast, light and heavy).	6. Play accompaniments to which child can respond. Be sure that rhythm is regular and easily detected. Ask child to listen first and then respond to the music. Avoid getting children on floor and saying, "Do what the music says" without first giving them an opportunity to listen. Avoid saying, "I am going to play some skipping music" (or galloping music). Children may respond to the music by walking, running, whirling, skipping, galloping, or in many other ways. Let the child choose response to the music.
8. Acquiring musical concepts of terms—high-low, short-long, fast-slow, and expressing them through movement.	7. Play very high and very low tones. Ask the child to show where each tone is by raising or lowering arms. After listening, ask the child where the light, heavy loud tones were heard.

---

[49] A. T. Jersild and Sylvia F. Beinstock, *Development of Rhythm in Young Children* (New York: Teachers College, 1937), p. 96.
[50] Ibid., p. 71.

Rhythmic Experiences

Developmental Sequence	Suggestions to the Teacher
	8. Do not expect same response of all children. a. Some will respond individually or in small groups—not even all kindergarteners are ready to participate in a large group. b. Skipping requires greater skill in muscular control than some of the other activities such as walking or running. Not all fours or even fives can skip. This is another reason for letting a child choose own response rather than asking everyone to skip.

Playing Instruments

Developmental Sequence	Suggestions to the Teacher
The Child: 1. Manipulates and experiments with instruments; becomes aware of differences in sounds in relation to ways in which the instruments are played; comes to recognize sounds of various instruments. 2. Listens to instrument played skillfully by a person or on recording. 3. Uses instrument as accompaniment to his or her movements—beats rhythm sticks as he or she marches, but not necessarily in time with his or her steps. 4. Listens to music and is able to identify the instrument that makes the appropriate sound. 5. Plays instrument and responds accurately to tempo of a recording or another instrument. 6. Plays instrument along with a small group of other children. 7. Is interested in and curious about instruments that adults play. 8. Learns names of several of the better known instruments, such as the violin or trumpet. 9. Listens and identifies sound of different instruments. Knows when certain instruments are playing in a musical selection.	1. Place instruments so they are available to children. A special music area may be arranged. Provide opportunity for children to experiment freely. Expect "noise" at first. Use instruments both inside and out-of-doors. Avoid showing child "how to hold instrument." Help child evaluate sound in relation to way tambourine or triangle is held. "Which way sounds better?" Help child discover how to hold an instrument in order to get the best tone. Help child discover tonal qualities of instrument. Which instrument has the highest sound? the lowest? Play the drum with hand, a wooden mallet, a yarn mallet. How does it sound? 2. Accept gifts or donations of real instruments, such as drums, string instruments. Make available to children to use experimentally. 3. Play music and ask child to listen and to decide which instrument will be appropriate. Play music again and child accompanies with his or her instrument. Let child choose instrument appropriate for a certain rhythm, such as a rain dance or a Funny Clown, or one that has a certain tone color such as one that sounds like an airplane or the wind. Avoid such statements as "All drums play" or "All

Playing Instruments

Developmental Sequence	Suggestions to the Teacher
	together, play." Listening and responding creatively help the child to develop sensitivity to mood, and good listening habits as well as auditory acuity and discrimination.
	Such procedure is followed first for individual children and later for the group.
	The formal rhythm band often requires strict conformity and adherence to the pattern designed by the teacher, which may tend to discourage creative listening and responses.
	Bring real instruments to school for children to see and touch. Invite an adult or a youth to play for the children. Children may visit an orchestra rehearsal.
	4. Provide recordings of instrumental music.
	5. Tuned bells and the autoharp are effective instruments for exploring music.

Jim and Lois became aware of the quality of sounds and gained in auditory acuity as they experimented with instruments.

Creating

Developmental Sequence	Suggestions to the Teacher
The Child: 1. Chants as he or she swings, piles blocks, or pulls the wagon. This may be a play on words, experimenting with sounds. 2. Experiments with instruments and sounds. 3. Suggests a new word for a song; for example, in the song "Do you know what says, Quack! Quack!?" Child may substitute "bow-wow." or "mew, mew," etc.[51] 4. Makes up extra verses for a song. 5. Chooses an appropriate instrument and accompanies a song or a recording. 6. Interprets the mood of music in rhythmic movement. Moves expressively. 7. Dramatizes a song. 8. Makes up a song cooperatively and later individually. Sings the words in developing tune. 9. Creates an original melody or tune.	1. Although suggestions here are limited largely to singing, this is not intended to imply that this is the only musical experience that lends itself to the creative approach. Other suggestions are made specifically for rhythmic experiences. 2. Create a permissive atmosphere in which the child feels free to chant and sing as he or she works and plays. 3. Select songs containing words and phrases for which other words may be substituted. 4. Sing animal song to child. Then ask a question such as "Can you think of another animal that makes a sound? Sing it." 5. Permit child to listen to song or recording, and then select instrument for accompaniment. 6. Play recordings characterized by a mood or moods. Let child listen and respond. Properties such as scarves or flags may be helpful in interpreting the mood. 7. Use songs with words that give clues to movement or singing games. For example, in the song "This Old Man," children may choose to have the old man come "hopping" or "skipping" home.[52] Another example might be "Community Helpers."[53] 8. Creating a song may be a group activity. Joe brought a "possum" to the kindergarten. As a group gathered around the piano, he asked Miss T., "Do you know a song about a possum?" Miss T.: "No, Joe, I don't, but perhaps we could make up a song about the possum." To the group Miss T. said, "Let's see if we can make a song about the possum. What would you want to sing first?" Sally: "We could tell his name." Miss T.: "Yes, we could, Sing it for us, Sally." Sally sang, "Pete the Possum."

---

[51] Mary J. Nelson and Gladys Tipton, *Music for Early Childhood* (New York: Silver Burdett, 1952), p. 16.

[52] Ibid., p. 43.

[53] Ibid., p. 19.

Creating

Developmental Sequence	Suggestions to the Teacher
	Miss T. repeated Sally's phrase. This procedure was continued until the following song was completed.
	Pete the Possum, in a cage, His tail is long, His nose is sharp.
	Miss T. played the tune on the piano and recorded the notes. If she had not been able to play the tune, she could have sung it several times in order to remember the tune.

"There are many different sounds at school—I can find soft sounds, loud sounds, scratchy sounds, and ringing sounds."

As the child progresses through the developmental sequences described for singing, listening, rhythmic experiences, and creating, musical experiences can help him or her to develop in many ways. For certain children music has special advantages. The overactive, aggressive child can be helped to become relaxed and less tense; the shy, timid child can be helped to become involved in group experience. For each child music can

1. Promote appreciation and enjoyment.
2. Encourage discrimination in the choice of music and other aesthetic experiences.
3. Develop an awareness of and sensitivity to sounds as well as auditory acuity.
4. Develop and extend voice range.
5. Provide experiences in listening.
6. Promote growth in motor control.
7. Develop intellectual and emotional capacities.

MOVEMENT

Movement comes very naturally to children. Observe children shopping with their parents in the grocery store or waiting for the bus; you will usually see them moving. Children love to run, hop, bounce, skip, and slide rather than walk. "Movement in itself is educative and movement is essential to learning in early childhood."[54]

Fundamental activities include walking, running, jumping, galloping, hopping, skipping, sliding, and leaping. These activities are included in both movement education and rhythmic activities, or rhythms. Rhythmic body movement may or may not be accompanied by music. However, when walking or when one of the fundamental activities is done "to music," it is usually considered a rhythmic activity. Activities in movement usually precede rhythmic activities. Movement education may be carried on with the entire group, several children, or an individual child. Space is needed both indoors and outdoors.

Movement patterns of children appear at different times in their lives. Some appear in infancy; some, later at two, three, or even four years. The child at two can usually walk up the stairs, but he or she may not be hopping until the age of four. Skipping may not be achieved until four and one half or five years.[55] Movement patterns should be appropriate to the child's developmental level. Let the child set the pace.

Much of the spontaneous movement of children includes the fundamental activities of walking, running, jumping, galloping, skipping, sliding, and leaping. In

[54] Caroline B. Sinclair, *Movement of the Young Child* (Columbus Ohio: Merrill, 1973), p. 10.
[55] Ibid., p. 27.

In this movement activity the teacher asked one child to stand in front of another. Much of children's movement, however, is spontaneous.

addition, however, the teacher may find the following suggestions helpful.[56] The teacher may ask the child (or children) to

Walk without touching another child.
Walk and change direction when a signal is given.
Walk as if you are happy, tired.
Walk as if you were the rain.
Touch your shoulders (and various parts of the body).
Show how many ways you can move your head, arms, legs, and feet.
Touch your knee with your elbow.
Jump over the string.
Jump up high.
Bounce a ball and catch it.

[56] Barbara Day, *Open Learning in Early Childhood* (New York: Macmillan, 1975), pp. 120–132.

"We can share one bucket and catch three balls."

Sit on the floor and bounce a ball.
Move your ball in as many different ways as you can.
Make a circle with the rope.
Move over the rope in as many ways as you can.
Sit inside the circle.
Toss and catch beanbag with different parts of your body.
Use imitation:
　Act out a word,
　Imitate an animal,
　Imitate an emotion,
　Pretend to be an inanimate object,
　Let children work in pairs and imitate each other's movements.
Encourage free movement:
　Put on a record of music, and let the children move their bodies around the
　room,

Play music, and let the children draw figures in the air with parts of their body, Let them dance freestyle to some pop music.

USING ART, MUSIC, AND MOVEMENT IN OTHER CURRICULAR AREAS

Integrating art, music, and movement into all curricular areas has many advantages. The arts can enhance learning and introduce the children to areas that they might never encounter otherwise and make learning multisensory and more meaningful.[57]

Art, movement, and music can communicate ideas and feelings and thus fit well into the language arts. Movement can be used to act out stories to make them come alive. Children use art, drawing and painting, to illustrate stories. Music and movement can motivate and help the child to increase his or her vocabulary as he or she uses and adds words like *imitate, glide, inside, toss;* provide opportunities for oral communication; and develop aural discrimination skills as the child speaks like an animal or makes the sound of a plane.[58]

[57] List, op. cit., p. 7.
[58] McDonald, op. cit., pp. 191–192.

A group of three is just the right number for throwing and catching a ball!

Singing is an extension of speech.[59] Singing can help a child develop flexibility and expression, which encourage development of speech. Some students who stutter do not stutter while singing. Teaching them to sing can help build their confidence in expressing themselves, and they feel more comfortable while learning.

Children can learn science concepts as they sing songs about animals, the weather, and body parts. They can dramatize activities relating to various seasons. In social studies the children may make pictures related to trips and stories, sing songs related to children of other lands and to persons who work in the community such as the police or traffic officer.

Suggested Activities

1. Visit a center for young children, and describe the approach to art or the philosophy of the teacher regarding the art of the young child. What evidence do you see that the philosophy and practices are consistent? What is your philosophy? Discuss your observations with your class.
2. Visit a children's center. Observe children engaged in art activities. Describe the activity and indicate the stage of art development in which several children seem to be.
3. Use one of the recipes, in this chapter, and prepare a medium for use by children. Experiment with ways of using the medium. Name the values that you feel the children gained from participating in this activity.
4. Examine one of the scales or studies listed in this chapter. Use the information in relation to drawings of several children. How do you feel the scale helped you gain insight into the child's product?
5. Observe a group of young children, and note any peer pressures that seem to affect a child's choice of activity or actions. How do you feel such conformity may influence a child's creative activities? What do you feel is the teacher's role in such situations?
6. Make a list of art supplies and materials that you might order for your classroom. Compile a list of sources of art supplies. List materials that may be made by the teacher and/or parents.
7. Observe a child's movements and tempo. Accompany child with a percussion instrument or by clapping hands. Follow the child's tempo.
8. Listen to and evaluate five recordings for use with young children.
9. Learn five songs appropriate for use with young children. Teach them to members of the class and to young children.
10. Reread the suggestions for "creating" in music listed in this chapter. Select one suggestion, and use it with a small group of young children. Do you feel that you accomplished your goals? What changes might you make when you use this activity again?
11. Make a list of instruments appropriate for use with children. Make an instrument to be used by a child.[60]
12. Make a list of ways in which a teacher helps a child or a group of children develop an

[59] List, op. cit., p. 10.
[60] Day, op. cit., p. 64.

awareness of sounds in the environment. Did you note additional opportunities that might have been utilized?

13. Formulate some learning objectives of a teacher for using movement education with young children.

14. Listen to Palmer, Hap. *Records for Music and Movement.* Freeport, N.Y.: Educational Activities. Select a record and use with a small group of children. Evaluate.

15. Use some of the suggestions for movement in this chapter with a small group of children. Evaluate.

16. View the film *Dance With Joy.* (Documentary Films, 3217 Trout Gulch Rd., Aptos, Calif., 95003).

Related Readings

Akman, Susan H., and Lynne Sherald. *Woodworking: Processes and Procedures.* College Park: U. of Maryland, 1973.

Andrews, Palmyra. "Music and Motion: The Rhythmic Language of Children." *Young Children,* **32:**1 (1976), pp. 14–19.

Bayless, Kathleen M., and Marjorie E. Ramsey. *Music a Way of Life for the Young Child.* St. Louis: C. V. Mosby Co., 1978.

Birkenshaw, Lois. *Music for Fun: Music for Learning.* Toronto: Holt, Rinehart and Winston of Canada, 1976.

Brand, Manny, and D. E. Fernie. "Music in the Early Childhood Curriculum." *Child. Educ.* **59:**5 (1983), pp. 321–326.

Brittain, W. L. *Creativity, Art, and the Young Child.* New York: Macmillan, 1979.

Cohen, Elaine P., and Ruth S. Gainer. "Art as Communication with Children." *Child. Educ.,* **53:**4 (1977), pp. 199–202.

———. "Does Art Matter in the Education of the Black Ghetto Child?" *Young Children* **29:**3 (1974), pp. 170–181.

Curtis, Sandra R. *The Joy of Movement in Early Childhood.* New York: Teachers College Press, 1982.

Francks, Olive R. "Scribbles? Yes They Are Art!" In *Curriculum Planning for Young Children,* ed. by Janet F. Brown, Washington, D.C.: NAEYC, 1982, pp. 178–186.

Danoff, Judith. "Children's Art: The Creative Process," *Children Today,* **4:**4 (1975), pp. 7–10.

Dimondstein, G. *Exploring the Arts with Children.* New York: Macmillan, 1974.

Eisner, E. W. *Educating Artistic Vision.* New York: Macmillan, 1972.

Fox, Marian N. "Creativity and Intelligence." *Child. Educ.,* **57:**4 (1981), pp. 227–232.

Hattwick, Melvin S. "The Role of Pitch Level and Range in Singing of Preschool, First Grade and Second Grade Children." *Child Develop.,* **4:**4 (1933), pp. 281–291.

Herberholz, Barbara. *Early Childhood Art.* Dubuque, Iowa: Brown, 1974.

Jersild, A. T., and Sylvia F. Beinstock. "The Influence of Training on the Vocal Ability of Three-Year-Old Children." *Child Develop.,* **11:**4 (1931), pp. 272–291.

Johnson, Harriet M. "The Art of Block Building." In *The Block Book,* ed. by Elisabeth Hirsch. Washington, D.C.: NAEYC, 1974. Pp. 9–24.

Kellogg, Rhoda, "Understanding Children's Art." In *Readings in Psychology Today,* 2d ed. Del Mar, Calif.: CRM Books, 1972.

Langstaff, Nancy, and Adelaide Sproul. *Exploring With Clay*. Washington, D.C.: ACEI, 1979.

McDonald, Dorothy T., and Jonny Ramsey. "Awakening the Artist: Music for Young Children." In *Curriculum Planning for Young Children*, ed. by Janet F. Brown, Washington, D.C.: NAEYC, 1982, pp. 187–193.

Nelson, Mary J., and G. Tipton. *Music in Early Childhood*. New York: Silver Burdette, 1952.

Nye, Vernice. *Music for Young Children*. New York: Brown, 1975.

Pile, Naomi, *Art Experience for Young Children*. N.Y.: Macmillan 1973.

Rafael, Berta. "Art Activities for Children With Special Needs." *Child. Educ.* **57**:3 (1981), pp. 149–155.

Rinehart, Caroll A. "Music: A Basic for the 1980s (The State of the Arts)." *Child. Educ.* **56**:3 (1980), pp. 140–145.

Seefeldt, Carol. "Art." In *Curriculum for the Preschool—Primary Child*, ed. by Carol Seefeldt, Columbus, Ohio: Merrill, 1976.

Shelley, Shirley J. "Music." In *Curriculum for the Preschool—Primary Child*, ed. by Carol Seefeldt, Columbus, Ohio: Merrill, 1976.

Stecher, Miriam B., and H. McElheny. *Music and Movement Improvisation*. Threshold Early Learning Library, Vol. 4. New York: Macmillan, 1972.

Stinson, Susan W. "Movement as Creative Interaction with the Child." *Young Children*, **32**:6 (1977), pp. 49–53.

Werner, P. H. *A Movement Approach to Games for Children*. St. Louis: C. V. Mosby, 1979.

PART THREE

Early Childhood Education: Making It Work

CHAPTER 15

Involving Parents As Partners

The involvement of parents in early childhood education attempts to provide opportunities for parents to have a more significant role in the development and education of their children and themselves. According to Morrison, as the process of parenting is improved, as parents grow in meaningful interaction with their children, the school achievement of children increases, and their daily lives are enriched. Parents will be more involved and self-fulfilled as they discover and use their strengths and talents.[1] White found that parent involvement in the first three years of life was critical not only for so-called disadvantaged children but for all children to be able to get the most from their early experiences.[2]

The process should be a reciprocal one, involving help for the parents and their children as well as help for the school. As parents serve as aides and volunteers, work with one child or a small group, and provide other assistance, they can help

---

[1] G. S. Morrison, *Parent Involvement in the Home, School, and Community* (Columbus, Ohio: Merrill, 1978), pp. 21–22.

[2] Burton L. White, *The First Three Years of Life* (Englewood Cliffs, N.J.: Prentice-Hall, 1978), preface, p. xiii.

421

the teacher to be more efficient and more effective. The teacher can come to have a better understanding of the family and the child in the family setting.[3]

PARENT INVOLVEMENT

In earlier times parents were the educators of their children. Over the years, however, as society changed, major responsibility for the education of children shifted to the schools. Since the 1960s there have been important developments regarding the role of parents in the education of their young children. One of the most important factors was political in nature, resulting in a demand, growing out of the civil rights movement, on the part of low-income and minority groups that control of the education of their children be returned to them. This demand resulted from the fact that children of such groups had not been able to succeed in the public schools and at the same time retain pride in their respective cultural heritage. A second factor was the mounting research evidence pointing to the importance of parent-child interactions in bringing about conditions, the exact variables of which are not yet clearly understood, that are necessary for the stimulation of early cognitive development. Theoretically, at least, such stimulation is necessary if children are to be able to cope with the expectations of the public schools.

So great was the conviction of the importance of these factors that federally sponsored programs such as Head Start, Follow Through, and the Parent Child Center mandated parent involvement. The implementation of these mandates varied from complete control, including conducting the instructional program itself, to more or less superficial participation in occasional meetings, invited classroom visits, and field trips. As a further safeguard to be sure parents were involved, half the members of advisory councils or committees had to be parents of the children served. As time went on, poor people were learning to have a part in the destiny of their children.

The seeds of the point of view described at the beginning of this chapter had been sown in earlier educational literature. Both Froebel and Montessori believed that parents were an integral and important part of early education. However, the present concept of involvement, giving parents an important role, had not evolved until recently.

During the past three decades, recognition of the changing role of parents in their relationships to the school has been pointed out by many educators.[4] As parents become involved, they may assume one or more of the following roles: audi-

---

[3] Morrison, op. cit., pp. 150–152.

[4] U. Bronfenbrenner, "Reality and Research in the Ecology of Human Development," *Proceedings of the American Philosophical Association*, **119** (1975), pp. 433–469; I. J. Gordon, *On the Continuity of Development*, ACEI Position Paper (Washington, D.C.: ACEI, 1976); Robert D. Hess, et al., "Parent Involvement in Early Education," in *Day Care: Resources for Decisions*, ed. by Edith H. Grotberg (Washington: D.C.: Office of Economic Opportunity, 1971), p. 267.

Parents play an important role in the education of their children. This dad reads with his son.

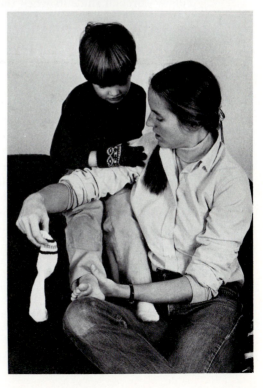

The mother helps by explaining, "Socks are to feet as mittens are to hands."

ence, learner, teacher of own child, classroom volunteer, decision maker, para-professional.[5]

Although parent involvement certainly is educational in nature for parents, a clear distinction should be made between parent involvement, and parent education as the concept appears in much of the earlier educational literature. The term *parent education* connotes that the parents are learners being "taught." *Parent involvement,* however, is comprehensive. The process includes helping parents discover and develop their strengths, potentialities, and talents and using them for the benefit of themselves and their children.[6] The results of this process are evident in the school achievement of children whose parents have been involved. Research reports of the positive relationship between child achievement and parent participation are presented in Chapter 4.

When parents have become involved in their child's educational process, certain ripple effects have been observed. Many families have shown changes in their social and economic goals. For example, families have been able to come off of welfare. Many parent educators in the federal Follow Through program have not only finished their high school equivalency test but have also graduated from college. Several have returned to teach in the classrooms in which they began as volunteers. Another noticeable ripple effect has been the advanced level of younger siblings of Follow Through students when they enter preschool.[7]

PARENTS AND TEACHERS COMMUNICATE AND WORK TOGETHER

Placing emphasis on parents and teachers working together, Washington[8] reports on an effective approach for helping urban children develop positive "I can" concepts. Paramount is a systematic approach designed to help parents improve their effectiveness as builders of self-esteem in their children. Enabling parents to accept responsibility as educators of their children, especially in the affective area, and to realize that success or failure in life for their children may depend on their effectiveness in this role is one of the major goals of the SUCCESS program.

Contact between parents and teacher should be a two-way process, from home to school and from school to home. Parents may want to know what they can do to help their children at home. Teachers want information that will help them provide

---

[5] Patricia P. Olmsted et al., *An Overview of the Parent Education Follow Through Program* (Chapel Hill, N.C.: University of North Carolina School of Education, March 1980), p. 22.

[6] Morrison, op. cit., pp. 22–23.

[7] Patricia P. Olmsted, *The Parent Education Follow Through Newsletter* (Chapel Hill, N.C.: U. of North Carolina 1:2 (May 1979), pp. 1–3.

[8] K. R. Washington, "SUCCESS: A Parent Effectiveness Approach for Developing Urban Children's Self-Concepts," *Young Children,* **32**:5 (July 1977), pp. 5–10.

a needed support system and improve opportunities for educational experiences for the child.[9] Often, however, one or the other party is hesitant to make the initial contact.

According to Leonard, Vandeman, and Miles, "When school and home enjoy understanding it is comparatively easy for one to approach the other in any individual or group situation that may exist.[10] What appears to be parental indifference is often in reality insecurity and low self-esteem. Thus, reaching and knowing such a parent may become a challenge to the teacher. Providing transportation, arranging meeting times suitable to the parents, avoiding formal meetings, and encouraging participation may be ways to involve such parents.

Even though all parents are different, they are alike in their desire to secure the best education for their child. They may also share the fear that their child is not like other children. Many parents are concerned that they are not providing adequately for their child. They need assistance and guidance in understanding what to provide and what not to provide. The wise teacher utilizes these concerns and builds upon the similarity of parents as plans are made for parent meetings and group study. Because the program needs to be concerned about differing social status, it provides an excellent opportunity for parents and children to have social experiences that will make it possible for the children to learn to live and work together with people from different backgrounds.

Nedler[11] explains and directly attacks the problem of why parents do not participate more in parent-teacher endeavors. For some time now it has been known that "parents on the run," as Nedler puts it, simply cannot take part because of the time schedule traditionally used by schools. These parents are working or otherwise detained with family responsibilities at scheduled times. What Nedler's suggestions boil down to is the simple fact that if parents are to participate in center or school activities, schedules must be flexible and personalized enough to make the school or center personnel and facilities available at night and during the weekends.

Morrison emphasizes the importance of attitudes in the process of parent involvement.[12] The school must be ready for parents and be willing to recognize their contribution. A decision must be made about what parents are to do and how they will be regarded. The teacher must really want parents to participate and not feel threatened. She or he must be willing to plan enthusiastically and effectively for their involvement.

There are many ways in which teachers and parents can communicate and work together. Suggestions follow.

[9]*Personalizing the Home–School Partnership* (Chapel Hill, N.C.: U. of North Carolina, 1982), p. 66.

[10] Edith M. Leonard, Dorothy D. Vandeman, and Lillian E. Miles, *Counseling with Parents in Early Childhood Education* (New York: Macmillan, 1954), p. 2.

[11] Shari Nedler, "Working with Parents on the Run," *Childhood Educ.*, **53**:3 (January 1977), pp. 128–132.

[12] Morrison, op. cit., pp. 134–137.

Home visits

Too often plans are made for the parents to come to the school for a visit, and yet no recognition is given to the need for the teacher to become acquainted with the child in his or her own home. A family interview, in order to fill out a child's history, is a helpful way to learn the home surroundings. The child becomes better acquainted with the teacher by actually seeing her or him visit in the child's home. The parent is more at ease in familiar surroundings and more likely to verbalize problems or questions. The teacher gains much through actually seeing how the family lives and how they feel about sending the child to school. Insight into feelings between family members may result from such a home visit.

Teachers usually find a home visit will be more profitable if (1) the visit is arranged at the convenience of the parents, (2) there is adequate time for both teacher and parent to talk uninterruptedly, and (3) the child is playing nearby where he or she can be observed, yet not always within hearing distance of the adults' discussion.

Home visits before the child enters school are valuable for the teacher and the parent in becoming acquainted and in giving insight into the background of the child. A friendly social visit will make the child, as well as the parent, more comfortable on the first day at school. The visit will make the child feel important in the eyes of the teacher, and it will help him or her to feel secure as the circle of peers at school is enlarged.

Today, many children have had one, two, or more years of preschool group experience before entering public kindergarten or first grade. In Home Start, Head Start, Parent Child Centers, and other such approaches, much of the instructional program may have been carried out in the home by the staff members as well as by the parents. Wise public school leadership will find ways to continue this close working relationship with parents.

School visits

The parent, accompanied by the child, needs to visit the school before the child enters to become acquainted with the facilities and to encourage the child to anticipate entering the program. These visits also make it possible for the parent to learn about the program and to assist the teacher in orienting the child to her or his first days at school. Communication between parents and teacher needs to be encouraged when the parent brings the child to school each morning. Both the teacher and the parent may gain further insight into the child's behavior through a conference held soon after a scheduled visit or planned observation. Scheduling the visits so that only one child's parents observe and visit the school on a given day will be more profitable and less disturbing to the children and the activities under the teacher's direction than if several parents visit on the same day. The teacher needs

When a parent comes to visit in this classroom for three-year-olds, it is a special treat, especially for one child.

to (1) develop an understanding of the place for and the importance of a planned visit to the school, (2) plan ahead, setting the actual time and date of the visit, (3) plan the procedures for the visit with both the child and the parent, and (4) provide for free time to discuss the child's activities as the parent observes the child or at an early time shortly after the visit.

If a simple observation guide in the form of suggestions for the visit is provided, the parent will feel more comfortable, and the first observations may be more profitable. Written suggestions may be profitable at each visit if they are planned to point out certain phases and aspects of the program or to assist the parents in gaining deeper insight into their child's development as he or she works, plays, and lives in a school situation. Some teachers do not find it desirable to prepare an observation guide; they prefer to make accessible pad and pencil so that the parents may jot down questions or comments to be discussed later in the follow-up conference.

For example, one teacher planned for parent observations to follow a group meeting that was devoted to the specific topic "The Child's Adjustment at School." Following a discussion of the topic, the teacher talked with the parents about planned observations at school and distributed "guides" pointing out various aspects of adjustment to be observed. A school visit was then scheduled for each parent, to be followed by an individual conference.

Observation form for parent

A short observation form may be helpful to both the teacher and the parent to use as a guide in a conference after the parent has observed the children in a group situation. A tentative form that could be useful follows.

AIMS OF THE PARENT OBSERVATION

1. To understand what children are like who are the same age as your child.
2. To know the daily schedule and the why's of various activities.
3. To learn how the teacher guides each child.
4. To attain insights as your child relates to the other children.

As you observe, try to be objective and avoid seeking out your child. Instead observe as many children as you can. Think of this experience as a learning one; stay in the background; write down questions or points as they occur. A planned conference will follow your observation.

POINTS TO OBSERVE

1. Observe the teacher in a variety of activities.
   a. Note how children's questions are answered.
   b. Watch how she or he relates to each child, what is said and done.
   c. How is she or he alert to any and all situations?
   d. How is the group guided smoothly into other activities?
   e. How are difficult situations handled?
2. Would you have handled activities in the same way or what would you have done differently? Why?
3. Observe certain children other than your own.
Note the following:
   a. How they respond to other children. Examples of sharing, trying to join a group, difficult behavior.
   b. How independent are they in activities?
   c. Are there special abilities shown by certain children in art, music?
   d. Use of language, number of questions.
   e. Length of time the child stays with an activity.

Telephone Conversations

Frequently a telephone conversation is thought to substitute for a scheduled conference. Like casual visits, these conversations make a definite contribution and have a place in communicating with parents. Minor routine situations, unexpected developments such as illness or a visit to the doctor, or some item that the teacher does not wish to discuss before the child may be discussed on the telephone. Scheduled conferences can be confirmed by the teacher with the parent in a telephone conversation, especially if the parent does not have the opportunity or does not avail herself or himself of the privilege of casual contacts.

Casual Visits

Parents communicate much information to the teacher and to other parents as they bring children to school or call for them later. The teacher can secure many cues as to a child's behavior and parent's attitude through analyzing remarks made in these casual contacts. It is necessary for the teacher to be alert to these cues because they may aid in gaining insight into how to work most profitably with the child during the day. The mother who states "We are running late this morning. We all overslept as we had unexpected relatives arrive late last night," may be giving many hints of how this will affect her child's day at school.

These casual contacts also give the teacher an opportunity to comment to the parent about the child. For example, she or he may say, "Janie seemed tired today. Did she watch television after her bedtime last night?" or "Jimmy sang alone in music today."

The value of casual contacts should not be underestimated; they make a significant contribution to the parent-teacher relationship by establishing rapport, paving the way and providing a means for scheduling the planned conference at a later date. Through these contacts, the teacher, the parent, and the child share moments of unified interest and learn to talk freely, one with the other.

Parent-teacher conferences

Through frequent, casual contacts, many so-called conferences are held by parents and teacher. However, they should not replace the scheduled conference. Sometimes teachers feel that it is not necessary to hold regularly scheduled conferences if they know the family and can develop an understanding of the child's home background through these informal discussions. Too often the true feelings of the parent or the teacher or the child may not be revealed in a casual visit; the problems needing discussion may be of the nature that the parent and the teacher do not wish those nearby to overhear. In addition, the teacher has not had time to study the child's record and to prepare for the conference; and the time is too limited to discuss problems, plans, purposes, procedures, progress, and follow-up activities. Many more areas can be discussed; recorded information, studied; and feelings, communicated in a planned conference.

The teacher needs to build an understanding of the need for and the purpose of a regular conference with the parent whether it be held only once during the year or more often. Each child as an individual needs to be carefully considered; and some tentative plans made by the teacher prior to the conference in order to discuss progress with the parents.

An individual folder for each child is recommended in which the teacher may insert short notes from time to time. Many teachers keep a written account of a child's reactions, achievements, and problems during the day; these are added to the collection in the folder. By reviewing each child's folder frequently, a teacher can discover children for whom there have accumulated valuable materials and those for whom there is little information. For the latter, the teacher needs to plan for closer observation and recording of information so that a conference about such a child may have more meaning. The teacher may have recorded little about some children because of being absorbed in helping a difficult child or one who is more interesting. Through analyzing the children's records, the teacher can plan to balance her or his time and attention to record activities of all children.

The planned conference should be a two-way affair in which the parent may not only learn of the child's progress, but may also have an opportunity to discuss differences of beliefs and procedures relative to working with the child. In many instances, the child may not have made much progress or change. Although the teacher recognizes the child as a growing, maturing individual, there are times when there appears to be little or no growth or change. The parent may not understand that this is satisfactory progress for the child at this time. The teacher needs to interpret what the behavior in the school situation means to the total growth of children.

Many teachers ask how they can actually communicate with a parent in a conference. A teacher needs to

> Recognize that each parent is an individual with personal needs, attitudes, values, and beliefs and accept the parent as a person even though differing with his or her beliefs. Remember, the parent may feel insecure.
>
> Accept the responsibility to plan and prepare for the conference by organizing thoughts and materials prior to the conference. Have records and samples of the child's work available.
>
> Arrange for a place for the conference where there will be no interruptions.
>
> Provide uninterrupted time, and give the impression of being unhurried and interested in the child and the parent and of being informed as to goals for the progress of the child. Ask if the parent has any special goals for the child. Begin with a positive comment about the child.
>
> Be warmly accepting of what the parent has to contribute.
>
> Be honest and truthful; keep personal feelings, facial expressions out of the situation, and avoid appearing shocked.
>
> Listen and find out why the parent feels or thinks as he or she does.
>
> Encourage the parent to work out possible ways of meeting problems. Suggest possible alternatives.
>
> Avoid destructive criticism.
>
> Allow time for changed thinking; do not force thinking or advice on parent.

Remember that the conference should be kept strictly confidential, and treat a parental or child problem in confidence.

Conclude the conference on a helpful and professional basis by discussing suggestions
the parent has for follow-through or further work with the child at school, as well
as planning with the parent for home activities and for future conferences.

Reassure the parent that the teacher and the parent are partners in planning for and
working with the child at all times. Invite the parent to call if questions or problems
arise.

Set a time to check back with the parent if a problem has been discussed.[13]

The teacher can communicate by means of such phrases as "Have you noticed how
well Susan can walk the planks now?" or "I have been so proud of Harold lately,
he is beginning to share the tricycle more readily." The way a teacher phrases
statements and the tone of voice used will assist her or him in talking easily and
profitably with any parent, and especially with one who may be on the defensive
worrying over what problems the teacher has encountered with his or her child.

Because communication between teachers and parents is a two-way process, the
following positive suggestions may assist the adults in gaining insight into relationships with each other.

Show genuine interest in the child.

Avoid being authoritative or too "teaching."

Avoid educational jargon.

Avoid arguments, becoming defensive over the way activities are carried through.

Listen for small cues about the child; then ask for clarification of certain points.

Avoid labeling or jumping to conclusions too quickly.

Offer several suggestions as to action rather than just telling what to do.

Attempt to arrive at some conclusions or points to be carried through by all concerned.

If meetings become repetitive, with little attention paid to the needs of parents,
low attendance can be expected. Few fathers can attend parent meetings if they
are at inconvenient times. A short social period designed to see that all parents
become acquainted will help provide more and better meetings.

Some program personnel may feel it is only necessary to have a meeting of parents at the beginning of the year to "inform the parents" of various policies and
another meeting at the end of the school year as a demonstration ceremony "to
show the parents" how the child can perform. Such demonstrations may be over-
stimulating to children and really serve little purpose. Graduation ceremonies for
young children may have meaning to adults but hold no place in good programs for
young children.

The most successful meetings are ones in which parents help plan and actually
participate in the meeting itself. A questionnaire sent home to parents with a list
of topics as an "interest finder" may provide helpful information for a parent committee in organizing these meetings. It is important that all the members have an

---

[13]*Personalizing the Home-School Partnership*, op. cit., p. 143.

opportunity at the first meeting to list problems according to interests and to plan an agenda of topics. Usually, a series of five or six discussion or study meetings will hold the interest better than a large number. Some topics that might lead to continuing group discussion are Helping Children Learn to Share, How to Prepare the Preschool Child for the Arrival of a New Baby, The Grandparents' Role in the Child's Home, Facing Crises in the Home, How to Handle TV in the Home, How to Buy Safe and Appropriate Toys, Health and Safety Information, A First-Aid Course, Child Resources in the Community, and so on.[14] The presentation of mental health plays related to one of these topics adds interest and variety.

As a way to provide good group discussion, it may be advisable to utilize additional human or material resources. Advance planning with members to bring in pertinent material or information about a topic, circulating reading material ahead of time, using bulletin board displays prior to the day of the meeting of the study group are all essential activities for the leader's preparation to produce a good flow of discussion from all members.

Study groups

A group of parents and teachers may wish to plan a few short discussion groups whereby all may study various aspects of child development or behavior. These groups may meet weekly or monthly, usually in a series consisting of planned meetings. One of the teachers or another adult who has been successful with group discussions may wish to begin the planning, leading, and organizing of such a group.

A few parents think that they or their child are the only ones who have a certain problem. Parents often find it very reassuring to discuss common problems. Most study groups have difficulty in finding a suitable meeting time because today's parents are so involved with many outside activities. The success of such a series of discussions comes from finding out ahead of time when the majority who are interested in a given problem can meet. Good leadership is very important. Interesting topics for discussion that will appeal to all attending will avoid turning the discussion into an information type of service. Adults benefit more from study through discussion groups because they have actually participated and voiced opinions, as well as shared experiences.

The planned parent meeting

Many teachers plan meetings regularly to bring parents and teachers together. The purpose of a meeting may be to communicate school policies to parents, to let

---

[14]Patricia P. Olmsted, *The Parent Education Follow Through Newsletter.* (Chapel Hill, N.C.: U. of North Carolina), 1:1 (April 1979), p. 3.

adults know what the daily program may be or what types of activities or seasonal events are planned, to view a good film, to hear an authority on some phase of child development, or to hold a meeting to get parent input on policy matters. Parent support groups may be organized for parents whose children have a similar problem. The parent who previously has had children in school can be used as a resource person.

Parent participation

There are many meaningful activities in which parents can participate. The school must take the lead in involving them. The decision to involve parents should be one in which the school administration, the director or principal, and teachers participate.

Parents can serve on advisory committees or councils. Such groups usually meet on a regular basis and advise with school personnel on matters of policy, program, problems, and plans. Parents may also serve as volunteers and aides. Training for these individuals and for their participation should be carefully planned. Such planning includes writing the philosophy and rationale for the program and the specific activity and developing an orientation and training program. Plans for supervising the volunteer and evaluating the performance by the children, the volunteer, and the teacher should also be made. A parent who has worked with the teacher earlier may serve as a parent coordinator. Some parents are able to participate on a regularly scheduled basis whereas others help on occasion.

The type and the amount of the participation should be carefully considered. Areas in which parent participation is particularly helpful include storytelling, music and art activities, field trips, group parties and picnics, library activities, celebration of special events or holidays, and parent work parties. Or a parent could be a resource person in a specialized area or activity. As the parents work and talk together with the teacher and the children, they develop a greater interest in and a deeper understanding of the program. In each group of children there will be some parents who have special talents or hobbies and who have the time and facilities to profitably enrich the lives of all the children through use of this talent. Opportunities for all parents to contribute in a variety of activities will build pride in the child's heritage and appreciation of the worth and dignity of all occupations. Examples of invitations to parents to participate follow.

September 29

Dear Parents,

On Saturday, October 2, the kindergarten is receiving a truckload of new sand for our playground. (Hooray!)

Parent helpers provide an opportunity for a child to have one-to-one interaction with an adult.

Fingerpainting or playing the game of naming body parts are examples of ways parents can help.

We very much need the helping hands of some of our mothers and fathers to move the sand from the box area to the swing and climbing areas. You would need to bring your own shovel, and we would need a few wheelbarrows.

If enough helping hands appear, we could do the job in an hour or so. The *teachers* and *children* would certainly appreciate your help!! Please return this note with your child on Friday if you are willing, and meet us at 10:00 a.m.

Most sincerely,

I can help on Saturday, October 2, at 10:00 a.m.

SIGNED: _____

P.S. Children are welcome!

February 19

Dear Parents,

Next week we will be learning about light, where it comes from, and how shadows are made by blocking the light. As one of the highlights of the week, we will be taking a walk on Friday to look for shadows. Please call the center if you can accompany us on our walk.

Sincerely,

In the parent-cooperative school it is expected that each parent will participate at specific times during the week as an assistant teacher. In all the participation of adults in programs for young children, a plan of weekly discussions between the directing teacher and the parents is essential for good management.

Parents may feel inferior to their child's teacher. The teacher may need to involve the parents in certain ways in order to know them better and to help them feel more at ease. Learning the skills and abilities of the parents can be a beginning in knowing the parents. A parent who plays a musical instrument or who has a special talent as well as the one who is willing to share in other ways may feel more needed. A broader concept of parent involvement has evolved with Head Start. Parents participate not only as helpers and in parent meetings but also in decision making that involves certain policies that concerns the program as related to their own children. Included is the parents' responsibility for carrying out the program both at home and school so that each supplements and supports the other.

In some regions, non-English-speaking parents may need interpretation through a teacher skilled in their language. Also, adult classes in English may have to be arranged.

FACILITIES AND MATERIALS FOR PARENTS

A special room for parents at the school where they may spend time looking over books or other materials is important as a parent center for many occasions. In such a room several parents may visit together or a parent conference can be held. Children's art or other creative achievements can be displayed, or a lending library of materials for parents can be arranged.

Many directors and principals have found that rooms used for other purposes, such as storage of obsolete and unused equipment, outdated materials, or just "trash" in general can be easily converted for parent use.

Parents should be given a free hand, within fire and safety requirements, in making the room attractive and suitable for their activities. The addition of newspapers, clipping and filmstrip files, tape recorders and, if possible, the use of a video camera and projector, at least on a scheduled basis, and a radio and a television set will add hominess to such a room. Records and a record player, instructional kits, and any specially developed instructional materials will add significance to, and interest in, the program.

Newsletters

Some programs send out weekly or monthly newsletters to parents; others distribute letters semiannually. As parents and teachers work together on this project, they will find that sharing experiences can be meaningful.

Brochures and bulletins as well as the informal newsletter have an important place in keeping parents informed and assisting them to understand and assume responsibility for extending the child's school experiences so that there is no conflict of goal or method between the home and the school. Special bulletins can be prepared as new developments indicate a need; for example, during an epidemic a bulletin might give information and policies relating to school attendance or it might serve the purpose of informing the parents that their child had been exposed to a certain disease and indicate procedures to be observed in safeguarding the child and other children. Examples of excerpts from newsletters follow.

February 19

Dear Families,

This has been an exciting week filled with all sorts of space adventures! On Monday we learned about astronauts, their qualification, equipment, and work. Tuesday we were ready to "blast off" in our rockets. Since then, we have discovered the feeling of weightlessness, explored the concept of gravity, and learned through the use of new "space" terms and activities.

Favorite activities have been constructing space helmets, parachutes, rockets, and moon surface. Science learnings were emphasized using the lightweight properties of styrofoam, balloons, and parachutes, and using the balloon as a rocket. It was fun to play with the real parachute in our classroom as we worked together and used our big muscles.

Skills and Concepts:

1. Gravity pulls objects toward the earth.
2. Objects are weightless when there is no gravity.
3. Rockets propel forward as gases expel backward—like a released balloon.
4. New space terms and concepts are learned.

Notes about holiday celebrations help parents in planning with their children. Two examples follow. These were included in newsletters. The first is from a center involving children ages two through six years. The second pertains to only one group.

 VALENTINE PARTIES

The 4's, 5's, and 6's will enjoy Valentine parties in their rooms Monday, February 14th. They will exchange Valentines. *DO NOT* address the Valentines, but *DO* sign your child's name or let your child do it. Please send a valentine for *every* child in the room.

The 2's and 3's will also have small parties but they *DO NOT* exchange valentines.

Valentine's Day provides a wonderful opportunity to discuss friendships. We will celebrate all week. Please help in the following way:

1. Tuesday, Feb. 9: Send in a shoebox or tissue box (to be used to collect Valentines).
2. Wednesday, Feb. 10, Thursday, Feb. 11, or Friday, Feb. 12: Please send in Valentines. Please do *not* address them (this makes distribution much simpler).
3. Please have your child help with the Valentines by signing his or her name, decorating them, or just putting them in the envelope. Valentines are a wonderful way to encourage an interest in reading and writing a child's name.

Parent Handbooks

Through handbooks, parents learn about school policies related to school entrance, size of groups, purposes, special services, fees, health provisions, school calendar and plans for parent contacts, participation, and visits, as well as of special activities scheduled throughout the year. Printed or mineographed bulletins assist in interpreting the school program and in building understanding of the purpose and plan for the activities in the school year.

One kindergarten handbook includes the following: kindergarten staff, school calendar, schedule, health policies, tuition and other fees, car pools, information regarding the newsletter, children's clothing, insurance, bringing toys to school, the kindergarten council, and the kindergarten program.

GUIDE FOR PARENTS IN SELECTING A PROGRAM

A parent's selection of a program for a child under six years of age should be regarded as an important decision in terms of what will contribute most effectively to mental, social, physical, and emotional development. The task is a difficult one as there are no set standards or guarantees as to the qualifications of the program personnel. Here is a list of generally accepted information of use to parents in identifying suitable programs for their children.

PURPOSE

Is the primary purpose to provide a program that fosters the total development of the child?

PROGRAM

Is the primary purpose of the program to provide an organized, continuous experience suited to the maturity level and growth pattern of the children attending?

Is the program so designed that regular continuous attendance is expected of each child?

Does the program provide for continuous uninterrupted growth of the child as he or she progresses to other units within the center and to units outside the center?

Are the records of each child systematically kept and available to the next unit?

Is the period scheduled for operation adequate for such a program?

Does the daily period of operation require additional plans for child care? If so, are these planned to be developmental, and are additional staff and facilities provided for this service?

Are there adequate provisions for the planned educational program? Health program? Nutritional program? Social services?

PERSONNEL

Are the adults in charge professionally competent?

Do teachers meet the certification requirements for specialization in early childhood education?

Are associates, aides, and volunteers utilized?

Is the adult-child ratio adequate so that individual and group experiences are provided for young children under proper guidance?

Are teachers pleasant, caring, and involved with the children?

FACILITIES

Is the center easily accessible?
Is adequate space indoors and outdoors provided?
Are facilities carefully maintained according to best practices for health and sanitation?
Are adequate and appropriate equipment and materials provided?

HEALTH AND SAFETY

Are there adequate provisions for health and safety?
Are food services available, adequately supervised, and sanitary?
Is the food nutritious?
Are health records kept of employees and children?
What plans are made for children who become ill at school or center?

SPECIAL SERVICES

What types of special services are provided?
How are these offered?
Are persons rendering this service fully qualified and certified?

Parents and teachers will find discussions of these questions in Parts II and III of this book.

Harms has developed a new home environment scale that will help parents who are going back to work to evaluate a home day care situation.[15] She has also prepared a checklist for *Evaluating Settings for Learning* from the child's point of view.[16]

SUMMARY

Involving parents as partners and friends in the program of educating the child is an important goal of early childhood education. Many feel this goal can best be met by ensuring parents of a larger role in determining and carrying out opportunities for educational experiences of their young children. Parents have become active partners with schools and centers in the early education of their children. Instructional materials and strategies designed to be carried out in the home or begun in the center or school and continued in the home have become a major influence in early education. Parents working with professionals on advisory committees or as aides, volunteers, or teachers have become a vital force in Early Childhood Education. These innovations, resulting mainly from research findings indicating parent-child interaction as an essential ingredient of early foundation cognitive development have placed new and major responsibilities on families, particularly on the parents of low-income families. In turn, the need for further education of the par-

---

[15] Thelma Harms, et al., *The Day Care Home Environment Rating Scale*, an adaptation of The Early Childhood Environment Scale—Harms and Clifford (New York: Teachers College, 1980).
[16] Thelma Harms, "Evaluating Settings for Learning," *Young Children* **25**:5 (1970), pp. 304–306.

ents themselves has increased. Day care and child development centers and schools for young children are becoming true partnership ventures with parents sharing equal responsibilities with staff personnel.

As children enter the public kindergarten and first grade, it is important that these responsibilities continue to be shared. Some of the ways to enhance this sharing are home visits, school visits, establishment of parent advisory committees, telephone conversations, casual visits, planned conferences, study groups and parent meetings, parent participation in the classroom, sharing of materials designed for parents, and periodic newsletters and other evaluative materials.

The outcome of early education may well rest primarily on the success or failure of parent involvement in the programs. Every good teacher hopes to help each child with whom she or he works and to challenge the child to learn and to prepare for more complex tasks. These desires are fundamentally the same as those of the parents. The task of the school is one of finding ways through which the drive to reach the goals of both groups may be integrated into a common endeavor.

Suggested Activities

1. Talk with a teacher of young children as to the procedure used in making home visits or holding parent conferences. Determine the frequency of such visits and the attitude of the teacher concerning them. Evaluate your own feelings in regard to the value of these visits or conferences.
2. Attend a parent meeting held by a child development center, nursery school, or kindergarten. Observe the reactions of parents, and note types of questions asked by parents. Determine frequency of meetings and types of usual programs. Evaluate these meetings.
3. Observe the teacher–parent contacts when children are brought to the day care center, nursery school, or kindergarten or when children are called for at the close of the school session. Note types of information obtained through such contacts for further insight into children's actions at school or center.
4. Arrange a parent bulletin board in a center or school for young children.
5. Make a list of five titles appropriate for a parent bookshelf.
6. Participate in a parent conference with the teacher with whom you are doing student teaching.
7. Select a topic, and develop a guide for parent observation to be used in a kindergarten.
8. Examine samples of parent newsletters. Plan one, and distribute it to parents. Ask them for suggestions and reactions.
9. Attend a parent advisory council. Observe how parents are involved.

Related Readings

Briggs, Dorothy Corkille. *Your Child's Self-Esteem.* Garden City, N.Y.: Dolphin, 1975.
Duff, R. Eleanor, Martha C. Heinz, and Charlena Husband. "Toy Lending Library: Linking Home and School." *Young Children.* **33**:4, 1978, pp. 16–22.

Haskins, R. (Ed.). *Parent Education and Public Policy.* Norwood, N.J.: Ablex, 1983.

Henderson, Ann. *Parent Participation—Student Achievement—The Evidence Grows.* Columbia, Md.: National Committee for Citizens in Education, 1981.

Honig, Alice S. *Parent Involvement in Early Childhood Education.* NAEYC, 1979.

Hymes, J. L., Jr. *Effective Home-School Relations.* Englewood Cliffs, N.J.: Prentice-Hall, 1953.

Jenkins, Gladys G. "For Parents Particularly." *Child. Educ.,* **56**:3 (1980), pp. 164–165.

Kaecher, Dan. "Preschool Education: A Good Idea for your Child?" *Better Homes and Gardens,* **60**:10, (1982).

Katz, Lillian G., ed. *Current Topics in Early Childhood Education.* Vol. 1. Norwood, N.J.: Ablex, 1977. Pp. 165–178.

Kelly, Francis J. "Guiding Groups of Parents of Young Children." *Young Children* **37**:1 (1981), pp. 28–32.

Leach, Penelope. *Your Baby and Child from Birth to Five.* New York: Knopf, 1981.

Marjoribanko, K. *Families and Their Learning Environments.* London: Routledge & Kegan Paul, 1979.

McCoy, Elin. "Is School Necessary?" *Parents,* **57**:4, (1982).

Moles, O. C. "Synthesis of Recent Research on Parent Participation in Children's Education." *Educational Leadership,* 1982, pp. 42–47.

Olmsted, P. P., and R. I. Rubin. "Linking Parent Behaviors to Child Achievement: Four Evaluation Studies From the Parent Education Follow Through Program." *Studies in Educational Evaluation,* 1983, **8**, 317–325.

Olmsted, Patricia P., Roberta I. Rubin, Joan H. True, and Dennis Revicki. *Parent Education: The Contributions of Ira J. Gordon.* Washington, D.C.: ACEI, 1980.

Orange County Mental Health Association, Parent Education Manual, panel discussion, *Parent Education: What Is It? Who Needs It? Where Do You Get It?* Chapel Hill, N.C., Sept. 27, 1978.

Osman, Betty B. *Learning Disabilities—A Family Affair.* New York: Random, 1979.

Reeves, Ramela. "A Daycare Place Where Children Thrive." *Working Mother,* **5**:9 (1982).

Rosin, Mark. "The Family of the Future" (from Alvin Toffler), *Parents,* **57**:3 (March, 1982).

Swick, K. J., and R. Eleanor Duff. *The Parent-Teacher Bond: Relating-Responding-Rewarding.* Dubuque, Iowa: Kendall-Hunt, 1978.

Thibault, Jonelle P., and Judy S. McKee. "Practical Parenting with Piaget." *Young Children* **38**:1 (1982), pp. 18–27.

Tway, Eileen. "When Will My Child Write?" *Child. Educ.* **59**:5 (1983), pp. 332–335.

CHAPTER 16

Guidance and Discipline of the Young Child

"You know . . . that the beginning is the most important part of any work, especially in the case of a young and tender thing; for that is the time at which the character is being formed." These words, as expressed by the philosopher Plato, have been emphasized by the findings of research in the areas of child growth and development. The early years are particularly important because habits and attitudes formed at this time may affect many aspects of a child's later life. The guidance given the child at the time that he or she has an experience may determine whether the resulting habits and attitudes are good or bad, even in adult life. Children learn, with or without instruction, and persons working closely with young children often are not aware that they offer guidance almost continuously. The effectiveness of this guidance depends on an understanding of the young child, the environment, and the goals and aspirations of the adults with whom the child comes in contact.

Problems related to the guidance of behavior and to discipline do not solve themselves. In order to enhance wholesome behavioral development the teacher must have clearly in mind the behavior it is hoped that the child will acquire. It is important, then, to consider such related factors as objectives and values, the environment, and the behavior that is considered normal and healthy for the age of the child.

OBJECTIVES AND VALUES

Attitudes and habits are developed as children work and play together in an environment that provides opportunities for physical, mental, and social growth. "Understanding," "getting along," and "cooperating" are not taught during designated periods of the day but are experienced as the child participates in such activities as science experiments or getting ready for lunch. The concern is not only for the experiences that a child may have, but also for what happens to the child while participating in these experiences. For example, as the child plays with other children, certain questions arise. Is the youngster developing the ability to "trust others," "get along," "take turns," or "have fun" and, as a result, learning to like people and to feel adequate as a person? Or are the other children too much for the child? Are they a threat? Is the child becoming bossy, aggressive, or withdrawn? What is happening to the child's self-concept? Is the child coming to think of himself or herself as a person who can tackle hard jobs or one who says, "I can't"? As one who tries new activities or one who hangs back? As one who has friends or one whom nobody likes?

If objectives and values are to be realized, there is need for consistency between purposes and actions, both verbal and nonverbal. The teacher should be a behavior model.

Children learn from watching how the teacher reacts toward them and toward other children. Adults who guide the behavior of children need to examine their values and goals in relation to practice. A thoughtful consideration of the following questions is helpful: What are the values it is hoped the child will come to accept? Are they, for example, honesty, cooperation, and respect for the worth and dignity of the individual? What type of person will the child become? Will he or she be understanding, adequate, cooperative, enthusiastic, aggressive, submissive, self-directing, or inquiring? Answers to questions such as these can serve as guidelines for examining practices. It is important that every teacher answer them. Teachers of young children will find a basis for answering such questions in Chapter 7. As teachers answer the questions for themselves, they may find that procedures are inconsistent with the desired ends or values. It is easy to say one thing and do something else. The following example illustrates how conflicts between purposes and practices may result in undesirable outcomes in the behavior of children.

In a meeting of kindergarten teachers, one member asked, "How do you make children sit still during story time?" There were several questions in reply. "What types of stories do you read?" "How long are the stories?" "When do you have story time?" The first teacher, impatient with the questions, replied, "It doesn't matter when or what I read. I intend to see that the children sit still and listen when I read a story." If one were to ask this teacher her purposes in reading the story, the following would probably be included: (1) to develop an appreciation of good literature, (2) to stimulate interest in reading, and (3) to provide pleasure and information. Her actions, however, tended to defeat the objectives she was trying to accomplish. By giving little or no attention to the selection read, by insisting that children sit and listen to material that might have little meaning for them, story time was becoming not only an ordeal for the teacher but a very uninteresting activity for the children. Such emphasis could easily cancel the values of appreciation and pleasure.

Values, however, can reinforce each other. A story, carefully chosen and well read, can provide pleasure and information, as well as develop interest, appreciation, and listening skills. In recognizing the importance of a consistent approach to goals, values, and practice in guiding behavior, we must examine the opportunities during the school day for learning values and the ways in which concepts are acquired.

At times children have not shown much ambition or enthusiasm for learning what has been expected of them. The "natural" learning capabilities and aspirations of each child must be considered.[1] The way in which children perceive a situation also affects their learning. As a child perceives, so a child behaves. A new baby in the home may be perceived as a threat by the child even though no threat is involved. The success of guiding young children in acquiring self-discipline is influenced by how the child feels toward or perceives the adult's actions—as those of a hostile, indifferent adult or as one who is warm, loving, and caring.[2]

There are two major ways of disciplining children. One way, love-oriented discipline, implies a bond of warmth between the adult and child. This type of discipline leads more rapidly to the development of a conscience. The child is given reasons for doing things or not doing things. The teacher is a model of a reasonable approach to life. The second way of disciplining children is power-assertive discipline. In this method the adult uses a loud threatening voice and spanking. Harms points out that if the child's only reason for not doing something is fear of punishment, then after the punishment he or she may feel that the wrongdoing has been paid for and he or she is free in beginning over again with a clean slate. Children who experience the power-oriented discipline seem to become more aggressive toward other children.[3]

THE ENVIRONMENT

The school environment can help or hinder the realization of goals for young children. The environment may be loving or frightening, stimulating or boring, conducive or inhibiting to the development of purposes and goals. What makes the

[1] D. Russell, "Goals for American Education: The Individual Focus," *Educ. Leadership*, **28**:6 (1971), pp. 592–594.
[2] D. K. Osborn and Janie D. Osborn, *Discipline and Classroom Management* (Athens, Ga.: Education Associates, 1977), p. 34.
[3] Thelma Harms, "Discipline—A Positive Approach," Frank Porter Graham Child Development Center, U. of North Carolina at Chapel Hill (1974), p. 6.

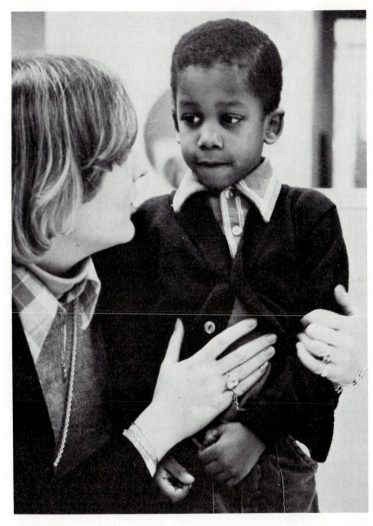

An atmosphere in which the self-concept may be enhanced is one in which the child can make an error and not lose face, one in which each child can participate and be a leader.

difference? No one single factor can be identified; for it is the interaction, the cause-and-effect relationship, of many elements that characterizes the total situation. John Dewey said that we educate indirectly, not directly, by means of the environment. The environment designed for the purpose of educating children can make a great difference.[4]

The effect of group size on the behavior of children is significant. McConkie and Hughes studied two groups, one with thirty-seven and one with twenty-six chil-

[4]John Dewey, quoted in Patricia L. Howell, and Robert G. Howell, Jr., *Discipline in the Classroom: Solving the Teaching Puzzle*, (Reston, Va.: Reston, 1979), p. 34.

dren, each attending school for a half-day, occupying the same room space, and taught by the same teacher. It was found that the larger group had less opportunity to work at its own problems and received less individual guidance. More aggressive behavior was also observed in the larger group. Its tempo revealed greater excitement, more noise, and a less permissive atmosphere. Twenty per cent of the children in the larger group initiated no personal contact with the teacher, whereas only 4 per cent of the smaller group had no such contact. The smaller group utilized space and materials better and played more cooperatively.[5]

A review of research related to kindergarten class size showed support for smaller class size as being more beneficial than larger classes in the areas of cognitive, academic, social, and emotional development; teacher effectiveness; and teacher satisfaction. The studies reviewed did not indicate a specific size for the kindergarten, but authors felt that it should not exceed twenty children. An optimal number of fifteen to eighteen children was recommended.[6]

Teacher behavior is also an important factor. Perkins studied two day care environments and found that when adults participated more often with the children and were less directive the children showed significantly higher levels of cognitive play, task involvement, and verbal interaction and lower levels of passive negative behavior. In the day care environment in which the adult was predominately uninvolved and directive, the antisocial behavior of children was significantly higher.[7]

The size of the group, then, should be considered in relation to the realization of the goals desired. If children are to grow in self-direction, wise use of materials, and cooperative behavior, provision should be made for a group situation small enough in number to make such behavior possible.

Another factor concerns the availability of materials and equipment. If the child is to grow in decision making, opportunities for choice are important. Interest or learning centers can offer the child possibilities for working at the easel, with blocks, or even with puzzles. Storage space must be accessible to the child to encourage independence and responsibility in the use and care of materials.

The extent of aggressive behavior may be influenced by the play material and space available. Two earlier studies report findings that are applicable today. Johnson reported her observation of nursery school children on the playground under different conditions. When only the stationary equipment (slides, climbing apparatus) was available, the children seemed to engage in more quarrels and to require more teacher intervention and direction than when movable equipment and toys

[5] Gwen W. McConkie and Marie M. Hughes, "Quality of Classroom Living Related to Size of Kindergarten Group," *Child Educ.*, **32**:9 (1956), pp. 428–432.

[6] Tamyra L. Beckner and Others, "A Study of the Relationship of Kindergarten Class Size, Length and Scheduling of the Kindergarten Day and Teacher Self-Concept to School Success," ERIC Reports, ED 165 891, (Arlington, Va.: Computer Microfilm International Corp., 1978), pp. 2–6.

[7] E. Phyfe Perkins, *An Ecological Assessment of Two Preschool Environments*, cited in Elizabeth Phyfe-Perkins, "Effects of Teacher Behavior on Preschool Children: A Review of Research," ERIC Reports, ED 211 176 (Arlington, Va.: Computer Microfilm International Corp., 1981), pp. 25–26.

were also available.[8] Jersild and Markey found that where play space was most restricted, conflicts were greatest in number.[9]

Rechsteiner, in a more recent study, found a significant relationship between the amount of social play observed and the amount of available play material. Less social play was observed when the amount of play material available was reduced. She recommends that more emphasis should be placed on the quality than on the quantity of play material for the classroom.[10]

The influence of the home

The home environment also has an influence on the child and the realization of goals. Before children enter nursery school or kindergarten, they have experienced various types of behavior in response to parental guidance and expectations. Some children have become independent, while others are unable to make decisions. Some have become submissive, and others are rebellious. Certain behaviors may be highly acceptable in one ethnic or social group, yet be considered unacceptable in another. The teacher, then, should be alert to the fact that the children have experienced different types of parental guidance that may have been influenced by various factors and in several ways.

One factor that may influence a child's behavior and socialization in school is maternal employment. Lower-class boys seem to develop more conflicts when mothers work than do middle-class boys. The father-son relationship in lower-class families may become strained because the fact that the mother works may imply that the father is a failure. Girls do not seem to be adversely affected by working mothers; in so far as higher achievement later in life is concerned.[11]

Divorce can cause fears and problems within the home that can affect a child's ability to handle school goals. How parents handle divorce is the key in determining how a child will handle divorce. Children who have had a divorce in their family were observed, and a report of the study indicated that disturbances may be evident in their play. They may no longer enjoy stories that deal with family relationships, and some children seem to dread playing house. During the divorce period a child may hit others, knock down block structures that others have built, or show other aggressive behaviors.[12]

---

[8] Marguerite W. Johnson, "The Effect on Behavior of Variation in the Amount of Play Equipment," *Child Develop.*, **6**:1 (1935), pp. 56–68.

[9] A. T. Jersild and F. V. Markey, "Conflicts Betwen Preschool Children," *Child Develop. Monogr.*, **21** (1935).

[10] Ann E. Rechsteiner, "The Effect of Variation in the Amount of Play Materials on the Play Behavior of the Preschool Child," Ph.D. dissertation, University of Maryland, College Park, 1978.

[11] Robert F. Biehler, *Child Development: An Introduction* (Boston: Houghton, 1981), p. 424.

[12] Mark J. Kittleson, "Children and Divorce," ERIC Reports, ED 169 026 (Arlington, Va.: Computer Microfilm International Corp., 1979), pp. 10–12.

How adults were reared as children plays an important part in how they treat their children. The adult may have come from a home where a strict father insisted that the child obey instantly or from a very lenient home where neither parent could agree as to what the child was permitted to do. Thus, adults may carry over certain feelings from their own childhood that give direction in dealing with their children. Parents may have resented how they were treated as children and may now attempt to direct their children differently. One may be an outgoing person who yells at a child but quickly gets over one's anger. Another parent may show no anger but demand that the child obey without question.

The parent may have read much of the literature written during the years when permissiveness without limits was in vogue and may have been influenced by ideas of permitting children to do exactly as they please. Feelings regarding the words *guidance* or *discipline* play an important part in dealing with children. The word *discipline* has different connotations. Some people feel that it means keeping order in a group, and others interpret it as a technique of maintaining order. To still others, discipline means punishment. The authors see discipline as a means of helping the child develop inner controls to do what is approved and act in approved ways. This goal may be shared by parents and teacher, but what is meant by the goal and how to achieve it may be completely different. Discipline should be discussed with parents. Children often find themselves in conflict when the guidance given at home and school is inconsistent. Both parents and teachers should realize that controls or limits are necessary for children to adjust to societal standards. Children feel more secure if they know what is expected of them and understand what conformity means.

The child may come from a home in which he or she has learned to expect physical punishment, threats, and abuse. This child may have difficulty in adjusting to a teacher who does not shout, threaten, or hit. This child may need help in learning to make decisions, having been told quite firmly how to behave at home. Because our society leans toward independent decision making and choice of behavior, such a child may have ambivalent feelings and difficulty in adjusting to the expected behavior for school and peers. Other children, having received much attention and constant direction, may have become overly dependent upon what the parents think is correct behavior. Still other children are insecure and appear shy and withdrawn. They need activities to help them develop a feeling of security and self-confidence.

There has been a tendency to equate certain modes of behavior with social classes. Although the socioeconomic level of the family can either limit or extend the opportunities of the child, it is the emotional and intellectual climate that determines the child's outlook. Home environment may be so harmful with regard to physical punishment that a family welfare agency may have to intervene. Today child abuse has been openly recognized by the courts and the medical profession. There still are parents who are unable to restrain themselves physically and as a result there are some unfortunate instances of bodily injury to children.[13] Bain points out that "gross physical abuse is only one segment of a much wider problem of parental neglect. The unloved child, the emotionally deprived child, becomes part of our group of neurotic, disturbed, retarded, or delinquent adults."[14]

Parents are entrusted by nature and society to care for the child and provide appropriate limits for behavior. However, there are times when families cannot fulfill their responsibilities alone. When children's needs are unmet, who takes responsibility?

Child advocacy is the term being used to describe the growing emphasis placed on identifying unmet needs of children, suggesting ways to meet these needs, and on stimulating public support for projects already in operation.[15] Child advocacy is a concept and a process designed to make the needs of children real to the public, to give us, at local and national levels, a structure with which to deal with these problems, and to insure needed services to children, youth, and their families.[16]

The ultimate goal for the child and all individuals is the acquiring of self-discipline. Gradually, children learn how to make decisions and to know whether their behavior is acceptable to others. At first the teacher or parent may help the child to make wise choices by offering two definite alternatives where either one is acceptable. Gradually, the child can move to more difficult decision making where the alternatives are less clear. For example, it is raining, and yet, with proper clothing, Charles may play out in the rain. The adult might say, "It is raining, but if you wear your boots and raincoat, you can go out to play in the rain, or you can stay inside and play with your trucks. You decide which you'd rather do."

Young children need to move toward independent thinking, for as they mature, they move away from the parental home to the school, to peers, and to a larger society. They will no longer have an adult always beside them to make choices. It will be easier to know which path to take as they approach adolescence and adulthood if they have begun to make appropriate decisions in their early years.

LEVEL OF MATURITY

Time is an important dimension in a child's behavior, for a relationship exists between a child's behavior and level of maturity. If the adult recognizes that each child develops at a different rate, the same behavior will not be expected of each child in the group. Opportunities for experiences appropriate to the child's level of

---

[13] M. G. Paulsen, "Legal Protections Against Child Abuse," *Children,* **13**:2 (1966), pp. 43–48.

[14] Katherine Bain, "Commentary: The Physically Abused Child," *Pediatrics,* **31**:6 (1963), p. 897.

[15] Shelia B. Kamerman, A. J. Kahn, and Brenda G. McGowan, "Research and Advocacy," *Children Today,* 1:2 (1972), pp. 35–36.

[16] S. A. Ward, "Components of a Child Advocacy Program," *Children Today,* 1:2, (1972), pp. 38–40.

maturity will be planned. There will be differences in many abilities. Examples follow.

1. *The ability to share and wait for turns.* One child may be able to take turns with four other children in riding a tricycle, but be unable to wait for twenty children to ride before having another chance.
2. *The ability to listen attentively.* The length of time one can listen varies, as does the content one has the background to enjoy.
3. *The ability to participate in a group.* Some children are comfortable in small group activities, but are not yet ready to cope with the total group of twenty-five children. Refusal to come "to a group story" may not indicate lack of interest in stories on the part of a child, nor an inappropriate story, but could indicate fear of the large group.
4. *Muscular coordination.* Some children can skip, while others can only run; some can cut exactly on the line, yet others can only tear paper.
5. *Reaction time.* Some children take longer to respond or react than others.

The good teacher provides opportunities for the child to engage in activities in terms of these differences. As certain behavior such as negativism or inattention appears, the teacher remembers that these are to be expected of children at certain stages of development.

The very young child of two or three may be extremely negative to any and all requests. This negative "No, I don't want to!" or "No, I won't" is expected at this age. The child is beginning to be self-assertive and may express this self-awareness in a negative way. The power of "no" has been discovered. The child begins to realize that adults are disturbed by "no" and thus uses it constantly, even when he or she really would like to carry out the activity requested. The wise teacher either rephrases the request, ignores the negativism, or redirects the activity. The teacher makes no issue when announcing, "Time to eat lunch," but simply takes the child by the hand and together they go to eat. The child is not indulged by being allowed not to eat; neither is he or she punished for saying no when in reality the child may not mean "no" at all. The child is helped to do what needs to be done.

Knowing that manners cannot always be counted on with four-year-olds does not mean that manners are ignored. It simply means, for example, that on leaving a party, the parent does not ask the child, "What do you say?" and risk a scene and embarrassment. Rather, the adult may say, "Jerry and I enjoyed the party. Thank you for inviting us." The adult sets the example, which later the child will make a part of his or her own behavior.

Knowing that most five-year-olds can listen in a group for only ten to fifteen minutes, the teacher should plan listening experiences involving stories, sharing, and music accordingly. To expect the child to sit attentively for a longer period is to expect more than he or she is capable of doing. One teacher kept five-year-olds in a circle for forty-five minutes. After the first few minutes they were very restless,

The teacher and child observe and talk about how the two children play together.

falling out of chairs, playing and wrestling with their neighbors. By insisting that they remain for that length of time, the teacher was not only causing difficulties in the form of discipline problems, but was teaching children to be rude, impolite listeners rather than to listen attentively while others were speaking.

Hymes, however, warns that the teacher must be careful not to become too easygoing and content with too little on the one hand or become too demanding and maintain unrealistic expectations on the other. For example, if the children are wiggling, it may be because of their age or their maturity level. Yet the reason may be entirely different. The children may be bored. The teacher, then, must determine the cause of the behavior and take action that is consistent with the cause.[17]

The developmental point of view is based on knowledge and understanding of the growth and development of the child. According to Hymes, this approach does not mean that anything goes; nor does it call for lowering of standards. Teachers have the highest possible standards for the age group they teach. The child development approach means accepting the behavior that is normal and healthy for a specific age. The teacher recognizes the maturity level of each child and lives with it.[18]

GUIDANCE AND DISCIPLINE

Although each teacher may have special strategies and techniques, it is important that teachers understand something of the philosophy of the approach they choose as the basis for guidance and discipline.

Butler reports that techniques advocated during the past several years come from two quite divergent sources.[19] One point of view, expressed by Maslow, Rogers, Kelley, and Combs in *Perceiving, Behaving, Becoming,* holds that the way a person behaves at a given moment is a direct expression of the way things seem to that person at that particular moment. Thus, the child does not behave according to the facts as they seem to an outsider. The child behaves in terms of how things seem to be or how they are perceived at that moment.[20]

These authors believe that the attributes of dignity, integrity, and autonomy are concomitants of the environment which impinges positively on the individual. They hold that "situations where the conditions for social development are kept open and fluid are most favorable for the development of these characteristics."[21] An atmosphere in which the self-concept may be enhanced is one in which

> Human development in dignity and honesty is put first.
> Each child's spiritual integrity—his or her right to be—is recognized.
> Individuality is considered an asset rather than a liability.
> Genetic growth patterns are respected and used as a basis for teaching.
> Each child helps to purpose and plan.
> Each can act freely, knowing those around him or her accept him or her as he or she is.

---

[17] J. L. Hymes, Jr., *Behavior and Misbehavior* (Englewood Cliffs, N.J.: Prentice-Hall, 1955), p. 53.
[18] Ibid., p. 52.
[19] Annie L. Butler, *Current Research in Early Childhood Education: A Compilation and Analysis for Program Planners* (Washington, D.C.: American Association of Elementary-Kindergarten-Nursery Educators, 1970), p. 117.
[20] A. W. Combs, (chm.), *Perceiving, Behaving, Becoming,* 1962 Yearbook (Alexandria, Va.: ASCD; 1962), pp. 67–68.
[21] Ibid., p. 221.

Peer relationships are important for handicapped as well as for nonhandicapped children. These children are expressing their friendship for each other.

Each can make an error—or even do wrong, and not lose face thereby.
Each child can grow each day and know that he or she is growing.
Each can hold his or her head up high and meet the other's gaze.
Each can make friends, enjoy other people, learn how to extend a hand to help.
Each can learn the warm flood of gratitude that comes from being regarded with warmth.
Each can venture into unknown worlds and stretch his or her wings to find new truths.
Above all where each child can experience success in subject matter, human relationships, and the discovery of self as a person of worth and dignity.[22]

"From a quite different point of view the theory of operant conditioning sees a preschool as essentially a behavior-modifying environment in which the teacher

[22] Ibid., pp. 232–233.

plays an important role in choosing behavior that will be systematically reinforced," says Butler.[23] Operant conditioning is usually based on the use of consequences to strengthen or weaken behavior in such areas as decreasing aggressive responses and threatening or violent behavior, increasing social skills, and learning to take responsibility for simple tasks. The behavior that is compatible with desired ends is reinforced.[24]

The first step in planning a behavior change program is to identify the problem. The teacher should describe what observable and countable actions make a behavior problem. Observable actions may include talking out during times when he or she should be quiet, not taking turns, hitting other children, or throwing blocks. Once the problem behaviors have been identified, the teacher can proceed to plan a program for eliminating them.[25]

Katz points out, however, that the application of these techniques must be thought through carefully. She says, "Stop, look, and listen before you condition."[26] Limitations of this approach are seen in the example described by Katz. Three children manifest disruptive behavior for which behavior modification is likely to work. When used without concern for the origins of the behavior, however, the positive results may be questioned.

> Child 1 learned to be disruptive because such behavior resulted in attention or some other reinforcement. For this child operant conditioning seems appropriate. The reinforcement that usually followed his disruptive behavior could be consciously withheld.
>
> Child 2's disruptive behavior may express some kind of emotional injury, some kind of internal stress. Although behavior modification may work and the undesirable behavior disappear, the injury could remain. A new manifestation of the stress may appear. A therapeutic response seems indicated in this case.
>
> Child 3 may lack the social skills or alternative ways of responding to the situation. This child can be helped by clarifying or explaining alternative solutions for solving the problem at hand. The teaching strategy appears to be appropriate.

Katz does not reject the principles of behavior modification but warns against the indiscriminate application of conditioning techniques. She emphasizes the fact that before applying the principles the teacher should know the child.[27]

For the teacher who decides to use reinforcement techniques, Osborn and Osborn make suggestions:[28]

[23] Butler, op. cit., p. 120.
[24] W. C. Becker, D. R. Thomas, and D. Carnine, *Reducing Behavior Problems: An Operant Conditioning Guide for Teachers* (Urbana: ERIC Clearinghouse University of Illinois, 1969), pp. 4–5.
[25] J. Mark Ackerman, *Operant Conditioning Techniques for the Classroom Teacher* (Glenview, Ill.: Scott, Foresman, 1972), p. 33.
[26] Lillian G. Katz, "Stop, Look, and Listen Before You Condition," *ERIC/ECE Newsletter*, **5**:6 (1971), pp. 1–2.
[27] Ibid.
[28] Osborn and Osborn, op. cit., pp. 40–49.

1. The child should be observed carefully.
2. The behavior to be changed should be identified and attainable goals set up.
3. The desired behavior should be rewarded.
4. The undesirable behavior should be ignored.
5. The reward (or reinforcement) should follow closely after the appropriate behavior.
6. Reinforcement, in the beginning, should be continuous.
7. Reinforcement should be consistent.
8. The child should be reobserved and goals evaluated.

Different approaches to guidance and discipline come from different philosophies and beliefs. Butler concludes, however, that

The important question is how one goes about building satisfying interpersonal relationships: whether one chooses to develop the relationships that encourage the child to want to change his or her behavior and give the guidance and support necessary to do this, or whether steps must be taken to urge him or her forward in the desired direction; whether the child should be motivated by some real desire to change, or

A gentle touch means I like you . . .

whether he or she responds to tangible rewards for desired behavior until the behavior becomes a habit.[29]

In guiding behavior, then, the teacher recognizes that options are available. One can choose to develop relationships within the classroom that encourage the child to want to change behavior. Likewise, the teacher may choose to encourage the formation of desirable habits of behavior by providing rewards or reinforcement.

Siegel's influence technique helps teachers to influence the behavior of a child. He says that the child is more likely to comply if the influence technique is clear and consistent; offers the child an alternate; and informs him or her of future consequences, reflects feelings, so that the child may respond in kind, and provides a "cushion."[30]

Kounin's influence techniques deal with the effect that control techniques exert on the other children in the classroom. He says that when the influence technique is clear and firm, the audience child responds with increased conformance; when rough, the audience children become upset.[31]

Another management strategy is Glasser's reality therapy that helps individuals to take responsibility for solving their own problems. Reality therapy is based on six principles: Human involvement, examination of current behaviors, student examination of behavior to determine if it is beneficial for self-needs; teacher assistance in making realistic plans to change behavior; student commitment; no student excuses for not changing behavior; and no punishment.[32]

Glasser stresses the importance of success experiences. To encourage such experiences, the school staff must be positively involved with each other, have a cooperative working relationship, care about each other, and work and plan together in the best interests of the child.[33] In order for children to experience success, schools must be a place in which they may experience happiness, comfort, and safety, and feel loved and worthwhile. The following example demonstrates some of Glasser's principles:

> Mike is pushing Sam. The teacher approaches the boys and says to Mike.
>
> Teacher: What are you doing right now? [present behavior]
> Mike: He won't let me have the box of colored crayons.
> Teacher: That's what he's doing, but what are you doing right now? [return to present behavior]
> Mike: I pushed him.

---

[29] Butler, op. cit., p. 121.

[30] A. E. Siegel, quoted in D. K. Osborn and Janie D. Osborn, *Discipline and Clasroom Management* (Athens, Ga.: Education Associates, 1981), pp. 68–73.

[31] J. S. Kounin, quoted in D. K. Osborn and Janie D. Osborn, ibid., pp. 73–77.

[32] William Glasser, quoted in Richard C. Callahn, Robert J. Harder, Dorothy I. Hellene, Donald P. Kauchak, Andrew J. Keogh, Constance H. Kravas, Donald C. Orlich, and R. A. Pendergrass, *Teaching Strategies: A Guide to Better Instruction* (Lexington, Mass.: Heath, 1980), pp. 386–389.

[33] Richard L. Curwin and Allen N. Modler, *The Discipline Book: A Complete Guide to School and Classroom Management* (Reston, Va.: Reston, 1980), p. 100.

Teacher: I'm glad to see that you know what you did. [positive reinforcement] Is pushing Sam helping you? [value judgment]

Mike: Well, he won't let me have the crayons.

Teacher: Let's see if there are other things that you could have done to get the crayons without pushing Sam. [plan] In this classroom we don't solve problems by pushing [rule].

Mike: I tried to talk to him, but he wouldn't listen.

Teacher: I'd like to suggest [plan] that you tell Sam that you'd like to share the crayons with him. If he refuses, then let me know. Do you have any other ideas?

Mike: No, that's OK with me. [commitment]

Teacher: The next time you don't get what you want, you'll tell Sam or any other child that you'd like to share the materials. If he or she refuses, then you'll tell me. [restating plan]

Mike: Yes, I'll do that. [seals the plan][34]

Helping the child become a group member

The transition from home to school may bring many new or different activities for the child. Being a part of a group is definitely one of them. A child new to the group may withdraw and watch the others or become aggressive and push and grab toys. Too often the teacher may not realize that children new to the group need more individual help as well as introduction to various group activities. Some children require a longer period of adjustment to become a part of the group, but others feel at home almost immediately.

Some of the difficulties that teachers encounter with young children are related to different behavior expectations of the home and the school. At home the child may have been encouraged or at least permitted to fight; use the language heard; take things without asking. The teacher, then, accepts the child and begins at the child's level in helping him or her learn to take turns, to share toys, and to become an active participant in a group. The child may use words for which he or she does not know the meaning:

> Tip, a four-year-old boy, called out happily to the teacher, "You look like a bastard!" The teacher, somewhat taken aback, responded by asking, "What do you mean when you say that I look like a bastard?" Tip replied, "You look funny." "Tip," said the teacher, "You need to explain what you mean when you say, 'Bastard.' People don't know that you mean *funny*." Tip said, "OK I'll just say, 'You have a funny face.'"

Other difficulties are related to assisting the child in learning to take turns, to share toys, to become an active participant in a group. Children need this kind of guidance, for most of them have been the center of attention at home. They have lived in a family setting where the other members were not of the same age as themselves. Thus, we find some three- and four-year-olds grabbing toys from others

[34] Ibid. (adapted), p. 102.

and hitting, pinching, biting, or using physical force to obtain what they want. Others stand back, watching, or withdrawing, or appealing to an adult for help. Comments frequently heard are "Tommy won't let me ride the tricycle" and "Nancy doesn't want me to be the daddy." The teacher can help the children suggesting, "Tommy, you've had the tricycle quite a while; two more trips around the circle; then it's Billy's turn." In other activities the teacher can often guide a child by merely saying, "You could try it this way." So often the manner in which the teacher suggests new ideas to children will encourage them to tackle a project or stick to one they are working on.

Establishing routines

When entering one of the many programs, children who are unaccustomed to group activities may find it hard to engage in the expected routines, such as washing, toileting, going out or coming indoors, resting, and eating at lunch time. Many of the children will imitate the others, yet usually there are a few who need help in adjusting to a daily schedule.

Furthermore, some children come from homes where there are few, if any, routines other than doing whatever they find to do at whatever time is convenient for the parents. They are not accustomed to washing their hands before eating. Meals have not been served according to a schedule. Resting is unimportant. These boys and girls must first have help in understanding the "why" of doing things. They need encouragement and support while they are in the process of acquiring the desired behavior. In helping the child, the teacher will find it important to consider the possible effect of guidance on the child's concept of self and his or her home.

Children often become confused when an activity is shifted because of weather conditions, a field trip, or special event. Explaining the necessity for a shift in plans or letting children know ahead that a routine will be shifted helps avoid confusion.

Younger children who have never had a chance to engage in water play may enjoy spending a longer time washing hands and face than the teacher has counted on. The teacher may need to give such a child a special "water play" time. Some children may be hesitant about going to the toilet when others are in the bathroom or may refuse to go at all. A teacher may need to supervise such children carefully until they become accustomed to groups in a bathroom. Some schools are equipped with child-size lavatories that may be a novelty to a child, who thus spends a longer time in the bathroom. The teacher must be aware of the home training in regard to toileting, as some parents have probably stressed modesty and others may have been rather free. New children are likely to have more frequent need to use the toilet facilities because of the newness of the situation, nervousness, or the weather's becoming colder. Therefore, in planning a daily schedule, the teacher would need to include more frequent toileting with new or younger children.

Teachers of young children consider it a part of their function to help children establish routines and habits dealing with dressing, cleanliness, elimination, eating, and rest.

The rigid conformance once required in nursery school or kindergarten routines has given way to a more relaxed and informal pattern that permits children to establish these requirements at their own pace, consistent with the demands of maturation attained at the time. Like most learned activities, changes occur gradually in keeping with the stage of development. It is, therefore, undesirable to expect the same level of conformity and perfection from all children.

These pictures illustrate activities characteristic of those in centers with a well-planned program designed to help children establish basic routines.

The routine of the rest period can provide a relaxing time, or it may produce only a group of squirming, restless children. The length and number of rest periods should be determined by the length of time children are in school, how much sleep they get at home, when they go to bed, and when they get up in the morning. For children who are in the center for only two or three hours, the fifteen-to-twenty-minute period may be considered a quiet time. Some children may need or want to lie down on mats, and others may choose a quiet activity, such as listening to music or looking at a book.

It is important for the teacher to remember that such a period provides not only physical relaxation but also a time for the child to be by herself or himself: in the group, yes, but not an active part of it. Rhodes found that when children in a morning kindergarten were provided with a rest period, there were fewer signs of fatigue.[35]

For children who are in the center all day, nap time is usually arranged just after lunch. Children seem to rest and sleep better if the amount of activity is reduced prior to nap time. Some children may sleep for an hour whereas others may not nap at all. They may spend the time relaxing on their cots and engaging in a quiet activity. The teacher's attitude about rest makes a difference as to whether the children are able to relax. Some teachers feel that soft music and darkened rooms are conducive to rest whereas in other schools the quiet attitude of the teacher with an expectation of relaxation may provide a better atmosphere.

The routine of eating should be considered in relation to both the midmorning snack and the noon lunch. Some children have not been used to washing hands before eating, to sitting down with a group their own age to eat, to a variety of foods, to conversation with other children while eating, or to behavior appropriate for mealtime. The lunch hour can be a pleasant experience instead of a nagging time. Small portions and the teacher's expectancy that the children will feed themselves and complete their meals without undue urging will be conducive in helping those children who are having difficulty at meal time.

Throughout the school day children become engrossed in their work and play and are not conscious of time. Many teachers encounter difficulty with children who are not ready to put blocks away, to stop their activity at the work bench or to return indoors for a story. Some children have become accustomed to what comes next in the daily routine and yet rebel at moving on to the next activity. Teachers can help children by warning them a few minutes prior to change of activity by quietly commenting, "It is almost juice time; we will need to start putting the blocks away very soon now." Sometimes there are too many blocks, and the job is too big for the child. The teacher can help by gaining the cooperation of other

[35] Frances Rhodes, "A Study of the Effects of Various Types of Rest Periods in a Morning Kindergarten on the Behavior Characteristics of Five-Year-Olds," unpublished graduate paper, Florida State University, Tallahassee, August 1954.

children as well as assisting in the putting away. Research suggests that smooth transitions enhance work involvement and lessen deviancy.[36]

Recognizing that each child may be accustomed at home to a variety of differences in routines is important in helping children know what is expected in a school group.

Teaching techniques

Diverting the child by redirecting unfavorable behavior into more constructive channels is a challenge to every adult, whether parent or teacher. It sometimes takes foresight or ingenuity for the adult to use favorable diversion in suggesting to the child other ways of handling situations. Sometimes a reminder may be used, such as "Remember we said the shovel is used to dig with. How about getting the wagon and filling it with dirt?"

Sometimes children who are overstimulated need quiet time to look at books or to play alone. The difficult child who disturbs the entire group may need to be removed from the group for a short period of time. Acherman points out that being removed from enjoyable activities and having to sit on the sidelines can be effective for the disruptive child. This technique is called "benching."[37] This removal should not be in the form of a threat, such as "If you don't behave, I'll have to put you in another room." Rather, the teacher should suggest, "You seem to be having trouble playing with Bob. Perhaps you should play by yourself for a while." If a child is extremely difficult or disturbing to a group, the teacher may need to isolate the youngster in another room in order to calm the entire situation. If the child is removed from the group, there are several factors to be considered:

1. *Length of time.* Briefness of isolation is extremely important because of the child's short span of attention. Five minutes can be a long time for a child.
2. *The child's understanding of purpose.* It is important that the child knows why he or she was removed, because many times he or she does not understand. Learning reasons for removal from the group can be helpful in preventing further behavior difficulties.
3. *Safety.* The safety and supervision of the child while outside the group should be assured.
4. *The child's reaction.* If the child is alone in a room or hall, is his or her security threatened? Is he or she frightened? Does the child enjoy the experience?
5. *Provision for learning.* If frequently excluded, does the child ever learn that the activity from which he or she was excluded can be an interesting and happy

[36] Osborn and Osborn, op. cit., p. 125.
[37] J. Mark Acherman, *Operant Conditioning Techniques for the Classroom Teacher* (Glenville, Illinois: Scott, Foresman, 1972). p. 98.

one? Is the child being helped to learn "what to do" and "how to behave" in order to remain in the group?

6. *Reinstatement in the group.* When does the child return to the group? Does the child or the teacher decide? Is the child told, "Come back when you can behave," or does the teacher reinstate the child within the group by saying, "Jim is ready to hear the story now"?

One of the most important traits in a teacher of young children is sensitivity to each child's needs and how these needs relate to the group as a whole. Knowing the developmental characteristics of children at each age level will assist the teacher in becoming aware of these needs. When guiding the behavior of children under six in group situations, the teacher needs to be aware that[38]

1. The tone of voice used should be positive yet not demanding, pleasant yet firm, calm yet forceful and matter-of-fact.
2. The teacher should give a feeling of expectancy that the request needs to be carried to completion. If he or she has to leave the group because of an unexpected situation, the children will know that the teacher will return and follow through with the activity.
3. The nonverbal behavior of the teacher should be consistent with his or her verbal behavior. The effects of a positive comment may be minimized if the teacher does not look directly at the child whereas the effects may be reinforced if the teacher places a hand on the child's shoulder.
4. The teacher places himself or herself so as to be able to see the entire group at all times to know where they are and what they are doing. In giving directions, the teacher may find it helpful to stand near the child who has difficulty in listening.
5. Reasons, rules, and directions should be clearly stated.
6. The teacher should be consistent in relations with the children. They learn what to expect and are more likely to comply.
7. The teacher should offer the child alternative solutions. Suggest acceptable behavior rather than merely prohibiting actions.
8. The teacher gives suggestions rather than commands; for example, "How about trying to do it this way?" or "You might ask Larry to to help you."
9. The teacher avoids favoritism by not giving too much attention to an attractive, a talented, a handicapped, or a disturbing child because doing so may result in neglect of others in the group.

It is expected that in a school situation teachers will not use threats with young children, nor will they use physical punishment. Parents may feel that these are necessary forms of punishment; nevertheless, they should not be used by teachers. The teacher who understands children is aware of other methods of guiding the child and does not have to resort to physical punishment. The personal approval of the teacher is one of the most effective rewards.[39]

---

[38] Osborn and Osborn, op. cit., pp. 61–63.

[39] Charles H. Madsen, Jr., and Clifford K. Madsen, *Teaching Discipline: A Positive Approach for Educational Development* (Boston: Allyn, 1981), p. 11.

Children often become engrossed in their work and play and are not conscious of time. Teachers can help in the routines of putting materials away by quietly commenting a few minutes prior to change of activity, "It is almost time for lunch. We will need to start putting the blocks away very soon."

Giving young children special privileges or attention may be legitimate if such practices do not become crutches on which teachers lean to gain cooperation from youngsters. Older children in elementary school are more likely to be helped in the area of discipline by the withdrawing of privileges than are preschool children. Praise, too, is an effective method of control. However, some teachers tend to use it too frequently, especially with the so-called "good children." Too often praise is withheld from those difficult children who really need more attention and would profit by having their efforts accepted.

Some teachers find it helpful to talk with kindergarten children about "how we act in kindergarten." Goals and rules are more effective when the children are involved in their formulation. Posters with pictures and suggestive slogans such as, *Listen, Use soft voices,* and *Find a job* may be effective.[40]

For some children in the group, the activities may be too difficult, either because the child does not know what is expected or because he or she may be slower in some aspects of development. Insight may be gained through study of the home situation, or it may be necessary to secure outside assistance from a child guidance clinic in cooperation with the parents. Too often teachers are afraid to admit failure with a child; in reality, however, the admission of the need for help is an indication of a professional teacher. Recognition of serious behavior difficulties and prompt referral can ensure early treatment for the child.

Through careful analysis of the child's feelings, attitudes, and reactions, appropriate steps in guiding behavior can be evolved. In the following paragraphs, two different types of school situations involving the behavior of children are described as illustrations of the application of guidance principles. No attempt is made to answer all questions but rather to suggest a process that may be used by the teacher in answering questions.

Total Group Situation. The teacher determines the goals for behavior in a group situation such as music or story time. For example,

> Each child will be a good listener; participate in group activity; share turns; show consideration for others in group.

In working to achieve these goals, the teacher plans and provides for

1. The activities to be within the attention span of the group and individuals in the group.
2. A balance of types of activities within the period—active and quiet, listening with participating.
3. Physical arrangements that are comfortable; seating arrangements so that children can see the leader and are not directly facing the light; proper temperature.
4. Content of the group activity appropriate for maturity level of the children. Adaptations made for individuals.

Even with all the planning, there still may be need for guidance on the part of the teacher. For example,

> It is story time. Fred, a five-year-old, is wiggling and squirming. He annoys the children next to him by an occasional kick, a slap on the back, a whisper, or a pinch. Should the teacher reprimand, ignore, or send Fred from the group? To do any one of the three is to disrupt the listening climate for the group. Yet something needs to be done for the sake of the group as well as for Fred.

[40] Carmen A. Morales, "Posters Pay Off in Classroom Control," *Education,* **102:**3 (1982), pp. 236–237.

Before the teacher makes the decision, it will be well to remember that Fred's behavior may have any number of causes and that it is important to ask, "Why?" If he needs to be excused from the group, the way in which it is done and the follow-up will vary according to the cause of the behavior. The teacher considers, Is Fred tired? He was listening to a recording during the free activity period. This is much the same type of activity. Perhaps he has done enough listening for now. The teacher might say, "Fred, you have listened to the story on the record, and you may find something else to do now. Remember, the rest of us are listening to the story. If you want to listen with us, you are welcome; but if not, choose something that will not disturb us."

Is Fred insecure in total group situations? Is such behavior evidence of his inadequacy to cope with the group? It is important that the treatment of this behavior not create more insecure feelings. Fred may be excused in much the same manner as just described. It is important, however, that Fred not be deprived of hearing stories and that he be helped to grow in his ability to participate within the group. The teacher may accomplish this by (1) finding time to read to Fred alone or with one or two other children, helping him to make "friends" with one of these children, (2) helping him to participate in an activity—in block building or in playing in the doll corner with a few other children, and (3) gradually increasing the size of the group in which Fred participates. The quality of the teacher's interaction with Fred is very important.

Is the content of the activity too difficult or perhaps boring for Fred? Does the vocabulary of the story relate to concepts and experiences that are not yet Fred's? If so, perhaps using pictures, a model, or giving an explanation might help.

The Activity or Work Period.   The teacher determines goals for behavior during work time or the activity period. For example, each child will

1. Find a job to do.
2. Gain satisfaction from the job or activities.
3. Take turns.
4. Put away materials.
5. Show consideration for others in the group.

There is much that the teacher can do in advance to set up an environment conducive to the desired behavior, such as the following:

1. Set up several centers of interest or activities in which the children can participate. For the youngest, these will be set up on arrival. The child simply goes to the activity of choice. The five-year-olds may participate in group planning and choose a job for which materials are available and accessible.
2. Balance activities to provide several that require a minimum of teacher supervision, thus enabling the teacher to give guidance in new activities or in those requiring more supervision.

3. Plan activities that are interesting and challenging but not too difficult or frustrating. Provide a variety of activities of varying difficulty so that each child can find something satisfying to do.
4. Provide materials in amounts that encourage sharing. For example, there need not be a pair of scissors for every child, but neither will the child's capacity to wait and take turns be strained by insisting that the youngster wait while five other children cut. Perhaps the child begins sharing most easily by using the scissors with one or two others. To share, then, does not mean waiting indefinitely or losing one's turn completely.

Despite this planning, Paul, age four, knocks down the block structure that three other boys have built. The teacher questions, Was it an accident? If not, was it an attempt to play with the others? Is Paul's aggressiveness perhaps due to a change in routines at home? Is his place in the family threatened by the new baby? Did a visit from relatives keep him up late last night? Has Daddy or Mother lost a job? Was there food for breakfast? Is there money for the rent? To scold or exclude Paul may cause him to think, "Not even the teacher cares any more." Certainly, Paul cannot be permitted to annoy the other boys, but the treatment should not make him more aggressive. A quiet comment, such as "Paul, you were angry and knocked down the blocks. Pat and Hugh worked hard to build the house. They will build it again. You can work over here." Thus, Paul is directed to an activity such as painting at the easel, pounding clay, or using hammer and nails. The teacher recognized that Paul felt aggressive but did not condone his behavior. She set the limits with positive guidance. "They will build it again. You can work over here."

Could Paul's aggressiveness be a way of saying, "I want to play with you"? If so, he needs help in learning acceptable ways of getting into a group. The teacher may say, "Boys, Paul wants to play with you. He will help you build the house again." In this instance, the teacher did not ask Paul, "What do you say when you want to play with the boys?" If he had been able to say it, he would not have resorted to the behavior he used. Rather, the teacher will supply the verbal request, "Boys, Paul really wants to play with you, but he had a strange way of showing it, didn't he?" Paul has experience, then, in another way of joining in play with the boys.

SUMMARY

Guiding the behavior of children, helping them develop a core of values, fostering good human relationships, and building healthy personalities are important yet exacting tasks for the teacher. Suggestions for this task, which have been presented, include the following:

1. Know the children. Review the general characteristics of children at this age level. Study each child's home environment, health status, goals, and interests.
2. Determine goals and values.

3. Plan a school environment and a program conducive to the understandings, attitudes, and habits that it is hoped the children will develop. As Hymes has said, "A program in school that is dull and dreary, uninteresting and boring, makes it harder for children to be good."[41]

4. Establish positive, friendly relationships between the teacher and the children. Keep verbal and nonverbal behavior consistent.

5. When an incident does arise, remember the following steps in guiding the child:
   a. Realistically accept the child's feelings through the use of verbalizations.
   b. Set up the necessary limits for the child, so he or she does not and cannot continue to build up unacceptable behavior patterns.
   c. Provide the necessary release for unacceptable feelings at the moment they occur through the use of materials appropriate for release of tense and difficult feelings.
   d. Encourage and support the child while he or she is in the process of getting release.[42]

6. Try to find the cause of the child's behavior difficulty.

7. Plan a course of action that is appropriate for the cause of the behavior and consistent with the goals sought for the child.

8. Show concern for the children's emotional health. Children must feel that the teacher likes them. Talk to the children about their feelings.

9. Remember to be objective and maintain a sense of humor.[43] Today, the child development point of view emphasizes the importance of helping the child become a self-directing individual. Both inner urges and outer pressures need to be considered.

Suggested Activities

1. Observe teacher–child contacts in a center for young children. Note the number of ways the teacher insists the child carry through on requests, when the teacher gives choices, when the child refuses, and the outcome of such.

2. Observe teacher–child contacts. Note the tone of voice used by the teacher when speaking to a child, the wording of requests, the teacher's poise, and the children's behavior in terms of requests completed, requests refused. Analyze why the children behaved as they did during such contacts.

3. Select one child to observe, either in a home or at a center. Note the number of "don'ts" used, the number of "would you like to's" or direct commands given the child by an adult. Analyze how this child behaved as a result of the way the teacher or parent communicated with the child.

[41] J. Hymes, "They Act Their Age," in *Discipline* (Washington, D.C.: ACEI, 1957), p. 22.
[42] Eleanor Evans, "Vents for Children's Feelings," in *Discipline* (Washington, D.C.: ACEI, 1957), p. 26.
[43] C. M. Charles, "Building Classroom Discipline: From Models to Practice," (New York: Longman, 1981), p. 45.

4. Observe children who are having difficulty belonging to or getting into groups. Note leadership qualities of certain children, shyness of others, aggressiveness, and the general outcome of "groupness" among the children. Did adults interfere or assist children or did the children handle the situations without adult help?

5. Observe a child who manifests aggressive behavior. Seek to determine the cause. Does the application of behavior modification techniques seem appropriate? Why? Discuss your reasons with the class.

6. Observe one child in a center for young children. Identify ways in which his or her self-concept was enhanced. Share your observations with the class.

7. Visit a center for young children. Note ways in which the teacher guides the interactions among children. How are children guided in the use of materials? Note instances in which children were involved in making decisions. How were children helped to enhance their self-concepts?

8. The way in which a skilled teacher talks to children can help in teaching them how to discipline themselves. Formulate statements that could be used by a teacher when a child is angry, hits another child, grabs a toy, or kicks the teacher.

9. Take pictures of young children in a center. Mount them on paper. Write each child's name under the picture. Read stories and sing songs using children's names. How can this teaching enhance a child's self-concept and help the child to identify with the group? In how many other places in the room do you see children's names?

10. There are routine jobs in the classroom in which children participate. Observe in a center, and note examples of children participating in routines. How did the teacher handle routines?

11. View the film *Discipline and Self-Control* Modern Talking Pictures, 2323 New Hyde Park Rd. New Hyde Park, N.Y. 11040).

Related Readings

Axline, Virginia. *Dibs in Search of Self.* Boston: Houghton, 1964.

Baker, Katherine Read, and Xenia F. Fane. *Understanding and Guiding Young Children.* Englewood Cliffs, N.J.: Prentice-Hall, 1970.

Caldwell, Bettye M. "Aggression and Hostility in Young Children." *Young Children,* **32**:2 (1977), pp. 4–13.

Castle, Kathryn. "A Language Model for Moral Development." In *Exploring Early Childhood: Readings in Theory and Practice.* New York: Macmillan, 1981.

Davidson, Jane. "Wasted Time: The Ignored Dilemma." In *Curriculum Planning for Young Children,* ed. by Janet F. Brown, Washington, D.C.: NAEYC, 1982, pp. 196–204.

DeJames, Patricia L. "Discipline: The Unsolved Dilemma." *Education,* **102**:4 (1982), pp. 420–422.

Epstein, Charlotte. *Classroom Management and Teaching: Persistent Problems and Rational Solutions.* Reston, Va., 1979.

Essa, Eva L. *Practical Guide for Solving Preschool Behavior Problems.* Albany, N.Y.: Delmar, 1983.

Gilstrap, Robert (ed.). *Toward Self-Discipline: A Guide for Parents and Teachers.* Washington, D.C.: ACEI, 1981.

Hartup, W. W. "Peer Relations: Developmental Implications and Interaction in Same- and Mixed-age Situations." *Young Children*, **32**:3 (1977), pp. 4–13.

House, Ernest R., and Stephen D. Lapan. *Survival in the Classroom*. Boston: Allyn, 1978.

Hughes, Marie M. "Teacher Behavior and Concept of Self." *Child Educ.*, **41**:1 (1964), pp. 29–33.

Hurlock, Elizabeth B. *Child Development*. New York: McGraw-Hill, 1978.

Jones, Louise S., and Vernon F. Jones. *Responsible Classroom Discipline. Creative Positive Learning Environments and Solving Problems*. Boston: Allyn, 1981.

Katz, Lillian G. "Condition with Caution." *Young Children*, **27**:5 (1972), pp. 277–280.

Leiserson, Marion Laurence. *Creating a "Loving" Environment for Young Children*. College Park, Md.: U. of Maryland, 1971.

Lipton, A. "Classroom Behavior: Messages from Children." *Elem. Sch. J.*, **7**:15 (1971), pp. 254–261.

Mead, Margaret, "Rearing Children to Live in a Changing World." *Parents Magazine*, **41**:1 (1966), pp. 33–35.

Miel, Alice. "Relating Freedom and Responsibility." *Child Educ.*, **52**:5 (1976), pp. 234–237.

Moore, Shirley. "Research in Review—Considerateness and Helpfulness in Children." *Young Children*, **32**:4 (1977), pp. 73–76.

Mowbray, Jean K., and Helen H. Salisbury. *Diagnosing Individual Needs for Early Childhood Education*. Columbus, Ohio: Merrill, 1975, pp. 109–120, 145–160.

Osborn, D. K., and Janie D. Osborn. *Discipline and Classroom Management*. Athens, Ga.: Education Associates, 1977.

Robinson, B. E., Patsy Skeen, and Carol Frate-Hobson, "Sex-Role Contributions of Male Teachers in Early Education Settings." *Child. Educ.* **57**:1 (1980), pp. 33–40.

Schaar, Karen. "Corporal Punishment Foes Strike Out." *Children Today*, **6**:5 (1977), p. 16.

Stipek, Deborah J. "Work Habits Begin in Preschool." In *Curriculum Planning for Young Children*, ed. by Janet F. Brown, Washington, D.C.: NAEYC, 1982, pp. 205–212.

Suchara, Helen T. "The Child's Right to Humane Treatment." *Child. Educ.*, **53**:6 (1977), pp. 290–296.

Todd, Virginia E., and Helen Heffernan. *The Years Before School—Guiding Preschool Children*, 3d ed. New York: Macmillan, 1977, pp. 561–563, 687–698.

Vartuli, Sue, and Carol Phelps. "Classroom Transitions." *Child. Educ.* **57**:2 (1980), pp. 94–96.

Veach, Davia M. "Choice with Responsibility." *Young Children*, **32**:4 (1977), pp. 22–25.

Walker, Hill M. *The Acting-Out Child: Coping with Classroom Disruption*. Boston: Allyn, 1979.

Wilcox, Mary M. *Developmental Journey: A Guide to the Development of Logical and Moral Reasoning and Social Perspective*. Nashville: Abingdon, 1979.

CHAPTER 17

The Exceptional Child: Providing for Children with Special Needs

Notable progress has been made in the early education of the exceptional child. Early childhood special education is a new field of study that has emerged with the increasing interest and concern for the exceptional child during the early years of life. The knowledge, understandings, and practices from both fields are needed because the early periods of rapid development may be even more crucial in the life of the handicapped child than in that of the normal child.[1]

Every child is exceptional in that he or she is unique. Children differ in levels and quality of development. Because of this, equal educational opportunity implies a diversity within a program rather than a similarity if each child is to reach his or her own maximum potential. Because exceptional children have the same basic needs as other children, except that these needs may be more or less intensive in specific ways, they provide a challenging opportunity for the educational system. This chapter presents help for the early childhood teacher in providing for young children with special needs.

[1] Janet Lerner, Carol Mardell-Czudnowski, and Dorothea Goldenberg, *Special Education for the Early Childhood Years* (Englewood Cliffs, N.J.: Prentice-Hall, 1981), pp. 4–5.

FEDERAL PARTICIPATION

As has been true in many areas of innovation in Early Childhood Education, Head Start took the lead when amendments to the Head Start authorization law in 1972 made it a requirement that all Head Start programs have at least a 10 per cent enrollment of children with severe handicapping conditions. The law specifically defined handicapped children as "mentally retarded, hard of hearing, deaf, speech impaired, visually handicapped, seriously emotionally disturbed, crippled, or other health impaired children who by reason thereof require special education and related services."[2] Most Head Start personnel were not equipped either by training or experience to cope with children with severe special needs. Experience has shown, however, that when classroom teachers and caregivers receive the support and guidance of professionally trained persons along with continuous and intensive in-service efforts by special agencies and consultants, the results can be most encouraging.

Many laws deal with specific pieces of the total problem of providing education and services to children with specific and different needs, but the most far-reaching one is Public Law 94-142, enacted on November 29, 1975, which amended the previous "Education of the Handicapped Act."[3] This law specifically requires the approval of state plans to be made effective in 1977 and thereafter, which guarantees a free public education to all handicapped children between three and eighteen years of age beginning in September 1978. It further requires that such education be provided in settings that include nonhandicapped children, hence, the interest in "mainstreaming." In addition, the law provides that academic and nonacademic services equal those provided other children.

Another provision of the law is the development of an Individualized Education Program (IEP) for each handicapped child. This is necessary for federal funding purposes. The IEP describes the educational objectives for and services to be provided for each handicapped child. The team approach is required for the evaluation and writing of the plan. The team includes a person qualified to teach or supervise special education from the school system, one or both parents of the child, the child, if appropriate, and other persons as requested by the parents or the school.[4]

PARENT INVOLVEMENT

Involvement of parents in the education of children with special needs is not an easy undertaking. The parents' process of adjustment to the child's disability is slow and usually involves three broad stages. The stage of denial comes first, and in-

[2] Jenny W. Klein, "Mainstreaming the Preschooler," *Young Children*, **30**:5 (July 1975), p. 319.
[3] "Education of Handicapped Children: Assistance to States," *Federal Register* (Washington, D.C.: DHEW, O.E., November 29, 1976.)
[4] Lerner, op. cit., p. 254.

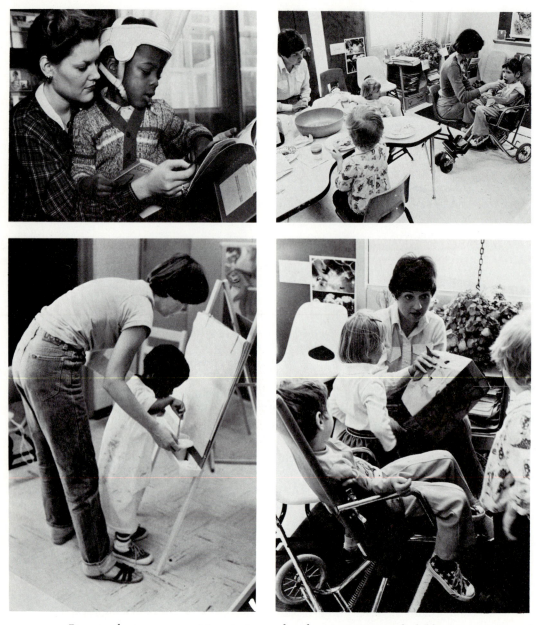

Parent volunteers can assist mainstreamed and nonmainstreamed children in a variety of activities. These activities can be a source of learning for parents as well as a source of assistance to the teacher.

cludes pretending the diagnosis never was made, shopping for a cure, and attempting to train the child in order to disprove the diagnosis. During the next stage, that of intellectual awareness, the parent manifests feelings of anger, guilt, and disappointment. When the parent reaches the stages of intellectual and emotional adjustment or acceptance, he or she shows realistic expectations for the child and cooperates in the child's program. The teacher, understanding the parents' adjustment, needs to encourage them to participate in the program, support them emotionally, share information, and work to improve parent-child interactions.[5]

Although most deviant children can benefit from participation in group programs along with so-called normal children, there are always those whose handicap is so severe that special rooms, special equipment, and specially trained teachers are required. There are also those whose handicapping condition is such that service must be provided for them in their homes. In such programs, the personnel must have an acute sensitivity to the rights and needs of parents. It is essential that the parents be made to feel that the responsibility for the child's development always remains with them, not with the program personnel. All involved parties must cultivate an attitude of trust on the part of both the parent and the child if the program is to be successful. Program personnel serve as resources, not only of information and the development of specific skills, but also as aids to the development of a feeling of security and confidence on the part of the parents.[6] Rejection, lack of reinforcement, and other negative attitudes in the home can seriously hinder progress that could be made for the handicapped child and the family. (See also Chapter 15).

MEETING THE NEEDS OF THE EXCEPTIONAL CHILD

Many children with special needs profit greatly from a form of grouping known as "mainstreaming" (being a part of a regular group) for at least some portion of each day.

For some children the extent of being exceptional is such that it is necessary to make special educational provisions for them. As different expectancies are set for children in terms of their capacities, varied teaching procedures, materials, and facilities are provided. These are selected in terms of the level of capacity, the limitations, and the characteristics of the individual child.

It is never too early for the exceptional child to have opportunities to become friends and to play with other children. All children learn from each other how to give and to take, the rules to follow, and to share and to have things shared with them. The physically handicapped, the intellectually handicapped, the malad-

---

[5] Ibid., pp. 230–232.

[6] Edith Levitt and Shirley Cohen, "Educating Parents of Children with Special Needs: Approaches and Issues," *Young Children,* **31**:4 (May 1976), pp. 263–274.

justed, and the gifted child need to, and should wish to, be treated in the same manner as other children and be given a chance to share in those tasks they are able to participate in. This is necessary in order to develop the skills and ability to have experiences that are adapted and designed to promote optimum development in relation to the special needs of each child concerned.

The teacher is always the primary factor in the learning situation in any classroom. Recognition of this fact becomes increasingly important when the teacher is expected to meet the demands of one or more children who need something different from or in addition to the planned program for the usual group. Additional qualifications and specialized training are essential for the teacher required to guide the deviations. Because of the specialized demands of working with these children, teachers and leaders in schools for young children find it desirable to establish some criteria to assist in determining how many and which atypical children can be included satisfactorily within the group.

In the admission of exceptional children, as with all children, the needs of the child and the school's ability to serve them are the primary factors in determining whether the child can be accepted in a group.

All teachers of young children have the responsibility of identifying the child within the group who needs special assistance and guidance over and beyond what can be provided. Through early identification, diagnosis, and treatment, many deviations can be corrected or adjustments can be made that are difficult if not impossible to make at a later date. Through counsel with the parents, plans can be developed to provide for the special needs of the exceptional child. In the classroom the special differences within the children can be identified and the decision made as to the best school situation for each child's guidance.

According to Olson, "It has become less and less customary to isolate exceptional children, and the tendency is to provide opportunities for work and play among children of all types so they can profit by such association. There is no fixed pattern and there probably should be none at our present state of knowledge. . . . A lush environment has in it both the qualitative and quantitative opportunities for the learning and growth of the least and the most able in any type of activity."[7]

Whenever appropriate, handicapped children should live with, play with, and go to school with "normal" children.[8] The arguments concern whether it is in the best interests for the gifted and for the intellectually handicapped to remain in the regular classroom. The relative values of the provision for the growth of these children within the regular school and within a special school are constantly under study. Research today indicates the acceptance by the normal group of the mentally or physically handicapped child. However, it appears that the mentally retarded child often has difficulty in adjusting to the regular classroom and also in securing accep-

---

[7] W. C. Olson, *Child Development*, 2d ed. (Boston: Heath, 1959), p. 343.
[8] *The Report to the President*, White House Conference on Children (Washington, D.C.: Superintendent of Documents, U.S. Government Printing Office, 1970), pp. 199–206.

The New Friends Program guides parents and teachers through the process of making dolls with various disabilities and then takes them into the classroom, where the dolls are introduced to children. The goal of the dolls' visit is to provide children with information about myths and stereotypes associated with disabilities.

tance. The physically handicapped usually encounters neither of these problems to a great degree. The demands of the child on the teacher because of the physical handicap will need to be carefully studied and measures provided to relieve the extra demand so that services to the total group are not curtailed.

For an interesting and lucid history of mainstreaming and ingredients that make it work successfully, see Dunlop's article in *Young Children*.[9]

The following section examines what mainstreaming means for educators, parents, and children.

Mainstreaming

Public Law 94-142 requires that a free public education be provided for all handicapped children in the least restrictive environment appropriate to the child's needs and abilities at no cost to the child's parents or guardians. The law does not mean that special education programs will be abandoned and that all exceptional children will be integrated randomly into general education classes. It does mean that handicapped children will receive appropriate schooling in the least restrictive environment possible.[10]

[9] Kathleen H. Dunlop. "Mainstreaming: Valuing Diversity in Children," *Young Children*, **30**:4 (1977), pp. 26–32.
[10] Lita Linzer Schwarts, *The Exceptional Child* (Belmont, Calif.: Wadsworth, 1979), pp. 3–4.

Unless a child is going to be in a special setting all his or her life, that child should be exposed to normal life experiences as soon as possible. There is a danger, however, that mainstreaming can be misused if a child is placed in an inappropriate class grouping. Not only would the handicapped child be frustrated but the entire class could be disrupted. The teacher might be forced to give a few students a disproportionate amount of time. Appropriate placement of a child being mainstreamed is extremely important.

When teachers and resource personnel plan to mainstream a child in a regular class certain behaviors and attitudes must be taken into account. The child must have some self-control and have learned to wait and to find alternate activities until the teacher can assist him or her. There should be an opportunity for the child to experience some success. The child should also have acceptable social skills. All persons involved, including the child, need to have a positive attitude toward the placement. A child who has these basic behaviors and attitudes is likely to be mainstreamed successfully.

The following factors are important in considering placement in a regular class setting: the teacher's strengths and weaknesses; the concepts that are being taught in the class; and the peers in the prospective class and guidance for them in accepting the handicapped or special child. The special child needs to be prepared for the new placement and to have an opportunity to become familiar with classroom materials before entering the class. The receiving teacher should have an IEP (Individual Education Plan), and continuous lines of communication should be open among all persons involved.[11]

In placing the exceptional child the severity of the disability, the child's age, the nature of the handicapping condition, and the facilities available in the school and the community must be considered.[12] PL 94-142 requires that placement be in the least restrictive environment, but this concept is not a mandate for mainstreaming. When appropriate, handicapped children should be placed with nonhandicapped children in a regular classroom. There are, however, several placement alternatives for these special children.

Educational alternatives

Once a special needs child is identified, the law requires an evaluation through the use of an Individualized Education Program. The IEP includes educational objectives, for the child, and it must be approved by the child's parents or guardians. When the educational objectives are mapped out, there are several placement options at the early childhood level: the regular classroom with access to support

---

[11] B. S. Nissman, *Mainstreaming: Who? Why? When? How?* (Trenton, N.J.: Guidance Awareness, 1980), pp. 4–5.

[12] Lerner et al., p. 246.

personnel; a small group of children who need additional evaluation and observation while they receive instruction on a daily basis; or a group of children with a common type of exceptionality, such as deaf or hearing impaired children, who need specialized instruction. A severely handicapped preschooler might be placed in the home with support personnel and with training for the family or principal caretaker. A last option would be combinations of these programs.[13] Other resources should also be considered, such as mental health agencies, private agencies, Head Start Programs, and hospital programs.

THE GIFTED CHILD

The public often assumes that creative and gifted children need no special help. This opinion is no more accurate for this group of exceptional children than for any other group.[14] When the gifted are segregated, their achievements may be spectacular in special areas. However, there appears to be no real evidence that they have gained materially over what they would have acquired in a heterogeneous group working in a rich environmment under capable guidance. Any good program for children allows and provides for differences, and the curriculum is developed to meet the needs of the gifted as well as the average and the retarded. The needs of these individuals are identified and planned for in such a way that each child becomes an accepted, contributing member of the group.

All children have gifts. The task of the teacher is to identify and to provide a suitable climate for their growth. As special abilities of children are noticed, records are made so that they may continue to receive guidance in terms of their special gift whether the child be intellectually gifted or specially talented. In identifying these children, the teacher does not place total dependence upon her or his own observation and test data but seeks counsel and assistance from other professional sources. Traits of creativity and inventiveness in problem solving are important cues in identifying the gifted.[15]

According to Passow, "There are no unique methods for teaching gifted children. In some ways, the apparent differences stem not so much from what the teacher does as from what the gifted child brings to the situation. One's ability to think, understand, create, initiate, relate, and imagine gives a qualitative dimension to the teaching-learning situation which may contrast visibly with the classroom environment of the average student."[16]

These gifted children have needs common to all children, including the development of the beginnings of basic concepts in all areas. They need provision for

---

[13] Ibid., pp. 246–247.
[14] Lita Linzer Schwartz, *The Exceptional Child* (Belmont, Calif.: Wadsworth, 1979), p. 15.
[15] Lerner et al., op. cit., p. 53.
[16] A. H. Passow, "Enrichment of Education for the Gifted," *Education for the Gifted*, 57th Yearbook, Part II, NSSE (Chicago: U. of Chicago, 1958), p. 198.

many stimulating and varied opportunities that develop initiative; to have the range and scope of their knowledge increased; to develop the power of working independently; to avoid the danger of becoming "one-sided" or interested in only a limited area; to have the acceptance of their peers even though they have superior ability in one or more areas; to overcome emotional stress in a socially acceptable manner and not to seek refuge in daydreaming. With these children the teacher places stress on independent thinking and action and on building relationships and concepts as opposed to learning multiple facts. Challenging situations are provided to develop critical thinking.

It is generally agreed that enrichment is the best method of working with intellectually accelerated children. Program personnel will find it helpful to utilize the many available resources—human and physical—to aid and to supplement the instructional process. They do this by implementing plans made in cooperation with parents and sometimes with other community and agency leaders. They know that the child may lose the genuine respect of peers when permitted to "always know the answers," to dictate what needs to be done, to be impatient with slower learners, or to draw attention constantly to self. The teacher may contribute to the antisocial attitude by always holding the child up as an example. However, flexible

The gifted-handicapped program provides these three- to five-year-old children with a balance between stimulating enrichment activities and therapy and remediation in developmental areas, delayed because of specific modality deficits or limited environmental experiences.

grouping plans and individual instruction in use today emphasize independent activities and put less emphasis on group participation.[17] One must be mindful that the child may become a "mental giant yet be a moral dwarf," and thereby not be capable, as a mature person, to make a real contribution to society. A good school for young children will provide adequate challenge for the superior child without "special" consideration and at the same time use these provisions for the enrichment of the educational experiences of the other children.

CHILDREN WITH MENTAL RETARDATION

In working with the child who has difficulty in learning, the teacher needs insight into how to help the child discover strengths as well as to assist him or her with liabilities; the teacher needs to accept him or her as a person as well as a child to be taught. It is important that this child's exception be noted in the early years and that a plan be made for his or her particular educational needs.

The degree of retardation is a significant factor in determining the placement of the intellectually handicapped child. If the retarded child is retained in a regular group, progress will be slower than that of the other members of the group; more praise and extrinsic rewards will be needed for successes; tasks will need to be briefer, less complex, and more routine with greater repetition—this repetition may, and should, be in varied situations. Many more and different concrete materials and experiences are required for this child. It will take longer to succeed; more time will be needed to make adjustments socially and emotionally. Serenity, happiness, and acceptance are essential.

Because it is difficult to predict how well a retarded child will fit into a group, many schools accept these children on a trial basis. The parents will need guidance as to further school plans if the child cannot be retained in the school. Most states have some provision for the child whose retardation is such that he or she cannot be absorbed within a group. Some communities have a school program for the children who are capable of benefiting from instruction but not with the regular group. Materials on these programs and suggestions for guidance in counseling parents of retarded children may be secured from the National Association for Retarded Citizens of the United States, 2501 Avenue J East, Arlington, Texas 76011. Private residential schools have been available for retarded children for many years. A listing of these schools is published annually by the American Association on Mental Deficiency, 5101 Wisconsin Avenue, NW, Washington, D.C. 22015.

Early congressional acts have given impetus to work with mental retardation and have provided opportunities for assistance to the preschool teacher of the mentally retarded child. Public Law 88-164, the Mental Retardation Facilities and Community Health Centers Construction Act passed by the 88th Congress and signed by

---

[17] Lerner et al., op. cit, p. 54.

Volunteers can be recruited through various community resources. They may provide a supportive one-to-one relationship with a handicapped child, or produce materials designed for a particular handicap.

President Kennedy, October 31, 1963, provided for (1) research centers, grants for the construction of university affiliated facilities and the construction of state centers maintained by the state; (2) the construction of community health centers; and (3) the training of teachers of the mentally retarded and other handicapped children as well as for research and demonstration projects in the education of the handicapped child. Public Law 88-156, the Maternal Health and Mental Retardation Amendments of 1963, provides an increase in child health and crippled children's services.[18]

The President's Panel on Mental Retardation in 1962 reported that the symptoms of the mentally retarded child are not always obvious but that early recognition and treatment offer the best prognosis. About 85 per cent of the retarded children can benefit from special education. Many children who are considered retarded are later found to be emotionally disturbed rather than having a mental defect existing from birth.

In the life of every parent of a retarded child there comes a time when plans must be made for schooling. "Mental retardation is a very complex problem, and many of these complexities make a difference in how the retarded child is educated."[19] Retarded children have special educational needs in terms of understanding, specially prepared and skilled teachers, and a specially developed curriculum. Because of their difficulty in learning, they need and learn best by special methods. Avery found that benefits from attendance at preschool would seem to indicate that a good preschool is worth a trial even though some people question whether young children of this type suffer by separation from home.[20]

Going to school is a time of many adjustments for all children, and it is more complicated for the mentally retarded. Safety, conformity to routines, languages and social readiness, ability in self-help activities, and stability and emotional adaptability need to be considered carefully. It is important to plan for admission of a mentally retarded child and to determine how his or her best interests as well as those of the other children in the group are to be served. Kirk suggests that certain educable children should be placed in a special preschool program at as early an age as possible.[21] All personnel in the program should be alert to behavioral cues associated with mental retardation. Here are some of the things to watch for:

Inability to follow multistep directions.
Little self-direction in choosing activities.

[18] *Mental Retardation, Plans and Programs* (Washington, D.C.: Department of Health, Education and Welfare, June 1965).
[19] H. M. Williams, *The Retarded Child Goes to School*, No. 123 (Washington, D.C.: U.S. Dept. of Health, Education, and Welfare, 1960), p. 1.
[20] Charlotte B. Avery, "Social Competence of Pre-School, Acoustically Handicapped Children," *Exceptional Child*, **15** (1948), pp. 71–73, 88.
[21] S. A. Kirk, *Early Education of Mentally Retarded: An Experimental Study* (Urbana, Ill.: U. of Illinois 1958), pp. 121–122.

Tendency to imitate rather than to create.

Poor abstract reasoning ability.

Difficulties in concentrating and learning.

Inability to apply learning from one situation to another or to anticipate consequences.

Inability to see similarities and differences in objects or situations.

Slower development than other children (walking, talking, and toilet training).

Delayed to poor motor coordination.

Poor eye–hand coordination.[22]

To assist in identifying the retarded child, the teacher needs (1) a record of age of development of such skills as creeping, crawling, standing, and talking; (2) an analysis of motor coordination of the child; (3) a record of vocabulary, interest in books, speech habits or impediments, memory span, ability to generalize, perceptual difficulties; (4) a history of physical difficulties, illnesses; and (5) a record of his or her ability to socialize; acceptance and rejection by peers. When the retarded child is located, the teacher works with the parents and with agencies that are skilled in diagnosing such problems. The ratio of pupil to teacher needs to be reduced to provide time for individual guidance; extra space is needed to avoid pushing or crowding and to provide for greater opportunities for creative play.

LEARNING DISABLED CHILDREN

A relatively new category of uniquely different need children has been labeled "learning disabilities." Although there have been many different definitions of this problem, it would appear that there is a growing feeling that the following qualities characterize the child with learning disabilities:

Does not benefit from classroom instruction that aids most children.

Possesses an average or better than average level of intelligence.

There are no evident physical, emotional, or cultural handicaps.

This means that a learning-disabled child is not mentally retarded, is not emotionally disturbed, and is not culturally disadvantaged. All it means is that the child does not respond to the usual classroom instruction. However, given the appropriate instruction for the particular child in question, the learning disability disappears.[23]

Many terms have been used to characterize children with learning problems. Children who are different in terms of learning have been called dullards, underachievers, school failures, minimally brain damaged, dyslexic, and many other pe-

[22]*Day Care: Serving Children with Special Needs.* (Washington, D.C.: U.S. DHEW, OCD, OE Bureau of Education for the Handicapped, 1972), p. 49.

[23]A. O. Ross. *Learning Disability: The Unrealized Potential* (New York: McGraw-Hill, 1977).

joratives. Today, it is estimated that there are more than 7 million children in America with this special problem, and many approaches from medical to genetic have been applied to an understanding of it. It stands to reason that because the problem involves the learning process, the point of attack should be at the level of the learning program, and as early as possible. For an interesting, instructive, illuminating, up-to-date, and helpful discussion of learning disabilities, you are heartily encouraged to read Ross's excellent work. Program personnel should suspect some degree of learning disability in children who exhibit any combination of the following characteristics:

Poor visual discrimination: difficulty distinguishing between shapes, letters, and numbers.
Poor visual memory: forgetting what is seen and read.
Poor auditory discrimination: inability to distinguish between different sounds or words.
Poor kinesthesia: difficulty distinguishing different objects by feeling.
Poor eye—hand muscle coordination: difficulty making hand do what eyes see.
Poor spatial orientation: difficulty remembering spacial differences.
Poor figure-ground: difficulty selecting one thing from a group.
Perseveration: difficulty shifting from one activity to another.
Hyperactivity: inability to concentrate on a structured activity.
Disinhibition: tendency to be lethargic or hyperactive.
Poor self-image: views herself or himself as anything but normal.[24]

THE PHYSICALLY HANDICAPPED CHILD

The orthopedically handicapped child is the least difficult to absorb within a regular group. However, the crippling defect must be minor, or special provision must be made for handling the child. Overprotectiveness on the part of the children, teacher, or other adults is one of the problems encountered in working with this type of child. The greatest problem may be the overprotectiveness of the parents. Even though at times it is difficult to enforce, the child must become independent through use of his or her own resources.

The type and degree of the handicap determines the program. Some of these children were born with a handicap; others have acquired it after birth. Some of these handicaps may be fully corrected; however, many children with severe handicaps need to be provided with special kinds of educational services. It is extremely important that handicapped children receive help before starting regular school. If the child is successfully helped at an early age, the problems for the parent as well as for the child are lessened. The opportunities for the child are expanded because

[24]*Day Care: Serving Children with Special Needs*, op. cit., p. 53.

A variety of mobility devices are used to help children in walking—some with and some without wheels.

of early acceptance of the handicap and participation in a planned educational program to utilize all the child's assets. Because of the flexibility and work with individuals in programs for young children, an excellent opportunity for such growth is available. Parents of these children increase their ability to help their child by assisting, observing, and working with the teacher. Through conferences, teachers and parents may give each other ideas, that will be helpful in working with the child.

Defective vision

The blind or partially seeing child will need to learn through the other senses; however, he or she must learn to do all things that he or she can do safely and successfully. Children with partial sight need different books, periods of frequent rest for their eyes, and a greater provision for safety. The environment should be made safe in order that these children can be encouraged to experiment and ex-

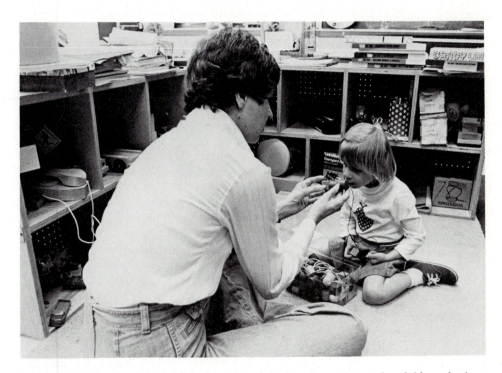

Visually impaired children need modification of the learning activity. This child needs close proximity to the materials.

plore. They also need encouragement and a sense of belonging, because they are delayed in developing self-awareness.[25] Often they can excel in games requiring auditory acuity. Many opportunities should be provided for them to develop and use this skill, thereby securing recognition and experiencing success within their peer group.

Children who are having difficulty with vision may rub their eyes frequently or blink when attempting to see objects; they frequently sit in a tense position or make facial expressions indicating intense effort to see. Children exhibiting these characteristics should be referred for testing by competent individuals. In the classroom they should have frequent rest periods and protection from glare or from work requiring close vision.

Impaired hearing

The child with impaired hearing will need help according to the type of hearing impairment. The child who has never heard has a greater problem than one who has lost his or her hearing after acquiring speech. Both of these groups have greater needs than the partially hearing-impaired child. The young child needs his or her hearing tested frequently; often correction can be made if impairment is discovered soon enough. The child with impaired hearing should at all times be seated so as to see the teacher's lips. Careful observation of the child's participation with the group will avoid his or her forming habits of withdrawal because of an inability to hear.

A program for hearing-impaired children was developed at The Florida State University Institute of Human Development in cooperation with personnel from the Department of Education Services for Exceptional Children, and the Speech and Hearing Clinic. Aware of the importance of an early educational start for these children (otherwise the hearing-impaired child will not learn language or achieve social and personal skills possessed by other children of this age), it was decided to place one such child in each of the Institute's preschool age groups. A teacher with specialized training in the field devoted half her time to the four children and also served as a consultant to the regular teachers. One of the major problems faced by atypical children is the difficulty of achieving group acceptance. How this was accomplished for one totally hearing-impaired child is described:

> Larry did not enter the group without considerable thought and preparation. Since each group of children in the school was to have a hearing-impaired child, decisions had to be made as to the group in which each child should be placed. This decision fell to the speech and hearing therapist who had worked closely with the children and their parents. Armed with the information and insights she had gained plus extensive clinical findings, she visited each group to see which group of children and teacher

[25] Lerner et al., op. cit., pp. 31–32.

might offer the best school environment for each child. Larry, age four, who is totally hearing-impaired, was placed in the four-year-old group.

The week before Larry was to join the group was a busy one for teacher and children. The teacher felt that the children should have some sense of the world, different from their own, in which Larry lived. They also needed to understand that he had not had the 4½ months of playing together which they had shared so he would be lacking in the degree of social living they had obtained. It was decided that an approach to sounds around them might be an opening wedge in evolving this awareness. The children listened to the sounds around them during sharing period. They talked about what they heard. Stories were read, like "Muffin" the little black dog who got a cinder in his eye and couldn't see, but could hear. When the children's interest was high, the teacher asked the children to tell her what they heard when they put their hands over their ears tightly. In unison they replied, "Nothing."

Then the teacher told them about Larry who couldn't hear yet wanted to come to school. She asked them how they could talk to him if he couldn't hear. Don said, "We could show him," and began to point directions. The children eagerly took up the suggestion and began to communicate with each other by gestures.

Larry entered school, a welcome addition to the group. His welcome was short-lived, however. He was not accustomed to such social acceptance and before long was entering each group like a friendly puppy, knocking down block houses with a wide friendly grin or grabbing a doll from the doll house and running to the far end of the yard. The warm acceptance changed to resentment and isolation for Larry by the group.

A week later at discussion time, while Larry was attending speech class, the teacher asked them what they thought of Larry. "We don't like him," came the reply. "Why?" asked the teacher. "He knocks down our blocks," was a quick response. "Why do you suppose he does that?" she asked them. For a minute there was silence, and then Susan said, "Maybe he doesn't know how to play with us. Tom used to knock them down too." The rest of the group agreed. The conversation turned to what they could do to help him. "We could tell him not to knock down our blocks by shaking our heads," Tom suggested. This was tried, but Larry thought the children were playing again. The children smiled as they shook their heads. Another discussion brought out the need for a serious face as the negative head shake was given.

Despite these initial difficulties, after four months in nursery school, Larry is an accepted member of the group, with no more than the usual four-year-old setbacks for outbursts of destruction. The warmth of acceptance permeates the group. This warmth was shown one day as Larry entered the door of the nursery school and met Tom coming out. Impulsively Tom threw his arms around Larry and kissed him on the cheek. Larry smiled in happy surprise, and both boys went their individual ways.

Each of the hearing-impaired children made a surprisingly good adjustment to the group and, as a result of intensive therapy, attained language facility. It is likely that these children will experience much less retardation during later school years than is common for children with severe or total hearing handicaps. The responsibility of the teacher in charge, in adapting to the needs of these children, is to

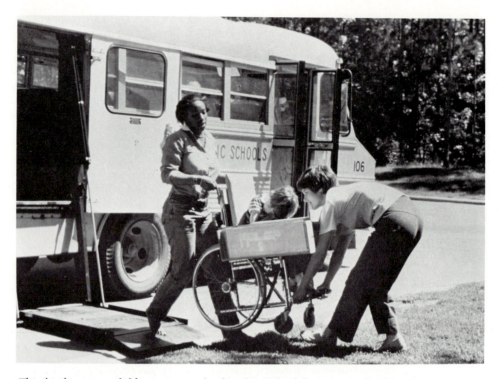

This kindergarten child comes to school in her wheelchair on a school bus.

provide constant language stimulation—sometimes referred to as auditory bombardment.[26] Through the use of a wide variety of art materials, dramatic play, structured music experiences, story sharing, and an assortment of toys, expressive outlets are provided for the frustrations experienced by the child.

Children with mild hearing loss do not usually need special placement, but children with a moderate hearing loss (55–69 dB) sometimes do. They usually need special assistance with language as well. The severely hearing impaired and the profoundly hearing impaired children routinely require special classes, language assistance, and educational assistance.

There is concern about the value of mainstreaming for hearing handicapped children if the curriculum and the needed support services are not available.[27]

[26] Alicia Hamilton, "A Preschool Program for Children with Limited Hearing," *Young Children*, **21**:5 (1966), p. 267.
[27] Schwartz, op. cit., pp. 49–50.

Impaired speech

The majority of cases of impaired speech involve faulty articulation. Most of these articulatory speech difficulties occur at an early age. Stuttering and nonfluency rate are other commonly found forms of speech impairment. The teacher needs to distinguish between actual speech impairment and speech difficulties that are a normal part of the child's developmental sequence. The child with impaired speech will need special help apart from the group even though he or she benefits from participating with the regular group. Physical defects such as cleft palate and harelip will need medical attention and correction.

Whatever the speech problem, personnel should identify the children who need help; secure counsel and assistance; provide special help to the child to the degree that training, experience, and teaching load permit; and work with parents and other agencies in providing for the total needs of the child.

A calm, helpful, and accepting manner in a relaxed climate is an effective method of work with children with speech difficulties. The teacher must be careful not to embarrass the child. In a classroom where a free, spontaneous atmosphere prevails, where tension is dispelled with a friendly remark or humorous situation, the speech of many children will improve. However, there are special skills and procedures for which the teacher must have training. If the teacher does not have this competency, she or he may secure assistance from individuals with special training.

The teacher is ever alert to ensure that problems of these children are not being developed in the other members of the group. For example, the attention and help on a speech problem with one child may encourage imitation on the part of another child in order to secure the desired attention.

THE MALADJUSTED CHILD

The child who experiences social and emotional conflict situations often has problems of personal and group adjustment. All children have conflicts, but most children develop the ability to resolve these conflicts through socially approved activities and procedures. The release of tensions through dramatics, play experiences, or creative activities has been discussed in previous chapters. A few children need help from adults to release their tensions and to resolve their conflicts. Careful guidance by the teacher may be all that is required. However, if these problems continue and are serious, the teacher and the parents need and should have the help of a specially trained person. The teacher identifies these children and refers them to the proper agencies. The teacher then cooperates in working out a satisfactory solution. In working with children who can be retrained in the group, the teacher will find helpful suggestions in the material in Chapter 16.

PROFESSIONAL RESOURCES AND PROGRAMS

There are numerous local, state, and national professional organizations concerned with children who have uniquely different needs. The following list is not comprehensive. It is intended as a starting point from which information can be secured about locating other resources at the local, state, and national levels.

Council for Exceptional Children
1920 Association Drive
Reston, Virginia 22091

Association for Childhood Education International (ACEI)
11141 Georgia Avenue
Wheaton, Maryland 20902

National Association for the Education of Young Children (NAEYC)
1834 Connecticut Avenue, NW
Washington, D.C. 20009

National Association for Retarded Citizens
P.O. Box 6109
Arlington, Texas 76011

National Association of Private Schools for Exceptional Children
P.O. Box 34293
Bethesda, Maryland 20817

Association for Children with Learning Disabilities
5246 Clarwin St.
Pittsburgh, Pennsylvania 15229

National Easter Seal Society
2023 West Ogden Avenue
Chicago, Illinois 60612

Association for Education of the Visually Handicapped
206 North Washington St.
Alexandria, Va. 22314

The American Speech and Hearing Association
10801 Rockville Pike
Rockville, Maryland 20852

National Association for Mental Health
418 South Washington St.
Alexandria, Va. 22314.

SUMMARY

Children can be exceptional in many ways, and they are found in almost every learning situation at the preschool level. These children might be gifted, learning disabled, physically handicapped, emotionally troubled, socially maladjusted, or language handicapped. Recent legislation, Public Law 94-142, requires that handicapped children be provided a free, appropriate education in the least restrictive setting possible. Intervention and proper placement in the preschool years are crucial in reducing or eliminating the effects of the children's handicaps. With proper planning, good communication, and positive attitudes on the part of all involved, educators, with help from parents and other resource persons, can continue to offer more and better opportunities for these children to learn and to reach their potentials as human beings.

Suggested Activities

1. Observe a group of children. List ways the teacher adjusts activities for exceptional children. List activities in which exceptional children participate as regular members of the group. Discuss the value of both types of activities.
2. Read and discuss in class references available in your library that are related to work with children who are uniquely different in their early years.
3. Make a list of special services available for assisting the teacher as she or he works with children who are uniquely different as members of a regular group. Describe how these are selected, contacted, and used with special children. Indicate how this special assistance is valuable.
4. List guides for the teachers in schools for young children in identifying and working with exceptional children—the gifted, the emotionally disturbed, the mentally retarded, the hearing-impaired, the partially sighted, the speech defective, the physically handicapped, and the culturally deprived.
5. Determine the provisions made for children who are uniquely different in your community.
6. Visit such a center and describe how the program is adjusted to the level of each of the differences observed.
7. Secure from your State Department of Education a copy of the approved state plan for mainstreaming children who require uniquely different educational services. Become familiar with the details of the plan including implementation. Arrange a seminar in order to acquaint all members of your class with the details of how your state provides educa-

tional services to its children whose needs differ greatly from those of the majority of children in the group.

8. Call Crippled Children's Services through your local health department and ask for printed materials about local services.

9. View the following films:

    Reading Potential. Encyclopaedia Britannica Educational Corp., 425 N. Michigan Avenue, Chicago, Ill. 60611.

    First Steps. CRM/McGraw-Hill Films, 110 15th Street, Del Mar, Calif. 92014.

    It Could Have Been Your Child. Aims Media, Inc., 626 Justin Avenue, Glendale, Calif. 91201.

    Across the Silence Barrier. Time-Life Films, 100 Eisenhower Drive, P.O. Box 644, Paramus, N.J. 07654.

Related Readings

Allen, Eileen K. *Mainstreaming in Early Childhood Education.* Albany, N.Y.: Delmar Publishers, 1980.

Askew, Judy, N. Rayder, and T. A. Taylor. "The 'Diff-enfranchised' Return to the Mainstream." *Child. Educ.* **57**:5 (1981), pp. 276–281.

Bleck, E. E., and D. A. Nagel. *Physically Handicapped Children—A Medical Atlas for Teachers.* New York: Grune and Stratton, 1975.

Bosco, J. J., and S. S. Fobin. *The Hyperactive Child and Stimulant Drugs.* Chicago: U. of Chicago, 1977.

Braun, Samual J., and Miriam G. Lasher. *Are You Ready to Mainstream?* Columbus, Ohio: Merrill, 1978.

Burns, P. C., and Betty Broman. "Language Arts for Exceptional Children." In *Language Arts in Childhood Education.* Chicago: Rand McNally College Publishing Co., 1979, pp. 505–551.

Cohen, S., M. Semmes, and M. J. Guralnick. "Public Law 94-142 and the Education of Exceptional Children." In *Exceptional Children* **45**:4 (1979), pp. 279–284.

Engel, Rosalind. "Understanding the Handicapped Through Literature." *Young Children* **35**:3 (1980), pp. 27–32.

French, A. P. *Disturbed Children and Their Families: Innovations in Evaluation and Treatment.* New York: Human Sciences, 1977.

Gearheart, B. R. *Learning Disabilities: Educational Strategies.* St. Louis: Mosby, 1977.

Hart, Verna. *Mainstreaming Children with Special Needs.* New York: Longman, 1981.

Hagino, Janice L. "Educating Children About Handicaps." *Child. Educ.* **57**:2 (1980), pp. 97–100.

Hayden, A. H., and E. B. Edgar. Identification, Screening, and Assessment." in *Early Childhood Education for Exceptional Children.* Ed. by J. B. Jordan and others. Reston, Va.: Council for Exceptional Children, 1977.

Jones, R. L. *Mainstreaming and the Minority Child.* Reston Va.: Council for Exceptional Child, 1976.

Jordan, June E., et al. (eds.). *Early Childhood Education for Exceptional Children: A Handbook of Ideas and Exemplary Practices.* Reston, Va.: *Council for Exceptional Child,* 1977.

Levin, J. R., and V. L. Allen. *Teaching Exceptional Children*. New York: Academic, 1976.

Linder, Toni W. *Early Childhood Special Education*. Baltimore, MD.: P. H. Brookes Publishers, 1983.

Meier, J. *Developmental and Learning Disabilities*. College Park: U. of Maryland, 1976.

Newton, Mariana. *Speech, Hearing, and Language Problems*. Lincoln, Neb.: *Professional Educator's Publications, 1977.*

Piazza, R. Readings in Preschool Education for the Handicapped. Guildford, CT.: Special Learning Corporation, 1978.

Project Head Start. Head Start Mainstreaming Preschoolers Series. Washington, D.C., HEW, 1978. Publication numbers: (OHDS 78-3115), (OHDS 78-31111), (OHDS 78-3114), (OHDS 78-3112), (OHDS 78-3116), (OHDS 78-31110), (OHDS 78-3113), (OHDS 78-3117).

Rafael, Berta. "Art Activities for Children with Special Needs." *Child. Educ.* **57**:3 (1981), pp. 149–155.

Taylor-Hershel, Denise, and Regine Webster. "Mainstreaming: A Case in Point." *Child. Educ.*, **59**:3 (1983), pp. 175–179.

Weston, A. J. *Articulation Disorders: Methods of Evaluation and Therapy*. Lincoln, Neb.: Professional Publisher's Publications, 1975.

Wishon, Phillip M., "Serving Handicapped Young Children: Six Imperatives." *Young Children* **38**:1 (1982), pp. 28–32.

Wood, Mary M., and O. L. Hurley. "Curriculum and Instruction." in *Early Childhood Education for Exceptional Children*. Reston, Va.: The Council for Exceptional Children, 1977. Pp. 132–157.

Yearbook of Special Education, 1977–1978. Chicago: Marquis Academic Media, 1977.

Zeitlin, Shirley, *Kindergarten Screening: Early Identification of Potential High Risk Learners*. Springfield, Ill.: Thomas, 1976.

CHAPTER 18

Providing Qualified Personnel and Maintaining Standards in Preschool Programs

Teachers and all adult personnel involved in the education of young children are regarded as the most significant factor in determining the quality of experience that a child will have in any program. Yet, it is still possible for persons without even minimal educational and personal qualifications to establish and operate programs for infants and young children. Assuring qualified teachers, caregivers, and other involved adults in programs for young children is one of today's greatest challenges, for the need still far exceeds the availability of good personnel.

Developing a high quality of teachers of young children is a continuous process. The quality depends on many factors, and one of these is that of attracting and holding qualified students in teacher education programs in colleges and universities.

Certification of educational personnel and licensing of centers are the usual means of attempting to ensure safety for the children and some degree of competence in teachers, administrators, and other educational personnel. Regardless of the licensing and certification standards, professionals and especially parents must always be on the alert that these standards are being met, reporting any concern to the appropriate licensing or certification authority.

CHARACTERISTICS OF GOOD ADULT PERSONNEL

Throughout the years, love of children has been recognized as basic to successful work with them. However, love is not enough. The adults must also enjoy working with children, and the love of such adults should be different from that of the mother. Patience and understanding not only for what is happening, but why it is happening, are essential to guiding the development of the young child. Only an adult who is secure can build security within children.[1] A warm, outgoing, but not dominating, person can work well with children and parents.

In the selection of teachers for preschool children, special attention is given to

[1] Dorothy Gross, "Teachers of Young Children Need Basic Inner Qualities," *Young Children*, **23**:2 (1967), pp. 107–110.

Patience and understanding not only of what is happening but why it is happening are essential to guiding the development of the young child.

personal qualities, such as warmth, openness, humor, efficiency, confidence, appearance, creativity, speech, voice, and the ability to communicate well by speaking clearly and choosing words carefully. Lay and Dopyers[2] stress as the major categories of qualifications for early childhood teachers commitment, sensitivity, resourcefulness, and organizational ability. However, a teacher may have all the desirable personal qualities, yet not be a good teacher. Basic information, understanding, knowledge, skill, competencies, and appreciations can only be secured through training and experience. The teacher must apply this knowledge in daily work with children. Many programs that prepare one for teaching in the field of Early Childhood Education provide counseling and guidance in the development of these essential qualities while the training and experience are secured.

Credentialing teachers today, however, places emphasis on the demonstration of professional competencies as well as personal qualities.[3] The competencies may be acquired in a variety of settings, including teacher education institutions, on the job training, and in the community through the utilization of human resources. The new direction is away from inflexible adherence to regulatory functions and toward constructive dynamic leadership at the local level. Widespread exploration and change is indicated. Among the changes are earlier exposure to teaching situations and a shifting in preparation from the campus to the school systems,[4] and other programs for young children.

Licensing standards for directors of child-care center staff vary from state to state. The director or head teacher is usually a college graduate with professional study in Early Childhood Education. Staff training is one of her or his responsibilities. The age for the director varies from sixteen years in four states to twenty-one years in the other states. The requirements also vary from high school graduation or its equivalent to four years of college. However, all states do require experience and also that the individual be equipped to do the work required. The qualifications of the other staff members also vary from state to state. The staff-in-training must be capable of doing work required and must have a sensitivity to children and their needs.[5]

As the need for full-day services for young children from low-income families, from families whose mother and father both work, from one-parent families, and from families of varied ethnic and cultural backgrounds increases, colleges and universities charged with the responsibility of providing for the preparation of teachers have responded by drastically changing the traditional "lab school" program and

[2] Margaret V. Lay and J. C. Dopyers, *Becoming A Teacher of Young Children* (Lexington, Mass: Heath, 1977).
[3] W. C. Allen, et al., "Performance Criteria for Education Personnel Development: A State Approach to Standards." *J. Teacher Educ.*, **20**:2 (1969), pp. 133–135. See also D. W. Allen and P. Wagschal, "New Look in Credentialing, *Clearing House*, **44**:3 (1969), pp. 137–140.
[4] *A Manual on Certification Requirements for School Personnel in the United States*, 1970 ed. (Washington, D.C.: National Commission on Teacher Education and Professional Standards, NEA, 1970).
[5] *Child Care Data and Materials*, Committee on Finance, U.S. Senate, June 16, 1971.

functions. There is a trend toward field-based teacher education where students are placed in actual, on-going children's programs.

CHILD DEVELOPMENT ASSOCIATE

A pilot program for training Child Development Associates (CDAs) was initiated in the fall of 1972, and the first CDA was credentialed on July 24, 1976. By April 1977, 1,000 CDAs had been approved,[6] and by November 1982, there were 11,000 credentialed CDAs in the nation. Initially, the credential was awarded by the Child Development Associate Consortium (CDAC) after the individual had been assessed by examining teams employed and selected by the consortium. The CDAC was a nonprofit organization funded by the Office of Child Development, DHEW, now The Administration For Children, Youth and Families, Office of Human Development Services, U.S. Department of Health and Human Services, for the purpose of providing competent personnel to work in preschool programs including Head Start.

The CDA training program is a competency-based program and consists of acquiring competencies that have been prescribed and can be assessed. Candidates must receive academic credit for courses to supplement their practicum experiences. Fifty per cent of the training must be field-based, and the program is not time-circumscribed. Bank Street College of Education in New York is now the grantee for assessing the credentials of the candidates. The CDA National Credentialing Program does not have the authority of law that certification of teachers does. Nevertheless, the promoters of the program envision wide national acceptance of the CDA Credential as appropriate preparation for personnel in meeting state standards. Currently 27 states and the District of Columbia recognize this credential in their guides for personnel in child care regulations.[7]

PARAPROFESSIONALS AND VOLUNTEERS

A pilot study reported by Prescott[8] gives a factual description of day care facilities and the requirements for day care leaders and volunteers. It has long been recognized that one teacher cannot do all that is needed for each child. Paraprofessionals render many services under the supervision and direction of the head teacher.[9]

---

[6] "CDAC Reaches New Milestone: Thousandth Credential," *Dateline* CDAC **3**:2 (May 1977), p. 1.

[7] Margaret Lay-Dopyera and John Dopyera, *Becoming a Teacher of Young Children* (Lexington, Mass.: Heath, 1982), pp. 103–104.

[8] Elizabeth Prescott, *A Pilot Study of Day Care Centers and Their Clientele* (Washington, D.C.: Children's Bureau, Welfare Division, U.S. Department of Health Education and Welfare, 1965).

[9] D. Findley and K. Henson, "Teacher Aides: Should They Be Certified?" *Contemporary Education*, **42**:4 (1971, pp. 177–180. See also A. J. Mauser, "The Paraprofessional: Panacea or Frankenstein?" *Contemporary Education*, **42**:3 (1970), pp. 139–141.

Teachers who model positive reinforcement and assistance to others find that this is reflected in children's behavior toward one another. Cindy is taking the hand of her friend to help guide her finger painting activity.

Aides can assist with clerical services, housekeeping activities, group supervision, technical assistance, and some instructional activities as assigned by the teacher.[10]

Volunteers may or may not be trained personnel. They assist the trained teacher and also help with community service. They share what they can do best. The trend is to involve *parents* and *community groups* in the instruction and care of children.

All personnel must have an understanding of the objectives and concepts of Early Childhood Education, a personality that children and adults respond to readily, and an intense interest in the development of the children.

[10] Sylvia Sunderlin and B. Willis, *Aides to Teachers and Children* (Washington, D.C.: ACEI, 1968).

The number of persons working in a center depends on the number of children and the maturity of the children. The type of head teacher also affects the enrollment. However, all centers should have at least one qualified person.

Other personnel may include a career assistant, a career community assistant, career health specialist as well as trainees or aides, the volunteer worker, and paraprofessional personnel. Trainees or aides may assume office or administrative responsibilities as a part of their duties or they may have this type of work exclusively.[11] As the personnel give evidence of continued interest in children, every opportunity should be given them to have additional responsibilities and additional work in courses and experience, as well as opportunities for developing career ladders for paraprofessionals.[12]

As the need and demand for the education of prekindergarten-age children continues to grow, concern for properly prepared teachers, caregivers, and other adult personnel increases. The extensive use of untrained paraprofessionals, parents, volunteers, and elementary teachers without specialized preparation in Early Childhood Education may result in inadequate programs for young children. This is not to say that this approach is necessarily unsatisfactory. What is needed in such cases is a carefully planned system of undifferentiated staffing, extensive preservice and in-service training, and retraining. Because of the nature of the needs of very young children, the contributions of professionals from varied disciplines, including psychology, sociology, health education, nutrition, anthropology, pediatrics, nursing, and possibly others, are needed. The most successful programs have this interdisciplinary instruction built into the program content, instead of having to depend on the "volunteer" efforts of professionals in these fields on a one-shot class-lecture basis.

CERTIFICATION OF TEACHERS

A number of reports concerning the preparation of teachers have been made.[13] In 1967 the Association for Childhood Education International identified the areas to be included in the preparation of teachers for children three to eight years of age. The areas included (1) liberal education, (2) foundations of Early Childhood Education, (3) child growth and development, (4) nature of the learning process, (5) small group dynamics, (6) curriculum and method, and (7) professional laboratory experiences. These areas were again included in an ACEI Position Paper in 1983.[14]

---

[11] Project Head Start, *Career Planning and Progression for a Child Development Center* (Washington, D.C.: U.S. Department of Health and Welfare, 1970).

[12] Margaret Malone, *Summary of Selected Proposals Related to Child Care* (Washington, D.C.: Library of Congress, Congressional Research Service, Education and Welfare, June 1971).

[13] *Preparation Standards for Teachers in Early Childhood Education* (Washington, D.C.: ACEI, 1967).

[14] Nita H. Barbour and Don Pease, "Preparation of Early Childhood Teachers," *Child. Educ.*, 59:5 (1983), pp. 301–306.

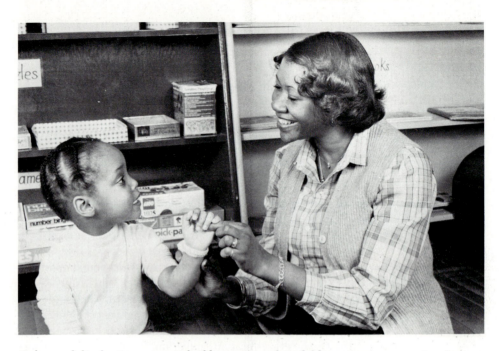

Only an adult who is secure can build security within children. A warm, outgoing, but not dominating individual can work well with children and parents.

The Ad Hoc Joint Committee on the Preparation of Nursery and Kindergarten Teachers of the National Commission on Teacher Education included desirable goals in its report for both preservice and in-service education.[15] These included independence, positive self-image, intellectual stimulations, creativity, socialization, physical development, emotional development, and staff collaboration and cooperation. The committee also sets forth proposals on personnel selection and programs for personnel at different levels.

By 1975, forty-eight states and territories had mandated certification for kindergarten teachers and administrators in the public schools. However, only eight states did not accept elementary certification for kindergarten teachers, seven required elementary plus minimal early childhood preparation, and twenty-nine required only an elementary certificate. Most states had no form of certification for paraprofessionals.[16]

[15]*Preliminary Report of Ad Hoc Joint Committee on the Preparation of Nursery and Kindergarten Teachers* (Washington, D.C.: National Commission on Teacher Education and Professional Standards, NEA, 1969).

[16]*Early Childhood Programs: A State Survey 1974–5*, Report No. 65 (Denver, Colo.: The Education Commission of the States, 1975).

In 1982, the National Association for the Education of the Young Children developed and endorsed guidelines for use by Early Childhood teacher education programs in institutions offering baccalaureate degrees. The purpose of these guidelines was to establish a standard of excellence for new and existing Early Childhood teacher education programs.[17] The nine guideline components include (1) curriculum, (2) instructional methods, (3) resources, (4) faculty qualifications, (5) professional relationships, (6) cultural diversity, (7) enrollment, (8) administrative structure, and (9) evaluation and constituent responsiveness.

STANDARDS AND LICENSING

Responsibility for regulating child care in the United States has always been with the state and local government. However, with increased federal funds for child care in the 1960s there was an increase in the government's role in establishing and enforcing child care requirements.

The Economic Opportunity Act of 1964 required that a set of standards be established by the Secretary of DHEW and the Director of OEO. The result was the publication in 1968 of a set of standards for Day Care (FIDCR).[18] Since its inception there have been many attempts at revision of the requirements. Title XX of the Social Security Act was passed in 1975, making the educational requirements of FIDCR optional but the staffing of adult-child ratios mandatory.

By 1980 new child care regulations to replace FIDCR had been developed and most of the provisions went into effect in October 1980. However, in response to concerns about the potential cost of the new requirements, subsequent actions of Congress in 1981 effectively eliminated any federal child care regulations. Child care services carried out with funds from block grants must now meet standards of state and local laws. State and local regulations are very important.

The Comparative Licensing study, begun in 1976, included information on laws and regulations pertaining to child care centers, group day care homes, and family day care homes. This study has been updated and includes state licensing requirements as of March 1981. No requirements were specified for group size related to four-year-olds in thirty-three states, Guam, Puerto Rico, and the Virgin Islands. In the other twenty-one states and the District of Columbia the size of the group ranged from a low of ten to a high of forty-five children to one caregiver. States that require the bachelor's degree for teachers are beginning to specify that the degree be in early childhood/child development. Other states are moving to adopt the CDA Credential.[19]

[17] *Early Childhood Teacher Education Guidelines*, Position Statement of the National Association for the Education of Young Children (Washington, D.C.: NAEYC, 1982), p. xi.
[18] C. L. Rampton (ed.), *Early Childhood Development, Alternatives for the Program Implementation in the States* (Denver, CO: Education Commission of States, 1971), pp. 4, 6, 13.
[19] Raymond C. Collins, "Child Care and the States: The Comparative Licensing Study," *Young Children* 38:5 (1983), pp. 3–11.

Through programs of cooperative action, plans suitable for a given locality are developed and put into effect. Participants often include leaders from public, private, and church-related schools, and federal programs, as well as social workers, doctors, psychologists, directors of educational programs for teachers, and other community leaders. Through educational and interpretive programs on television and radio, and through newspapers and magazine articles, the general public is being informed as to values and problems of good schools for young children. As a result, parents are becoming more and more discriminating toward the schools their young children attend. They are cooperating with leaders in the movement to ensure that all schools for young children meet minimum standards.

Licensing is one form of ensuring standards in preschool centers. It does not guarantee optimum conditions but indicates a level at which a center can operate safely and efficiently. Many persons consider the licensing of child care facilities as the responsibility of departments of welfare. In some situations, however, other agencies cooperate or assume the responsibility.[20]

Readers are urged to contact local or state agencies and area colleges or universities for current information regarding licensing legislation.

ORGANIZATIONS CONCERNED WITH YOUNG CHILDREN

Participation in the programs of professional organizations can be very rewarding to teachers, caregivers, and other personnel working with young children. One of the greatest benefits is getting to know others in the same type of responsibility and sharing ideas with them. Most organizations help people keep up to date through conferences and publications. Organizations that have been influential in influencing the quality and type of services and educational programs available to young children today include the following.

Association for Childhood Education International (ACEI) 11141 Georgia Avenue, Wheaton, MD 20902

The major purpose of ACEI is to work for the education and well-being of children from birth to fourteen years of age. Publications include *Childhood Education*, the official journal, and bulletins on current topics in education.

---

[20] E. Class, *Licensing of Child Care Facilities by State Welfare Departments*. Washington, D.C.: *U.S. Department of Health, Education and Welfare, Social and Rehabilitation Service* Children's Bureau, 1968.

National Association for the Education of Young Children (NAEYC), 1834 Connecticut Avenue, NW, Washington, D.C. 20009

The expressed purpose of NAEYC focuses on the provision of educational services and resources for children from birth to eight years. Publications include the magazine, *Young Children*, books, and pamphlets on topics concerned with young children.

World Organization for Early Childhood Education P.O. Box 931, Fresno, Calif. 93714

The World Organization for Early Childhood Education, known as OMEP after the initials of the French translation, Organisation Mondiale pour l'Education Prescolaire, is an educational organization that promotes the study and education of young children, fosters happy childhood and home life, and thus contributes to world peace. The *International Journal of Early Childhood* is published by OMEP.

Other national organizations

Though the professional groups mentioned may be thought of as the "old standbys," many other groups afford valuable assistance to programs for young children and to the personnel involved. Programs for young children have broadened in purpose and scope in recent years, among which the following serve as significant examples.

Alexander Graham Bell Association for the Deaf, Inc.
3417 Volta Place, NW,
Washington, D.C. 20007

The Alexander Graham Bell Association for the Deaf acts as an information center for parents. This association has as its purpose the promotion of speech and lipreading with the use of residual hearing. It publishes the *Volta Review* as well as many educational materials.

Bureau of Education for the Handicapped
U.S. Office of Education, Department of Health and Human Services
7th and D Streets, SW, Washington, D.C. 20036

The Bureau of Education for the Handicapped is the official arm of the federal government dealing with the education of children with handicaps of all kinds.

Black Child Development Institute
1463 Rhode Island Avenue NW, Washington, D.C. 20005

The Black Child Development Institute focuses on black child development through technical assistance to predominantely black day care centers.

Child Welfare League of America
67 Irving Place, New York, N.Y. 10013

The Child Welfare League involves itself in all phases of child welfare, including adoption, day care, and foster family care. The league publishes *Child Welfare* and many educational materials.

Council for Exceptional Children
1920 Association Drive, Reston, Virginia 22091

The Council for Exceptional Children is a major professional association for those involved with handicapped and gifted children and youth. The council publishes *Exceptional Children* and *Teaching Exceptional Children*.

Education Commission of the States, Early Childhood Project
300 Lincoln Tower, 1860 Lincoln Street, Denver, Colo. 80295

The Early Childhood Project gathers, interprets, and disseminates findings concerning all phases of Early Childhood Education throughout the nation, serving as a valuable resource to persons in the field. The Commission's Early Childhood Project publishes *Early Childhood Project Newsletter* and numerous study reports.

National Association for Retarded Citizens
Post Office Box 6109, Arlington, Tex. 76011

The National Association for Retarded Citizens is largely for parents of mentally retarded children. Other members and volunteers are interested persons with concerns for the mentally retarded people.

National Association of Private Schools for Exceptional Children (NAPSEC)
P.O. Box 34293
West Bethesda, Md 20817

NAPSEC, encourages cooperation among educational facilities serving exceptional students and provides a vehicle for intercommunication directed toward enhancing the role of these facilities.

National Congress of Parents and Teachers
700 North Rush Street, Chicago, Ill. 61611–2571

The National Congress of Parents and Teachers publishes *PTA Today*, which includes study guides for parent meetings and study groups.

The Administration For Children, Youth and Families
Office of Human Development Services
U.S. Department of Health and Human Services
P.O. Box 1182
Washington, D.C. 20013

The Administration for Children, Youth and Families is the federal agency most involved with programs for children and youth, especially those dealing with children of low-income families.

The Children's Defense Fund
122 C Street NW
Washington, D.C. 20001

The Children's Defense Fund is a national public charity created to provide a long-range and systematic voice on behalf of the nation's children. Subscriptions are available to *CDF Reports*, a monthly newsletter.

The preceding list of services, though they were carefully selected for their importance to readers of this text, represents only a sample of the organizations and agencies at the national level concerned with programs for young children. It does not mean that those omitted are not important, especially if they emphasize a particular area of concern. Following is a list of organizations having concerns and resources related to a specific area of early childhood.

Action for Children's Television (ACT)
46 Austin Street
Newtonville, Mass. 02160

American Academy of Pediatrics (AAP)
1801 Hinman Avenue
Evanston, Ill. 60204

American Association for Gifted Children (AAGC)
15 Gramercy Park
New York, N. Y. 10003

American Education Research Association (AERA)
Early Childhood SIG Group
% Educational Testing Service
Rosedale Road
Princeton, J. J. 08541

American Home Economics Association (AHEA)
2010 Massachusetts Avenue N. W.
Washington, D. C. 20036

American Library Association/Association for
Library Service to Children (ALA)
50 E. Huron Street
Chicago, Ill. 60611

American Montessori Society (AMS)
150 Fifth Avenue, Suite 203
New York, N. Y. 10011

Association Montessori Int'l/USA (AMI)
780 West End Avenue, Apt. 4E
New York, N. Y. 10025

Bank Street College of Education
610 W. 112th Street
New York, N. Y. 10025

CDA National Credentialing Program (CDA)
1341 G Street N. W., #802
Washington, D. C. 20005

ERIC Clearinghouse on Elementary and
Early Childhood Education (ERIC/EECE)
College of Education
University of Illinois
805 W. Pennsylvania Avenue
Urbana, Ill. 61801

National Association of Early Childhood
Teacher Educators (NAECTE)
Family and Child Ecology
Michigan State University
East Lansing, Mich. 48824

National Council of Churches of
Christ in the U.S.A.
475 Riverside Drive, Room 572
New York, N. Y. 10115

Society for Research in Child Development (SRCD)
Institute of Human Development
1209 Tolman Hall
University of California
Berkeley, Calif. 94720

Southern Association on Children Under
Six (SACUS)
P. O. Box 5403, Brady Station
Little Rock, Ark. 72215

Sources for films on early childhood

Contacts should be made with media centers at the various state universities, state departments of education, and the National Audio-Visual Center, National Archives and Records Service, General Services Administration, Washington, D.C. 20409. Information regarding films may be secured from these sources. For example, films suitable for Head Start and other Child Development Programs may be obtained from this source.

Suggested Activities

1. Discuss requirements for teacher certification in your area.
2. Have a panel discussion on relative merits of different organizations and contributions of each to teacher certification and standards for preschool children.
3. List and discuss local organizations interested in schools for young children in your area. Invite members of these organizations and groups to share their plan of action, problems encountered, and progress being made in their efforts to provide good preschools for all young children in your area.
4. Discuss how the preschools in your area are financed. List financial costs for full-time and part-time attendance in the preschools in the area.
5. List requirements for joining and participating in professional and community organizations in your area.
6. Select an instrument for the evaluation of teacher interaction with children. Analyze your interaction with a group of children using the instrument.
7. If possible, find an employed CDA in the community, visit that program, and invite her or him to participate in a class discussion on the pros and cons of the effectiveness of the credentialed CDA with children.

Related Readings

Carlson, Nancy A., Alice Whiren, and Donna Howe. "After-Kindergarten Day Care: A Challenge to the Community." *Young Children*, **36**:1 (1980), pp. 13–20.

Class, N. and R. Orton, "Day Care Regulation: The Limits of Licensing." *Young Children*, **35**:6 (1980), pp. 12–17.

Fuller, F. F., and O. H. Brown. "Becoming A Teacher," in *Teacher Education, The Seventy-fourth Yearbook of NSSE, Part II*, edited by K. Ryan. Chicago: The University of Chicago Press, 1975.

Greenman, J.. "Day Care in the Schools? A Response to the Position of the AFT. *Young Children*, **33**:4 (1978), pp. 4–13.

Grosse, Susan J. "Burn-out Prevention." *The Delta Kappa Gamma Bulletin*, **49**:2 (1983), pp. 45–48.

Hartman, Karen. "How Do I Teach Children in a Future-Shocked World?" *Young Children*, **32**:3 (March 1977), pp. 32–36.

————. "As I See It: Teachers Must Not Be Intimidated." *Educ. Leadership*, **39**:6 (1982), p. 447.

Katz, Lillian, and Evangeline Ward. "A Case of Ethics: The Hallmark of a Profession." In *Ethical Behavior in Early Childhood Education*. Washington, D. C. NAEYC, 1978. pp. 20–21.

Kilmer, S. (Ed.). *Advances in Early Education and Day Care*, Volume 2. Greenwich, Conn: JAI Press, 1981.

Long, Edna L. "A New Teacher 1928." *Child. Educ.* **57**:1 (1980), pp. 18–21.

Morales, Carmen A. "Teacher Certification at the Threshold in Florida." *The Delta Kappa Gamma Bulletin* **49**:3 (1983), pp. 35–39.

Orstein, A. C. "Do Teachers Make a Difference?" *Child. Educ.* **59**:5 (1983), pp. 342–349.

Pofahl, D., and Sister Rochelle Potaracke, FSPA. "Staff Development: A Cooperative Approach." *Young Children* **38**:5 (1983), pp. 14–20.

Raines, Shirley C. "Developing Professionalism: Shared Responsibility." *Child Educ.* **59**:3 (1983), pp. 151–153.

Riley, Roberta D. B. E. Robinson. "A Teaching/Learning Center for Teacher Education." *Young Children* **36**1 (1980), pp. 3–12.

Sarver, M L. "10,000 CDAs . . . Caring for Children." *Child. Educ.* **59**:3 (1983), pp. 154–156.

Stevens, J. H. Jr. "Parent Education Programs: What Determines Effectiveness?" *Young Children* **33**:4 (1978), pp. 59–65.

Welty, D. A., and Dorothy R. Welty, *The Teacher Aide in the Instructional Team*, New York: McGraw-Hill Book Co. 1976.

Wilson, LaVisa Cam. *Caregiver for Child Care*. Columbus, Ohio: Charles E. Merrill Publishing Co., 1977.

CHAPTER 19

Physical Facilities, Equipment, and Materials

Physical facilities should be functional for the developmental level of the children and should be selected to allow for a wide range of abilities and growth patterns. *Children are alike, yet different.* Most young children are active and vigorous, curious about the environment, and more likely to learn through concrete rather than abstract experiences. Provisions for the handicapped child must be made.

PHYSICAL FACILITIES: THEIR VALUE

A model child-oriented environment should consider the multisensory approach to learning. What the child sees, hears, touches, smells, and tastes helps him or her gather information and form concepts.[1]

Safety of all children and staff members is of the upmost importance when setting

---

[1] Anne P. Taylor and George Vlastos, *School Zone: Learning Environments for Children* (New York: Van Nostrand Reinhold, 1975, pp. 28–61.

up a learning environment. Fire-resistant materials, fire extinguishers on walls, fire alarm systems, and proper emergency hardware on doors must be installed.[2]

The design of a center should fit the goals for the center. The physical facilities for a "model" early childhood environment should include the following: a well-organized activity room with interest centers situated about; a storage and display area; a dining area that is bright, cheerful, and airy; an isolation area for ill or sick children; restrooms that are cheerful with windows for sunlight and ventilation; a well-planned adult area that includes a parent reception area, staff and parent lounge, office, and workroom; a resource room is needed for programs involved in mainstreaming handicapped children; and an aesthetically pleasing outdoor area that can be easily entered from the classroom.[3]

The early childhood physical environment must be a flexible one, making it possible for the site and space, as well as furniture and equipment, to be free to expand, shrink, disappear completely, or move outdoors if necessary. Although physical facilities do not determine the environment, satisfactory facilities greatly assist in developing a challenging and satisfactory learning situation. Either the absence of adequate facilities and materials or the provision of quantities of inappropriate materials may curtail the effectiveness of the learning. Good lighting is necessary whether the center is a new or a remodeled building. Before deciding on the facilities needed, the characteristics, objectives, and purposes of the program should be outlined. The number of children, teachers, aides, parents, and other adults to be accommodated should then be decided.[4]

The ratio between adults and students affects the room arrangement and choice of activities. The planning for and arrangement of facilities should take into account interrelated activities and housekeeping responsibilities so as to make for smooth operation of the child's day of play and work times, transition times, and eating and resting periods.[5]

The adults who play a major role in shaping the preschool child's environment include the teacher, parents, director, principal, caregiver, doctor, nurse, social worker, secretary, custodian, nutritionist, aide, and the volunteers. When all work as an effectively coordinated team with mutual respect and understanding of children, they become a vital part of the child's learning environment. This environment is one in which teachers, parents, children, and other adults can learn from one another.[6]

"The learning environment is the atmosphere one senses when approaching a

[2] Celia A. Decker and John R. Decker, *Planning and Administering Early Childhood Programs*, 2d ed. 1980, pp. 122–182.

[3] Decker, op. cit., pp. 122–182.

[4] Minnie P. Berson and William H. Chase, "Planning Preschool Facilities," *Amer. Educ.*, **2**:10 (1966), pp. 7–11.

[5] Clara Coble, "Teacher–Planner of the Nursery School," in *Space Arrangement Beauty in School* (Washington, D.C.: ACEI, 1958), p. 6.

[6] Barbara Day, *Open Learning in Early Childhood*, (New York: Macmillan; 1975, p. 4.

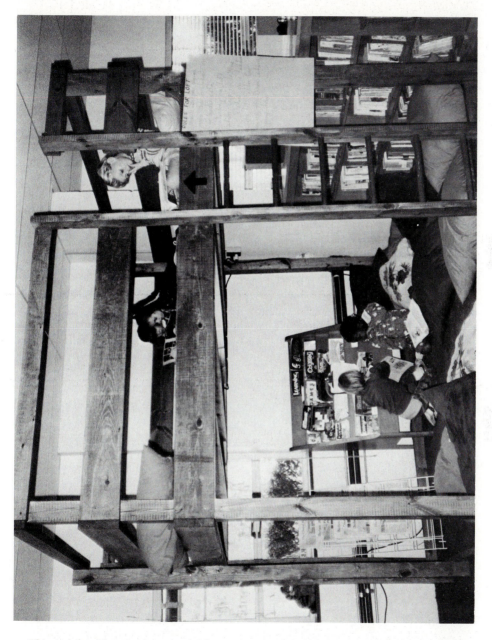

This multilevel learning center provides opportunities for small group and individual learning in a variety of areas: sharing a book with a friend, reading alone, or looking at children's magazines. The ladder calls for climbing.

school or looking in the door of a classroom.[7] This learning environment, this atmosphere, is important to the attitudes and feelings of children in their first educational adventure. The environment should invite the child to participate in activities and to have experiences through which may be learned the joy of discovering, of exploring, of creating, of experimenting and of observing. This requires many types of materials and equipment in a suitable space; however, the amounts, the variety, and the timing for use should not be such that they overpower the child. The skillful teacher retains some materials and draws upon them throughout the year in order to provide new, richer, and more challenging experiences. The teacher continues the use of many materials over an extended period and adds or takes away others as situations and timing make it advisable.

A room that is "efficiently organized in terms of space, orderliness, and convenience gives the children better opportunity for working effectively and creatively."[8] Suggestions for this type of organization include the following: (1) Equipment and materials requiring close eyework should be in the best light; (2) creative work, block building, and so on, need protection from traffic; (3) space for quiet activities should be provided together, and space for noisy activities should be together and removed from quiet areas; and (4) all equipment and material should be appropriate and in good condition.[9]

Because the room is for the child, it should reflect children's tastes, interests, and activities. Brightness and balance in tone, beauty and hygiene, friendliness and warmth, freedom for movement, places to be alone, arrangements for small cluster groups and for the total group to work, are requisites. The wise teacher includes the challenge of color in a room that by shape and layout makes provision for exploration, play, and rest, as well as crannies and nooks for quiet thinking and work.

Rooms of simple, free flowing lines, natural materials, and an absence of ostentation are preferred.[10] Converted buildings are being used in many programs.

The philosophy and objectives for the local program should determine the inside and outside equipment and facilities. The building should, whenever possible, serve the purpose of the program. Some facilities have been renovated and the programs have made very successful adaptations.[11]

Clean air, adequate lighting, temperature within a satisfactory range for children, a sound level that does not demand competition from external or internal noises, and convenient movable furniture are major specifications for the physical environment.

In planning for space, consideration must be given to the provision for adequate

[7] Robert R. Leeper (ed.), *Creating a Good Environment for Learning* 1954 Yearbook, ASCD (Alexandria, Va.: ASCD, 1954), p. 3.

[8] Vivienne Hochman, "Kindergarten—Primary Rooms Reflect Interests," in *Space Arrangement Beauty in School*, (Washington, D.C.: ACEI, 1958), p. 7.

[9] Coble, op. cit., p. 6.

[10] Minnie P. Berson, *Kindergarten, Your Child's Big Step* (New York: Dutton, 1959), p. 81.

[11] Decker and Decker, op. cit., pp. 122–182.

amounts of indoor and outdoor areas according to location, situation, and climate. The proportionate relationship between indoor and outdoor space will differ also in terms of the program to be developed. The location should be accessible to the children and on a site that is drained satisfactorily, is away from distracting noises, and is removed from people who will be annoyed by the children's voices while at play. Adequate and safe parking while vehicles take on and discharge children is essential. The outdoor area needs to be regular in outline so that outdoor play can be supervised satisfactorily. The number of children that should be enrolled depends on the amount of space that can be provided in relation to the number of qualified personnel employed.

The building needs to be adaptable for use, properly insulated against heat and cold, fireproofed and soundproofed, built close to the ground, free from exposed wires, and accessible for delivery for supplies as well as for garbage and disposal.

Suitable light, both artificial and natural, is required for program development, but it should be used wisely in order to safeguard the child's eyesight. Room arrangements that make satisfactory use of available light are especially important for activities requiring concentration, such as painting and looking at books. Adequate space will make this possible.

Heat and ventilation, sanitary facilities including drinking fountains, lockers, storage for children's wraps and possessions, the walls, the floors, furniture and equipment, dining facilities, space for isolation of a sick child including toilet facilities, storage space for teacher use, space for conferences—all require careful consideration and planning as the provision for space is made.

CRITERIA FOR SELECTION OF FACILITIES, EQUIPMENT, AND MATERIALS

The following questions may be helpful in looking at physical facilities in schools for young children:[12]

1. Is the indoor and outdoor space large enough to permit each child to investigate, explore, and experiment?
2. Does the room arrangement provide for a traffic pattern that permits children to move about with freedom and safety?
3. Is there a sufficient variety of equipment and materials so that some children may play alone, some engage in parallel play and others in groups?
4. Are there materials and equipment for active work and play as well as for quiet work and play?
5. Is each article adaptable to many uses or limited to one? For example, a climbing tower can be used for several purposes; a slide, for only one.

[12] Adapted from an address by Dr. Hazel Gabbard, reprinted in *Good Schools for Children Under Six in Florida* (Tallahassee: Florida State University, 1955), pp. 29–30.

6. Is the article so finished and constructed that it will withstand vigorous use by many young children?
7. Must the article be permanently placed or can it be removed when the children have lost interest in it or need stimulation? Is there adequate storage space for such articles when not in use?
8. If adequate equipment and material cannot be supplied, what makeshift article has the teacher provided that will ensure a well-rounded program? (If only temporary storage space is possible, what improvised arrangements have been made to help children develop desirable work habits and orderliness?)
9. Does each article of material and equipment have a specific educational objective appropriate to the development and needs of the children?
10. Are there enough materials available to promote development of fine and gross motor skills?
11. Are these materials, facilities, and equipment adaptable to children with different interests, abilities, and maturity levels?
12. Is there enough storage space for every child to put away his or her coats, wraps, and personal belongings?
13. Are there adequate and convenient toilet and water facilities?
14. Is the room well heated, lighted, and ventilated?

INDOOR SPACE

Children move through and use space in a different way from adults. They are smaller and more agile and when permitted, move through space much more rapidly than adults.[13] The schoolroom should be large enough for children to live and work together without being regimented. The inside work space should be adaptable, flexible, livable, and homelike. The shape and layout are significant. A rectangular room may lend itself more readily to activities than a square one. The room should be on the ground floor and have no hidden areas so that it can be easily supervised. It should also be adjacent to toilet facilities. The entrance should be near the street level. The amount of space should be adequate for the children to move about easily so they may use large muscles; approximately 40 to 60 square feet per child is recommended. More space would be recommended for those living in a colder climate and who have to stay indoors longer. When weather permits, outdoors can provide even more space.[14] If there is no space to grow plants outdoors, opportunities for this activity should be provided indoors.

An area for individual work is needed so that the child may be free from peers and devote full time to special tasks while working with teacher or consultant. This area also can be used for testing of individual children or a small group or for small group or individual activities. This area may be arranged by the use of bookcases

[13] Taylor and Vlastos, op. cit., pp. 28–61.
[14] Ibid.

and dividers on casters; however, the walls should be transparent or low enough for supervision if there is only one teacher for the center. Space should take into account the number of adults in the program. One large room is preferable to several small rooms because supervision and teaching cannot be as easily performed in several rooms.

Level changes within the classroom can utilize empty and nonfunctional areas, thus making additional space available. A balcony can provide a quiet place for a child to hear a story. The ladder for climbing to the balcony must be fastened securely. Lowering the ceiling in certain parts of the room helps to scale the space to the child's level.

There should be learning centers or areas of interest set up around the classroom. Before the teacher sets up these areas, one should visualize how he or she wants the children to move around the room. The best possible arrangement would be made by deciding the easiest pattern for the children to remember and by minimizing the confusion of the children getting into one another's way.[15]

There are many different ways to set up learning centers in a classroom.[16] Bookcases put together around a rug, rocking chairs, and dolls to read to can provide a book center. A tall bookcase or box between two tables gives two more learning centers. Space on the back of teacher's desk, on bookcases, and pianos may be used for instructions. A large appliance box is useful for storage, table space, or covering projects left spread out on the floor.

The teacher should remember to place top priority on space. Furniture and equipment should not be as important as open space. The centers should also be flexible, in that when children tire of a center, or a new center needs adding, they can be changed or added with ease.

Ideas for classroom designs can be seen in Day's *Open Learning in Early Childhood*. The teacher should remember, however, that some or part of these designs might not necessarily work for the space he or she has available. The teacher should design the room to fit the space available, utilizing the space in the most productive way possible.[17]

Rest or sleeping facilities

Provision for rest is recognized as important in schools for young children; hence, rest facilities are considered essential. These facilities are discussed in detail in Chapter 13 on Health and Safety.

[15]Verna Hildebrand, *Introduction to Early Childhood Education* (New York: Macmillan, 1976), pp. 67–71.

[16]Imogene Forte and Joy Mackenzie, *Nooks, Crannies and Corners Learning Centers for Creative Classrooms* (Nashville, Tenn.: Incentive Publications, 1972), pp. 169–171.

[17]Day, op. cit., pp. 194–197.

Lockers and storage space

Well-planned storage space assists the child in learning to accept responsibility for caring for floor equipment. Each child needs a place of his or her own to store wraps and personal belongings. Locker space may take many forms, but all types should provide for easy usability by the child. Usually 10 to 15 inches is adequate for depth and 10 to 12 inches for width. The height may total 35 inches with rod or hooks for clothing and include a shelf 7 inches from the top and a rack for shoes 10 inches from the floor. The actual space for hanging coats must be adequate for the child who uses the locker. If the coats and rest pads are stored in the individual lockers, the space should be increased in height and width accordingly. Many nursery schools and kindergartens provide special coat facilities. Locker spaces should be close to the door that parents will enter to call for the child. If lockers are in out-of-the-way places, children are likely to forget their belongings. Each child needs a box for his or her little treasures. Each child's name should be printed on his or her locker and box. A symbol beside the name will help the child to recognize his or her name.[18]

The necessary supply cabinets may need to have doors; however, many cupboards and shelves can be built in sections and can be easily moved to make work centers or be used as screens. These will need to be equipped with casters, drawers, and trays, as well as open shelves, according to plans for use. Storage space should be provided for large toys, large paper, blocks, and supplies as well as for the smaller articles. All storage space should be well ventilated. Unit storage seems to work best. When similar playthings or materials for a center are kept together, it is easier for the child to clean up.[19]

There must be storage space for art materials. Arrangements should be made for both large and standard sized materials. Smaller materials, such as scissors and paints, need separate storage space.

The adults need storage space too. This should include a storage space for wraps; space for a lavatory, commode, and possibly a shower; a table or desk; a comfortable chair and something to "stretch out" on. The space should allow for privacy for the adult and also for conferences with child, parent, or fellow workers.

Sanitary facilities

Running water and sinks are essentials in preparing for and cleaning up after activities in the school. The toilet and handwashing facilities should be adjacent to or

[18] Hildebrand, op. cit., pp. 67–71.
[19] E. M. Matterson, *Play and Playthings for the Preschool Child* (Baltimore, Md.: Penguin, 1965), p. 18.

easily accessible both to the outdoor and the indoor space. One large or two smaller rooms are needed. One for boys and one for girls are provided in some localities; in other localities a large one is used by both groups. Exhaust fans in toilet facilities and an outside window are requisites. The toilet floor should be of ceramic or washable tile. One lavatory and one toilet for every ten children is essential, but a ratio of one toilet for five children is preferred. Total fixtures with seats varying from 10 to 13 inches from the floor and lavatories 23 to 24 inches from the floor are desirable if four- and five-year-olds are included. The sizes will vary according to the sizes of the children who will use them. However, steps can be used for the smaller children to adjust the higher fixtures for their use. Provision for the fixture of suitable size assists in the development of routines and also promotes a feeling of self-confidence and independence within the child. The lavatory should be placed near the door as a reminder to the child to use it after toileting. The sink in the bathroom and playroom should be large, have automatic tepid water—no hot water— and be equipped with a disposal drain to catch clay, sand, and so on, before draining into the regular disposal unit. Requirements vary from place to place. The local health officials should be contacted for specific requirements.

A low sink in the creative arts center can be used to mix paints and moisten sponges. Children can clean up here without interfering with the bathroom routine.

Drinking fountains, if used, should be accessible to indoor and outdoor space, or fountains for both spaces should be made available.[20] Steps may be used for the smaller children. It is important that the child be taught to drink so as not to put his or her mouth on the fountain. This is not easy for the child, and supervision is necessary. For these reasons, individual paper cups are used in some schools.

Acoustics

Recent information concerning the effect of noise on people both physically and psychologically has pointed to the need for providing satisfactory acoustics in schools for young children. Provision for appropriate communication is difficult when noises from air conditioning and other mechanical equipment, as well as noise of cars and other unwanted sounds, come into the classroom. To eliminate some of the sound, draperies, carpets on floors, and soft materials on walls and ceilings may be added.

Acoustical absorption underfoot appears to be more efficient per dollar invested than materials placed overhead. A carpeted floor is attractive and easy to maintain. It provides a comfortable surface on which the child may work. However, there should be a hard, uncarpeted surface for art work. This area needs to be cleaned daily with water and after any spill during the day. Using carpet of different colors helps to separate the areas of work and provides a pleasing appearance.

Noise from tables and chairs may be reduced by padding with pieces of carpeting

[20] Hildebrand, op. cit., pp. 67–71.

on furniture legs. Tablecloths on luncheon tables to reduce clatter, area rugs, removable pads on surface of tables used for pounding and hammering, and a door or movable screen to keep out kitchen noises are some inexpensive ways to eliminate unnecessary sounds. Some suggested acoustical principles include provision of fewer and movable walls, acoustical flooring, a luminous ceiling, semi-insulation to soften the most fundamental sound-reflecting surfaces, satisfactory room arrangements, and isolation of plumbing piping.[21]

Acoustical ceilings ranging from 10 to 11 feet high are desirable to relieve noise and to provide for a feeling of freedom.

Walls

The wall space should be usable and employed to further ongoing activities and not to exhibit the best work of a few children. An abundance of "pinning space" at the eye level of the child is desirable.

The arrangement of windows and doors should allow large spaces for bulletin boards, for attaching things to pull on, and for a small amount of chalkboard. However, portable chalkboards are generally considered preferable to those fastened to the wall because they can be used more functionally. If movable, they may also serve as room dividers or screens. Green chalkboards are more aesthetic and generally considered to be better for the eyes.

The walls may be a type of vinyl porous material, soft pine, or of some material that will deaden the noise and can be used for bulletin space. Walls that are washable, especially to the height of the child, are recommended. Shifting inside walls provide for a wider variety of activities and a greater use of space. According to type, the walls, floor, and ceiling will either subdue or add to the noise and thereby contribute to or detract from the provision for a classroom climate suitable for work and play. Carefully selected colors can add to the light available in the room.

Rooms with walls in a variety of colors provide beauty and challenge as well as add to the feeling of spaciousness. This challenge of color and space is a requisite in the well-planned schoolroom. Upon entering the room, the child, the parent, and the teacher should have a feeling of relaxation as well as challenge; however, the primary colors and challenging situations should be skillfully used so that they do not overstimulate the child. Primary colors, which children like, need to be carefully selected and utilized for toys and equipment to add brightness and to provide accent in an environment of the more subdued tones of the walls and the plain floors.

[21] D. W. Rapp, "Noise in the Nursery School," unpublished paper, Human Development Institute, Florida State University, 1966.

Floors

The floors should be sanitary and of a material that can easily be kept clean. Flooring material needs to deaden sound and be suited to hard wear. Because, in schools for young children, much of the child's activity is on the floor, provision for warmth and freedom from drafts is a necessity. No bare concrete flooring should be allowed in the floor space. Popular floor converings include linoleum, a variety of woods, and rubber or plastic tiles.

The dining area may also be the playroom. The floors in this dining space, the tables, and the chairs should be of materials that can be easily cleaned and the space should be adequately ventilated. All food preparation and serving centers should conform to the standards established by the local and state boards of health.

Windows and doors

The exits and windows are an important part of the learning environment. Therefore, their placement and type need careful consideration. The windows should be low enough so that a child can see out. They should be fitted with shades or blinds. Translucent shades or venetian blinds assist in regulating the light; however, care must be exercised in adjusting venetian blinds in order to avoid bonds of bright light or direct sunlight. An overhanging roof or awnings or both help regulate glare. All windows should be fitted with guards, screens, or both. The windows in the area used for dining must be screened. If any windows look out on a brick wall or unsightly area, this space may be covered and used advantageously for classroom displays.

All outside doors should be light in weight so that the children can handle them easily. They should be hung so as to open out of the building. Double doors leading to the playground are desirable. The doorknobs should be low enough to be in easy reach of the child and be of the type that he or she can readily turn. No self-locking or swinging doors should be included. Ramps should be available for children who need them.

Ventilation, heat, lighting

Draftfree cross ventilation by open windows is desirable. However, climatic conditions in given areas need to be considered. The windows should be easily operated and screened with screens hooked beyond the child's reach. Humidity should range between 50 per cent and 65 per cent, and the temperature should be maintained evenly throughout the room at approximately 70°F.[22] The use of radiant heat

[22] In the event that fuel shortages necessitate a lower temperature, children should be dressed warmly.

has become more widespread, even in climates that require little heat. Thermostats and thermometers should be located at the child's eye level or breathing level when seated. These are not for child use, however, and provision should be made to protect them. This will make it possible for them to also be used as a functional part of the curriculum. Electric outlets are needed every 10 to 12 feet. They should be covered and above the reach of the child. The fuse box should be convenient to the teacher but beyond the child's reach.

Although specialists plan the lighting, the teacher should be alert to the need for control of light in terms of changing conditions and activities throughout the day. Plans must be made for light control in order to ensure ample quantity of good light evenly distributed over the room. Too bright a light is distracting and frustrating to the child. Paint may be used in making dark areas brighter and in controlling the areas which are too bright. Skylights and translucent walls help to maintain an effective light situation. Natural light is better for displays of work.

Furniture

The furniture should be movable, durable, comfortable, attractive, child-sized, storable, and easy to clean. Single-purpose furniture restricts the child and takes up needed play space.

Tables should be varied as to height, ranging from 15 to 22 inches high to fit the sizes of the children. Differing shapes provide for a variety of uses; for example, small tables for book corners. Tables should be easy to move and, if possible, stackable and with formica tops. Some need to have large working surfaces. A few tables that can be hinged to the wall and put back up can be useful.

Raised platforms, about 5 feet by 3 feet 6 inches, and 1 foot from the floor, with easily cleaned surfaces, can be used for art activities.

Chairs should be stackable, light enough for children to handle, movable without undue noise. Chairs should be in varied sizes, from 14 to 20 inches high, depending on ages and sizes of children. Check by placing hand, palm down, between front of chair seat and upper part of child's leg; space will not be adequate for adult hand if height is correct. Larger chairs for teacher and other adults are needed.

Benches, cushions, rugs, carpets, child size rocker, adult rocker, and upholstered furniture in various centers make for an interesting, homelike environment. The use of different kinds of fabrics on seating equipment can add color and texture.

Display racks and bookshelves are preferably movable on casters—shelves easily accessible to child.

The clock should have a large face with arabic numerals, preferably black hands on white face.

Easels should be easily adjustable to child's size (so that elbows are even with bottom of paper), portable with washable surface and include trays to hold cans of paint and clips to hold paper.

For equipment to make its contribution to child development, it must be educationally sound. For example, the tone quality of the piano must be good, the books suitably illustrated, and the tools usable (not toy saws and hammer). All equipment and materials have many uses; therefore, no definite plan for exclusive use to develop a single concept or skill is planned. Dangerous swinging objects, apparatus that requires taking turns, and single use equipment restrict a child's ability to create his or her own play or to work creatively in a group.

Parents and children benefit from building or preparing equipment and facilities. For example, pens, cages, and aquariums are essential equipment for a school. They may be purchased; however, there are values to be obtained from building them cooperatively or from sharing one that is brought from a home.

EQUIPMENT AND MATERIALS

There should be a close relationship between the equipment and materials provided and the curriculum objectives. The purposes and goals of the program give direction to the use of the equipment and materials. In chapter 13, "Health and Safety," the selection and use of equipment and materials are presented as they would be used in the development of that phase of the program. Provision for rest is recognized as important in schools for young children; hence, rest facilities are considered essential and are treated there. Likewise, as each curriculum area is presented, the equipment and materials needed and their use are discussed.

Some of the equipment and materials usually found in facilities for young children are included in the following list. It should be noted that one or more of each type will be found in most schools but not all that are listed may be found in any given school. In addition, many others are available. This is a general list, not comprehensive, and no item should be included unless it is functional to the program. The amount and quality will vary with the size and type of group, with activity underway at the time, and with teachers. The list includes the following:

Art Materials and Supplies. Brushes varying in size and length of handle, easels, clay, crayons, powder paint, finger paint; muslin, oilcloth, paper for finger painting and crayons, newsprint, tagboard; paste and brush, blunt scissors; yarn, sewing basket with varying sizes of thread, and large-eyed needles.

Woodworking. Claw hammers, nails of assorted sizes, files and cards for cleaning files, scraps of soft wood and beaver board, saws, screwdrivers and screws of assorted size, workbench with clamps, yardstick and rulers, hand drill, monkey wrench, planes, sandpaper, dowel rods, screw eyes, pliers, paint, varnish, shellac, brushes, linseed oil, and paint remover.

Science. Aquarium and herbarium with cover (material for making), barometer,

This movable equipment for climbing can be used indoors on cold and rainy days.

thermometer, compass, cage for pets, magnifying glass and access to microscope, horseshoes, glass jars with lids, preserving fluid for specimens, tuning fork, prisms, collection of various types of magnets, iron filings, blotters, seeds, gardening tools, watering cans, weathervane and weather glass, measuring vessels, and spoons, batteries, and pulleys.

Music and musical instruments. Autoharp, drum, rhythm sticks, songbells, tuned time bells, tom-tom, triangle, tone blocks, xylophone, piano and bench, record player and recordings, tape recorder and tapes (blank and prepared); also radio and television available for special purposes and for special occasions.

Water Play. A wading pool, hoses, a tube, a table with metal or plastic pans, plastic dishes, and a place to wash doll clothes.

Toys. Playhouse toys, puzzles of varying types and difficulty, games, transportation toys of all types, and other manipulative construction toys.

Wheel Toys. Wagons, tricycles, "kiddie-kar," wheelbarrow, trucks, tractors, boards equipped with large casters.

Stationary Play Equipment. Jungle gym, climbers of different varieties, slides, swings, bridges, ladders, boards, mazes, gangplanks, pools, sandbox, platforms. Sandbox. (See "Outdoor Play— Space" later in this chapter.)

Numbers. Dominoes, calendar, measuring cups, containers, measuring spoons, play money, scales, rulers, yardstick, tape measure, peg boards, games, abacus, collection of articles for counting such as beads, buttons, sticks.

Audiovisual Facilities. United States flag, films and filmstrips; record player and recordings; globe, maps, pictures, picture books, magazines and catalogs, puppets, and access to projectors, screen, and tape recorder.

Dramatic Play. See Chapter 8.

Animals. See Chapter 12. "Science: Investigating and Discovering."

Housekeeping and Cooking Equipment and Supplies. Suitable and in sufficient quantity—stove and refrigerator may be on casters. If stove not available, a hot plate can be substituted. Equipment for cleaning up "spills" and for child care of room; tissues, paper towels, and roll of brown paper.

Storage. Discussed under physical facilities.

First Aid and Safety. Large Red Cross first-aid kit for emergency and smaller kit for daily use. Fire extinguisher easily accessible and in good condition at all times.

Miscellaneous Supplies. The teacher will need forms for admitting child, for recording progress and personal data, and for transmitting child's record. The teacher will also need a pencil for china marking, twine, pencils, paste and pastebrushes, boxes for storing, beads and beadlaces, chart rack, large scissors, colored and white tissue, colored construction paper, cleaning tissue, paper towels; roll of 36-inch brown paper, materials for making finger paint and other art media; adhesive and mending tape, scotch tape, masking tape, chalk, erasers, stationery and envelopes, stamps, a marking pad and pencil, erasers, paper clips, large crayons of black and primary colors, pencil sharpener, pen holder and assorted sizes of lettering pens, India ink, felt-tip marking pen, pins (straight and safety), stapler and staples, eyelet punch and eyelets, reinforcements, and rubber bands. The teacher will need access to a primer-sized typewriter, typewriter ribbons, paper and carbons, and to a duplicator, carbon, and paper for duplicating.

Sources for securing these supplies and a more detailed list of materials and equipment for an infant, nursery, or kindergarten group, according to age and size of the group, is published by the Association for Childhood Education International.[23] A list of manufacturers and distributors is included. Many of the items may be secured locally.

A teacher will need some commercial materials for the classroom, but an early childhood classroom should have many raw materials or open-ended materials available or both. Such materials may include rocks, pieces of fabric, egg cartons, wood shavings, old clothes, popsicle sticks, buttons, seeds, and endless other items that can be classified, counted, made into various art projects, or used in learning centers. Children should be encouraged to supply some of these raw materials or open-ended materials or both.

[23]*Selecting Educational Equipment and Materials for Home and School* (Washington, D.C.: ACEI, 1976).

In selecting materials and equipment, the teacher should make sure they will be useful for different ages, abilities, and interests. Materials available should help children improve their gross and fine motor control, help them become more independent, and help them to better act and interact with their environment.[24]

Use and care of equipment

The children need to learn to use and to care for the equipment and materials. Equipment and materials can be coded so that if pieces are misplaced they can easily be put back where they belong. Establishing routines and procedures for use and storing will assist the child and the teacher as they develop such helpful patterns of behavior as

1. Wearing aprons or coveralls when painting.
2. Returning all tools, scissors, crayons, blocks, toys to designated storage space when not in use. (Cleaning all paint brushes and modeling boards before storing.)
3. Cleaning up all spilled paint, shellac, or varnish immediately. Learning what to use for each. For example, cold water for water paint, turpentine for varnish or paint, and alcohol for shellac.
4. Storing oil rags or cloths with shellac on them in metal containers away from heat or papers.
5. Repairing toys or equipment that need mending immediately. They should not be used until this repair is completed.
6. Cleaning and picking up in the play space after activity.
7. Storing hats and coats in a definite place and in an orderly manner.

THE ROLE OF ADULTS

Parent volunteers and teacher's aides can be very important to an early childhood classroom. They should work closely with the teacher and discuss common goals that the teacher wishes to accomplish with the children. The teacher should also work closely with all parents.[25] Some activities require an adult to participate, others require an adult to observe, and others may be initiated by the child. An adult must be able to see the children as they use equipment. The placement and arrangement of equipment contribute greatly to its use. Accessibility and easy use in an uncluttered environment is the goal of each teacher. Neatness can be a virtue, but also it can detract from the use of equipment. A certain amount of orderliness is required or the environment will be confusing to the child. The children soon

[24] Day, op. cit., p. 189.
[25] Taylor and Vlastos, op. cit., p. 60.

learn the places for things and enjoy using them and replacing them. Frequently, teachers rearrange the equipment; the children will need reorientation to this change unless the teacher and the children together planned and made the change.

Many teachers find it desirable to use a limited amount of movable equipment at one time and add to it as the weeks go by. They and the children plan together for the use, the placing, and the care of this additional material. This type of planning provides for new and challenging experiences with the added equipment and permits the child to have a part in the plans for arrangement. Thus, the classroom truly becomes the children's and the teacher's work-play space.

As opportunities for more complex experiences are offered, other materials and equipment may be needed. As the child uses these materials in work-play activities, he or she makes the equipment or material into whatever the child perceives them to be. Through observation of the child at this work-play, the teacher gains greater insight for further planning of activities, for determining what additional materials will be desirable, and what materials are not suitable for the child at this time.

Regardless of the type and amount of physical facilities, equiment, and materials available and used, the teacher's resourcefulness, vision, initiative, and creativity are the most important learning materials in any classroom. It is the use of the space, equipment, and materials that determines the teaching effectiveness. Responsibility and ingenuity are developed through the functional use of buildings, equipment, and materials as teacher and children discover better ways of arranging and using them for a given purpose. Many opportunities for new learnings are provided as teacher and child explore together. The curriculum then challenges and guides the use of materials and resources; it does not limit or curtail the learning activities; neither are materials and resources permitted to limit or to warp the curriculum.

SELECTION OF PLAY EQUIPMENT AND MATERIALS

The goals of the program and the activities planned for the child indicate the basis for selecting equipment and materials for play. This selection should not be a haphazard process but one that is shared by all members of the staff and parents.

A variety of materials are provided. These are the media through which children develop physical strength and motor coordination, dramatic play, creative activities, and social skills. The variety is also necessary to meet the needs of children from different cultural and ethnic groups. Plans must be made for children with special needs, such as handicapping conditions.

An ingenious teacher with imagination can improvise and collect materials that children greatly enjoy. Toys, especially wagons and tricycles in good repair and outgrown by older children, may be donated to the school. Parents handy with tools can contribute equipment. Before deciding to make, rather than buy equipment, one should consider the cost, durability, and safety. There are some intangible values, however, that may accrue from using homemade materials, and these should not be overlooked, for example, parent involvement and conservation.[26]

However, there are equipment and supplies that must be purchased. Other materials, such as art supplies should be included in the yearly budget. Items to be bought as a part of a longtime purchasing plan include wheel toys, blocks, puzzles, equipment for dramatic play, musical instruments, and stationary outdoor equipment such as the jungle gym. The stationary equipment is expensive and should be selected carefully in terms of the total amount of money available.

Criteria for selection and purchase are needed. Questions that may be asked in evaluating equipment and materials have been adapted from the ACEI criteria for selection.[27]

> For what age level is the item most suitable?
> Is the material of which it is made durable, resistant to effects of weather, easy to maintain, store?
> Is the size correct?
> Is the article strong enough?
> Are the edges rounded, not sharp? Are there protruding parts? splinters? electrical and mechanical hazards?[28]
> Is the paint nonpoisonous?
> Is the article flame-resistant?
> Is it nonsexist?
> Is the item suitable to the child's culture and environment?
> Can the article be used for more than one purpose? By more than one child?
> Does the article stimulate in children curiosity, interest, manipulation, initiative, resourcefulness, problem solving, imagination, creativity?
> Does it develop muscular coordination, freedom of movement, manual skills?
> Does it develop techniques in reading, writing, numbers?
> Does it promote growth toward independence, exploration, group activity, social relationships, international relationships?

OUTDOOR PLAY

Outdoor play can help lessen the pressures on children that often result from living under crowded conditions. "Healthy children," says Baker, "are likely to be those

---

[26] Oralie McAfee, "To Make or Buy?" in *Selecting Educational Equipment and Materials for Home and School*, ed. M. Cohen (Washington, D.C.; ACEI, 1976), pp. 25–27.

[27] *Selecting Educational Equipment and Materials for Home and School* (Washington, D.C.: ACEI, 1976), p. 28.

[28] Contact the U.S. Consumer Product Safety Commission, Washington, D.C., for suggestions on safety in play and materials.

Play equipment must be carefully and safely installed and maintained in good repair. Strong muscles, creative activities, and social relationships are all developed when proper outdoor facilities are provided.

who spend a great deal of time outdoors where they can play actively and imaginatively."[29] "Baker continues,

> For a child, time spent watching clouds in the sky or the patterns of light and shadow through trees or discovering some of the many objects to be found outdoors are experiences of wonder. They feed the eager curiosity of childhood which is the basis for learning.

Children need to play outdoors. The children who live in apartments or crowded housing units especially need to have opportunities for outdoor play; they need to feel the wind on their faces or hair, to see blossoms floating by, to watch things grow, to feel the grass under their feet.

The outdoor environment offers many opportunities for physical activity, for exploring, discovering and learning. Outdoor play is not always vigorous. Provision should be made for outdoor play that involves musical instruments, easel painting, clay modeling, or even following a slow moving animal. Boxes and crates are simple outdoor equipment that provide a challenge and an opportunity for the young child to imagine, to recreate, and to enjoy the land of make believe.

[29] Katherine Read Baker, "Extending the Indoors Outside," in *Housing for Early Childhood Education* (Washington, D.C.: ACEI, 1968), p. 59.

Space

Outdoor space should be so arranged and equipped that it provides opportunities for enriching experiences rather than restricting activities. If the outdoor space is adjacent to indoor play space, much of the equipment can be used in either indoor or outdoor activities. A minimum of 75 to 100 square feet of play area per child should be provided for outdoor play. If several groups of children use the area and the space is limited, a schedule for using the yard should be provided so that all children are not outdoors at one time.[30] This space should be adjacent to the playroom and located on one side of the building so as to be easily supervised. The covering of outdoor space may vary and include both grass and paved surfaces. All play space should be durable and easily cleaned, be able to shed water and dry quickly, be free from safety or fire hazards, and be made of resilient surface so it will not injure a child if he or she falls on it. Shade is essential, and a balance between sun and shade should be established. Trees are valuable for shade, light, and sound control.

Bengtsson points out, however, the importance of the playground itself and suggests that consideration be given to the proportions of the area.[31] There may be need for some type of enclosing wall, screen, or shrubs to create some secluded areas and give a feeling of security and intimacy. A clear view for supervision is important, but at times children like to carry on play free from interruption. The smaller units within the area can provide shelter from the wind and the sun.

In hot, extremely cold, and rainy climates it is well to have a part of the space covered. Shelters from prevailing winds can be provided. A covered terrace or porch should be approached by a ramp (no steps) located near the playroom and entered through double doors off the playroom.

Landscaping is particularly important for the young child. Children need to have corners for play, secret places for being alone and for small group activities but not away from the watchful eyes of the teacher. Hardy plants that bloom at different seasons provide a pleasing effect but they should be placed so as not to interfere with the child's play. Adequate landscaping helps to provide for protection from the weather.

The surface of the outdoor play area is particularly important. Grass is the best possible surface and some grassy surface should be provided for all centers. A part of the area may be sloping, but all areas should be well drained. Surfaces for wheel toys, which are important to the child's development, need a hard base.

Outdoor space should be securely fenced with a nonsplintering material and kept in good repair. The construction should be such that it will have childproof exits. It needs to be sufficiently high and constructed so that it will not invite climbing. A gate that can be locked should be provided.

[30]*Plan of Action for Children 1953–55* (Washington, D.C.: ACEI, 1953).

[31]A. Bengtsson, *Environmental Planning for Children's Play* (New York: Praeger, 1970), 154.

All play space should be free from rocks and glass. All sandboxes or places reserved for digging need to be protected from animals and covered when not in use. Concrete sandboxes which may be emptied and covered when not in use are cheaper if used over a long period of time. However, this type of sandbox should have adequate drainage before pouring. A digging area that is not part of the formal garden provides freedom for use and yet protects the child.

Features such as slopes and mounds or even an undulating asphalt surface provide variety and help make the area more interesting. For the safety of children a fence with adequate fastenings on the gate is essential.

Baker suggests that the area be located on the south side of the building where there will be sun and light throughout the day.[32] The play area should include:

1. A balance of space in the sun and shade.
2. A hard surface area where wheel toys can be used, balls bounced, and block structures built.
3. A balance of open and secluded areas.
4. A grassy plot for playing, running, and romping.
5. A spot for pets, gardens, and digging.
6. An area for sand play and manipulative activities.
7. A space for water play.

This outdoor space should be used as an integral part of the school.

Play equipment and materials

For selecting appropriate equipment and supplies, the maturity level of the child furnishes one fundamental criterion. As children mature, they may continue to use familiar materials, but in a different manner. In order, however, to challenge improved skills, new, fresh materials and more complex equipment are also needed. The many ways in which children actually use play equipment are sometimes quite different from what the designers had in mind.[33] The young child likes to work and rework materials. The observations seem to suggest that the provision of simple, manipulable, and imaginative materials is important.

Stationary equipment should be placed and installed around the outer edge of the yard so that supervision is easy and each separate piece is far enough apart to prevent accidents. The equipment must be carefully and safely installed and maintained in good repair. Sand, sawdust, or tanbark should be placed under all climbing and swinging apparatus in order to break falls.

Because of the expense and space involved, few play yards can include all items listed here or available on the market today. Those chosen should be carefully

---

[32] Baker, op. cit., p. 60.
[33] Jeanette Galambos Stone, *Play and Playgrounds* (Washington: D.C.: NAEYC, 1970), pp. 15–63.

selected in terms of the criteria listed earlier and the total budget. Items that encourage large muscle development that are usually included on the play area are listed as follows.

1. The Jungle Gym. The jungle gym is an arrangement of strong metal pipes or wooden rungs. For outdoor use a metal gym is recommended; a wooden structure may be used indoors. The distance between rungs of the gym should be such that it can be managed by the children using the gym. Also useful are modifications of the gym—the climbing frame and a rope with knots tied about 18 in. apart suspended from a well-braced frame.

2. The Sand Area. The sandbox should be large enough for children to get into. A minimum of 50 to 60 square feet of space is desirable. A ledge or shelf around the edge helps to keep the sand contained and may be used as a seat or walking board. The sandbox must be covered when not in use in order to keep dirt, refuse, and animals out of the sand. In constructing a sandbox it is recommended that the floor be covered with brick or about 4 inches of gravel to facilitate drainage and then filled with from 18 to 24 in. of sand. The outdoor sandbox should be located so as to be in the sun for a part of the day. Utensils for sand play, such as shovels, pails, and small dishes are needed. Inspect these utensils frequently and discard broken or rusty toys.

3. Swings. Some teachers prefer not to include swings because of the safety hazards involved. As the younger child jumps from the swing, he or she may fall and be struck by the seat of the swing. Even a five-year-old is likely to forget and run in front of the swing. A safer type of swing for the younger child has a canvas strip for the seat. For the four- or five-year-old a swing may be made by attaching an old tire (with holes punched to prevent accumulation of water), to the end of a strong rope, suspended from well-braced frames. On the playground, swings should be placed so as not to be in line of traffic as the children run from one piece of equipment to another. It is important to arrange for a protective barrier to prevent a child from accidentally running in front of the moving swings. A deep layer of soft sand under the swings is recommended.[34] The sand should extend well to the front and rear of the swings.

4. Slide. A standard slide that is metal and rust-proof with a safe climbing ladder is recommended. The height of the ladder and slide should be in relation to the age of the children. The slide should be placed so that it can be easily supervised, yet not in line of traffic to and from other equipment. A slide may be constructed as a part of a play platform.

   A slide of generous width does not require as much courage to climb and can be used in a variety of ways.[35] It is wise to arrange a slide so that a ladder is not needed, perhaps bedded in a natural slope of the ground.

5. Platforms. A play platform with a railing and fence around the top offers pos-

[34] Bengtsson, op. cit., pp. 203–205.
[35] Ibid., p. 200.

siblities for dramatic play. Suggested measurements are: height, 5 to 7 feet; platform, 4 by 6 feet. The steps may be from 20 to 36 inches wide, and the risers should be of appropriate height for the children using them—approximately 3 to 6 inches. Ladders are often used in place of steps.

6. Merry-Go-Round. Although this piece of equipment is popular with the children, it is one that requires very close and careful supervision to assure safety for those using it. The apparatus offers opportunity for pushing and running at the kindergarten level. Most younger children do not have the muscular control and coordination required.

7. Miscellaneous. For example, a large sewer pipe, set lengthwise and firmly in cement affords opportunities for climbing over and through it. A tree trunk can be used for the same purpose. Old tires may be used to make units to crawl and climb in, to roll, to lift, or to carry. Old equipment such as cars or boats, can stimulate eager minds and bodies.

Movable equipment for the playground includes the following:

1. Walking Boards. Cleats should be bolted to the bottom of the plank about 6 inches from the end to keep the plank from slipping when placed on boxes or sawhorses. It is suggested that planks be of varying lengths, ranging from 4 feet to 6 feet long, 1 inch thick, and from 8 inches to 10 inches wide. From 8 to 12 planks are needed for each group.

2. Sawhorses. A suggested size is from 1 foot 6 inches to 3 feet high and of varying widths, from 18 to 36 inches. These may be used with ladders for climbing and with cleated boards for walking. From 4 to 6 sawhorses are recommended for each group.

3. Ladders. These may be metal, rope, or wood but should be light and sturdy enough to be moved or dragged around easily by children. Cleats or hooks should be attached to each end. Recommended sizes include 3-, 4-, or 5-foot lengths by 14-inch width.

4. Balls. Lightweight balls in both medium and large sizes are recommended. Include rubber balls 8 to 24 inches in diameter. Beanbags may also be used for throwing and catching.

5. Jump Ropes. Include both long ones to be turned by an adult and short ones for individual children. For younger children not able to jump the rope, lengths of rope of various sizes have many play uses.

6. Wheel Toys. The wagon and tricycle (12-inch and 16-inch ball-bearing wheels) and a wheelbarrow may be used both indoors and outdoors.

7. Tools for Gardening. Include items such as shovels, rakes, watering cans, trowels, and hoes. These items should be durable and child-size.

8. Miscellaneous. Such items should include kegs, packing boxes, drag boxes, boats, car or jeep bodies, a large airplane or truck tire or tube. All such equipment should be safe for use—free of nails, splinters, glass, rough and broken edges, and rusted edges. Inspect often and discard equipment no longer safe

Block play extends to the outdoors. These five-year-old boys are on their way to the More-head Planetarium to see "Blast-off Into Space."

for children to use. Adequate provision needs to be made for storage of outdoor equipment when not in use. The storage area should be adjacent to the play area.

9. Building blocks and tools for woodworking may be used out-of-doors also.
10. A wading pool, hoses, a tube, and a table with metal or plastic pans provide opportunities for water play.

Games

Nursery school children are usually not ready for organized games, and only very simple games are appropriate for the kindergarten. Games suggested for use in the kindergarten include those that require little group cooperation, have few rules or directions, and do not include the competitive element or refined coordinated movements not yet developed by the child. Choose games in which many children can participate at the same time rather than those in which most children are inactive while only a few are active. Tag, Loobey Loo, Here We Go Round the Mulberry Bush, and Musical Chairs are examples of games that involve all children and are loosely organized. Imitative games, such as Follow the Leader and Simon Says, are also appropriate.

As the teacher begins using games, the directions should be given one at a time, followed by the activity. For example, the first direction may be, "Take hands and make a circle." The teacher then moves among the group helping each child as needed. This is done before the next direction is given. In games that involve choices, some children may not be chosen. In order that all children may have a chance to play the game, ask those who have not had a turn to raise their hands. Ask the child who is making the choice to select a child whose hand is raised.

Activities

Water play is enjoyed by children in whatever form it may be available. Hartley, Frank, and Goldenson say that water play offers more varied experience and keener pleasure to the development of sensation and feeling than any other material except finger-paint.[36] Water play offers opportunities for flexibility, experimentation, and exploration. Materials such as a spray, small buckets and pans, a water hose, are inexpensive and contribute much to the activity.

Many indoor activities such as the following, can be moved outdoors or to an open porch or patio. Using books and telling stories are discussed in Chapter 8. A table with books may be set up in a quiet, shaded spot. Small rugs or mats may be used for the children to sit on during a group story period.

Imitative activities include the imitation of actions or movements of another child or person, an animal, or a machine. The child gives his or her interpretation of the way another person or thing moves or acts. The teacher may name the activity by saying, "Show me how you would fly if you were a bird," and the child creates his or her own response. The child, however, may imitate a person, animal, or thing and ask others to name or identify it.

Story plays usually involve a series of bodily movements based on a story or a plot.[37] They are generally a sequence of events created by the teacher with the help of the children. All of the participants do all of the actions together as the story is told. Story plays are related to the experiences of the children, have a simple plot,

[36] Ruth Hartley, L. K. Frank, and R. M. Goldenson, *Understanding Children's Play* (New York: Columbia U.P., 1952), p. 185.
[37] Clarice D. Willis and Lucile Lindberg, *Kindergarten for Today's Children* (Chicago: Follett 1967), pp. 243–245.

and include activities that promote the use of large muscles. Story plays may be developed on topics such as playing on the beach or playing in the leaves.

Musical and rhythmical activities, art activities, and dramatic play are presented in other parts of this volume. Suggestions made in those sections are applicable for the outdoor play area.

Picnics and snacks may be enjoyed on the playground also.

Supervision

Children should be supervised on the playground at all times. The teacher must be alert to the entire situation. Even when talking or occupied with one child the teacher does not turn her or his back on or forget the group. Remove objects that might cause a child to trip and fall. Definite limits relating to the use of apparatus must be set and consistently maintained. For example,

1. We run on the grass, not in front of the swings.
2. We need both our hands for climbing on the jungle gym. We leave blocks, boards, and dolls on the ground.
3. We slide down the slide. We climb up the ladder.

Evaluation

Questions that may be used in evaluating outdoor activities include the following:

1. Are the equipment and space adequate for the development of motor skills and muscular coordination?
2. Is the equipment placed so as to facilitate supervision and minimize the possibility of accidents?
3. Is there a variety of play equipment available—both stationary and movable? Is it varied in size and complexity to challenge children and lead to the development of new skills?
4. Does the teacher's supervision and guidance of the activities result in the continued physical, social, emotional, and intellectual growth of the child?

INDOOR PLAY

Adequate supervision for indoor play requires consideration of such factors as the following.

Space

Indoor space required for good school living varies in each situation. For example, in warmer climates more time can be spent out-of-doors, and it is possible to place all climbing apparatus outside and to use porches and patios. Less indoor space may be necessary. Arrangement of furniture and equipment also affects the space available. It is important, however, that the space be adequate to provide for a variety of equipment and activities and to enable children to move about freely without feeling cramped or crowded.

According to Jefferson, authorities differ as to recommendations for indoor floor space, "but the range from 35 to 60 square feet per child will provide a fair-sized room for a group of from 15 to 25 children."[38]

Equipment, supplies, and activities

Climbing Apparatus. In sections where weather conditions necessitate children remaining indoors for a considerable part of the time, indoor apparatus should be provided. Hardwood, movable apparatus, such as a jungle gym or slide, may be used. Walking boards can be used indoors as well.

Blocks. Blocks are one of the basic play materials for young children. As children begin to use blocks, they are largely concerned with manipulating them—stacking, pushing, carrying, and lifting. After a time, this manipulation begins to be meaningful. A long row of blocks, carefully arranged on the floor, becomes a road; and a toy car, or even another block, is driven over the road. Gradually, the child begins to plan structures and to test her or his own ideas. "Look, I'm going to build a tall bridge."

Play with blocks can provide opportunities for the following:

1. Physical release and the development of muscular coordination through lifting, carrying, and pulling.
2. Emotional release through dramatic play. The child may express feelings of happiness, aggression, hostility, satisfaction of achievement, or fear.
3. Creative expression and the development of a sense of design and form.
4. Cognitive growth through the development of concepts and language opportunities.
5. Development of concepts of size, shape, and number values.
6. Development of readiness for reading through conversation, observation of size

---

[38] Ruth E. Jefferson, "Indoor Facilities," In *Housing for Early Childhood Education* (Washington, D.C.: ACEI, 1968), p. 41.

and shapes, and the need for additional information from books for his or her dramatic play.

In the guidance of block play, the teacher has an opportunity to observe what the child has absorbed of life going on around her or him as to ideas, information, relationships, and possible confusions. Rather than criticize or correct any errors, the teacher has the responsibility of creating a situation in which the child can learn and enrich his or her experiences. The child, however, does need to be held to the highest standards that he or she is able to attain. The teacher may use questions to help the child evaluate his or her structure. For example, "How do people get into your house?"

When cleanup time comes, the presence and help of the teacher or another adult makes the task easier. For example, the adult may hand down the "high" blocks to the child and thus avoid a collapse of the block structure. Other children who have finished cleanup may help put the blocks away. Indoors, blocks should be stored on open shelves near the floor area where they are used. Provide ample floor space for block play. Traffic patterns need to be considered in selecting the space for block play, avoiding entrances to the classroom or the bathroom.[39]

In the selection of blocks, it is recommended that they be hollow and large enough to make structures that children can actually use. Suggested numbers and sizes recommended for a group of children, ages four to six years, include

24 hollow blocks, $5\frac{1}{2}$ in. $\times$ 11 in. $\times$ 11 in., basic unit.
60 interlocking large floor blocks (to be added to original purchase).[40]
350 unit floor blocks, assorted shapes and sizes.[41]
1 set of building blocks, straight cuts, 500 or more, various sizes.
8 boards, 6 in. by 3 ft. long.
1 set of blocks which fasten together to make permanent structures large enough to accommodate children.
1 or 2 sets "stay-put" blocks fastening together with snaps, bolts, or pegs.

A waterproof finish will make the blocks suitable for outdoor use as well. Small trains, cars, farm animals, and people may be included in the block building area.

A good set of blocks represents a considerable financial investment but will last for many years. Cardboard blocks, which are much less expensive, are available and may be assembled for use. These are lighter in weight and do not provide the same experience in lifting as the heavier wooden blocks. There is one advantage, however; less noise is involved when they fall. A collection of wooden boxes can be assembled and used out-of-doors for building and construction.

Accessories for block building can contribute to the dramatic play in which the

---

[39] Elisabeth S. Hirsch, "Block Building—Practical Considerations for the Classroom Teacher," In *The Block Book*, ed. by Elisabeth S. Hirsch (Washington, D.C.: NAEYC, 1974), pp. 89–96.

[40] ACEI, *Selecting Educational Equipment and Materials*, op. cit., p. 62.

[41] For suggestions regarding Unit Blocks, see NAEYC, *The Block Book*, Hirsch, op. cit., pp. 105–108.

child may engage. These may include miniature family figures, community helpers, zoo and farm animals, transportation toys, and other unstructured materials such as spools, cans, baskets, boxes, or crates.[42]

Puzzles.   The wooden jigsaw puzzle, framed or interlocked, is preferred. For the youngest nursery school child, the puzzle may consist of two or three pieces, such as of an animal, to be fitted into a frame. The number of pieces increases with age and the fours can handle from five to eight pieces in the frame. Framed puzzles are still preferred for the fives, but some children of this age can handle puzzles of the interlocking type.

A frame into which the puzzle can be slipped for storage is recommended. Put the same color on the backs of all pieces of one puzzle. This helps in identifying the parts of one puzzle and minimizes confusion when several children are using puzzles at the same table. Values of puzzles include opportunities for eye-hand coordination, use of small muscles, recognition of shape and color, and use of visual memory.

Equipment for Dramatic Play.   The teacher's role in guiding dramatic play has been presented in Chapter 8. At this point, the emphasis is placed on materials and equipment conducive to dramatic play. Among the most important materials are blocks, mentioned earlier. Equipment conducive to dramatic play is not listed. Rather, suggestions are made to indicate the types of materials that may be used creatively. Equipment related to family living and housekeeping usually includes dolls and accessories. The dolls should be unbreakable and washable, both boys and girls, and representative of different races and occupations.

Include authentic multicultural materials. Often these can be supplied by the child or parents. These materials can help the child from a different background.

Clothing for the dolls as well as a bed (large and sturdy), a bathinette, and a carriage are all appropriate. Clothes for dressing up (including hats, gloves, pocket books, ties, and gloves) help children to assume various roles.

Materials for housekeeping include a variety of furniture, the amount depending on the space available. Children often find uses for a table, chairs (including a rocker), dishes, a sink, a stove and cooking utensils, and a broom and other cleaning supplies. The toy telephone encourages conversation and language development.

Games and toys may be used separately in relation to block play or other types of dramatic play. A cash register may be used at "the store." A set of family dolls and toy animals is frequently used. Accessories such as a fire fighter's hat, a conductor's or a painter's cap, or an astronaut's helmet contribute to the play of children. Wooden animals, people, airplanes, trucks, trains, and boats can be stimulating too. Color cones, peg boards, dominoes (picture or large size with regular dots),

---

[42]*A Guide for Early Childhood Education in Florida Schools* (Bull. 76) (Tallahassee, Florida State Department of Education, 1969), pp. 61–62.

pounding peg boards, picture lotto games, and wooden beads for stringing are only a few of the games and activities that can be provided.

The teacher's imagination and ingenuity offer many leads for creative materials. Although some equipment may be purchased, much can be improvised. Parent involvement can be especially helpful in this area.

Workbench and Tools. "Most children have a natural interest in working with wood and tools. It is one area of play content that most children do not have to be urged to try."[43] Early attempts at woodworking are largely manipulative. Have you observed a child drive one nail after another into a soft piece of wood or saw a board, just to be sawing? As in other activities, the manipulation begins to have meaning, and the child realizes that the board she or he has sawed looks like a boat. Then the child usually begins to have ideas that she or he wants to test. The results may be crude and show little similarity to the finished product they represent, but the value of the activity does not lie in the finished product. Woodworking provides opportunities for eye-hand coordination; use of large muscles; emotional and physical release; social growth through sharing, taking turns, working together, caring for tools; and experimentation.

Suggestions for the use of tools include the following:

1. Have an adult supervise the workbench at all times when it is in use by the children.
2. Arrange plenty of space for the child who is working.
3. Limit number of hammers and saws in use at one time.
4. Store tools in a safe place. A tool board (a peg board) may be mounted on the wall or on the inside of a door and serve as a convenient and safe way to care for tools. The shapes of tools may be outlined on the board in order to make storage easier. Hooks for tools should be strong.

In the selection of tools for use by young children, it is important to remember that they should be of excellent quality. Questions that may be used as criteria for the selection of tools are listed below:[44]

1. Are the tools suitable for the age and interests of the child using them? Consider the child's stage of motor control and muscular strength. Do they serve the number of children involved?
2. Are the tools of good quality, adequate for long and hard use? Can they be resharpened, reconditioned, and broken parts replaced?
3. Will they build a child's respect for tools as a functional means to an end, stimulate interest, and encourage a wide variety of experiences?
4. Do they afford the means for developing in children appreciation for fine furniture and construction, in wood, in many forms?

[43] Rowenna M. Shoemaker, *All in Play* (New York: Play Schools Association, 1958), p. 29.
[44] *Creating with Materials for Work and Play*, Leaflet 5 (Washington, D.C.: ACEI, 1957), p. 2.

Tools and supplies suggested for woodworking include the following:

Hammers (claw), 6 oz. to 10 oz. in weight for nursery school; 13 oz. to 16 0z. kindergarten.
Saws (crosscut) 12 in. and 16 in.
Screwdrivers.
Clamps.
Workbench—the bench should be the correct height for the children. If a carpenter's workbench is not available, use sturdy wooden worktables or low broad-topped sawhorses with vises.
Pliers, screwdriver, ruler, yardstick.
Hand drill and bits.
Soft wood.
Dowel rods, different sizes.
Nails—large heads, assorted sizes.

Games. The comments and suggestions for outdoor games are also applicable for indoor use.

Cooking. See chapter 6 "Planning for Learning."

Evaluation

The understanding of the importance of play in a child's life is closely related to the concern for the healthy development of all children. Play activities should be appropriate to the developmental level of the children in the group; and a balanced program, provided. Equipment should be carefully selected. Although play is fun for the children, it is also work for them. They need resourceful, creative guidance, adequate space, materials, and equipment.

Questions that may be used in evaluating and suggestions for encouraging and upgrading indoor play activities include the following:

1. Are materials and equipment conducive to dramatic play? Arrange them in such a way as to be available to the children. Provide space for several groups or centers of interest to be active at the same time.
2. Is there time for individual and small group play? Schedule opportunity for participation in play activities.
3. Is there a variety of play equipment available—wheel toys, blocks, games, dolls, housekeeping equipment? Provide materials of varying levels of complexity to challenge children and lead to new skills.
4. Does the teacher's guidance of the activities result in the continued physical, social, emotional, and intellectual growth of the child? For example, the children used blocks, barrels, and boxes in building a train. Encourage them to

explore this interest in trains and gain more information. Add accessories such as caps. Make recordings, books, and pictures available. Take a trip to see a train.

5. Are the experiences that children are having sufficiently rich and varied to provide a background for creative play? Make pictures and books available to help children recall and relive experiences.

Suggested Activities

1. Observe in a center for young children and describe how the physical environment seems to affect the development of the children, the activities planned, the use of equipment, and provision for individual differences. Note any materials you believe should be added or removed.

2. List and describe the ways in which teachers, parents, and interested community persons can work cooperatively to provide adequate physical facilities for centers for young children. Discuss the relative value of this cooperative effort.

3. Discuss how the environment contributes to the provision for individual differences among young children.

4. Make a list of equipment and supplies essential to the development of a good center for three-, four-, and five-year-olds. Describe how these may be provided. Check local stores and recent catalogs, compare prices, and make a purchase order.

5. Draw a diagram of two classrooms and two playgrounds for young children, showing how learning opportunities may be provided in different settings.

6. View the following films: *Concepts Development in Outdoor Play.* (Campus Films, 2 Overhill Road, Scarsdale, N.Y. 10583). Compare and discuss in relation to your observations. *Creating a Playground, Making Things to Learn,* and *Setting Up a Classroom.* (Modern Talking Pictures, 2323 New Hyde Park Rd., New Hyde Park, N.Y. 11040).

7. Make some games for various interest centers.

8. Plan an open house for your school in which parents can observe the classroom facilities, equipment, and materials.

9. Check your classroom with the *Early Childhood Environment Scale* written by Thelma Harms and Richard C. Clifford. (*See Young Children,* **25**:5 (1970), pp. 304–306, 308.)

10. Examine a commercial catalog of equipment for centers. List purchases necessary for the first year of operation of the center.

11. Visit a local toy store. Select and evaluate five toys in terms of the criteria presented in this chapter. Share your findings with the class.

12. Construct a game or piece of equipment that may be used in dramatic play of a young child.

13. Visit a playground for young children and do the following:
    a. Evaluate the play area in terms of comments given earlier.
    b. Note any safety hazards.
    c. Describe any play materials or equipment that seems to be unusual or especially creative.
    d. Draw a diagram of the play area showing location of equipment. Comment.

14. Reread the opportunities for learning through block play. Observe children involved in block play. Note shapes of blocks and accessories used. Note teacher's role. Describe and give examples of learning that the children seem to be achieving.

Related Readings

Brown, Mary, and Norman Precious. *The Integrated Day in the Primary School*. New York: Agathon, 1968.

Butler, Annie L. *Early Childhood Education: Planning and Administering Programs*. New York: Van Nostrand Reinhold, 1974.

Cartwright, Sally. "Blocks and Learning." *Young Children*, **29**:3 (1974), pp. 141–146.

Cherry, Clare. *Nursery School Management Guide*. Belmont, Calif.: Fearon, 1974.

Decker, Celia A., and J. R. Decker. *Planning and Administering Early Childhood Programs*. Columbus, Ohio: Merrill, 1980.

Deutsch, M., et al. *Memorandum on Facilities for Early Childhood Education*. New York: Educational Facilities Laboratories, 1970.

Ford, Bonny E. "The Extended School Day: Privilege, Not Punishment." *Child. Educ.*, **53**:6 (1977), pp. 297–301.

Frost, Joe L., and Barry L. Klein. *Children's Play and Playgrounds*. Boston, Allyn, 1979.

Frost, Joe L., and Joan B. Kissinger. *The Young Child and the Educative Process*. New York: Holt, 1976. Chapter 9, "Creating the Classroom Environment," pp. 217–233.

Haase, Ronald W. *Designing the Child Development Center*. Washington: HEW, U.S. Government Printing Office, 1969. No. 0-369-699.

————, and Richard M. Clifford. *Early Childhood Environment Rating Scale*. New York Teachers College; Frank Porter Graham Development Center, U. of North Carolina at Chapel Hill, 1980.

Hill, Dorothy M. *Mud, Sand, and Water*. Washington, D.C.: NAEYC, 1977.

Hirsch, Elisabeth S. (ed.). *The Block Book*. Washington, D.C.: NAEYC, 1974.

Jones, Margaret H. "Physical Facilities and Environments." In *Early Childhood Education for Exceptional Children*. Reston, Va.: Council for Exceptional Children, 1977. Pp. 182–207.

Kinsman, Cheryl A., and Laura E. Berk. "Joining the Block and Housekeeping Areas: Changes in Play and Social Behavior." *Young Children* **35**:1 (1979), pp. 66–75.

Kritchevsky, Sybil, and Elizabeth Prescott. *Planning Environments for Young Children— Physical Space*, 2d ed. Washington, D.C.: NAEYC, 1977.

LaCrosse, E. R. "Thoughts for New Administrators." *Young Children*, **32**:6 (1977), pp. 4–13.

Lipson, Rosella. "A Mobile Preschool." *Young Children*, **24**:3 (1969), pp. 154–156.

Markum, Patricia M. *Playscapes*. Washington, D.C.: ACEI, 1973.

Mitchell, D. "Equipping the Child-Care Center: Some Precautionary Notes." In *Selecting Educational Equipment and Materials for School and Home*. Washington, D.C.: ACEI, 1976. Pp. 31–39.

Neterer, Elizabeth, et al. "The Developmental Needs of All Children." In *Selecting Educational Equipment and Materials for School and Home*. Washington, D.C.: AECI, 1976. Pp. 31–39.

Stevens, J. H., Jr., and Edith E. King. *Administering Early Childhood Education Programs.* Boston: Little, Brown, 1976.

Streets, D. T. *Administering Day Care and Preschool Programs.* Boston: Allyn and Bacon, Inc., 1982.

Suter, Antoinette B. "A Playground—Why Not Let the Children Create It?" *Young Children,* **32**:3 (1977), pp. 64–69.

Taylor, Anne P., and G. Vlastos. *School Zone: Learning Environments for Children.* New York: Van Nostrand Reinhold, 1975.

CHAPTER 20

A Look to the Future

What will the school that the child will enter be like? In trying to answer this question, parents and adults often resort to recalling their own early school experiences. A look, however, at the present curriculum will reveal changes that have occurred and others that are dictated by the present scene and the future. Some of these follow.

1. The days of a single total curriculum required of all children at the same time are past. The child needs to build on all that has gone before. He or she enters school wanting to learn and will not be helped by being pushed beyond his or her level of maturity or by being bored by practicing skills already acquired.
2. The development of values is urgent in order that through the choices they make children and youth can maintain a framework of worthwhile goals. The need for personal fulfillment will continue.
3. The emphasis on literacy will have high priority. Not only will literacy in reading and mathematics be important, but computer literacy is becoming essential also.
4. Another major emphasis must be on learning to deal with one another. Children and youth need help in developing responsibility for and sensitivity to social interaction.

5. The school must concentrate on developing the ability to solve problems using higher-level thinking skills.
6. Conservation of natural resources and concern for the environment are essential. Most of the earth's resources are finite. How these resources are to be used poses a major problem to be solved.
7. The classroom situation must encourage children to inquire, to study, and to become lifelong learners.

In order to help to make the child's entry into first grade happy and successful, the adults in the child's kindergarten, the parents or parent, and the first-grade teacher need to provide help, support, and cooperation.

1. Many kindergartens provide opportunities for children to visit the school they will be attending, to talk to the teacher and children, to become familiar with the facilities, and to see the fascinating materials and equipment they will use.
2. A conference between the parents and the first-grade teacher helps provide for satisfactory adjustment to the new situation and tends to maintain parent interest in the school, setting up lines of communication between home and school. Among the topics that can be discussed are transportation plans and the child's previous experiences, health records, and special interests and problems.
3. The kindergarten should provide certain basic information to the school the child will enter and should forward each child's record to the school the child is to attend.

It is hoped that each child has been helped to live richly and fully each school day as a three-, four-, and five-year-old child. This we believe to be the very best preparation both for first grade and for the future.

Related Readings

Biehler, R. F. *Child Development, An Introduction,* 2nd ed. Boston: Houghton Mifflin, 1981.

Dittmann, Laura L., and Marjorie E. Ramsey, eds. *Their Future Is Now: Today Is for Children.* Washington, D.C.: ACEI, 1982.

"Children in the Age of Microcomputers." *Child. Educ.* **59**:4 (1983).

Combs, Arthur W. "What the Future Demands of Education." *Phi Delta Kappan,* **62** (Jan. 1981), pp. 369–372.

Cornish, Edward. *The Study of the Future.* Washington, D.C.: World Future Society, 1977.

Frazier, A. *Adventuring, Mastering, Associating: New Strategies for Teaching Children.* Alexandria, Va.: ASCD, 1976.

Goodlad, John I. *Facing The Future: Issues in Education and Schooling.* New York: McGraw-Hill, 1976.

Purkey, W. W. *Inviting School Success: A Self-Concept Approach to Teaching and Learning.* Belmont, CA.: Wadsworth Publishing Co., Inc., 1978.

Shane, Harold G. "A Curriculum for the New Century." *Phi Delta Kappan,* **62** (Jan. 1981), pp. 256–351.

Author Index

Subject Index

Abstract reasoning, cognitive development and, 192

Abt Associates, Follow Through and, 18, 19

Academic approach, for curriculum, 191–194

Academic learnings, curriculum achieving, 181

Accidents at school, 365, 366
  see also Safety

Accountability, of programs, 115
  see also Record keeping

Achievement, 136
  assessing, 136–137
    Achievement Checklist for, 137, 138–141
  recording, *see* Record keeping

Achievement Checklist, 137, 138–141

Acoustics, equipment for proper, 517–518

Acquisition concept, of learning, 107

Action for Children's Television (ACT), 505

Active listening, by teacher, 333–334

Activity period, discipline for, 465–466

Administration for Children, Youth, and Families, 100, 505

Adventure play, 127–128

Affective development, 82–83, 92
  art activities fostering, 382
  curriculum achieving, 180, 189–190
  maladjustment in, 489
  reading readiness and, 225

Age, reading readiness and, 220, 221

Aggressive behavior, school environment influencing, 446–447
  see also Discipline

Aides, 498, 499
  parents as, 433
  physical examination of, 364
  physical facilities and, 524

Alexander Graham Bell Association for the Deaf, 503

American Academy of Pediatrics (AAP), 505